Density Ratio Estimation in Machine Learning

Machine learning is an interdisciplinary field of science and engineering that studies mathematical theories and practical applications of systems that learn. This book introduces theories, methods, and applications of density ratio estimation, which is a newly emerging paradigm in the machine learning community. Various machine learning problems such as non-stationarity adaptation, outlier detection, dimensionality reduction, independent component analysis, clustering, classification, and conditional density estimation can be systematically solved via the estimation of probability density ratios. The authors offer a comprehensive introduction of various density ratio estimators including methods via density estimation, moment matching, probabilistic classification, density fitting, and density ratio fitting as well as describing how these can be applied to machine learning. The book also provides mathematical theories for density ratio estimation including parametric and non-parametric convergence analysis and numerical stability analysis to complete the first and definitive treatment of the entire framework of density ratio estimation in machine learning.

Dr. Masashi Sugiyama is an Associate Professor in the Department of Computer Science at the Tokyo Institute of Technology.

Dr. Taiji Suzuki is an Assistant Professor in the Department of Mathematical Informatics at the University of Tokyo, Japan.

Dr. Takafumi Kanamori is an Associate Professor in the Department of Computer Science and Mathematical Informatics at Nagoya University, Japan.

Density Ratio Estimation in Machine Learning

MASASHI SUGIYAMA

Tokyo Institute of Technology

TAIJI SUZUKI

The University of Tokyo

TAKAFUMI KANAMORI

Nagoya University

CAMBRIDGE
UNIVERSITY PRESS

CAMBRIDGE
UNIVERSITY PRESS

University Printing House, Cambridge CB2 8BS, United Kingdom

One Liberty Plaza, 20th Floor, New York, NY 10006, USA

477 Williamstown Road, Port Melbourne, VIC 3207, Australia

314-321, 3rd Floor, Plot 3, Splendor Forum, Jasola District Centre, New Delhi - 110025, India

79 Anson Road, #06-04/06, Singapore 079906

Cambridge University Press is part of the University of Cambridge.

It furthers the University's mission by disseminating knowledge in the pursuit of education, learning and research at the highest international levels of excellence.

www.cambridge.org
Information on this title: www.cambridge.org/9781108461733

First published 2012
First paperback edition 2018

A catalogue record for this publication is available from the British Library

ISBN 978-0-521-19017-6 Hardback
ISBN 978-1-108-46173-3 Paperback

Contents

Foreword

Estimating probability distributions is widely viewed as a central question in machine learning. The whole enterprise of probabilistic modeling using probabilistic graphical models is generally addressed by learning marginal and conditional probability distributions. Classification and regression – starting with Fisher's fundamental contributions – are similarly viewed as problems of estimating conditional densities.

The present book introduces an exciting alternative perspective – namely, that virtually all problems in machine learning can be formulated and solved as problems of estimating *density ratios* – the *ratios* of two probability densities. This book provides a comprehensive review of the elegant line of research undertaken by the authors and their collaborators over the last decade. It reviews existing work on density-ratio estimation and derives a variety of algorithms for directly estimating density ratios. It then shows how these novel algorithms can address not only standard machine learning problems – such as classification, regression, and feature selection – but also a variety of other important problems such as learning under a covariate shift, multi-task learning, outlier detection, sufficient dimensionality reduction, and independent component analysis.

At each point this book carefully defines the problems at hand, reviews existing work, derives novel methods, and reports on numerical experiments that validate the effectiveness and superiority of the new methods. A particularly impressive aspect of the work is that implementations of most of the methods are available for download from the authors' web pages.

The last part of the book is devoted to mathematical analyses of the methods. This includes not only an analysis for the case where the assumptions underlying the algorithms hold, but also situations in which the models are misspecified. Careful study of these results will not only provide fundamental insights into the problems and algorithms but will also provide the reader with an introduction to many valuable analytic tools.

In summary, this is a definitive treatment of the topic of density-ratio estimation. It reflects the authors' careful thinking and sustained research efforts. Researchers and students alike will find it an important source of ideas and techniques. There is no doubt that this book will change the way people think about machine learning and stimulate many new directions for research.

Thomas G. Dietterich
School of Electrical Engineering
Oregon State University, Corvallis, OR, USA

Preface

Machine learning is aimed at developing systems that learn. The mathematical foundation of machine learning and its real-world applications have been extensively explored in the last decades. Various tasks of machine learning, such as regression and classification, typically can be solved by estimating probability distributions behind data. However, estimating probability distributions is one of the most difficult problems in statistical data analysis, and thus solving machine learning tasks *without* going through distribution estimation is a key challenge in modern machine learning.

So far, various algorithms have been developed that do not involve distribution estimation but solve target machine learning tasks directly. The *support vector machine* is a successful example that follows this line – it does not estimate data-generating distributions but directly obtains the class-decision boundary that is sufficient for classification. However, developing such an excellent algorithm for each of the machine learning tasks could be highly costly and difficult.

To overcome these limitations of current machine learning research, we introduce and develop a novel paradigm called *density-ratio estimation* – instead of probability distributions, the *ratio* of probability densities is estimated for statistical data processing. The density-ratio approach covers various machine learning tasks, for example, non-stationarity adaptation, multi-task learning, outlier detection, two-sample tests, feature selection, dimensionality reduction, independent component analysis, causal inference, conditional density estimation, and probabilitic classification. Thus, density-ratio estimation is a versatile tool for machine learning. This book is aimed at introducing the mathematical foundation, practical algorithms, and applications of density-ratio estimation.

Most of the contents of this book are based on the journal and conference papers we have published in the last couple of years. We acknowledge our collaborators for their fruitful discussions: Hirotaka Hachiya, Shohei Hido, Yasuyuki Ihara, Hisashi Kashima, Motoaki Kawanabe, Manabu Kimura, Masakazu Matsugu, Shin-ichi Nakajima, Klaus-Robert Müller, Jun Sese, Jaak Simm, Ichiro Takeuchi, Masafumi

Picture taken in Nagano, Japan, in the summer of 2009. From left to right, Taiji Suzuki, Masashi Sugiyama, and Takafumi Kanamori.

Takimoto, Yuta Tsuboi, Kazuya Ueki, Paul von Bünau, Gordon Wichern, and Makoto Yamada.

Finally, we thank the Ministry of Education, Culture, Sports, Science and Technology; the Alexander von Humboldt Foundation; the Okawa Foundation; Microsoft Institute for Japanese Academic Research Collaboration Collaborative Research Project; IBM Faculty Award; Mathematisches Forschungsinstitut Oberwolfach Research-in-Pairs Program; the Asian Office of Aerospace Research and Development; Support Center for Advanced Telecommunications Technology Research Foundation; and the Japan Science and Technology Agency for their financial support.

Masashi Sugiyama, Taiji Suzuki, and Takafumi Kanamori

Part I

Density-Ratio Approach to Machine Learning

1

Introduction

The goal of *machine learning* is to extract useful information hidden in data (Hastie et al., 2001; Schölkopf and Smola, 2002; Bishop, 2006). This chapter is devoted to describing a brief overview of the machine learning field and showing our focus in this book – *density-ratio methods*. In Section 1.1, fundamental machine learning frameworks of *supervised learning*, *unsupervised learning*, and *reinforcement learning* are briefly reviewed. Then we show examples of machine learning problems to which the density-ratio methods can be applied in Section 1.2 and briefly review methods of density-ratio estimation in Section 1.3. A brief overview of theoretical aspects of density-ratio estimation is given in Section 1.4. Finally, the organization of this book is described in Section 1.5.

1.1 Machine Learning

Depending on the type of data and the purpose of the analysis, machine learning tasks can be classified into three categories:

Supervised learning: An input–output relation is learned from input–output samples.

Unsupervised learning: Some interesting "structure" is found from input-only samples.

Reinforcement learning: A decision-making policy is learned from reward samples.

In this section we briefly review each of these tasks.

1.1.1 Supervised Learning

In the *supervised learning* scenario, data samples take the form of input–output pairs and the goal is to infer the input–output relation behind the data. Typical examples of supervised learning problems are *regression* and *classification* (Figure 1.1):

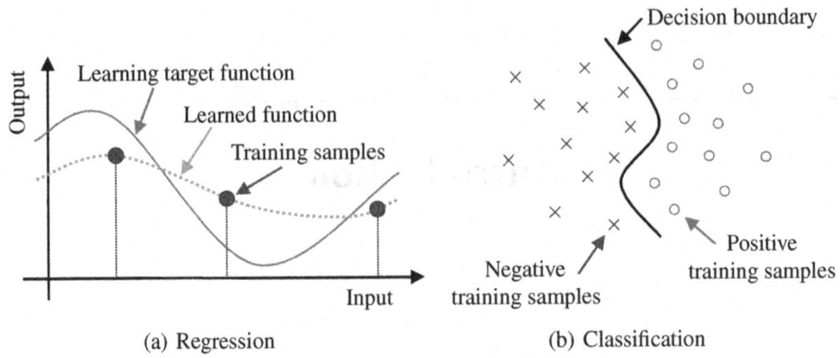

Figure 1.1. Regression and classification tasks in supervised learning. The goal of regression is to learn the target function from training samples, while the goal of classification is to learn the decision boundary from training samples.

Regression: Real-valued output values are predicted. A distance structure exists in the output space, thus making it important that the prediction be "close" to the true output.

Classification: Categorical output values are predicted. No distance structure exists in the output space, and thus the only thing that matters is whether the prediction is correct.

Designing learning algorithms for making good predictions is the central research topic in supervised learning. Beyond that, there are various challenging research issues such as *model selection*, *active learning*, and *dimensionality reduction* (Figure 1.2):

Model selection: To obtain good prediction performance in supervised learning, it is critical to control the *complexity* of models appropriately. Here a *model* refers to a set of functions from which a learned function is searched (Akaike, 1970, 1974, 1980; Mallows, 1973; Takeuchi, 1976; Schwarz, 1978; Rissanen, 1978; Craven and Wahba, 1979; Rissanen, 1987; Shibata, 1989; Wahba, 1990; Efron and Tibshirani, 1993; Murata et al., 1994; Konishi and Kitagawa, 1996; Ishiguro et al., 1997; Vapnik, 1998; Sugiyama and Ogawa, 2001b; Sugiyama and Müller, 2002; Sugiyama et al., 2004).

Active learning: When users are allowed to design the location of training input points, it is desirable to design the location so that the prediction performance is maximized (Fedorov, 1972; Pukelsheim, 1993; Cohn et al., 1996; Fukumizu, 2000; Wiens, 2000; Sugiyama and Ogawa, 2000, 2001a; Kanamori and Shimodaira, 2003; Sugiyama, 2006; Kanamori, 2007; Sugiyama and Nakajima, 2009). Active learning is also called the *experiment design* in statistics. The challenging problem of solving active learning and model selection simultaneously has also been explored (Sugiyama and Ogawa, 2003; Sugiyama and Rubens, 2008).

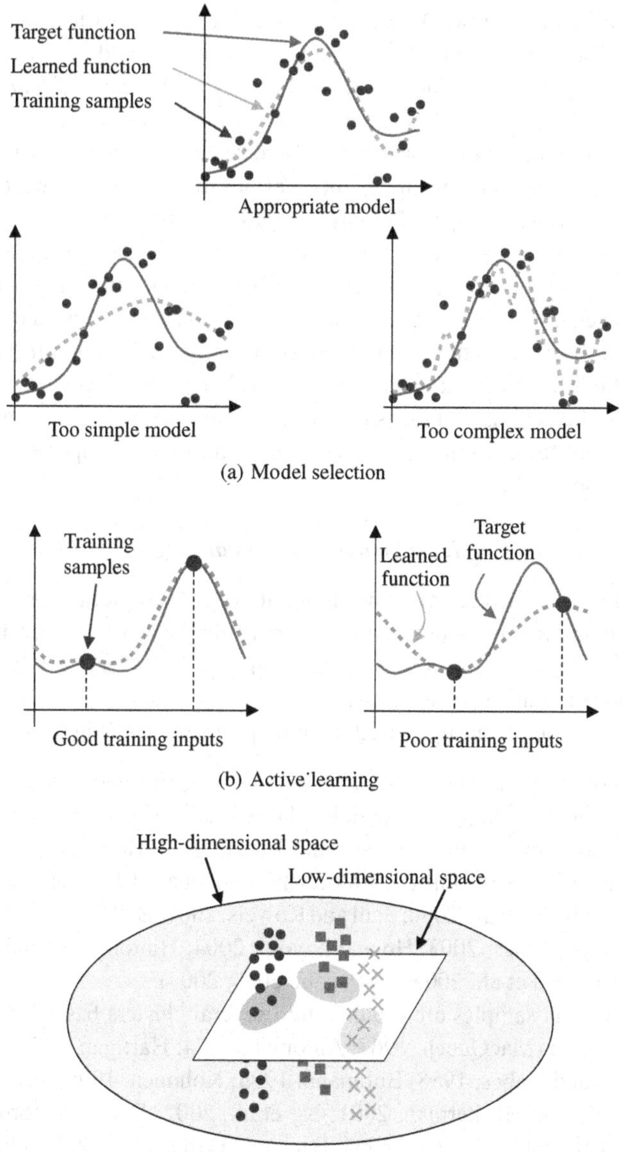

Figure 1.2. Research topics in supervised learning. The goal of model selection is to appropriately control the complexity of a function class from which a learned function is searched. The goal of active learning is to find good location of training input points. The goal of dimensionality reduction is to find a suitable low-dimensional expression of training samples for predicting output values.

Dimensionality reduction: As the dimensionality of input variables gets higher, the supervised learning problem becomes more and more difficult. Because of its hardness, this phenomenon is often referred to as the *curse of dimensionality* (Bellman, 1961; Vapnik, 1998). One way to mitigate the curse of dimensionality is to assume that the data at hand are redundant in some sense and try to remove such redundant components. Various dimensionality reduction techniques have been developed (Fukunaga, 1990; Li, 1991, 1992; Fukumizu et al., 2004; Weinberger et al., 2006; Globerson and Roweis, 2006; Sugiyama, 2007, 2009; Davis et al., 2007; Song et al., 2007b; Suzuki and Sugiyama, 2010; Sugiyama et al., 2010c). Dimensionality reduction is also referred to as *feature extraction*. If the reduction is confined to choosing a subset of attributes of the original high-dimensional input vector, it is called *feature selection* or *variable selection*. Unsupervised dimensionality reduction methods (i.e., output information is not utilized) are also often employed, even in supervised learning scenarios (see Section 1.1.2).

1.1.2 Unsupervised Learning

In contrast to supervised learning, where input–output samples are provided, data samples containing only input information are available in an unsupervised learning scenario. The goal of *unsupervised learning* is to discover some "interesting" structure hidden in the input-only data.

Typical examples of unsupervised learning problems are (Figure 1.3)

Visualization: High-dimensional data samples are projected onto a space with dimension no more than 3. Essentially, data visualization is almost the same as dimensionality reduction (Friedman and Tukey, 1974; Huber, 1985; Friedman, 1987; Oja, 1982, 1989; Jolliffe, 1986; Schölkopf et al., 1998; Roweis and Saul, 2000; Tenenbaum et al., 2000; Saul and Roweis, 2003; Belkin and Niyogi, 2003; Donoho and Grimes, 2003; He and Niyogi, 2004; Hinton and Salakhutdinov, 2006; Blanchard et al., 2006; Kawanabe et al., 2007).

Clustering: Data samples are grouped into several clusters based on their similarity/distance (MacQueen, 1967; Antoniak, 1974; Hartigan, 1975; Kohonen, 1988; Jain and Dubes, 1988; Buhmann, 1995; Kohonen, 1995; Shi and Malik, 2000; Meila and Heckerman, 2001; Ng et al., 2002; Bach and Jordan, 2006; Dhillon et al., 2004; Xu et al., 2005; Bach and Harchaoui, 2008; Zelnik-Manor and Perona, 2005; Blei and Jordan, 2006; Song et al., 2007a; Faivishevsky and Goldberger, 2010; Kimura and Sugiyama, 2011; Agakov and Barber, 2006; Gomes et al., 2010; Sugiyama et al., 2011d).

Outlier detection: In real-world problems, data samples often contain *outliers* (i.e., "irregular" samples) because of measurement error or human mislabeling. The goal of outlier detection is to identify outliers in a dataset (Breunig et al., 2000; Schölkopf et al., 2001; Tax and Duin, 2004; Hodge and Austin, 2004; Hido et al., 2011). The problem of outlier detection is also referred to as *anomaly detection*, *novelty detection*, and *single-class classification*.

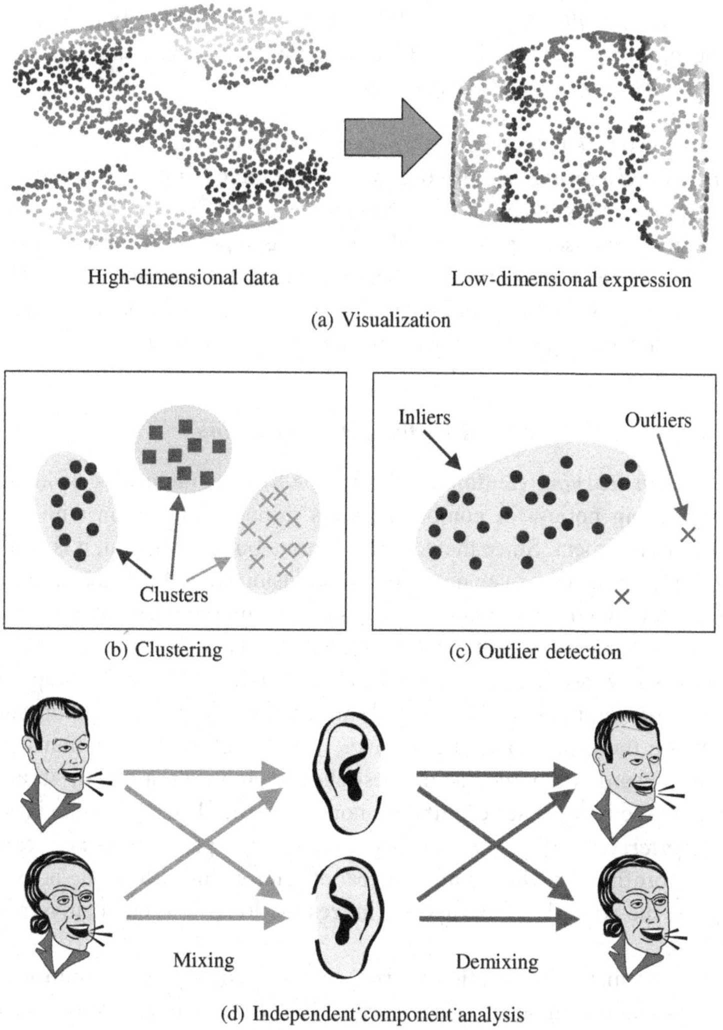

Figure 1.3. Research topics in unsupervised learning. The goal of visualization is to find a low-dimensional expression of samples that provides us some intuition behind the data. The goal of clustering is to group samples into several clusters. The goal of outlier detection is to identify "irregular" samples. The goal of independent component analysis is to extract original source signals from their mixed signals.

Independent component analysis: Independent component analysis is a machine learning approach to the problem of *blind source separation*, which is also known as the *cocktail party problem*. The goal of blind source separation is to extract the original source signals from their mixed signals. Independent component analysis methods tackle this problem based on the statistical independence among the source signals (Jutten and Herault, 1991; Cardoso and Souloumiac,

1993; Comon, 1994; Amari et al., 1996; Amari, 1998, 2000; Hyvaerinen, 1999; Cardoso, 1999; Lee et al., 1999; Hyvärinen et al., 2001; Bach and Jordan, 2002; Hulle, 2008; Suzuki and Sugiyama, 2011).

An intermediate situation between supervised and unsupervised learning called *semi-supervised learning* has also become a major topic of interest recently, where input–output samples and input-only samples are given (Chapelle et al., 2006). The goal of semi-supervised learning is still the same as supervised learning. Thus, the only difference between semi-supervised learning and supervised learning is that, in semi-supervised learning, additional input-only samples are provided, based on which we expect that prediction performance can be improved.

1.1.3 Reinforcement Learning

Reinforcement learning (Sutton and Barto, 1998) is a framework of learning a decision-making policy for computer agents through interaction with the surrounding environment. Since the goal is to learn a policy function, it is similar to supervised learning. However, no explicit supervision is available, that is, an action to take is not explicitly provided. Thus, it is also similar to unsupervised learning.

Without any supervision, it is not possible to learn a policy function in a meaningful way. A key assumption in reinforcement learning is that implicit supervision called *rewards* is provided. The reward information reflects the appropriateness of the action the agent takes at that time. Thus, intuitively, the action with the maximum reward is regarded as the best choice. However, a greedy strategy of maximizing the immediate reward does not necessarily lead to the maximization of the *long-term cumulative rewards*. For example, a prior investment can produce more profits in the long run. The goal of reinforcement learning is to let the agent learn the control policy that maximizes the long-term cumulative rewards (Figure 1.4).

Regression methods are often utilized to solve efficiently the reinforcement learning problem (Lagoudakis and Parr, 2003). Furthermore, various machine learning techniques such as clustering, active learning, and dimensionality

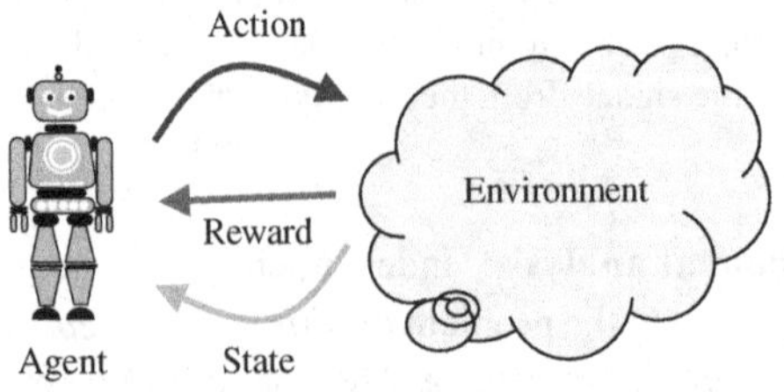

Figure 1.4. Reinforcement learning. If the agent takes some action, then the next state and the reward are given from the environment. The goal of reinforcement learning is to let the agent learn the control policy that maximizes the long-term cumulative rewards.

reduction are highly useful for solving realistic reinforcement learning problems. Thus, reinforcement learning can be regarded as a challenging application of machine learning methods. Following the rapid advancement of machine learning techniques and computer environments in the last decade, reinforcement learning algorithms have become capable of handling large-scale, complex, real-world problems. For this reason, reinforcement learning has gathered considerable attention recently in the machine learning community.

1.2 Density-Ratio Approach to Machine Learning

As described in the previous section, machine learning includes various kinds of important and practical data-processing tasks. For this reason, machine learning become one of the most challenging and growing research fields in the areas of computer science and related data processing fields. Among the various approaches, statistical methods have particularly achieved great success in the last decade, when the size, dimension, and complexity of the data have grown explosively.

In a statistical approach, the data samples are assumed to be drawn from an underlying probability distribution. Thus, the most fundamental statistical approach tries to estimate the underlying probability distribution from samples. Indeed, virtually all machine learning problems can be solved via probability distribution estimation. However, since probability distribution estimation is known to be one of the most difficult problems (Vapnik, 1998), solving a target machine learning task via probability distribution estimation can be highly erroneous.

Recently, an alternative framework of machine learning based on the *ratio* of probability densities has been proposed and has gathered a great deal of attention (Sugiyama et al., 2009). The purpose of this book is to give an overview of the density-ratio framework including algorithms, applications, and theories.

The density-ratio framework of machine learning includes various statistical data-processing tasks, which are extensively covered in Part III of this book.

Non-stationarity adaptation (Section 9.1): Ordinary supervised learning methods have been developed under the assumption that samples used for training a regressor/classifier follow the same probability distribution as test samples whose outputs are predicted. Under the common distribution assumption, ordinary learning algorithms are designed to have good theoretical properties such as *consistency* and *asymptotic unbiasedness*.

However, this fundamental assumption is often violated in real-world problems such as robot control, speech recognition, image recognition, brain-signal analysis, natural language processing, bioinformatics, and computational chemistry. The goal of non-stationarity adaptation research is to develop learning algorithms that perform well even when the training and test samples follow different probability distributions. If the problem domains of the training and test data are different, the adaptation problem is called *domain adaptation* or *transfer learning*. In econometrics, this problem has been studied under the name of *sample selection bias* (Heckman, 1979).

When the training and test distributions have nothing in common, it is not possible to learn anything about the test distribution from the training samples. Thus, some similarity between training and test distributions needs to be assumed to make the discussion meaningful. Here we focus on the situation called a *covariate shift*, where the training and test *input* distributions are different but the conditional distribution of outputs given inputs is common to the training and test samples (Shimodaira, 2000). Note that "covariate" refers to an input variable in statistics.

Under the covariate shift setup, the density ratio between the training and test densities can be used as the measure of the "importance" of each training sample in the test domain. This approach can be regarded as an application of the *importance sampling* technique in statistics (Fishman, 1996). By weighting the training loss function according to the importance value, ordinary supervised learning techniques can be systematically modified so that suitable theoretical properties such as consistency and asymptotic unbiasedness can be properly achieved even under covariate shift (Shimodaira, 2000; Zadrozny, 2004; Sugiyama and Müller, 2005; Sugiyama et al., 2007, 2008; Storkey and Sugiyama, 2007; Huang et al., 2007; Yamazaki et al., 2007; Bickel et al., 2007; Kanamori et al., 2009; Quiñonero-Candela et al., 2009; Sugiyama and Kawanabe, 2011).

Multi-task learning (Section 9.2): When one wants to solve many supervised learning problems, each of which contains a small number of training samples, solving them simultaneously could be more promising than solving them independently if the learning problems possess some similarity. The goal of multi-task learning is to solve multiple related learning problems accurately based on task similarity (Caruana et al., 1997; Baxter, 1997, 2000; Ben-David et al., 2002; Bakker and Heskes, 2003; Ben-David and Schuller, 2003; Evgeniou and Pontil, 2004; Micchelli and Pontil, 2005; Yu et al., 2005; Ando and Zhang, 2005; Xue et al., 2007; Kato et al., 2010).

The essence of multi-task learning is data sharing among different tasks, which can also be carried out systematically by using the *importance sampling* technique (Bickel et al., 2008). Thus, a multi-task learning problem can be handled in the same way as non-stationarity adaptation in the density ratio framework.

Outlier detection (Section 10.1): The goal of outlier detection is to identify outliers in a dataset. In principle, outlier-detection problems can be solved in a supervised way by learning a classification rule between the outliers and inliers based on outlier and inlier samples. However, because outlier patterns are often so diverse and their tendency may change over time in practice, such a supervised learning approach is not necessarily appropriate. *Semi-supervised* approaches are also being explored (Gao et al., 2006a, 2006b) but they still suffer from the same limitation. For this reason, it is common to tackle the outlier-detection problems as *one-class classifications* in an unsupervised way. However, solving the unsupervised outlier detection problem is hard due to lack of prior knowledge about outliers.

Here we suppose that a set of inlier samples is given in addition to the test dataset from which we want to find outliers. Then the density ratio between the inlier dataset and the test dataset can be used for outlier detection; if the density-ratio value for a test sample is far from one, the test sample is plausible to an outlier (Smola et al., 2009; Hido et al., 2011). This setup is called *inlier-based outlier detection*. In the framework of inlier-based outlier detection, outliers are explicitly defined as samples "far" from inliers. As such, the density-ratio approach to outlier detection can overcome the ill-posedness of unsupervised outlier detection in which the definition of the outliers is implicit and unclear.

Two-sample test (Section 10.2): Given two sets of samples, testing whether probability distributions behind the samples are equivalent is a fundamental task in statistical data analysis. This problem is referred to as the *two-sample test* or the *homogeneity test* (Kullback, 1959).

A standard approach to the two-sample test is to estimate a divergence between two probability distributions (Keziou and Leoni-Aubin, 2005; Kanamori et al., 2011a). A key observation is that a general class of divergences (Ali and Silvey, 1966; Csiszár, 1967), including the *Kullback–Leibler divergence* (Kullback and Leibler, 1951) and the *Pearson divergence* (Pearson, 1900), can be approximated accurately via density-ratio estimation (Nguyen et al., 2010; Sugiyama et al., 2011c), resulting in better test accuracy than estimating the two distributions separately.

Change-point detection in time series: The goal of change-point detection is to identify time points at which properties of time series data change (Basseville and Nikiforov, 1993; Brodsky and Darkhovsky, 1993; Guralnik and Srivastava, 1999; Gustafsson, 2000; Yamanishi and Takeuchi, 2002; Ide and Kashima, 2004; Kifer et al., 2004). This problem is also referred to as *event detection*. If vectorial samples are extracted from time series data in a sliding-window manner, then change-point detection is reduced to a distribution comparison. (Kawahara and Sugiyama, 2011).

Conditional density estimation (Section 12.1): Estimating the conditional mean of an input–output relation is the goal of regression. However, the regression analysis is not sufficiently informative if the conditional distribution has multi-modality, is highly asymmetric, or contains heteroscedastic noise. In such scenarios, estimating the conditional density itself would be more useful (Bishop, 2006; Takeuchi et al., 2006, 2009; Li et al., 2007). Since the conditional density is expressed as the joint probability of inputs and outputs over the marginal probability of inputs, *conditional density estimation* can be carried out by direct application of density-ratio estimators (Sugiyama et al., 2010b).

Probabilistic classification (Section 12.2): The goal of classification is to predict class labels for test patterns. Depending on the application, one may also want to know the *confidence* of the class prediction (Hastie et al., 2001); for example, when the confidence of class prediction is low, one may decide to label the test pattern manually. The confidence of class prediction can be obtained by the class-posterior probability given the test patterns. A classification based on the class-posterior probability is called *probabilistic classification*. Because the class-posterior probability is expressed as the joint probability of patterns and labels over the marginal probability of patterns, probabilistic classification can be carried out by direct application of density-ratio estimators (Sugiyama, 2010).

Furthermore, density-ratio methods can be used directly for approximating *mutual information* (Suzuki et al., 2008, 2009a). Mutual information plays a central role in *information theory* (Cover and Thomas, 2006) and can be used as a measure of statistical independence among random variables. As will be shown later, mutual information estimators based on density ratios are useful for solving various machine learning tasks.

Independence test: Given input–output samples, testing whether the input and output are statistically independent is an important task in statistical data analysis. This problem is referred to as the *independence test*. A standard approach to the independence test is to estimate the degree of independence between the inputs and outputs. Mutual information estimators based on density ratios can be used for this purpose (Sugiyama and Suzuki, 2011).

Variable selection: The goal of *variable selection* or *feature selection* in supervised learning is to find a subset of attributes of the original input vector that are responsible for predicting the output values. This can be carried out by measuring the independence between a subset of input features and outputs. Thus, mutual information estimators based on density ratios can be used for this purpose (Suzuki et al., 2009b).

Clustering: The goal of *clustering* is to group data samples into several disjoint clusters based on their pairwise similarity. This can be carried out by determining the cluster labels (i.e., group indices) so that the dependence on input patterns is maximized (Song et al., 2007a; Faivishevsky and Goldberger, 2010). Mutual information estimators based on density ratios can be used as a dependence measure (Kimura and Sugiyama, 2011).

Object matching: The goal of *object matching* is to find a correspondence between two sets of objects in different domains in an unsupervised way. Object matching is typically formulated as finding a mapping from objects in one domain to objects in the other domain so that the pairwise dependency is maximized (Jebara, 2004; Quadrianto et al., 2010). Mutual information estimators based on density ratios can be used as a dependence measure (Yamada and Sugiyama, 2011a).

Dimensionality reduction (Section 11.2): The goal of *dimensionality reduction* or *feature extraction* is the same as feature selection. However, instead of subsets, linear combinations of input features are searched. Similarly to feature selection, feature extraction can be carried out by measuring the independence between linear combinations of input features and outputs. Thus, mutual information estimators based on density ratios can be effectively utilized for this purpose (Suzuki and Sugiyama, 2010).

Independent component analysis (Section 11.3): The goal of *independent component analysis* is to separate mixed-source signals into statistically independent ones, by which the original source signals can be recovered under some assumption. Here, signals are separated so that they are as independent of each other as possible. Thus, mutual information estimators based on density ratios can be utilized for this purpose (Suzuki and Sugiyama, 2011).

Causality learning: The goal of *causality learning* is to discover a causal relation in data (Pearl, 2000). Under some additive noise assumptions, such causal relations can be identified by investigating the dependency between one of the variables and the residual of the prediction of the other variable (Hoyer et al., 2009). Mutual information estimators based on density ratios are useful for this purpose (Yamada and Sugiyama, 2010).

1.3 Algorithms of Density-Ratio Estimation

As was shown in the previous section, the use of density ratios allows us to solve a wide range of machine learning problems in a unified manner. Part II of this book is devoted to introducing various algorithms for density-ratio estimation. These algorithms are aimed at estimating the density ratio $r^*(\boldsymbol{x})$ between the probability densities $p^*_{\mathrm{nu}}(\boldsymbol{x})$ and $p^*_{\mathrm{de}}(\boldsymbol{x})$ from samples $\{\boldsymbol{x}_i^{\mathrm{nu}}\}_{i=1}^{n_{\mathrm{nu}}}$ and $\{\boldsymbol{x}_j^{\mathrm{de}}\}_{j=1}^{n_{\mathrm{de}}}$:

$$r^*(\boldsymbol{x}) := \frac{p^*_{\mathrm{nu}}(\boldsymbol{x})}{p^*_{\mathrm{de}}(\boldsymbol{x})},$$

where "nu" and "de" indicate "numerator" and "denominator," respectively.

A naive approach to estimating the density ratio $r^*(\boldsymbol{x})$ is based on density estimation of $p^*_{\mathrm{nu}}(\boldsymbol{x})$ and $p^*_{\mathrm{de}}(\boldsymbol{x})$:

Density estimation (Chapter 2): Each density function is estimated separately from the corresponding samples, and then the ratio of the estimated densities is computed.

However, density estimation is known to be a hard problem, and thus this two-step approach may not be reliable in practice.

Vapnik (1998) advocated that

> One should avoid solving more difficult intermediate problems when solving a target problem.

This statement is sometimes referred to as *Vapnik's principle*. The *support vector machine* (SVM; Cortes and Vapnik, 1995; Vapnik, 1998; Schölkopf and Smola, 2002) would be a successful realization of this principle. Indeed, an SVM directly models the decision boundary that is sufficient for pattern recognition instead of solving a more general and thus difficult problem of estimating the data-generation probability.

Vapnik's principle in the context of density ratio estimation may be interpreted as follows:

> One should avoid estimating the two densities $p^*_{\text{nu}}(\boldsymbol{x})$ and $p^*_{\text{de}}(\boldsymbol{x})$ when estimating the ratio $r^*(\boldsymbol{x})$.

This statement sounds reasonable because knowing the two densities $p^*_{\text{nu}}(\boldsymbol{x})$ and $p^*_{\text{de}}(\boldsymbol{x})$ implies knowing the ratio $r^*(\boldsymbol{x})$. However, the opposite is not necessarily true, because the ratio $r^*(\boldsymbol{x})$ cannot be uniquely decomposed into the two densities $p^*_{\text{nu}}(\boldsymbol{x})$ and $p^*_{\text{de}}(\boldsymbol{x})$ (Figure 1.5). Thus, directly estimating the ratio $r^*(\boldsymbol{x})$ would be a more sensible and promising approach than estimating the two densities $p^*_{\text{nu}}(\boldsymbol{x})$ and $p^*_{\text{de}}(\boldsymbol{x})$ separately.

Following this idea, various direct density-ratio estimation methods have been proposed so far, which are summarized in the following.

Moment matching (Chapter 3): Two distributions are equivalent if and only if all *moments* agree with each other and the numerator density $p^*_{\text{nu}}(\boldsymbol{x})$ can be expressed in terms of the ratio $r^*(\boldsymbol{x})$ as

$$p^*_{\text{nu}}(\boldsymbol{x}) = r^*(\boldsymbol{x})p^*_{\text{de}}(\boldsymbol{x}). \tag{1.1}$$

Thus, if a density-ratio model $r(\boldsymbol{x})$ is learned so that the moments of $p^*_{\text{nu}}(\boldsymbol{x})$ and $r(\boldsymbol{x})p^*_{\text{de}}(\boldsymbol{x})$ agree with each other, a good approximation to the true density ratio $r^*(\boldsymbol{x})$ may be obtained. This is the basic idea of the moment-matching approach (see Figure 1.6).

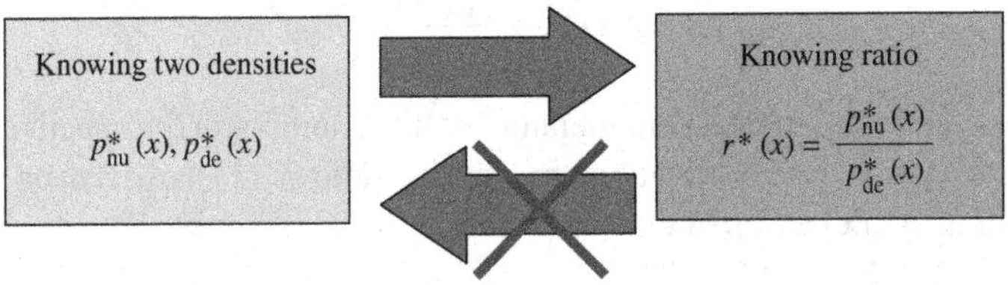

Figure 1.5. Knowing the two densities $p^*_{\text{nu}}(\boldsymbol{x})$ and $p^*_{\text{de}}(\boldsymbol{x})$ implies knowing their ratio $r^*(\boldsymbol{x})$. However, the ratio $r^*(\boldsymbol{x})$ cannot be uniquely decomposed into the two densities $p^*_{\text{nu}}(\boldsymbol{x})$ and $p^*_{\text{de}}(\boldsymbol{x})$.

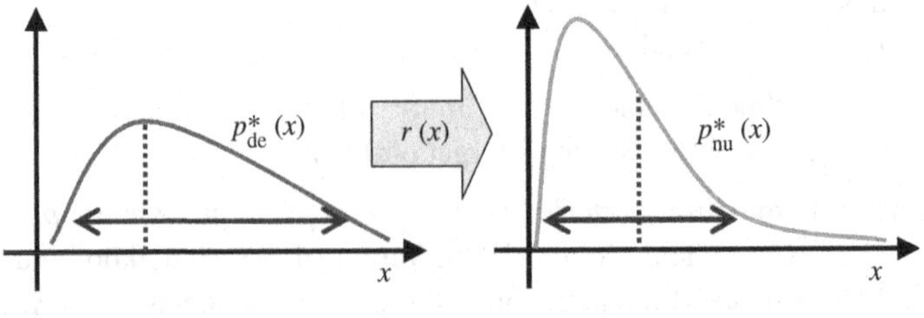

Figure 1.6. The idea of moment matching.

However, directly matching all (i.e., infinitely many) moments is not possible in reality, and hence one may choose a finite number of moments and match them. Although this results in a computationally tractable algorithm, *consistency* is not guaranteed (i.e., even in the limit of a large sample size, the optimal solution cannot be necessarily obtained).

An alternative approach is to employ a *universal reproducing kernel Hilbert space* (Steinwart, 2001); the *Gaussian* reproducing kernel Hilbert space is a typical example. It was shown that mean matching in a universal reproducing kernel Hilbert space leads to a consistent estimator (Huang et al., 2007; Quiñonero-Candela et al., 2009). This gives a computationally efficient and consistent algorithm for density-ratio estimation.

Probabilistic classification (Chapter 4): An alternative approach to density-ratio estimation is to use a probabilistic classifier. A key fact is that the density ratio $r^*(\boldsymbol{x})$ can be expressed as

$$r^*(\boldsymbol{x}) = \frac{p^*(y=\mathrm{de})}{p^*(y=\mathrm{nu})}\frac{p^*(y=\mathrm{nu}|\boldsymbol{x})}{p^*(y=\mathrm{de}|\boldsymbol{x})}.$$

Thus, if a probabilistic classifier that separates numerator samples and denominator samples can be obtained, the density rato can be estimated (Qin, 1998; Cheng and Chu, 2004; Bickel et al., 2007). For example, a *logistic regression classifier* (Hastie et al., 2001) and a *least-squares probabilistic classifier* (LSPC; Sugiyama, 2010) can be employed for this purpose (see Figure 1.7).

The logistic regression approach is shown to be optimal among a class of semi-parametric estimators under a correct model assumption (Qin, 1998), while an LSPC is computationally more efficient than logistic regression and is thus applicable to massive datasets.

Density fitting (Chapter 5): In the moment matching approach described previously, density ratios are estimated so that the moments of $p^*_{\mathrm{nu}}(\boldsymbol{x})$ and $r(\boldsymbol{x})p^*_{\mathrm{de}}(\boldsymbol{x})$ are matched via Eq. (1.1). On the other hand, in the density-fitting approach, density ratios are estimated so that the *Kullback–Leibler* divergence from $p^*_{\mathrm{nu}}(\boldsymbol{x})$ to $r(\boldsymbol{x})p^*_{\mathrm{de}}(\boldsymbol{x})$ is minimized. This framework is called the *KL importance estimation procedure* (KLIEP; Sugiyama et al., 2008). The "importance" is another name for the density ratio.

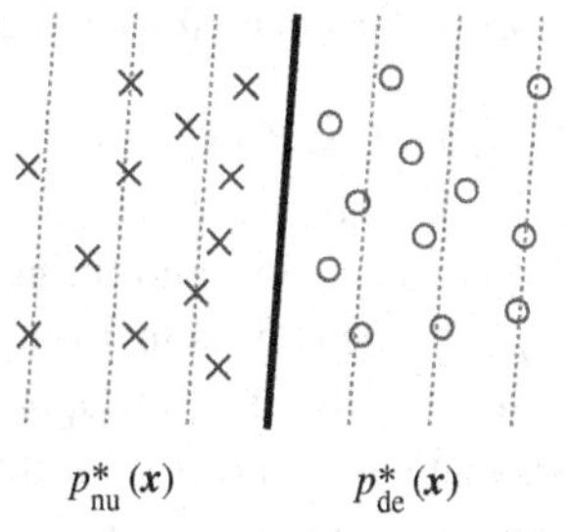

Figure 1.7. Probabilistic classification of samples drawn from $p^*_{\mathrm{nu}}(\boldsymbol{x})$ and $p^*_{\mathrm{de}}(\boldsymbol{x})$.

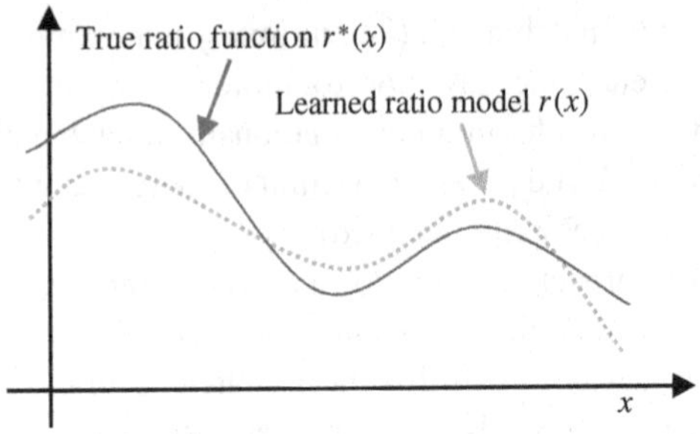

Figure 1.8. The idea of density-ratio fitting.

Practical implementations of KLIEP for various density-ratio models have been developed, including linear, kernel, log-liner, Gaussian mixture, and principal–component–analyzer mixture models (Sugiyama et al., 2008; Tsuboi et al., 2009; Yamada and Sugiyama, 2009; Nguyen et al., 2010; Yamada et al., 2010a). We will describe the ideas and derivations of these algorithms with numerical examples.

Density-ratio fitting (Chapter 6): A direct approach to density-ratio estimation would be to fit a density-ratio model $r(\boldsymbol{x})$ to the true density-ratio function $r^*(\boldsymbol{x})$ [see Figure 1.8]. A *least-squares* fitting framework of density ratios was proposed in Kanamori et al. (2009), which is called *least-squares importance fitting* (LSIF).

At a glance, the LSIF framework may look equivalent to *regression* [see Section 1.1.1 and Figure 1.1(a)]. However, density-ratio fitting is essentially different from regression because samples from the target function (the true density-ratio function in this case) are not available.

Computationally efficient algorithms of LSIF have been developed (Kanamori et al., 2009). Because a *regularization-path* tracking algorithm is available if the ℓ_1-regularizer is used (Best, 1982; Efron et al., 2004; Hastie et al., 2004), it is computationally efficient. Furthermore, an unconstrained variant of LSIF allows one to learn the density-ratio estimator *analytically*, which can be computed efficiently and stably. Moreover, the analytic-form solution can be utilized for various purposes such as *dimensionality reduction*, *independent component analysis*, and *causality learning* (see Section 1.2).

In Chapter 7, a unified framework of density-ratio estimation by *density-ratio fitting* (Sugiyama et al., 2011a) is introduced. This is a natural extension of the previously mentioned least-squares density-ratio fitting approach to the *Bregman* divergence (Bregman, 1967). The density-ratio fitting framework includes the moment matching approach, the logistic regression approach, the KLIEP approach, and the LSIF approach as special cases and is substantially more general. Thus, the density-ratio fitting framework provides a unified view of various density-ratio estimation approaches. The density-ratio fitting approach can also be interpreted as *divergence estimation* (Nguyen et al., 2010) based on the *Ali–Silvey–Csiszár* divergence (a.k.a. *f-divergence*; Ali and Silvey, 1966; Csiszár, 1967).

The direct density-ratio estimation approaches described previously are shown to compare favorably with the naive density estimation methods in experiments. However, these direct density-ratio estimation methods still perform rather poorly when the dimensionality of the data domain is high. To cope with this problem, a framework of *direct density-ratio estimation with dimensionality reduction* (D^3; pronounced "D-cube") was introduced in Sugiyama et al. (2010a). The basic idea of D^3 is to find a subspace in which the numerator and denominator densities are significantly different, and then carry out density-ratio estimation only within this subspace. Methods based on discriminant analysis and divergence maximization have been proposed (Sugiyama et al., 2010a, 2011b). These methods will be covered in Chapter 8.

Although we do not go into detail in this book, the density-ratio approach was shown to be useful in various real-world applications including brain–computer interface (Sugiyama et al., 2007; Y. Li et al., 2010), robot control (Hachiya et al., 2009; Akiyama et al., 2010; Sugiyama et al., 2010b; Hachiya et al., 2011b), speaker identification (Yamada et al., 2010b), audio tagging (Wichern et al., 2010), natural language processing (Tsuboi et al., 2009), semiconductor wafer alignment (Sugiyama and Nakajima, 2009), human age prediction (Ueki et al., 2011), bioinformatics (Suzuki et al., 2009b), visual inspection of precision instruments (Takimoto et al., 2009), spam filtering (Bickel et al., 2007), human activity recognition (Hachiya et al., 2011a), and HIV therapy screening (Bickel et al., 2008). Thus, the density-ratio approach is a novel and promising paradigm in machine learning and data mining.

1.4 Theoretical Aspects of Density-Ratio Estimation

In Part IV theoretical aspects of density ratio estimation are explored.

Parametric convergence analysis (Chapter 13): One of the main statistical concerns about density-ratio estimation is the *consistency* (does the estimator converges to the optimal solution in the limit of large sample size?) and *convergence rate* (how fast does the estimator converge to the optimal solution?). In Chapter 13, such convergence issues are theoretically investigated for the density-fitting method (Chapter 5) and the density-ratio fitting method (Chapter 6) in the parametric setup, showing that both methods are consistent and achieve the optimal parametric convergence rate (Sugiyama et al., 2008; Kanamori et al., 2009).

Also, the optimality of the probabilistic classification method based on logistic regression (Chapter 4) is established. More specifically, if the logistic regression model is *correctly specified* (i.e., the true function is included in the parametric model), logistic regression asymptotically gives the minimum variance estimator among a wide class of estimators (Qin, 1998).

We also theoretically compare the performances of the density estimation method (Chapter 2), the logistic regression method (Chapter 4), and the Kullback–Leibler density-fitting method (Chapter 5). If both numerator and denominator density models are *correctly specified* (i.e., the true density is included in the parametric model), the density estimation approach is shown to be the most accurate method (Kanamori et al., 2010). However, if the model is *misspecified* (which would be the case in practice), the Kullback–Leibler density-fitting method is shown to be the most promising approach (Kanamori et al., 2010).

Non-parametric convergence analysis (Chapter 14): In Chapter 14, non-parametric convergence rates of the density fitting method (Chapter 5) and the density-ratio fitting method (Chapter 6) are elucidated. More specifically, both of the methods are shown to achieve the optimal non-parametric convergence rate in the *mini-max* sense (Sugiyama et al., 2008; Kanamori et al., 2011b).

Parametric two-sample test (Chapter 15): In Chapter 15 we consider a divergence-based two-sample test (Section 10.2), where the divergence is approximated based on parametric density-ratio estimation. More specifically, an optimal estimator of the divergence in the sense of the asymptotic variance is derived, and a statistic for a two-sample test based on the optimal divergence estimator is provided, which is shown to dominate the existing empirical likelihood-score test (Kanamori et al., 2011a).

Non-parametric numerical stability analysis (Chapter 16): In Chapter 16, the numerical stabilities of the density-ratio fitting and the moment matching methods are theoretically analyzed. Actually, the least-squares density-ratio fitting method (Chapter 6) and the kernel-based moment matching method (Chapter 3) share the same solution in theory (Chapter 7). However, their optimization criteria are substantially different. Here the *condition number* of the *Hessian matrix* is theoretically analyzed, and the least-squares density-ratio fitting method is shown to be more favorable than kernel-based moment matching (Kanamori et al., 2011c).

1.5 Organization of this Book at a Glance

The rest of chapters of this book are organized as follows (Figure 1.9):

Part II of this book introduces various methods of density-ratio estimations. These methods are arranged into five chapters: density estimation (Chapter 2), moment matching (Chapter 3), probabilistic classification (Chapter 4), density fitting (Chapter 5), and density-ratio fitting (Chapter 6). Because these methods form the basis of the density-ratio framework, we explain not only the algorithms but also their ideas and derivations in detail. For an intuitive understanding of the behavior of each method, illustrative numerical examples are also provided in each chapter. In Chapter 7, a unified framework of density-ratio estimation by density-ratio fitting is introduced, which accommodates various density-ratio estimation methods and is substantially more general. The final chapter of Part II, Chapter 8,

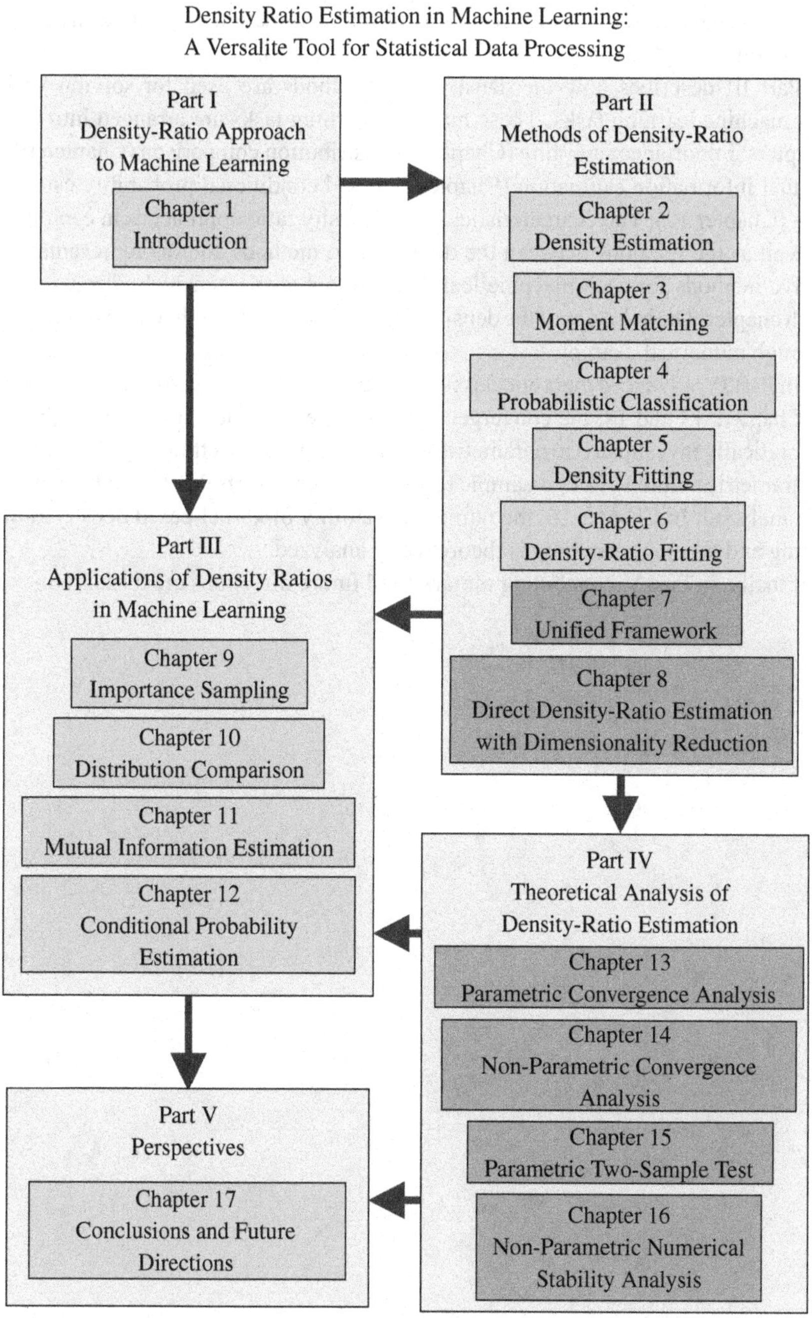

Figure 1.9. Organization of chapters. Chapters 7, 8, 13, 14, 15, and 16 contain advanced materials, and thus beginners may skip these chapters at first.

covers an advanced topic of direct density-ratio estimation with dimensionality reduction for high-dimensional density ratio estimation.

Part III describes how the density-ratio methods are used for solving various machine learning tasks. These machine learning tasks are arranged into four chapters: importance sampling (Chapter 9), distribution comparison (Chapter 10), mutual information estimation (Chapter 11), and conditional probability estimation (Chapter 12). The characteristics of the density ratio approaches in each task as well as the relations between the density ratio methods and the representative native methods for each machine learning task are also extensively discussed in each chapter. The behavior of the density ratio and the native methods are illustrated through numerical examples.

In Part IV, advanced theoretical issues of density-ratio estimation are explained. In Chapters 13 and 14, the convergence rates of density-ratio fitting methods are theoretically investigated in parametric and non-parametric settings. In Chapter 15, a parametric method of a two-sample test is described, and its theoretical properties are analyzed. In Chapter 16, the numerical stability of kernel-based density-ratio fitting and moment matching is theoretically analyzed.

Finally, in Part V, concluding remarks and future directions are discussed.

Part II

Methods of Density-Ratio Estimation

In this part we discuss the problem of estimating the ratio of two probability density functions from samples.

First we formulate the problem of density-ratio estimation. Let $\mathcal{X}$ $(\subset \mathbb{R}^d)$ be the data domain, and suppose we are given *independent and identically distributed (i.i.d.)* samples $\{\boldsymbol{x}_i^{\text{nu}}\}_{i=1}^{n_{\text{nu}}}$ from a distribution with density $p_{\text{nu}}^*(\boldsymbol{x})$ and i.i.d. samples $\{\boldsymbol{x}_j^{\text{de}}\}_{j=1}^{n_{\text{de}}}$ from another distribution with density $p_{\text{de}}^*(\boldsymbol{x})$:

$$\{\boldsymbol{x}_i^{\text{nu}}\}_{i=1}^{n_{\text{nu}}} \overset{\text{i.i.d.}}{\sim} p_{\text{nu}}^*(\boldsymbol{x}) \quad \text{and} \quad \{\boldsymbol{x}_j^{\text{de}}\}_{j=1}^{n_{\text{de}}} \overset{\text{i.i.d.}}{\sim} p_{\text{de}}^*(\boldsymbol{x}).$$

We assume that $p_{\text{de}}^*(\boldsymbol{x})$ is strictly positive over the domain $\mathcal{X}$, that is, $p_{\text{de}}^*(\boldsymbol{x}) > 0$ for all $\boldsymbol{x} \in \mathcal{X}$. Our goal is to estimate the density ratio

$$r^*(\boldsymbol{x}) := \frac{p_{\text{nu}}^*(\boldsymbol{x})}{p_{\text{de}}^*(\boldsymbol{x})}$$

from the samples $\{\boldsymbol{x}_i^{\text{nu}}\}_{i=1}^{n_{\text{nu}}}$ and $\{\boldsymbol{x}_j^{\text{de}}\}_{j=1}^{n_{\text{de}}}$, "nu" and "de" indicate "numerator" and "denominator," respectively.

This part contains seven chapters. In Chapter 2, density-ratio estimation based on a separate density estimation is explained. Parametric and nonparametric density estimation methods are covered here. In the two-step approach of first estimating the numerator and denominator densities and then plugging the estimated densities into the ratio, the error caused by the second step (plug-in) is not taken into account in the first step (density estimation). Thus, a more promising approach would be a one-shot procedure of directly estimating the density ratio *without* going through density estimation. Methods following this idea will be explained in detail in the following chapters.

In Chapter 3, the framework of density-ratio estimation based on *moment matching* is explained. The basic idea of moment matching is to obtain a "transformation" function $r(\boldsymbol{x})$ that matches moments of the denominator density $p_{\text{de}}^*(\boldsymbol{x})$ with those of the numerator density $p_{\text{nu}}^*(\boldsymbol{x})$. Along this line, finite-order and infinite-order moment matching methods are explained here.

In Chapter 4, the framework of density-ratio estimation based on *probabilistic classification* is explained. The density ratio can be expressed in terms of the class-posterior probability whether a point $\boldsymbol{x}$ is drawn from $p^*_{\mathrm{nu}}(\boldsymbol{x})$ or $p^*_{\mathrm{de}}(\boldsymbol{x})$. Density-ratio estimation methods based on *logistic regression*, the *least-squares probabilistic classifier*, and the *support vector machine* are covered here.

In Chapter 5, the framework of density-ratio estimation based on *density fitting* is explained. The basic idea of density fitting is to minimizes the *Kullback–Leibler* (KL) divergence from the true numerator density $p^*_{\mathrm{nu}}(\boldsymbol{x})$ to its estimator $r(\boldsymbol{x})p^*_{\mathrm{de}}(\boldsymbol{x})$. This framework is called the *KL importance estimation procedure* (KLIEP), and we describe practical implementations of KLIEP for various density-ratio models including *linear/kernel* models, *log-linear* models, *Gaussian-mixture* models, and *probabilistic principal–component–analyzer mixture* models.

In Chapter 6, the framework of density-ratio estimation based on *density-ratio fitting* is explained. The basic idea of this framework, called *least-squares importance fitting* (LSIF), is to fit a density-ratio model $r(\boldsymbol{x})$ to the true density-ratio function $r^*(\boldsymbol{x})$ by *least-squares* estimation. We cover two implementations of LSIF for linear/kernel models.

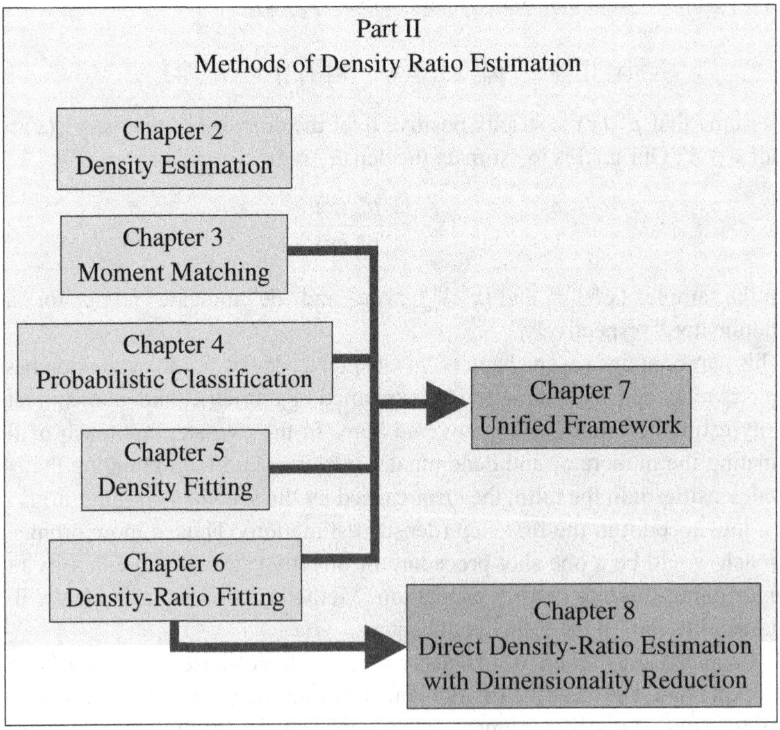

Figure 1.10. Structure of Part II. Chapters 7 and 8 contain advanced materials, and thus beginners may skip these chapters at first.

In Chapter 7 we describe a unified framework of density-ratio estimation that is based on *density-ratio fitting* under the *Bregman* divergence. This framework is a natural extension of the least-squares approach described in Chapter 6, and it includes various existing approaches as special cases. Furthermore, a novel instance of this framework such as robust density-ratio estimation is also described here.

The direct density-ratio estimation methods introduced in the preceding are shown to compare favorably with the separate density estimation methods in experiments. However, there is still room for further improvement when the dimensionality of the data space is high. In Chapter 8, the framework of *direct density-ratio estimation with dimensionality reduction* (D^3; pronounced "D-cube") is described. In this framework, a subspace in which the numerator and denominator densities are significantly different is first identified, and then density-ratio estimation is carried out only within this low-dimensional subspace. Methods based on discriminant analysis and density fitting are covered here.

The structure of the chapters in Part II is illustrated in Figure 1.10. The most important chapters in Part II are Chapters 5 and 6. Chapters 7 and 8 deal with advanced topics, and thus beginners may skip these chapters at first.

2

Density Estimation

In this chapter, density-ratio estimation through *density estimation* is explained. In Section 2.1, basic ideas of density estimation approaches are explained, including the ratio of density estimators in Section 2.1.1 and *uniformized* density estimation in Section 2.1.2. Then, parametric and non-parametric density estimation methods are explained in Sections 2.2 and 2.3, respectively. Numerical examples are shown in Section 2.4, and the chapter is concluded in Section 2.5.

2.1 Basic Framework

Suppose i.i.d. samples $\{\boldsymbol{x}_k\}_{k=1}^{n}$ following a probability distribution with density function $p^*(\boldsymbol{x})$ are given:

$$\{\boldsymbol{x}_k\}_{k=1}^{n} \overset{\text{i.i.d.}}{\sim} p^*(\boldsymbol{x}).$$

The goal of density estimation is to obtain an estimator $\widehat{p}(\boldsymbol{x})$ of the true density $p^*(\boldsymbol{x})$ from $\{\boldsymbol{x}_k\}_{k=1}^{n}$.

Here we describe two approaches to density-ratio estimation based on density estimation: ratio of density estimators in Section 2.1.1 and uniformized density estimation in Section 2.1.2

2.1.1 Ratio of Density Estimators

Density estimation methods can be used for density-ratio estimation by first obtaining density estimators $\widehat{p}_{\mathrm{nu}}(\boldsymbol{x})$ and $\widehat{p}_{\mathrm{de}}(\boldsymbol{x})$ *separately* from $\{\boldsymbol{x}_i^{\mathrm{nu}}\}_{i=1}^{n_{\mathrm{nu}}}$ and $\{\boldsymbol{x}_j^{\mathrm{de}}\}_{j=1}^{n_{\mathrm{de}}}$, and then estimating the density ratio by plugging the density estimators into the ratio as

$$\widehat{r}(\boldsymbol{x}) = \frac{\widehat{p}_{\mathrm{nu}}(\boldsymbol{x})}{\widehat{p}_{\mathrm{de}}(\boldsymbol{x})}.$$

This density estimation approach would be an easy and handy method for density-ratio estimation. However, division by an estimated density $\widehat{p}_{\mathrm{de}}(\boldsymbol{x})$ may magnify the estimation error included in $\widehat{p}_{\mathrm{nu}}(\boldsymbol{x})$.

2.1.2 Uniformized Density Estimation

When the denominator density $p^*_{\mathrm{de}}(\boldsymbol{x})$ is uniform, the density ratio $r^*(\boldsymbol{x})$ is proportional to the numerator density $p^*_{\mathrm{nu}}(\boldsymbol{x})$:

$$r^*(\boldsymbol{x}) \propto p^*_{\mathrm{nu}}(\boldsymbol{x}).$$

Thus, if we transform the input variable $\boldsymbol{x}$ to another domain so that the denominator density becomes uniform, we may simply approximate the density ratio by a standard density estimation method (Ćwik and Mielniczuk, 1989; Chen et al., 2009). We refer to this method as *uniformized density estimation*.

When the dimensionality of the input domain is $d = 1$ with a finite domain $[a, b]$, where $-\infty < a < b < \infty$, the above uniformization idea can be implemented using the cumulative distribution function $P^*_{\mathrm{de}}(x)$ of p^*_{de}:

$$P^*_{\mathrm{de}}(x) := \int_a^x p^*_{\mathrm{nu}}(x)\mathrm{d}x.$$

That is, if the denominator input variable x^{de} is transformed to $\widetilde{x}^{\mathrm{de}}$ by $P^*_{\mathrm{de}}(x)$ as $\widetilde{x}^{\mathrm{de}} = P^*_{\mathrm{de}}(x^{\mathrm{de}})$, then $\widetilde{x}^{\mathrm{de}}$ has the uniform density, as illustrated in Figure 2.1.

In practice, the cumulative distribution function $P^*_{\mathrm{de}}(x)$ is unknown, so we may instead use the empirical cumulative distribution function $\widehat{P}_{\mathrm{de}}(x)$ for $\{x^{\mathrm{de}}_j\}_{j=1}^{n_{\mathrm{de}}}$:

$$\widehat{P}_{\mathrm{de}}(x) := \begin{cases} 0 & \text{if } x \leq x^{\mathrm{de}}_1, \\ j/n_{\mathrm{de}} & \text{if } x^{\mathrm{de}}_j < x \leq x^{\mathrm{de}}_{j-1}, \\ 1 & \text{if } x > x^{\mathrm{de}}_{n_{\mathrm{de}}}, \end{cases}$$

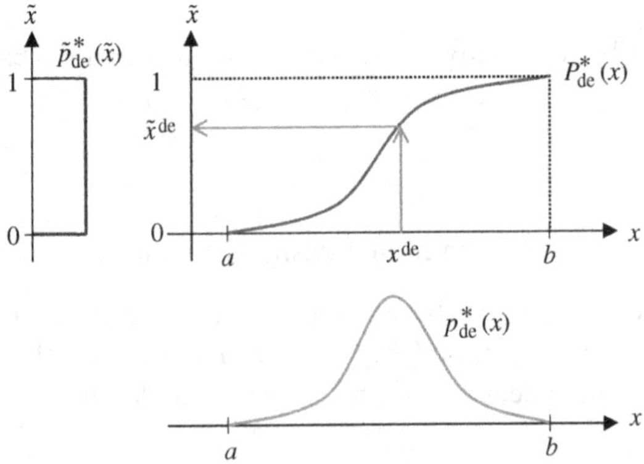

Figure 2.1. Let $\widetilde{x}^{\mathrm{de}} = P^*_{\mathrm{de}}(x^{\mathrm{de}})$, where $P^*_{\mathrm{de}}(x)$ is the cumulative distribution function of $p^*_{\mathrm{nu}}(x)$. When x^{de} follows $p^*_{\mathrm{de}}(x)$, $\widetilde{x}^{\mathrm{de}}$ has a uniform density.

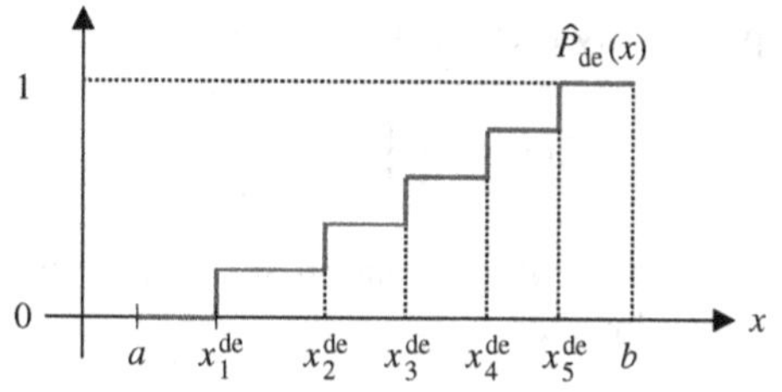

Figure 2.2. Empirical cumulative distribution function $\widehat{P}_{\mathrm{de}}(x)$ for $x_1^{\mathrm{de}} \leq \cdots \leq x_{n_{\mathrm{de}}}^{\mathrm{de}}$.

where we assume that $x_1^{\mathrm{de}} \leq \cdots \leq x_{n_{\mathrm{de}}}^{\mathrm{de}}$ without loss of generality (see Figure 2.2).

Since no division by an estimated quantity is included in the uniformized density estimation approach, it is expected to be more accurate than the ratio of density estimations explained in Section 2.1.1. However, as shown in Ćwik and Mielniczuk (1989) and Chen et al. (2009), these two approaches possess the same non-parametric convergence rate.

2.1.3 Summary

As shown in the previous subsections, density estimation can be used for estimating density ratios. In the rest of this chapter, we consider a standard density estimation problem of estimating $p^*(\boldsymbol{x})$ from its i.i.d. samples $\{\boldsymbol{x}_k\}_{k=1}^n$ and review two approaches to density estimation: the *parametric* approach (Section 2.2) and the *non-parametric* approach (Section 2.3).

2.2 Parametric Approach

The parametric approach to density estimation uses a *parametric model* of probability density functions: $p(\boldsymbol{x};\boldsymbol{\theta})$, where $\boldsymbol{\theta}$ is a parameter in some parameter space Θ. A parametric model $p(\boldsymbol{x};\boldsymbol{\theta})$ is a set of probability density functions specified by $\boldsymbol{\theta}$. Thus, it satisfies $p(\boldsymbol{x};\boldsymbol{\theta}) \geq 0$ and $\int p(\boldsymbol{x};\boldsymbol{\theta})\mathrm{d}\boldsymbol{x} = 1$ for all $\boldsymbol{\theta}$ in Θ.

The goal of *parametric density estimation* is to learn the parameter $\boldsymbol{\theta}$ so that the true density $p^*(\boldsymbol{x})$ is accurately approximated. In the following, we explain two methods: *maximum likelihood estimation* in Section 2.2.1 and *Bayes estimation* in Section 2.2.2. Then the issue of model selection is discussed in Section 2.2.3.

2.2.1 Maximum Likelihood Estimation

The main idea of *maximum likelihood (ML) estimation* is to determine the parameter $\boldsymbol{\theta}$ so that the data at hand are most likely to be generated. To this end, the probability of obtaining $\{\boldsymbol{x}_k\}_{k=1}^n$ from the model $p(\boldsymbol{x};\boldsymbol{\theta})$ needs to be evaluated as a function of $\boldsymbol{\theta}$. Because the samples $\{\boldsymbol{x}_k\}_{k=1}^n$ are assumed to be i.i.d. (see Section 2.1), the data-generating probability is expressed as

$$L(\boldsymbol{\theta}) := \prod_{k=1}^{n} p(\boldsymbol{x}_k;\boldsymbol{\theta}).$$

This is called the *likelihood*. In ML estimation, the parameter $\boldsymbol{\theta}$ is learned so that the likelihood $L(\boldsymbol{\theta})$ is maximized:

$$\widehat{\boldsymbol{\theta}}_{\mathrm{ML}} := \underset{\boldsymbol{\theta}\in\Theta}{\operatorname{argmax}}\ L(\boldsymbol{\theta}).$$

Then the ML density estimator $\widehat{p}_{\mathrm{ML}}(\boldsymbol{x})$ is given by $\widehat{p}_{\mathrm{ML}}(\boldsymbol{x}) = p(\boldsymbol{x};\widehat{\boldsymbol{\theta}}_{\mathrm{ML}})$.

When the number n of samples is large, the likelihood often takes an extremely small value. To avoid any numerical instability caused by this, the *log-likelihood* is often used instead:

$$\log L(\boldsymbol{\theta}) = \sum_{k=1}^{n} \log p(\boldsymbol{x}_k;\boldsymbol{\theta}). \tag{2.1}$$

Because the log function is monotone increasing, the same ML estimator can be obtained by maximizing the log-likelihood, which may be numerically more preferable:

$$\widehat{\boldsymbol{\theta}}_{\mathrm{ML}} = \underset{\boldsymbol{\theta}\in\Theta}{\operatorname{argmax}}\ \log L(\boldsymbol{\theta}).$$

Under some mild assumptions, the ML estimator was shown to possess the following properties:

Consistency: The ML estimator converges in probability to the optimal parameter in the model (i.e., the projection of the true probability density function onto the model) under the *Kullback–Leibler* (KL) divergence (see Section 2.2.3).

Asymptotic unbiasedness: The expectation of the ML estimator converges in probability to the optimal parameter in the model.

Asymptotic efficiency: The ML estimator has the smallest variance among all asymptotic unbiased estimators.[1]

Thus, the ML approach would be a useful method for parametric density estimation. However, the previously mentioned asymptotic properties do not necessarily imply that the ML estimator is accurate in small sample cases.

2.2.2 Bayes Estimation

In the framework of *Bayes estimation* (Bishop, 2006) the parameter $\boldsymbol{\theta}$ is treated as a random variable. Then, the following probabilities can be considered for $\boldsymbol{\theta}$:

$$\pi(\boldsymbol{\theta})\text{: Prior probability,}$$

[1] More precisely, the ML estimator asymptotically achieves the *Cramér-Rao lower bound* for the variance (Cramér, 1946; Rao, 1945).

$p(\boldsymbol{\theta}|D)$: Posterior probability,

$p(D|\boldsymbol{\theta})$: Likelihood,

where $D := \{\boldsymbol{x}_k\}_{k=1}^n$. The likelihood is given in the same way as the ML case:

$$p(D|\boldsymbol{\theta}) = \prod_{k=1}^{n} p(\boldsymbol{x}_k|\boldsymbol{\theta}),$$

where the parametric model is denoted as a conditional density $p(\boldsymbol{x}|\boldsymbol{\theta})$ in the Bayesian approach.

In Bayes estimation, the posterior probability $p(\boldsymbol{\theta}|D)$ corresponds to a learned result because this describes the behavior of parameter $\boldsymbol{\theta}$ *after* knowing the samples D. On the other hand, the prior probability $\pi(\boldsymbol{\theta})$ represents our "belief" in the target learning problem.

By Bayes's theorem, the posterior probability $p(\boldsymbol{\theta}|D)$ can be expressed as

$$p(\boldsymbol{\theta}|D) = \frac{p(D|\boldsymbol{\theta})\pi(\boldsymbol{\theta})}{\int p(D|\boldsymbol{\theta}')\pi(\boldsymbol{\theta}')\mathrm{d}\boldsymbol{\theta}'} = \frac{\prod_{k=1}^{n} p(\boldsymbol{x}_k|\boldsymbol{\theta})\pi(\boldsymbol{\theta})}{\int \prod_{k'=1}^{n} p(\boldsymbol{x}_{k'}|\boldsymbol{\theta}')\pi(\boldsymbol{\theta}')\mathrm{d}\boldsymbol{\theta}'}. \tag{2.2}$$

Based on this expression, the *Bayesian predictive distribution* $\widehat{p}_{\mathrm{Bayes}}(\boldsymbol{x})$ is given as

$$\begin{aligned}\widehat{p}_{\mathrm{Bayes}}(\boldsymbol{x}) &:= \int p(\boldsymbol{x}|\boldsymbol{\theta})p(\boldsymbol{\theta}|D)\mathrm{d}\boldsymbol{\theta} \\ &= \frac{\int p(\boldsymbol{x}|\boldsymbol{\theta})\prod_{k=1}^{n} p(\boldsymbol{x}_k|\boldsymbol{\theta})\pi(\boldsymbol{\theta})\mathrm{d}\boldsymbol{\theta}}{\int \prod_{k'=1}^{n} p(\boldsymbol{x}_{k'}|\boldsymbol{\theta}')\pi(\boldsymbol{\theta}')\mathrm{d}\boldsymbol{\theta}'}. \end{aligned} \tag{2.3}$$

Thus, the parametric model $p(\boldsymbol{x}|\boldsymbol{\theta})$ is averaged over the posterior probability $p(\boldsymbol{\theta}|D)$. This averaging nature would be a peculiarity of Bayes estimation: $\widehat{p}_{\mathrm{Bayes}}(\boldsymbol{x})$ does not necessarily belong to the original parametric model $p(\boldsymbol{x}|\boldsymbol{\theta})$ because a parametric model often forms a *curved* manifold in the space of probability densities (Amari and Nagaoka, 2000). See Figure 2.3 for illustration.

Bayes estimation was shown to be a powerful alternative to ML density estimation. However, its computation is often cumbersome as a result of the integrals involved in Eq. (2.3). To ease this problem, an approximation method called *maximum a posteriori (MAP) estimation* comes in handy – the integral over the posterior probability $p(\boldsymbol{\theta}|D)$ is approximated by the single maximizer of $p(\boldsymbol{\theta}|D)$. Because the denominator $\int \prod_{k'=1}^{n} p(\boldsymbol{x}_{k'}|\boldsymbol{\theta}')\pi(\boldsymbol{\theta}')\mathrm{d}\boldsymbol{\theta}'$ in Eq. (2.2) is independent of $\boldsymbol{\theta}$, the posterior probability $p(\boldsymbol{\theta}|D)$ can be expressed as

$$p(\boldsymbol{\theta}|D) \propto \prod_{k=1}^{n} p(\boldsymbol{x}_k|\boldsymbol{\theta})\pi(\boldsymbol{\theta}),$$

where $\propto$ means "proportional to." Thus, the maximizer of the posterior probability $p(\boldsymbol{\theta}|D)$ is given by

$$\widehat{\boldsymbol{\theta}}_{\mathrm{MAP}} := \underset{\boldsymbol{\theta}\in\Theta}{\mathrm{argmax}} \prod_{k=1}^{n} p(\boldsymbol{x}_k|\boldsymbol{\theta})\pi(\boldsymbol{\theta}).$$

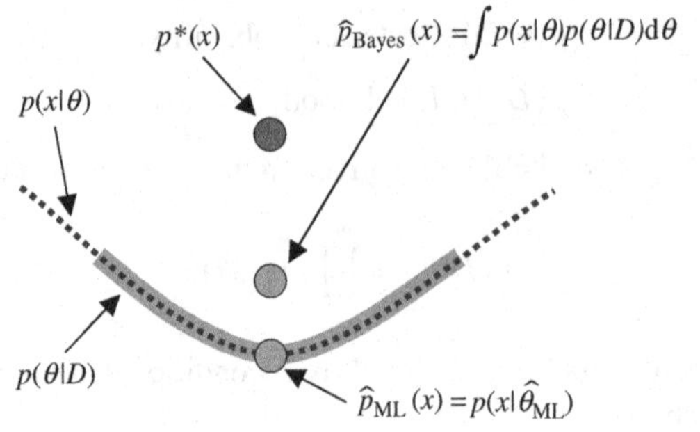

Figure 2.3. The Bayes solution does not necessarily belong to the original parametric model.

Then the MAP solution $\widehat{p}_{\text{MAP}}(\boldsymbol{x})$ is given by $\widehat{p}_{\text{MAP}}(\boldsymbol{x}) := p(\boldsymbol{x}|\widehat{\boldsymbol{\theta}}_{\text{MAP}})$. Because the integral is approximated by a single point, MAP estimation loses the peculiarity of Bayes estimation – the MAP solution is always a member of the parametric model.

The MAP estimator may also be obtained in the "log" domain, possibly in a numerically stable manner:

$$\widehat{\boldsymbol{\theta}}_{\text{MAP}} = \underset{\boldsymbol{\theta}\in\Theta}{\text{argmax}} \left[\prod_{k=1}^{n} p(\boldsymbol{x}_k|\boldsymbol{\theta}) + \log \pi(\boldsymbol{\theta}) \right].$$

Because the first term is the log-likelihood, the MAP solution can be regarded as a variant of the ML method with a "penalty" induced by the prior probability $\pi(\boldsymbol{\theta})$. For this reason, MAP estimation is also called *penalized ML estimation*.

2.2.3 Model Selection

Parametric estimation works very well when the model at hand is *correctly specified*, that is, there exists a parameter $\boldsymbol{\theta}^*$ such that $p(\boldsymbol{x};\boldsymbol{\theta}^*) = p^*(\boldsymbol{x})$. Otherwise, a good approximator of the true density in the model may be obtained.[2] However, when the model at hand is strongly *misspecified*, the best solution in the model is still a poor approximation, and thus the parametric method is not reliable. In such cases, different models may be used for obtaining better approximations. Here we show how appropriate models are chosen based on data samples.

Akaike Information Criterion

When choosing an appropriate model, it is important to evaluate how good a candidate model is. As a performance measure, let us employ the *Kullback–Leibler* (KL) divergence (Kullback and Leibler, 1951) from the true density $p^*(\boldsymbol{x})$ to its

[2] As explained in Section 2.2.2, the estimated density is not necessarily included in the model in the case of Bayes estimation.

approximation $\widehat{p}(\boldsymbol{x})$:

$$\mathrm{KL}(p^*\|\widehat{p}) := \int p^*(\boldsymbol{x}) \log \frac{p^*(\boldsymbol{x})}{\widehat{p}(\boldsymbol{x})} \mathrm{d}\boldsymbol{x}. \tag{2.4}$$

The use of the KL divergence as a performance measure would be natural in the ML framework because it is consistent with the log-likelihood. That is, the KL divergence from $p^*(\boldsymbol{x})$ to $p(\boldsymbol{x};\boldsymbol{\theta})$ can be regarded as the expectation of $\log \frac{p^*(\boldsymbol{x})}{p(\boldsymbol{x};\boldsymbol{\theta})}$ over the true density $p^*(\boldsymbol{x})$. If this expectation is approximated by the empirical average over i.i.d. samples $\{\boldsymbol{x}_k\}_{k=1}^n$, we have

$$\begin{aligned}\widehat{\mathrm{KL}}(p^*\|p) &:= \frac{1}{n}\sum_{k=1}^n \log \frac{p^*(\boldsymbol{x}_k)}{p(\boldsymbol{x}_k;\boldsymbol{\theta})} \\ &= \frac{1}{n}\sum_{k=1}^n \log p^*(\boldsymbol{x}_k) - \frac{1}{n}\sum_{k=1}^n \log p(\boldsymbol{x}_k;\boldsymbol{\theta}). \end{aligned} \tag{2.5}$$

Note that, by the *law of large numbers*, $\widehat{\mathrm{KL}}(p^*\|p)$ converges in probability to $\mathrm{KL}(p^*\|p)$ as n tends to infinity. Since the first term in Eq. (2.5) does not depend on the parameter $\boldsymbol{\theta}$, minimizing $\widehat{\mathrm{KL}}(p^*\|p)$ with respect to $\boldsymbol{\theta}$ is equivalent to maximizing the log-likelihood [see Eq. (2.1)]:

$$\underset{\boldsymbol{\theta}\in\Theta}{\operatorname{argmax}}\ \widehat{\mathrm{KL}}(p^*\|p) = \underset{\boldsymbol{\theta}\in\Theta}{\operatorname{argmax}}\ \log L(\boldsymbol{\theta}).$$

From this, consistency of the ML estimator under the KL divergence may be intuitively understood.

Under the above setup, the model that minimizes the KL divergence may be regarded as the best model. However, the KL divergence cannot be computed directly because it includes the unknown true density $p^*(\boldsymbol{x})$. Let us decompose the KL divergence as

$$\mathrm{KL}(p^*\|\widehat{p}) = \int p^*(\boldsymbol{x}) \log p^*(\boldsymbol{x}) \mathrm{d}\boldsymbol{x} - \int p^*(\boldsymbol{x}) \log \widehat{p}(\boldsymbol{x}) \mathrm{d}\boldsymbol{x},$$

where the first term is the negative *entropy* of $p^*(\boldsymbol{x})$ and is independent of $\widehat{p}(\boldsymbol{x})$. Since we are interested in estimating the KL divergence as a function of $\widehat{p}(\boldsymbol{x})$, the entropy term can be safely ignored. Thus, the model that minimizes the second term (denoted by KL′) is now regarded as the best one:

$$\mathrm{KL}' := -\int p^*(\boldsymbol{x}) \log \widehat{p}(\boldsymbol{x}) \mathrm{d}\boldsymbol{x}. \tag{2.6}$$

KL′ may be estimated by the negative log-likelihood (2.1). However, simply using the negative log-likelihood as an approximation to KL′ for model selection is not appropriate because the more complex the model is, the smaller the negative log-likelihood is. Thus, model selection based on the negative log-likelihood merely ends up always choosing the most complex model at hand, which is meaningless in practice.

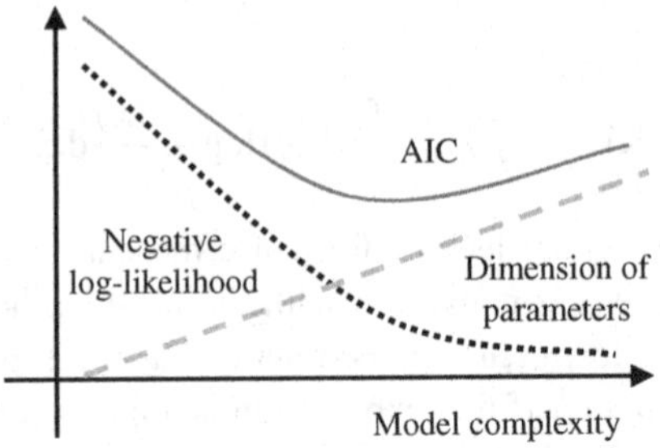

Figure 2.4. Akaike information criterion.

A more sensible and accurate approximation to KL′ is given by the *Akaike information criterion*[3] (AIC; Akaike, 1974):

$$\mathrm{AIC} := -\sum_{k=1}^{n} \log p(\boldsymbol{x}_k; \widehat{\boldsymbol{\theta}}_{\mathrm{ML}}) + \dim \boldsymbol{\theta},$$

where $\dim \boldsymbol{\theta}$ denotes the dimensionality of parameter $\boldsymbol{\theta}$. Since the first term of the AIC is the negative log-likelihood, the AIC can be regarded as an additive modification of the negative log-likelihood by the dimensionality of parameters. By this modification, the AIC can avoid always resulting in choosing the most complex model (Figure 2.4). The implementation of the AIC is very simple, and thus is practically useful. Various generalizations and extensions of the AIC have been proposed by several researchers (e.g., Takeuchi, 1976; Shibata, 1989; Murata et al., 1994; Konishi and Kitagawa, 1996; Ishiguro et al., 1997).

Empirical Bayes Method and Bayesian Information Criterion

In the Bayesian framework, the choice of the prior probability is as critical as the choice of parametric models. Let us use a prior probability parameterized by a hyperparameter $\boldsymbol{\beta}$: $\pi(\boldsymbol{\theta}; \boldsymbol{\beta})$. The hyperparameter may be optimized based on the likelihood principle; that is, it is determined so that the probability of obtaining the current data $D := \{\boldsymbol{x}_k\}_{k=1}^{n}$ is maximized:

$$\boldsymbol{\beta}_{\mathrm{EB}} := \underset{\boldsymbol{\theta} \in \Theta}{\mathrm{argmax}}\ p(D; \boldsymbol{\beta}).$$

This approach is called the *empirical Bayes* method or *type II maximum likelihood estimation*. $p(D; \boldsymbol{\beta})$ is called the *evidence* or the *marginal likelihood* (Bishop, 2006).

The marginal likelihood can be expressed as

$$p(D; \boldsymbol{\beta}) = \int \prod_{k=1}^{n} p(\boldsymbol{x}_k | \boldsymbol{\theta}) \pi(\boldsymbol{\theta}; \boldsymbol{\beta}) \mathrm{d}\boldsymbol{\theta},$$

[3] Although the criterion multiplied by 2 is the original AIC, we omitted the factor 2 for simplicity.

which can be directly used for model selection. However, computing the marginal likelihood is often cumbersome because of the integral. To ease this problem, the *Laplace approximation* is commonly used in practice (MacKay, 2003). The Laplace approximation is based on the second-order Taylor expansion of $\log p(D;\boldsymbol{\beta})$ around the MAP solution $\widehat{\boldsymbol{\theta}}_{\mathrm{MAP}}$. The Laplace approximation of the log-marginal-likelihood is given by

$$\log p(D;\boldsymbol{\beta}) \approx \sum_{k=1}^{n} \log p(\boldsymbol{x}_k|\widehat{\boldsymbol{\theta}}_{\mathrm{MAP}}) + \log \pi(\widehat{\boldsymbol{\theta}}_{\mathrm{MAP}};\boldsymbol{\beta}) + \frac{\log(2\pi)}{2}\dim\boldsymbol{\theta} - \frac{1}{2}\log\det(-\boldsymbol{H}), \tag{2.7}$$

where $\det(\cdot)$ denotes the determinant of a matrix. $\boldsymbol{H}$ is the matrix of size $\dim\boldsymbol{\theta} \times \dim\boldsymbol{\theta}$ with the (ℓ,ℓ')-th element given by

$$H_{\ell,\ell'} := \frac{\partial}{\partial\theta_\ell}\frac{\partial}{\partial\theta_{\ell'}}\left(\sum_{k=1}^{n}\log p(\boldsymbol{x}_k|\boldsymbol{\theta}) + \log\pi(\boldsymbol{\theta};\boldsymbol{\beta})\right)\Bigg|_{\boldsymbol{\theta}=\widehat{\boldsymbol{\theta}}_{\mathrm{MAP}}},$$

where θ_ℓ denotes the ℓ-th element of $\boldsymbol{\theta}$. Note that $\boldsymbol{H}$ corresponds to the *Hessian matrix* of $\log p(\boldsymbol{\theta}|D)$.

If higher order terms are ignored in Eq. (2.7), a much simpler criterion can be obtained. The negative of the remaining lower order terms is called the *Bayesian information criterion* (BIC; Schwarz, 1978):

$$\mathrm{BIC} := -\sum_{k=1}^{n}\log p(\boldsymbol{x}_k|\widehat{\boldsymbol{\theta}}_{\mathrm{ML}}) + \frac{\log n}{2}\dim\boldsymbol{\theta}.$$

It is noteworthy that the first term of the BIC is the negative log-likelihood, which is the same as the AIC. Thus, the difference between the AIC and the BIC is only the second term. However, because the framework of the AIC and the BIC is completely different, one cannot simply conclude that one is better than the other (Shibata, 1981).

2.3 Non-Parametric Approach

The parametric approach would be a useful method of density estimation when combined with model selection. Another possible approach is not to use parametric models, but *directly* approximate a density function. Such an approach is called *non-parametric density estimation* (Härdle et al., 2004).

The basic idea of non-parametric density estimation is to consider a local region $\mathcal{R}$ in the domain $\mathcal{X}$. Let V be the *volume* of the region $\mathcal{R}$, and let P be the probability that a random sample following $p^*(\boldsymbol{x})$ falls into the region $\mathcal{R}$ [Figure 2.5(a)]. Then, using a point $\boldsymbol{x}'$ in the region $\mathcal{R}$, P can be approximated as $P \approx Vp^*(\boldsymbol{x}')$ [see Figure 2.5(b)].

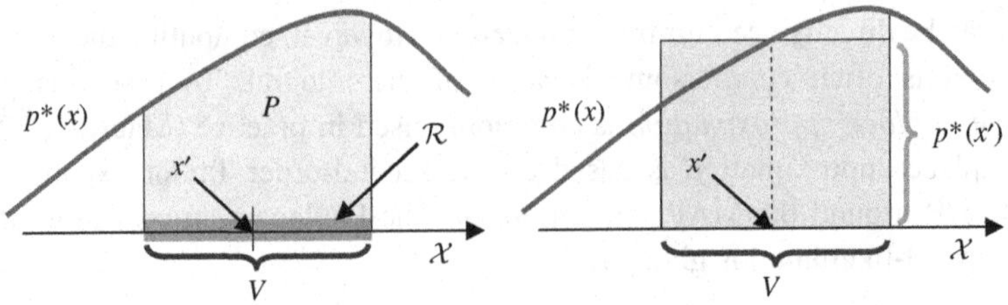

(a) Notation (b) Rectangle approximation

Figure 2.5. Non-parametric density estimation.

Similarly, for m being the number of samples falling into the region $\mathcal{R}$ among $\{\boldsymbol{x}_k\}_{k=1}^n$, P can be approximated as $P \approx m/n$. Together, the probability density $p^*(\boldsymbol{x}')$ at a point $\boldsymbol{x}'$ in the region $\mathcal{R}$ can be approximated as $p^*(\boldsymbol{x}') \approx m/(nV)$.

The approximation quality depends on the choice of the local region $\mathcal{R}$ (and thus V and m). In the following, we describe two approaches to determining $\mathcal{R}$: *kernel density estimation* in Section 2.3.1 and *nearest neighbor density estimation* in Section 2.3.2. Then the issue of hyperparameter selection is discussed in Section 2.3.3.

2.3.1 Kernel Density Estimation

Let us employ a hypercube with edge length h as a local region $\mathcal{R}$. Then its volume V is given by $V = h^d$, where d is the dimensionality of the input domain $\mathcal{X}$ and

$$m = \sum_{k=1}^{n} W\left(\frac{\boldsymbol{x} - \boldsymbol{x}_k}{h}\right),$$

where, for $\boldsymbol{x} = (x^{(1)}, \ldots, x^{(d)})^\top$, $W(\boldsymbol{x})$ is the *Parzen window function* defined as

$$W(\boldsymbol{x}) = \begin{cases} 1 & \text{if } \max(|x^{(1)}|, \ldots, |x^{(d)}|) \leq 1/2, \\ 0 & \text{otherwise.} \end{cases}$$

This method is called *Parzen window estimation*.

A drawback of Parzen window estimation is its discrete nature caused by the Parzen window function. *Kernel density estimation* (KDE) is a "smooth" variant of Parzen window estimation, where the Parzen window function is replaced by a smooth *kernel function* such as the *Gaussian kernel*:

$$K(\boldsymbol{x}, \boldsymbol{x}') = \exp\left(-\frac{\|\boldsymbol{x} - \boldsymbol{x}'\|^2}{2\sigma^2}\right).$$

The KDE solution for the Gaussian kernel is given by

$$\widehat{p}_{\mathrm{KDE}}(\boldsymbol{x}) := \frac{1}{n(2\pi\sigma^2)^{d/2}} \sum_{k=1}^{n} K(\boldsymbol{x}, \boldsymbol{x}_k).$$

2.3.2 Nearest Neighbor Density Estimation

Nearest neighbor density estimation (NNDE) uses the hypersphere with radius τ as a local region $\mathcal{R}$. Its volume V is given by

$$V = \frac{\pi^{\frac{d}{2}}\tau^d}{\Gamma(\frac{d}{2}+1)},$$

where $\Gamma(\alpha)$ denotes the *gamma function*:

$$\Gamma(\alpha) := \int_0^\infty u^{\alpha-1}e^{-u}du.$$

Since $\Gamma(t) = (t-1)!$ for any positive integer t, the gamma function can be regarded as an extension of the *factorial* to real numbers. The radius τ is set to the distance to the m-th closest sample to the center (i.e., the hypersphere has the minimum radius with m samples being contained). Then NNDE is expressed as

$$\widehat{p}_{\mathrm{NNDE}}(\boldsymbol{x}) = \frac{m\Gamma(\frac{d}{2}+1)}{n\pi^{\frac{d}{2}}\tau^d}.$$

2.3.3 Cross-Validation

The performance of KDE and NNDE depends on the choice of hyperparameters such as the kernel width σ in KDE or the number m of nearest neighbors in NNDE. For choosing the hyperparameter values appropriately, it is important to evaluate how good a candidate the hyperparameter value is. As a performance measure, let us again use the KL divergence defined by Eq. (2.4).

Cross-validation (CV) is a general method of estimating the second term of the KL divergence [KL$'$ in Eq. (2.6)] as follows: First, the samples $D = \{\boldsymbol{x}_k\}_{k=1}^n$ are divided into T disjoint subsets $\{D_t\}_{t=1}^T$ of approximately the same size. Then a density estimator $\widehat{p}_t(\boldsymbol{x})$ is obtained from $D \backslash D_t$ (i.e., all samples without D_t), and its log-likelihood for the hold-out samples D_t is computed (see Figure 2.6):

$$\widetilde{\mathrm{KL}}'_t := \frac{1}{|D_t|}\sum_{\boldsymbol{x}\in D_t}\log\widehat{p}_t(\boldsymbol{x}).$$

This procedure is repeated for $t = 1, \ldots, T$, and the average of the above hold-out log-likelihood over all t is computed as

$$\widetilde{\mathrm{KL}}' := \frac{1}{T}\sum_{t=1}^T \widetilde{\mathrm{KL}}'_t.$$

Then the hyperparameter value that maximizes $\widetilde{\mathrm{KL}}'$ is chosen. Note that the above $\widetilde{\mathrm{KL}}'$ (and also each $\widetilde{\mathrm{KL}}'_t$) is an almost unbiased estimator of KL$'$ (Härdle et al., 2004).

Asymptotically, the AIC and CV were shown to behave similarly (Stone, 1974). However, CV is more widely applicable and often accurate, although it

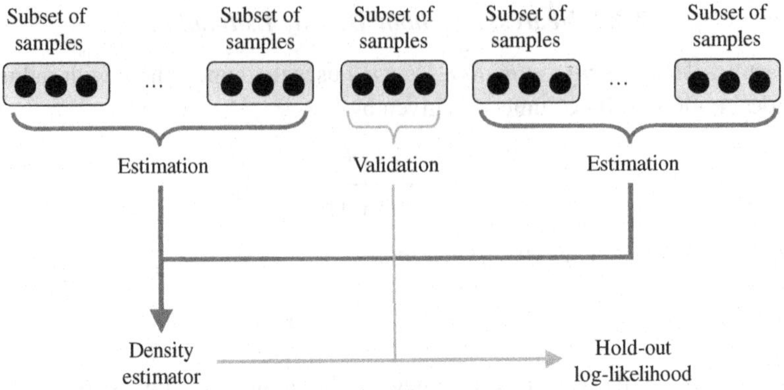

Figure 2.6. Cross-validation. Hold-out estimation is carried out for all subsets, and the average hold-out log-likelihood is output as an estimator of KL′.

is computationally more expensive than the AIC as a result of the necessity of repetitions.

2.4 Numerical Examples

In this section we illustrate the numerical behavior of KDE-based density-ratio estimation described in Section 2.3.1.

Let us consider a one-dimensional example (i.e., $d = 1$) and suppose that the two densities $p^*_{\mathrm{nu}}(x)$ and $p^*_{\mathrm{de}}(x)$ are defined as

$$p^*_{\mathrm{nu}}(x) = N(x;1,1^2) \quad \text{and} \quad p^*_{\mathrm{de}}(x) = N(x;0,2^2),$$

where $N(x;\mu,\sigma^2)$ denotes the Gaussian density with mean μ and variance σ^2. The true densities are plotted in Figure 2.7(a), while the true density ratio $r^*(x)$ is plotted in Figure 2.7(b).

Let $n_{\mathrm{nu}} = n_{\mathrm{de}} = 200$. For density-ratio estimation we use Gaussian kernel KDE: $\widehat{r}(x) = \widehat{p}_{\mathrm{nu}}(x)/\widehat{p}_{\mathrm{de}}(x)$, where

$$\widehat{p}_{\mathrm{nu}}(x) = \frac{1}{n_{\mathrm{nu}}(2\pi\sigma^2_{\mathrm{nu}})^{d/2}} \sum_{\ell=1}^{n_{\mathrm{nu}}} \exp\left(-\frac{(x - x^{\mathrm{nu}}_{\ell})^2}{2\sigma^2_{\mathrm{nu}}}\right),$$

$$\widehat{p}_{\mathrm{de}}(x) = \frac{1}{n_{\mathrm{de}}(2\pi\sigma^2_{\mathrm{de}})^{d/2}} \sum_{\ell=1}^{n_{\mathrm{de}}} \exp\left(-\frac{(x - x^{\mathrm{de}}_{\ell})^2}{2\sigma^2_{\mathrm{de}}}\right).$$

The Gaussian widths σ_{nu} and σ_{de} are chosen by 5-fold cross-validation (see Section 2.3.3). The density functions estimated by KDE, $\widehat{p}_{\mathrm{nu}}(x)$ and $\widehat{p}_{\mathrm{de}}(x)$, are illustrated in Figure 2.7(a), and the density-ratio function estimated by KDE, $\widehat{r}(x)$, is plotted in Figure 2.7(b). The results show that KDE gives reasonably good approximations to the true density functions and thus the true density-ratio function.

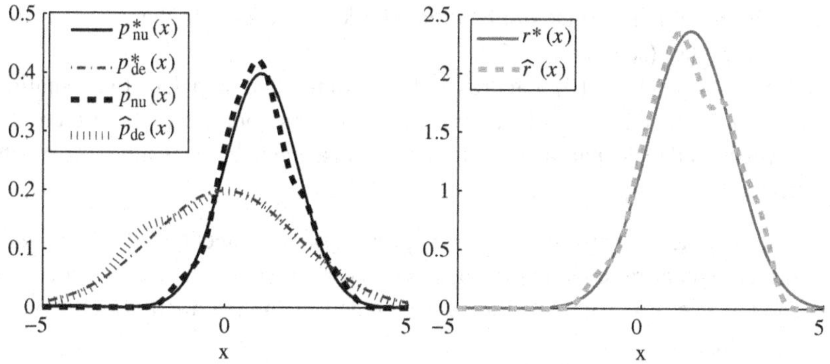

(a) True and estimated densities (b) True and estimated density ratios

Figure 2.7. Numerical example of KDE.

2.5 Remarks

Density-ratio estimation based on density estimation would be an easy and convenient approach: just estimating the numerator and denominator densities separately from their samples and taking the ratio of the estimated densities. However, its two-step structure may not be suitable because density estimation in the first step is carried out without regard to the second step of taking their ratio. For example, optimal model/hyperparameter selection in density estimation is not necessarily the best choice for density-ratio estimation. Furthermore, the approximation error produced in the density estimation step can be increased by taking the ratio – division by an estimated quantity often makes an estimator unreliable. This problem seems to be critical when the dimension of the input domain is high, because density values tend to be small in high-dimensional cases, and thus its reciprocal is vulnerable to a small error.

To overcome these limitations of the density estimation approach, one-shot procedures of directly estimating the density ratio *without* going through density estimation would be sensible and more promising. Methods following this idea will be described in the following chapters.

It was advocated that one should avoid solving more difficult intermediate problems when solving a target problem (Vapnik, 1998). This statement is sometimes referred to as *Vapnik's principle*, and the *support vector machine* (SVM; Cortes and Vapnik, 1995; Vapnik, 1998; Schölkopf and Smola, 2002) would be a successful example of this principle – instead of estimating a data-generation model, SVM directly models the decision boundary, which is sufficient for pattern recognition. Density estimation (estimating the data-generation model) is a more general and thus difficult problem than pattern recognition (learning the decision boundary).

If we followed Vapnik's principle, directly estimating the ratio $r^*(\boldsymbol{x})$ would be more promising than estimating the two densities $p^*_{\mathrm{nu}}(\boldsymbol{x})$ and $p^*_{\mathrm{de}}(\boldsymbol{x})$, because knowing two densities $p^*_{\mathrm{nu}}(\boldsymbol{x})$ and $p^*_{\mathrm{de}}(\boldsymbol{x})$ implies knowing the ratio $r^*(\boldsymbol{x})$, but not vice versa; the ratio $r^*(\boldsymbol{x})$ cannot be uniquely decomposed into the two densities $p^*_{\mathrm{nu}}(\boldsymbol{x})$ and $p^*_{\mathrm{de}}(\boldsymbol{x})$ (see Figure 1.5).

In Kanamori et al. (2010), the pros and cons of the two-step density estimation approach and one-shot direct density ratio estimation approaches were theoretically investigated in the parametric framework. In a nutshell, the theoretical results showed the following:

- The two-step density estimation approach is more accurate than one-shot direct density-ratio estimation approaches when *correctly specified* density models (i.e., the true densities are included in the parametric models) are available.
- The one-shot direct density-ratio estimation approach shown in Chapter 5 is more accurate than the two-step density estimation approach when density/density-ratio models are misspecified.

These theoretical results will be explained in more detail in Chapter 13.

Since correctly specified density models may not be available in practice, the one-shot direct density-ratio estimation approaches explained in the following chapters would be more promising than the two-step density estimation approach described.

3

Moment Matching

In this chapter we describe a framework of density-ratio estimation without going through density estimation based on *moment matching*. In Section 3.1, the framework of moment matching is explained. Then, a finite-order approach to moment matching is introduced in Section 3.2, and an infinite-order moment matching method is shown in Section 3.3. Numerical examples of moment matching methods are shown in Section 3.4, and the chapter is concluded in Section 3.5.

3.1 Basic Framework

Suppose that a one-dimensional random variable x is drawn from a probability distribution with density $p^*(x)$. Then the k-th order moment of x about the origin is defined by

$$\int x^k p^*(x)\mathrm{d}x.$$

Note that two distributions are equivalent if and only if all moments (i.e., for $k = 1, 2, \ldots$) agree with each other.

The moment matching approach to density-ratio estimation tries to match the moments of $p^*_{\mathrm{nu}}(\boldsymbol{x})$ and $p^*_{\mathrm{de}}(\boldsymbol{x})$ via a "transformation" function $r(\boldsymbol{x})$ (Qin, 1998). More specifically, using the true density ratio $r^*(\boldsymbol{x})$, $p^*_{\mathrm{nu}}(\boldsymbol{x})$ can be expressed as

$$p^*_{\mathrm{nu}}(\boldsymbol{x}) = r^*(\boldsymbol{x})p^*_{\mathrm{de}}(\boldsymbol{x}).$$

Thus, for a density-ratio model $r(\boldsymbol{x})$, matching the moments of $p^*_{\mathrm{nu}}(\boldsymbol{x})$ and $r(\boldsymbol{x})p^*_{\mathrm{de}}(\boldsymbol{x})$ gives a good approximation to the true density ratio $r^*(\boldsymbol{x})$. A schematic illustration of the moment-matching approach is described in Figure 3.1.

3.2 Finite-Order Approach

In this section we describe methods of finite-order moment matching for density-ratio estimation. In Section 3.2.1, the case of a *fixed design*, that is, estimating

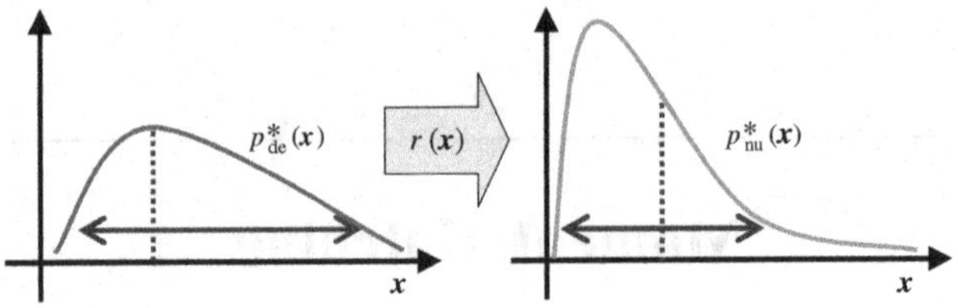

Figure 3.1. The idea of moment matching. The moments of $r(\boldsymbol{x})p^*_{\mathrm{de}}(\boldsymbol{x})$ are matched with those of $p^*_{\mathrm{nu}}(\boldsymbol{x})$.

density ratio values only at sample points, is considered. In Section 3.2.2, the case of *induction*, that is, estimating the entire density ratio function, is considered.

3.2.1 Fixed Design

Here, we describe a finite-order moment matching method under the *fixed-design* setup, where density-ratio values only at the denominator sample points $\{\boldsymbol{x}_j^{\mathrm{de}}\}_{j=1}^{n_{\mathrm{de}}}$ are estimated.

The simplest implementation of moment matching would be to match the first-order moment (i.e., the mean):

$$\underset{r}{\mathrm{argmin}} \left\| \int \boldsymbol{x} r(\boldsymbol{x}) p^*_{\mathrm{de}}(\boldsymbol{x}) \mathrm{d}\boldsymbol{x} - \int \boldsymbol{x} p^*_{\mathrm{nu}}(\boldsymbol{x}) \mathrm{d}\boldsymbol{x} \right\|^2,$$

where $\|\cdot\|$ denotes the Euclidean norm. Its non-linear variant can be obtained using some non-linear function $\phi(\boldsymbol{x}) : \mathbb{R}^d \to \mathbb{R}$ as

$$\underset{r}{\mathrm{argmin}} \left(\int \phi(\boldsymbol{x}) r(\boldsymbol{x}) p^*_{\mathrm{de}}(\boldsymbol{x}) \mathrm{d}\boldsymbol{x} - \int \phi(\boldsymbol{x}) p^*_{\mathrm{nu}}(\boldsymbol{x}) \mathrm{d}\boldsymbol{x} \right)^2.$$

This non-linear method can be easily extended to multiple components by using a vector-valued function $\boldsymbol{\phi}(\boldsymbol{x}) : \mathbb{R}^d \to \mathbb{R}^t$ as

$$\underset{r}{\mathrm{argmin}}\ \mathrm{MM}'(r),$$

where

$$\mathrm{MM}'(r) := \left\| \int \boldsymbol{\phi}(\boldsymbol{x}) r(\boldsymbol{x}) p^*_{\mathrm{de}}(\boldsymbol{x}) \mathrm{d}\boldsymbol{x} - \int \boldsymbol{\phi}(\boldsymbol{x}) p^*_{\mathrm{nu}}(\boldsymbol{x}) \mathrm{d}\boldsymbol{x} \right\|^2.$$

"MM" stands for "moment matching." Let us ignore the irrelevant constant in $\mathrm{MM}'(r)$ and define the rest as $\mathrm{MM}(r)$:

$$\begin{aligned} \mathrm{MM}(r) := & \left\| \int \boldsymbol{\phi}(\boldsymbol{x}) r(\boldsymbol{x}) p^*_{\mathrm{de}}(\boldsymbol{x}) \mathrm{d}\boldsymbol{x} \right\|^2 \\ & - 2 \left\langle \int \boldsymbol{\phi}(\boldsymbol{x}) r(\boldsymbol{x}) p^*_{\mathrm{de}}(\boldsymbol{x}) \mathrm{d}\boldsymbol{x}, \int \boldsymbol{\phi}(\boldsymbol{x}) p^*_{\mathrm{nu}}(\boldsymbol{x}) \mathrm{d}\boldsymbol{x} \right\rangle, \end{aligned}$$

where $\langle \cdot, \cdot \rangle$ denotes the inner product.

In practice, the expectations over $p^*_{\mathrm{nu}}(\boldsymbol{x})$ and $p^*_{\mathrm{de}}(\boldsymbol{x})$ in $\mathrm{MM}(r)$ are replaced by sample averages. That is, for an n_{de}-dimensional vector

$$\boldsymbol{r}^*_{\mathrm{de}} := (r^*(\boldsymbol{x}^{\mathrm{de}}_1), \ldots, r^*(\boldsymbol{x}^{\mathrm{de}}_{n_{\mathrm{de}}}))^\top,$$

where $^\top$ denotes the transpose, an estimator $\widehat{\boldsymbol{r}}_{\mathrm{de}}$ of $\boldsymbol{r}^*_{\mathrm{de}}$ can be obtained by solving the following optimization problem:

$$\widehat{\boldsymbol{r}}_{\mathrm{de}} := \underset{\boldsymbol{r} \in \mathbb{R}^{n_{\mathrm{de}}}}{\mathrm{argmin}}\ \widehat{\mathrm{MM}}(\boldsymbol{r}), \tag{3.1}$$

where

$$\widehat{\mathrm{MM}}(\boldsymbol{r}) := \frac{1}{n^2_{\mathrm{de}}} \boldsymbol{r}^\top \boldsymbol{\Phi}^\top_{\mathrm{de}} \boldsymbol{\Phi}_{\mathrm{de}} \boldsymbol{r} - \frac{2}{n_{\mathrm{de}} n_{\mathrm{nu}}} \boldsymbol{r}^\top \boldsymbol{\Phi}^\top_{\mathrm{de}} \boldsymbol{\Phi}_{\mathrm{nu}} \boldsymbol{1}_{n_{\mathrm{nu}}}. \tag{3.2}$$

$\boldsymbol{1}_n$ denotes the n-dimensional vector with all ones, and $\boldsymbol{\Phi}_{\mathrm{nu}}$ and $\boldsymbol{\Phi}_{\mathrm{de}}$ are the $t \times n_{\mathrm{nu}}$ and $t \times n_{\mathrm{de}}$ *design matrices* defined by

$$\boldsymbol{\Phi}_{\mathrm{nu}} := (\boldsymbol{\phi}(\boldsymbol{x}^{\mathrm{nu}}_1), \ldots, \boldsymbol{\phi}(\boldsymbol{x}^{\mathrm{nu}}_{n_{\mathrm{nu}}})),$$
$$\boldsymbol{\Phi}_{\mathrm{de}} := (\boldsymbol{\phi}(\boldsymbol{x}^{\mathrm{de}}_1), \ldots, \boldsymbol{\phi}(\boldsymbol{x}^{\mathrm{de}}_{n_{\mathrm{de}}})),$$

respectively. Taking the derivative of the objective function (3.2) with respect to $\boldsymbol{r}$ and setting it to zero, we have

$$\frac{2}{n^2_{\mathrm{de}}} \boldsymbol{\Phi}^\top_{\mathrm{de}} \boldsymbol{\Phi}_{\mathrm{de}} \boldsymbol{r} - \frac{2}{n_{\mathrm{de}} n_{\mathrm{nu}}} \boldsymbol{\Phi}^\top_{\mathrm{de}} \boldsymbol{\Phi}_{\mathrm{nu}} \boldsymbol{1}_{n_{\mathrm{nu}}} = \boldsymbol{0}_t,$$

where $\boldsymbol{0}_t$ denotes the t-dimensional vector with all zeros. Solving this equation with respect to $\boldsymbol{r}$, one can obtain the solution analytically as

$$\widehat{\boldsymbol{r}}_{\mathrm{de}} = \frac{n_{\mathrm{de}}}{n_{\mathrm{nu}}} (\boldsymbol{\Phi}^\top_{\mathrm{de}} \boldsymbol{\Phi}_{\mathrm{de}})^{-1} \boldsymbol{\Phi}^\top_{\mathrm{de}} \boldsymbol{\Phi}_{\mathrm{nu}} \boldsymbol{1}_{n_{\mathrm{nu}}}.$$

One may add a normalization constraint $\frac{1}{n_{\mathrm{de}}} \boldsymbol{1}^\top_{n_{\mathrm{de}}} \boldsymbol{r} = 1$ to the optimization problem (3.1). Then the optimization problem becomes a *convex linearly constrained quadratic program*. Because there is no known method for obtaining the analytic-form solution for general convex linearly constrained quadratic programs, a numerical solver may be needed to compute the solution. Furthermore, a non-negativity constraint $\boldsymbol{r} \geq \boldsymbol{0}_{n_{\mathrm{de}}}$ and/or an upper bound for a positive constant B, that is, $\boldsymbol{r} \leq B\boldsymbol{1}_{n_{\mathrm{de}}}$, may also be incorporated in the optimization problem (3.1), where inequalities for vectors are applied in the element-wise manner. Even with these modifications, the optimization problem is still a convex, linearly constrained quadratic program. Therefore, its solution can be computed numerically by standard optimization software.

3.2.2 Induction

The fixed-design method described in the previous section gives estimates of the density-ratio values only at the denominator sample points $\{\boldsymbol{x}^{\mathrm{de}}_j\}^{n_{\mathrm{de}}}_{j=1}$. Here we describe a finite-order moment matching method under the *induction* setup, where the entire density-ratio function $r^*(\boldsymbol{x})$ is estimated.

We use the following linear density-ratio model for density-ratio function learning:

$$r(\boldsymbol{x}) = \sum_{\ell=1}^{b} \theta_\ell \psi_\ell(\boldsymbol{x}) = \boldsymbol{\psi}(\boldsymbol{x})^\top \boldsymbol{\theta},$$

where $\boldsymbol{\psi}(\boldsymbol{x}) : \mathbb{R}^d \to \mathbb{R}^b$ is a basis function vector and $\boldsymbol{\theta}$ $(\in \mathbb{R}^b)$ is a parameter vector. We assume that the basis functions are non-negative: $\boldsymbol{\psi}(\boldsymbol{x}) \geq \boldsymbol{0}_b$. Then model outputs at $\{\boldsymbol{x}_j^{\mathrm{de}}\}_{j=1}^{n_{\mathrm{de}}}$ are expressed in terms of the parameter vector $\boldsymbol{\theta}$ as

$$(r(\boldsymbol{x}_1^{\mathrm{de}}), \ldots, r(\boldsymbol{x}_{n_{\mathrm{de}}}^{\mathrm{de}}))^\top = \boldsymbol{\Psi}_{\mathrm{de}}^\top \boldsymbol{\theta},$$

where $\boldsymbol{\Psi}_{\mathrm{de}}$ is the $b \times n_{\mathrm{de}}$ *design matrix* defined by

$$\boldsymbol{\Psi}_{\mathrm{de}} := (\boldsymbol{\psi}(\boldsymbol{x}_1^{\mathrm{de}}), \ldots, \boldsymbol{\psi}(\boldsymbol{x}_{n_{\mathrm{de}}}^{\mathrm{de}})). \tag{3.3}$$

Then, following Eq. (3.1), the parameter $\boldsymbol{\theta}$ is learned as

$$\widehat{\boldsymbol{\theta}} := \underset{\boldsymbol{\theta} \in \mathbb{R}^b}{\mathrm{argmin}} \left[\frac{1}{n_{\mathrm{de}}^2} \boldsymbol{\theta}^\top \boldsymbol{\Psi}_{\mathrm{de}} \boldsymbol{\Phi}_{\mathrm{de}}^\top \boldsymbol{\Phi}_{\mathrm{de}} \boldsymbol{\Psi}_{\mathrm{de}}^\top \boldsymbol{\theta} - \frac{2}{n_{\mathrm{de}} n_{\mathrm{nu}}} \boldsymbol{\theta}^\top \boldsymbol{\Psi}_{\mathrm{de}} \boldsymbol{\Phi}_{\mathrm{de}}^\top \boldsymbol{\Phi}_{\mathrm{nu}} \boldsymbol{1}_{n_{\mathrm{nu}}} \right]. \tag{3.4}$$

Taking the derivative of the above objective function with respect to $\boldsymbol{\theta}$ and setting it to zero, we have the solution $\widehat{\boldsymbol{\theta}}$ analytically as

$$\widehat{\boldsymbol{\theta}} = \frac{n_{\mathrm{de}}}{n_{\mathrm{nu}}} (\boldsymbol{\Psi}_{\mathrm{de}} \boldsymbol{\Phi}_{\mathrm{de}}^\top \boldsymbol{\Phi}_{\mathrm{de}} \boldsymbol{\Psi}_{\mathrm{de}}^\top)^{-1} \boldsymbol{\Psi}_{\mathrm{de}} \boldsymbol{\Phi}_{\mathrm{de}}^\top \boldsymbol{\Phi}_{\mathrm{nu}} \boldsymbol{1}_{n_{\mathrm{nu}}}.$$

One may include a normalization constraint, a non-negativity constraint (given that the basis functions are non-negative), and a regularization constraint in the optimization problem (3.4):

$$\frac{1}{n_{\mathrm{de}}} \boldsymbol{1}_{n_{\mathrm{de}}}^\top \boldsymbol{\Psi}_{\mathrm{de}}^\top \boldsymbol{\theta} = 1, \quad \boldsymbol{\theta} \geq \boldsymbol{0}_b, \quad \text{and} \quad \boldsymbol{\theta} \leq B \boldsymbol{1}_b.$$

Then the optimization problem becomes a convex, linearly constrained quadratic program whose solution can be obtained by a standard numerical solver.

The upper-bound parameter B, which works as a regularizer, may be optimized by *cross-validation* (CV). That is, the numerator and denominator samples $\mathcal{D}^{\mathrm{nu}} = \{\boldsymbol{x}_i^{\mathrm{nu}}\}_{i=1}^{n_{\mathrm{nu}}}$ and $\mathcal{D}^{\mathrm{de}} = \{\boldsymbol{x}_j^{\mathrm{de}}\}_{j=1}^{n_{\mathrm{de}}}$ are first divided into T disjoint subsets $\{\mathcal{D}_t^{\mathrm{nu}}\}_{t=1}^{T}$ and $\{\mathcal{D}_t^{\mathrm{de}}\}_{t=1}^{T}$, respectively. Then a density-ratio estimator $\widehat{r}_t(\boldsymbol{x})$ is obtained from $\mathcal{D}^{\mathrm{nu}} \backslash \mathcal{D}_t^{\mathrm{nu}}$ and $\mathcal{D}^{\mathrm{de}} \backslash \mathcal{D}_t^{\mathrm{de}}$ (i.e., all samples without $\mathcal{D}_t^{\mathrm{nu}}$ and $\mathcal{D}_t^{\mathrm{de}}$), and its moment matching error is computed for the hold-out samples $\mathcal{D}_t^{\mathrm{nu}}$ and $\mathcal{D}_t^{\mathrm{de}}$:

$$\widetilde{\mathrm{MM}}_t(\widehat{r}) := \left(\frac{1}{|\mathcal{D}_t^{\mathrm{de}}|} \sum_{\boldsymbol{x}^{\mathrm{de}} \in \mathcal{D}_t^{\mathrm{de}}} \boldsymbol{\phi}(\boldsymbol{x}^{\mathrm{de}}) \widehat{r}_t(\boldsymbol{x}^{\mathrm{de}}) \right)^2$$

$$-\frac{2}{|D_t^{\mathrm{de}}||D_t^{\mathrm{nu}}|}\left(\sum_{x^{\mathrm{de}}\in D_t^{\mathrm{de}}}\boldsymbol{\phi}(\boldsymbol{x}^{\mathrm{de}})\widehat{r}_t(\boldsymbol{x}^{\mathrm{de}})\right)^{\top}\left(\sum_{x^{\mathrm{nu}}\in D_t^{\mathrm{nu}}}\boldsymbol{\phi}(\boldsymbol{x}^{\mathrm{nu}})\right),$$

where $|D|$ denotes the number of elements in the set D. This procedure is repeated for $t = 1,\ldots,T$, and the average of the hold-out moment matching error over all t is computed as

$$\widetilde{\mathrm{MM}} := \frac{1}{T}\sum_{t=1}^{T}\widetilde{\mathrm{MM}}_t.$$

Then the upper-bound parameter B that minimizes $\widetilde{\mathrm{MM}}$ is chosen. The availability of CV would be one of the advantages of the inductive method (i.e., learning the entire density-ratio function).

3.3 Infinite-Order Approach: KMM

Matching a finite number of moments does not necessarily lead to the true density-ratio function $r^*(\boldsymbol{x})$, even if infinitely many samples are available. To guarantee that the true density-ratio function can always be obtained in the large-sample limit, all moments up to the infinite order need to be matched.

In this section we describe a method of infinite-order moment matching called *kernel mean matching* (KMM), which allows one to efficiently match all the moments using kernel functions (Huang et al., 2007; Gretton et al., 2009). The fixed-design case is considered in Section 3.3.1, and the induction case is considered in Section 3.3.2.

3.3.1 Fixed Design

The basic idea of KMM is essentially the same as the finite-order approach, but a *universal reproducing kernel* $K(\boldsymbol{x},\boldsymbol{x}')$ (Steinwart, 2001) is used as a non-linear transformation. The *Gaussian kernel*

$$K(\boldsymbol{x},\boldsymbol{x}') = \exp\left(-\frac{\|\boldsymbol{x}-\boldsymbol{x}'\|^2}{2\sigma^2}\right)$$

is an example of universal reproducing kernels. It has been shown that the solution of the following optimization problem agrees with the true density-ratio function (Huang et al., 2007; Gretton et al., 2009):

$$\min_{r\in\mathcal{R}}\left\|\int K(\boldsymbol{x},\cdot)p_{\mathrm{nu}}^*(\boldsymbol{x})\mathrm{d}\boldsymbol{x} - \int K(\boldsymbol{x},\cdot)r(\boldsymbol{x})p_{\mathrm{de}}^*(\boldsymbol{x})\mathrm{d}\boldsymbol{x}\right\|_{\mathcal{R}}^2,$$

where $\mathcal{R}$ denotes a universal reproducing kernel Hilbert space and $\|\cdot\|_{\mathcal{R}}$ denotes its norm.

An empirical version of the problem is expressed as

$$\min_{\boldsymbol{r}\in\mathbb{R}^{n_{\mathrm{de}}}}\left[\frac{1}{n_{\mathrm{de}}^2}\boldsymbol{r}^\top\boldsymbol{K}_{\mathrm{de,de}}\boldsymbol{r}-\frac{2}{n_{\mathrm{de}}n_{\mathrm{nu}}}\boldsymbol{r}^\top\boldsymbol{K}_{\mathrm{de,nu}}\boldsymbol{1}_{n_{\mathrm{nu}}}\right],$$

where $\boldsymbol{K}_{\mathrm{de,de}}$ and $\boldsymbol{K}_{\mathrm{de,nu}}$ denote the kernel Gram matrices defined by

$$[\boldsymbol{K}_{\mathrm{de,de}}]_{j,j'}=K(\boldsymbol{x}_j^{\mathrm{de}},\boldsymbol{x}_{j'}^{\mathrm{de}})\quad\text{and}\quad[\boldsymbol{K}_{\mathrm{de,nu}}]_{j,i}=K(\boldsymbol{x}_j^{\mathrm{de}},\boldsymbol{x}_i^{\mathrm{nu}}),$$

respectively. In the same way as the finite-order case, the solution can be obtained analytically as

$$\widehat{\boldsymbol{r}}_{\mathrm{de}}=\frac{n_{\mathrm{de}}}{n_{\mathrm{nu}}}\boldsymbol{K}_{\mathrm{de,de}}^{-1}\boldsymbol{K}_{\mathrm{de,nu}}\boldsymbol{1}_{n_{\mathrm{nu}}}.$$

If necessary, one may include a non-negativity constraint, a normalization constraint, and an upper bound in the same way as the finite-order case. Then the solution can be obtained numerically by solving a convex linearly constrained quadratic programming problem.

3.3.2 Induction

For a linear density-ratio model

$$r(\boldsymbol{x})=\sum_{\ell=1}^{b}\theta_\ell\psi_\ell(\boldsymbol{x})=\boldsymbol{\psi}(\boldsymbol{x})^\top\boldsymbol{\theta},$$

where $\boldsymbol{\psi}(\boldsymbol{x}):\mathbb{R}^d\rightarrow\mathbb{R}^b$ is a non-negative basis function vector and $\boldsymbol{\theta}$ $(\in\mathbb{R}^b)$ is a parameter vector, an inductive variant of KMM is formulated as

$$\min_{\boldsymbol{\theta}\in\mathbb{R}^b}\left[\frac{1}{n_{\mathrm{de}}^2}\boldsymbol{\theta}^\top\boldsymbol{\Psi}_{\mathrm{de}}\boldsymbol{K}_{\mathrm{de,de}}\boldsymbol{\Psi}_{\mathrm{de}}^\top\boldsymbol{\theta}-\frac{2}{n_{\mathrm{de}}n_{\mathrm{nu}}}\boldsymbol{\theta}^\top\boldsymbol{\Psi}_{\mathrm{de}}\boldsymbol{K}_{\mathrm{de,nu}}\boldsymbol{1}_{n_{\mathrm{nu}}}\right],$$

and the solution $\widehat{\boldsymbol{\theta}}$ is given by

$$\widehat{\boldsymbol{\theta}}=\frac{n_{\mathrm{de}}}{n_{\mathrm{nu}}}(\boldsymbol{\Psi}_{\mathrm{de}}\boldsymbol{K}_{\mathrm{de,de}}\boldsymbol{\Psi}_{\mathrm{de}})^{-1}\boldsymbol{\Psi}_{\mathrm{de}}\boldsymbol{K}_{\mathrm{de,nu}}\boldsymbol{1}_{n_{\mathrm{nu}}}.$$

3.4 Numerical Examples

In this section we illustrate the numerical behavior of the fixed-design KMM algorithm described in Section 3.3.1.

Let us consider a one-dimensional example (i.e., $d=1$), and suppose that the two densities $p_{\mathrm{nu}}^*(x)$ and $p_{\mathrm{de}}^*(x)$ are defined as

$$p_{\mathrm{nu}}^*(x)=N(x;1,1^2)\quad\text{and}\quad p_{\mathrm{de}}^*(x)=N(x;0,2^2),$$

where $N(x;\mu,\sigma^2)$ denotes the Gaussian density with mean μ and variance σ^2. The true densities are plotted in Figure 3.2(a), while the true density ratio $r^*(x)$ is plotted in Figure 3.2(b).

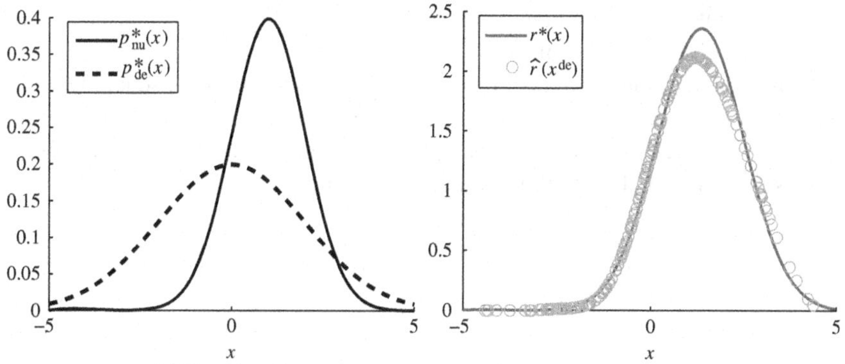

(a) True densities (b) True and estimated density ratios

Figure 3.2. Numerical example of KMM.

Let $n_{nu} = n_{de} = 200$. For density-ratio estimation, we use the fixed-design KMM algorithm with the Gaussian kernel:

$$K(x,x') = \exp\left(-\frac{(x-x')^2}{2\sigma^2}\right).$$

The Gaussian kernel width σ is set to the median distance between all samples, which is a popular heuristic in kernel methods (Schölkopf and Smola, 2002).

The density-ratio function estimated by KMM, $\widehat{r}(x)$, is described in Figure 3.2(b), showing that KMM gives a reasonably good approximation to the true density-ratio function $r^*(x)$.

3.5 Remarks

Density-ratio estimation by moment matching can successfully avoid density estimation.

The finite-order moment matching method (Section 3.2) is simple and computationally efficient, if the number of matching moments is kept reasonably small. However, the finite-order approach is not necessarily *consistent*, that is, in the limit of a large sample size, the solution does not necessarily converge to the true density ratio. On the other hand, the infinite-order moment matching method (Section 3.3), *kernel mean matching* (KMM), can efficiently match all the moments by making use of universal reproducing kernels. Indeed, KMM has the excellent theoretical property that it is consistent (Huang et al., 2007; Gretton et al., 2009). However, KMM has a limitation in model selection – there is no known method for determining the kernel parameter (i.e., the Gaussian kernel width in the case of Gaussian kernels). A popular heuristic of setting the Gaussian width to the median distance between samples (Schölkopf and Smola, 2002) would be useful in some cases, but this may not always be reasonable.

In this chapter moment matching was performed in terms of the squared norm, which led to an analytic-form solution (if no constraint is imposed). As shown in Kanamori et al. (2011b), moment matching can be generalized systematically to various divergences. This will be explained in detail in Chapter 16.

4

Probabilistic Classification

In this chapter we describe a framework of density-ratio estimation via *probabilistic classification*.

We begin by describing a basic framework in Section 4.1. Then, a probabilistic classification algorithm called *logistic regression* is explained in Section 4.2, an alternative probabilistic classification algorithm called *least-squares probabilistic classifier* is explained in Section 4.3, and a large-margin classification method called the *support vector machine* is explained in Section 4.4. A model selection issue is addressed in Section 4.5, and numerical examples are shown in Section 4.6. Finally, Section 4.7 concludes the chapter.

4.1 Basic Framework

The basic idea of the probabilistic classification approach to density-ratio estimation is to learn a probabilistic classifier that separates numerator samples $\{\boldsymbol{x}_i^{\mathrm{nu}}\}_{i=1}^{n_{\mathrm{nu}}}$ and denominator samples $\{\boldsymbol{x}_j^{\mathrm{de}}\}_{j=1}^{n_{\mathrm{de}}}$ (see Figure 4.1).

Let us assign labels $y=+1$ to $\{\boldsymbol{x}_i^{\mathrm{nu}}\}_{i=1}^{n_{\mathrm{nu}}}$ and $y=-1$ to $\{\boldsymbol{x}_j^{\mathrm{de}}\}_{j=1}^{n_{\mathrm{de}}}$, respectively. Then the two densities $p_{\mathrm{nu}}^*(\boldsymbol{x})$ and $p_{\mathrm{de}}^*(\boldsymbol{x})$ are written as

$$p_{\mathrm{nu}}^*(\boldsymbol{x}) = p^*(\boldsymbol{x}|y=+1) \quad \text{and} \quad p_{\mathrm{de}}^*(\boldsymbol{x}) = p^*(\boldsymbol{x}|y=-1),$$

respectively. Note that y is regarded as a random variable here. An application of Bayes' theorem,

$$p^*(\boldsymbol{x}|y) = \frac{p^*(y|\boldsymbol{x})p^*(\boldsymbol{x})}{p^*(y)},$$

yields that the density ratio $r^*(\boldsymbol{x})$ can be expressed in terms of y as

$$\begin{aligned} r^*(\boldsymbol{x}) = \frac{p_{\mathrm{nu}}^*(\boldsymbol{x})}{p_{\mathrm{de}}^*(\boldsymbol{x})} &= \left(\frac{p^*(y=+1|\boldsymbol{x})p^*(\boldsymbol{x})}{p^*(y=+1)}\right)\left(\frac{p^*(y=-1|\boldsymbol{x})p^*(\boldsymbol{x})}{p^*(y=-1)}\right)^{-1} \\ &= \frac{p^*(y=-1)}{p^*(y=+1)}\frac{p^*(y=+1|\boldsymbol{x})}{p^*(y=-1|\boldsymbol{x})}. \end{aligned}$$

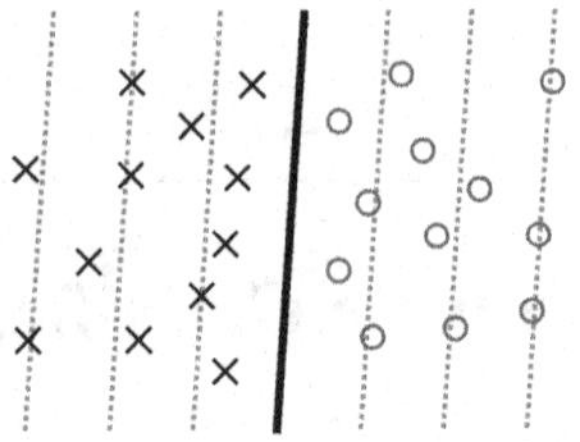

Figure 4.1. Probabilistic classification of samples drawn from $p^*_{\mathrm{nu}}(\boldsymbol{x})$ and $p^*_{\mathrm{de}}(\boldsymbol{x})$.

The prior ratio $p^*(y=-1)/p^*(y=+1)$ may be approximated simply by the ratio of the sample size:

$$\frac{p^*(y=-1)}{p^*(y=+1)} \approx \frac{n_{\mathrm{de}}/(n_{\mathrm{nu}}+n_{\mathrm{de}})}{n_{\mathrm{nu}}/(n_{\mathrm{nu}}+n_{\mathrm{de}})} = \frac{n_{\mathrm{de}}}{n_{\mathrm{nu}}}.$$

The "class"-posterior probability $p^*(y|\boldsymbol{x})$ may be approximated by separating $\{\boldsymbol{x}_i^{\mathrm{nu}}\}_{i=1}^{n_{\mathrm{nu}}}$ and $\{\boldsymbol{x}_j^{\mathrm{de}}\}_{j=1}^{n_{\mathrm{de}}}$ using a probabilistic classifier. Thus, given an estimator of the class-posterior probability, $\widehat{p}(y|\boldsymbol{x})$, a density-ratio estimator $\widehat{r}(\boldsymbol{x})$ can be constructed as

$$\widehat{r}(\boldsymbol{x}) = \frac{n_{\mathrm{de}}}{n_{\mathrm{nu}}} \frac{\widehat{p}(y=+1|\boldsymbol{x})}{\widehat{p}(y=-1|\boldsymbol{x})}. \tag{4.1}$$

A practical advantage of the probabilistic classification approach is its easy implementability. Indeed, one can directly use standard probabilistic classification algorithms for density-ratio estimation. In the following, we describe representative classification algorithms including *logistic regression*, the *least-squares probabilistic classifier*, and *support vector machines*. For notational brevity, let $n := n_{\mathrm{nu}} + n_{\mathrm{de}}$ and we consider a set of paired samples $\{(\boldsymbol{x}_k, y_k)\}_{k=1}^n$, where

$$(\boldsymbol{x}_1,\ldots,\boldsymbol{x}_n) := (\boldsymbol{x}_1^{\mathrm{nu}},\ldots,\boldsymbol{x}_{n_{\mathrm{nu}}}^{\mathrm{nu}},\boldsymbol{x}_1^{\mathrm{de}},\ldots,\boldsymbol{x}_{n_{\mathrm{de}}}^{\mathrm{de}}),$$

$$(y_1,\ldots,y_n) := (\underbrace{+1,\ldots,+1}_{n_{\mathrm{nu}}},\underbrace{-1,\ldots,-1}_{n_{\mathrm{de}}}).$$

4.2 Logistic Regression

In this section, a popular classification algorithm called *logistic regression* (Hastie et al., 2001) is explained.

A logistic regression classifier employs a parametric model of the following form for expressing the class-posterior probability $p^*(y|\boldsymbol{x})$:

$$p(y|\boldsymbol{x};\boldsymbol{\theta}) = \frac{1}{1+\exp\left(-y\boldsymbol{\psi}(\boldsymbol{x})^\top\boldsymbol{\theta}\right)},$$

where $\boldsymbol{\psi}(\boldsymbol{x}) : \mathbb{R}^d \rightarrow \mathbb{R}^b$ is a basis function vector and $\boldsymbol{\theta}$ ($\in \mathbb{R}^b$) is a parameter vector. The parameter vector $\boldsymbol{\theta}$ is learned so that the *penalized log-likelihood* is maximized, which can be expressed as the following minimization problem:

$$\widehat{\boldsymbol{\theta}} := \underset{\boldsymbol{\theta} \in \mathbb{R}^b}{\operatorname{argmin}} \left[\sum_{k=1}^{n} \log\left(1 + \exp\left(-y_k \boldsymbol{\psi}(\boldsymbol{x}_k)^\top \boldsymbol{\theta}\right)\right) + \lambda \boldsymbol{\theta}^\top \boldsymbol{\theta} \right], \tag{4.2}$$

where $\lambda \boldsymbol{\theta}^\top \boldsymbol{\theta}$ is a penalty term included for regularization purposes. In this optimization problem, $\boldsymbol{\psi}(\boldsymbol{x}_k)^\top \boldsymbol{\theta}$ can be regarded as an estimator of y_k: $\widehat{y}_k = \boldsymbol{\psi}(\boldsymbol{x}_k)^\top \boldsymbol{\theta}$. Thus, in logistic regression, the *log-loss* is employed for measuring the loss of estimating y_k by $\widehat{y}_k$:

$$\operatorname{loss}(y_k, \widehat{y}_k) := \log\left(1 + \exp(-y_k \widehat{y}_k)\right),$$

where $y_k \widehat{y}_k$ is called the *margin* for the sample $\boldsymbol{x}_k$ (Schapire et al., 1998). A profile of a log-loss function is illustrated in Figure 4.2.

Because the objective function in Eq. (4.2) is convex, the global optimal solution can be obtained by a standard non-linear optimization technique such as the *gradient descent method* or *(quasi-)Newton methods* (Hastie et al., 2001; Minka, 2007). A logistic regression model classifies a new input sample $\boldsymbol{x}$ by choosing the most probable class as

$$\widehat{y} = \underset{y=\pm 1}{\operatorname{argmax}}\ p(y|\boldsymbol{x}; \widehat{\boldsymbol{\theta}}).$$

Finally, a density-ratio estimator $\widehat{r}_{\mathrm{LR}}(\boldsymbol{x})$ is given by

$$\widehat{r}_{\mathrm{LR}}(\boldsymbol{x}) = \frac{n_{\mathrm{de}}}{n_{\mathrm{nu}}} \frac{1 + \exp\left(\boldsymbol{\psi}(\boldsymbol{x})^\top \widehat{\boldsymbol{\theta}}\right)}{1 + \exp\left(-\boldsymbol{\psi}(\boldsymbol{x})^\top \widehat{\boldsymbol{\theta}}\right)}$$

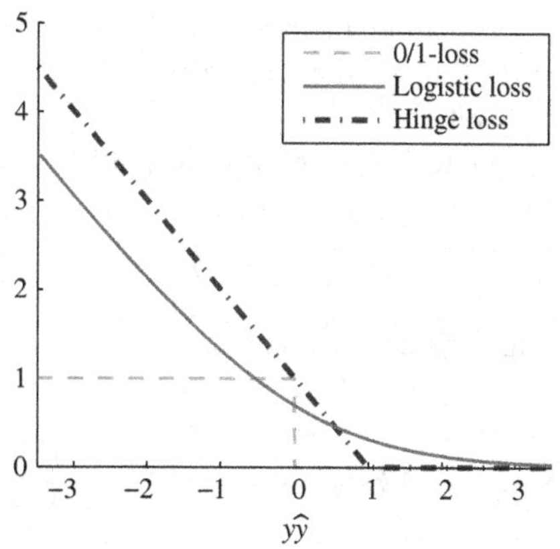

Figure 4.2. Loss functions for classification.

$$= \frac{n_{\mathrm{de}}}{n_{\mathrm{nu}}} \frac{\exp\left(\boldsymbol{\psi}(\boldsymbol{x})^\top \widehat{\boldsymbol{\theta}}\right)\left(\exp\left(-\boldsymbol{\psi}(\boldsymbol{x})^\top \widehat{\boldsymbol{\theta}}\right)+1\right)}{1+\exp\left(-\boldsymbol{\psi}(\boldsymbol{x})^\top \widehat{\boldsymbol{\theta}}\right)}$$

$$= \frac{n_{\mathrm{de}}}{n_{\mathrm{nu}}} \exp\left(\boldsymbol{\psi}(\boldsymbol{x})^\top \widehat{\boldsymbol{\theta}}\right),$$

where “LR” stands for “logistic regression.”

4.3 Least-Squares Probabilistic Classifier

Although the performance of general-purpose non-linear optimization techniques has been improved along with the evolution of computer environments, training logistic regression classifiers is still computationally expensive. In this sections, an alternative probabilistic classification algorithm called the *least-squares probabilistic classifier* (LSPC; Sugiyama, 2010) is described. The LSPC is computationally more efficient than logistic regression, with comparable accuracy. The LSPC is actually based on the density-ratio estimation method described in Section 6.2.2, and a detailed explanation of the LSPC will be provided in Section 12.2. For this reason, we only briefly describe the algorithm of the LSPC here.

In the LSPC, the class-posterior probability $p^*(y|\boldsymbol{x})$ is modeled as

$$p(y|\boldsymbol{x};\boldsymbol{\theta}) := \sum_{\ell=1}^{b} \theta_\ell \psi(\boldsymbol{x}, y) = \boldsymbol{\psi}(\boldsymbol{x}, y)^\top \boldsymbol{\theta},$$

where $\boldsymbol{\psi}(\boldsymbol{x}, y)$ $(\in \mathbb{R}^b)$ is a non-negative basis function vector and $\boldsymbol{\theta}$ $(\in \mathbb{R}^b)$ is a parameter vector. The class label y takes a value in $\{1,\ldots,c\}$, where c denotes the number of classes.

The basic idea of the LSPC is to express the class-posterior probability $p^*(y|\boldsymbol{x})$ in terms of the equivalent density-ratio expression:

$$p^*(y|\boldsymbol{x}) = \frac{p^*(\boldsymbol{x}, y)}{p^*(\boldsymbol{x})}. \tag{4.3}$$

Then the density-ratio estimation method called *unconstrained least-squares importance fitting* (uLSIF; Kanamori et al., 2009; see also Section 6.2.2) is used for estimating this density ratio.

As explained in Section 12.2, the solution of the LSPC can be obtained by solving the following system of linear equations:

$$(\widehat{\boldsymbol{H}} + \lambda \boldsymbol{I}_b)\widehat{\boldsymbol{\theta}} = \widehat{\boldsymbol{h}},$$

where λ (≥ 0) is the regularization parameter, $\boldsymbol{I}_b$ is the b-dimensional identity matrix,

$$\widehat{\boldsymbol{H}} := \frac{1}{n}\sum_{k=1}^{n}\sum_{y=1}^{c} \boldsymbol{\psi}(\boldsymbol{x}_k, y)\boldsymbol{\psi}(\boldsymbol{x}_k, y)^\top, \quad \text{and} \quad \widehat{\boldsymbol{h}} := \frac{1}{n}\sum_{k=1}^{n} \boldsymbol{\psi}(\boldsymbol{x}_k, y_k).$$

Thus, the solution $\widehat{\boldsymbol{\theta}}$ is given *analytically* as $\widehat{\boldsymbol{\theta}} = (\widehat{\boldsymbol{H}} + \lambda \boldsymbol{I}_b)^{-1}\widehat{\boldsymbol{h}}$.

To assure that the LSPC produces a probability, the outputs are normalized and negative outputs are rounded up to zero (Yamada et al., 2011a); thus, the final LSPC solution is given by

$$\widehat{p}(y|\boldsymbol{x}) = \frac{\max(0, \boldsymbol{\psi}(\boldsymbol{x},y)^\top \widehat{\boldsymbol{\theta}})}{\sum_{y'=1}^{c} \max(0, \boldsymbol{\psi}(\boldsymbol{x},y')^\top \widehat{\boldsymbol{\theta}})}.$$

A standard choice of basis functions $\boldsymbol{\psi}(\boldsymbol{x},y)$ would be a *kernel* model:

$$p(y|\boldsymbol{x};\boldsymbol{\theta}) = \sum_{\ell=1}^{n} \theta_\ell^{(y)} K(\boldsymbol{x},\boldsymbol{x}_\ell),$$

where $K(\boldsymbol{x},\boldsymbol{x}')$ is some kernel function such as the *Gaussian kernel*:

$$K(\boldsymbol{x},\boldsymbol{x}') = \exp\left(-\frac{\|\boldsymbol{x}-\boldsymbol{x}'\|^2}{2\sigma^2}\right).$$

As just described, the LSPC solution can be computed *analytically* simply by solving a regularized system of linear equation. Thus, its computation is highly efficient and stable. A MATLAB® implementation of the LSPC is available from http://sugiyama-www.cs.titech.ac.jp/~sugi/software/LSPC/.

4.4 Support Vector Machine

The *support vector machine* (SVM) is a popular classification technique in the machine learning community (Cortes and Vapnik, 1995; Vapnik, 1998; Schölkopf and Smola, 2002). The SVM finds the hyperplane that separates samples from different classes with maximum *margin* (see Figure 4.3).

The SVM models the separating hyperplane by

$$\boldsymbol{w}^\top \boldsymbol{x} - w_0 = 0,$$

where $\boldsymbol{w} = (w_1, \ldots, w_d)^\top$ ($\in \mathbb{R}^d$) and w_0 ($\in \mathbb{R}$) are parameters to be learned. For this model, the margin is expressed as $1/\|\boldsymbol{w}\|$, and thus the maximum margin

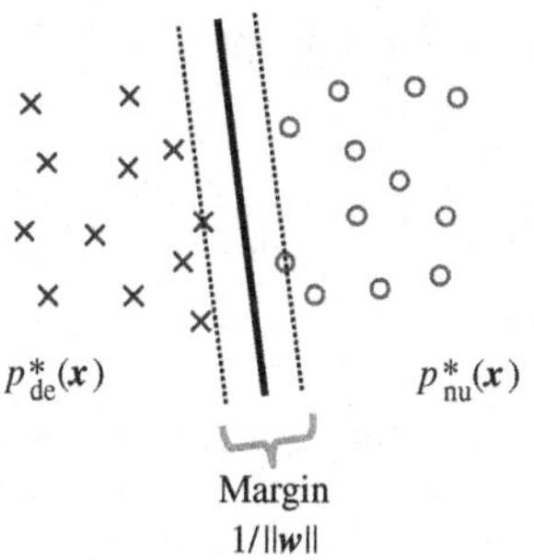

Figure 4.3. Margin of a separating hyperplane.

hyperplane is given as the solution of the following *convex quadratic program*:

$$\min_{\boldsymbol{w}\in\mathbb{R}^d, w_0\in\mathbb{R}} \quad \boldsymbol{w}^\top \boldsymbol{w}$$

$$\text{s.t.} \quad y_k(\boldsymbol{w}^\top \boldsymbol{x}_k - w_0) \geq 1 \text{ for } k = 1, \ldots, n.$$

If samples $\{\boldsymbol{x}_k | y_k = +1\}$ and $\{\boldsymbol{x}_k | y_k = -1\}$ are not *linearly separable*, then the *soft-margin* variant may be employed instead:

$$\min_{\boldsymbol{w}\in\mathbb{R}^d, w_0\in\mathbb{R}} \left[\sum_{k=1}^{n} \xi_k + \lambda \boldsymbol{w}^\top \boldsymbol{w} \right]$$

$$\text{s.t.} \quad y_k(\boldsymbol{w}^\top \boldsymbol{x}_k - w_0) \geq 1 - \xi_k \text{ and } \xi_k \geq 0 \text{ for } k = 1, \ldots, n,$$

where $\{\xi_k\}_{k=1}^n$ are *slack* variables and λ (> 0) is a regularization parameter.

By eliminating the slack variables $\{\xi_k\}_{k=1}^n$, this optimization problem can be equivalently expressed as

$$\min_{\boldsymbol{w}\in\mathbb{R}^d, w_0\in\mathbb{R}} \left[\sum_{k=1}^{n} \max\left(0, 1 - y_k(\boldsymbol{w}^\top \boldsymbol{x}_k - w_0)\right) + \lambda \boldsymbol{w}^\top \boldsymbol{w} \right].$$

In this optimization problem, $\boldsymbol{w}^\top \boldsymbol{x}_k - w_0$ can be regarded as an estimator of y_k: $\widehat{y}_k = \boldsymbol{w}^\top \boldsymbol{x}_k - w_0$. Thus the SVM can be regarded as employing the *hinge-loss* for measuring the loss of estimating y_k by $\widehat{y}_k$:

$$\text{loss}(y_k, \widehat{y}_k) := \max\left(0, 1 - y_k \widehat{y}_k\right).$$

A profile of a hinge-loss function is described in Figure 4.2.

The *dual* expression of the soft-margin SVM problem is expressed as

$$\max_{\{\theta_k\}_{k=1}^n} \left[\sum_{k=1}^{n} \theta_k - \frac{1}{2} \sum_{k,k'=1}^{n} \theta_k \theta_{k'} y_k y_{k'} \boldsymbol{x}_k^\top \boldsymbol{x}_{k'} \right]$$

$$\text{s.t.} \quad 0 \leq \theta_k \leq \frac{1}{\lambda} \text{ for } k = 1, \ldots, n, \text{ and } \sum_{k=1}^{n} \theta_k y_k = 0,$$

where $\{\theta_k\}_{k=1}^n$ are Lagrange multipliers. This formulation allows one to obtain a non-linear method by replacing the inner product $\boldsymbol{x}^\top \boldsymbol{x}'$ with a reproducing kernel function $K(\boldsymbol{x}, \boldsymbol{x}')$:

$$\max_{\boldsymbol{\theta}\in\mathbb{R}^n, b\in\mathbb{R}} \left[\sum_{k=1}^{n} \theta_k - \frac{1}{2} \sum_{k,k'=1}^{n} \theta_k \theta_{k'} y_k y_{k'} K(\boldsymbol{x}_k, \boldsymbol{x}_{k'}) \right]$$

$$\text{s.t.} \quad 0 \leq \theta_k \leq \frac{1}{\lambda} \text{ for } k = 1, \ldots, n, \text{ and } \sum_{k=1}^{n} \theta_k y_k = 0.$$

The SVM was shown to converge to the *Bayes optimal classifier* as the number of training samples tends to infinity (Lin, 2002). However, the SVM does not give probabilistic outputs and thus it cannot be directly employed for density-ratio estimation. Platt (2000) and Wu et al. (2004) proposed heuristic methods for computing the class-posterior probability from the SVM solution, by which density ratios may be approximated.

4.5 Model Selection by Cross-Validation

An important advantage of the probabilistic classification approach is that *model selection* (i.e., choice of the basis functions and the regularization parameter) is possible by ordinary *cross-validation*, because the learning problem involved in this framework is a standard supervised classification problem.

More specifically, the numerator and denominator samples $\mathcal{D}^{\mathrm{nu}} = \{\boldsymbol{x}_i^{\mathrm{nu}}\}_{i=1}^{n_{\mathrm{nu}}}$ and $\mathcal{D}^{\mathrm{de}} = \{\boldsymbol{x}_j^{\mathrm{de}}\}_{j=1}^{n_{\mathrm{de}}}$ are divided into T disjoint subsets $\{\mathcal{D}_t^{\mathrm{nu}}\}_{t=1}^{T}$ and $\{\mathcal{D}_t^{\mathrm{de}}\}_{t=1}^{T}$, respectively. Then a probabilistic classifier $\widehat{p}_{\mathcal{D}_t^{\mathrm{nu}},\mathcal{D}_t^{\mathrm{de}}}(y|\boldsymbol{x})$ is obtained using $\mathcal{D}^{\mathrm{nu}}\backslash\mathcal{D}_t^{\mathrm{nu}}$ and $\mathcal{D}^{\mathrm{de}}\backslash\mathcal{D}_t^{\mathrm{de}}$ (i.e., all samples without $\mathcal{D}_t^{\mathrm{nu}}$ and $\mathcal{D}_t^{\mathrm{de}}$), and its misclassification error (ME) for the hold-out samples $\mathcal{D}_t^{\mathrm{nu}}$ and $\mathcal{D}_t^{\mathrm{de}}$ is computed[1]:

$$\widetilde{\mathrm{ME}}_t := \frac{1}{|\mathcal{D}_t^{\mathrm{nu}}|}\sum_{\boldsymbol{x}^{\mathrm{nu}}\in\mathcal{D}_t^{\mathrm{nu}}} I\left(\operatorname*{argmax}_{y=\pm1}\widehat{p}_{\mathcal{D}_t^{\mathrm{nu}},\mathcal{D}_t^{\mathrm{de}}}(y|\boldsymbol{x}^{\mathrm{nu}}) = +1\right)$$
$$+\frac{1}{|\mathcal{D}_t^{\mathrm{de}}|}\sum_{\boldsymbol{x}^{\mathrm{de}}\in\mathcal{D}_t^{\mathrm{de}}} I\left(\operatorname*{argmax}_{y=\pm1}\widehat{p}_{\mathcal{D}_t^{\mathrm{nu}},\mathcal{D}_t^{\mathrm{de}}}(y|\boldsymbol{x}^{\mathrm{de}}) = -1\right),$$

where $I(\cdot)$ is the indicator function:

$$I(c) = \begin{cases} 1 & \text{if } c \text{ is true,} \\ 0 & \text{otherwise.} \end{cases}$$

This procedure is repeated for $t = 1,\ldots,T$, and the average misclassification error over all t is computed as

$$\widetilde{\mathrm{ME}} := \frac{1}{T}\sum_{t=1}^{T}\widetilde{\mathrm{ME}}_t.$$

Then the model that minimizes $\widetilde{\mathrm{ME}}$ is chosen.

4.6 Numerical Examples

In this section we illustrate the numerical behavior of the logistic-regression–based density-ratio estimation algorithm described in Section 4.2.

[1] For probabilistic classifiers, a hold-out likelihood may also be used as the error metric in cross-validation.

Let us consider a one-dimensional example (i.e., $d = 1$) and suppose that the two densities $p^*_{\mathrm{nu}}(x)$ and $p^*_{\mathrm{de}}(x)$ are defined as

$$p^*_{\mathrm{nu}}(x) = N(x;1,1^2) \quad \text{and} \quad p^*_{\mathrm{de}}(x) = N(x;0,2^2),$$

where $N(x;\mu,\sigma^2)$ denotes the Gaussian density with mean μ and variance σ^2. The true densities are plotted in Figure 4.4(a), while the true density ratio $r^*(x)$ is plotted in Figure 4.4(c).

Let $n_{\mathrm{nu}} = n_{\mathrm{de}} = 200$, $n = n_{\mathrm{nu}} + n_{\mathrm{de}} = 400$, and

$$(x_1,\ldots,x_n) := (x_1^{\mathrm{nu}},\ldots,x_{n_{\mathrm{nu}}}^{\mathrm{nu}},x_1^{\mathrm{de}},\ldots,x_{n_{\mathrm{de}}}^{\mathrm{de}}),$$
$$(y_1,\ldots,y_n) := (\underbrace{+1,\ldots,+1}_{n_{\mathrm{nu}}},\underbrace{-1,\ldots,-1}_{n_{\mathrm{de}}}).$$

For density-ratio estimation, we use logistic regression with the Gaussian kernel:

$$p(y|x) = \frac{1}{1+\exp\left(-y\left(\sum_{\ell=1}^{n}\theta_\ell \exp\left(-\frac{(x-x_\ell)^2}{2\sigma^2}\right)\right)\right)}.$$

The Gaussian width σ and the regularization parameter λ are chosen by 5-fold cross-validation (see Section 4.5). The true class-posterior probabilities and their estimates obtained by logistic regression are described in Figure 4.4(b), and the density-ratio function estimated by logistic regression, $\widehat{r}(x)$, is described in Figure 4.4(c). The results show that reasonably good approximations were obtained by the logistic regression approach.

4.7 Remarks

Density-ratio estimation by probabilistic classification can successfully avoid density estimation by casting the problem of density ratio estimation as the problem of learning the class-posterior probability. The availability of cross-validation for model selection is an advantage of the probabilistic classification approach over the infinite-order moment matching approach described in Section 3.3. Furthermore, the probabilistic classification approach is convenient practically because existing software packages of probabilistic classifiers can be used directly for density-ratio estimation.

The probabilistic classification approach with logistic regression actually has a superior theoretical property: If the logistic regression model is *correctly specified*, the logistic regression approach gives the optimal estimator among a class of semi-parametric estimators in the sense that the *asymptotic variance* is minimal (Qin, 1998). However, when the model is *misspecified* (which would be the case in practice), this strong theoretical property is not true and the *density fitting approach* explained in Chapter 5 is more preferable (Kanamori et al., 2010). Details of these theoretical analyses will be explained in Chapter 13.

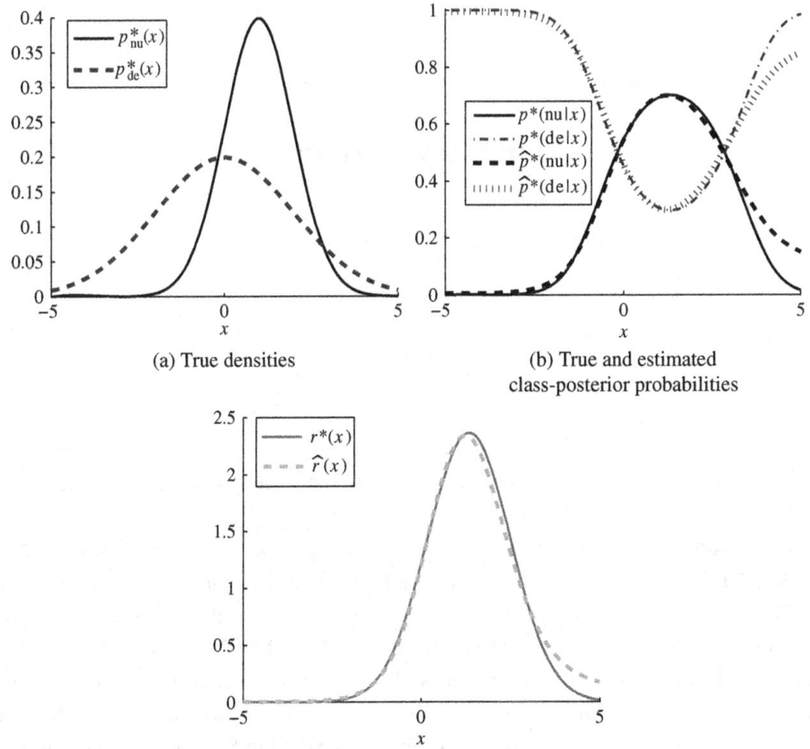

(a) True densities

(b) True and estimated class-posterior probabilities

(c) True and estimated density ratios

Figure 4.4. Numerical example of density-ratio estimation by logistic regression.

Another advantage of the probabilistic classification approach is that it can be used for estimating density ratios among *multiple* densities by a multi-class probabilistic classifier. In this context, the *least-squares probabilistic classifier* (LSPC; see Section 12.2) will be particularly useful because of its high computational efficiency.

5

Density Fitting

In this chapter we describe a framework of density-ratio estimation by *density fitting*.

In Section 5.1 we first describe a basic framework of density fitting under the *Kullback–Leibler* (KL) divergence (Kullback and Leibler, 1951) called the *KL importance estimation procedure* (KLIEP; Sugiyama et al., 2008). Then, in Section 5.2, we describe implementations of the KLIEP for various density-ratio models including *linear/kernel* models, *log-linear* models, *Gaussian mixture* models, and *probabilistic principal–component–analyzer mixture* models. Model selection of the KLIEP by cross-validation is explained in Section 5.3, and numerical examples are shown in Section 5.4. Finally, the chapter is concluded in Section 5.5.

5.1 Basic Framework

In this section we describe the framework of density-ratio estimation by density fitting under the KL divergence.

Let $r(\boldsymbol{x})$ be a model of the true density ratio

$$r^*(\boldsymbol{x}) = \frac{p^*_{\mathrm{nu}}(\boldsymbol{x})}{p^*_{\mathrm{de}}(\boldsymbol{x})}.$$

Then the numerator density $p^*_{\mathrm{nu}}(\boldsymbol{x})$ may be modeled by

$$p_{\mathrm{nu}}(\boldsymbol{x}) = r(\boldsymbol{x})p^*_{\mathrm{de}}(\boldsymbol{x}).$$

Now let us consider the KL divergence from $p^*_{\mathrm{nu}}(\boldsymbol{x})$ to $p_{\mathrm{nu}}(\boldsymbol{x})$:

$$\mathrm{KL}'(p^*_{\mathrm{nu}} \| p_{\mathrm{nu}}) := \int p^*_{\mathrm{nu}}(\boldsymbol{x}) \log \frac{p^*_{\mathrm{nu}}(\boldsymbol{x})}{p_{\mathrm{nu}}(\boldsymbol{x})} \mathrm{d}\boldsymbol{x} = C - \mathrm{KL}(r),$$

where $C := \int p^*_{\text{nu}}(\boldsymbol{x}) \log \frac{p^*_{\text{nu}}(\boldsymbol{x})}{p^*_{\text{de}}(\boldsymbol{x})} \mathrm{d}\boldsymbol{x}$ is a constant irrelevant to r and $\text{KL}(r)$ is the relevant part:

$$\text{KL}(r) := \int p^*_{\text{nu}}(\boldsymbol{x}) \log r(\boldsymbol{x}) \mathrm{d}\boldsymbol{x}.$$

An empirical approximation $\widehat{\text{KL}}(r)$ of $\text{KL}(r)$ is given by

$$\widehat{\text{KL}}(r) := \frac{1}{n_{\text{nu}}} \sum_{i=1}^{n_{\text{nu}}} \log r(\boldsymbol{x}_i^{\text{nu}}).$$

Because $p_{\text{nu}}(\boldsymbol{x})$ is a probability density function, its integral should be one:

$$\int p_{\text{nu}}(\boldsymbol{x}) \mathrm{d}\boldsymbol{x} = \int r(\boldsymbol{x}) p^*_{\text{de}}(\boldsymbol{x}) \mathrm{d}\boldsymbol{x} = 1. \tag{5.1}$$

Its empirical approximation is given by $\frac{1}{n_{\text{de}}} \sum_{j=1}^{n_{\text{de}}} r(\boldsymbol{x}_j^{\text{de}}) = 1$. Furthermore, the density $p_{\text{nu}}(\boldsymbol{x})$ should be non-negative: $r(\boldsymbol{x}) \geq 0$ for all $\boldsymbol{x}$. Combining these equations together, we have the following optimization problem:

$$\max_r \ \frac{1}{n_{\text{nu}}} \sum_{i=1}^{n_{\text{nu}}} \log r(\boldsymbol{x}_i^{\text{nu}})$$

$$\text{s.t.} \ \frac{1}{n_{\text{de}}} \sum_{j=1}^{n_{\text{de}}} r(\boldsymbol{x}_j^{\text{de}}) = 1 \text{ and } r(\boldsymbol{x}) \geq 0 \text{ for all } \boldsymbol{x}.$$

This formulation is called the *KL importance estimation procedure* (KLIEP; Sugiyama et al., 2008).

5.2 Implementations of KLIEP

In this section we describe practical implementations of the KLIEP for various density-ratio models, including *linear/kernel* models (Section 5.2.1), *log-linear* models (Section 5.2.2), *Gaussian mixture* models (Section 5.2.3), and *probabilistic principal–component–analyzer mixture* models (Section 5.2.4).

5.2.1 Linear and Kernel Models

Let us employ a linear model for density-ratio estimation:

$$r(\boldsymbol{x}) = \sum_{\ell=1}^{b} \theta_\ell \psi_\ell(\boldsymbol{x}) = \boldsymbol{\psi}(\boldsymbol{x})^\top \boldsymbol{\theta},$$

where $\boldsymbol{\psi}(\boldsymbol{x}) : \mathbb{R}^d \rightarrow \mathbb{R}^b$ is a basis function vector and $\boldsymbol{\theta}$ ($\in \mathbb{R}^b$) is a parameter vector. We assume that the basis functions are non-negative. Then the KLIEP optimization problem for the linear model is expressed as follows (Sugiyama et al., 2008):

$$\max_{\boldsymbol{\theta} \in \mathbb{R}^b} \frac{1}{n_{\text{nu}}} \sum_{i=1}^{n_{\text{nu}}} \log(\boldsymbol{\psi}(\boldsymbol{x}_i^{\text{nu}})^\top \boldsymbol{\theta}) \quad \text{s.t.} \ \ \overline{\boldsymbol{\psi}}_{\text{de}}^\top \boldsymbol{\theta} = 1 \text{ and } \boldsymbol{\theta} \geq \boldsymbol{0}_b,$$

where $\overline{\boldsymbol{\psi}}_{\text{de}} := \frac{1}{n_{\text{de}}}\sum_{j=1}^{n_{\text{de}}} \boldsymbol{\psi}(\boldsymbol{x}_j^{\text{de}})$.

Because this optimization problem is *convex* (i.e., the objective function to be maximized is concave and the feasible set is convex), there exists the unique global optimum solution. Furthermore, the KLIEP solution tends to be *sparse*, that is, many parameters take exactly zero. Such sparsity would contribute to reducing the computation time when computing the estimated density-ratio values.

A pseudo code of the KLIEP for linear models is described in Figure 5.1. As can be confirmed from the pseudo code, the denominator samples $\{\boldsymbol{x}_j^{\text{de}}\}_{j=1}^{n_{\text{de}}}$ appear only in terms of the basis-transformed mean $\overline{\boldsymbol{\psi}}_{\text{de}}$. Thus, the KLIEP is computationally efficient even when the number n_{de} of denominator samples is very large.

The performance of the KLIEP depends on the choice of the basis functions $\boldsymbol{\psi}(\boldsymbol{x})$. As explained below, the use of the following Gaussian kernel model is reasonable:

$$r(\boldsymbol{x}) = \sum_{\ell=1}^{n_{\text{nu}}} \theta_\ell K(\boldsymbol{x}, \boldsymbol{x}_\ell^{\text{nu}}), \tag{5.2}$$

where $K(\boldsymbol{x}, \boldsymbol{x}')$ is the Gaussian kernel:

$$K(\boldsymbol{x}, \boldsymbol{x}') = \exp\left(-\frac{\|\boldsymbol{x} - \boldsymbol{x}'\|^2}{2\sigma^2}\right).$$

The reason why the numerator samples $\{\boldsymbol{x}_i^{\text{nu}}\}_{i=1}^{n_{\text{nu}}}$, and not the denominator samples $\{\boldsymbol{x}_j^{\text{de}}\}_{j=1}^{n_{\text{de}}}$, are chosen as the Gaussian centers is as follows. By definition, the

Input: Data samples $D^{\text{nu}} = \{\boldsymbol{x}_i^{\text{nu}}\}_{i=1}^{n_{\text{nu}}}$ and $D^{\text{de}} = \{\boldsymbol{x}_j^{\text{de}}\}_{j=1}^{n_{\text{de}}}$,
and basis functions $\boldsymbol{\psi}(\boldsymbol{x})$
Output: Density-ratio estimator $\widehat{r}(\boldsymbol{x})$

$\boldsymbol{\Psi}_{\text{nu}} \longleftarrow (\boldsymbol{\psi}(\boldsymbol{x}_1^{\text{nu}}), \ldots, \boldsymbol{\psi}(\boldsymbol{x}_{n_{\text{nu}}}^{\text{nu}}))^\top$;
$\overline{\boldsymbol{\psi}}_{\text{de}} \longleftarrow \frac{1}{n_{\text{de}}}\sum_{j=1}^{n_{\text{de}}} \boldsymbol{\psi}(\boldsymbol{x}_j^{\text{de}})$;
Initialize $\boldsymbol{\theta}$ $(> \mathbf{0}_b)$ and ε $(0 < \varepsilon \ll 1)$;
Repeat until convergence
  $\boldsymbol{\theta} \longleftarrow \boldsymbol{\theta} + \varepsilon \boldsymbol{\Psi}_{\text{nu}}^\top (\mathbf{1}_{n_{\text{nu}}} ./ \boldsymbol{\Psi}_{\text{nu}}\boldsymbol{\theta})$; % Gradient ascent
  $\boldsymbol{\theta} \longleftarrow \boldsymbol{\theta} + (1 - \overline{\boldsymbol{\psi}}_{\text{de}}^\top \boldsymbol{\theta})\overline{\boldsymbol{\psi}}_{\text{de}} / (\overline{\boldsymbol{\psi}}_{\text{de}}^\top \overline{\boldsymbol{\psi}}_{\text{de}})$; % Constraint satisfaction
  $\boldsymbol{\theta} \longleftarrow \max(\mathbf{0}_b, \boldsymbol{\theta})$; % Constraint satisfaction
  $\boldsymbol{\theta} \longleftarrow \boldsymbol{\theta} / (\overline{\boldsymbol{\psi}}_{\text{de}}^\top \boldsymbol{\theta})$; % Constraint satisfaction
end
$\widehat{r}(\boldsymbol{x}) \longleftarrow \boldsymbol{\psi}(\boldsymbol{x})^\top \boldsymbol{\theta}$;

Figure 5.1. Pseudo code of the KLIEP. "./" indicates the element-wise division and "$^\top$" denotes the transpose. Inequalities and the "max" operation for vectors are applied in the element-wise manner.

density ratio

$$r^*(\boldsymbol{x}) = \frac{p^*_{\mathrm{nu}}(\boldsymbol{x})}{p^*_{\mathrm{de}}(\boldsymbol{x})}$$

tends to take large values if $p^*_{\mathrm{nu}}(\boldsymbol{x})$ is large and $p^*_{\mathrm{de}}(\boldsymbol{x})$ is small. Conversely, $r^*(\boldsymbol{x})$ tends to be small (i.e., close to zero) if $p^*_{\mathrm{nu}}(\boldsymbol{x})$ is small and $p^*_{\mathrm{de}}(\boldsymbol{x})$ is large. When a non-negative function is approximated by a Gaussian kernel model, many kernels may be needed in the region where the output of the target function is large. On the other hand, only a small number of kernels would be enough in the region where the output of the target function is close to zero (see Figure 5.2). Following this heuristic, many kernels are allocated in the region where $p^*_{\mathrm{nu}}(\boldsymbol{x})$ takes large values, which can be achieved by setting the Gaussian centers to $\{\boldsymbol{x}^{\mathrm{nu}}_i\}_{i=1}^{n_{\mathrm{nu}}}$.

Alternatively, we may locate $(n_{\mathrm{nu}} + n_{\mathrm{de}})$ Gaussian kernels at both $\{\boldsymbol{x}^{\mathrm{nu}}_i\}_{i=1}^{n_{\mathrm{nu}}}$ and $\{\boldsymbol{x}^{\mathrm{de}}_j\}_{j=1}^{n_{\mathrm{de}}}$. However, this seems not to further improve the accuracy but slightly increases the computational cost. When n_{nu} is very large, using all the numerator samples $\{\boldsymbol{x}^{\mathrm{nu}}_i\}_{i=1}^{n_{\mathrm{nu}}}$ as Gaussian centers only is already computationally expensive. To ease this problem, a subset of $\{\boldsymbol{x}^{\mathrm{nu}}_i\}_{i=1}^{n_{\mathrm{nu}}}$ may be chosen in practice as Gaussian centers for computational efficiency, that is,

$$r(\boldsymbol{x}) = \sum_{\ell=1}^{b} \theta_\ell K(\boldsymbol{x}, \boldsymbol{c}_\ell),$$

where $\{\boldsymbol{c}_\ell\}_{\ell=1}^{b}$ are template points randomly chosen from $\{\boldsymbol{x}^{\mathrm{nu}}_i\}_{i=1}^{n_{\mathrm{nu}}}$ without replacement, and b $(\in \{1, \ldots, n_{\mathrm{nu}}\})$ is a prefixed number.

A MATLAB® implementation of the entire KLIEP algorithm (including model selection by cross-validation; see Section 5.3) is available from http://sugiyama-www.cs.titech.ac.jp/~sugi/software/KLIEP/.

The KLIEP methods for linear/kernel models are referred to as *linear KLIEP* (L-KLIEP) and *kernel KLIEP* (K-KLIEP), respectively.

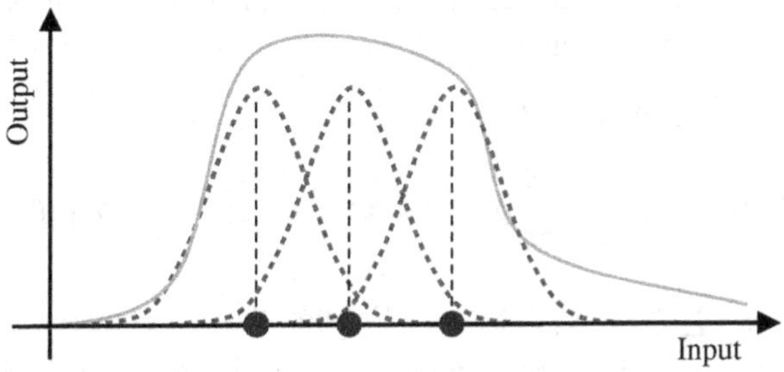

Figure 5.2. Heuristic of Gaussian kernel allocation.

5.2.2 Log-Linear Models

Another popular model choice is the *log-linear model* (Tsuboi et al., 2009; Kanamori et al., 2010):

$$r(\boldsymbol{x};\boldsymbol{\theta},\theta_0) = \exp\left(\boldsymbol{\psi}(\boldsymbol{x})^\top\boldsymbol{\theta} + \theta_0\right),$$

where θ_0 is a normalization parameter. From the normalization constraint

$$\frac{1}{n_{\mathrm{de}}}\sum_{j=1}^{n_{\mathrm{de}}} r(\boldsymbol{x}_j^{\mathrm{de}};\boldsymbol{\theta},\theta_0) = 1$$

derived from Eq. (5.1), θ_0 is determined as

$$\widehat{\theta}_0 = -\log\left(\frac{1}{n_{\mathrm{de}}}\sum_{j=1}^{n_{\mathrm{de}}}\exp\left(\boldsymbol{\psi}(\boldsymbol{x})^\top\boldsymbol{\theta}\right)\right).$$

Then the density-ratio model is expressed as

$$r(\boldsymbol{x};\boldsymbol{\theta}) = \frac{\exp\left(\boldsymbol{\psi}(\boldsymbol{x})^\top\boldsymbol{\theta}\right)}{\frac{1}{n_{\mathrm{de}}}\sum_{j=1}^{n_{\mathrm{de}}}\exp\left(\boldsymbol{\psi}(\boldsymbol{x})^\top\boldsymbol{\theta}\right)}.$$

By definition, outputs of the log-linear model $r(\boldsymbol{x};\boldsymbol{\theta})$ are non-negative for all $\boldsymbol{x}$. Thus, we do not need the non-negativity constraint on the parameter. Then the KLIEP optimization criterion is expressed as

$$\max_{\boldsymbol{\theta}\in\mathbb{R}^b} J(\boldsymbol{\theta}),$$

where

$$J(\boldsymbol{\theta}) := \overline{\boldsymbol{\psi}}_{\mathrm{nu}}^\top\boldsymbol{\theta} - \log\left(\frac{1}{n_{\mathrm{de}}}\sum_{j=1}^{n_{\mathrm{de}}}\exp(\boldsymbol{\psi}(\boldsymbol{x}_j^{\mathrm{de}})^\top\boldsymbol{\theta})\right),$$

$$\overline{\boldsymbol{\psi}}_{\mathrm{nu}} := \frac{1}{n_{\mathrm{nu}}}\sum_{i=1}^{n_{\mathrm{nu}}}\boldsymbol{\psi}(\boldsymbol{x}_i^{\mathrm{nu}}).$$

This is an unconstrained convex optimization problem, and thus the global optimal solution can be obtained by, for example, the gradient method or the (quasi-) Newton method. The gradient vector $\nabla J(\boldsymbol{\theta})$ and the Hessian matrix $\nabla\nabla J(\boldsymbol{\theta})$ of the objective function J are given by

$$\nabla J(\boldsymbol{\theta}) = \overline{\boldsymbol{\psi}}_{\mathrm{nu}} - \boldsymbol{\zeta}(\boldsymbol{\theta}),$$

$$\nabla\nabla J(\boldsymbol{\theta}) = -\frac{1}{n_{\mathrm{de}}}\sum_{j=1}^{n_{\mathrm{de}}}\boldsymbol{\psi}(\boldsymbol{x}_j^{\mathrm{de}})\boldsymbol{\psi}(\boldsymbol{x}_j^{\mathrm{de}})^\top r(\boldsymbol{x}_j^{\mathrm{de}};\boldsymbol{\theta}) + \boldsymbol{\zeta}(\boldsymbol{\theta})\boldsymbol{\zeta}(\boldsymbol{\theta})^\top,$$

where $\boldsymbol{\zeta}(\boldsymbol{\theta}) := \frac{1}{n_{\mathrm{de}}}\sum_{j=1}^{n_{\mathrm{de}}}\boldsymbol{\psi}(\boldsymbol{x}_j^{\mathrm{de}})r(\boldsymbol{x}_j^{\mathrm{de}};\boldsymbol{\theta})$. Because the numerator samples $\{\boldsymbol{x}_i^{\mathrm{nu}}\}_{i=1}^{n_{\mathrm{nu}}}$ appear only in terms of the basis-transformed mean $\overline{\boldsymbol{\psi}}_{\mathrm{nu}}$, the KLIEP for log-linear models is computationally efficient even when the number n_{nu} of numerator samples is large (cf. the KLIEP for linear/kernel models is computationally efficient when n_{de} is large; see Section 5.2.1).

The KLIEP method for log-linear models is called the *log-linear KLIEP* (LL-KLIEP).

5.2.3 Gaussian-Mixture Models

In the Gaussian kernel model (5.2), the Gaussian shape is spherical and its width is controlled by a single bandwidth parameter σ, which is chosen by *cross-validation* (see Section 5.3). Although it is possible to use correlated Gaussian kernels as a flexible alternative to spherical Gaussian kernels, choosing the covariance matrix via cross-validation is computationally intractable.

A practical approach to overcoming this problem is to also learn the covariance matrix directly from data. In this scenario, the *Gaussian mixture model* comes in handy (Yamada and Sugiyama, 2009):

$$r(\boldsymbol{x}; \{\theta_k, \boldsymbol{\mu}_k, \boldsymbol{\Sigma}_k\}_{k=1}^{c}) = \sum_{k=1}^{c} \theta_k N(\boldsymbol{x}; \boldsymbol{\mu}_k, \boldsymbol{\Sigma}_k), \tag{5.3}$$

where c is the number of mixing components, $\{\theta_k\}_{k=1}^{c}$ are mixing coefficients, $\{\boldsymbol{\mu}_k\}_{k=1}^{c}$ are means of Gaussian functions, $\{\boldsymbol{\Sigma}_k\}_{k=1}^{c}$ are covariance matrices of Gaussian functions, and $N(\boldsymbol{x}; \boldsymbol{\mu}, \boldsymbol{\Sigma})$ denotes the multi-dimensional Gaussian density with mean $\boldsymbol{\mu}$ and covariance matrix $\boldsymbol{\Sigma}$:

$$N(\boldsymbol{x}; \boldsymbol{\mu}, \boldsymbol{\Sigma}) := \frac{1}{(2\pi)^{\frac{d}{2}} \det(\boldsymbol{\Sigma})^{\frac{1}{2}}} \exp\left(-\frac{1}{2}(\boldsymbol{x} - \boldsymbol{\mu})^\top \boldsymbol{\Sigma}^{-1} (\boldsymbol{x} - \boldsymbol{\mu})\right), \tag{5.4}$$

where $\det(\cdot)$ denotes the determinant of a matrix. Note that $\boldsymbol{\Sigma}$ should be *positive definite*, that is, all the eigenvectors of $\boldsymbol{\Sigma}$ should be strictly positive.

For the Gaussian mixture model (5.3), the KLIEP optimization problem is expressed as

$$\begin{aligned}
&\max_{\{\theta_k, \boldsymbol{\mu}_k, \boldsymbol{\Sigma}_k\}_{k=1}^{c}} \ \frac{1}{n_{\mathrm{nu}}} \sum_{i=1}^{n_{\mathrm{nu}}} \log\left(\sum_{k=1}^{c} \theta_k N(\boldsymbol{x}_i^{\mathrm{nu}}; \boldsymbol{\mu}_k, \boldsymbol{\Sigma}_k)\right) \\
&\text{s.t.} \ \frac{1}{n_{\mathrm{de}}} \sum_{j=1}^{n_{\mathrm{de}}} \sum_{k=1}^{c} \theta_k N(\boldsymbol{x}_j^{\mathrm{de}}; \boldsymbol{\mu}_k, \boldsymbol{\Sigma}_k) = 1, \\
&\qquad \theta_k \geq 0 \text{ and } \boldsymbol{\Sigma}_k \succ \boldsymbol{O} \text{ for } k = 1, \ldots, c,
\end{aligned}$$

where $\boldsymbol{\Sigma}_k \succ \boldsymbol{O}$ means that $\boldsymbol{\Sigma}_k$ is positive definite.

This optimization problem is *non-convex*, and there is no known method for obtaining the global optimal solution. A *fixed-point iteration* gives an effective algorithm for obtaining a local optimal solution. A pseudo code is described in Figure 5.3. Practically, the *k-means clustering algorithm* may be used for effectively initializing the parameters (Bishop, 2006), and cross-validation (see

Section 5.3) may be used for determining the number of mixing components c and the regularization parameter λ (see the pseudo code in Figure 5.3).

The KLIEP method for Gaussian mixture models is called the *Gaussian-mixture KLIEP* (GM-KLIEP).

Input: Data samples $D^{\mathrm{nu}} = \{\boldsymbol{x}_i^{\mathrm{nu}}(\in \mathbb{R}^d)\}_{i=1}^{n_{\mathrm{nu}}}$ and $D^{\mathrm{de}} = \{\boldsymbol{x}_j^{\mathrm{de}}(\in \mathbb{R}^d)\}_{j=1}^{n_{\mathrm{de}}}$, and the number of mixing components c.
Output: Density-ratio estimator $\widehat{r}(\boldsymbol{x})$.

Initialization step: Initialize mixing coefficients $\{\theta_k(\geq 0)\}_{k=1}^{c}$, Gaussian means $\{\boldsymbol{\mu}_k(\in \mathbb{R}^d)\}_{k=1}^{c}$, and Gaussian covariance matrices $\{\boldsymbol{\Sigma}_k(\succ \boldsymbol{O})\}_{k=1}^{c}$.
Step 1: Evaluate the responsibility values $\{\gamma_{k,i}\}_{k=1,i=1}^{c\quad n_{\mathrm{nu}}}$ and $\{\beta_{k,j}\}_{k=1,j=1}^{c\quad n_{\mathrm{de}}}$ using the current parameters:

$$\gamma_{k,i} \longleftarrow \frac{\theta_k N(\boldsymbol{x}_i^{\mathrm{nu}};\boldsymbol{\mu}_k,\boldsymbol{\Sigma}_k)}{\sum_{k'=1}^{c}\theta_{k'} N(\boldsymbol{x}_i^{\mathrm{nu}};\boldsymbol{\mu}_{k'},\boldsymbol{\Sigma}_{k'})},$$

$$\beta_{k,j} \longleftarrow \frac{n_{\mathrm{nu}}}{n_{\mathrm{de}}}\theta_k N(\boldsymbol{x}_j^{\mathrm{de}}|\boldsymbol{\mu}_k,\boldsymbol{\Sigma}_k).$$

Step 2: Re-estimate the parameters $\{\theta_k,\boldsymbol{\mu}_k,\boldsymbol{\Sigma}_k\}_{k=1}^{c}$ using the current responsibility values $\{\gamma_{k,i}\}_{k=1,i=1}^{c\quad n_{\mathrm{nu}}}$:

$$\theta_k \longleftarrow \frac{n_{\mathrm{de}}\sum_{i=1}^{n_{\mathrm{nu}}}\gamma_{k,i}}{n_{\mathrm{nu}}\sum_{j=1}^{n_{\mathrm{de}}} N(\boldsymbol{x}_j^{\mathrm{de}};\boldsymbol{\mu}_k,\boldsymbol{\Sigma}_k)},$$

$$\boldsymbol{\mu}_k \longleftarrow \frac{\sum_{i=1}^{n_{\mathrm{nu}}}\gamma_{k,i}\boldsymbol{x}_i^{\mathrm{nu}} - \sum_{j=1}^{n_{\mathrm{de}}}\beta_{k,j}\boldsymbol{x}_j^{\mathrm{de}}}{\sum_{i'=1}^{n_{\mathrm{nu}}}\gamma_{k,i'} - \sum_{j'=1}^{n_{\mathrm{de}}}\beta_{k,j'}},$$

$$\boldsymbol{\Sigma}_k \longleftarrow \frac{\sum_{i=1}^{n_{\mathrm{nu}}}\gamma_{k,i}(\boldsymbol{x}_i^{\mathrm{nu}}-\boldsymbol{\mu}_k)(\boldsymbol{x}_i^{\mathrm{nu}}-\boldsymbol{\mu}_k)^\top}{\sum_{i'=1}^{n_{\mathrm{nu}}}\gamma_{k,i'} - \sum_{j'=1}^{n_{\mathrm{de}}}\beta_{k,j'}} - \frac{\sum_{j=1}^{n_{\mathrm{de}}}\beta_{k,j}(\boldsymbol{x}_j^{\mathrm{de}}-\boldsymbol{\mu}_k)(\boldsymbol{x}_j^{\mathrm{de}}-\boldsymbol{\mu}_k)^\top}{\sum_{i'=1}^{n_{\mathrm{nu}}}\gamma_{k,i'} - \sum_{j'=1}^{n_{\mathrm{de}}}\beta_{k,j'}} + \lambda\boldsymbol{I}_d,$$

where λ (> 0) is the regularization parameter and $\boldsymbol{I}_d$ denotes the d-dimensional identity matrix.
Evaluation step: Evaluate the objective value

$$\frac{1}{n_{\mathrm{nu}}}\sum_{i=1}^{n_{\mathrm{nu}}}\log\left(\sum_{k=1}^{c}\theta_k N(\boldsymbol{x}_i^{\mathrm{nu}};\boldsymbol{\mu}_k,\boldsymbol{\Sigma}_k)\right),$$

and repeat Steps 1 and 2 until the objective value converges.

Figure 5.3. Pseudo code of KLIEP for Gaussian-mixture models (GM-KLIEP).

5.2.4 Probabilistic PCA Mixture Models

The Gaussian mixture model explained in the previous subsection would be more flexible than linear, kernel, and log-linear models and suitable for approximating density-ratio functions with some correlation in input variables. However, when the target density-ratio function is (locally) rank-deficient, its behavior could be unstable because inverse covariance matrices are included in the Gaussian function [see Eq. (5.4)]. To cope with this problem, *probabilistic principal–component–analyzer mixture* (PPCA mixture) models (Tipping and Bishop, 1999) can be useful (Yamada et al., 2010a).

The PPCA mixture model is defined as

$$r(\boldsymbol{x}; \{\theta_k, \boldsymbol{\mu}_k, \sigma_k^2, \boldsymbol{W}_k\}_{k=1}^c) = \sum_{k=1}^{c} \theta_k N(\boldsymbol{x}; \boldsymbol{\mu}_k, \sigma_k^2, \boldsymbol{W}_k),$$

where c is the number of mixing components and $\{\theta_k\}_{k=1}^c$ are mixing coefficients. $N(\boldsymbol{x}; \boldsymbol{\mu}, \sigma^2, \boldsymbol{W})$ is a PPCA model defined by

$$N(\boldsymbol{x}; \boldsymbol{\mu}, \sigma^2, \boldsymbol{W}) = \frac{1}{(2\pi\sigma^2)^{\frac{d}{2}} \det(\boldsymbol{C})^{\frac{1}{2}}} \exp\left(-\frac{1}{2}(\boldsymbol{x}-\boldsymbol{\mu})^\top \boldsymbol{C}^{-1}(\boldsymbol{x}-\boldsymbol{\mu})\right),$$

where $\det(\cdot)$ denotes the determinant of a matrix. $\boldsymbol{\mu}$ is the mean of the Gaussian function, σ^2 is the variance of the Gaussian function, $\boldsymbol{W}$ is a $d \times m$ 'projection' matrix onto an m-dimensional *latent* space (where $m \leq d$), and $\boldsymbol{C} = \boldsymbol{W}\boldsymbol{W}^\top + \sigma^2 \boldsymbol{I}_d$.

Then the KLIEP optimization criterion is expressed as

$$\begin{aligned}
\max_{\{\theta_k, \boldsymbol{\mu}_k, \sigma_k^2, \boldsymbol{W}_k\}_{k=1}^c} \quad & \frac{1}{n_{\mathrm{nu}}} \sum_{i=1}^{n_{\mathrm{nu}}} \log\left(\sum_{k=1}^{c} \theta_k N(\boldsymbol{x}_i^{\mathrm{nu}}; \boldsymbol{\mu}_k, \sigma_k^2, \boldsymbol{W}_k)\right) \\
\text{s.t.} \quad & \frac{1}{n_{\mathrm{de}}} \sum_{j=1}^{n_{\mathrm{de}}} \sum_{k=1}^{c} \theta_k N(\boldsymbol{x}_j^{\mathrm{de}}; \boldsymbol{\mu}_k, \sigma_k^2, \boldsymbol{W}_k) = 1, \\
& \theta_k \geq 0 \text{ for } k = 1, \ldots, c.
\end{aligned}$$

This optimization is non-convex, and thus we may use the *fixed-point iteration* to obtain a local optimal solution in the same way as the GM-KLIEP (Yamada et al., 2010a).

When the dimensionality of the latent space m is equal to the entire dimensionality d, PPCA models are reduced to ordinary Gaussian models. Thus, PPCA models can be regarded as an extension of Gaussian models to (locally) rank-deficient data. The KLIEP method for PPCA mixture models is called the *PPCA-mixture KLIEP* (PM-KLIEP). The PM-KLIEP is suitable for learning locally rank-deficient density-ratio functions. On the other hand, methods for accurately learning *globally* rank-deficient density-ratio functions are explained in Chapter 8.

5.3 Model Selection by Cross-Validation

In the previous section we described implementations of the KLIEP for various models. In practice, estimation accuracy depends heavily on the choice of tuning parameters such as the regularization parameter and kernel parameters. Model selection of the KLIEP is possible based on *cross-validation* (CV), which is explained in this section.

In the CV procedure of the KLIEP, the numerator samples $\mathcal{D}^{\mathrm{nu}} = \{\boldsymbol{x}_i^{\mathrm{nu}}\}_{i=1}^{n_{\mathrm{nu}}}$ are divided into T disjoint subsets $\{\mathcal{D}_t^{\mathrm{nu}}\}_{t=1}^{T}$. Then a KLIEP solution $\widehat{r}_t(\boldsymbol{x})$ is obtained using $\mathcal{D}^{\mathrm{nu}} \backslash \mathcal{D}_t^{\mathrm{nu}}$ and $\mathcal{D}^{\mathrm{de}}$ (i.e., all numerator samples without $\mathcal{D}_t^{\mathrm{nu}}$ and all denominator samples), and its KL value for the hold-out numerator samples $\mathcal{D}_t^{\mathrm{nu}}$ is computed:

$$\widetilde{\mathrm{KL}}_t := \frac{1}{|\mathcal{D}_t^{\mathrm{nu}}|} \sum_{\boldsymbol{x}^{\mathrm{nu}} \in \mathcal{D}_t^{\mathrm{nu}}} \log \widehat{r}_t(\boldsymbol{x}^{\mathrm{nu}}).$$

This procedure is repeated for $t = 1, \ldots, T$, and the average of the hold-out KL values over all t is computed as

$$\widetilde{\mathrm{KL}} := \frac{1}{T} \sum_{t=1}^{T} \widetilde{\mathrm{KL}}_t.$$

Then the model that maximizes $\widetilde{\mathrm{KL}}$ is chosen.

A pseudo code of CV for KLIEP is summarized in Figure 5.4.

Input: Data samples $\mathcal{D}^{\mathrm{nu}} = \{\boldsymbol{x}_i^{\mathrm{nu}}\}_{i=1}^{n_{\mathrm{nu}}}$ and $\mathcal{D}^{\mathrm{de}} = \{\boldsymbol{x}_j^{\mathrm{de}}\}_{j=1}^{n_{\mathrm{de}}}$,
and a set of basis function candidates $\{\boldsymbol{\psi}_m(\boldsymbol{x})\}_{m=1}^{M}$.
Output: Density-ratio estimator $\widehat{r}(\boldsymbol{x})$.

Split $\mathcal{D}^{\mathrm{nu}}$ into T disjoint subsets $\{\mathcal{D}_t^{\mathrm{nu}}\}_{t=1}^{T}$;
for each model candidate $m = 1, \ldots, M$
  for each split $t = 1, \ldots, T$
    $\widehat{r}_t(\boldsymbol{x}) \longleftarrow \mathrm{KLIEP}(\mathcal{D}^{\mathrm{nu}} \backslash \mathcal{D}_t^{\mathrm{nu}}, \mathcal{D}^{\mathrm{de}}, \boldsymbol{\psi}(\boldsymbol{x}))$;
    $\widetilde{\mathrm{KL}}_t(m) \longleftarrow \frac{1}{|\mathcal{D}_t^{\mathrm{nu}}|} \sum_{\boldsymbol{x} \in \mathcal{D}_t^{\mathrm{nu}}} \log \widehat{r}_t(\boldsymbol{x})$;
  end
  $\widetilde{\mathrm{KL}}(m) \longleftarrow \frac{1}{T} \sum_{t=1}^{T} \widetilde{\mathrm{KL}}_t(m)$;
end
$\widehat{m} \longleftarrow \mathrm{argmax}_m \, \widetilde{\mathrm{KL}}(m)$;
$\widehat{r}(\boldsymbol{x}) \longleftarrow \mathrm{KLIEP}(\mathcal{D}^{\mathrm{nu}}, \mathcal{D}^{\mathrm{de}}, \boldsymbol{\psi}_{\widehat{m}}(\boldsymbol{x}))$;

Figure 5.4. Pseudo code of CV for KLIEP.

5.4 Numerical Examples

In this section we illustrate the numerical behavior of the KLIEP algorithm for the kernel models described in Section 5.2.1.

Let us consider a one-dimensional example (i.e., $d = 1$), and suppose that the two densities $p^*_{\mathrm{nu}}(x)$ and $p^*_{\mathrm{de}}(x)$ are defined as

$$p^*_{\mathrm{nu}}(x) = N(x; 1, 1^2) \quad \text{and} \quad p^*_{\mathrm{de}}(x) = N(x; 0, 2^2),$$

where $N(x; \mu, \sigma^2)$ denotes the Gaussian density with mean μ and variance σ^2. The true densities are plotted in Figure 5.5(a), while the true density ratio $r^*(x)$ is plotted in Figure 5.5(b).

Let $n_{\mathrm{nu}} = n_{\mathrm{de}} = 200$. For density-ratio estimation, we use the KLIEP algorithm with the following Gaussian kernel model:

$$r(x) = \sum_{\ell=1}^{n_{\mathrm{nu}}} \theta_\ell \exp\left(-\frac{(x - x_\ell^{\mathrm{nu}})^2}{2\sigma^2}\right).$$

The Gaussian width σ is chosen by 5-fold cross-validation (see Section 5.3). The density-ratio function estimated by the KLIEP algorithm, $\widehat{r}(x)$, is described in Figure 5.5(b), which shows that the KLIEP gives a reasonably good approximation to the true density-ratio function $r^*(x)$.

5.5 Remarks

Density-ratio estimation by density fitting under the KL divergence allows one to avoid density estimation when estimating density ratios (Section 5.1). Furthermore, cross-validation with respect to the KL divergence is available for model selection, as described in Section 5.3.

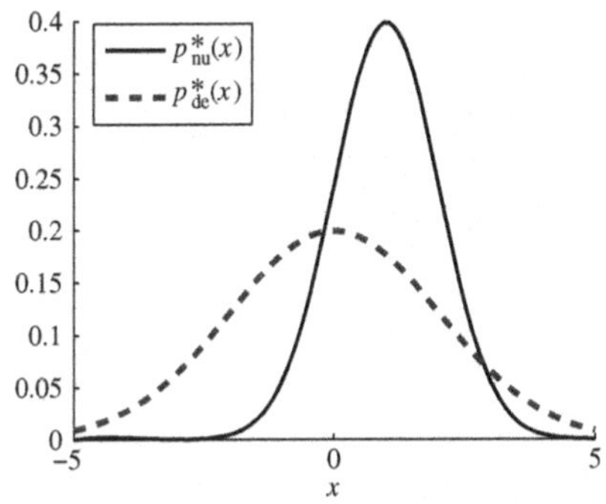

(a) True densities

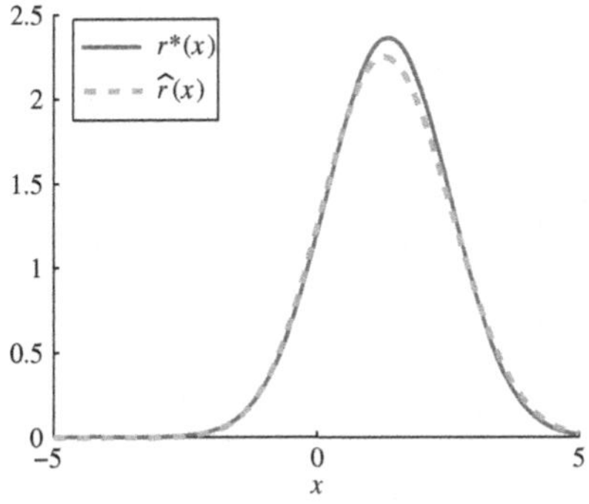

(b) True and estimated density ratios

Figure 5.5. Numerical example of the KLIEP.

The method, called the *KL importance estimation procedure* (KLIEP), is applicable to a variety of models such as linear models, kernel models, log-linear models, Gaussian mixture models, and probabilistic principal–component–analyzer mixture models (see Section 5.2).

Theoretical properties of the KLIEP such as parametric and non-parametric convergence rates have been studied in Sugiyama et al. (2008), which will be explained in Sections 13.1 and 14.2. Also, under a certain parametric setup, the KLIEP was proved to perform better than alternative approaches (Kanamori et al., 2010), which will be detailed in Section 13.4.

6

Density-Ratio Fitting

In this chapter we describe a framework of density-ratio estimation by least-squares density-ratio fitting (Kanamori et al., 2009).

We first give a basic framework for a least-squares fitting of density ratios called *least-squares importance fitting* (LSIF) in Section 6.1. Then, two practical implementation LSIFs *constrained LSIF* (cLSIF) and *unconstrained LSIF* (uLSIF) – are described in Section 6.2. In Section 6.3, model selection by cross-validation in the LSIF framework is explained. Also, we describe two schemes for speeding up model selection, that is, regularization path tracking for cLSIF and analytic computation of leave-one-out cross-validation scores for uLSIF. Numerical examples are shown in Section 6.4, and finally the chapter is concluded in Section 6.5.

6.1 Basic Framework

In this section we describe the framework of least-squares density-ratio fitting (Kanamori et al., 2009).

Let us model the true density-ratio function

$$r^*(\boldsymbol{x}) = \frac{p^*_{\mathrm{nu}}(\boldsymbol{x})}{p^*_{\mathrm{de}}(\boldsymbol{x})}$$

by a model $r(\boldsymbol{x})$. The model $r(\boldsymbol{x})$ is learned so that the following squared error SQ' is minimized:

$$\begin{aligned}\mathrm{SQ}'(r) &:= \frac{1}{2}\int \left(r(\boldsymbol{x}) - r^*(\boldsymbol{x})\right)^2 p^*_{\mathrm{de}}(\boldsymbol{x})\mathrm{d}\boldsymbol{x} \\ &= \frac{1}{2}\int r(\boldsymbol{x})^2 p^*_{\mathrm{de}}(\boldsymbol{x})\mathrm{d}\boldsymbol{x} - \int r(\boldsymbol{x}) p^*_{\mathrm{nu}}(\boldsymbol{x})\mathrm{d}\boldsymbol{x} + \frac{1}{2}\int r^*(\boldsymbol{x}) p^*_{\mathrm{nu}}(\boldsymbol{x})\mathrm{d}\boldsymbol{x},\end{aligned}$$

where the last term is a constant and therefore can be safely ignored. Let us denote the first two terms by SQ:

$$\mathrm{SQ}(r) := \frac{1}{2}\int r(\boldsymbol{x})^2 p^*_{\mathrm{de}}(\boldsymbol{x})\mathrm{d}\boldsymbol{x} - \int r(\boldsymbol{x}) p^*_{\mathrm{nu}}(\boldsymbol{x})\mathrm{d}\boldsymbol{x}.$$

Approximating the expectations in SQ by empirical averages, we obtain

$$\widehat{\mathrm{SQ}}(r) := \frac{1}{2n_{\mathrm{de}}}\sum_{j=1}^{n_{\mathrm{de}}} r(\boldsymbol{x}_j^{\mathrm{de}})^2 - \frac{1}{n_{\mathrm{nu}}}\sum_{i=1}^{n_{\mathrm{nu}}} r(\boldsymbol{x}_i^{\mathrm{nu}}).$$

Thus, the optimization problem is given as

$$\min_r \left[\frac{1}{2n_{\mathrm{de}}}\sum_{j=1}^{n_{\mathrm{de}}} r(\boldsymbol{x}_j^{\mathrm{de}})^2 - \frac{1}{n_{\mathrm{nu}}}\sum_{i=1}^{n_{\mathrm{nu}}} r(\boldsymbol{x}_i^{\mathrm{nu}})\right].$$

We refer to this formulation as *least-squares importance fitting* (LSIF).

6.2 Implementation of LSIF

In this section we describe two implementations of LSIF for the linear model

$$r(\boldsymbol{x}) = \sum_{\ell=1}^{b} \theta_\ell \psi_\ell(\boldsymbol{x}) = \boldsymbol{\psi}(\boldsymbol{x})^\top \boldsymbol{\theta},$$

where $\boldsymbol{\psi}(\boldsymbol{x}) : \mathbb{R}^d \to \mathbb{R}^b$ is a non-negative basis function vector and $\boldsymbol{\theta}$ ($\in \mathbb{R}^b$) is a parameter vector. Because this model is in the same form as that used in the KLIEP for linear/kernel models (Section 5.2.1), we may use the same basis design idea described there.

For the above linear model, SQ and $\widehat{\mathrm{SQ}}$ defined in Section 6.1 are expressed as

$$\mathrm{SQ}(\boldsymbol{\theta}) := \frac{1}{2}\boldsymbol{\theta}^\top \boldsymbol{H}\boldsymbol{\theta} - \boldsymbol{h}^\top\boldsymbol{\theta} \quad \text{and} \quad \widehat{\mathrm{SQ}}(\boldsymbol{\theta}) := \frac{1}{2}\boldsymbol{\theta}^\top \widehat{\boldsymbol{H}}\boldsymbol{\theta} - \widehat{\boldsymbol{h}}^\top\boldsymbol{\theta},$$

where

$$\boldsymbol{H} := \int p^*_{\mathrm{de}}(\boldsymbol{x})\boldsymbol{\psi}(\boldsymbol{x})\boldsymbol{\psi}(\boldsymbol{x})^\top \mathrm{d}\boldsymbol{x}, \quad \widehat{\boldsymbol{H}} := \frac{1}{n_{\mathrm{de}}}\sum_{j=1}^{n_{\mathrm{de}}} \boldsymbol{\psi}(\boldsymbol{x}_j^{\mathrm{de}})\boldsymbol{\psi}(\boldsymbol{x}_j^{\mathrm{de}})^\top, \tag{6.1}$$

$$\boldsymbol{h} := \int p^*_{\mathrm{nu}}(\boldsymbol{x})\boldsymbol{\psi}(\boldsymbol{x})\mathrm{d}\boldsymbol{x}, \quad \text{and} \quad \widehat{\boldsymbol{h}} := \frac{1}{n_{\mathrm{nu}}}\sum_{i=1}^{n_{\mathrm{nu}}} \boldsymbol{\psi}(\boldsymbol{x}_i^{\mathrm{nu}}). \tag{6.2}$$

Following Kanamori et al. (2009), we describe implementations of LSIF for linear models *with* and *without* non-negativity constraints in Sections 6.2.1 and 6.2.2.

6.2.1 Implementation with Non-Negativity Constraint

Here we describe an implementation of LSIF *with* a non-negativity constraint, called a *constrained LSIF* (cLSIF).

Let us impose the non-negativity constraint $\boldsymbol{\theta} \geq \boldsymbol{0}_b$ when minimizing $\widehat{\mathrm{SQ}}$, since the density-ratio function is non-negative by definition. Let us further add the following regularization term to the objective function:

$$\mathbf{1}_b^\top \boldsymbol{\theta} = \|\boldsymbol{\theta}\|_1 := \sum_{\ell=1}^{b} |\theta_\ell|.$$

The term $\mathbf{1}_b^\top \boldsymbol{\theta}$ works as the ℓ_1-regularizer if it is combined with the non-negativity constraint. Then the optimization problem is expressed as

$$\min_{\boldsymbol{\theta} \in \mathbb{R}^b} \left[\frac{1}{2} \boldsymbol{\theta}^\top \widehat{\boldsymbol{H}} \boldsymbol{\theta} - \widehat{\boldsymbol{h}}^\top \boldsymbol{\theta} + \lambda \mathbf{1}_b^\top \boldsymbol{\theta} \right] \quad \text{s.t.} \quad \boldsymbol{\theta} \geq \mathbf{0}_b,$$

where λ (≥ 0) is the regularization parameter. We refer to this method as a *constrained LSIF* (cLSIF). The cLSIF optimization problem is a convex quadratic program, and thus the unique global optimal solution can be obtained by a standard optimization software.

We can also use the ℓ_2-regularizer $\boldsymbol{\theta}^\top \boldsymbol{\theta}$, instead of the ℓ_1-regularizer $\mathbf{1}_b^\top \boldsymbol{\theta}$, without changing the computational property (i.e., the optimization problem is still a convex quadratic program). However, the ℓ_1-regularizer is more advantageous due to its *sparsity-inducing* property, that is, many parameters take exactly zero (Williams, 1995; Tibshirani, 1996; Chen et al., 1998). Furthermore, as explained in Section 6.3.2, the use of the ℓ_1-regularizer allows one to compute the entire *regularization path* efficiently (Best, 1982; Efron et al., 2004; Hastie et al., 2004), which highly improves the computational cost in the model selection phase.

6.2.2 Implementation without Non-Negativity Constraint

Here we describe another implementation of LSIF *without* the non-negativity constraint.

Without the non-negativity constraint, the linear regularizer $\mathbf{1}_b^\top \boldsymbol{\theta}$ used in cLSIF does not work as a regularizer. For this reason, a quadratic regularizer $\boldsymbol{\theta}^\top \boldsymbol{\theta}$ is adopted here. Then we have the following optimization problem:

$$\min_{\boldsymbol{\theta} \in \mathbb{R}^b} \left[\frac{1}{2} \boldsymbol{\theta}^\top \widehat{\boldsymbol{H}} \boldsymbol{\theta} - \widehat{\boldsymbol{h}}^\top \boldsymbol{\theta} + \frac{\lambda}{2} \boldsymbol{\theta}^\top \boldsymbol{\theta} \right]. \tag{6.3}$$

Equation (6.3) is an unconstrained convex quadratic program, and the solution can be computed *analytically* by solving the following system of linear equations:

$$(\widehat{\boldsymbol{H}} + \lambda \boldsymbol{I}_b) \boldsymbol{\theta} = \widehat{\boldsymbol{h}},$$

where $\boldsymbol{I}_b$ is the b-dimensional identity matrix. The solution $\widehat{\boldsymbol{\theta}}$ of this equation is given by $\widehat{\boldsymbol{\theta}} = (\widehat{\boldsymbol{H}} + \lambda \boldsymbol{I}_b)^{-1} \widehat{\boldsymbol{h}}$. This method is called an *unconstrained LSIF* (uLSIF). An advantage of uLSIF is that the solution can be analytically computed simply by solving a system of linear equations. Therefore, its computation is stable when λ is not too small.

Because the non-negativity constraint $\boldsymbol{\theta} \geq \mathbf{0}_b$ was dropped, estimated density-ratio values could be negative. To compensate for this, negative outputs may be rounded up to zero as follows (Kanamori et al., 2011b):

$$\widehat{r}(\boldsymbol{x}) = \max(0, \boldsymbol{\psi}(\boldsymbol{x})^\top \boldsymbol{\theta}).$$

6.3 Model Selection by Cross-Validation

Model selection of cLSIF and uLSIF (i.e., the choice of the basis functions and the regularization parameter) is possible by *cross-validation* based on the SQ criterion.

In Section 6.3.1 we first explain how cross-validation is performed for cLSIF and uLSIF. Then we describe two schemes for speeding up model selection: a *regularization-path* tracking algorithm for cLSIF (Section 6.3.2) and analytic computation of leave-one-out cross-validation scores for uLSIF (Section 6.3.3).

6.3.1 Cross-Validation

More specifically, the numerator and denominator samples $\mathcal{D}^{\mathrm{nu}} = \{\boldsymbol{x}_i^{\mathrm{nu}}\}_{i=1}^{n_{\mathrm{nu}}}$ and $\mathcal{D}^{\mathrm{de}} = \{\boldsymbol{x}_j^{\mathrm{de}}\}_{j=1}^{n_{\mathrm{de}}}$ are divided into T disjoint subsets $\{\mathcal{D}_t^{\mathrm{nu}}\}_{t=1}^T$ and $\{\mathcal{D}_t^{\mathrm{de}}\}_{t=1}^T$, respectively. Then a density-ratio estimator $\widehat{r}_t(\boldsymbol{x})$ is obtained using $\mathcal{D}^{\mathrm{nu}} \backslash \mathcal{D}_t^{\mathrm{nu}}$ and $\mathcal{D}^{\mathrm{de}} \backslash \mathcal{D}_t^{\mathrm{de}}$ (i.e., all samples without $\mathcal{D}_t^{\mathrm{nu}}$ and $\mathcal{D}_t^{\mathrm{de}}$), and its SQ value for the hold-out samples $\mathcal{D}_t^{\mathrm{nu}}$ and $\mathcal{D}_t^{\mathrm{de}}$ is computed:

$$\widetilde{\mathrm{SQ}}_t := \frac{1}{2|\mathcal{D}_t^{\mathrm{nu}}|} \sum_{\boldsymbol{x}^{\mathrm{nu}} \in \mathcal{D}_t^{\mathrm{nu}}} \widehat{r}_t(\boldsymbol{x}^{\mathrm{nu}})^2 - \frac{1}{|\mathcal{D}_t^{\mathrm{de}}|} \sum_{\boldsymbol{x}^{\mathrm{de}} \in \mathcal{D}_t^{\mathrm{de}}} \widehat{r}_t(\boldsymbol{x}^{\mathrm{de}}).$$

This procedure is repeated for $t = 1, \ldots, T$, and the average of these hold-out SQ values is computed as

$$\widetilde{\mathrm{SQ}} := \frac{1}{T} \sum_{t=1}^{T} \widetilde{\mathrm{SQ}}_t.$$

Then the model that minimizes $\widetilde{\mathrm{SQ}}$ is chosen.

6.3.2 Entire Regularization Path for cLSIF

The cLSIF solution $\widehat{\boldsymbol{\theta}}$ is shown to be *piecewise-linear* with respect to the regularization parameter λ (see Figure 6.1). Thus, the *regularization path* (i.e., solutions for all λ) can be computed efficiently based on the *parametric optimization technique* (Best, 1982; Efron et al., 2004; Hastie et al., 2004).

A basic idea of regularization-path tracking is to check the violation of the *Karush–Kuhn–Tacker (KKT) conditions* (Boyd and Vandenberghe, 2004), which are necessary and sufficient conditions for the optimality of convex programs, when the regularization parameter λ is changed. A pseudo code of the regularization-path tracking algorithm for cLSIF is described in Figure 6.2. Thanks to the regularization-path algorithm, model selection of cLSIF can be carried out efficiently.

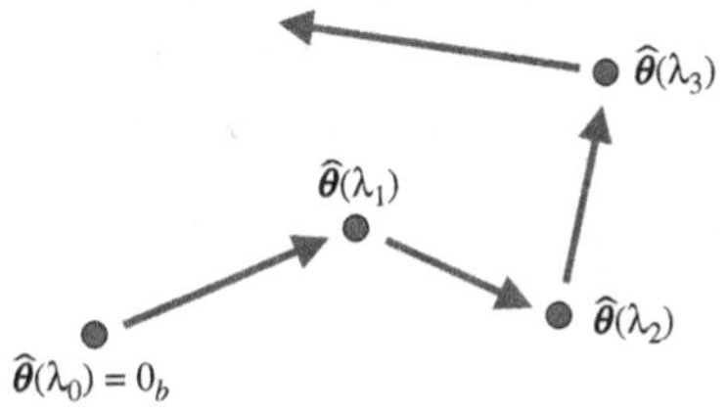

Figure 6.1. Regularization path tracking of cLSIF. The solution $\widehat{\boldsymbol{\theta}}(\lambda)$ is shown to be piecewise-linear in the parameter space as a function of λ. Starting from $\lambda = \infty$, the trajectory of the solution is traced as λ is decreased to zero. When $\lambda \geq \lambda_0$ for some $\lambda_0 \geq 0$, the solution stays at the origin $\mathbf{0}_b$. When λ gets smaller than λ_0, the solution departs from the origin. As λ is further decreased, for some λ_1 such that $0 \leq \lambda_1 \leq \lambda_0$, the solution goes straight to $\widehat{\boldsymbol{\theta}}(\lambda_1)$ with a constant 'speed'. Then the solution path changes its direction and, for some λ_2 such that $0 \leq \lambda_2 \leq \lambda_1$, the solution heads straight for $\widehat{\boldsymbol{\theta}}(\lambda_2)$ with a constant speed as λ is further decreased. This process is repeated until λ reaches zero.

The pseudo code implies that we no longer need a quadratic programming solver for obtaining the cLSIF solution; just computing matrix inverse is sufficient. Furthermore, the regularization-path algorithm is computationally more efficient when the solution is sparse (i.e., most of the elements are zero) because the number of change points tends to be small for such sparse solutions.

Although the regularization-path tracking algorithm is computationally efficient, it tends to be numerically unreliable, as experimentally shown in Kanamori et al. (2009). This numerical instability is caused by near singularity of the matrix $\widehat{\boldsymbol{G}}$ (see the pseudo code in Figure 6.2). When $\widehat{\boldsymbol{G}}$ is nearly singular, it is not easy to accurately obtain the solutions $\boldsymbol{u}$ and $\boldsymbol{v}$ in Figure 6.2. Then the change point $\lambda_{\tau+1}$ cannot be detected accurately, and the active set of the inequality constraints cannot be updated accurately. Consequently, the obtained solution $\widehat{\boldsymbol{\theta}}(\lambda)$ can become unreliable; furthermore, such numerical error tends to be accumulated through the path-tracking process. This instability issue seems to be a common pitfall of solution-path-tracking algorithms in general (Scheinberg, 2006).

Suppose that the basis design heuristic described in Section 5.2.1 (i.e., the Gaussian kernel model with Gaussian centers chosen from the numerator samples) is used. Then the matrix $\widehat{\boldsymbol{H}}$ tends to be nearly singular when the Gaussian width σ is very small or very large, which makes the matrix $\widehat{\boldsymbol{G}}$ also nearly singular. On the other hand, when the Gaussian width σ is not too small or too large compared with the dispersion of samples, the matrix $\widehat{\boldsymbol{G}}$ is well conditioned, and therefore the path-following algorithm performs well in a stable and reliable manner.

An R implementation of cLSIF with regularization path tracking is available from http://www.math.cm.is.nagoya-u.ac.jp/~kanamori/software/LSIF/.

6.3.3 Analytic Expression of Leave-One-Out Score

A practically important advantage of uLSIF over cLSIF is that the score of *leave-one-out cross-validation* (LOOCV) can be computed analytically (Kanamori

Input: $\widehat{\boldsymbol{H}}$ and $\widehat{\boldsymbol{h}}$ % see Eqs. (6.1) and (6.2) for their definitions

Output: Entire regularization path $\widehat{\boldsymbol{\theta}}(\lambda)$ for $\lambda \geq 0$

$\tau \longleftarrow 0$; $\quad k \longleftarrow \mathrm{argmax}_i\{\widehat{h}_i \mid i=1,\ldots,b\}$; $\quad \lambda_\tau \longleftarrow \widehat{h}_k$;

$\widehat{\mathcal{A}} \longleftarrow \{1,\ldots,b\}\backslash\{k\}$; $\quad \widehat{\boldsymbol{\theta}}(\lambda_\tau) \longleftarrow \boldsymbol{0}_b$;

While $\lambda_\tau > 0$

$\quad \widehat{\boldsymbol{E}} \longleftarrow \boldsymbol{O}_{|\widehat{\mathcal{A}}|\times b}$;

$\quad$ **For** $i=1,\ldots,|\widehat{\mathcal{A}}|$

$\quad\quad \widehat{E}_{i,\widehat{j}_i} \longleftarrow 1$; % $\widehat{\mathcal{A}}=\{\widehat{j}_1,\ldots,\widehat{j}_{|\widehat{\mathcal{A}}|} \mid \widehat{j}_1 < \cdots < \widehat{j}_{|\widehat{\mathcal{A}}|}\}$

$\quad$ **end**

$$\widehat{\boldsymbol{G}} \longleftarrow \begin{pmatrix} \widehat{\boldsymbol{H}} & -\widehat{\boldsymbol{E}}^\top \\ -\widehat{\boldsymbol{E}} & \boldsymbol{O}_{|\widehat{\mathcal{A}}|\times|\widehat{\mathcal{A}}|} \end{pmatrix}; \quad \boldsymbol{u} \longleftarrow \widehat{\boldsymbol{G}}^{-1}\begin{pmatrix} \widehat{\boldsymbol{h}} \\ \boldsymbol{0}_{|\widehat{\mathcal{A}}|} \end{pmatrix}; \quad \boldsymbol{v} \longleftarrow \widehat{\boldsymbol{G}}^{-1}\begin{pmatrix} \boldsymbol{1}_b \\ \boldsymbol{0}_{|\widehat{\mathcal{A}}|} \end{pmatrix};$$

$\quad$ **If** $\boldsymbol{v} \leq \boldsymbol{0}_{b+|\widehat{\mathcal{A}}|}$ % the final interval

$\quad\quad \lambda_{\tau+1} \longleftarrow 0$; $\quad \widehat{\boldsymbol{\theta}}(\lambda_{\tau+1}) \longleftarrow (u_1,\ldots,u_b)^\top$;

$\quad$ **else** % an intermediate interval

$\quad\quad k \longleftarrow \mathrm{argmax}_i\{u_i/v_i \mid v_i > 0,\ i=1,\ldots,b+|\widehat{\mathcal{A}}|\}$;

$\quad\quad \lambda_{\tau+1} \longleftarrow \max\{0, u_k/v_k\}$;

$\quad\quad \widehat{\boldsymbol{\theta}}(\lambda_{\tau+1}) \longleftarrow (u_1,\ldots,u_b)^\top - \lambda_{\tau+1}(v_1,\ldots,v_b)^\top$;

$\quad\quad$ **If** $1 \leq k \leq b$

$\quad\quad\quad \widehat{\mathcal{A}} \longleftarrow \widehat{\mathcal{A}} \cup \{k\}$;

$\quad\quad$ **else**

$\quad\quad\quad \widehat{\mathcal{A}} \longleftarrow \widehat{\mathcal{A}}\backslash\{\widehat{j}_{k-b}\}$;

$\quad\quad$ **end**

$\quad$ **end**

$\quad \tau \longleftarrow \tau + 1$;

end

$$\widehat{\boldsymbol{\theta}}(\lambda) \longleftarrow \begin{cases} \boldsymbol{0}_b & \text{if } \lambda \geq \lambda_0 \\ \frac{\lambda_{\tau+1}-\lambda}{\lambda_{\tau+1}-\lambda_\tau}\widehat{\boldsymbol{\theta}}(\lambda_\tau) + \frac{\lambda-\lambda_\tau}{\lambda_{\tau+1}-\lambda_\tau}\widehat{\boldsymbol{\theta}}(\lambda_{\tau+1}) & \text{if } \lambda_{\tau+1} \leq \lambda \leq \lambda_\tau \end{cases}$$

Figure 6.2. Pseudo code for computing the entire regularization path of cLSIF. When the computation of $\widehat{\boldsymbol{G}}^{-1}$ is numerically unstable, small positive diagonals may be added to $\widehat{\boldsymbol{H}}$ for stabilization.

et al., 2009). Thanks to this property, the computational complexity for performing LOOCV is the same order as just computing a single solution.

In the current setup, two sets of samples, $\{\boldsymbol{x}_i^{\mathrm{nu}}\}_{i=1}^{n_{\mathrm{nu}}}$ and $\{\boldsymbol{x}_j^{\mathrm{de}}\}_{j=1}^{n_{\mathrm{de}}}$, generally have different sample sizes. For $i=1,\ldots,n$, where $n := \min(n_{\mathrm{nu}}, n_{\mathrm{de}})$, suppose that the i-th numerator sample $\boldsymbol{x}_i^{\mathrm{nu}}$ and the i-th denominator sample $\boldsymbol{x}_i^{\mathrm{de}}$ are held out at the same time in the LOOCV procedure; the remaining numerator or numerator samples for $i > n$ are assumed to be always used for density-ratio estimation.

Note that the order of numerical samples can be changed without sacrificing the computational advantages.

Let $\widehat{r}_i(\boldsymbol{x})$ be a density-ratio estimate obtained without the i-th numerator sample $\boldsymbol{x}_i^{\mathrm{nu}}$ and the i-th denominator sample $\boldsymbol{x}_i^{\mathrm{de}}$. Then the LOOCV score is expressed as

$$\mathrm{LOOCV} = \frac{1}{n}\sum_{i=1}^{n}\left[\frac{1}{2}(\widehat{r}_i(\boldsymbol{x}_i^{\mathrm{de}}))^2 - \widehat{r}_i(\boldsymbol{x}_i^{\mathrm{nu}})\right].$$

A trick to efficiently compute the LOOCV score is to use the *Sherman–Woodbury–Morrison formula* (Golub and Loan, 1996) for computing matrix inverses: For an invertible square matrix $\boldsymbol{A}$ and vectors $\boldsymbol{u}$ and $\boldsymbol{v}$ such that $\boldsymbol{v}^\top \boldsymbol{A}^{-1}\boldsymbol{u} \neq -1$,

$$(\boldsymbol{A}+\boldsymbol{u}\boldsymbol{v}^\top)^{-1} = \boldsymbol{A}^{-1} - \frac{\boldsymbol{A}^{-1}\boldsymbol{u}\boldsymbol{v}^\top\boldsymbol{A}^{-1}}{1+\boldsymbol{v}^\top\boldsymbol{A}^{-1}\boldsymbol{u}}.$$

Efficient approximation schemes of LOOCV have been investigated under asymptotic setups (Stone, 1974; Larsen and Hansen, 1996). On the other hand, for uLSIF, the LOOCV score can be computed exactly, which follows the same line as that for *ridge regression* (Hoerl and Kennard, 1970; Wahba, 1990).

MATLAB® and R implementations of uLSIF are available from http://sugiyama-www.cs.titech.ac.jp/~sugi/software/uLSIF/ and http://www.math.cm.is.nagoya-u.ac.jp/~kanamori/software/LSIF/.

6.4 Numerical Examples

In this section we illustrate the numerical behavior of the uLSIF algorithm described in Section 6.2.2.

Let us consider a one-dimensional example (i.e., $d = 1$), and suppose that the two densities $p^*_{\mathrm{nu}}(x)$ and $p^*_{\mathrm{de}}(x)$ are defined as

$$p^*_{\mathrm{nu}}(x) = N(x;1,1^2) \quad \text{and} \quad p^*_{\mathrm{de}}(x) = p(x;0,2^2),$$

where $N(x;\mu,\sigma^2)$ denotes the Gaussian density with mean μ and variance σ^2. The true densities are plotted in Figure 6.3(a), while the true density ratio $r^*(x)$ is plotted in Figure 6.3(b).

Let $n_{\mathrm{nu}} = n_{\mathrm{de}} = 200$. For density-ratio estimation, we use the uLSIF algorithm with the following Gaussian kernel model:

$$r(x) = \sum_{\ell=1}^{n_{\mathrm{nu}}}\theta_\ell \exp\left(-\frac{(x-x_\ell^{\mathrm{nu}})^2}{2\sigma^2}\right).$$

The Gaussian width σ and the regularization parameter λ are chosen by 5-fold cross-validation (see Section 6.3). The density-ratio function estimated by uLSIF, $\widehat{r}(x)$, is described in Figure 6.3(b), which shows that uLSIF gives a good approximation to the true density-ratio function $r^*(x)$.

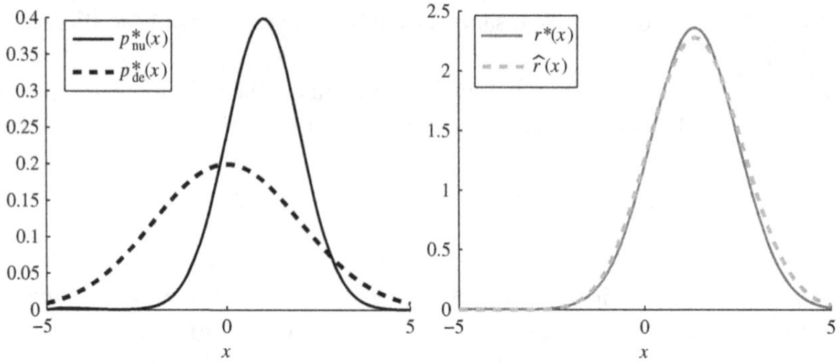

(a) True densities (b) True and estimated density ratios

Figure 6.3. Numerical example of uLSIF.

6.5 Remarks

The least-squares density-ratio fitting methods for linear/kernel models are computationally more advantageous than alternative approaches. Indeed, the constrained method (cLSIF) with the ℓ_1-regularizer is equipped with a regularization-path-tracking algorithm (Section 6.3.2). Furthermore, the unconstrained method (uLSIF) allows one to compute the density-ratio estimator *analytically* (Section 6.2.2); the leave-one-out cross-validation score can also be computed in a closed form (Section 6.3.3). Thus, the overall computation of uLSIF including model selection is highly efficient.

The fact that uLSIF has an analytic-form solution is actually very useful beyond its computational efficiency. When one wants to optimize some criterion defined using a density-ratio estimator, for example, *mutual information* (Cover and Thomas, 2006) or the *Pearson divergence* (Pearson, 1900), the analytic-form solution of uLSIF allows one to compute the *derivative* of the target criterion analytically. Then one can develop, for example, gradient-based and (quasi-) Newton algorithms for optimization. This property can be successfully utilized, for example, in identifying the central subspace in *sufficient dimension reduction* (Section 11.2), finding independent components in *independent component analysis* (Section 11.3), and identifying the heterodistributional subspace in *direct density-ratio estimation with dimensionality reduction* (Section 8.2).

Asymptotic convergence behavior of cLSIF and uLSIF in the parametric setup was elucidated in Kanamori et al. (2009), which is explained in Section 13.2. The asymptotic non-parametric convergence rate of uLSIF was studied in Kanamori et al. (2011b), which is explained in Section 14.3. Also, uLSIF was shown to be numerically stable and reliable under condition number analysis (Kanamori et al., 2011c), which will be detailed in Chapter 16.

7

Unified Framework

In this chapter we describe a framework of density-ratio estimation by *density-ratio fitting* under the *Bregman* divergence (Bregman, 1967). This framework is a natural extension of the least-squares approach described in Chapter 6, and it includes various existing approaches as special cases (Sugiyama et al., 2011a).

In Section 7.1 we first describe the framework of density-ratio fitting under the Bregman divergence. Then, in Section 7.2, we show that various existing approaches can be accommodated in this framework, such as *kernel mean matching* (see Section 3.3), *logistic regression* (see Section 4.2), *Kullback–Leibler importance estimation procedure* (see Section 5.1), and *least-squares importance fitting* (see Section 6.1). We then show other views of the density-ratio fitting framework in Section 7.3. Furthermore, in Section 7.4, a robust density-ratio estimator is derived as an instance of the density-ratio fitting approach based on Basu's *power* divergence (Basu et al., 1998). The chapter is concluded in Section 7.5.

7.1 Basic Framework

A basic idea of density-ratio fitting is to fit a density ratio model $r(\boldsymbol{x})$ to the true density-ratio function $r^*(\boldsymbol{x})$ under some divergence (Figure 7.1). At a glance, this density-ratio fitting problem may look equivalent to the *regression problem*, which is aimed at learning a real-valued function [see Section 1.1.1 and Figure 1.1(a)]. However, density-ratio fitting is essentially different from regression because samples of the true density-ratio function are not available. Here we employ the *Bregman* (BR) divergence (Bregman, 1967) for measuring the discrepancy between the true density-ratio function and the density-ratio model.

The BR divergence is an extension of the *Euclidean distance* to a class of distances that share similar properties. Let f be a differentiable and *strictly*

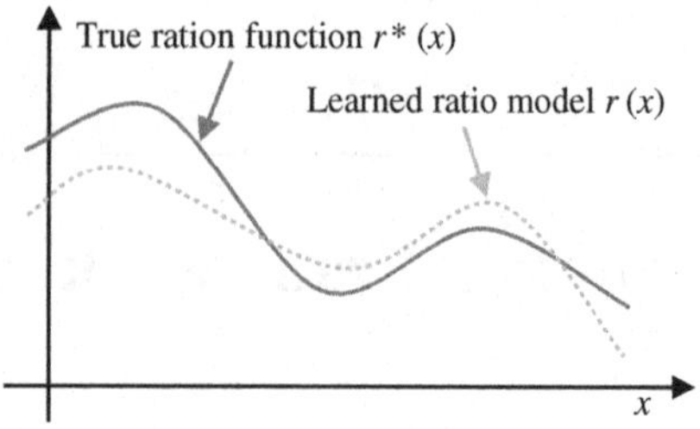

Figure 7.1. The idea of density-ratio fitting.

convex[1] function. Then the BR divergence from t^* to t associated with f is defined as

$$\mathrm{BR}'_f(t^* \| t) := f(t^*) - f(t) - \partial f(t)(t^* - t),$$

where ∂f is the derivative of f. Note that

$$f(t) + \partial f(t)(t^* - t)$$

is the value of the first-order *Taylor expansion* of f around t evaluated at t^*. Thus the BR divergence evaluates the difference between the value of f at point t^* and its linear extrapolation from t (Figure 7.2). Note that the BR divergence $\mathrm{BR}'_f(t^* \| t)$ is a convex function with respect to t^*, but it is not necessarily convex with respect to t.

Here the discrepancy from the true density-ratio function r^* to a density ratio model r is measured using the BR divergence as

$$\mathrm{BR}'_f\left(r^* \| r\right) := \int p^*_{\mathrm{de}}(\boldsymbol{x})\Big(f(r^*(\boldsymbol{x})) - f(r(\boldsymbol{x})) \\ - \partial f(r(\boldsymbol{x}))(r^*(\boldsymbol{x}) - r(\boldsymbol{x}))\Big)\mathrm{d}\boldsymbol{x}. \qquad (7.1)$$

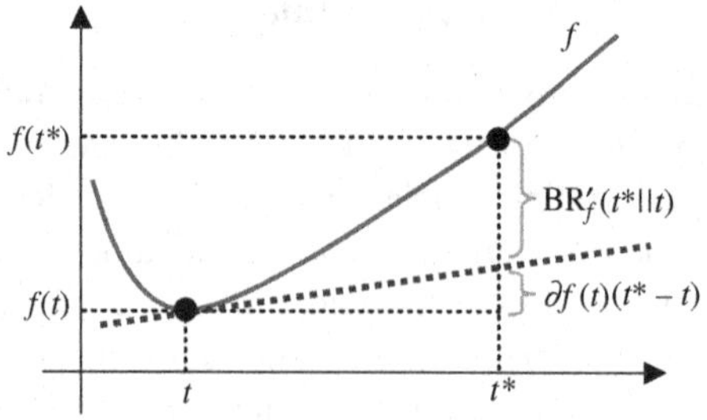

Figure 7.2. Bregman divergence $\mathrm{BR}'_f(t^* \| t)$.

[1] A function f is said to be *convex* if

$$f(\alpha t + (1-\alpha)t') \leq \alpha f(t) + (1-\alpha) f(t')$$

holds for any $t < t'$ and any $\alpha \in (0,1)$. If the above inequality holds without equality (i.e., with '$<$'), f is said to be *strictly convex*.

A motivation for this choice is that the BR divergence allows one to directly obtain an *empirical approximation* for any f. Let us extract a relevant part of the BR divergence, BR_f, as

$$\begin{aligned}\mathrm{BR}'_f\left(r^* \| r\right) &= C - \int p^*_{\mathrm{de}}(\boldsymbol{x}) f(r(\boldsymbol{x}))\mathrm{d}\boldsymbol{x} - \int p^*_{\mathrm{de}}(\boldsymbol{x}) \partial f(r(\boldsymbol{x})) r^*(\boldsymbol{x})\mathrm{d}\boldsymbol{x} \\ &\quad + \int p^*_{\mathrm{de}}(\boldsymbol{x}) \partial f(r(\boldsymbol{x})) r(\boldsymbol{x})\mathrm{d}\boldsymbol{x} \\ &= C + \mathrm{BR}_f(r),\end{aligned}$$

where $C := \int p^*_{\mathrm{de}}(\boldsymbol{x}) f(r^*(\boldsymbol{x}))\mathrm{d}\boldsymbol{x}$ is a constant independent of r and

$$\begin{aligned}\mathrm{BR}_f(r) &:= \int p^*_{\mathrm{de}}(\boldsymbol{x}) \partial f(r(\boldsymbol{x})) r(\boldsymbol{x})\mathrm{d}\boldsymbol{x} - \int p^*_{\mathrm{de}}(\boldsymbol{x}) f(r(\boldsymbol{x}))\mathrm{d}\boldsymbol{x} \\ &\quad - \int p^*_{\mathrm{nu}}(\boldsymbol{x}) \partial f(r(\boldsymbol{x}))\mathrm{d}\boldsymbol{x}. \end{aligned} \tag{7.2}$$

Then an empirical approximation $\widehat{\mathrm{BR}}_f(r)$ of $\mathrm{BR}_f(r)$ is given by

$$\begin{aligned}\widehat{\mathrm{BR}}_f(r) &:= \frac{1}{n_{\mathrm{de}}} \sum_{j=1}^{n_{\mathrm{de}}} \partial f(r(\boldsymbol{x}^{\mathrm{de}}_j)) r(\boldsymbol{x}^{\mathrm{de}}_j) - \frac{1}{n_{\mathrm{de}}} \sum_{j=1}^{n_{\mathrm{de}}} f(r(\boldsymbol{x}^{\mathrm{de}}_j)) \\ &\quad - \frac{1}{n_{\mathrm{nu}}} \sum_{i=1}^{n_{\mathrm{nu}}} \partial f(r(\boldsymbol{x}^{\mathrm{nu}}_i)). \end{aligned} \tag{7.3}$$

This immediately gives the following optimization criterion:

$$\min_r \widehat{\mathrm{BR}}_f(r).$$

7.2 Existing Methods as Density-Ratio Fitting

In this section we show that various density-ratio estimation methods explained in the previous chapters can actually be accommodated in the density-ratio fitting framework described in the previous section. The methods we explain in this section are *least-squares importance fitting* (Section 7.2.1), *kernel mean matching* (Section 7.2.2), *logistic regression* (Section 7.2.3), and the *Kullback–Leibler importance estimation procedure* (Section 7.2.4).

7.2.1 Least-Squares Importance Fitting

Here we show that the *least-squares importance fitting* (LSIF) approach introduced in Section 6.1 is an instance of density-ratio fitting. More specifically, there exists a BR divergence such that the optimization problem of density-ratio fitting is reduced to that of LSIF.

When

$$f(t) = \frac{1}{2}(t-1)^2,$$

BR (7.1) is reduced to the squared (SQ) distance:

$$\mathrm{SQ}'(t^* \| t) := \frac{1}{2}(t^* - t)^2.$$

Following Eqs. (7.2) and (7.3), let us denote SQ$'$ without an irrelevant constant term by $\mathrm{SQ}(r)$ and its empirical approximation by $\widehat{\mathrm{SQ}}(r)$, respectively:

$$\mathrm{SQ}(r) := \frac{1}{2}\int p^*_{\mathrm{de}}(\boldsymbol{x}) r(\boldsymbol{x})^2 \mathrm{d}\boldsymbol{x} - \int p^*_{\mathrm{nu}}(\boldsymbol{x}) r(\boldsymbol{x}) \mathrm{d}\boldsymbol{x},$$

$$\widehat{\mathrm{SQ}}(r) := \frac{1}{2n_{\mathrm{de}}}\sum_{j=1}^{n_{\mathrm{de}}} r(\boldsymbol{x}_j^{\mathrm{de}})^2 - \frac{1}{n_{\mathrm{nu}}}\sum_{i=1}^{n_{\mathrm{nu}}} r(\boldsymbol{x}_i^{\mathrm{nu}}).$$

This agrees with the LSIF formulation given in Section 6.1.

7.2.2 Kernel Mean Matching

In this subsection we show that the solution of the infinite-order moment matching method, *kernel mean matching* (KMM), introduced in Section 3.3 actually agrees with that of an *unconstrained LSIF* (uLSIF; see Section 6.2.2) for a specific kernel model. Because uLSIF was shown to be an instance of density-ratio fitting in Section 7.2.1, the KMM solution can also be obtained in the density-ratio fitting framework.

Let us consider the following kernel density-ratio model:

$$r(\boldsymbol{x}) = \sum_{\ell=1}^{n_{\mathrm{de}}} \theta_\ell K(\boldsymbol{x}, \boldsymbol{x}_\ell^{\mathrm{de}}), \tag{7.4}$$

where $K(\boldsymbol{x}, \boldsymbol{x}')$ is a *universal reproducing kernel* (Steinwart, 2001) such as the Gaussian kernel:

$$K(\boldsymbol{x}, \boldsymbol{x}') = \exp\left(-\frac{\|\boldsymbol{x} - \boldsymbol{x}'\|^2}{2\sigma^2}\right).$$

Note that the original uLSIF and KLIEP use the numerator samples $\{\boldsymbol{x}_i^{\mathrm{nu}}\}_{i=1}^{n_{\mathrm{nu}}}$ as Gaussian centers (see Section 5.2.1), while the model (7.4) adopts the denominator samples $\{\boldsymbol{x}_j^{\mathrm{de}}\}_{j=1}^{n_{\mathrm{de}}}$ as Gaussian centers.

For the density-ratio model (7.4), the matrix $\widehat{\boldsymbol{H}}$ defined by Eq. (6.1) and the vector $\widehat{\boldsymbol{h}}$ defined by Eq. (6.2) are expressed as

$$\widehat{\boldsymbol{H}} = \frac{1}{n_{\mathrm{de}}}\boldsymbol{K}^2_{\mathrm{de,de}} \quad \text{and} \quad \widehat{\boldsymbol{h}} = \frac{1}{n_{\mathrm{nu}}}\boldsymbol{K}_{\mathrm{de,nu}}\boldsymbol{1}_{n_{\mathrm{nu}}},$$

where $\mathbf{1}_{n_{\mathrm{nu}}}$ denotes the n_{nu}-dimensional vector with all ones, and $\boldsymbol{K}_{\mathrm{de,de}}$ and $\boldsymbol{K}_{\mathrm{de,nu}}$ are the $n_{\mathrm{de}} \times n_{\mathrm{de}}$ and $n_{\mathrm{de}} \times n_{\mathrm{nu}}$ matrices defined by

$$[\boldsymbol{K}_{\mathrm{de,de}}]_{j,j'} = K(\boldsymbol{x}_j^{\mathrm{de}}, \boldsymbol{x}_{j'}^{\mathrm{de}}) \quad \text{and} \quad [\boldsymbol{K}_{\mathrm{de,nu}}]_{j,i} = K(\boldsymbol{x}_j^{\mathrm{de}}, \boldsymbol{x}_i^{\mathrm{nu}}).$$

Then the (unregularized) uLSIF solution (see Section 6.2.2 for details), $\widehat{\boldsymbol{\theta}} = \widehat{\boldsymbol{H}}^{-1}\widehat{\boldsymbol{h}}$, is expressed as

$$\widehat{\boldsymbol{\theta}} = \frac{n_{\mathrm{de}}}{n_{\mathrm{nu}}} \boldsymbol{K}_{\mathrm{de,de}}^{-2} \boldsymbol{K}_{\mathrm{de,nu}} \mathbf{1}_{n_{\mathrm{nu}}}. \tag{7.5}$$

On the other hand, let us consider an inductive variant of KMM for the kernel model (7.4) (see Section 3.3.2). For the density-ratio model (7.4), the matrix $\boldsymbol{\Psi}_{\mathrm{de}}$ defined by Eq. (3.3) is expressed as $\boldsymbol{\Psi}_{\mathrm{de}} = \boldsymbol{K}_{\mathrm{de,de}}$. Then the KMM solution (see Section 3.3.2 for details),

$$\widehat{\boldsymbol{\theta}} = \frac{n_{\mathrm{de}}}{n_{\mathrm{nu}}} (\boldsymbol{\Psi}_{\mathrm{de}} \boldsymbol{K}_{\mathrm{de,de}} \boldsymbol{\Psi}_{\mathrm{de}})^{-1} \boldsymbol{\Psi}_{\mathrm{de}} \boldsymbol{K}_{\mathrm{de,nu}} \mathbf{1}_{n_{\mathrm{nu}}},$$

is reduced to Eq. (7.5).

Thus, KMM and uLSIF share the same solution. However, it is important to note that the optimization criteria of the two approaches differ. As will be shown in Chapter 16, this fact makes a significant difference in *numerical stability*. More specifically, the density-ratio fitting method has a smaller *condition number* than the generalized moment-matching method (Kanamori et al., 2011c). Thus, the density-ratio fitting approach is numerically more stable and computationally more efficient than the moment matching method if solutions are computed by numerical algorithms such as quasi-Newton methods.

7.2.3 Logistic Regression

Here we show that the *logistic regression* approach introduced in Section 4.2 is an instance of density-ratio fitting. More specifically, there exists a BR divergence such that the optimization problem of density-ratio fitting is reduced to that of the logistic regression approach.

When

$$f(t) = t \log t - (1+t)\log(1+t),$$

BR (7.1) is reduced to the *binary Kullback–Leibler* (BKL) divergence:

$$\mathrm{BKL}'(t^* \| t) := (1+t^*)\log\frac{1+t}{1+t^*} + t^* \log\frac{t}{t^*}.$$

The name BKL comes from the fact that $\mathrm{BKL}'(t^* \| t)$ is expressed as

$$\mathrm{BKL}'(t^* \| t) = (1+t^*)\mathrm{KL}_{\mathrm{bin}}\left(\frac{1}{1+t^*} \middle\| \frac{1}{1+t}\right),$$

where $\mathrm{KL}_{\mathrm{bin}}$ is the KL divergence for binary random variables defined as

$$\mathrm{KL}_{\mathrm{bin}}(p,q) := p \log \frac{p}{q} + (1-p)\log \frac{1-p}{1-q}$$

for $0 < p,q < 1$. Thus, BKL' agrees with $\mathrm{KL}_{\mathrm{bin}}$ up to the scaling factor $(1+t^*)$.

Following Eqs. (7.2) and (7.3), let us denote BKL' without an irrelevant constant term by $\mathrm{BKL}(r)$ and its empirical approximation by $\widehat{\mathrm{BKL}}(r)$, respectively:

$$\mathrm{BKL}(r) := -\int p^*_{\mathrm{de}}(\boldsymbol{x}) \log \frac{1}{1+r(\boldsymbol{x})} \mathrm{d}\boldsymbol{x} - \int p^*_{\mathrm{nu}}(\boldsymbol{x}) \log \frac{r(\boldsymbol{x})}{1+r(\boldsymbol{x})} \mathrm{d}\boldsymbol{x},$$

$$\widehat{\mathrm{BKL}}(r) := -\frac{1}{n_{\mathrm{de}}} \sum_{j=1}^{n_{\mathrm{de}}} \log \frac{1}{1+r(\boldsymbol{x}_j^{\mathrm{de}})} - \frac{1}{n_{\mathrm{nu}}} \sum_{i=1}^{n_{\mathrm{nu}}} \log \frac{r(\boldsymbol{x}_i^{\mathrm{nu}})}{1+r(\boldsymbol{x}_i^{\mathrm{nu}})}. \tag{7.6}$$

The density-ratio model r is learned so that $\widehat{\mathrm{BKL}}(r)$ is minimized.

Equation (7.6) is a generalized expression of logistic regression (Qin, 1998). Indeed, the ordinary logistic regression formulation can be obtained from Eq. (7.6) as follows: Let us consider a set of paired samples $\{(\boldsymbol{x}_k, y_k)\}_{k=1}^n$, where, for $n = n_{\mathrm{nu}} + n_{\mathrm{de}}$,

$$(\boldsymbol{x}_1,\ldots,\boldsymbol{x}_n) := (\boldsymbol{x}_1^{\mathrm{nu}},\ldots,\boldsymbol{x}_{n_{\mathrm{nu}}}^{\mathrm{nu}},\boldsymbol{x}_1^{\mathrm{de}},\ldots,\boldsymbol{x}_{n_{\mathrm{de}}}^{\mathrm{de}}),$$
$$(y_1,\ldots,y_n) := (+1,\ldots,+1,-1,\ldots,-1).$$

We employ the following log-linear density-ratio model:

$$r(\boldsymbol{x}) = \exp(\boldsymbol{\psi}(\boldsymbol{x})^\top \boldsymbol{\theta}).$$

Then $\widehat{\mathrm{BKL}}$ is expressed as

$$\begin{aligned}\widehat{\mathrm{BKL}}(\boldsymbol{\theta}) &= \frac{1}{n_{\mathrm{de}}} \sum_{j=1}^{n_{\mathrm{de}}} \log\left(1+\exp(\boldsymbol{\psi}(\boldsymbol{x}_j^{\mathrm{de}})^\top\boldsymbol{\theta})\right) \\ &\quad + \frac{1}{n_{\mathrm{nu}}} \sum_{i=1}^{n_{\mathrm{nu}}} \log\left(1+\exp(-\boldsymbol{\psi}(\boldsymbol{x}_i^{\mathrm{nu}})^\top\boldsymbol{\theta})\right) \\ &= \sum_{k=1}^{n} \log\left(1+\exp\left(-y_k\boldsymbol{\psi}(\boldsymbol{x}_k)^\top\boldsymbol{\theta}\right)\right).\end{aligned}$$

When $n_{\mathrm{nu}} = n_{\mathrm{de}}$, this agrees with Eq. (4.2) up to a regularizer.

7.2.4 Kullback–Leibler Importance Estimation Procedure

We now show that the *KL importance estimation procedure* (KLIEP) introduced in Section 5.1 is an instance of density-ratio fitting. More specifically, there exists a BR divergence such that the optimization problem of density-ratio fitting is reduced to that of the KLIEP approach.

When

$$f(t) = t\log t - t,$$

BR (7.1) is reduced to the *unnormalized Kullback–Leibler* (UKL) divergence[2]:

$$\mathrm{UKL}'(t^*\|t) := t^*\log\frac{t^*}{t} - t^* + t.$$

Following Eqs. (7.2) and (7.3), let us denote UKL′ without an irrelevant constant term by $\mathrm{UKL}(r)$ and its empirical approximation by $\widehat{\mathrm{UKL}}(r)$, respectively:

$$\mathrm{UKL}(r) := \int p^*_{\mathrm{de}}(\boldsymbol{x})r(\boldsymbol{x})\mathrm{d}\boldsymbol{x} - \int p^*_{\mathrm{nu}}(\boldsymbol{x})\log r(\boldsymbol{x})\mathrm{d}\boldsymbol{x},$$

$$\widehat{\mathrm{UKL}}(r) := \frac{1}{n_{\mathrm{de}}}\sum_{j=1}^{n_{\mathrm{de}}} r(\boldsymbol{x}_j^{\mathrm{de}}) - \frac{1}{n_{\mathrm{nu}}}\sum_{i=1}^{n_{\mathrm{nu}}}\log r(\boldsymbol{x}_i^{\mathrm{nu}}). \tag{7.7}$$

The density-ratio model r is learned so that $\widehat{\mathrm{UKL}}(r)$ is minimized. Here, we further impose that the ratio model $r(\boldsymbol{x})$ is non-negative for all $\boldsymbol{x}$ and is normalized with respect to $\{\boldsymbol{x}_j^{\mathrm{de}}\}_{j=1}^{n_{\mathrm{de}}}$:

$$\frac{1}{n_{\mathrm{de}}}\sum_{j=1}^{n_{\mathrm{de}}} r(\boldsymbol{x}_j^{\mathrm{de}}) = 1.$$

Then the optimization criterion is reduced to

$$\max_r \ \frac{1}{n_{\mathrm{nu}}}\sum_{i=1}^{n_{\mathrm{nu}}}\log r(\boldsymbol{x}_i^{\mathrm{nu}})$$

$$\text{s.t.} \ \frac{1}{n_{\mathrm{de}}}\sum_{j=1}^{n_{\mathrm{de}}} r(\boldsymbol{x}_j^{\mathrm{de}}) = 1 \text{ and } r(\boldsymbol{x}) \geq 0 \text{ for all } \boldsymbol{x}.$$

This agrees with the KLIEP formulation explained in Section 5.1.

7.3 Interpretation of Density-Ratio Fitting

In this section we give interpretations of the density-ratio fitting approach. In Section 7.3.1, we show that the density-ratio fitting approach can be interpreted as divergence estimation. In Section 7.3.2, the correspondence between the density-ratio fitting approach and the moment-matching approach (Chapter 3) is described.

[2] The UKL divergence from $p(\boldsymbol{x})$ and $q(\boldsymbol{x})$ is reduced to the ordinary KL divergence if $p(\boldsymbol{x})$ and $q(\boldsymbol{x})$ are normalized (i.e., integrated to one):

$$\int p(\boldsymbol{x})\log\frac{p(\boldsymbol{x})}{q(\boldsymbol{x})}\mathrm{d}\boldsymbol{x} - \int p(\boldsymbol{x})\mathrm{d}\boldsymbol{x} + \int q(\boldsymbol{x})\mathrm{d}\boldsymbol{x} = \int p(\boldsymbol{x})\log\frac{p(\boldsymbol{x})}{q(\boldsymbol{x})}\mathrm{d}\boldsymbol{x}.$$

7.3.1 Divergence Estimation View

Here we show that the density-ratio fitting formulation can be interpreted as *divergence estimation* based on the *Ali–Silvey–Csiszár* (ASC) divergence (a.k.a. the *f-divergence*).

Let us consider the ASC divergence (Ali and Silvey, 1966; Csiszár, 1967) for measuring the discrepancy between two probability density functions. An ASC divergence is defined using a *convex function* f such that $f(1) = 0$ as follows:

$$\mathrm{ASC}_f(p^*_{\mathrm{nu}} \| p^*_{\mathrm{de}}) := \int p^*_{\mathrm{de}}(\boldsymbol{x}) f\left(\frac{p^*_{\mathrm{nu}}(\boldsymbol{x})}{p^*_{\mathrm{de}}(\boldsymbol{x})}\right) \mathrm{d}\boldsymbol{x}. \tag{7.8}$$

The ASC divergence is reduced to the *Kullback–Leibler* (KL) divergence (Kullback and Leibler, 1951) if $f(t) = t \log t$, and the *Pearson* (PE) divergence (Pearson, 1900) if $f(t) = (t-1)^2/2$.

Let $\partial f(t)$ be the *sub-differential* of f at a point t $(\in \mathbb{R})$, which is a set defined as follows (Rockafellar, 1970):

$$\partial f(t) := \{z \in \mathbb{R} \mid f(s) \geq f(t) + z(s-t),\ \forall s \in \mathbb{R}\}.$$

If f is differentiable at t, then the sub-differential is reduced to the ordinary derivative. Although the sub-differential is a set in general, for simplicity, we treat $\partial f(r)$ as a single element if there is no confusion. In the following we assume that f is *closed*, that is, its *epigraph* is a closed set (Rockafellar, 1970).

Let f^* be the *conjugate dual function* associated with f defined as

$$f^*(u) := \sup_t [tu - f(t)] = -\inf_t [f(t) - tu].$$

Because f is a closed convex function, we also have

$$f(t) = -\inf_u [f^*(u) - tu]. \tag{7.9}$$

For the KL divergence where $f(t) = t\log t$, the conjugate dual function is given by $f^*(u) = \exp(u-1)$. For the PE divergence where $f(t) = (t-1)^2/2$, the conjugate dual function is given by $f^*(u) = u^2/2 + u$.

Substituting Eq. (7.9) into Eq. (7.8), we have the following lower bound (Keziou, 2003a):

$$\mathrm{ASC}_f(p^*_{\mathrm{nu}} \| p^*_{\mathrm{de}}) = -\inf_g \mathrm{ASC}'_f(g),$$

where

$$\mathrm{ASC}'_f(g) := \int f^*(g(\boldsymbol{x})) p^*_{\mathrm{de}}(\boldsymbol{x}) \mathrm{d}\boldsymbol{x} - \int g(\boldsymbol{x}) p^*_{\mathrm{nu}}(\boldsymbol{x}) \mathrm{d}\boldsymbol{x}. \tag{7.10}$$

According to the *variational principle* (Jordan et al., 1999), the infimum of ASC'_f is attained at g such that

$$\partial f^*(g(\boldsymbol{x})) = \frac{p^*_{\mathrm{nu}}(\boldsymbol{x})}{p^*_{\mathrm{de}}(\boldsymbol{x})} = r^*(\boldsymbol{x}).$$

Thus, minimizing $\mathrm{ASC}'_f(g)$ yields the true density-ratio function $r^*(\boldsymbol{x})$.

In the following we derive a more explicit expression of $\mathrm{ASC}'_f(g)$. For some g, there exists r such that $g = \partial f(r)$. Then $f^*(g)$ is expressed as

$$f^*(g) = \sup_s \left[s\partial f(r) - f(s) \right].$$

According to the variational principle, the supremum in the right-hand side of the equation is attained at $s = r$. Thus we have

$$f^*(g) = r\partial f(r) - f(r).$$

Then the lower bound $\mathrm{ASC}'_f(g)$ defined by Eq. (7.10) can be expressed as

$$\mathrm{ASC}'_f(g) = \int p^*_{\mathrm{de}}(\boldsymbol{x})\Big(r(\boldsymbol{x})\partial f(r(\boldsymbol{x})) - f(r(\boldsymbol{x}))\Big)\mathrm{d}\boldsymbol{x} - \int \partial f(r(\boldsymbol{x}))p^*_{\mathrm{nu}}(\boldsymbol{x})\mathrm{d}\boldsymbol{x}.$$

This is equivalent to the criterion BR_f defined by Eq. (7.2) in Section 7.1. Thus, density-ratio fitting under the BR divergence can be interpreted as divergence estimation under the ASC divergence.

7.3.2 Moment-Matching View

Let us investigate the correspondence between the density-ratio fitting approach and the moment-matching approach (Chapter 3). To this end, we focus on the ideal situation where the true density-ratio function r^* is included in the density-ratio model r.

The non-linear version of finite-order moment matching (see Section 3.2.1) learns the density-ratio model r so that the following criterion is minimized:

$$\left\| \int \boldsymbol{\phi}(\boldsymbol{x})r(\boldsymbol{x})p^*_{\mathrm{de}}(\boldsymbol{x})\mathrm{d}\boldsymbol{x} - \int \boldsymbol{\phi}(\boldsymbol{x})p^*_{\mathrm{nu}}(\boldsymbol{x})\mathrm{d}\boldsymbol{x} \right\|^2,$$

where $\boldsymbol{\phi}(\boldsymbol{x}) : \mathbb{R}^d \to \mathbb{R}^m$ is some vector-valued function. Under the assumption that the density-ratio model r can represent the true density ratio r^*, we have the following estimation equation:

$$\int \boldsymbol{\phi}(\boldsymbol{x})r(\boldsymbol{x})p^*_{\mathrm{de}}(\boldsymbol{x})\mathrm{d}\boldsymbol{x} - \int \boldsymbol{\phi}(\boldsymbol{x})p^*_{\mathrm{nu}}(\boldsymbol{x})\mathrm{d}\boldsymbol{x} = \boldsymbol{0}_m, \tag{7.11}$$

where $\boldsymbol{0}_m$ denotes the m-dimensional vector with all zeros.

On the other hand, the density-ratio fitting approach described in Section 7.1 learns the density-ratio model r so that the following criterion is minimized:

$$\int p^*_{\mathrm{de}}(\boldsymbol{x})\partial f(r(\boldsymbol{x}))r(\boldsymbol{x})\mathrm{d}\boldsymbol{x} - \int p^*_{\mathrm{de}}(\boldsymbol{x})f(r(\boldsymbol{x}))\mathrm{d}\boldsymbol{x} - \int p^*_{\mathrm{nu}}(\boldsymbol{x})\partial f(r(\boldsymbol{x}))\mathrm{d}\boldsymbol{x}.$$

Taking the derivative of the above criterion with respect to parameters in the density-ratio model r and equating it to zero, we have the following estimation equation:

$$\int p^*_{\mathrm{de}}(\boldsymbol{x})r(\boldsymbol{x})\nabla r(\boldsymbol{x})\partial^2 f(r(\boldsymbol{x}))\mathrm{d}\boldsymbol{x} - \int p^*_{\mathrm{nu}}(\boldsymbol{x})\nabla r(\boldsymbol{x})\partial^2 f(r(\boldsymbol{x}))\mathrm{d}\boldsymbol{x} = \boldsymbol{0}_b,$$

where ∇ denotes the differential operator with respect to parameters in the density-ratio model r, and b is the number of parameters. This implies that putting

$$\boldsymbol{\phi}(\boldsymbol{x}) = \nabla r(\boldsymbol{x})\partial^2 f(r(\boldsymbol{x}))$$

in Eq. (7.11) gives the same estimation equation as density-ratio fitting, resulting in the same optimal solution.

7.4 Power Divergence for Robust Density-Ratio Estimation

In this section we introduce a new instance of density-ratio fitting based on Basu's *power* divergence (BA divergence; Basu et al., 1998).

In Section 7.4.1 we derive a density-ratio estimation method based on density-ratio fitting under the BA divergence. In Section 7.4.2, the method based on the BA divergence is shown to be robust against outliers. In Section 7.4.3 we show some numerical examples.

7.4.1 Derivation

For $\alpha > 0$, let

$$f(t) = \frac{t^{1+\alpha} - t}{\alpha}.$$

Then BR (7.1) is reduced to the BA divergence:

$$\mathrm{BA}'_\alpha(t^* \| t) := t^\alpha(t - t^*) - \frac{t^*(t^\alpha - (t^*)^\alpha)}{\alpha}.$$

Following Eqs. (7.2) and (7.3), let us denote BA'_α without an irrelevant constant term by $\mathrm{BA}_\alpha(r)$ and its empirical approximation by $\widehat{\mathrm{BA}}_\alpha(r)$, respectively:

$$\mathrm{BA}_\alpha(r) := \int p^*_{\mathrm{de}}(\boldsymbol{x})r(\boldsymbol{x})^{\alpha+1}\mathrm{d}\boldsymbol{x} - \left(1 + \frac{1}{\alpha}\right)\int p^*_{\mathrm{nu}}(\boldsymbol{x})r(\boldsymbol{x})^{\alpha}\mathrm{d}\boldsymbol{x} + \frac{1}{\alpha},$$

$$\widehat{\mathrm{BA}}_\alpha(r) := \frac{1}{n_{\mathrm{de}}}\sum_{j=1}^{n_{\mathrm{de}}} r(\boldsymbol{x}_j^{\mathrm{de}})^{\alpha+1} - \left(1 + \frac{1}{\alpha}\right)\frac{1}{n_{\mathrm{nu}}}\sum_{i=1}^{n_{\mathrm{nu}}} r(\boldsymbol{x}_i^{\mathrm{nu}})^{\alpha} + \frac{1}{\alpha}.$$

The density-ratio model r is learned so that $\widehat{\mathrm{BA}}_\alpha(r)$ is minimized.

When $\alpha = 1$, the BA divergence is reduced to the twice SQ divergence (see Section 7.2.1):

$$\widehat{\mathrm{BA}}_1 = 2\widehat{\mathrm{SQ}}.$$

Similarly, the fact

$$\lim_{\alpha \to 0} \frac{t^{\alpha} - 1}{\alpha} = \log t$$

implies that the BA divergence tends to the UKL divergence (see Section 7.2.4) as $\alpha \to 0$:

$$\lim_{\alpha \to 0} \widehat{\mathrm{BA}}_{\alpha}(r) = \frac{1}{n_{\mathrm{de}}} \sum_{j=1}^{n_{\mathrm{de}}} r(\boldsymbol{x}_j^{\mathrm{de}}) - \frac{1}{n_{\mathrm{nu}}} \sum_{i=1}^{n_{\mathrm{nu}}} \log r(\boldsymbol{x}_i^{\mathrm{nu}}) = \widehat{\mathrm{UKL}}(r).$$

Thus, the BA divergence essentially includes the SQ and UKL divergences as special cases, and is substantially more general.

7.4.2 Robustness

Let us take the derivative of $\widehat{\mathrm{BA}}_{\alpha}(r)$ with respect to parameters included in the density-ratio model r and equate it to zero. Then we have the following estimation equation:

$$\frac{1}{n_{\mathrm{de}}} \sum_{j=1}^{n_{\mathrm{de}}} r(\boldsymbol{x}_j^{\mathrm{de}})^{\alpha} \nabla r(\boldsymbol{x}_j^{\mathrm{de}}) - \frac{1}{n_{\mathrm{nu}}} \sum_{i=1}^{n_{\mathrm{nu}}} r(\boldsymbol{x}_i^{\mathrm{nu}})^{\alpha-1} \nabla r(\boldsymbol{x}_i^{\mathrm{nu}}) = \boldsymbol{0}_b, \tag{7.12}$$

where ∇ is the differential operator with respect to parameters in the density-ratio model r, b denotes the number of parameters, and $\boldsymbol{0}_b$ denotes the b-dimensional vector with all zeros.

As explained in Section 7.4.1, the BA method with $\alpha \to 0$ corresponds to the KLIEP (using the UKL divergence). According to Eq. (7.7), the estimation equation of the KLIEP is given as follows [this also agrees with Eq. (7.12) with $\alpha = 0$]:

$$\frac{1}{n_{\mathrm{de}}} \sum_{j=1}^{n_{\mathrm{de}}} \nabla r(\boldsymbol{x}_j^{\mathrm{de}}) - \frac{1}{n_{\mathrm{nu}}} \sum_{i=1}^{n_{\mathrm{nu}}} r(\boldsymbol{x}_i^{\mathrm{nu}})^{-1} \nabla r(\boldsymbol{x}_i^{\mathrm{nu}}) = \boldsymbol{0}_b.$$

Comparing this with Eq. (7.12), we see that the BA method can be regarded as a weighted version of the KLIEP according to $r(\boldsymbol{x}_j^{\mathrm{de}})^{\alpha}$ and $r(\boldsymbol{x}_i^{\mathrm{nu}})^{\alpha}$. When $r(\boldsymbol{x}_j^{\mathrm{de}})$ and $r(\boldsymbol{x}_i^{\mathrm{nu}})$ are less than 1, the BA method downweights the effect of those samples. Thus, "outlying" samples relative to the density-ratio model r tend to have less influence on parameter estimation, which will lead to *robust* estimators (Basu et al., 1998).

Since LSIF corresponds to $\alpha = 1$, it is more robust against outliers than the KLIEP (which corresponds to $\alpha \to 0$) in the above sense, and BA with $\alpha > 1$ would be even more robust.

7.4.3 Numerical Examples

Let the numerator and denominator densities be defined as follows [Figure 7.3(a)]:

$$p^*_{\mathrm{nu}}(x) = 0.7N\left(x;0,\frac{1}{16}\right) + 0.3N\left(x;1,\frac{1}{4}\right),$$

$$p^*_{\mathrm{de}}(x) = N(x;0,1),$$

where $N(x;\mu,\sigma^2)$ denotes the Gaussian density with mean μ and variance σ^2. We draw $n_{\mathrm{nu}} = n_{\mathrm{de}} = 300$ samples from each density, which are illustrated in Figure 7.3(b).

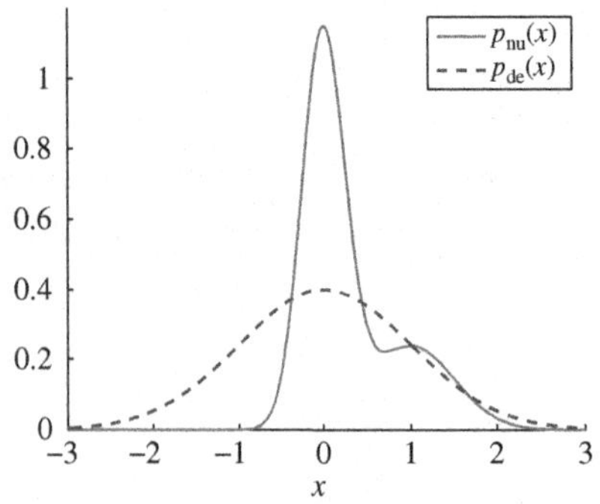

(a) Numerator and denominator density functions

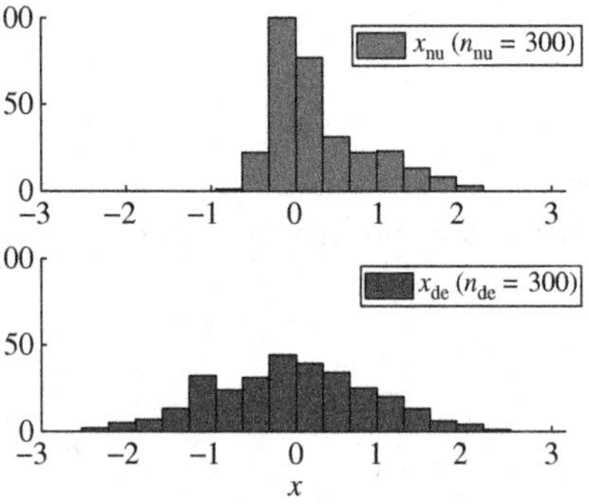

(b) Numerator and denominator sample points

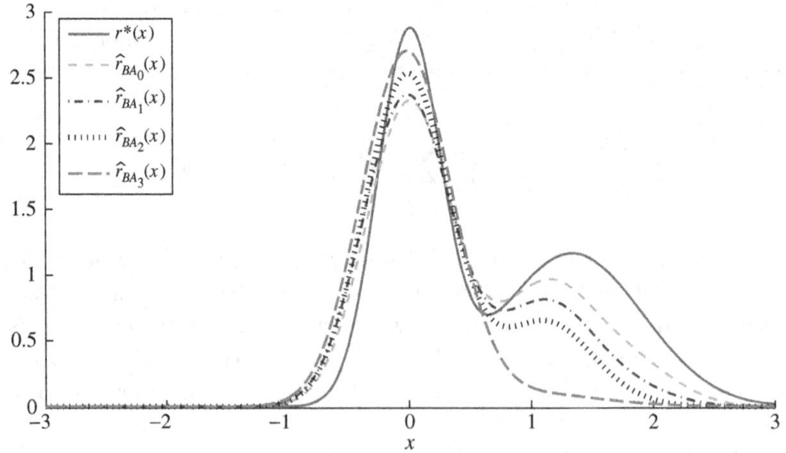

(c) True and learned density-ratio functions

Figure 7.3. Numerical examples.

Here we employ the Gaussian kernel density-ratio model:

$$r(\boldsymbol{x}) = \sum_{\ell=1}^{n_{\mathrm{nu}}} \theta_\ell K(\boldsymbol{x}, \boldsymbol{x}_\ell^{\mathrm{nu}}),$$

where $K(\boldsymbol{x}, \boldsymbol{x}')$ is the Gaussian kernel with kernel width σ:

$$K(\boldsymbol{x}, \boldsymbol{x}') = \exp\left(-\frac{\|\boldsymbol{x} - \boldsymbol{x}'\|^2}{2\sigma^2}\right).$$

The model parameter $\boldsymbol{\theta}$ is learned so that $\widehat{\mathrm{BA}}_\alpha(r)$ with a quadratic regularizer is minimized under the non-negativity constraint:

$$\begin{aligned} \min_{\boldsymbol{\theta} \in \mathbb{R}^b} \Bigg[& \frac{1}{n_{\mathrm{de}}} \sum_{j=1}^{n_{\mathrm{de}}} \left(\sum_{\ell=1}^{n_{\mathrm{nu}}} \theta_\ell K(\boldsymbol{x}_j^{\mathrm{nu}}, \boldsymbol{x}_\ell^{\mathrm{nu}}) \right)^{\alpha+1} \\ & - \left(1 + \frac{1}{\alpha}\right) \frac{1}{n_{\mathrm{nu}}} \sum_{i=1}^{n_{\mathrm{nu}}} \left(\sum_{\ell=1}^{n_{\mathrm{nu}}} \theta_\ell K(\boldsymbol{x}_i^{\mathrm{de}}, \boldsymbol{x}_\ell^{\mathrm{nu}}) \right)^{\alpha} + \lambda \boldsymbol{\theta}^\top \boldsymbol{\theta} \Bigg] \\ \text{s.t. } & \boldsymbol{\theta} \geq \boldsymbol{0}_b. \end{aligned} \tag{7.13}$$

Note that this optimization problem is convex for $0 < \alpha \leq 1$. In our implementation, we solve the above optimization problem by gradient projection, that is, the parameters are iteratively updated by gradient descent with respect to the objective function, and the solution is projected back to the feasible region by rounding up negative parameters to zero. Before solving the optimization problem (7.13), we run uLSIF (see Section 6.2.2) and obtain cross-validation estimates of the Gaussian width σ and the regularization parameter λ. We then fix the Gaussian width and the regularization parameter in the BA method to these values and solve the optimization problem (7.13) by gradient-projection with $\boldsymbol{\theta} = \boldsymbol{1}_b / b$ as the initial solution.

Figure 7.3(c) shows the true and estimated density-ratio functions by the BA methods for $\alpha = 0, 1, 2, 3$. The true density-ratio function has two peaks: higher one at $x = 0$ and a lower one at around $x = 1.2$. The graph shows that, as α increases, the estimated density-ratio functions tend to focus on approximating the higher peak and ignore the lower peak.

7.5 Remarks

In this chapter we introduced a framework of density-ratio estimation by *density-ratio fitting* under the *Bregman* divergence. This is a natural extension of the least-squares approach described in Chapter 6 and includes various existing approaches such as *kernel mean matching* (see Section 3.3), *logistic regression* (see Section 4.2), *Kullback–Leibler importance estimation procedure* (see Section 5.1), and *least-squares importance fitting* (see Section 6.1). We also gave interpretations of the density-ratio fitting approach as divergence estimation and moment-matching in Section 7.3.

This general framework allows one to derive novel density-ratio estimation methods based on various instances of the Bregman divergence. Indeed, we showed in Section 7.4 that the use of Basu's *power* divergence yields a robust density-ratio estimation method.

In the power divergence method, the choice of the robustness parameter α is an open issue. Although there seems to be no universal way of doing this (Basu et al., 1998; Jones et al., 2001; Fujisawa and Eguchi, 2008), a practical approach would be to use cross-validation over a fixed divergence such as the squared distance.

8

Direct Density-Ratio Estimation with Dimensionality Reduction

The approaches of direct density-ratio estimation explained in the previous chapters were shown to be promising in experiments with naive kernel density estimation in experiments. However, these methods still perform rather poorly when the dimensionality of the data domain is high.

The purpose of this chapter is to introduce ideas for mitigating this weakness, following Sugiyama et al. (2010a, 2011b). A basic assumption behind the approaches explained here is that the difference between the two distributions in the density ratio (i.e., the distributions corresponding to the numerator and denominator of the density ratio) does not spread over the entire data domain, but is confined in a low-dimensional *subspace* – which we refer to as the *heterodistributional subspace*. Once the heterodistributional subspace can be identified, the density ratio is estimated only within this subspace. This will lead to more stable and reliable estimations of density ratios. Such an approach is called *direct density-ratio estimation with dimensionality reduction* (D^3; pronounced "D-cube").

In this chapter, two approaches to D^3 are described. In Section 8.1, a heuristic method based on discriminant analysis is explained. This method is shown to be computationally very efficient, and thus is very practical. On the other hand, in Section 8.2, a more theory-oriented approach based on divergence maximization is introduced. This method is justifiable under general settings, and thus it has a wider applicability. Numerical examples are shown in Section 8.3, and the chapter is concluded in Section 8.4.

8.1 Discriminant Analysis Approach

In this section, a D^3 method based on discriminant analysis is explained (Sugiyama et al., 2010a). The D^3 approach based on discriminant analysis is formulated in Section 8.1.1, where the *heterodistributional subspace* plays an essential role. In Section 8.1.2, the heterodistributional subspace is characterized in terms of *bi-orthogonal bases*. In Section 8.1.3, a method of heterodistributional subspace search based on supervised dimensionality reduction is explained. Finally, in

Section 8.1.4, an entire algorithm of the D^3 method based on discriminant analysis is described.

8.1.1 Hetero- and Homodistributional Subspaces

The basic assumption behind the D^3 approach is that the two densities $p^*_{\mathrm{nu}}(\boldsymbol{x})$ and $p^*_{\mathrm{de}}(\boldsymbol{x})$ in the density ratio

$$r^*(\boldsymbol{x}) = \frac{p^*_{\mathrm{nu}}(\boldsymbol{x})}{p^*_{\mathrm{de}}(\boldsymbol{x})}$$

are different not in the entire domain but only in some *subspace*. This assumption can be formulated mathematically using the following linear mixing model.

Let $\{\boldsymbol{u}^{\mathrm{nu}}_i\}_{i=1}^{n_{\mathrm{nu}}}$ be i.i.d. samples drawn from an m-dimensional distribution with density $p^*_{\mathrm{nu}}(\boldsymbol{u})$, where $m \in \{1,\ldots,d\}$. Let $\{\boldsymbol{u}^{\mathrm{de}}_j\}_{j=1}^{n_{\mathrm{de}}}$ be i.i.d. samples drawn from another m-dimensional distribution with density $p^*_{\mathrm{de}}(\boldsymbol{u})$, which is assumed to be strictly positive. Let $\{\boldsymbol{v}^{\mathrm{nu}}_i\}_{i=1}^{n_{\mathrm{nu}}}$ and $\{\boldsymbol{v}^{\mathrm{de}}_j\}_{j=1}^{n_{\mathrm{de}}}$ be i.i.d. samples drawn from a $(d-m)$-dimensional *common* distribution with density $p^*(\boldsymbol{v})$, which is also assumed to be strictly positive. Let $\boldsymbol{A}$ be a $d \times m$ matrix and $\boldsymbol{B}$ be a $d \times (d-m)$ matrix such that the column vectors of $\boldsymbol{A}$ and $\boldsymbol{B}$ span the entire space. Based on these quantities, we consider the case where the samples $\{\boldsymbol{x}^{\mathrm{nu}}_i\}_{i=1}^{n_{\mathrm{nu}}}$ and $\{\boldsymbol{x}^{\mathrm{de}}_j\}_{j=1}^{n_{\mathrm{de}}}$ are generated as

$$\boldsymbol{x}^{\mathrm{nu}}_i = \boldsymbol{A}\boldsymbol{u}^{\mathrm{nu}}_i + \boldsymbol{B}\boldsymbol{v}^{\mathrm{nu}}_i \quad \text{and} \quad \boldsymbol{x}^{\mathrm{de}}_j = \boldsymbol{A}\boldsymbol{u}^{\mathrm{de}}_j + \boldsymbol{B}\boldsymbol{v}^{\mathrm{de}}_j.$$

Thus, $p^*_{\mathrm{nu}}(\boldsymbol{x})$ and $p^*_{\mathrm{de}}(\boldsymbol{x})$ are expressed as

$$p^*_{\mathrm{nu}}(\boldsymbol{x}) = c\, p^*_{\mathrm{nu}}(\boldsymbol{u})p^*(\boldsymbol{v}) \quad \text{and} \quad p^*_{\mathrm{de}}(\boldsymbol{x}) = c\, p^*_{\mathrm{de}}(\boldsymbol{u})p^*(\boldsymbol{v}), \tag{8.1}$$

where c is the *Jacobian* between the observation $\boldsymbol{x}$ and $(\boldsymbol{u},\boldsymbol{v})$. We call the ranges of $\boldsymbol{A}$ and $\boldsymbol{B}$ – denoted by $\mathcal{R}(\boldsymbol{A})$ and $\mathcal{R}(\boldsymbol{B})$, respectively – the *heterodistributional subspace* and the *homodistributional subspace*, respectively. Note that $\mathcal{R}(\boldsymbol{A})$ and $\mathcal{R}(\boldsymbol{B})$ are not generally orthogonal to each other (see Figure 8.1).

Under this decomposability assumption, the density ratio is simplified as

$$r^*(\boldsymbol{x}) = \frac{p^*_{\mathrm{nu}}(\boldsymbol{x})}{p^*_{\mathrm{de}}(\boldsymbol{x})} = \frac{c\, p^*_{\mathrm{nu}}(\boldsymbol{u})p^*(\boldsymbol{v})}{c\, p^*_{\mathrm{de}}(\boldsymbol{u})p^*(\boldsymbol{v})} = \frac{p^*_{\mathrm{nu}}(\boldsymbol{u})}{p^*_{\mathrm{de}}(\boldsymbol{u})} = r^*(\boldsymbol{u}). \tag{8.2}$$

This means that the density ratio does not have to be estimated in the entire d-dimensional space, but only in the heterodistributional subspace of dimensionality $m\ (\leq d)$.

Now we want to extract the heterodistributional components $\boldsymbol{u}^{\mathrm{nu}}_i$ and $\boldsymbol{u}^{\mathrm{de}}_j$ from $\boldsymbol{x}^{\mathrm{nu}}_i$ and $\boldsymbol{x}^{\mathrm{de}}_j$, which allows estimation of the density ratio only in $\mathcal{R}(\boldsymbol{A})$ via Eq. (8.2). As illustrated in Figure 8.1, the *oblique projection* of $\boldsymbol{x}^{\mathrm{nu}}_i$ and $\boldsymbol{x}^{\mathrm{de}}_j$ onto $\mathcal{R}(\boldsymbol{A})$ along $\mathcal{R}(\boldsymbol{B})$ gives $\boldsymbol{u}^{\mathrm{nu}}_i$ and $\boldsymbol{u}^{\mathrm{de}}_j$.

8.1.2 Characterization of Heterodistributional Subspace

Let us denote the oblique projection matrix onto $\mathcal{R}(\boldsymbol{A})$ along $\mathcal{R}(\boldsymbol{B})$ by $\boldsymbol{P}_{\mathcal{R}(\boldsymbol{A}),\mathcal{R}(\boldsymbol{B})}$. To characterize the oblique projection matrix $\boldsymbol{P}_{\mathcal{R}(\boldsymbol{A}),\mathcal{R}(\boldsymbol{B})}$, let us consider *dual bases*

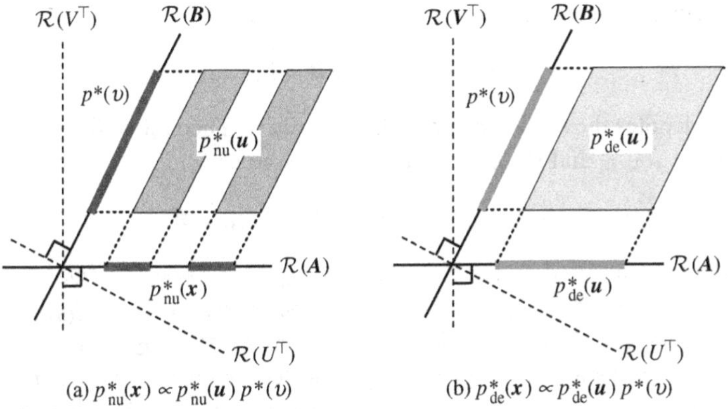

Figure 8.1. A schematic picture of the heterodistributional subspace for $d = 2$ and $m = 1$. Let $\boldsymbol{A} \propto (1,0)^\top$ and $\boldsymbol{B} \propto (1,2)^\top$. Then $\boldsymbol{U} \propto (2,-1)$ and $\boldsymbol{V} \propto (0,1)$. $\mathcal{R}(\boldsymbol{A})$ and $\mathcal{R}(\boldsymbol{B})$ are called the heterodistributional subspace and the homodistributional subspace, respectively. If a data point $\boldsymbol{x}$ is projected onto $\mathcal{R}(\boldsymbol{A})$ along $\mathcal{R}(\boldsymbol{B})$, the homodistributional component $\boldsymbol{v}$ is eliminated and the heterodistributional component $\boldsymbol{u}$ is extracted.

$\boldsymbol{U}$ and $\boldsymbol{V}$ for $\boldsymbol{A}$ and $\boldsymbol{B}$, respectively; that is, $\boldsymbol{U}$ is an $m \times d$ matrix and $\boldsymbol{V}$ is a $(d-m)\times d$ matrix such that they are *bi-orthogonal* to each other:

$$\boldsymbol{U}\boldsymbol{B} = \boldsymbol{O}_{m\times(d-m)} \quad \text{and} \quad \boldsymbol{V}\boldsymbol{A} = \boldsymbol{O}_{(d-m)\times m},$$

where $\boldsymbol{O}_{m\times m'}$ denotes the $m \times m'$ matrix with all zeros. Thus, $\mathcal{R}(\boldsymbol{B})$ and $\mathcal{R}(\boldsymbol{U}^\top)$ are orthogonal to each other and $\mathcal{R}(\boldsymbol{A})$ and $\mathcal{R}(\boldsymbol{V}^\top)$ are orthogonal to each other. When $\mathcal{R}(\boldsymbol{A})$ and $\mathcal{R}(\boldsymbol{B})$ are orthogonal to each other, $\mathcal{R}(\boldsymbol{U}^\top)$ agrees with $\mathcal{R}(\boldsymbol{A})$ and $\mathcal{R}(\boldsymbol{V}^\top)$ agrees with $\mathcal{R}(\boldsymbol{B})$. However, they are different in general, as illustrated in Figure 8.1.

The relation between $\boldsymbol{A}$ and $\boldsymbol{B}$ and the relation between $\boldsymbol{U}$ and $\boldsymbol{V}$ can be characterized in terms of the covariance matrix $\boldsymbol{\Sigma}$ (of either $p^*_{\text{nu}}(\boldsymbol{x})$ or $p^*_{\text{de}}(\boldsymbol{x})$) as

$$\boldsymbol{A}^\top\boldsymbol{\Sigma}^{-1}\boldsymbol{B} = \boldsymbol{O}_{(d-m)\times m} \quad \text{and} \quad \boldsymbol{U}\boldsymbol{\Sigma}\boldsymbol{V}^\top = \boldsymbol{O}_{m\times(d-m)}. \tag{8.3}$$

These orthogonarilies in terms of $\boldsymbol{\Sigma}$ follow from the statistical independence between the components in $\mathcal{R}(\boldsymbol{A})$ and $\mathcal{R}(\boldsymbol{B})$. More specifically, the left equation in Eq. (8.3) follows from the facts that the *sphering* operation (transforming samples $\boldsymbol{x}$ by $\boldsymbol{\Sigma}^{-1/2}$ in advance) orthogonalizes independent components $\boldsymbol{u}$ and $\boldsymbol{v}$ (Hyvärinen et al., 2001) and the right equation in Eq. (8.3) is its dual expression (Kawanabe et al., 2007). After sphering, the covariance matrix becomes identity and all the discussions become simpler. However, estimating the covariance matrix from samples is erroneous, and taking its inverse tends to further magnify the estimation error. For this reason, we deal directly with non-orthogonal $\boldsymbol{A}$ and $\boldsymbol{B}$ in the following.

For normalization purposes, we further assume that

$$UA = I_m \quad \text{and} \quad VB = I_{d-m},$$

where I_m denotes the m-dimensional identity matrix. Then the oblique projection matrices $P_{\mathcal{R}(A),\mathcal{R}(B)}$ and $P_{\mathcal{R}(B),\mathcal{R}(A)}$ can be expressed as

$$P_{\mathcal{R}(A),\mathcal{R}(B)} = AU \quad \text{and} \quad P_{\mathcal{R}(B),\mathcal{R}(A)} = BV,$$

which can be confirmed by the facts that $P^2_{\mathcal{R}(A),\mathcal{R}(B)} = P_{\mathcal{R}(A),\mathcal{R}(B)}$ (*idempotence*), the null space of $P_{\mathcal{R}(A),\mathcal{R}(B)}$ is $\mathcal{R}(B)$, and the range of $P_{\mathcal{R}(A),\mathcal{R}(B)}$ is $\mathcal{R}(A)$; the same goes for $P_{\mathcal{R}(B),\mathcal{R}(A)}$. These expressions of $P_{\mathcal{R}(A),\mathcal{R}(B)}$ and $P_{\mathcal{R}(B),\mathcal{R}(A)}$ imply that U plays a role of expressing projected images in an m-dimensional coordinate system within $\mathcal{R}(A)$, and V plays a role of expressing projected images in a $(d-m)$-dimensional coordinate system within $\mathcal{R}(B)$. U and V are called the the *heterodistributional mapping* and the *homodistributional mapping*, respectively.

Now u_i^{nu}, u_j^{de}, v_i^{nu}, and v_j^{de} are expressed as

$$u_i^{\mathrm{nu}} = Ux_i^{\mathrm{nu}}, \quad u_j^{\mathrm{de}} = Ux_j^{\mathrm{de}}, \quad v_i^{\mathrm{nu}} = Vx_i^{\mathrm{nu}}, \quad \text{and} \quad v_j^{\mathrm{de}} = Vx_j^{\mathrm{de}}.$$

Thus, if the heterodistributional mapping U was estimated, estimation of the density ratio $r^*(x)$ could be carried out in a low-dimensional heterodistributional subspace via Eq. (8.2).

In the next subsection we explain how to estimate the heterodistributional mapping U. For a while, we assume that the dimensionality m of the heterodistributional subspace is known. We explain how m is estimated in Section 8.1.4.

8.1.3 Estimating the Heterodistributional Subspace by Supervised Dimensionality Reduction

To estimate the heterodistributional subspace, we need a criterion that reflects the degree of distributional difference in a subspace. Here we explain that the heterodistributional subspace can be estimated by using supervised dimensionality reduction methods.

Basic Idea

A key observation in identifying the heterodistributional subspace is that the existence of distributional difference can be checked whether samples from the two distributions can be *separated* from each other. That is, if the samples of one distribution could be distinguished from the samples of the other distribution, the two distributions would be different; otherwise, the distributions are similar. We employ this idea for finding the heterodistributional subspace. Let us denote the samples projected onto the heterodistributional subspace by

$$\{u_i^{\mathrm{nu}} \mid u_i^{\mathrm{nu}} = Ux_i^{\mathrm{nu}}\}_{i=1}^{n_{\mathrm{nu}}} \quad \text{and} \quad \{u_j^{\mathrm{de}} \mid u_j^{\mathrm{de}} = Ux_j^{\mathrm{de}}\}_{j=1}^{n_{\mathrm{de}}}.$$

Then our goal is to find the matrix $\boldsymbol{U}$ such that $\{\boldsymbol{u}_i^{\mathrm{nu}}\}_{i=1}^{n_{\mathrm{nu}}}$ and $\{\boldsymbol{u}_j^{\mathrm{de}}\}_{j=1}^{n_{\mathrm{de}}}$ are maximally separated from each other. To achieve this goal, we may use *any* supervised dimensionality reduction methods.

Among various supervised dimensionality reduction methods (e.g., Hastie and Tibshirani, 1996a, 1996b; Fukumizu et al., 2004; Goldberger et al., 2005; Globerson and Roweis, 2006), we decided to use *local Fisher discriminant analysis* (LFDA; Sugiyama, 2007), which is an extension of the classical *Fisher discriminant analysis* (FDA; Fisher, 1936). LFDA has various practically useful properties; for example, there is no limitation on the dimensionality of the reduced subspace,[1] it works well even when the data have a multimodal structure (such as separate clusters), it is robust against outliers, its solution can be analytically computed using eigenvalue decomposition in a numerically stable and computationally efficient manner, and its experimental performance was shown to be better than competitive methods. In the following we briefly review the LFDA method, and show how it can be used for finding the heterodistributional subspace.

Let us consider a set of binary-labeled training samples

$$\{(\boldsymbol{x}_k, y_k) \mid \boldsymbol{x}_k \in \mathbb{R}^d, y_k \in \{+1, -1\}\}_{k=1}^{n},$$

and reduce the dimensionality of $\boldsymbol{x}_k$ by $\boldsymbol{T}\boldsymbol{x}_k$, where $\boldsymbol{T}$ is an $m \times d$ transformation matrix. Effectively, the training samples $\{(\boldsymbol{x}_k, y_k)\}_{k=1}^{n}$ correspond to the following setup: For $n = n_{\mathrm{nu}} + n_{\mathrm{de}}$,

$$(\boldsymbol{x}_1, \ldots, \boldsymbol{x}_n) = (\boldsymbol{x}_1^{\mathrm{nu}}, \ldots, \boldsymbol{x}_{n_{\mathrm{nu}}}^{\mathrm{nu}}, \boldsymbol{x}_1^{\mathrm{de}}, \ldots, \boldsymbol{x}_{n_{\mathrm{de}}}^{\mathrm{de}}),$$
$$(y_1, \ldots, y_n) = (\underbrace{+1, \ldots, +1}_{n_{\mathrm{nu}}}, \underbrace{-1, \ldots, -1}_{n_{\mathrm{de}}}).$$

Fisher Discriminant Analysis (FDA)

Because LFDA is an extention of FDA (Fisher, 1936), we first briefly review the original FDA.

Let n_+ and n_- be the number of samples in classes $+1$ and -1, respectively. Let $\boldsymbol{\mu}$, $\boldsymbol{\mu}_+$, and $\boldsymbol{\mu}_-$ be the means of $\{\boldsymbol{x}_k\}_{k=1}^{n}$, $\{\boldsymbol{x}_k | y_k = +1\}_{k=1}^{n}$, and $\{\boldsymbol{x}_k | y_k = -1\}_{k=1}^{n}$, respectively:

$$\boldsymbol{\mu} := \frac{1}{n}\sum_{k=1}^{n} \boldsymbol{x}_k, \quad \boldsymbol{\mu}_+ := \frac{1}{n_+}\sum_{k:y_k=+1} \boldsymbol{x}_k, \quad \text{and} \quad \boldsymbol{\mu}_- := \frac{1}{n_-}\sum_{k:y_k=-1} \boldsymbol{x}_k.$$

Let $\boldsymbol{S}^{(\mathrm{b})}$ and $\boldsymbol{S}^{(\mathrm{w})}$ be the *between-class scatter matrix* and the *within-class scatter matrix*, defined as

$$\boldsymbol{S}^{(\mathrm{b})} := n_+(\boldsymbol{\mu}_+ - \boldsymbol{\mu})(\boldsymbol{\mu}_+ - \boldsymbol{\mu})^\top + n_-(\boldsymbol{\mu}_- - \boldsymbol{\mu})(\boldsymbol{\mu}_- - \boldsymbol{\mu})^\top,$$
$$\boldsymbol{S}^{(\mathrm{w})} := \sum_{k:y_k=+1} (\boldsymbol{x}_k - \boldsymbol{\mu}_+)(\boldsymbol{x}_k - \boldsymbol{\mu}_+)^\top + \sum_{k:y_k=-1} (\boldsymbol{x}_k - \boldsymbol{\mu}_-)(\boldsymbol{x}_k - \boldsymbol{\mu}_-)^\top.$$

[1] FDA can only find a subspace with dimensionality less than the number of classes (Fukunaga, 1990). Thus, in the binary classification scenario that we are dealing with here, the maximum dimensionality of the subspace that FDA can find is only one.

The FDA transformation matrix $\boldsymbol{T}_{\mathrm{FDA}}$ is defined as

$$\boldsymbol{T}_{\mathrm{FDA}} := \underset{\boldsymbol{T}\in\mathbb{R}^{m\times d}}{\operatorname{argmax}} \left[\operatorname{tr}(\boldsymbol{T}\boldsymbol{S}^{(\mathrm{b})}\boldsymbol{T}^\top(\boldsymbol{T}\boldsymbol{S}^{(\mathrm{w})}\boldsymbol{T}^\top)^{-1})\right].$$

That is, FDA seeks a transformation matrix $\boldsymbol{T}$ such that between-class scatter is maximized and within-class scatter is minimized in the embedding space $\mathbb{R}^m$.

Let $\{\boldsymbol{\phi}_l\}_{l=1}^d$ be the generalized eigenvectors associated with the generalized eigenvalues $\{\lambda_l\}_{l=1}^d$ of the following generalized eigenvalue problem:

$$\boldsymbol{S}^{(\mathrm{b})}\boldsymbol{\phi} = \lambda\boldsymbol{S}^{(\mathrm{w})}\boldsymbol{\phi}.$$

Without loss of generality, we assume that the generalized eigenvalues are sorted as $\lambda_1 \geq \cdots \geq \lambda_d$. Then a solution $\boldsymbol{T}_{\mathrm{FDA}}$ is analytically given as $\boldsymbol{T}_{\mathrm{FDA}} = (\boldsymbol{\phi}_1|\cdots|\boldsymbol{\phi}_m)^\top$ (e.g., Duda et al., 2001).

FDA works very well if the samples in each class have Gaussian distributions with a common covariance structure. However, it tends to give undesired results if the samples in a class form several separate clusters or there are outliers. Furthermore, the between-class scatter matrix $\boldsymbol{S}^{(\mathrm{b})}$ is known to have rank one in the current setup (see e.g., Fukunaga, 1990), implying that we can obtain only a single meaningful feature $\boldsymbol{\phi}_1$ through the FDA criterion; the remaining features $\{\boldsymbol{\phi}_l\}_{l=2}^d$ found by FDA are arbitrary in the null space of $\boldsymbol{S}^{(\mathrm{b})}$. This is an essential limitation of FDA in dimensionality reduction.

Local Fisher Discriminant Analysis (LFDA)

To overcome the weaknesses of FDA explained above, LFDA has been introduced (Sugiyama, 2007). Here we briefly explain the main idea of LFDA.

The scatter matrices $\boldsymbol{S}^{(\mathrm{b})}$ and $\boldsymbol{S}^{(\mathrm{w})}$ in the original FDA can be expressed in a pairwise manner as

$$\boldsymbol{S}^{(\mathrm{b})} = \frac{1}{2}\sum_{k,k'=1}^{n} W_{k,k'}^{(\mathrm{b})}(\boldsymbol{x}_k - \boldsymbol{x}_{k'})(\boldsymbol{x}_k - \boldsymbol{x}_{k'})^\top,$$

$$\boldsymbol{S}^{(\mathrm{w})} = \frac{1}{2}\sum_{k,k'=1}^{n} W_{k,k'}^{(\mathrm{w})}(\boldsymbol{x}_k - \boldsymbol{x}_{k'})(\boldsymbol{x}_k - \boldsymbol{x}_{k'})^\top,$$

where

$$W_{k,k'}^{(\mathrm{b})} := \begin{cases} 1/n - 1/n_+ & \text{if } y_k = y_{k'} = +1, \\ 1/n - 1/n_- & \text{if } y_k = y_{k'} = -1, \\ 1/n & \text{if } y_k \neq y_{k'}, \end{cases}$$

$$W_{k,k'}^{(\mathrm{w})} := \begin{cases} 1/n_+ & \text{if } y_k = y_{k'} = +1, \\ 1/n_- & \text{if } y_k = y_{k'} = -1, \\ 0 & \text{if } y_k \neq y_{k'}. \end{cases}$$

Based on this pairwise expression, let us define the *local* between-class scatter matrix $\boldsymbol{S}^{(\mathrm{lb})}$ and the *local* within-class scatter matrix $\boldsymbol{S}^{(\mathrm{lw})}$ as

$$\boldsymbol{S}^{(\mathrm{lb})} := \frac{1}{2}\sum_{k,k'=1}^{n} W_{k,k'}^{(\mathrm{lb})}(\boldsymbol{x}_k - \boldsymbol{x}_{k'})(\boldsymbol{x}_k - \boldsymbol{x}_{k'})^\top,$$

$$\boldsymbol{S}^{(\mathrm{lw})} := \frac{1}{2}\sum_{k,k'=1}^{n} W_{k,k'}^{(\mathrm{lw})}(\boldsymbol{x}_k - \boldsymbol{x}_{k'})(\boldsymbol{x}_k - \boldsymbol{x}_{k'})^\top,$$

where

$$W_{k,k'}^{(\mathrm{lb})} := \begin{cases} A_{k,k'}(1/n - 1/n_+) & \text{if } y_k = y_{k'} = +1, \\ A_{k,k'}(1/n - 1/n_-) & \text{if } y_k = y_{k'} = -1, \\ 1/n & \text{if } y_k \neq y_{k'}, \end{cases}$$

$$W_{k,k'}^{(\mathrm{lw})} := \begin{cases} A_{k,k'}/n_+ & \text{if } y_k = y_{k'} = +1, \\ A_{k,k'}/n_- & \text{if } y_k = y_{k'} = -1, \\ 0 & \text{if } y_k \neq y_{k'}. \end{cases}$$

$A_{k,k'}$ is the affinity value between $\boldsymbol{x}_k$ and $\boldsymbol{x}_{k'}$, for example, defined based on the *local scaling heuristic* (Zelnik-Manor and Perona, 2005):

$$A_{k,k'} := \exp\left(-\frac{\|\boldsymbol{x}_k - \boldsymbol{x}_{k'}\|^2}{\eta_k \eta_{k'}}\right).$$

η_k is the local scaling factor around $\boldsymbol{x}_k$ defined by $\eta_k := \|\boldsymbol{x}_k - \boldsymbol{x}_k^{(K)}\|$, where $\boldsymbol{x}_k^{(K)}$ denotes the K-th nearest neighbor of $\boldsymbol{x}_k$. A heuristic choice of $K = 7$ was shown to be useful through extensive simulations (Zelnik-Manor and Perona, 2005; Sugiyama, 2007). Note that the local scaling factors are computed in a classwise manner in LFDA.

Based on the local scatter matrices $\boldsymbol{S}^{(\mathrm{lb})}$ and $\boldsymbol{S}^{(\mathrm{lw})}$, the LFDA transformation matrix $\boldsymbol{T}_{\mathrm{LFDA}}$ is defined as

$$\boldsymbol{T}_{\mathrm{LFDA}} := \underset{\boldsymbol{T}\in\mathbb{R}^{m\times d}}{\mathrm{argmax}} \left[\mathrm{tr}(\boldsymbol{T}\boldsymbol{S}^{(\mathrm{lb})}\boldsymbol{T}^\top(\boldsymbol{T}\boldsymbol{S}^{(\mathrm{lw})}\boldsymbol{T}^\top)^{-1})\right].$$

The definitions of $\boldsymbol{S}^{(\mathrm{lb})}$ and $\boldsymbol{S}^{(\mathrm{lw})}$ imply that LFDA seeks a transformation matrix $\boldsymbol{T}$ such that *nearby* data pairs in the same class are made close to each other and the data pairs in different classes are made apart from each other; *far apart* data pairs in the same class are not imposed to be close to each other.

By this localization effect, LFDA can overcome the weakness of the original FDA against clustered data and outliers. When $A_{k,k'} = 1$ for all k, k' (i.e., no locality), $\boldsymbol{S}^{(\mathrm{lw})}$ and $\boldsymbol{S}^{(\mathrm{lb})}$ are reduced to $\boldsymbol{S}^{(\mathrm{w})}$ and $\boldsymbol{S}^{(\mathrm{b})}$, respectively. Thus, LFDA could be regarded as a localized variant of FDA. The between-class scatter matrix $\boldsymbol{S}^{(\mathrm{b})}$ in the original FDA has only rank one, while its local counterpart $\boldsymbol{S}^{(\mathrm{lb})}$ in LFDA usually has full rank with no multiplicity in eigenvalues (given $n \geq d$). Therefore, LFDA can be practically applied to dimensionality reduction in *any* dimensional subspaces, which is a significant advantage over the original FDA.

A solution $\boldsymbol{T}_{\mathrm{LFDA}}$ can be computed in the same way as the original FDA; namely, the LFDA solution is given as

$$\boldsymbol{T}_{\mathrm{LFDA}} = (\boldsymbol{\varphi}_1|\cdots|\boldsymbol{\varphi}_m)^\top,$$

where $\{\boldsymbol{\varphi}_l\}_{l=1}^d$ are the generalized eigenvectors associated with the generalized eigenvalues $\{\gamma_l\}_{l=1}^d$ of the following generalized eigenvalue problem:

$$\boldsymbol{S}^{(\mathrm{lb})}\boldsymbol{\varphi} = \gamma \boldsymbol{S}^{(\mathrm{lw})}\boldsymbol{\varphi}. \tag{8.4}$$

Without loss of generality, we assume that the generalized eigenvalues are sorted as $\gamma_1 \geq \cdots \geq \gamma_d$. Thus, LFDA is computationally as efficient as the original FDA.

A pseudo code of LFDA is summarized in Figure 8.2. A MATLAB® implementation of LFDA is available from http://sugiyama-www.cs.titech.ac.jp/~sugi/software/LFDA/.

Use of LFDA for Heterodistributional Subspace Search

Finally, we show how to obtain an estimate of the transformation matrix $\boldsymbol{U}$ needed in the D^3 procedure from the LFDA transformation matrix $\boldsymbol{T}_{\mathrm{LFDA}}$.

First, an orthonormal basis $\{\widetilde{\boldsymbol{\varphi}}_l\}_{l=1}^m$ of the LFDA subspace is computed from the generalized eigenvectors $\{\boldsymbol{\varphi}_l\}_{l=1}^m$ so that the span of $\{\widetilde{\boldsymbol{\varphi}}_l\}_{l=1}^{m'}$ agrees with the span of $\{\boldsymbol{\varphi}_l\}_{l=1}^{m'}$ for all m' $(1 \leq m' \leq m)$. This can be carried out, for example, by the *Gram–Schmidt orthonormalization* (see e.g., Golub and Loan, 1996). Then an estimate $\widehat{\boldsymbol{U}}$ is given as

$$\widehat{\boldsymbol{U}} := (\widetilde{\boldsymbol{\varphi}}_1|\cdots|\widetilde{\boldsymbol{\varphi}}_m)^\top,$$

and the samples are transformed as

$$\widehat{\boldsymbol{u}}_i^{\mathrm{nu}} := \widehat{\boldsymbol{U}}\boldsymbol{x}_i^{\mathrm{nu}} \quad \text{for } i = 1,\ldots,n_{\mathrm{nu}}, \tag{8.5}$$

$$\widehat{\boldsymbol{u}}_j^{\mathrm{de}} := \widehat{\boldsymbol{U}}\boldsymbol{x}_j^{\mathrm{de}} \quad \text{for } j = 1,\ldots,n_{\mathrm{de}}. \tag{8.6}$$

This expression of $\widehat{\boldsymbol{U}}$ implies another useful advantage of LFDA. In this D^3 procedure, we need the LFDA solution for each reduced dimensionality $m = 1,\ldots,d$. However, we do not have to compute the LFDA solution for each m – we only have to solve the generalized eigenvalue problem (8.4) once for $m = d$ and compute the orthonormal basis $\{\widetilde{\boldsymbol{\varphi}}_l\}_{l=1}^d$; the solution for $m < d$ can be obtained simply by taking the first m basis vectors $\{\widetilde{\boldsymbol{\varphi}}_l\}_{l=1}^m$.

8.1.4 D^3 via LFDA and uLSIF

Given that the heterodistributional subspace has been successfully estimated, the final step is to estimate the density ratio within the subspace.

Here we use *unconstrained least-squares importance fitting* (uLSIF; Kanamori et al., 2009) – a ratio fitting method based on the *squared distance* (see Section 6.2.2) – because it has several advantages over other methods; for example,

Input: Two sets of samples $\{\boldsymbol{x}_i^{\mathrm{nu}}\}_{i=1}^{n_{\mathrm{nu}}}$ and $\{\boldsymbol{x}_j^{\mathrm{de}}\}_{j=1}^{n_{\mathrm{de}}}$ on $\mathbb{R}^d$
Dimensionality of embedding space $m \in \{1,\ldots,d\}$
Output: $m \times d$ transformation matrix $\widehat{\boldsymbol{U}}$

$\widetilde{\boldsymbol{x}}_i^{\mathrm{nu}} \longleftarrow$ 7th nearest neighbor of $\boldsymbol{x}_i^{\mathrm{nu}}$ among $\{\boldsymbol{x}_{i'}^{\mathrm{nu}}\}_{i'=1}^{n_{\mathrm{nu}}}$ for $i = 1,\ldots,n_{\mathrm{nu}}$;
$\widetilde{\boldsymbol{x}}_j^{\mathrm{de}} \longleftarrow$ 7th nearest neighbor of $\boldsymbol{x}_j^{\mathrm{de}}$ among $\{\boldsymbol{x}_{j'}^{\mathrm{de}}\}_{j'=1}^{n_{\mathrm{de}}}$ for $j = 1,\ldots,n_{\mathrm{de}}$;
$\eta_i^{\mathrm{nu}} \longleftarrow \|\boldsymbol{x}_i^{\mathrm{nu}} - \widetilde{\boldsymbol{x}}_i^{\mathrm{nu}}\|$ for $i = 1,\ldots,n_{\mathrm{nu}}$;
$\eta_j^{\mathrm{de}} \longleftarrow \|\boldsymbol{x}_j^{\mathrm{de}} - \widetilde{\boldsymbol{x}}_j^{\mathrm{de}}\|$ for $j = 1,\ldots,n_{\mathrm{de}}$;
$A_{i,i'}^{\mathrm{de}} \longleftarrow \exp\left(-\frac{\|\boldsymbol{x}_i^{\mathrm{de}} - \boldsymbol{x}_{i'}^{\mathrm{de}}\|^2}{\eta_i^{\mathrm{de}}\eta_{i'}^{\mathrm{de}}}\right)$ for $i,i' = 1,\ldots,n_{\mathrm{nu}}$;
$A_{j,j'}^{\mathrm{de}} \longleftarrow \exp\left(-\frac{\|\boldsymbol{x}_j^{\mathrm{de}} - \boldsymbol{x}_{j'}^{\mathrm{de}}\|^2}{\eta_j^{\mathrm{de}}\eta_{j'}^{\mathrm{de}}}\right)$ for $j,j' = 1,\ldots,n_{\mathrm{de}}$;
$\boldsymbol{X}^{\mathrm{nu}} \longleftarrow (\boldsymbol{x}_1^{\mathrm{nu}}|\cdots|\boldsymbol{x}_{n_{\mathrm{nu}}}^{\mathrm{nu}})$;
$\boldsymbol{X}^{\mathrm{de}} \longleftarrow (\boldsymbol{x}_1^{\mathrm{de}}|\cdots|\boldsymbol{x}_{n_{\mathrm{de}}}^{\mathrm{de}})$;
$\boldsymbol{G}^{\mathrm{nu}} \longleftarrow \boldsymbol{X}^{\mathrm{nu}}\mathrm{diag}(\boldsymbol{A}^{\mathrm{nu}}\boldsymbol{1}_{n_{\mathrm{nu}}})\boldsymbol{X}^{\mathrm{nu}\top} - \boldsymbol{X}^{\mathrm{nu}}\boldsymbol{A}^{\mathrm{nu}}\boldsymbol{X}^{\mathrm{nu}\top}$;
$\boldsymbol{G}^{\mathrm{de}} \longleftarrow \boldsymbol{X}^{\mathrm{de}}\mathrm{diag}(\boldsymbol{A}^{\mathrm{de}}\boldsymbol{1}_{n_{\mathrm{de}}})\boldsymbol{X}^{\mathrm{de}\top} - \boldsymbol{X}^{\mathrm{de}}\boldsymbol{A}^{\mathrm{de}}\boldsymbol{X}^{\mathrm{de}\top}$;
$\boldsymbol{S}^{(\mathrm{lw})} \longleftarrow \frac{1}{n_{\mathrm{nu}}}\boldsymbol{G}^{\mathrm{nu}} + \frac{1}{n_{\mathrm{de}}}\boldsymbol{G}^{\mathrm{de}}$;
$n \longleftarrow n_{\mathrm{nu}} + n_{\mathrm{de}}$;
$\boldsymbol{S}^{(\mathrm{lb})} \longleftarrow (\frac{1}{n} - \frac{1}{n_{\mathrm{nu}}})\boldsymbol{G}^{\mathrm{nu}} + (\frac{1}{n} - \frac{1}{n_{\mathrm{de}}})\boldsymbol{G}^{\mathrm{de}} + \frac{n_{\mathrm{de}}}{n}\boldsymbol{X}^{\mathrm{nu}}\boldsymbol{X}^{\mathrm{nu}\top} + \frac{n_{\mathrm{nu}}}{n}\boldsymbol{X}^{\mathrm{de}}\boldsymbol{X}^{\mathrm{de}\top}$
$\quad -\frac{1}{n}\boldsymbol{X}^{\mathrm{nu}}\boldsymbol{1}_{n_{\mathrm{nu}}}(\boldsymbol{X}^{\mathrm{de}}\boldsymbol{1}_{n_{\mathrm{de}}})^\top - \frac{1}{n}\boldsymbol{X}^{\mathrm{de}}\boldsymbol{1}_{n_{\mathrm{de}}}(\boldsymbol{X}^{\mathrm{nu}}\boldsymbol{1}_{n_{\mathrm{nu}}})^\top$;
$\{(\gamma_l,\boldsymbol{\varphi}_l)\}_{l=1}^m \longleftarrow$ generalized eigenvalues and eigenvectors of
$\boldsymbol{S}^{(\mathrm{lb})}\boldsymbol{\varphi} = \gamma\boldsymbol{S}^{(\mathrm{lw})}\boldsymbol{\varphi}$; % $\gamma_1 \geq \cdots \geq \gamma_d$
$\{\widetilde{\boldsymbol{\varphi}}_l\}_{l=1}^m \longleftarrow$ orthonormal basis of $\{\boldsymbol{\varphi}_l\}_{l=1}^m$;
% $\mathrm{span}(\{\widehat{\boldsymbol{\varphi}}_l\}_{l=1}^{m'}) = \mathrm{span}(\{\boldsymbol{\varphi}_l\}_{l=1}^{m'})$ for $m' = 1,\ldots,m$
$\widehat{\boldsymbol{U}} \longleftarrow (\widetilde{\boldsymbol{\varphi}}_1|\cdots|\widetilde{\boldsymbol{\varphi}}_m)^\top$;

Figure 8.2. Pseudo code of LFDA. $\boldsymbol{1}_n$ denotes the n-dimensional vectors with all ones, and $\mathrm{diag}(\boldsymbol{b})$ denotes the diagonal matrix with diagonal elements specified by a vector $\boldsymbol{b}$.

its solution can be computed analytically by solving a system of linear equations in an efficient manner, model selection is possible via *cross-validation* (CV), the leave-one-out CV (LOOCV) score can be computed analytically without repeating hold-out loops, and it was reported to perform well in experiments.

For convenience, we summarize how to compute the uLSIF solution once again. In uLSIF, the linear model $r(\boldsymbol{u}) = \boldsymbol{\psi}(\boldsymbol{u})^\top\boldsymbol{\theta}$ is used for density-ratio estimation, where $\boldsymbol{\psi}(\boldsymbol{u}) : \mathbb{R}^m \to \mathbb{R}^b$ is a non-negative basis function vector and $\boldsymbol{\theta}$ $(\in \mathbb{R}^b)$ is a parameter vector. The uLSIF solution is given by

$$\widehat{\boldsymbol{\theta}} = (\widehat{\boldsymbol{H}} + \lambda\boldsymbol{I}_b)^{-1}\widehat{\boldsymbol{h}}, \tag{8.7}$$

where $\boldsymbol{I}_b$ is the b-dimensional identity matrix and

$$\widehat{\boldsymbol{H}} := \frac{1}{n_{\mathrm{de}}} \sum_{j=1}^{n_{\mathrm{de}}} \boldsymbol{\psi}(\widehat{\boldsymbol{u}}_j^{\mathrm{de}}) \boldsymbol{\psi}(\widehat{\boldsymbol{u}}_j^{\mathrm{de}})^\top \quad \text{and} \quad \widehat{\boldsymbol{h}} := \frac{1}{n_{\mathrm{nu}}} \sum_{i=1}^{n_{\mathrm{nu}}} \boldsymbol{\psi}(\widehat{\boldsymbol{u}}_i^{\mathrm{nu}}).$$

$\{\widehat{\boldsymbol{u}}_i^{\mathrm{nu}} (\in \mathbb{R}^m)\}_{i=1}^{n_{\mathrm{nu}}}$ and $\{\widehat{\boldsymbol{u}}_j^{\mathrm{de}} (\in \mathbb{R}^m)\}_{j=1}^{n_{\mathrm{de}}}$ are dimensionality-reduced samples given by Eqs. (8.5) and (8.6).

Thus far we have assumed that the dimensionality m of the heterodistributional subspace is known. In practice, the CV score of the uLSIF algorithm (see Section 6.3.3 for details) may be used for determining m. More specifically, let $n := \min(n_{\mathrm{nu}}, n_{\mathrm{de}})$, and let $\widehat{r}^{(k)}$ ($k \in \{1, \ldots, n\}$) be a density-ratio estimator obtained by uLSIF with $\{\widehat{\boldsymbol{u}}_i^{\mathrm{nu}}\}_{i=1}^{n_{\mathrm{nu}}} \backslash \widehat{\boldsymbol{u}}_k^{\mathrm{nu}}$ and $\{\widehat{\boldsymbol{u}}_j^{\mathrm{de}}\}_{j=1}^{n_{\mathrm{de}}} \backslash \widehat{\boldsymbol{u}}_k^{\mathrm{de}}$. Then the LOOCV score of uLSIF, given by

$$\widehat{J}^{\mathrm{LOOCV}} = \frac{1}{n} \sum_{k=1}^{n} \left[\frac{1}{2} (\widehat{r}^{(k)}(\widehat{\boldsymbol{u}}_k^{\mathrm{de}}))^2 - \widehat{r}^{(k)}(\widehat{\boldsymbol{u}}_k^{\mathrm{nu}}) \right],$$

is computed as a function of the reduced dimensionality m, and the one that minimizes the LOOCV score is chosen; we may use k-fold cross-validation instead of LOOCV.

The D^3 procedure explained here is referred to as *D^3-LFDA/uLSIF*, which effectively combines LFDA and uLSIF, both of which have analytic-form solutions. The pseudo code of D^3-LFDA/uLSIF is described in Figure 8.3.

```
Input:   Two sets of samples {x_i^nu}_{i=1}^{n_nu} and {x_j^de}_{j=1}^{n_de} on R^d
Output:  Density-ratio estimator r̂(x)

Obtain orthonormal basis {φ̃_l}_{l=1}^d by LFDA with {x_i^nu}_{i=1}^{n_nu} and {x_j^de}_{j=1}^{n_de};
For each reduced dimensionality m = 1,...,d
    Form projection matrix: Û_m = (φ̃_1|···|φ̃_m)^T;
    Project samples: {û_{i,m}^nu = Û_m x_i^nu}_{i=1}^{n_nu} and {û_{j,m}^de = Û_m x_j^de}_{j=1}^{n_de};
    For each candidate of Gaussian width σ
        For each candidate of regularization parameter λ
            Compute Ĵ^LOOCV(m,σ,λ) using {û_{i,m}^nu}_{i=1}^{n_nu} and {û_{j,m}^de}_{j=1}^{n_de};
        end
    end
end
Choose the best model: (m̂,σ̂,λ̂) ← argmin_{m,σ,λ} Ĵ^LOOCV(m,σ,λ);
Estimate density ratio by uLSIF for (σ̂,λ̂) using {û_{i,m̂}^nu}_{i=1}^{n_nu} and {û_{j,m̂}^de}_{j=1}^{n_de};
```

Figure 8.3. Pseudo code of D^3-LFDA/uLSIF.

8.2 Divergence Maximization Approach

The method of D^3-LFDA/uLSIF explained in the previous section was shown to be useful in high-dimensional density-ratio estimation (Sugiyama et al., 2010a). However, it possesses two potential weaknesses: the restrictive definition of the heterodistributional subspace and the limiting ability of its search method. In this section, an alternative approach to D^3 that can overcome these limitations (Sugiyama et al., 2011b) is introduced.

The basic idea of the alternative approach is explained in Section 8.2.1, and a generalized definition of heterodistributional subspaces is introduced in Section 8.2.2. Then, in Section 8.2.3, a criterion for heterodistributional subspace searches is given and how it is estimated from data is explained. In Section 8.2.4, algorithms for finding heterodistributional subspaces are described. Finally, in Section 8.2.5, the entire algorithm of heterodistributional subspace search for D^3 is described.

8.2.1 Basic Idea

In the D^3-LFDA/uLSIF method introduced in the previous section, the component inside the heterodistributional subspace and its complementary component are assumed to be statistically independent [see Eq. (8.1)]. This assumption is rather restrictive and can be violated in practice.

Furthermore, D^3-LFDA/uLSIF tries to find a subspace in which samples drawn from the numerator and denominator distributions are separated from each other. If samples drawn from the two distributions were separable, the two distributions would be significantly different. However, the opposite may not be always true; that is, non-separability does not necessarily imply that the two distributions are different (consider two similar distributions with a common support). Thus, LFDA (and any other supervised dimensionality reduction methods) does not necessarily identify the correct heterodistributional subspace.

Here, a more general definition of the heterodistributional subspace is adopted, where the independence assumption between the component inside the heterodistributional subspace and its complementary component is not imposed. This allows us to apply the concept of D^3 to a wider class of problems.

However, this general definition in turn makes the task of searching the heterodistributional subspace more challenging – supervised dimensionality reduction methods for separating samples drawn from the two distributions cannot be used anymore. Thus, we need an alternative method for identifying the largest subspace such that the two *conditional* distributions are equivalent in its complementary subspace.

To this end, it is proved that the heterodistributional subspace can be identified by finding a subspace in which two *marginal* distributions are maximally different under the *Pearson* (PE) divergence (Pearson, 1900), which is a squared-loss variant of the *Kullback–Leibler* (KL) divergence (Kullback and Leibler, 1951). Based on this characterization, a method called *least-squares heterodistributional subspace search* (LHSS) is introduced for searching a subspace such that the Pearson divergence between two marginal distributions is maximized (Sugiyama et al., 2011b).

An advantage of the LHSS method is that the subspace search (divergence estimation within a subspace) is carried out also using the density-ratio estimation method uLSIF (see Section 6.2.2). Thus, the two steps in the D^3 procedure (first identifying the heterodistributional subspace and then estimating the density ratio within the subspace) are merged into a single step. Thanks to this, the final density-ratio estimator can be obtained automatically without additional computation. This single-shot density-ratio estimation procedure is called *D^3 via LHSS* (D^3-LHSS). A summary of the density-ratio estimation methods is given in Figure 8.4.

8.2.2 Heterodistributional Subspaces Revisited

We now give a generalized definition of heterodistributional subspaces (cf. Section 8.1.1).

Let $\boldsymbol{u}$ be an m-dimensional vector ($m \in \{1,\ldots,d\}$) and $\boldsymbol{v}$ be a $(d-m)$-dimensional vector defined as

$$\begin{pmatrix} \boldsymbol{u} \\ \boldsymbol{v} \end{pmatrix} := \begin{pmatrix} \boldsymbol{U} \\ \boldsymbol{V} \end{pmatrix} \boldsymbol{x},$$

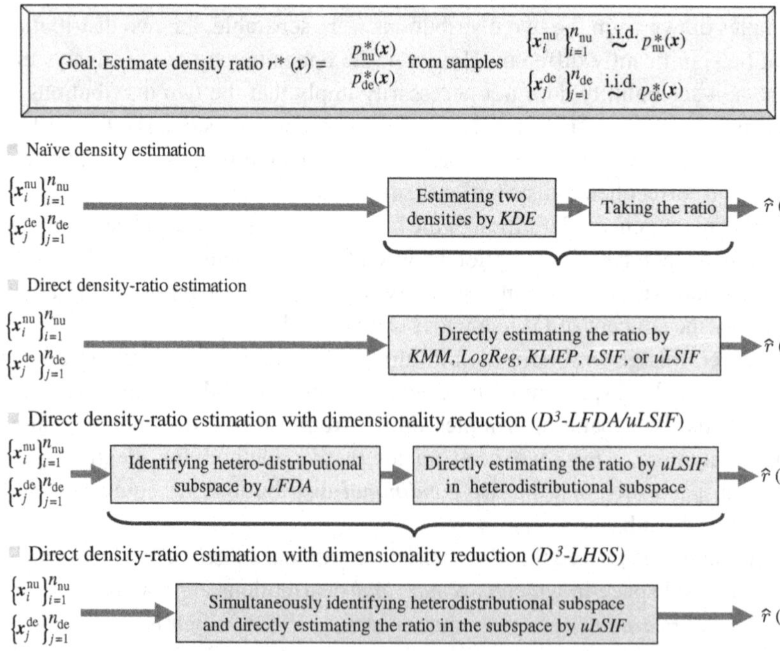

Figure 8.4. Summary of density-ratio estimation approaches.

where U is an $m \times d$ matrix and V is a $(d-m) \times d$ matrix. To ensure the uniqueness of the decomposition, we assume (without loss of generality) that the row vectors of U and V form an orthonormal basis, that is, U and V correspond to "projection" matrices that are orthogonally complementary to each other (see Figure 8.5). Then the two densities $p^*_{\mathrm{nu}}(\boldsymbol{x})$ and $p^*_{\mathrm{de}}(\boldsymbol{x})$ can be decomposed as

$$p^*_{\mathrm{nu}}(\boldsymbol{x}) = p^*_{\mathrm{nu}}(\boldsymbol{v}|\boldsymbol{u})p^*_{\mathrm{nu}}(\boldsymbol{u}) \quad \text{and} \quad p^*_{\mathrm{de}}(\boldsymbol{x}) = p^*_{\mathrm{de}}(\boldsymbol{v}|\boldsymbol{u})p^*_{\mathrm{de}}(\boldsymbol{u}).$$

The key theoretical assumption that forms the basis of the algorithm introduced here is that the conditional densities $p^*_{\mathrm{nu}}(\boldsymbol{v}|\boldsymbol{u})$ and $p^*_{\mathrm{de}}(\boldsymbol{v}|\boldsymbol{u})$ agree with each other; that is, the two densities $p^*_{\mathrm{nu}}(\boldsymbol{x})$ and $p^*_{\mathrm{de}}(\boldsymbol{x})$ are decomposed as

$$p^*_{\mathrm{nu}}(\boldsymbol{x}) = p(\boldsymbol{v}|\boldsymbol{u})p^*_{\mathrm{nu}}(\boldsymbol{u}) \quad \text{and} \quad p^*_{\mathrm{de}}(\boldsymbol{x}) = p(\boldsymbol{v}|\boldsymbol{u})p^*_{\mathrm{de}}(\boldsymbol{u}),$$

where $p(\boldsymbol{v}|\boldsymbol{u})$ is the common conditional density. This assumption implies that the marginal densities of $\boldsymbol{u}$ are different, but the conditional density of $\boldsymbol{v}$ given $\boldsymbol{u}$ is common to $p^*_{\mathrm{nu}}(\boldsymbol{x})$ and $p^*_{\mathrm{de}}(\boldsymbol{x})$. Then the density ratio is simplified as

$$r^*(\boldsymbol{x}) = \frac{p^*_{\mathrm{nu}}(\boldsymbol{u})}{p^*_{\mathrm{de}}(\boldsymbol{u})} =: r^*(\boldsymbol{u}).$$

Thus, the density ratio does not have to be estimated in the entire d-dimensional space; it is sufficient to estimate the density ratio only in the m-dimensional subspace specified by U.

In the following we will use the term *hetero-distributional subspace* to denote the subspace specified by U in which $p^*_{\mathrm{nu}}(\boldsymbol{u})$ and $p^*_{\mathrm{de}}(\boldsymbol{u})$ are different. More precisely, let $\mathcal{S}$ be a subspace specified by U and V such that

$$\mathcal{S} = \{U^\top U\boldsymbol{x} \mid p^*_{\mathrm{nu}}(\boldsymbol{v}|\boldsymbol{u}) = p^*_{\mathrm{de}}(\boldsymbol{v}|\boldsymbol{u}),\ \boldsymbol{u} = U\boldsymbol{x},\ \boldsymbol{v} = V\boldsymbol{x}\}.$$

Then the heterodistributional subspace is defined as the *intersection* of all subspaces $\mathcal{S}$. Intuitively, the heterodistributional subspace is the "smallest" subspace specified by U such that $p^*_{\mathrm{nu}}(\boldsymbol{v}|\boldsymbol{u})$ and $p^*_{\mathrm{de}}(\boldsymbol{v}|\boldsymbol{u})$ agree with each other. We refer to the orthogonal complement of the heterodistributional subspace as the *homodistributional subspace* (see Figure 8.5).

This formulation is a generalization of the one described in Section 8.1.1, where the components in the heterodistributional subspace and its complimentary subspace are assumed to be independent of each other. On the other hand, such an independence assumption is not imposed here. As will be demonstrated in Section 8.3, this generalization has the remarkable effect of extending the range of applications of D^3.

For the moment, we again assume that the true dimensionality m of the heterodistributional subspace is known. Later, how m is estimated from data is explained in Section 8.2.5.

8.2.3 Evaluating Distributional Difference by Pearson Divergence

Next we introduce a criterion for heterodistributional subspace searches, and explain how they are estimated from data.

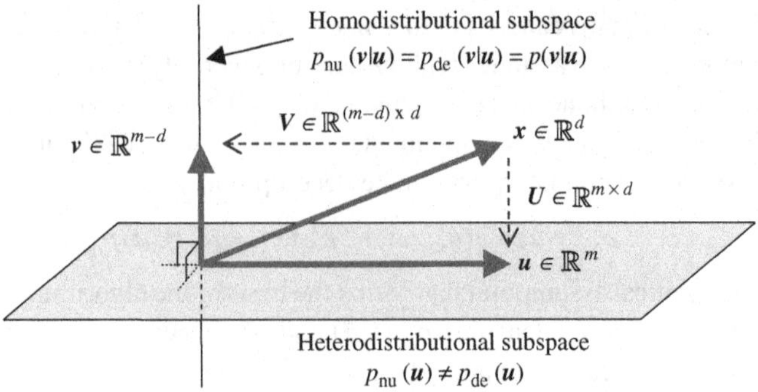

Figure 8.5. Heterodistributional subspace.

We use the *Pearson* (PE) divergence (Pearson, 1900) as our criterion for evaluating the discrepancy between two distributions. PE is a squared-loss variant of the *Kullback–Leibler* (KL) divergence (Kullback and Leibler, 1951). PE from $p^*_{\mathrm{nu}}(\boldsymbol{x})$ to $p^*_{\mathrm{de}}(\boldsymbol{x})$ is defined and expressed as

$$\begin{aligned}\mathrm{PE}[p^*_{\mathrm{nu}}(\boldsymbol{x}), p^*_{\mathrm{de}}(\boldsymbol{x})] &:= \frac{1}{2}\int \left(\frac{p^*_{\mathrm{nu}}(\boldsymbol{x})}{p^*_{\mathrm{de}}(\boldsymbol{x})} - 1\right)^2 p^*_{\mathrm{de}}(\boldsymbol{x})\mathrm{d}\boldsymbol{x}\\ &= \frac{1}{2}\int \frac{p^*_{\mathrm{nu}}(\boldsymbol{x})}{p^*_{\mathrm{de}}(\boldsymbol{x})} p^*_{\mathrm{nu}}(\boldsymbol{x})\mathrm{d}\boldsymbol{x} - \frac{1}{2}.\end{aligned}$$

$\mathrm{PE}[p^*_{\mathrm{nu}}(\boldsymbol{x}), p^*_{\mathrm{de}}(\boldsymbol{x})]$ vanishes if and only if $p^*_{\mathrm{nu}}(\boldsymbol{x}) = p^*_{\mathrm{de}}(\boldsymbol{x})$.

The following lemma (called the *data-processing inequality*) characterizes the heterodistributional subspace in terms of PE.

Lemma 8.1 (Sugiyama et al., 2011b). *Let*

$$\begin{aligned}\mathrm{PE}[p^*_{\mathrm{nu}}(\boldsymbol{u}), p^*_{\mathrm{de}}(\boldsymbol{u})] &= \frac{1}{2}\int \left(\frac{p^*_{\mathrm{nu}}(\boldsymbol{u})}{p^*_{\mathrm{de}}(\boldsymbol{u})} - 1\right)^2 p^*_{\mathrm{de}}(\boldsymbol{u})\mathrm{d}\boldsymbol{u}\\ &= \frac{1}{2}\int \frac{p^*_{\mathrm{nu}}(\boldsymbol{u})}{p^*_{\mathrm{de}}(\boldsymbol{u})} p^*_{\mathrm{nu}}(\boldsymbol{u})\mathrm{d}\boldsymbol{u} - \frac{1}{2}. \qquad (8.8)\end{aligned}$$

Then

$$\begin{aligned}&\mathrm{PE}[p^*_{\mathrm{nu}}(\boldsymbol{x}), p^*_{\mathrm{de}}(\boldsymbol{x})] - \mathrm{PE}[p^*_{\mathrm{nu}}(\boldsymbol{u}), p^*_{\mathrm{de}}(\boldsymbol{u})]\\ &= \frac{1}{2}\int \left(\frac{p^*_{\mathrm{nu}}(\boldsymbol{x})}{p^*_{\mathrm{de}}(\boldsymbol{x})} - \frac{p^*_{\mathrm{nu}}(\boldsymbol{u})}{p^*_{\mathrm{de}}(\boldsymbol{u})}\right)^2 p^*_{\mathrm{de}}(\boldsymbol{x})\mathrm{d}\boldsymbol{x} \geq 0. \qquad (8.9)\end{aligned}$$

Equation (8.9) is non-negative, and it vanishes if and only if

$$p^*_{\mathrm{nu}}(\boldsymbol{v}|\boldsymbol{u}) = p^*_{\mathrm{de}}(\boldsymbol{v}|\boldsymbol{u}). \qquad (8.10)$$

Because $\mathrm{PE}[p^*_{\mathrm{nu}}(\boldsymbol{x}), p^*_{\mathrm{de}}(\boldsymbol{x})]$ is a constant with respect to $\boldsymbol{U}$, maximizing $\mathrm{PE}[p^*_{\mathrm{nu}}(\boldsymbol{u}), p^*_{\mathrm{de}}(\boldsymbol{u})]$ with respect to $\boldsymbol{U}$ leads to Eq. (8.10) (Figure 8.6). That

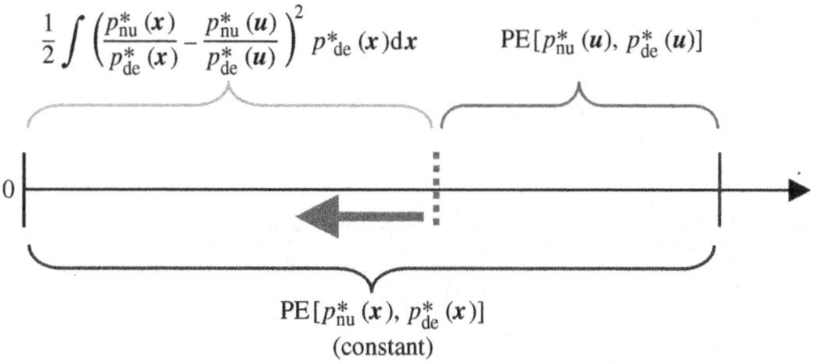

Figure 8.6. Because $\mathrm{PE}[p^*_{\mathrm{nu}}(\boldsymbol{x}), p^*_{\mathrm{de}}(\boldsymbol{x})]$ is a constant, minimizing $\frac{1}{2}\int \left(\frac{p^*_{\mathrm{nu}}(\boldsymbol{x})}{p^*_{\mathrm{de}}(\boldsymbol{x})} - \frac{p^*_{\mathrm{nu}}(\boldsymbol{u})}{p^*_{\mathrm{de}}(\boldsymbol{u})}\right)^2 p^*_{\mathrm{de}}(\boldsymbol{x})\mathrm{d}\boldsymbol{x}$ is equivalent to maximizing $\mathrm{PE}[p^*_{\mathrm{nu}}(\boldsymbol{u}), p^*_{\mathrm{de}}(\boldsymbol{u})]$.

is, the heterodistributional subspace can be characterized as the maximizer[2] of $\mathrm{PE}[p^*_{\mathrm{nu}}(\boldsymbol{u}), p^*_{\mathrm{de}}(\boldsymbol{u})]$.

However, we cannot directly find the maximizer of $\mathrm{PE}[p^*_{\mathrm{nu}}(\boldsymbol{u}), p^*_{\mathrm{de}}(\boldsymbol{u})]$ because $p^*_{\mathrm{nu}}(\boldsymbol{u})$ and $p^*_{\mathrm{de}}(\boldsymbol{u})$ are unknown. Here, we utilize a direct density-ratio estimator uLSIF (see Section 6.2.2) for approximating $\mathrm{PE}[p^*_{\mathrm{nu}}(\boldsymbol{u}), p^*_{\mathrm{de}}(\boldsymbol{u})]$ from samples. Let us replace the density ratio $p^*_{\mathrm{nu}}(\boldsymbol{u})/p^*_{\mathrm{de}}(\boldsymbol{u})$ in Eq. (8.8) by a density ratio estimator $\widehat{r}(\boldsymbol{u})$. Approximating the expectation over $p^*_{\mathrm{nu}}(\boldsymbol{u})$ by an empirical average over $\{\boldsymbol{u}_i^{\mathrm{nu}}\}_{i=1}^{n_{\mathrm{nu}}}$, we have the following PE estimator:

$$\widehat{\mathrm{PE}}[p^*_{\mathrm{nu}}(\boldsymbol{u}), p^*_{\mathrm{de}}(\boldsymbol{u})] := \frac{1}{2n_{\mathrm{nu}}}\sum_{i=1}^{n_{\mathrm{nu}}} \widehat{r}(\boldsymbol{u}_i^{\mathrm{nu}}) - \frac{1}{2}.$$

8.2.4 Least-Squares Heterodistributional Subspace Search (LHSS)

Given the uLSIF-based PE estimator $\widehat{\mathrm{PE}}[p^*_{\mathrm{nu}}(\boldsymbol{u}), p^*_{\mathrm{de}}(\boldsymbol{u})]$, our next task is to find a maximizer of $\widehat{\mathrm{PE}}[p^*_{\mathrm{nu}}(\boldsymbol{u}), p^*_{\mathrm{de}}(\boldsymbol{u})]$ with respect to $\boldsymbol{U}$ and identify the heterodistributional subspace (cf. the data-processing inequality given in Lemma 8.1). This procedure is called the *least-squares hetero-distributional subspace search* (LHSS).

We may employ various optimization techniques to find a maximizer of $\widehat{\mathrm{PE}}[p^*_{\mathrm{nu}}(\boldsymbol{u}), p^*_{\mathrm{de}}(\boldsymbol{u})]$. Here we describe several possibilities.

Plain Gradient Algorithm

A gradient ascent algorithm is a fundamental approach to non-linear smooth optimization. The gradient of $\widehat{\mathrm{PE}}[p^*_{\mathrm{nu}}(\boldsymbol{u}), p^*_{\mathrm{de}}(\boldsymbol{u})]$ with respect to $\boldsymbol{U}$ is expressed as

[2] As proved in Sugiyama et al. (2011b), the data-processing inequality holds not only for PE, but also for *any* f-divergence (Ali and Silvey, 1966; Csiszár, 1967). Thus, the characterization of the heterodistributional subspace is not limited to PE, but is applicable to all f-divergences.

follows (Sugiyama et al., 2011b):

$$\frac{\partial \widehat{\mathrm{PE}}}{\partial \boldsymbol{U}} = \sum_{\ell=1}^{b} \widehat{\theta}_\ell \frac{\partial \widehat{h}_\ell}{\partial \boldsymbol{U}} - \frac{1}{2} \sum_{\ell,\ell'=1}^{b} \widehat{\theta}_\ell \widehat{\theta}_{\ell'} \frac{\partial \widehat{H}_{\ell,\ell'}}{\partial \boldsymbol{U}}, \tag{8.11}$$

where $\widehat{\boldsymbol{\theta}}$ is the uLSIF solution given by Eq. (8.7) and

$$\frac{\partial \widehat{h}_\ell}{\partial \boldsymbol{U}} = \frac{1}{n_{\mathrm{nu}}} \sum_{i=1}^{n_{\mathrm{nu}}} \frac{\partial \psi_\ell(\boldsymbol{u}_i^{\mathrm{nu}})}{\partial \boldsymbol{U}},$$

$$\frac{\partial \widehat{H}_{\ell,\ell'}}{\partial \boldsymbol{U}} = \frac{1}{n_{\mathrm{de}}} \sum_{j=1}^{n_{\mathrm{de}}} \left(\frac{\partial \psi_\ell(\boldsymbol{u}_j^{\mathrm{de}})}{\partial \boldsymbol{U}} \psi_{\ell'}(\boldsymbol{u}_j^{\mathrm{de}}) + \psi_\ell(\boldsymbol{u}_j^{\mathrm{de}}) \frac{\partial \psi_{\ell'}(\boldsymbol{u}_j^{\mathrm{de}})}{\partial \boldsymbol{U}} \right),$$

$$\frac{\partial \psi_\ell(\boldsymbol{u})}{\partial \boldsymbol{U}} = -\frac{1}{\sigma^2} (\boldsymbol{u} - \boldsymbol{c}_\ell)(\boldsymbol{x} - \boldsymbol{c}'_\ell)^\top \psi_\ell(\boldsymbol{u}).$$

$\boldsymbol{c}'_\ell$ ($\in \mathbb{R}^d$) is a pre-image of $\boldsymbol{c}_\ell$ ($\in \mathbb{R}^m$), that is, $\boldsymbol{c}_\ell = \boldsymbol{U}\boldsymbol{c}'_\ell$. Note that $\{\widehat{\theta}_\ell\}_{\ell=1}^b$ in Eq. (8.11) depend on $\widehat{\boldsymbol{U}}$ through $\widehat{\boldsymbol{H}}$ and $\widehat{\boldsymbol{h}}$ in Eq. (8.7), which was taken into account when deriving the gradient. A plain gradient update rule is then given as

$$\boldsymbol{U} \longleftarrow \boldsymbol{U} + t \frac{\partial \widehat{\mathrm{PE}}}{\partial \boldsymbol{U}},$$

where t (> 0) is a learning rate. t may be chosen in practice by some approximate line search method such as *Armijo's rule* (Patriksson, 1999) or a *backtracking line search* (Boyd and Vandenberghe, 2004).

A naive gradient update does not necessarily fulfill the orthonormality $\boldsymbol{U}\boldsymbol{U}^\top = \boldsymbol{I}_m$, where $\boldsymbol{I}_m$ is the m-dimensional identity matrix. Thus, after every gradient step, $\boldsymbol{U}$ needs to be orthonormalized, for example, by the *Gram–Schmidt process* (Golub and Loan, 1996) to guarantee its orthonormality. However, this may be rather time-consuming.

Natural Gradient Algorithm

In the Euclidean space, the ordinary gradient $\frac{\partial \widehat{\mathrm{PE}}}{\partial \boldsymbol{U}}$ gives the steepest direction. On the other hand, in the current setup, the matrix $\boldsymbol{U}$ is restricted to be a member of the *Stiefel manifold* $\mathbb{S}_m^d(\mathbb{R})$:

$$\mathbb{S}_m^d(\mathbb{R}) := \{\boldsymbol{U} \in \mathbb{R}^{m \times d} \mid \boldsymbol{U}\boldsymbol{U}^\top = \boldsymbol{I}_m\}.$$

On a manifold, it is known that, not the ordinary gradient, but the *natural gradient* (Amari, 1998) gives the steepest direction. The natural gradient $\nabla \widehat{\mathrm{PE}}$ at $\boldsymbol{U}$ is the projection of the ordinary gradient $\frac{\partial \widehat{\mathrm{PE}}}{\partial \boldsymbol{U}}$ onto the tangent space of $\mathbb{S}_m^d(\mathbb{R})$ at $\boldsymbol{U}$.

If the tangent space is equipped with the canonical metric, that is, for any $\boldsymbol{G}$ and $\boldsymbol{G}'$ in the tangent space

$$\langle \boldsymbol{G}, \boldsymbol{G}' \rangle = \frac{1}{2} \mathrm{tr}(\boldsymbol{G}^\top \boldsymbol{G}'), \tag{8.12}$$

the natural gradient is given by

$$\nabla\widehat{\mathrm{PE}}(\boldsymbol{U}) = \frac{1}{2}\left(\frac{\partial\widehat{\mathrm{PE}}}{\partial\boldsymbol{U}} - \boldsymbol{U}\frac{\partial\widehat{\mathrm{PE}}}{\partial\boldsymbol{U}}^{\top}\boldsymbol{U}\right).$$

Then the *geodesic* from $\boldsymbol{U}$ to the direction of the natural gradient $\nabla\widehat{\mathrm{PE}}(\boldsymbol{U})$ over $\mathbb{S}_m^d(\mathbb{R})$ can be expressed using $t \in \mathbb{R}$ as

$$\boldsymbol{U}_t := \boldsymbol{U}\exp\left\{t\left(\boldsymbol{U}^{\top}\frac{\partial\widehat{\mathrm{PE}}}{\partial\boldsymbol{U}} - \frac{\partial\widehat{\mathrm{PE}}}{\partial\boldsymbol{U}}^{\top}\boldsymbol{U}\right)\right\},$$

where "exp" for a matrix denotes the *matrix exponential*, that is, for a square matrix $\boldsymbol{C}$,

$$\exp(\boldsymbol{C}) := \sum_{k=0}^{\infty}\frac{1}{k!}\boldsymbol{T}^k. \tag{8.13}$$

Thus, a line search along the geodesic in the natural gradient direction is equivalent to finding a maximizer from $\{\boldsymbol{U}_t \mid t \geq 0\}$. More details of the geometric structure of the Stiefel manifold can be found in Nishimori and Akaho (2005).

A natural gradient update rule is then given as $\boldsymbol{U} \longleftarrow \boldsymbol{U}_t$, where t (> 0) is the learning rate. Since the orthonormality of $\boldsymbol{U}$ is automatically satisfied in the natural gradient method, it is computationally more efficient than the plain gradient method. However, optimizing the $m \times d$ matrix $\boldsymbol{U}$ is still computationally expensive.

Givens Rotation

Another simple strategy for optimizing $\boldsymbol{U}$ is to rotate the matrix in the plane spanned by two coordinate axes (which is called the *Givens rotations*; see Golub and Loan, 1996). That is, a two-dimensional subspace spanned by the i-th and j-th variables is randomly chosen, and the matrix $\boldsymbol{U}$ is rotated within this subspace:

$$\boldsymbol{U} \longleftarrow \boldsymbol{R}_\theta^{(i,j)}\boldsymbol{U},$$

where $\boldsymbol{R}_\theta^{(i,j)}$ is the rotation matrix by angle θ within the subspace spanned by the i-th and j-th variables. $\boldsymbol{R}_\theta^{(i,j)}$ is equal to the identity matrix except that its elements (i,i), (i,j), (j,i), and (j,j) form a two-dimensional rotation matrix:

$$\begin{pmatrix} [\boldsymbol{R}_\theta^{(i,j)}]_{i,i} & [\boldsymbol{R}_\theta^{(i,j)}]_{i,j} \\ [\boldsymbol{R}_\theta^{(i,j)}]_{j,i} & [\boldsymbol{R}_\theta^{(i,j)}]_{j,j} \end{pmatrix} = \begin{pmatrix} \cos\theta & \sin\theta \\ -\sin\theta & \cos\theta \end{pmatrix}.$$

The rotation angle θ $(0 \leq \theta \leq \pi)$ may be optimized by some *secant* method (Press et al., 1992).

As shown above, the update rule of the Givens rotations is computationally very efficient. However, because the update direction is not optimized as in the plain/natural gradient methods, the Givens rotation method could be potentially less efficient as an optimization strategy.

Subspace Rotation

Because we are searching for a subspace, rotation *within* the subspace does not have any influence on the objective value $\widehat{\mathrm{PE}}$ (see Figure 8.7). This implies that the number of parameters to be optimized in the gradient algorithm can be reduced.

For a *skew-symmetric* matrix $\boldsymbol{M}$ ($\in \mathbb{R}^{d\times d}$), that is, $\boldsymbol{M}^\top = -\boldsymbol{M}$, rotation of $\boldsymbol{U}$ can be expressed as (Plumbley, 2005)

$$\left(\boldsymbol{I}_m \; \boldsymbol{O}_{m,(d-m)}\right) \exp(\boldsymbol{M}) \begin{pmatrix} \boldsymbol{U} \\ \boldsymbol{V} \end{pmatrix},$$

where $\boldsymbol{O}_{d,d'}$ is the $d \times d'$ matrix with all zeros, and $\exp(\boldsymbol{M})$ is the matrix exponential of $\boldsymbol{M}$ [see Eq. (8.13)]. $\boldsymbol{M} = \boldsymbol{O}_{d,d}$ (i.e., $\exp(\boldsymbol{O}_{d,d}) = \boldsymbol{I}_d$) corresponds to no rotation.

An update formula of $\boldsymbol{U}$ through the matrix $\boldsymbol{M}$ is as follows.

Let us adopt Eq. (8.12) as the inner product in the space of skew-symmetric matrices. Then the following lemma holds.

Lemma 8.2 (Sugiyama et al., 2011b). *The derivative of* $\widehat{\mathrm{PE}}$ *with respect to* $\boldsymbol{M}$ *at* $\boldsymbol{M} = \boldsymbol{O}_{d,d}$ *is given by*

$$\left.\frac{\partial \widehat{\mathrm{PE}}}{\partial \boldsymbol{M}}\right|_{\boldsymbol{M}=\boldsymbol{O}_{d,d}} = \begin{pmatrix} \boldsymbol{O}_{m,m} & \frac{\partial \widehat{\mathrm{PE}}}{\partial \boldsymbol{U}} \boldsymbol{V}^\top \\ -\left(\frac{\partial \widehat{\mathrm{PE}}}{\partial \boldsymbol{U}} \boldsymbol{V}^\top\right)^\top & \boldsymbol{O}_{(d-m),(d-m)} \end{pmatrix}. \tag{8.14}$$

The block structure of Eq. (8.14) has an intuitive explanation: The non-zero off-diagonal blocks correspond to the rotation angles *between* the heterodistributional subspace and its orthogonal complement that affect the objective function $\widehat{\mathrm{PE}}$. On the other hand, the derivative of the rotation *within* the two subspaces vanishes because this does not change the objective value. Thus, the only variables to be optimized are the angles corresponding to the non-zero off-diagonal blocks $\frac{\partial \widehat{\mathrm{PE}}}{\partial \boldsymbol{U}} \boldsymbol{V}^\top$, which includes only $m(d-m)$ variables. In contrast, the plain/natural gradient algorithms optimize the matrix $\boldsymbol{U}$ consisting of md variables. Thus, when m is

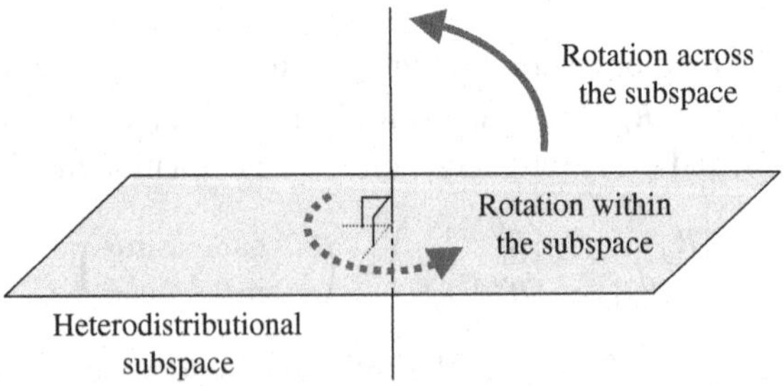

Figure 8.7. In the heterodistributional subspace search, only rotation that changes the subspace matters (the solid arrow); rotation within the subspace (dotted arrow) can be ignored because this does not change the subspace. Similarly, rotation within the orthogonal complement of the heterodistributional subspace can also be ignored (not depicted in the figure).

large, the subspace rotation approach may be computationally more efficient than the plain/natural gradient algorithms.

The gradient ascent update rule of $\boldsymbol{M}$ is given by

$$\boldsymbol{M} \longleftarrow t \frac{\partial \widehat{\mathrm{PE}}}{\partial \boldsymbol{M}}\bigg|_{\boldsymbol{M}=\boldsymbol{O}_{d,d}},$$

where t is a step size. Then $\boldsymbol{U}$ is updated as

$$\boldsymbol{U} \longleftarrow \left(\boldsymbol{I}_m\ \boldsymbol{O}_{m,(d-m)}\right) \exp(\boldsymbol{M}) \begin{pmatrix} \boldsymbol{U} \\ \boldsymbol{V} \end{pmatrix}.$$

The *conjugate gradient* method (Golub and Loan, 1996) may be used for the update of $\boldsymbol{M}$.

Following the update of $\boldsymbol{U}$, its counterpart $\boldsymbol{V}$ also needs to be updated accordingly, because the heterodistributional subspace and its complement specified by $\boldsymbol{U}$ and $\boldsymbol{V}$ should be orthogonal to each other (see Figure 8.5). This can be achieved by setting

$$\boldsymbol{V} \longleftarrow \left(\boldsymbol{\varphi}_1 | \cdots | \boldsymbol{\varphi}_{d-m}\right)^\top,$$

where $\boldsymbol{\varphi}_1, \ldots, \boldsymbol{\varphi}_{d-m}$ are orthonormal basis vectors in the orthogonal complement of the heterodistributional subspace.

8.2.5 The D³-LHSS Algorithm

Finally, we describe a method of estimating the density ratio in the heterodistributional subspace detected by the above LHSS procedure.

A notable fact of the LHSS algorithm is that the density-ratio estimator in the heterodistributional subspace has already been obtained during the heterodistributional subspace search procedure. Thus, an additional estimation procedure is not necessary – the final solution is simply given by

$$\widehat{r}(\boldsymbol{x}) = \sum_{\ell=1}^{b} \widehat{\theta}_\ell \psi_\ell(\widehat{\boldsymbol{U}}\boldsymbol{x}),$$

where $\widehat{\boldsymbol{U}}$ is a projection matrix obtained by the LHSS algorithm. $\{\widehat{\theta}_\ell\}_{\ell=1}^{b}$ are the learned parameters for $\widehat{\boldsymbol{U}}$ that were obtained and used when computing the gradient.

This expression implies that if the dimensionality is not reduced (i.e., $m = d$), the density-ratio estimator obtained by the above procedure agrees with that of the original uLSIF. Thus, the above method could be regarded as a natural extension of uLSIF to high-dimensional data.

Given the true dimensionality m of the heterodistributional subspace, the heterodistributional subspace can be estimated by the LHSS algorithm. When m is unknown, the best dimensionality based on the CV score of the uLSIF estimator may be used. This entire procedure is called *D³-LHSS* (D-cube LHSS;

Input: Two sets of samples $\{x_i^{\mathrm{nu}}\}_{i=1}^{n_{\mathrm{nu}}}$ and $\{x_j^{\mathrm{de}}\}_{j=1}^{n_{\mathrm{de}}}$ on $\mathbb{R}^d$
Output: Density-ratio estimator $\widehat{r}(x)$

For each reduced dimensionality $m = 1,\ldots,d$
  Initialize embedding matrix U_m ($\in \mathbb{R}^{m\times d}$);
  Repeat until U_m converges
    Choose Gaussian width σ and regularization parameter λ by CV;
    Update U by some optimization method (see Section 8.2.4);
  end
  Obtain embedding matrix $\widehat{U}_m$ and density-ratio estimator $\widehat{r}_m(x)$;
  Compute its CV value as a function of m;
end
Choose the best reduced dimensionality $\widehat{m}$ that minimizes the CV score;
Set $\widehat{r}(x) = \widehat{r}_{\widehat{m}}(x)$;

Figure 8.8. Pseudo code of D^3-LHSS.

direct density-ratio estimation with dimensionality reduction via a least-squares heterodistributional subspace search).

The complete procedure of D^3-LHSS is summarized in Figure 8.8. A MATLAB® implementation of D^3-LHSS is available from http://sugiyama-www.cs.titech.ac.jp/~sugi/software/D3LHSS/.

8.3 Numerical Examples

In this section numerical examples of the D^3 methods are shown. The subspace rotation algorithm explained in Section 8.2.4 was used in the D^3-LHSS implementation. In uLSIF, the number of parameters is fixed to $b = 100$; the Gaussian width σ and the regularization parameter λ are chosen based on cross-validation.

8.3.1 Illustrative Examples

First we illustrate the behavior of the D^3 algorithms using toy datasets.

As explained in Section 8.2, the D^3-LFDA/uLSIF method introduced in Section 8.1 has two potential weaknesses:

- The component $\boldsymbol{u}$ inside the heterodistributional subspace and its complementary component $\boldsymbol{v}$ are assumed to be statistically independent.
- Separability of samples drawn from two distributions implies that the two distributions are different, but non-separability does not necessarily imply that the two distributions are equivalent. Thus, D^3-LFDA/uLSIF may not be

able to detect the subspace in which the two distributions are different, but the samples are not really separable.

Here, through numerical examples, we illustrate these weaknesses of D^3-LFDA/uLSIF as well as how D^3-LHSS can overcome them.

Let us consider two-dimensional examples (i.e., $d = 2$), and suppose that the two densities $p^*_{\mathrm{nu}}(\boldsymbol{x})$ and $p^*_{\mathrm{de}}(\boldsymbol{x})$ are different only in the one-dimensional subspace (i.e., $m = 1$) spanned by $(1,0)^\top$:

$$p^*_{\mathrm{nu}}(\boldsymbol{x}) = p(v|u)p^*_{\mathrm{nu}}(u) \quad \text{and} \quad p^*_{\mathrm{de}}(\boldsymbol{x}) = p(v|u)p^*_{\mathrm{de}}(u),$$

where $\boldsymbol{x} = (x^{(1)}, x^{(2)})^\top = (u, v)^\top$. Let $n_{\mathrm{nu}} = n_{\mathrm{de}} = 1000$. The following three datasets are used:

Rather-separate **dataset (Figure 8.9):**

$$p(v|u) = p(v) = N(v;0,1^2), \quad p^*_{\mathrm{nu}}(u) = N(u;0,0.5^2), \quad \text{and}$$
$$p^*_{\mathrm{de}}(u) = 0.5N(u;-1,1^2) + 0.5N(u;1,1^2),$$

where $N(u;\mu,\sigma^2)$ denotes the Gaussian density with mean μ and variance σ^2 with respect to u. This is an easy and simple dataset for the purpose of illustrating the usefulness of the idea of D^3.

Highly-overlapped **dataset (Figure 8.10):**

$$p(v|u) = p(v) = N(v;0,1^2),$$
$$p^*_{\mathrm{nu}}(u) = N(u;0,0.6^2), \quad \text{and} \quad p^*_{\mathrm{de}}(u) = N(u;0,1.2^2).$$

Because v is independent of u, D^3-LFDA/uLSIF is still applicable in principle. However, u^{nu} and u^{de} are highly overlapped and are not clearly separable. Thus, this dataset would be hard for D^3-LFDA/uLSIF.

Dependent **dataset (Figure 8.11):**

$$p(v|u) = N(v;u,1^2), \quad p^*_{\mathrm{nu}}(u) = N(u;0,0.5^2), \quad \text{and}$$
$$p^*_{\mathrm{de}}(u) = 0.5N(u;-1,1^2) + 0.5N(u;1,1^2).$$

In this dataset, the *conditional* distribution $p(v|u)$ is common, but the *marginal* distributions $p^*_{\mathrm{nu}}(v)$ and $p^*_{\mathrm{de}}(v)$ are different. Because v is not independent of u, this dataset would be out of scope for D^3-LFDA/uLSIF.

The true heterodistributional subspace for the *rather-separate* dataset is depicted by the dotted line in Figure 8.9(a); the solid line and the dashed line depict the heterodistributional subspace found by LHSS and LFDA with reduced dimensionality $m = 1$, respectively. This graph shows that LHSS and LFDA both give very good estimates of the true heterodistributional subspace. In Figure 8.9(c)–(e), density-ratio functions estimated by the plain uLSIF without dimensionality reduction, D^3-LFDA/uLSIF, and D^3-LHSS for the *rather-separate* dataset are depicted. These graphs show that both D^3-LHSS and D^3-LFDA/uLSIF give much better

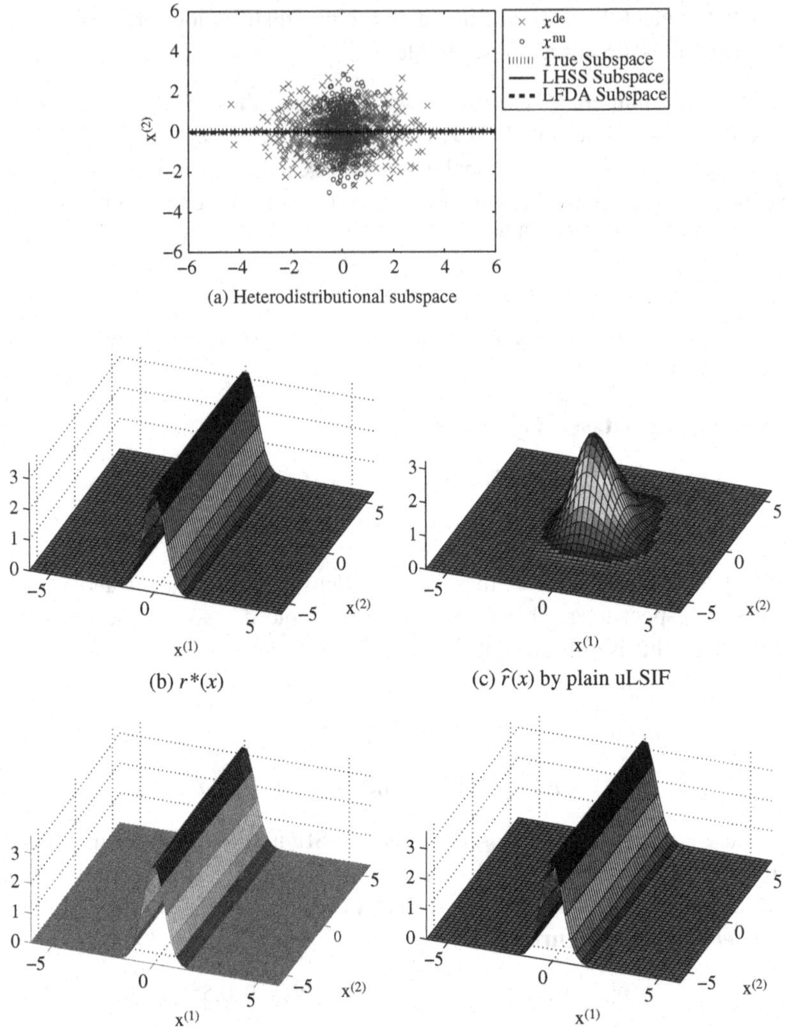

(a) Heterodistributional subspace

(b) $r^*(x)$

(c) $\widehat{r}(x)$ by plain uLSIF

(d) $\widehat{r}(x)$ by D^3-LFDA/uLSIF

(e) $\widehat{r}(x)$ by D^3-LHSS

Figure 8.9. *Rather-separate* dataset.

estimates of the density-ratio function [see Figure 8.9(b) for the profile of the true density-ratio function] than the plain uLSIF without dimensionality reduction. Thus, the usefulness of D^3 was illustrated.

For the *highly-overlapped* dataset (Figure 8.10), LHSS gives a reasonable estimate of the heterodistributional subspace, while LFDA is highly erroneous due to less separability. As a result, the density-ratio function obtained by D^3-LFDA/uLSIF does not reflect the true redundant structure appropriately. On the other hand, D^3-LHSS still works well.

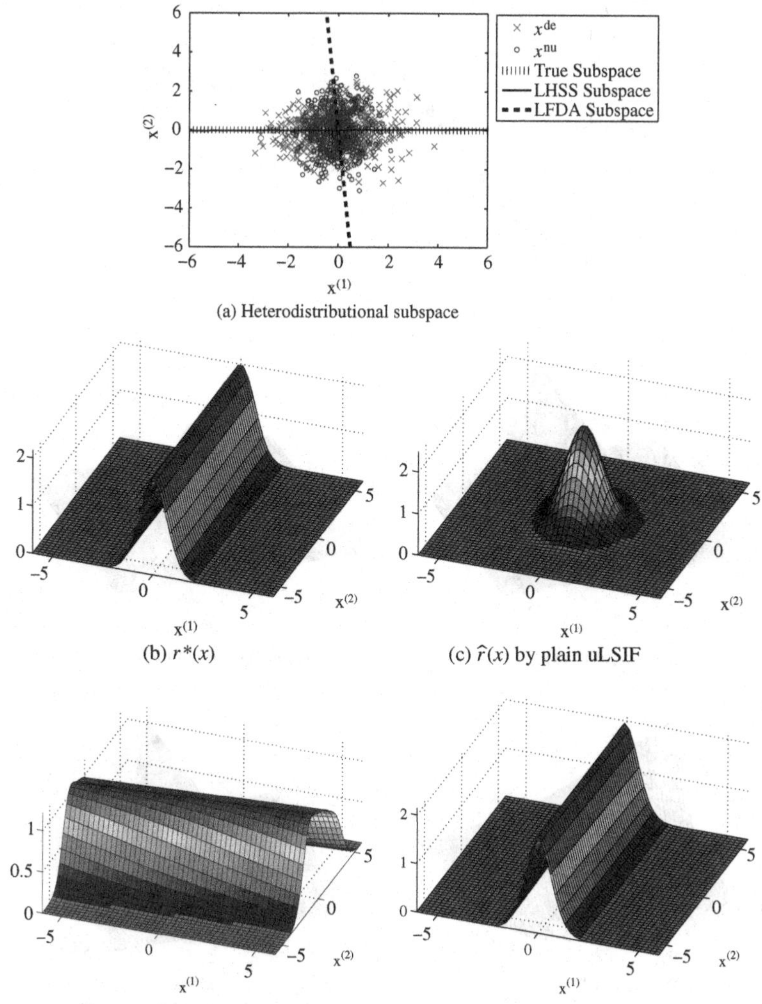

(a) Heterodistributional subspace

(b) $r^*(x)$

(c) $\widehat{r}(x)$ by plain uLSIF

(d) $\widehat{r}(x)$ by D^3-LFDA/uLSIF

(e) $\widehat{r}(x)$ by D^3-LHSS

Figure 8.10. *Highly overlapped* dataset.

Finally, for the *dependent* dataset (Figure 8.11), LHSS gives an accurate estimate of the heterodistributional subspace. However, LFDA gives a highly biased solution because the marginal distributions $p^*_{\mathrm{nu}}(v)$ and $p^*_{\mathrm{de}}(v)$ are no longer common in the *dependent* dataset. Consequently, the density-ratio function obtained by D^3-LFDA/uLSIF is highly erroneous. In contrast, D^3-LHSS still works very well for the *dependent* dataset.

The experimental results for the *highly-overlapped* and *dependent* datasets illustrated typical failure modes of LFDA, and LHSS was shown to be able to successfully overcome these weaknesses of LFDA. Note, however, that one can

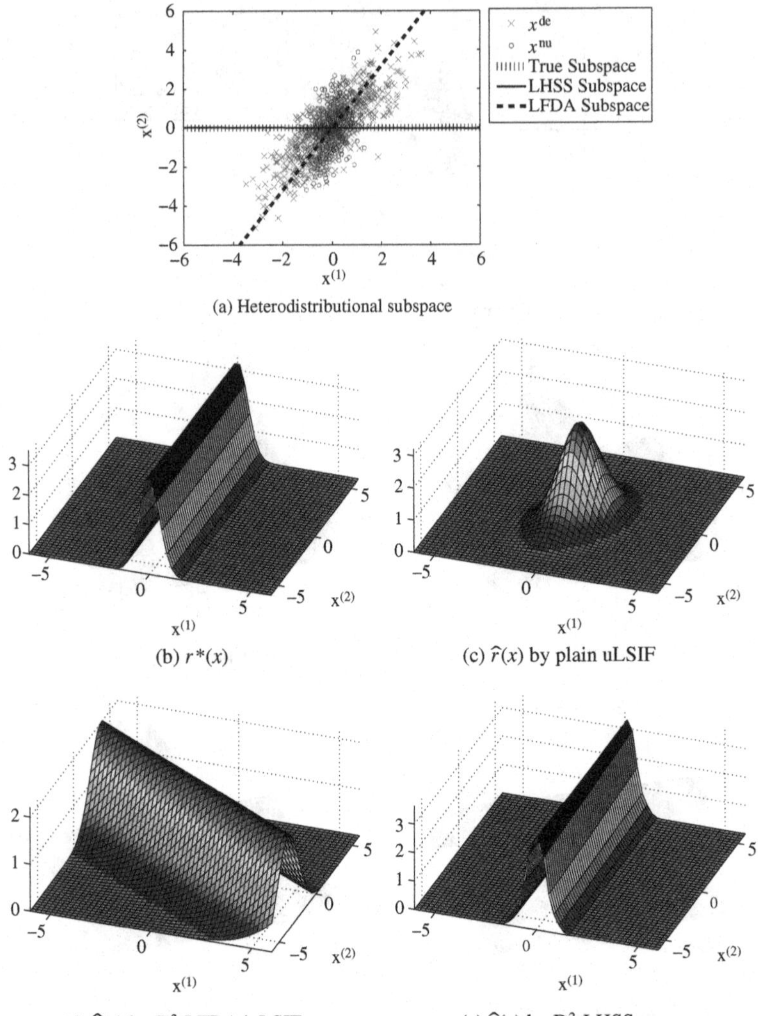

(a) Heterodistributional subspace

(b) $r^*(x)$

(c) $\widehat{r}(x)$ by plain uLSIF

(d) $\widehat{r}(x)$ by D^3-LFDA/uLSIF

(e) $\widehat{r}(x)$ by D^3-LHSS

Figure 8.11. *Dependent* dataset.

obtain only a local optimal solution in D^3-LHSS, while D^3-LFDA/uLSIF gives the global optimal solution with high computational efficiency.

8.3.2 Evaluation on Artificial Data

Next we compare the performance of D^3-LHSS with that of the plain uLSIF and D^3-LFDA/uLSIF for high-dimensional artificial data.

For the three datasets used in the previous experiments, the entire dimensionality is increased as $d = 2, 3, \ldots, 10$ by adding dimensions consisting of standard normal noise. The dimensionality of the heterodistributional subspace is estimated based on the CV score of uLSIF. The error of a density-ratio estimator $\widehat{r}(\boldsymbol{x})$ is evaluated by

$$\text{Error} := \frac{1}{2}\int \left(\widehat{r}(\boldsymbol{x}) - r^*(\boldsymbol{x})\right)^2 p^*_{\text{de}}(\boldsymbol{x})\mathrm{d}\boldsymbol{x}, \tag{8.15}$$

which uLSIF tries to minimize (see Section 6.2.2).

The top graphs in Figures 8.12, 8.13, 8.14 show the density-ratio estimation error averaged over 100 runs as functions of the entire input dimensionality d. The best method in terms of the mean error and comparable methods according to the *t-test* (Henkel, 1976) at the 1% significance level are specified by "o"; the other methods are specified by "×".

These plots show that, while the error of the plain uLSIF increases rapidly as the entire dimensionality d increases, that of D^3-LHSS is kept moderate. Consequently, D^3-LHSS consistently outperforms the plain uLSIF. D^3-LHSS is

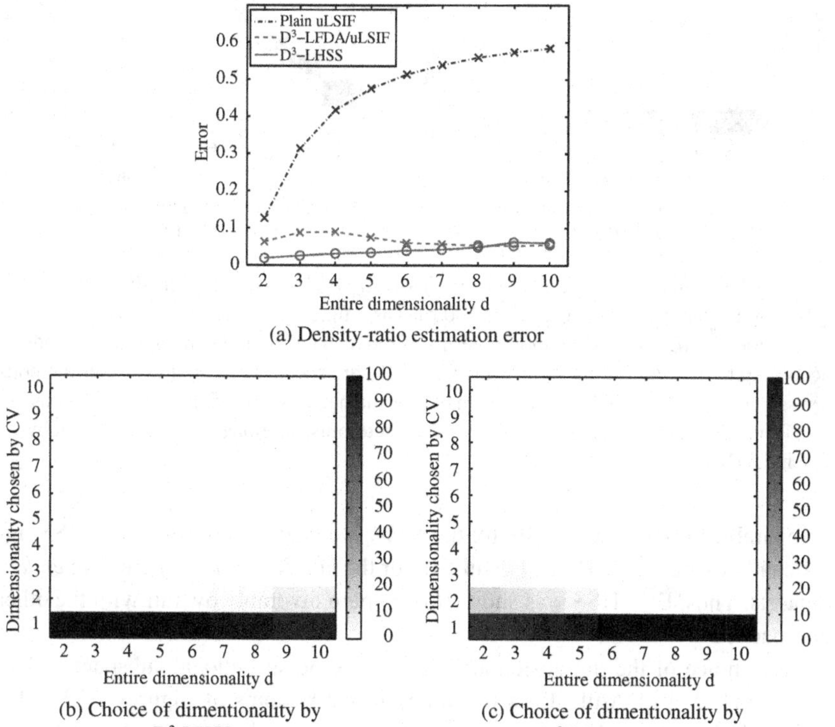

(a) Density-ratio estimation error

(b) Choice of dimentionality by D^3-LHSS

(c) Choice of dimentionality by D^3-LFDA/uLSIF

Figure 8.12. Experimental results for *rather-separate* dataset. (a) Density-ratio estimation error (8.15) averaged over 100 runs as a function of the entire data dimensionality d. The best method in terms of the mean error and comparable methods according to the *t-test* at the significance level 1% are specified by "o"; the other methods are specified by "×". (b) The dimensionality of the heterodistributional subspace chosen by CV in LHSS. (c) The dimensionality of the heterodistributional subspace chosen by CV in LFDA.

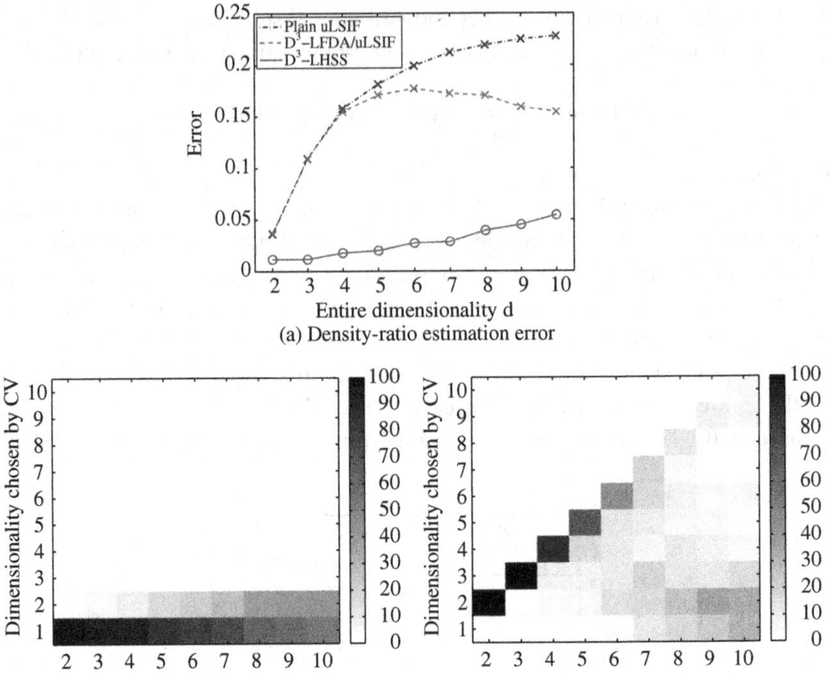

(a) Density-ratio estimation error

(b) Choice of dimentionality by D^3-LHSS

(c) Choice of dimentionality by D^3-LFDA/uLSIF

Figure 8.13. Experimental results for *highly-overlapped* dataset. (a) Density-ratio estimation error (8.15) averaged over 100 runs as a function of the entire data dimensionality d. The best method in terms of the mean error and comparable methods according to the *t-test* at the significance level 1% are specified by "o"; the other methods are specified by "×". (b) The dimensionality of the heterodistributional subspace chosen by CV in LHSS. (c) The dimensionality of the heterodistributional subspace chosen by CV in LFDA.

comparable to D^3-LFDA/uLSIF for the *rather-separate* dataset, and D^3-LHSS significantly outperforms D^3-LFDA/uLSIF for the *highly-overlapped* and *dependent* datasets. Thus, D^3-LHSS was shown to compare favorably overall with the other approaches.

The choice of the dimensionality of the heterodistributional subspace in D^3-LHSS and D^3-LFDA/uLSIF is illustrated in the bottoms of Figures 8.12, 8.13, and 8.14; the darker the color is, the more frequently the corresponding dimensionality is chosen. The plots show that D^3-LHSS reasonably identifies the true dimensionality ($m = 1$ in the current setup) for all three datasets, while D^3-LFDA/uLSIF performs well only for the *rather-separate* dataset. This occurred because D^3-LFDA/uLSIF could not find appropriate low-dimensional subspaces for the *highly-overlapped* and *dependent* datasets, and therefore the CV scores misled the choice of subspace dimensionality.

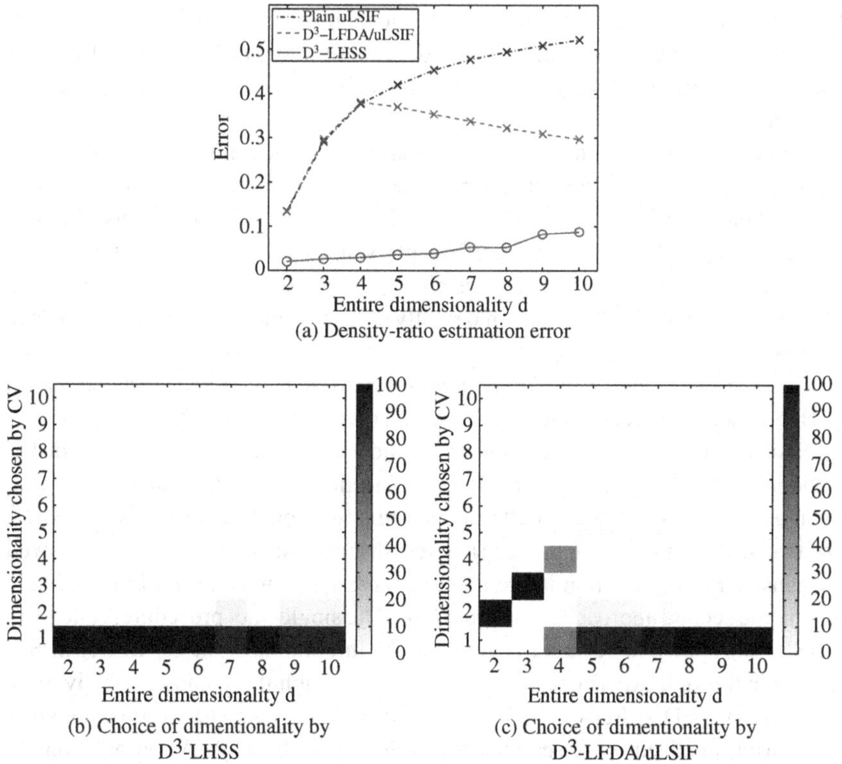

Figure 8.14. Experimental results for *dependent* dataset. (a) Density-ratio estimation error (8.15) averaged over 100 runs as a function of the entire data dimensionality d. The best method in terms of the mean error and comparable methods according to the *t-test* at the significance level 1% are specified by "o"; the other methods are specified by "×". (b) The dimensionality of the heterodistributional subspace chosen by CV in LHSS. (c) The dimensionality of the heterodistributional subspace chosen by CV in LFDA.

8.4 Remarks

In this chapter we explained two approaches to estimating density ratios in high-dimensional spaces called *direct density-ratio estimation with dimensionality reduction* (D^3). The basic idea of D^3 was to identify a subspace called the *heterodistributional subspace*, in which two distributions (corresponding to the numerator and denominator of the density ratio) are different.

In the first approach introduced in Section 8.1, the heterodistributional subspace was identified by finding a subspace in which samples drawn from the two distributions are maximally separated from each other. To this end, supervised dimensionality reduction methods such as *local Fisher discriminant analysis* (LFDA; Sugiyama, 2007) were utilized. This approach, called D^3-LFDA/uLSIF, is computationally very efficient because analytic-form solutions are available. It has been shown to work well when the components inside and outside the heterodistributional subspace are statistically independent and samples drawn from the two distributions are highly separable from each other in the heterodistributional subspace.

However, violation of these conditions can cause significant performance degradation, as numerically illustrated in Section 8.3. This drawback can be overcome in principle by finding a subspace such that the two *conditional* distributions are similar to each other in its complementary subspace. To implement this idea, the heterodistributional subspace was characterized as the subspace in which the two *marginal* distributions are maximally different under *Pearson* divergence (Lemma 8.1). Based on this lemma, an algorithm for finding the heterodistributional subspace called the *least-squares hetero-distributional subspace search* (LHSS) was introduced in Section 8.2 as an alternative approach to D^3.

Because a density-ratio estimation method is utilized during a heterodistributional subspace search in the LHSS procedure, an additional density-ratio estimation step is not needed after a heterodistributional subspace search. Thus, the two steps in the first approach (heterodistributional subspace search followed by density-ratio estimation in the identified subspace) were merged into a single step in the second approach (see Figure 8.4). The single-shot procedure, called D^3-LHSS, was shown to be able to overcome the limitations of the D^3-LFDA/uLSIF approach through experiments in Section 8.3, although it is computationally more expensive than D^3-LFDA/uLSIF. Thus, improving the computation cost for a heterodistributional subspace search is an important future work. A computationally efficient way to find a heterodistributional subspace is studied in Yamada and Sugiyama (2011b).

Part III

Applications of Density Ratios in Machine Learning

In this part we show how density-ratio estimation methods can be used for solving various machine learning problems.

In the context of *importance sampling* (Fishman, 1996), where the expectation over one distribution is computed by the *importance-weighted* expectation over another distribution, density ratios play an essential role. In Chapter 9, the importance sampling technique is applied to *non-stationarity/domain adaptation* in the semi-supervised learning setup (Shimodaira, 2000; Zadrozny, 2004; Sugiyama and Müller, 2005; Storkey and Sugiyama, 2007; Sugiyama et al., 2007; Quiñonero-Candela et al., 2009; Sugiyama and Kawanabe, 2011). It is also shown that the same importance-weighting idea can be used for solving *multi-task learning* (Bickel et al., 2008).

Another major usage of density ratios is *distribution comparisons*. In Chapter 10, two methods of distribution comparison based on density-ratio estimation are described: *inlier-base outlier detection*, where distributions are compared in a pointwise manner (Smola et al., 2009; Hido et al., 2011), and *two-sample tests*, where the overall difference between distributions is compared within the framework of hypothesis testing (Sugiyama et al., 2011c).

In Chapter 11 we show that density-ratio methods allow one to accurately estimate *mutual information* (Suzuki et al., 2008, 2009a). Mutual information is a key quantity in *information theory* (Cover and Thomas, 2006), and it can be used for detecting statistical independence between random variables. Mutual information estimators have various applications in machine learning, including *independence tests* (Sugiyama and Suzuki, 2011), *variable selection* (Suzuki et al., 2009b), *supervised dimensionality reduction* (Suzuki and Sugiyama, 2010), *independent component analysis* (Suzuki and Sugiyama, 2011), *clustering* (Kimura and Sugiyama, 2011; Sugiyama et al., 2011d), *object matching* (Yamada and Sugiyama, 2011a), and *causal inference* (Yamada and Sugiyama, 2010).

Finally, in Chapter 12, density-ratio methods are applied to *conditional probability estimation*. When the output variable is continuous, this corresponds to *conditional density estimation* (Sugiyama et al., 2010b). On the other hand, when the output variable is categorical, conditional probability estimation is reduced to a *probabilistic classification* (Sugiyama, 2010). Density-ratio methods systematically provide computationally efficient algorithms for these tasks.

Each of the four chapters in this part is self-contained and is not dependent on the others. Thus, readers may choose to read one of the chapters independently.

9

Importance Sampling

In this chapter the usage of density ratio estimation in *importance sampling* (Fishman, 1996) is explained.

The following identity shows the essence of importance sampling:

$$\mathbb{E}_{x^{\mathrm{nu}}\sim p^*_{\mathrm{nu}}(x)}[g(x^{\mathrm{nu}})] = \int g(x)p^*_{\mathrm{nu}}(x)\mathrm{d}x$$
$$= \int g(x)\frac{p^*_{\mathrm{nu}}(x)}{p^*_{\mathrm{de}}(x)}p^*_{\mathrm{de}}(x)\mathrm{d}x = \mathbb{E}_{x^{\mathrm{de}}\sim p^*_{\mathrm{de}}(x)}\left[g(x^{\mathrm{de}})\frac{p^*_{\mathrm{nu}}(x^{\mathrm{de}})}{p^*_{\mathrm{de}}(x^{\mathrm{de}})}\right],$$

where $\mathbb{E}_{x^{\mathrm{nu}}\sim p^*_{\mathrm{nu}}(x)}$ and $\mathbb{E}_{x^{\mathrm{de}}\sim p^*_{\mathrm{de}}(x)}$ denote the expectations over x^{nu} following $p^*_{\mathrm{nu}}(x)$ and x^{de} following $p^*_{\mathrm{de}}(x)$, respectively. In the context of importance sampling, the density ratio $p^*_{\mathrm{nu}}(x)/p^*_{\mathrm{de}}(x)$ is called the *importance*. The above identity shows that the expectation of a function $g(x)$ over $p^*_{\mathrm{nu}}(x)$ can be computed by the importance-weighted expectation of $g(x)$ over $p^*_{\mathrm{de}}(x)$. Thus, the difference of distributions can be adjusted systematically by importance weighting.

In Section 9.1, density-ratio estimation is used for semi-supervised non-stationarity adaptation under the *covariate shift* model, where input distributions change between the training and test phases but the conditional distribution of outputs given inputs remains unchanged. In Section 9.2, the problem of *multi-task learning* is addressed, where many similar supervised learning tasks are solved simultaneously with the hope that better prediction performance can be achieved than solving the tasks separately. A similar importance sampling idea is shown to provide a useful approach to multi-task learning.

9.1 Covariate Shift Adaptation

In this section we consider a particular *semi-supervised learning* setup under non-stationarity called a *covariate shift*, which is also called *domain adaptation* and *transfer learning* depending on the context and research areas.

After an introduction in Section 9.1.1, the problem of semi-supervised learning under a covariate shift is formulated in Section 9.1.2. Then, learning methods under covariate shifts are introduced in Section 9.1.3, and the issue of model selection under a covariate shift is addressed in Section 9.1.4; numerical examples are also provided for illustrating the behavior of covariate-shift adaptation techniques. Finally, the section is concluded in Section 9.1.5.

9.1.1 Introduction

The goal of *supervised learning* is to infer an unknown input–output dependency from training samples, by which output values for unseen test input points can be predicted (see Section 1.1.1). When developing a method of supervised learning, it is commonly assumed that the input points in the training set and the input points used for testing follow the *same* probability distribution (Wahba, 1990; Bishop, 1995; Vapnik, 1998; Duda et al., 2001; Hastie et al., 2001; Schölkopf and Smola, 2002). However, this common assumption is not fulfilled, for example, when the area outside of the training region is *extrapolated* or when the training input points are designed by an *active learning* (a.k.a. *experimental design*) algorithm (Wiens, 2000; Kanamori and Shimodaira, 2003; Sugiyama, 2006; Kanamori, 2007; Sugiyama and Nakajima, 2009).

Situations where training and test input points follow different probability distributions but the conditional distributions of output values given input points are unchanged are called *covariate shifts*[1] (Shimodaira, 2000). In this section we introduce covariate shift adaptation techniques based on density-ratio estimation.

Under covariate shifts, standard learning techniques such as maximum likelihood estimation are biased. It was shown that the bias caused by a covariate shift can be asymptotically canceled by weighting the loss function according to the *importance* – the ratio of test and training input densities (Shimodaira, 2000; Zadrozny, 2004; Sugiyama and Müller, 2005; Sugiyama et al., 2007; Quiñonero-Candela et al., 2009; Sugiyama and Kawanabe, 2011). Similarly, standard model selection criteria such as cross-validation (Stone, 1974; Wahba, 1990) and Akaike's information criterion (Akaike, 1974) lose their unbiasedness under covariate shifts. It was shown that proper unbiasedness can also be recovered by modifying the methods based on importance weighting (Shimodaira, 2000; Zadrozny, 2004; Sugiyama and Müller, 2005; Sugiyama et al., 2007).

Examples of successful real-world applications of covariate shift adaptations include brain–computer interfaces (Sugiyama et al., 2007; Y. Li et al., 2010), robot control (Hachiya et al., 2009; Akiyama et al., 2010; Hachiya et al., 2011b), speaker identification (Yamada et al., 2010b), audio tagging (Wichern et al., 2010), age prediction from face images (Ueki et al., 2011), wafer alignment in semiconductor exposure apparatus (Sugiyama and Nakajima, 2009), human activity recognition

[1] Note that the term "covariate" refers to an input variable in statistics. Thus, a "covariate shift" indicates a situation where input-data distributions shift.

from accelerometric data (Hachiya et al., 2011a), and natural language processing (Tsuboi et al., 2009). Details of those real-world applications as well as technical details of covariate-shift adaptation techniques are covered extensively in Sugiyama and Kawanabe (2011).

9.1.2 Problem Formulation

We formulate the problem of supervised learning under covariate shifts.

Let us consider the supervised learning problem of estimating an unknown input–output dependency from training samples. Let

$$\{(\boldsymbol{x}_i^{\mathrm{tr}}, y_i^{\mathrm{tr}}) | \boldsymbol{x}_i^{\mathrm{tr}} \in \mathcal{X} \subset \mathbb{R}^d, y_i^{\mathrm{tr}} \in \mathcal{Y} \subset \mathbb{R}\}_{i=1}^{n_{\mathrm{tr}}}$$

be the training samples, where $\boldsymbol{x}_i^{\mathrm{tr}}$ is a training input point drawn from a probability distribution with density $p_{\mathrm{tr}}^*(\boldsymbol{x})$, and y_i^{tr} is a training output value following a conditional probability distribution with conditional density $p^*(y|\boldsymbol{x} = \boldsymbol{x}_i^{\mathrm{tr}})$. $p^*(y|\boldsymbol{x})$ may be regarded as the superposition of the true output $f^*(\boldsymbol{x})$ and noise ϵ:

$$y = f^*(\boldsymbol{x}) + \epsilon.$$

This formulation for $\mathcal{Y}$ as a continuous set (i.e., *regression*) is illustrated in Figure 9.1.

Let $(\boldsymbol{x}^{\mathrm{te}}, y^{\mathrm{te}})$ be a test sample that is not given to us in the training phase but will be provided in the test phase in the future. $\boldsymbol{x}^{\mathrm{te}} \in \mathcal{X}$ is a test input point following a probability distribution with density $p_{\mathrm{te}}^*(\boldsymbol{x})$, which is generally different from the training-data distribution. $y^{\mathrm{te}} \in \mathcal{Y}$ is a test output value following $p^*(y|\boldsymbol{x} = \boldsymbol{x}^{\mathrm{te}})$, which is the same conditional density as the training phase.

The goal of supervised learning is to obtain an approximation $\widehat{f}(\boldsymbol{x})$ to the true function $f^*(\boldsymbol{x})$ for predicting the test output value y^{te}. More formally, we would like to obtain the approximation $\widehat{f}(\boldsymbol{x})$ that minimizes the test error expected over all test samples (which is called the *generalization error* or the *risk*):

$$G := \mathbb{E}_{\boldsymbol{x}^{\mathrm{te}} \sim p_{\mathrm{te}}^*(\boldsymbol{x})} \mathbb{E}_{y^{\mathrm{te}} \sim p^*(y|\boldsymbol{x}=\boldsymbol{x}^{\mathrm{te}})} \left[\mathrm{loss}(\widehat{f}(\boldsymbol{x}^{\mathrm{te}}), y^{\mathrm{te}}) \right],$$

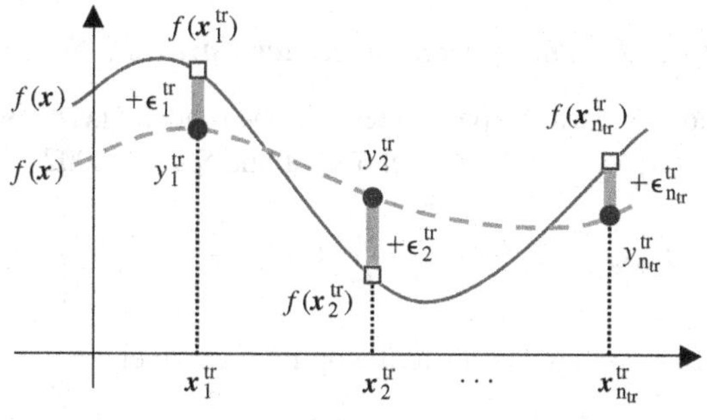

Figure 9.1. Framework of supervised learning.

where $\mathbb{E}_{\boldsymbol{x}^{\mathrm{te}} \sim p^*_{\mathrm{te}}(\boldsymbol{x})}$ denotes the expectation over $\boldsymbol{x}^{\mathrm{te}}$ drawn from $p^*_{\mathrm{te}}(\boldsymbol{x})$ and $\mathbb{E}_{y^{\mathrm{te}} \sim p^*(y|\boldsymbol{x}=\boldsymbol{x}^{\mathrm{te}})}$ denotes the expectation over y^{te} drawn from $p^*(y|\boldsymbol{x}=\boldsymbol{x}^{\mathrm{te}})$.

The term $\mathrm{loss}(\widehat{y}, y)$ denotes the *loss* function that measures the discrepancy between the true output value y and its estimate $\widehat{y}$. When the output domain $\mathcal{Y}$ is continuous, the problem is called *regression* and the *squared loss* is a standard choice:

$$\mathrm{loss}(\widehat{y}, y) = (\widehat{y} - y)^2. \tag{9.1}$$

On the other hand, when the output domain $\mathcal{Y}$ is binary categories (i.e., $\mathcal{Y} = \{+1, -1\}$), the problem is called binary *classification* and the *0/1-loss* is a typical choice:

$$\mathrm{loss}(\widehat{y}, y) = \begin{cases} 0 & \text{if } \mathrm{sgn}(\widehat{y}) = y, \\ 1 & \text{otherwise,} \end{cases}$$

where $\mathrm{sgn}(y) = +1$ if $y \geq 0$ and $\mathrm{sgn}(y) = -1$ if $y < 0$. Note that the generalization error with the 0/1-loss corresponds to the *misclassification rate*.

We use a parametric function $f(\boldsymbol{x};\boldsymbol{\theta})$ for learning, where $\boldsymbol{\theta}$ is a parameter. A model $f(\boldsymbol{x};\boldsymbol{\theta})$ is said to be *correctly specified* if there exists a parameter $\boldsymbol{\theta}^*$ such that $f(\boldsymbol{x};\boldsymbol{\theta}^*) = f^*(\boldsymbol{x})$; otherwise the model is said to be *misspecified*. In practice, the model used for learning is misspecified to a greater or less extent because we do not generally have enough prior knowledge for correctly specifying the model. Thus, learning theories specialized to correctly specified models are less useful in practice; it is important to explicitly consider the case where our model at hand is misspecified to some extent when developing machine learning algorithms.

In standard supervised learning theories (Wahba, 1990; Bishop, 1995; Vapnik, 1998; Duda et al., 2001; Hastie et al., 2001; Schölkopf and Smola, 2002), the test input point $\boldsymbol{x}^{\mathrm{te}}$ is assumed to follow the same probability distribution as the training input point $\boldsymbol{x}^{\mathrm{tr}}$, that is, $p^*_{\mathrm{tr}}(\boldsymbol{x}) = p^*_{\mathrm{te}}(\boldsymbol{x})$. On the other hand, in this section we consider the situation called a covariate shift (Shimodaira, 2000); that is, the training input point $\boldsymbol{x}^{\mathrm{tr}}$ and the test input point $\boldsymbol{x}^{\mathrm{te}}$ have different probability densities (i.e., $p^*_{\mathrm{tr}}(\boldsymbol{x}) \neq p^*_{\mathrm{te}}(\boldsymbol{x})$). Under a covariate shift, most of the standard learning techniques do not work well due to differing distributions. In the following, we introduce *importance sampling* techniques for mitigating the influence of covariate shifts.

9.1.3 Learning Methods under Covariate Shifts

A standard method to learn the parameter $\boldsymbol{\theta}$ in the model $f(\boldsymbol{x};\boldsymbol{\theta})$ is *empirical risk minimization* (ERM; Vapnik, 1998; Schölkopf and Smola, 2002):

$$\widehat{\boldsymbol{\theta}}_{\mathrm{ERM}} := \operatorname*{argmin}_{\boldsymbol{\theta}} \left[\frac{1}{n_{\mathrm{tr}}} \sum_{i=1}^{n_{\mathrm{tr}}} \mathrm{loss}(f(\boldsymbol{x}_i^{\mathrm{tr}};\boldsymbol{\theta}), y_i^{\mathrm{tr}}) \right].$$

If $p^*_{\mathrm{tr}}(\boldsymbol{x}) = p^*_{\mathrm{te}}(\boldsymbol{x})$, $\widehat{\boldsymbol{\theta}}_{\mathrm{ERM}}$ converges to the optimal parameter $\boldsymbol{\theta}^*$:

$$\boldsymbol{\theta}^* := \operatorname*{argmin}_{\boldsymbol{\theta}} [G].$$

However, under a covariate shift where $p^*_{\mathrm{tr}}(\boldsymbol{x}) \neq p^*_{\mathrm{te}}(\boldsymbol{x})$, $\widehat{\boldsymbol{\theta}}_{\mathrm{ERM}}$ does not necessarily converge to $\boldsymbol{\theta}^*$ if the model is misspecified.[2] Here we explain parameter learning methods for covariate-shift adaptations and show numerical examples.

Importance-Weighted Empirical Risk Minimization

The inconsistency of ERM is due to the difference between the training and test input distributions. *Importance sampling* (Fishman, 1996) is a standard technique to compensate for the difference of distributions:

$$\mathbb{E}_{\boldsymbol{x}^{\mathrm{te}} \sim p^*_{\mathrm{te}}(\boldsymbol{x})}[g(\boldsymbol{x}^{\mathrm{te}})] = \mathbb{E}_{\boldsymbol{x}^{\mathrm{tr}} \sim p^*_{\mathrm{tr}}(\boldsymbol{x})}\left[g(\boldsymbol{x}^{\mathrm{tr}})\frac{p^*_{\mathrm{te}}(\boldsymbol{x}^{\mathrm{tr}})}{p^*_{\mathrm{tr}}(\boldsymbol{x}^{\mathrm{tr}})}\right],$$

where $\mathbb{E}_{\boldsymbol{x}^{\mathrm{tr}} \sim p^*_{\mathrm{tr}}(\boldsymbol{x})}$ and $\mathbb{E}_{\boldsymbol{x}^{\mathrm{te}} \sim p^*_{\mathrm{te}}(\boldsymbol{x})}$ denote the expectations over $\boldsymbol{x}^{\mathrm{tr}}$ drawn from $p^*_{\mathrm{tr}}(\boldsymbol{x})$ and $\boldsymbol{x}^{\mathrm{te}}$ drawn from $p^*_{\mathrm{te}}(\boldsymbol{x})$, respectively. The density ratio

$$\frac{p^*_{\mathrm{te}}(\boldsymbol{x})}{p^*_{\mathrm{tr}}(\boldsymbol{x})}$$

is referred to as the *importance* in the context of importance sampling. The above identity shows that the expectation of a function $g(\boldsymbol{x})$ over $p^*_{\mathrm{te}}(\boldsymbol{x})$ can be computed by the *importance-weighted* expectation of $g(\boldsymbol{x})$ over $p^*_{\mathrm{tr}}(\boldsymbol{x})$. Thus, the difference of distributions can be systematically adjusted by importance weighting.

Applying the above importance weighting technique to ERM, we obtain *importance-weighted ERM* (IWERM):

$$\widehat{\boldsymbol{\theta}}_{\mathrm{IWERM}} := \underset{\boldsymbol{\theta}}{\mathrm{argmin}}\left[\frac{1}{n_{\mathrm{tr}}}\sum_{i=1}^{n_{\mathrm{tr}}}\frac{p^*_{\mathrm{te}}(\boldsymbol{x}_i^{\mathrm{tr}})}{p^*_{\mathrm{tr}}(\boldsymbol{x}_i^{\mathrm{tr}})}\mathrm{loss}(f(\boldsymbol{x}_i^{\mathrm{tr}};\boldsymbol{\theta}), y_i^{\mathrm{tr}})\right].$$

$\widehat{\boldsymbol{\theta}}_{\mathrm{IWERM}}$ converges to $\boldsymbol{\theta}^*$ under a covariate shift, even if the model is misspecified (Shimodaira, 2000). In practice, IWERM may be *regularized*, for example, by slightly flattening the importance weight and/or adding a penalty term as

$$\underset{\boldsymbol{\theta}}{\mathrm{argmin}}\left[\frac{1}{n_{\mathrm{tr}}}\sum_{i=1}^{n_{\mathrm{tr}}}\left(\frac{p^*_{\mathrm{te}}(\boldsymbol{x}_i^{\mathrm{tr}})}{p^*_{\mathrm{tr}}(\boldsymbol{x}_i^{\mathrm{tr}})}\right)^{\gamma}\mathrm{loss}(f(\boldsymbol{x}_i^{\mathrm{tr}};\boldsymbol{\theta}), y_i^{\mathrm{tr}}) + \lambda\boldsymbol{\theta}^{\top}\boldsymbol{\theta}\right], \tag{9.2}$$

where $0 \leq \gamma \leq 1$ is the *flattening* parameter, $\lambda \geq 0$ is the regularization parameter, and $^{\top}$ denotes the transpose.

Numerical Examples

Here we illustrate the behavior of IWERM using toy regression and classification datasets.

First, let us consider a one-dimensional regression problem. Let the learning target function be

$$f^*(x) = \mathrm{sinc}(x),$$

[2] If the model is correctly specified, $\widehat{\boldsymbol{\theta}}_{\mathrm{ERM}}$ still converges to $\boldsymbol{\theta}^*$ even under a covariate shift. However, we may not be able to assume the availability of a correctly specified model in practice.

and let the training and test input densities be

$$p^*_{\mathrm{tr}}(x) = N(x;1,(1/2)^2) \quad \text{and} \quad p^*_{\mathrm{te}}(x) = N(x;2,(1/4)^2),$$

where $N(x;\mu,\sigma^2)$ denotes the Gaussian density with mean μ and variance σ^2. As illustrated in Figure 9.2, we are considering a (weak) extrapolation problem because the training input points are distributed on the left-hand side of the input domain and the test input points are distributed on the right-hand side.

We create the training output value $\{y_i^{\mathrm{tr}}\}_{i=1}^{n_{\mathrm{tr}}}$ as $y_i^{\mathrm{tr}} = f^*(x_i^{\mathrm{tr}}) + \epsilon_i^{\mathrm{tr}}$, where $\{\epsilon_i^{\mathrm{tr}}\}_{i=1}^{n_{\mathrm{tr}}}$ are i.i.d. noise drawn from $N(\epsilon;0,(1/4)^2)$. Let the number of training samples be $n_{\mathrm{tr}} = 150$, and use the following linear model for function approximation:

$$f(x;\boldsymbol{\theta}) = \theta_1 x + \theta_2.$$

The parameter $\boldsymbol{\theta}$ is learned by *importance-weighted least-squares* (IWLS), which is IWERM (9.2) with the squared loss (9.1).

We fix the regularization parameter to $\lambda = 0$ and compare the performance of IWLS for different flattening parameters $\gamma = 0, 0.5, 1$. When $\gamma = 0$, a good approximation of the left-hand side of the target function can be obtained [see Figure 9.2(b)]. However, this is not appropriate for estimating the test output values ("×" in the figure). Thus, IWLS with $\gamma = 0$ (i.e., ordinary LS) results in a

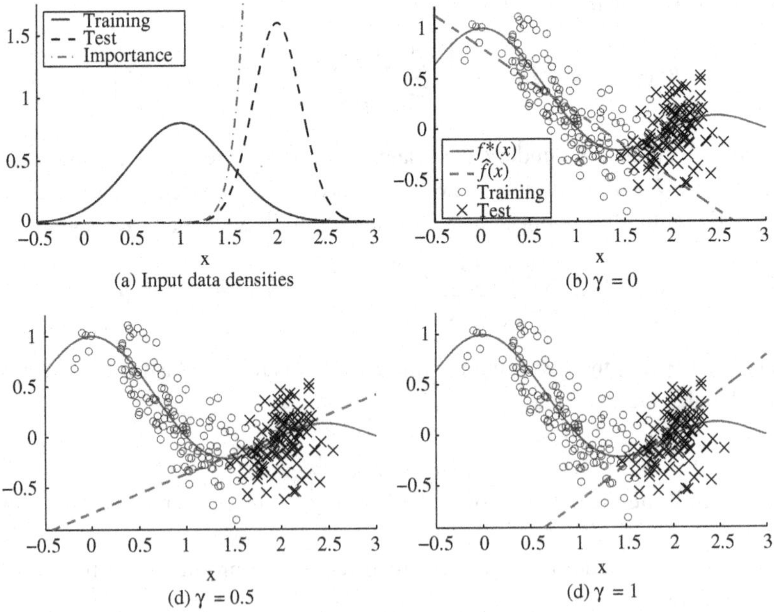

Figure 9.2. An illustrative regression example with covariate shifts. (a) The probability density functions of the training and test input points and their ratio (i.e., the importance). (b)–(d) The learning target function $f^*(x)$ (solid line), training samples (∘), a learned function $\widehat{f}(x)$ (dashed line), and test samples (×).

large test error under a covariate shift. Figure 9.2(d) depicts the learned function for $\gamma = 1$, which tends to approximate the test output values well. However, it tends to have a larger variance than the approximator obtained by $\gamma = 0$. Figure 9.2(c) depicts a learned function for $\gamma = 0.5$, which yields an even better estimation of the test output values for this particular data realization.

Next let us consider a binary classification problem on a two-dimensional input space. For $\boldsymbol{x} = (x^{(1)}, x^{(2)})^\top$, let the class-posterior probabilities given input $\boldsymbol{x}$ be

$$p^*(y = +1|\boldsymbol{x}) = \frac{1}{2}\left(1 + \tanh\left(x^{(1)} + \min(0, x^{(2)})\right)\right),$$
$$p^*(y = -1|\boldsymbol{x}) = 1 - p^*(y = +1|\boldsymbol{x}).$$

The optimal decision boundary, that is, a set of all $\boldsymbol{x}$ such that

$$p^*(y = +1|\boldsymbol{x}) = p^*(y = -1|\boldsymbol{x}) = \frac{1}{2},$$

is illustrated in Figure 9.3(a).

Let the training and test input densities be

$$p^*_{\mathrm{tr}}(\boldsymbol{x}) = \frac{1}{2}N\left(\boldsymbol{x}; \begin{bmatrix}-2\\3\end{bmatrix}, \begin{bmatrix}1 & 0\\0 & 4\end{bmatrix}\right) + \frac{1}{2}N\left(\boldsymbol{x}; \begin{bmatrix}2\\3\end{bmatrix}, \begin{bmatrix}1 & 0\\0 & 4\end{bmatrix}\right),$$
$$p^*_{\mathrm{te}}(\boldsymbol{x}) = \frac{1}{2}N\left(\boldsymbol{x}; \begin{bmatrix}0\\-1\end{bmatrix}, \begin{bmatrix}1 & 0\\0 & 1\end{bmatrix}\right) + \frac{1}{2}N\left(\boldsymbol{x}; \begin{bmatrix}4\\-1\end{bmatrix}, \begin{bmatrix}1 & 0\\0 & 1\end{bmatrix}\right),$$

where $N(\boldsymbol{x}; \boldsymbol{\mu}, \boldsymbol{\Sigma})$ is the multivariate Gaussian density with mean $\boldsymbol{\mu}$ and covariance matrix $\boldsymbol{\Sigma}$. This setup implies that we are considering a (weak) extrapolation problem. Contours of the training and test input densities are illustrated in Figure 9.3(a).

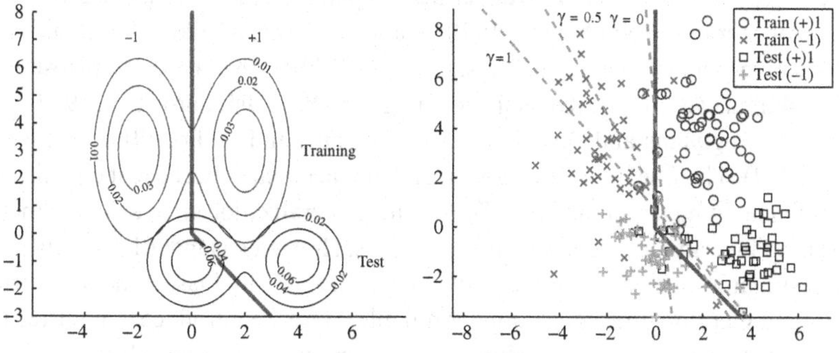

(a) Optimal decision boundary (the thick solid line) and contours of training and test input densities (thin solid lines).

(b) Optimal decision boundary (solid line) and learned boundaries (dashed line). "o" and "x" denote the positive and negative training samples, while "□" and "+" denote the positive and negative test samples.

Figure 9.3. An illustrative classification example with covariate shift.

Let the number of training samples be $n_{\mathrm{tr}} = 500$; we then create training input points $\{\boldsymbol{x}_i^{\mathrm{tr}}\}_{i=1}^{n_{\mathrm{tr}}}$ following $p_{\mathrm{tr}}^*(\boldsymbol{x})$ and each training output label y_i^{tr} following $p^*(y|\boldsymbol{x} = \boldsymbol{x}_i^{\mathrm{tr}})$. Similarly, let the number of test samples be $n_{\mathrm{te}} = 500$ and create n_{te} test input points $\{\boldsymbol{x}_j^{\mathrm{te}}\}_{j=1}^{n_{\mathrm{te}}}$ following $p_{\mathrm{te}}^*(\boldsymbol{x})$ and each test output label y_j^{te} following $p^*(y|\boldsymbol{x} = \boldsymbol{x}_j^{\mathrm{te}})$. We use the following linear model for learning:

$$f(\boldsymbol{x};\boldsymbol{\theta}) = \theta_1 x^{(1)} + \theta_2 x^{(2)} + \theta_3.$$

The parameter $\boldsymbol{\theta}$ is learned by *importance-weighted Fisher discriminant analysis* (IWFDA; Sugiyama et al., 2007), which is IWERM (9.2) with the squared loss (9.1).

Now we fix the regularization parameter to $\lambda = 0$ and compare the performance of IWFDA for different flattening parameters $\gamma = 0, 0.5, 1$. Figure 9.3(b) depicts a realization of training and test samples, and decision boundaries obtained by IWFDA with $\gamma = 0, 0.5, 1$. For this particular realization of data samples, $\gamma = 0.5$ and 1 work better than $\gamma = 0$.

9.1.4 Model Selection under Covariate Shifts

As illustrated in the previous subsection, importance weighting is a promising approach to covariate-shift adaptation, given that the flattening parameter γ is chosen appropriately. Although $\gamma = 0.5$ worked well both for the previous toy regression and classification experiments, $\gamma = 0.5$ may not always be the best choice. Indeed, an appropriate value of γ depends on various factors such as the learning target function, models, and the noise level in the training samples. Therefore, *model selection* needs to be appropriately carried out for enhancing the generalization capability under covariate shifts.

The goal of model selection is to determine the model (e.g., basis functions, the flattening parameter γ, and the regularization parameter λ) so that the generalization error is minimized (Akaike, 1970; Mallows, 1973; Akaike, 1974; Takeuchi, 1976; Craven and Wahba, 1979; Shibata, 1989; Wahba, 1990; Efron and Tibshirani, 1993; Murata et al., 1994; Konishi and Kitagawa, 1996; Ishiguro et al., 1997; Vapnik, 1998; Sugiyama and Ogawa, 2001b; Sugiyama and Müller, 2002; Sugiyama et al., 2004). The true generalization error is not accessible because it contains the unknown learning target function. Thus, some generalization error estimator needs to be used instead for model selection purposes. However, standard generalization error estimators such as *cross-validation* (CV) are heavily biased under covariate shifts, and therefore they are no longer reliable. Here we introduce a modified CV method that possesses proper unbiasedness even under covariate shifts.

Importance-Weighted Cross-Validation

One of the popular techniques for estimating the generalization error is CV (Stone, 1974; Wahba, 1990), which has been shown to give an *almost* unbiased estimate of the generalization error with finite samples (Luntz and Brailovsky, 1969;

Schölkopf and Smola, 2002). However, such almost unbiasedness is no longer fulfilled under covariate shifts.

To cope with this problem, a variant of CV called an *importance-weighted CV* (IWCV) has been proposed (Sugiyama et al., 2007). Let us randomly divide the training set $\mathcal{Z} = \{(\boldsymbol{x}_i^{\mathrm{tr}}, y_i^{\mathrm{tr}})\}_{i=1}^{n_{\mathrm{tr}}}$ into k disjoint non-empty subsets $\{\mathcal{Z}_i\}_{i=1}^{k}$ of (approximately) the same size. Let $\widehat{f}_{\mathcal{Z}_i}(\boldsymbol{x})$ be a function learned from $\mathcal{Z}\backslash\mathcal{Z}_i$ (i.e., without $\mathcal{Z}_i$). Then the *k-fold IWCV* (kIWCV) estimate of the generalization error G is given by

$$\widehat{G}_{k\mathrm{IWCV}} = \frac{1}{k}\sum_{i=1}^{k}\frac{1}{|\mathcal{Z}_i|}\sum_{(x,y)\in\mathcal{Z}_i}\frac{p_{\mathrm{te}}^*(\boldsymbol{x})}{p_{\mathrm{tr}}^*(\boldsymbol{x})}\mathrm{loss}(\widehat{f}_{\mathcal{Z}_i}(\boldsymbol{x}), y),$$

where $|\mathcal{Z}_i|$ is the number of samples in the subset $\mathcal{Z}_i$.

When $k = n_{\mathrm{tr}}$, kIWCV is particularly called *leave-one-out IWCV* (LOOIWCV):

$$\widehat{G}_{\mathrm{LOOIWCV}} = \frac{1}{n_{\mathrm{tr}}}\sum_{i=1}^{n_{\mathrm{tr}}}\frac{p_{\mathrm{te}}^*(\boldsymbol{x}_i^{\mathrm{tr}})}{p_{\mathrm{tr}}^*(\boldsymbol{x}_i^{\mathrm{tr}})}\mathrm{loss}(\widehat{f}_i(\boldsymbol{x}_i^{\mathrm{tr}}), y_i^{\mathrm{tr}}),$$

where $\widehat{f}_i(\boldsymbol{x})$ is a function learned from $\mathcal{Z}\backslash(\boldsymbol{x}_i^{\mathrm{tr}}, y_i^{\mathrm{tr}})$ [i.e., without $(\boldsymbol{x}_i^{\mathrm{tr}}, y_i^{\mathrm{tr}})$]. It was proved that LOOIWCV gives an *almost* unbiased estimate of the generalization error even under covariate shifts (Sugiyama et al., 2007). More precisely, LOOIWCV for n_{tr} training samples gives an unbiased estimate of the generalization error for $n_{\mathrm{tr}} - 1$ training samples:

$$\begin{aligned}\mathbb{E}_{\{\boldsymbol{x}_i^{\mathrm{tr}}\}_{i=1}^{n_{\mathrm{tr}}}}\mathbb{E}_{\{y_i^{\mathrm{tr}}\}_{i=1}^{n_{\mathrm{tr}}}}\left[\widehat{G}_{\mathrm{LOOIWCV}}\right] &= \mathbb{E}_{\{\boldsymbol{x}_i^{\mathrm{tr}}\}_{i=1}^{n_{\mathrm{tr}}}}\mathbb{E}_{\{y_i^{\mathrm{tr}}\}_{i=1}^{n_{\mathrm{tr}}}}[G'] \\ &\approx \mathbb{E}_{\{\boldsymbol{x}_i^{\mathrm{tr}}\}_{i=1}^{n_{\mathrm{tr}}}}\mathbb{E}_{\{y_i^{\mathrm{tr}}\}_{i=1}^{n_{\mathrm{tr}}}}[G],\end{aligned}$$

where $\mathbb{E}_{\{\boldsymbol{x}_i^{\mathrm{tr}}\}_{i=1}^{n_{\mathrm{tr}}}}$ denotes the expectation over $\{\boldsymbol{x}_i^{\mathrm{tr}}\}_{i=1}^{n_{\mathrm{tr}}}$ drawn independently from $p_{\mathrm{tr}}^*(\boldsymbol{x})$, $\mathbb{E}_{\{y_i^{\mathrm{tr}}\}_{i=1}^{n_{\mathrm{tr}}}}$ denotes the expectation over $\{y_i^{\mathrm{tr}}\}_{i=1}^{n_{\mathrm{tr}}}$ with each drawn from $p^*(y|\boldsymbol{x} = \boldsymbol{x}_i^{\mathrm{tr}})$, and G' denotes the generalization error for $n_{\mathrm{tr}} - 1$ training samples. A similar proof is also possible for kIWCV, but the bias is slightly larger (Hastie et al., 2001).

The almost unbiasedness of IWCV holds for any loss function, any model, and any learning method; even *non-identifiable models* (Watanabe, 2009) and *non-parametric learning methods* (Schölkopf and Smola, 2002) are allowed. Thus, IWCV is a highly flexible model selection technique under covariate shifts. For other model selection criteria under covariate shifts, see Shimodaira (2000) for regular models with smooth losses and Sugiyama and Müller (2005) for linear models with a squared loss.

A MATLAB® implementation of a regression method for covariate shift adaptation – combining an importance-weighted version of kernel *least-squares regression*, IWCV, and uLSIF (Section 6.2.2) – is available from http://sugiyama-www.cs.titech.ac.jp/~sugi/software/IWLS.

A MATLAB® implementation of a classification method for covariate shift adaptation – combining an importance-weighted version of *logistic regression*

(Section 4.2) and KLIEP (Section 5.2.1) – is available from http://sugiyama-www.cs.titech.ac.jp/~yamada/iwklr.html.

A MATLAB® implementation of a classification method for covariate shift adaptation – combining an importance-weighted version of the *least-squares probabilistic classifier* (Section 12.2), IWCV, and uLSIF – is available from http://sugiyama-www.cs.titech.ac.jp/~hachiya/software/IWLSPC/.

Numerical Examples

Here we illustrate the behavior of IWCV using the same toy datasets as in Section 9.1.3.

Let us continue the one-dimensional regression simulation in Section 9.1.3. As illustrated in Figure 9.2, IWLS with a flattening parameter $\gamma = 0.5$ appears to work well for that particular realization of data samples. However, the best value of γ depends on the realization of samples. To systematically investigate this issue, let us run the simulation 1000 times with different random seeds; that is, in each run, input–output pairs $\{(x_i^{\mathrm{tr}}, \epsilon_i^{\mathrm{tr}})\}_{i=1}^{n_{\mathrm{tr}}}$ are randomly drawn and the scores of 10-fold IWCVs and 10-fold ordinary CVs are calculated for $\gamma = 0, 0.1, 0.2, \ldots, 1$. The means and standard deviations of the generalization error G and its estimate by each method are depicted as functions of γ in Figure 9.4. The graphs show that IWCV gives accurate estimates of the generalization error, while ordinary CV is heavily biased.

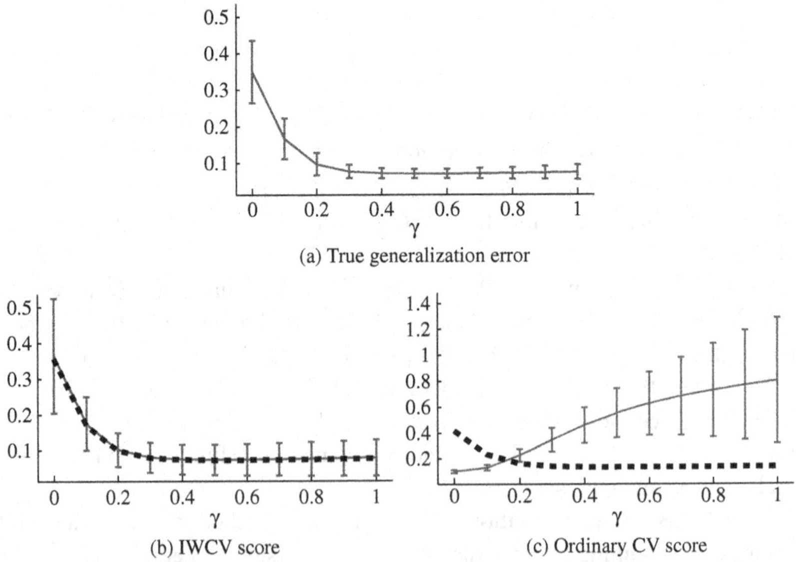

Figure 9.4. Generalization error and its estimates obtained by IWCV and ordinary CV as functions of the flattening parameter γ in IWLS for the regression examples in Figure 9.2. The thick dashed curves in the bottom graphs depict the true generalization error for a clear comparison.

Table 9.1. The mean and standard deviation of the generalization error G obtained by each method for the toy regression dataset. The best method and comparable ones by the t-test at the significance level 5% are indicated by "∘." For reference, the generalization error obtained with the optimal γ (i.e., the minimum generalization error) is described as "Optimal."

IWCV	Ordinary CV	Optimal
$^\circ 0.077 \pm 0.020$	0.356 ± 0.086	0.069 ± 0.011

We then investigate the model selection performance. The flattening parameter γ is chosen from $\{0, 0.1, 0.2, \ldots, 1\}$ so that the score of each model selection criterion is minimized. The means and standard deviations of the generalization error G of the learned function obtained by each method over 1000 runs are described in Table 9.1. This shows that IWCV gives a significantly smaller generalization error than ordinary CV, under the *t-test* (Henkel, 1976) at the 5% significance level. For reference, the generalization error when the flattening parameter γ is chosen optimally (i.e., in each trial, γ is chosen so that the true generalization error is minimized) is described as "optimal" in the table. The result shows that the performance of IWCV is rather close to that of the optimal choice.

Next, let us continue the toy classification simulation in Section 9.1.3. In Figure 9.3(b), IWFDA with a middle/large flattening parameter γ appears to work well for that particular realization of samples. Here we investigate the choice of the flattening parameter value by IWCV and ordinary CV. Figure 9.5 depicts the means and standard deviations of the generalization error G (i.e., the misclassification rate) and its estimate by each method over 1000 runs, as functions of the flattening parameter γ in IWFDA. The graphs clearly show that IWCV gives much better estimates of the generalization error than ordinary CV.

Finally, we investigate the model selection performance. The flattening parameter γ is chosen from $\{0, 0.1, 0.2, \ldots, 1\}$ so that the score of each model selection criterion is minimized. The means and standard deviations of the generalization error G of the learned function obtained by each method over 1000 runs are described in Table 9.2. The table shows that IWCV gives significantly smaller test errors than ordinary CV, and the performance of IWCV is rather close to that of the optimal choice.

9.1.5 Remarks

In standard supervised learning theories (Wahba, 1990; Bishop, 1995; Vapnik, 1998; Duda et al., 2001; Hastie et al., 2001; Schölkopf and Smola, 2002), test input points are assumed to follow the same probability distribution as training

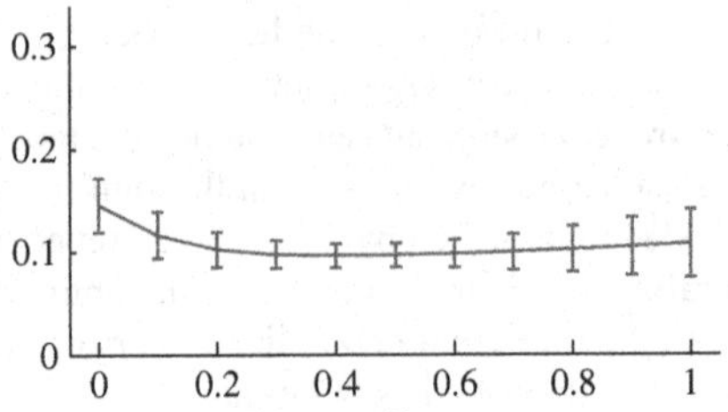

(a) True generalization error

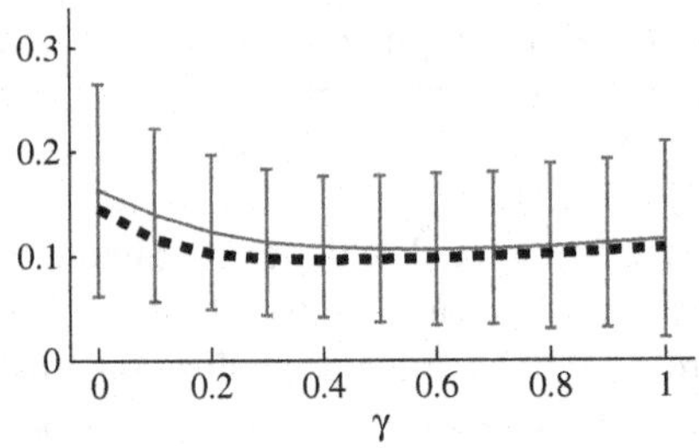

(b) IWCV score

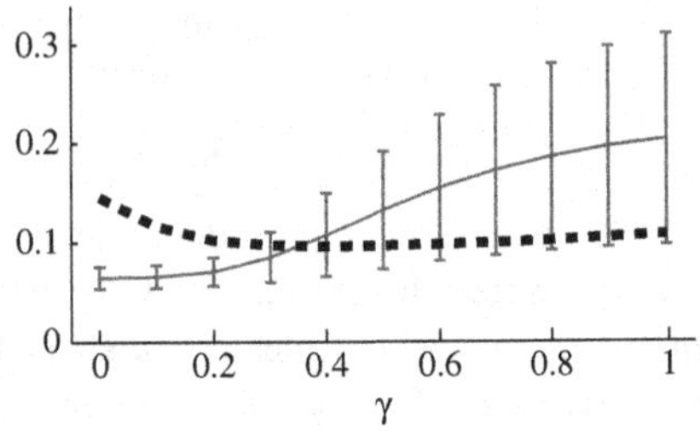

(c) Ordinary CV score

Figure 9.5. The generalization error G (i.e., the misclassification rate) and its estimates obtained by IWCV and ordinary CV as functions of the flattening parameter γ in IWFDA for the toy classification examples in Figure 9.3. The thick dashed curves in the bottom graphs depict the true generalization error for clear comparison.

Table 9.2. The mean and standard deviation of the generalization error G (i.e., the misclassification rate) obtained by each method for the *toy classification* dataset. The best method and comparable ones by the t-test at the significance level 5% are indicated by "∘." For reference, the generalization error obtained with the optimal γ (i.e., the minimum generalization error) is described as "Optimal."

IWCV	Ordinary CV	Optimal
$^{\circ}0.108 \pm 0.027$	0.131 ± 0.029	0.091 ± 0.009

input points. However, this assumption is often violated in real-world learning problems. In this section, we introduced importance-weighting techniques for covariate-shift adaptations. Details of real-world applications as well as technical details of covariate-shift adaptation techniques are extensively explained in Sugiyama and Kawanabe (2011).

Recently, Elkan (2011) proposed using importance sampling techniques in *privacy-preserving data mining* (Aggarwal and Yu, 2008). Privacy-preserving data mining is a novel paradigm in the area of data mining aimed at performing some data-processing operation (the most fundamental one would be to compute the mean of data) with the data kept *confidential* to the public. The density-ratio methods explained in Part II will play a central role in this line of research.

9.2 Multi-Task Learning

In this section we consider a problem of *multi-task learning* under supervised learning. After an introduction in Section 9.2.1, we formulate the problem of multi-task learning in Section 9.2.2. Then, a multi-task learning approach that explicitly shares data samples across different tasks based on *importance sampling* is introduced in Section 9.2.3. In Section 9.2.4, we describe another practical approach to multi-task learning that implicitly shares information from different tasks by *regularization*.

9.2.1 Introduction

Multi-task learning deals with a situation where multiple related learning tasks exist. The rationale behind multi-task learning is that, rather than solving such related learning tasks separately, solving them simultaneously by sharing some common information behind the tasks may improve the prediction accuracy (Caruana et al., 1997; Baxter, 1997, 2000; Ben-David et al., 2002; Bakker and Heskes, 2003; Ben-David and Schuller, 2003; Evgeniou and Pontil, 2004; Micchelli and Pontil, 2005; Yu et al., 2005; Ando and Zhang, 2005; Xue et al., 2007; Bonilla et al., 2008; Kato et al., 2010; Simm et al., 2011).

In Section 9.2.3 we describe multi-task learning methods that *explicitly* share training samples with other tasks. We first introduce a naive approach that merely borrows training samples from related tasks. This approach is useful if the other tasks are very similar to the target task. On the other hand, if the other tasks are rather similar but substantially different, the use of *importance sampling* for absorbing differing distributions would be technically more sound (Bickel et al., 2008).

Another line of research tries to *implicitly* share data samples in different tasks. If prior knowledge that some parameters can be shared across different tasks (e.g., the class-wise variance of the data is common to all tasks), such a parametric form can be utilized for improving the prediction accuracy. However, such "hard" data-sharing models may not always be appropriate in practice.

More general approaches that do not require data-sharing models assume the common prior distribution across different tasks in the *Bayesian framework* (Yu et al., 2005; Xue et al., 2007; Bonilla et al., 2008) or impose solutions of different tasks to be close to each other in the *regularization* framework (Evgeniou and Pontil, 2004; Lapedriza et al., 2007; Kato et al., 2010; Simm et al., 2011). These implicit data-sharing approaches are more flexible than the explicit data-sharing approach. The regularization-based approach is described in Section 9.2.3.

In multi-task learning, the computational cost is a key issue to be addressed in general because many related tasks should be solved at the same time. Thus, the number of training samples as well as the number of parameters tend to be much larger than single-task learning problems. In Section 9.2.3 we introduce a computationally efficient multi-task learning method that uses a probabilistic classifier based on density-ratio estimation described in Section 12.2.

9.2.2 *Problem Formulation*

In this subsection we formulate the problem of multi-task supervised learning.

Suppose there are m supervised learning tasks, each of which has different but similar learning target functions. The training samples in the multi-task learning setup are accompanied with the task index, that is,

$$\{(\boldsymbol{x}_k, y_k, t_k)\}_{k=1}^{n},$$

where t_k ($\in \{1,\ldots,m\}$) denotes the index of the task to which the input–output sample $(\boldsymbol{x}_k, y_k)$ belongs. The training input point $\boldsymbol{x}_k$ ($\in \mathcal{X} \subset \mathbb{R}^d$) is drawn from a probability distribution with density $p^*_{t_k}(\boldsymbol{x})$, and the training output value y_k ($\in \mathcal{Y} \subset \mathbb{R}$) follows a conditional probability distribution with conditional density $p^*_{t_k}(y|\boldsymbol{x}=\boldsymbol{x}_k)$. $p^*_t(y|\boldsymbol{x})$ for the t-th task, which may be regarded as the superposition of the true output $f^*_t(\boldsymbol{x})$ and noise ϵ:

$$y = f^*_t(\boldsymbol{x}) + \epsilon.$$

Let $p^*_t(\boldsymbol{x}, y)$ be the joint density of input $\boldsymbol{x}$ and output y for the t-th task.

9.2.3 *Explicit Sample Sharing*

Now we introduce multi-task approaches based on explicit sample sharing.

Naive Sample Sharing

Suppose we have prior knowledge that other tasks are very similar to the target task t. Then we may directly use all samples $\{(\boldsymbol{x}_k, y_k, t_k)\}_{k=1}^{n}$, including samples that belong to other tasks as

$$\min_{\boldsymbol{\theta}^{(t)}} \left[\sum_{k=1}^{n} \mathrm{loss}(f(\boldsymbol{x}_k; \boldsymbol{\theta}^{(t)}), y_k) \right], \tag{9.3}$$

where $f(\boldsymbol{x}; \boldsymbol{\theta}^{(t)})$ is a model of the t-th target function $f^*_t(\boldsymbol{x})$ and $\mathrm{loss}(\widehat{y}, y)$ is the *loss* function that measures the discrepancy between the true output value y and its estimate $\widehat{y}$, for example, the squared loss (9.1).

Such a naive data-sharing approach is useful when the number of training samples for each task is very small. For example, in an application of multi-task learning to *optical surface profiling* (Sugiyama et al., 2006), three parameters in the model

$$f(x;\boldsymbol{\theta}^{(t)}) = \theta_0^{(t)} + \theta_1^{(t)}\cos(x) + \theta_2^{(t)}\sin(x)$$

should be learned from only a *single* training sample. Because this is an ill-posed problem, directly solving this task may not provide a useful solution. In such applications, borrowing data samples from "vicinity" tasks is essential, and the above simple multi-task approach was shown to work well. See Yokota et al. (2009), Kurihara et al. (2010), and Mori et al. (2011) for further developments along this line of research, such as how the vicinity tasks are chosen and how model selection is carried out.

Adaptive Sample Sharing by Importance Sampling

When other tasks have some similarity to the target task but they are substantially different from the target task, using *importance weighting* (Fishman, 1996) would be technically more sound:

$$\min_{\boldsymbol{\theta}^{(t)}} \left[\sum_{k=1}^{n} \frac{p_t^*(\boldsymbol{x}_k, y_k)}{p_{t_k}^*(\boldsymbol{x}_k, y_k)} \text{loss}(f(\boldsymbol{x}_k;\boldsymbol{\theta}^{(t)}), y_k) \right]. \tag{9.4}$$

A notable difference from the *covariate shift adaptation* methods shown in Section 9.1 is that the importance in Eq. (9.4) is defined over both input $\boldsymbol{x}$ and output y.

In the multi-task setup, it is essential to use *multiple* density ratios,

$$\frac{p_t^*(\boldsymbol{x}, y)}{p_{t'}^*(\boldsymbol{x}, y)} \quad (\forall t, t' \in \{1, \dots, m\}),$$

for mutual data sharing. For estimating the density ratios $p_t^*(\boldsymbol{x}, y)/p_{t'}^*(\boldsymbol{x}, y)$ we can use any of the various density-ratio estimators described in Part II. Among them, an approach based on *probabilistic classification* described in Chapter 4 is particularly useful in the context of multi-task learning, because density-ratio estimators for multiple density ratios $\{p_t^*(\boldsymbol{x}, y)/p_{t'}^*(\boldsymbol{x}, y)\}_{t,t'=1}^m$ can be obtained *simultaneously* using multi-class probabilistic classifiers (Bickel et al., 2008).

Although the importance-based multi-task learning approach is highly flexible, estimating the importance weights over both $\boldsymbol{x}$ and y is a hard problem. Thus, this approach could be unreliable if the number of training samples in each task is limited.

9.2.4 Implicit Sample Sharing

Another popular idea of multi-task learning is to impose solutions of different tasks to be similar to each other (Evgeniou and Pontil, 2004; Lapedriza et al., 2007; Kato et al., 2010; Simm et al., 2011), by which common information behind different tasks can be effectively shared.

Basic Formulation

The parameter for the task t ($\in \{1,\ldots,m\}$) is decomposed into the *common* part $\boldsymbol{\theta}^{(0)}$ that is shared for all tasks and an individual part $\boldsymbol{\theta}^{(t)}$ that can be different for each task (see Figure 9.6):

$$\boldsymbol{\theta}^{(0)} + \boldsymbol{\theta}^{(t)}.$$

Then the parameters for all the tasks are learned simultaneously as

$$\min_{\{\boldsymbol{\theta}^{(t)}\}_{t=0}^{m}} \left[\sum_{k=1}^{n} \mathrm{loss}(f(\boldsymbol{x}_k;\boldsymbol{\theta}^{(0)} + \boldsymbol{\theta}^{(t_k)}), y_k) \right.$$
$$\left. + \frac{\lambda}{2}\|\boldsymbol{\theta}^{(0)}\|^2 + \frac{\gamma}{2m}\sum_{t=1}^{m}\|\boldsymbol{\theta}^{(t)}\|^2 \right], \qquad (9.5)$$

where λ (≥ 0) is the regularization parameter for the shared (i.e., task-independent) parameter $\boldsymbol{\theta}^{(0)}$, and γ (≥ 0) is the regularization parameter for the individual (i.e., task-specific) parameters $\{\boldsymbol{\theta}^{(t)}\}_{t=1}^{m}$. λ controls the strength of the regularization effect for all of the entire solutions, while γ controls how close to each other the solution of each task should be.

If λ is large, the shared component $\boldsymbol{\theta}^{(0)}$ tends to vanish and thus we merely have m separate single-task learning problems with a common regularizer $\frac{\gamma}{2m}\|\boldsymbol{\theta}^{(t)}\|^2$ for each task. On the other hand, if γ is large, the solutions for all tasks tend to $\boldsymbol{\theta}^{(0)}$; that is, all tasks are jointly solved as a single task.

In the naive data-sharing approach (9.3) and the importance-weighting approach (9.4), the optimization problems one needs to solve were task-wise. Thus, the computational cost may be linear with respect to the number of tasks, m. On the other hand, in the regularization approach (9.5), one needs to optimize all the parameters $\{\boldsymbol{\theta}^{(t)}\}_{t=0}^{m}$ simultaneously, which will cause computational challenges when a large number of tasks are handled. So far, the idea of regularization-based multi-task learning has been applied to a deterministic classifier such as the *support vector machine* (Evgeniou and Pontil, 2004; Kato et al., 2010) and a

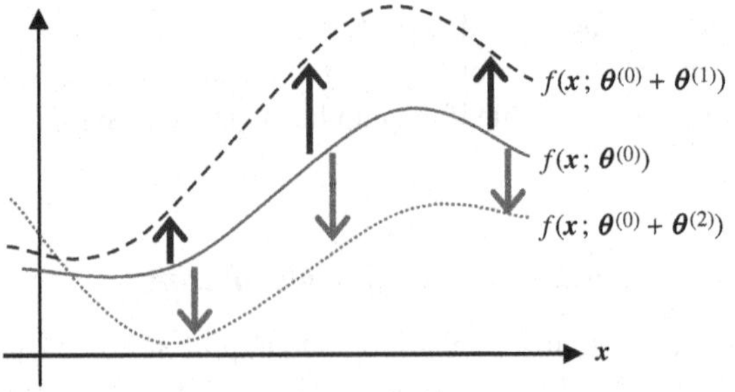

Figure 9.6. Decomposition of model parameters into the common part $\boldsymbol{\theta}^{(0)}$ and individual parts $\boldsymbol{\theta}^{(1)}$ and $\boldsymbol{\theta}^{(2)}$.

probabilistic classifier such as *logistic regression* (Lapedriza et al., 2007), and both were shown to improve the prediction accuracy. Although optimization techniques for the support vector machine have been studied extensively and highly improved (Platt, 1999; Joachims, 1999; Chang and Lin, 2001; Collobert and Bengio., 2001; Suykens et al., 2002; Rifkin et al., 2003; Tsang et al., 2005; Fung and Mangasarian, 2005; Fan et al., 2005; Tang and Zhang, 2006; Joachims, 2006; Teo et al., 2007; Franc and Sonnenburg, 2009), training logistic regression classifiers for large-scale problems is still computationally expensive (Hastie et al., 2001; Minka, 2007).

Computationally Efficient Multi-Task Classification

Sugiyama (2010) developed a computationally efficient probabilistic classification method called the *least-squares probabilistic classifier* (LSPC), which is based on density-ratio estimation (see Section 12.2). Simm et al. (2011) built up the LSPC a computationally efficiently multi-task algorithm for probabilistic classification, which is explained here.

The multi-task LSPC models the *class-posterior probability* $p_t^*(y|\boldsymbol{x})$ for each task $t \in \{1,\ldots,m\}$ and each class $y \in \{1,\ldots,c\}$ by the following linear model[3]:

$$p(y|\boldsymbol{x};\boldsymbol{\theta}^{(0,y)} + \boldsymbol{\theta}^{(t,y)}) = \boldsymbol{\psi}(\boldsymbol{x})^\top(\boldsymbol{\theta}^{(0,y)} + \boldsymbol{\theta}^{(t,y)}),$$

where $\boldsymbol{\psi}(\boldsymbol{x}) = (\psi_1(\boldsymbol{x}),\ldots,\psi_b(\boldsymbol{x}))^\top$ is a basis function. As detailed in Section 12.2.2, the LSPC adopts the empirical squared difference between the true class-posterior probability $p_t^*(y|\boldsymbol{x})$ and its model $p(y|\boldsymbol{x};\boldsymbol{\theta}^{(t,y)})$ as the loss function. The multi-task LSPC learns the parameters $\{\boldsymbol{\theta}^{(t,y)}\}_{t=0}^m$ by Eq. (9.5) with this loss function for each class y, which is formulated as

$$\begin{aligned}\min_{\{\boldsymbol{\theta}^{(t,y)}\}_{t=0}^m} \Bigg[& \frac{1}{2n}\sum_{k=1}^{n}\left(\boldsymbol{\psi}(\boldsymbol{x}_k)^\top(\boldsymbol{\theta}^{(0,y)} + \boldsymbol{\theta}^{(t_k,y)})\right)^2 \\ & - \frac{1}{n}\sum_{k:y_k=y}\boldsymbol{\psi}(\boldsymbol{x}_k)^\top(\boldsymbol{\theta}^{(0,y)} + \boldsymbol{\theta}^{(t_k,y)}) \\ & + \frac{\lambda}{2}\|\boldsymbol{\theta}^{(0,y)}\|^2 + \frac{\gamma}{2m}\sum_{t=1}^{m}\|\boldsymbol{\theta}^{(t,y)}\|^2\Bigg].\end{aligned}$$

This is a convex optimization problem and the final solution is given *analytically* as follows (Simm et al., 2011):

$$\widehat{p}_t(y|\boldsymbol{x}) \propto \max\left(0, \sum_{k:y_k=y}[\boldsymbol{A}^{-1}\boldsymbol{g}(\boldsymbol{x},t)]_k\right),$$

[3] More precisely, the model is referred to as LSPC(full); see Section 12.2.3.

where

$$A_{k,k'} := \left(\frac{\gamma}{m\lambda} + \delta_{t_k,t_{k'}}\right) \boldsymbol{\psi}(\boldsymbol{x}_k)^\top \boldsymbol{\psi}(\boldsymbol{x}_{k'}) + \frac{\gamma n}{m}\delta_{k,k'},$$

$$g_k(\boldsymbol{x},t) := \left(\frac{\gamma}{m\lambda} + \delta_{t,t_k}\right) \boldsymbol{\psi}(\boldsymbol{x})^\top \boldsymbol{\psi}(\boldsymbol{x}_k).$$

$\delta_{t,t'}$ denotes the *Kronecker delta*:

$$\delta_{t,t'} = \begin{cases} 1 & \text{if } t = t', \\ 0 & \text{otherwise.} \end{cases}$$

Numerical Examples

Here we evaluate experimentally the performance of multi-task learning methods.

In the first set of experiments, we use the *UMIST face recognition* dataset (Graham and Allinson, 1998), which contains images of 20 different people 575 images in total. Each face image was appropriately cropped into 112×92 (= 10304) pixels, and each pixel takes 8-bit intensity values from 0 to 255.

The database contains 4 female subjects among the 20 subjects. In this experiment, a male subject is chosen from the 16 male subjects for each of the 4 female subjects, and we construct 4 binary classification tasks between male (class $+1$) and female (class -1). We expect that multi-task learning captures some common structure behind the different male–female classifiers. As inputs, the raw pixel values of the grayscale images are directly used, that is, $\boldsymbol{x} \in \mathbb{R}^{10304}$. The training images are chosen randomly from the images of the target male and female subjects, and the rest of the images are used as test samples. In each task, the numbers of male and female samples are set to be equal for both training and testing.

We compare the classification accuracies and computation times of the multi-task LSPC (MT-LSPC) method with the multi-task kernel logistic regression (MT-KLR) method (Lapedriza et al., 2007) as functions of the number of training samples. As baselines, we also include their single-task counterparts: i-LSPC, i-KLR, c-LSPC, and c-KLR, where the "i" indicates "independent," meaning that each task is treated independently and a classifier is trained for each task using only samples of that task [this corresponds to setting λ in Eq. (9.5) large enough]. On the other hand, "c" denotes "combined," meaning that all tasks are combined together and a single common classifier is trained using samples from all tasks [this corresponds to setting γ in Eq. (9.5) large enough].

In all six methods, MT-LSPC, MT-KLR, i-LSPC, i-KLR, c-LSPC, and c-KLR, the Gaussian kernel

$$K(\boldsymbol{x},\boldsymbol{x}') = \exp\left(-\frac{\|\boldsymbol{x}-\boldsymbol{x}'\|^2}{2\sigma^2}\right)$$

is adopted as the basis function. five-fold cross-validation (CV) with respect to the classification accuracy is used to choose the regularization parameter λ and the Gaussian kernel bandwidth σ. Additionally, for MT-LSPC and MT-KLR, the multi-task parameter γ is also selected based on CV.

All the methods are implemented using MATLAB®. KLR solutions are numerically computed by the *limited-memory Broyden–Fletcher–Goldfarb–Shanno* (L-BFGS) method using the *minFunc* package (Schmidt, 2005). The experiments are repeated 50 times with different random seeds, and the mean accuracy and computation time are evaluated. The classification accuracy is summarized in Figure 9.7, showing that both multi-task learning methods significantly outperform the single-task learning counterparts. The accuracies of MT-LSPC and MT-KLR are comparable to each other. Figure 9.7 summarizes the computation times, showing that LSPCs are two to three times faster than KLRs, respectively.

In the second set of experiments, we use the *Landmine image classification* dataset (Xue et al., 2007). The *Landmine* dataset consists of 29 binary classification tasks about various landmine fields. Each input sample $\boldsymbol{x}$ is a nine-dimensional feature vector corresponding to a region of landmine fields, and the binary class y corresponds to whether there is a landmine in that region. The feature vectors are extracted from radar images, which concatenate four moment-based features, three correlation-based features, one energy ratio feature, and one spatial variance feature (see Xue et al., 2007, for details). The goal is to estimate whether a test landmine field contains landmines based on the region features. In the 29 landmine classification tasks, the first 15 tasks are highly foliated and the last 14 tasks are regions that are bare earth or desert. All 15 highly foliated regions and the first 2 tasks from the bare earth regions are used for experiments. We completely reverse the class labels in the latter two datasets and evaluate the robustness of the multi-task methods against noisy tasks.

We again compare the performance of MT-LSPC, MT-KLR, i-LSPC, i-KLR, c-LSPC, and c-KLR. The experimental setup is the same as the previous UMIST experiments, except that, instead of the classification accuracy, the *area under the*

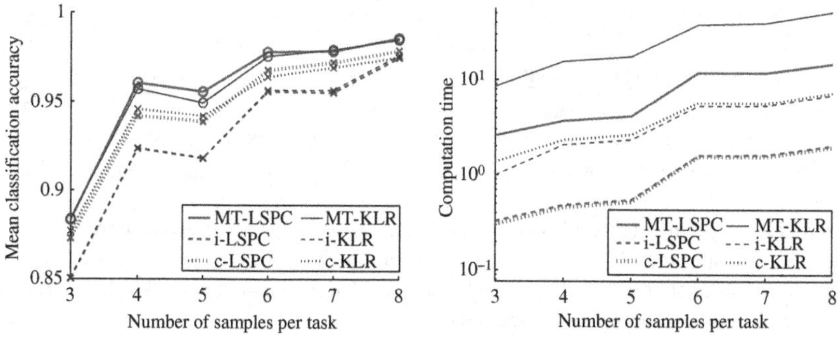

(a) Accuracy (b) Computation time

Figure 9.7. Experimental results for the UMIST dataset. (a) Mean accuracy over 50 runs. "∘" indicates the best performing method or a tie with the best performance (by t-test with 1% level of significance). "×" indicates that the method is weaker than the best one. (b) The computation time (in seconds).

receiver operating characteristic curve (AUC; Bradley, 1997) is adopted as the performance measure. The reason for this choice is as follows. In the landmine datasets, only about 6% of the samples are from the landmine class and the rest are from the non-landmine class. For such *imbalanced classification* problems (Chawla et al., 2004), using only classification accuracy is not appropriate because just predicting all test samples to be non-landmine achieves 94% accuracy, which is obviously nonsense. In imbalanced classification scenarios, it is important to take into account the *coverage* of true landmine fields, in addition to the classification accuracy. Because there is a trade-off between the coverage and the classification accuracy, we decided to adopt the AUC as our error metric here, which reflects all possible trade-offs. In the experiments, the AUC score on the test samples is first calculated for each task separately, and then the mean of the AUC values over all tasks is computed.[4]

The number of landmine samples contained in each task is 445–690. A subset of the samples is randomly selected for training and the rest are used as test data for evaluating the AUC score. The experiments are repeated 50 times with different random seeds, and the mean AUC score and computation time are evaluated.

Figure 9.8(a) summarizes the AUC scores. The results show that the AUC scores of MT-LSPC and MT-KLR are comparable to each other, and the multi-task learning methods are significantly better than the single-task learning counterparts. Figure 9.8(b) summarizes the computation time, showing that MT-LSPC is faster than MT-KLR in two orders of magnitude.

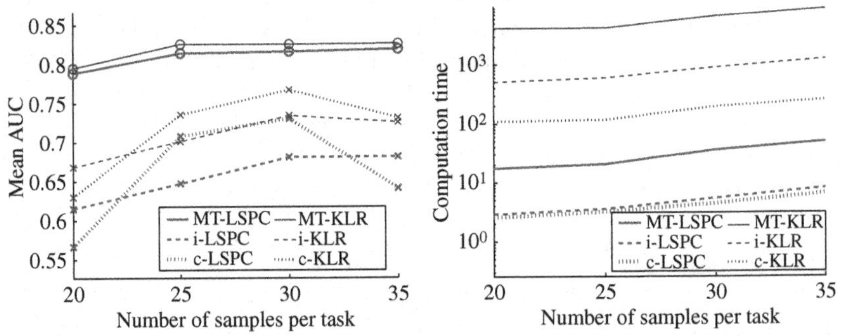

(a) AUC score (b) Computation time

Figure 9.8. Experimental results for the Landmine dataset. (a) Mean AUC score over 50 runs. "o" indicates the best performing method or a tie with the best performance (by t-test with 1% level of significance). "×" indicates that the method is weaker than the best one. (b) The computation time (in seconds).

4 To be consistent with the above performance measure, CV is also performed with respect to the AUC score. Because the landmine datasets are highly imbalanced, the validation data in the CV procedure can contain no landmine sample, which causes an inappropriate choice of tuning parameters. To avoid this problem, all estimated class-posterior probabilities from different tasks are combined and a single AUC score is calculated in the CV procedure, instead of merely taking the mean of the AUC scores over all tasks.

9.2.5 Remarks

Learning from a small number of training samples has been an important challenge in the machine learning community. Multi-task learning tries to overcome this difficulty by utilizing information brought by other related tasks. In this section we have described various multi-task learning methods by naive sample sharing, adaptive sample sharing with importance sampling, and implicit sample sharing using regularization.

The naive sample sharing without importance weighting is useful for overcoming the ill-posedness of learning problems under very small sample sizes. The adaptive sample sharing based on importance sampling would be theoretically more sound, but estimating importance weights defined over both input and output can induce another technical challenge. The implicit data sharing based on regularization is a heuristic, but it can be useful in practice due to its simple formulation. However, this makes optimization more challenging since all the task parameters need to be learned at the same time. For regression, one may use *ridge regression* (Hoerl and Kennard, 1970) as a building block for multi-task learning due to its computational efficiency. For classification, the *support vector machine* (SVM) and *least-squares probabilistic classifier* (LSPC) would produce computationally efficient multi-task learning algorithms.

10

Distribution Comparison

In this chapter we explain the usage of density-ratio estimation for comparing probability distributions.

In Section 10.1, the *pointwise* difference of two densities is considered for evaluating whether a sample drawn from one distribution is "typical" in the other distribution. This problem is referred to as *inliner-based outlier detection*, where the degree of outlyingness of samples in an evaluation dataset is examined based on another dataset that consists only of inlier samples (Smola et al., 2009; Hido et al., 2011).

In Section 10.2, the *overall* difference of two densities is considered, which basically corresponds to estimating a *divergence* between two densities. The estimated divergence can be used for a *two-sample test*, which is aimed at judging whether two distributions are the same within the framework of hypothesis testing (Sugiyama et al., 2011c).

10.1 Inlier-Based Outlier Detection

In this section we show how density-ratio methods can be used for *inlier-based outlier detection* (Smola et al., 2009; Hido et al., 2011). After an introduction in Section 10.1.1, we formulate the problem of inlier-based outlier detection and show how it can be solved via density-ratio estimation in Section 10.1.2. Various native outlier-detection methods are reviewed in Section 10.1.3, and experimental performance is compared in Section 10.1.4. Finally, the section is concluded in Section 10.1.5.

10.1.1 Introduction

The goal of *outlier detection* (a.k.a. *anomaly detection*, *novelty detection*, or *one-class classification*) is to find uncommon instances ("outliers") in a given dataset. Outlier detection has been used in various applications such as defect detection from behavior patterns of industrial machines (Fujimaki et al., 2005; Ide and Kashima, 2004), intrusion detection in network systems (Yamanishi et al.,

2004), and topic detection in news documents (Manevitz and Yousef, 2002). Recent studies include finding unusual patterns in time series (Yankov et al., 2008), discovery of spatio-temporal changes in time-evolving graphs (Chan et al., 2008), self-propagating worms detection in information systems (Jiang and Zhu, 2009), and identification of inconsistent records in construction equipment data (Fan et al., 2009). Because outlier detection is useful in various applications, it has been an active research topic in statistics, machine learning, and data mining communities for decades (Hodge and Austin, 2004).

A standard outlier-detection problem falls into the category of *unsupervised learning* (see Section 1.1.2), due to a lack of prior knowledge about the "anomalous data". In contrast, Goa et al. (2006a, 2006b) addressed the problem of *semi-supervised* outlier detection where some examples of outliers and inliers are available as a training set. The semi-supervised outlier detection methods perform better than unsupervised methods thanks to additional label information. However, such outlier samples for training are not always available in practice. Furthermore, the type of outliers may be diverse, and thus the semi-supervised methods – learning from *known* types of outliers – are not necessarily useful in detecting *unknown* types of outliers.

In this section we address the problem of *inlier-based* outlier detection where examples of inliers are available. More formally, the inlier-based outlier-detection problem is to find outlier instances in the test set based on the training set consisting only of inlier instances. The setting of inlier-based outlier detection is more practical than the semi-supervised setting because inlier samples are often available in abundance. For example, in defect detection of industrial machines, we know that there was no outlier (i.e., no defect) in the past because no failure has been observed in the machinery. Therefore, it is reasonable to separate the measurement data into a training set consisting only of inlier samples observed in the past and the test set consisting of recent samples from which we would like to find outliers.

As opposed to *supervised learning*, the outlier detection problem is often vague and it may not be possible to universally define what the outliers are. Here we consider a statistical framework and regard instances with low probability densities as outliers. In light of inlier-based outlier detection, outliers may be identified via density estimation of inlier samples. However, density estimation is known to be a hard task particularly in high-dimensional problems, and thus outlier detection via density estimation may not work well in practice.

To avoid density estimation, one can use a *one-class support vector machine* (OSVM; Schölkopf et al., 2001) or *support vector data description* (SVDD; Tax and Duin, 2004), which finds an inlier region containing a certain fraction of training instances; samples outside the inlier region are regarded as outliers. However, these methods cannot make use of inlier information available in the inlier-based settings. Furthermore, the solutions of OSVM and SVDD depend heavily on the choice of tuning parameters (e.g., the Gaussian kernel bandwidth), and there seems to be no reasonable method to appropriately determine the values of such tuning parameters.

In this section we explore an alternative approach to inlier-based outlier detection based on density-ratio estimation that can overcome the weakness of the above approaches. Among the various methods of density-ratio estimation reviewed in Part II, the *Kullback–Leibler importance estimation procedure* (KLIEP; see Chapter 5) and *unconstrained least-squares importance fitting* (uLSIF; see Section 6.2.2) are employed for outlier detection here. The reason for this choice is that KLIEP and uLSIF are equipped with cross-validation (CV), and hence values of the tuning parameters such as the kernel bandwidth and regularization strength can be objectively determined without subjective trial and error.

As explained in Section 7.4.2, uLSIF is more robust against outliers than KLIEP. This in turn means that KLIEP can provide a more *sensitive* outlier score than uLSIF. On the other hand, uLSIF is computationally more efficient than KLIEP thanks to the analytic-form solution of uLSIF. Furthermore, the leave-one-out CV (LOOCV) score can be computed analytically. Thus, uLSIF-based outlier detection is more scalable to massive datasets.

10.1.2 Formulation

Suppose we have two sets of samples – training samples $\{\boldsymbol{x}_i^{\mathrm{tr}}\}_{i=1}^{n_{\mathrm{tr}}}$ and test samples $\{\boldsymbol{x}_j^{\mathrm{te}}\}_{j=1}^{n_{\mathrm{te}}}$ on $\mathbb{R}^d$. The training samples $\{\boldsymbol{x}_i^{\mathrm{tr}}\}_{i=1}^{n_{\mathrm{tr}}}$ are all *inliers*, while the test samples $\{\boldsymbol{x}_j^{\mathrm{te}}\}_{j=1}^{n_{\mathrm{te}}}$ can contain some outliers. The goal of outlier detection here is to identify outliers in the test set based on the training set consisting only of inliers. More formally, we want to assign a suitable *outlier score* for the test samples – the larger the outlier score, the more plausible the sample is an outlier.

Let us consider a statistical framework of the inlier-based outlier-detection problem: Suppose training samples $\{\boldsymbol{x}_i^{\mathrm{tr}}\}_{i=1}^{n_{\mathrm{tr}}}$ are drawn independently from a training data distribution with density $p_{\mathrm{tr}}^*(\boldsymbol{x})$ and test samples $\{\boldsymbol{x}_j^{\mathrm{te}}\}_{j=1}^{n_{\mathrm{te}}}$ are drawn independently from a test data distribution with strictly positive density $p_{\mathrm{te}}^*(\boldsymbol{x})$. Within this statistical framework, test samples with low training data densities are regarded as outliers. However, the true density $p_{\mathrm{tr}}^*(\boldsymbol{x})$ is not accessible in practice, and estimating densities is known to be a hard problem. Therefore, merely using the training data density as an outlier score may not be reliable in practice.

So instead we employ the ratio of training and test data densities as an outlier score[1]:

$$r^*(\boldsymbol{x}) = \frac{p_{\mathrm{tr}}^*(\boldsymbol{x})}{p_{\mathrm{te}}^*(\boldsymbol{x})}.$$

If no outlier sample exists in the test set (i.e., the training and test data densities are equivalent), the density-ratio value is one. On the other hand, the density-ratio value tends to be small in the regions where the training data density is low and the test data density is high. Thus, samples with small density-ratio values are plausible to be outliers.

[1] Note that the definition of the density-ratio is inverted compared with the one used in covariate shift adaptation (see Chapter 9). We chose this definition because the test data domain may be wider than the training data domain in the context of inlier-based outlier detection.

One may suspect that this density-ratio approach is not suitable when there exist only a small number of outliers – because a small number of outliers cannot increase the values of $p^*_{\mathrm{te}}(\boldsymbol{x})$ significantly. However, this is not a problem because outliers are drawn from a region with small $p^*_{\mathrm{tr}}(\boldsymbol{x})$, and therefore a small change in $p^*_{\mathrm{te}}(\boldsymbol{x})$ significantly reduces the density-ratio value. For example, let the increase of $p^*_{\mathrm{te}}(\boldsymbol{x})$ be $\epsilon = 0.01$; then $\frac{1}{1+\epsilon} \approx 1$, but $\frac{0.001}{0.001+\epsilon} \ll 1$. Thus, the density-ratio $r^*(\boldsymbol{x})$ would be a suitable outlier score.

A MATLAB® implementation of inlier-based outlier detection based on KLIEP (see Section 5.2.1), called *maximum likelihood outlier detection* (MLOD), is available from http://sugiyama-www.cs.titech.ac.jp/~sugi/software/MLOD/. Similarly, a MATLAB® implementation of inlier-based outlier detection based on uLSIF (see Section 6.2.2), called *least-squares outlier detection* (LSOD), is available from http://sugiyama-www.cs.titech.ac.jp/~sugi/software/LSOD/.

10.1.3 Relation to Existing Methods

In this subsection we discuss the relation between the density-ratio–based outlier-detection approach and other native outlier-detection methods.

The outlier-detection problem addressed here is to find outliers in the test set $\{\boldsymbol{x}^{\mathrm{te}}_j\}_{j=1}^{n_{\mathrm{te}}}$ based on the training set $\{\boldsymbol{x}^{\mathrm{tr}}_i\}_{i=1}^{n_{\mathrm{tr}}}$ consisting only of inliers. On the other hand, the outlier-detection problem that the methods reviewed here are solving is to find outliers in the test set without the training set. Thus, the problem setup is slightly different. However, such native outlier-detection methods can also be employed in the inlier-based scenario by simply using the union of training and test samples as a test set:

$$(\boldsymbol{x}_1,\ldots,\boldsymbol{x}_n) = (\boldsymbol{x}^{\mathrm{tr}}_1,\ldots,\boldsymbol{x}^{\mathrm{tr}}_{n_{\mathrm{tr}}},\boldsymbol{x}^{\mathrm{te}}_1,\ldots,\boldsymbol{x}^{\mathrm{te}}_{n_{\mathrm{te}}}),$$

where $n := n_{\mathrm{tr}} + n_{\mathrm{te}}$.

Kernel Density Estimation

Kernel density estimation (KDE) is a non-parametric technique to estimate a density $p^*(\boldsymbol{x})$ from samples $\{\boldsymbol{x}_k\}_{k=1}^n$ (see Section 2.3.1). KDE with the Gaussian kernel is expressed as

$$\widehat{p}(\boldsymbol{x}) = \frac{1}{n(2\pi\sigma^2)^{d/2}} \sum_{k=1}^{n} K(\boldsymbol{x},\boldsymbol{x}_k),$$

where d is the dimensionality of $\boldsymbol{x}$ and $K(\boldsymbol{x},\boldsymbol{x}')$ is the Gaussian kernel:

$$K(\boldsymbol{x},\boldsymbol{x}') = \exp\left(-\frac{\|\boldsymbol{x}-\boldsymbol{x}'\|^2}{2\sigma^2}\right).$$

The performance of KDE depends on the choice of the kernel width σ, and its value can be determined based on CV (Härdle et al., 2004): A subset of $\{\boldsymbol{x}_k\}_{k=1}^n$ is used for density estimation and the rest is used for estimating the likelihood of the hold-out samples (see Section 2.3.1 for details). Note that this CV procedure corresponds to choosing σ such that the Kullback–Leibler divergence from $p^*(\boldsymbol{x})$ to $\widehat{p}(\boldsymbol{x})$ is minimized. The estimated density values could be used directly as an outlier score. A variation of the KDE approach has been studied in Latecki et al. (2007), where local outliers are detected from multi-modal datasets.

However, KDE is known to suffer from the *curse of dimensionality* (Vapnik, 1998), and therefore the KDE-based outlier-detection method may not be reliable in practice.

The density-ratio can also be estimated by KDE, that is, first estimating the training and test data densities separately and then taking the ratio of the estimated densities (see Section 2.3). However, the estimation error tends to be accumulated in this two-step procedure, and thus this approach is not reliable.

One-Class Support Vector Machine

The *support vector machine* (SVM; Cortes and Vapnik, 1995; Vapnik, 1998; Schölkopf and Smola, 2002; see also Section 4.4) is one of the most successful classification algorithms in machine learning. The core idea of SVM is to separate samples into different classes by the maximum-margin hyperplane in a kernel-induced feature space.

A *one-class SVM* (OSVM) is an extension of SVM to outlier detection (Schölkopf et al., 2001). The basic idea of OSVM is to separate data samples $\{\boldsymbol{x}_k\}_{k=1}^n$ into outliers and inliers by a hyperplane in a Gaussian reproducing kernel Hilbert space. More specifically, the solution of OSVM is given as the solution of the following *quadratic programming* problem:

$$\min_{\{\theta_k\}_{k=1}^n} \sum_{k,k'=1}^n \theta_k\theta_{k'} K(\boldsymbol{x}_k,\boldsymbol{x}_{k'}) \quad \text{s.t.} \sum_{k=1}^n \theta_k = 1 \text{ and } 0 \leq \theta_1,\ldots,\theta_n \leq \frac{1}{\nu n},$$

where ν $(0 \leq \nu \leq 1)$ is the maximum fraction of outliers.

The solution solution of OSVM is dependent on the outlier ratio ν and the Gaussian kernel width σ. A critical weakness of OSVM is that there is no systematic method to choose these tuning parameter values. In practice, these tuning parameters should be optimized manually, which is highly subjective and thus less reliable in unsupervised outlier detection. Furthermore, outlier scores cannot be directly obtained by OSVM; the distance from the separating hyperplane may be used as an outlier score, but its statistical meaning is not clear.

A similar algorithm named *support vector data description* (SVDD; Tax and Duin, 2004) is known to be equivalent to OSVM if the Gaussian kernel is used.

Local Outlier Factor

The *local outlier factor* (LOF) is an outlier score suitable for detecting local outliers around dense regions (Breunig et al., 2000). The LOF value of a sample $\boldsymbol{x}$ is defined using the ratio of the average distance from the nearest neighbors as

$$\mathrm{LOF}_T(\boldsymbol{x}) = \frac{1}{T}\sum_{t=1}^{T} \frac{\mathrm{LRD}_T(\mathrm{nearest}_t(\boldsymbol{x}))}{\mathrm{LRD}_T(\boldsymbol{x})},$$

where $\mathrm{nearest}_t(\boldsymbol{x})$ represents the t-th nearest neighbor of $\boldsymbol{x}$ and $\mathrm{LRD}_T(\boldsymbol{x})$ denotes the inverse of the average distance from the T nearest neighbors of $\boldsymbol{x}$ (LRD stands for local reachability density). If $\boldsymbol{x}$ lies around a high-density region and its nearest neighbor samples are close to each other in the high-density region, $\mathrm{LRD}_T(\boldsymbol{x})$ tends to become much smaller than $\mathrm{LRD}_T[\mathrm{nearest}_t(\boldsymbol{x})]$ for every t. Then, $\mathrm{LOF}_T(\boldsymbol{x})$ takes a large value and $\boldsymbol{x}$ is regarded as a local outlier.

Although the LOF values seem to be a reasonable outlier measure, its performance strongly depends on the choice of the locality parameter T. Unfortunately, there is no systematic method to select an appropriate value for T, and thus subjective tuning is necessary, which is not reliable in unsupervised outlier detection. In addition, the computational cost of the LOF score is expensive because it involves a number of nearest neighbor search procedures.

10.1.4 Experiments

Here, the performances of various outlier-detection methods are compared experimentally. In all the experiments, the statistical language environment *R* (R Development Core Team, 2009) is used. The comparison includes the following density-ratio estimators:

- Unconstrained least-squares importance fitting (uLSIF; see Section 6.2.2)
- Kullback–Leibler importance estimation procedure (KLIEP; see Section 5.2.1)
- Kernel logistic regression (KLR; see Section 4.2)
- Kernel mean matching (KMM; see Section 3.3)

In addition, the native outlier-detection methods KDE, OSVM, and LOF reviewed in Section 10.1.3 are included in the comparison. A package of the the *limited-memory Broyden–Fletcher–Goldfarb–Shanno quasi-Newton* method called *optim* is used for computing the KLR solution, and a quadratic program solver called *ipop* contained in the *kernlab* package (Karatzoglou et al., 2004) used for computing the KMM solution. The *ksvm* function contained in the *kernlab* package is used as an OSVM implementation, and the *lofactor* function included in the *dprep* package (Fernandez, 2005) is used as an LOF implementation.

Twelve datasets taken from the *IDA Benchmark Repository* (Rätsch et al., 2001) are used for experiments. Note that they are originally binary classification datasets – here, the positive samples are regarded as inliers and the negative samples are treated as outliers. All the negative samples are removed from the training set; that is, the training set contains only inlier samples. In contrast, a fraction ρ of randomly chosen negative samples are retained in the test set; that is, the test set includes all inlier samples and some outliers.

When evaluating the performance of outlier-detection algorithms, it is important to take into account both the *detection rate* (the amount of true outliers an outlier detection algorithm can find) and the *detection accuracy* (the amount of true inliers that an outlier detection algorithm misjudges as outliers). Because there is a trade-off between the detection rate and detection accuracy, the *area under the ROC curve* (AUC; Bradley, 1997) is adopted as the error metric.

The AUC values of the density-ratio–based methods (KMM, KLR, KLIEP, and uLSIF) and other methods (KDE, OSVM, and LOF) are compared. All the tuning parameters included in KLR, KLIEP, uLSIF, and KDE are chosen based on cross-validation (CV) from a wide range of values. CV is not available to KMM, OSVM, and LOF; the Gaussian kernel width in KMM and OSVM is set to the median distance between samples, which was shown to be a useful heuristic (Schölkopf and Smola, 2002). For KMM, the other tuning parameters are fixed to $B = 1000$ and $\epsilon = (\sqrt{n_{\mathrm{te}}} - 1)/\sqrt{n_{\mathrm{te}}}$ following Huang et al. (2007). For OSVM, the tuning parameter is set to $\nu = 0.1$. The number of basis functions in KLIEP and uLSIF is fixed to $b = 100$ (note that b can also be optimized by CV if necessary). For LOF, three candidate values 5, 30, and 50 are tested as the number T of nearest neighbors.

The mean AUC values over 20 trials as well as the computation time are summarized in Table 10.1, where the computation time is normalized so that uLSIF is one. Because the types of outliers may be diverse depending on the datasets, no single method may consistently outperform the others for all the datasets. To evaluate the overall performance, the average AUC values over all datasets are also described at the bottom of Table 10.1.

The results show that KLIEP is the most accurate on the whole, and uLSIF follows with a small margin. Because KLIEP can provide a more sensitive outlier score than uLSIF (see Section 7.4.2), this would be a reasonable result. On the other hand, uLSIF is computationally much more efficient than KLIEP. KLR works reasonably well overall, but it performs poorly for some datasets such as the *splice*, *twonorm*, and *waveform* datasets, and the average AUC performance is not as good as uLSIF and KLIEP.

KMM and OSVM are not comparable to uLSIF in terms of AUC, and they are computationally less efficient. Note that we also tested KMM and OSVM with several different Gaussian widths and experimentally found that the heuristic of using the median sample distance as the Gaussian kernel width works reasonably well in this experiment. Thus, the AUC values of KMM and OSVM are close to their optimal values.

LOF with large T is shown to work well, although it is not clear whether the heuristic of simply using large T is always appropriate. In fact, the average AUC values of LOF are slightly higher for $T = 30$ than $T = 50$, and there is no systematic way to choose the optimal value for T. LOF is very slow because nearest neighbor search is computationally expensive.

Table 10.1. Mean AUC values over 20 trials for the benchmark datasets

Dataset		uLSIF	KLIEP	KLR	KMM	OSVM	LOF			KDE
Name	ρ	(CV)	(CV)	(CV)	(med)	(med)	$T=5$	$T=30$	$T=50$	(CV)
	0.01	0.851	0.815	0.447	0.578	0.360	0.838	0.915	0.919	0.934
banana	0.02	0.858	0.824	0.428	0.644	0.412	0.813	0.918	0.920	0.927
	0.05	0.869	0.851	0.435	0.761	0.467	0.786	0.907	0.909	0.923
	0.01	0.463	0.480	0.627	0.576	0.508	0.546	0.488	0.463	0.400
b-cancer	0.02	0.463	0.480	0.627	0.576	0.506	0.521	0.445	0.428	0.400
	0.05	0.463	0.480	0.627	0.576	0.498	0.549	0.480	0.452	0.400
	0.01	0.558	0.615	0.599	0.574	0.563	0.513	0.403	0.390	0.425
diabetes	0.02	0.558	0.615	0.599	0.574	0.563	0.526	0.453	0.434	0.425
	0.05	0.532	0.590	0.636	0.547	0.545	0.536	0.461	0.447	0.435
	0.01	0.416	0.485	0.438	0.494	0.522	0.480	0.441	0.385	0.378
f-solar	0.02	0.426	0.456	0.432	0.480	0.550	0.442	0.406	0.343	0.374
	0.05	0.442	0.479	0.432	0.532	0.576	0.455	0.417	0.370	0.346
	0.01	0.574	0.572	0.556	0.529	0.535	0.526	0.559	0.552	0.561
german	0.02	0.574	0.572	0.556	0.529	0.535	0.553	0.549	0.544	0.561
	0.05	0.564	0.555	0.540	0.532	0.530	0.548	0.571	0.555	0.547
	0.01	0.659	0.647	0.833	0.623	0.681	0.407	0.659	0.739	0.638
heart	0.02	0.659	0.647	0.833	0.623	0.678	0.428	0.668	0.746	0.638
	0.05	0.659	0.647	0.833	0.623	0.681	0.440	0.666	0.749	0.638
	0.01	0.812	0.828	0.600	0.813	0.540	0.909	0.930	0.896	0.916
satimage	0.02	0.829	0.847	0.632	0.861	0.548	0.785	0.919	0.880	0.898
	0.05	0.841	0.858	0.715	0.893	0.536	0.712	0.895	0.868	0.892
	0.01	0.713	0.748	0.368	0.541	0.737	0.765	0.778	0.768	0.845
splice	0.02	0.754	0.765	0.343	0.588	0.744	0.761	0.793	0.783	0.848
	0.05	0.734	0.764	0.377	0.643	0.723	0.764	0.785	0.777	0.849
	0.01	0.534	0.720	0.745	0.681	0.504	0.259	0.111	0.071	0.256
thyroid	0.02	0.534	0.720	0.745	0.681	0.505	0.259	0.111	0.071	0.256
	0.05	0.534	0.720	0.745	0.681	0.485	0.259	0.111	0.071	0.256
	0.01	0.525	0.534	0.602	0.502	0.456	0.520	0.525	0.525	0.461
titanic	0.02	0.496	0.498	0.659	0.513	0.526	0.492	0.503	0.503	0.472
	0.05	0.526	0.521	0.644	0.538	0.505	0.499	0.512	0.512	0.433
	0.01	0.905	0.902	0.161	0.439	0.846	0.812	0.889	0.897	0.875
twonorm	0.02	0.896	0.889	0.197	0.572	0.821	0.803	0.892	0.901	0.858
	0.05	0.905	0.903	0.396	0.754	0.781	0.765	0.858	0.874	0.807
	0.01	0.890	0.881	0.243	0.477	0.861	0.724	0.887	0.889	0.861
waveform	0.02	0.901	0.890	0.181	0.602	0.817	0.690	0.887	0.890	0.861
	0.05	0.885	0.873	0.236	0.757	0.798	0.705	0.847	0.874	0.831
Average		0.661	0.685	0.530	0.608	0.596	0.594	0.629	0.622	0.623
Comp. time		1.00	11.7	5.35	751	12.4		85.5		8.70

KDE sometimes works reasonably well, but the performance fluctuates depending on the dataset. Therefore, its average AUC value is not comparable to uLSIF and KLIEP.

Overall, the uLSIF-based and KLIEP-based methods are shown to be promising in inlier-based outlier detection.

10.1.5 Remarks

In this section we discussed the problem of inlier-based outlier detection. Because inlier information can be taken into account in this approach, it tends to outperform unsupervised outlier-detection methods (if such inlier information is available). Furthermore, thanks to the density-ratio formulation, model selection is possible by cross-validation over the density-ratio approximation error. This is a significant advantage over purely unsupervised approaches. An inlier-based outlier-detection method based on the *hinge-loss* was also studied (see Smola et al., 2009).

The goal of *change detection* (a.k.a. *event detection*) is to identify time points at which properties of time series data change (Basseville and Nikiforov, 1993; Brodsky and Darkhovsky, 1993; Guralnik and Srivastava, 1999; Gustafsson, 2000; Yamanishi and Takeuchi, 2002; Ide and Kashima, 2004; Kifer et al., 2004). Change detection covers a broad range of real-world problems such as *fraud detection* in cellular systems (Murad and Pinkas, 1999; Bolton and Hand, 2002), *intrusion detection* in computer networks (Yamanishi et al., 2004), *irregular-motion detection* in vision systems (Ke et al., 2007), *signal segmentation* in data streams (Basseville and Nikiforov, 1993), and *fault detection* in engineering systems (Fujimaki et al., 2005). If vectorial samples are extracted from time series data in a sliding-window manner, one can apply density-ratio methods to change detection (Kawahara and Sugiyama, 2011).

10.2 Two-Sample Test

Given two sets of samples, testing whether the probability distributions behind the samples are equivalent is a fundamental task in statistical data analysis. This problem is referred to as the *two-sample test* or the *homogeneity test* (Kullback, 1959).

In this section we explain a density-ratio approach to two-sample testing. After an introduction in Section 10.2.1, we review the framework of *hypothesis testing* in Section 10.2.2. In hypothesis testing, the choice of test statistics and the way the null distribution is computed are the key components. In Section 10.2.3, we describe a density-ratio method of divergence estimation that is used as a test statistic. We then describe a two-sample test method called the *least-squares two-sample test* (LSTT; Sugiyama et al., 2011c) in Section 10.2.4, which uses the *permutation test* (Efron and Tibshirani, 1993) for computing the null distribution. In Section 10.2.5, we review a kernel-based two-sample test method called *maximum mean discrepancy* (MMD; see Borgwardt et al., 2006; Gretton et al., 2007; Sriperumbudur et al.,

2009), and we compare the experimental performance of the LSTT and MMD in Section 10.2.6. Finally, the section is concluded in Section 10.2.7.

10.2.1 Introduction

The two-sample test is useful in various practically important learning scenarios:

- When learning is performed in a non-stationary environment, for example, in brain–computer interfaces (Sugiyama et al., 2007) and robot control (Hachiya et al., 2009), testing the homogeneity of the data-generating distributions allows one to determine whether some adaptation scheme should be used or not. When the distributions are not significantly different, one can avoid using data-intensive non-stationarity adaptation techniques (such as *covariate shift adaptation* explained in Section 9.1). This can significantly contribute to stabilizing the performance.
- When multiple sets of data samples are available for learning, for example, biological experimental results obtained from different laboratories (Borgwardt et al., 2006), the homogeneity test allows one to make a decision as to whether all the datasets are analyzed jointly as a single dataset or they should be treated separately.
- Similarly, one can use the homogeneity test for deciding whether *multi-task learning* methods (Caruana et al., 1997, see also Section 9.2) are employed. The rationale behind multi-task learning is that when several related learning tasks are provided, solving them simultaneously can give better solutions than solving them individually. However, when the tasks are not similar to each other, using multi-task learning techniques can degrade the performance. Thus, it is important to avoid using multi-task learning methods when the tasks are not similar to each other. This may be achieved by testing the homogeneity of the datasets.

The *t-test* (Student, 1908) is a classical method for testing homogeneity that compares the means of two Gaussian distributions with a common variance; its multi-variate extension also exists (Hotelling, 1951). Although the t-test is a fundamental method for comparing the means, its range of application is limited to Gaussian distributions with a common variance, which may not be fulfilled in practical applications.

The *Kolmogorov–Smirnov test* and the *Wald–Wolfowitz runs test* are classical non-parametric methods for the two-sample problem; their multi-dimensional variants have also been developed (Bickel, 1969; Friedman and Rafsky, 1979). Since then, different types of non-parametric test methods have been studied (e.g., Anderson et al., 1994; Li, 1996).

Recently, a non-parametric extension of the t-test called *maximum mean discrepancy* (MMD) was proposed (Borgwardt et al., 2006; Gretton et al., 2007). The MMD compares the means of two distributions in a *universal reproducing kernel Hilbert space* (universal RKHS; Steinwart, 2001) – the Gaussian kernel is a typical example that induces a universal RKHS. The MMD does not require a restrictive parametric assumption, and hence it could be a flexible alternative to the t-test. The MMD was shown experimentally to outperform alternative homogeneity tests such as the *generalized Kolmogorov–Smirnov test* (Friedman and Rafsky, 1979), the *generalized Wald–Wolfowitz test* (Friedman and Rafsky, 1979), the *Hall–Tajvidi test* (Hall and Tajvidi, 2002), and the *Biau–Györfi test* (Biau and Györfi, 2005).

The performance of the MMD depends on the choice of universal RKHSs (e.g., the Gaussian bandwidth in the case of Gaussian RKHSs). Thus, the universal RKHS should be chosen carefully for obtaining good performance. The Gaussian RKHS with bandwidth set to the median distance between samples has been a popular heuristic in practice (Borgwardt et al., 2006; Gretton et al., 2007). Recently, a novel idea of using the universal RKHS (or the Gaussian widths) yielding the maximum MMD value was introduced and shown to work well (Sriperumbudur et al., 2009).

Another approach to the two-sample problem is to evaluate a divergence between two distributions. The divergence-based approach is advantageous in that cross-validation over the divergence functional is available for optimizing tuning parameters in a data-dependent manner. A typical choice of the divergence functional would be the f-divergences (Ali and Silvey, 1966; Csiszár, 1967), which include the *Kullback–Leibler* (KL) divergence (Kullback and Leibler, 1951) and the *Pearson* (PE) divergence (Pearson, 1900) as special cases.

Various methods for estimating the divergence functional have been studied so far (e.g., Darbellay and Vajda, 1999; Wang et al., 2005; Silva and Narayanan, 2007; Pérez-Cruz, 2008). Among them, approaches based on *density-ratio estimation* have been shown to be promising both theoretically and experimentally (Sugiyama et al., 2008; Gretton et al., 2009; Kanamori et al., 2009; Nguyen et al., 2010).

A parametric density-ratio estimator based on logistic regression (Qin, 1998; Cheng and Chu, 2004) has been applied to the homogeneity test (Keziou and Leoni-Aubin, 2005). Although the density-ratio estimator based on logistic regression was proved to achieve the smallest asymptotic variance among a class of semi-parametric estimators (Qin, 1998, see also Section 13.3), this theoretical guarantee is valid only when the parametric model is *correctly specified* (i.e., the target density-ratio is included in the parametric model at hand). However, when this unrealistic assumption is violated, a divergence-based density-ratio estimator (Sugiyama et al., 2008; Nguyen et al., 2010) was shown to perform better (Kanamori et al., 2010).

Among various divergence-based density-ratio estimators, *unconstrained least-squares importance fitting* (uLSIF) was demonstrated to be accurate and computationally efficient (Kanamori et al., 2009; see also Section 6.2.2). Furthermore, uLSIF was proved to possess the optimal non-parametric convergence rate (Kanamori et al., 2011b; see also Section 14.3) and optimal numerical stability (Kanamori et al., 2011c; see also Chapter 16). In this section, we describe a method for testing the homogeneity based on uLSIF.

Similarly to the MMD, the uLSIF-based homogeneity test processes data samples only through kernel functions. Thus, the uLSIF-based method can be used for testing the homogeneity of *non-vectorial structured objects* such as strings, trees, and graphs by employing kernel functions defined for such structured data (Lodhi et al., 2002; Duffy and Collins, 2002; Kashima and Koyanagi, 2002; Kondor and Lafferty, 2002; Kashima et al., 2003; Gärtner et al., 2003; Gärtner, 2003). This is an advantage over traditional two-sample tests.

10.2.2 Hypothesis Testing

A *hypothesis test* is a statistical method of decision making from data samples (Henkel, 1976). Here, we briefly review the framework of hypothesis testing (see Figure 10.1).

The hypothesis being tested is called the *null hypothesis* and denoted by H_0. Its complementary hypothesis is called the *alternative hypothesis* and denoted by H_1. In the case of two-sample tests, the null hypothesis H_0 is that the two data-generating distributions are equivalent, and the alternative hypothesis H_1 is that the two data-generating distributions are different. A decision is made whether the null hypothesis is *accepted* or *rejected* under a pre-specified *significance level* α. The significance level is conventionally set to $\alpha = 0.01$ or 0.05.

For testing, some test statistic η is considered; typically, an estimator of the "distance" between the two data-generating distributions is used. Then the distribution of the test statistic is computed under the assumption that the null hypothesis H_0 is correct.

Next, the value of the test statistic $\widehat{\eta}$ for the given data is computed, and its *ranking* in the null distribution is evaluated. If $\widehat{\eta}$ is in the *critical region*, which is a tail of the null distribution with probability α, the null hypothesis H_0 is rejected. Otherwise, there is not enough evidence to reject the null hypothesis H_0, and thus the null hypothesis H_0 is accepted.

A key component in this hypothesis testing procedure is the kind of test statistics that is used and how the null distribution of the test statistics is computed. In this section we use the uLSIF-based divergence estimator described in Section 10.2.3 as a test statistic. For computing the null distribution, we use a general-purpose numerical method called the *permutation test*, which is described in Section 10.2.4.

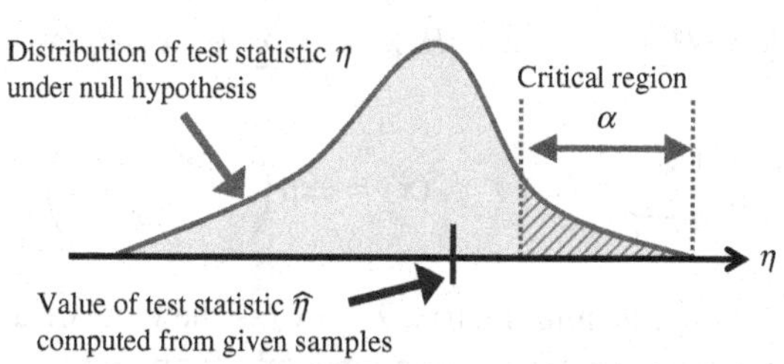

Figure 10.1. Framework of hypothesis testing.

10.2.3 Divergence Estimation

To describe a divergence estimator based on uLSIF, suppose we are given a set of samples $\mathcal{X} := \{\boldsymbol{x}_i | \boldsymbol{x}_i \in \mathbb{R}^d\}_{i=1}^n$ drawn independently from a probability distribution P^* with density $p^*(\boldsymbol{x})$, and another set of samples $\mathcal{X}' := \{\boldsymbol{x}'_j | \boldsymbol{x}'_j \in \mathbb{R}^d\}_{j=1}^{n'}$ drawn independently from (possibly) another probability distribution P'^* with density $p'^*(\boldsymbol{x})$:

$$\{\boldsymbol{x}_i\}_{i=1}^n \overset{\text{i.i.d.}}{\sim} P^* \quad \text{and} \quad \{\boldsymbol{x}'_j\}_{j=1}^{n'} \overset{\text{i.i.d.}}{\sim} P'^*.$$

Let us consider the *Pearson* (PE) divergence (Pearson, 1900) from P^* to P'^* as a discrepancy measure between P^* and P'^*, which is defined and expressed as

$$\begin{aligned} \mathrm{PE}(P^*, P'^*) &:= \frac{1}{2}\int \left(\frac{p^*(\boldsymbol{x})}{p'^*(\boldsymbol{x})} - 1\right)^2 p'^*(\boldsymbol{x})\mathrm{d}\boldsymbol{x} \\ &= \frac{1}{2}\int r^*(\boldsymbol{x})p^*(\boldsymbol{x})\mathrm{d}\boldsymbol{x} - \int r^*(\boldsymbol{x})p'^*(\boldsymbol{x})\mathrm{d}\boldsymbol{x} + \frac{1}{2}, \end{aligned} \tag{10.1}$$

where $r^*(\boldsymbol{x})$ is the density-ratio function defined by

$$r^*(\boldsymbol{x}) = \frac{p^*(\boldsymbol{x})}{p'^*(\boldsymbol{x})}.$$

$\mathrm{PE}(P^*, P'^*)$ vanishes if and only if $P^* = P'^*$. The PE divergence is a squared-loss variant of the *Kullback–Leibler* (KL) divergence (Kullback and Leibler, 1951) and is an instance of the f-divergences, which are also known as the *Ali–Silvey–Csiszár* (ASC) divergence (Csiszár, 1967; Ali and Silvey, 1966).

Let us replace the density-ratio function $r^*(\boldsymbol{x})$ by a uLSIF estimator $\widehat{r}(\boldsymbol{x})$ (see Section 6.2.2):

$$\widehat{r}(\boldsymbol{x}) = \sum_{\ell=1}^{b} \widehat{\theta}_\ell \psi_\ell(\boldsymbol{x}),$$

where b denotes the number of basis functions,

$$\widehat{\boldsymbol{\theta}} = (\widehat{\boldsymbol{H}} + \lambda \boldsymbol{I}_b)^{-1}\widehat{\boldsymbol{h}}, \quad \widehat{H}_{\ell,\ell'} = \frac{1}{n'}\sum_{j=1}^{n'} \psi_\ell(\boldsymbol{x}'_j)\psi_{\ell'}(\boldsymbol{x}'_j),$$

$$\widehat{h}_\ell = \frac{1}{n}\sum_{i=1}^{n} \psi_\ell(\boldsymbol{x}_i), \quad \psi_\ell(\boldsymbol{x}) = \exp\left(-\frac{\|\boldsymbol{x} - \boldsymbol{c}_\ell\|^2}{2\sigma^2}\right),$$

$\boldsymbol{I}_b$ is the b-dimensional identity matrix, λ (≥ 0) is the regularization parameter, and $\{\boldsymbol{c}_\ell\}_{\ell=1}^b$ are Gaussian centers chosen randomly from $\{\boldsymbol{x}_i\}_{i=1}^n$. To these kernel basis functions we may also add a constant basis function $\psi_0(\boldsymbol{x}) = 1$.

Approximating the expectations in Eq. (10.1) by empirical averages, we have the following PE divergence estimator:

$$\widehat{\mathrm{PE}}(\mathcal{X},\mathcal{X}') := \frac{1}{2n}\sum_{i=1}^{n}\widehat{r}(\boldsymbol{x}_i) - \frac{1}{n'}\sum_{j=1}^{n'}\widehat{r}(\boldsymbol{x}'_j) + \frac{1}{2}$$
$$= \frac{1}{2}\widehat{\boldsymbol{h}}^\top\widehat{\boldsymbol{\theta}} - \widehat{\boldsymbol{h}}'^\top\widehat{\boldsymbol{\theta}} + \frac{1}{2},$$

where $\widehat{h}'_\ell = \frac{1}{n'}\sum_{j=1}^{n'}\psi_\ell(\boldsymbol{x}'_j)$.

Note that $\widehat{\mathrm{PE}}(\mathcal{X},\mathcal{X}')$ can take a negative value, although the true $\mathrm{PE}(P^*, P'^*)$ is non-negative by definition. Thus, the estimation accuracy of $\widehat{\mathrm{PE}}(\mathcal{X},\mathcal{X}')$ can be improved by rounding up a negative estimate to zero. However, we do not employ this rounding-up strategy here because we are interested in the relative *ranking* of the divergence estimates, as explained in Section 10.2.4.

10.2.4 Least-Squares Two-Sample Test

Here we describe a two-sample test method based on $\widehat{\mathrm{PE}}(\mathcal{X},\mathcal{X}')$. We first describe a basic procedure of the two-sample test and show its theoretical properties. Then we illustrate its behavior using a toy dataset and discuss practical issues for improving the performance.

Permutation Test

The two-sample test described here is based on the *permutation test* (Efron and Tibshirani, 1993).

We first run the uLSIF-based PE divergence estimation procedure using the original datasets $\mathcal{X}$ and $\mathcal{X}'$ and obtain a PE divergence estimate $\widehat{\mathrm{PE}}(\mathcal{X},\mathcal{X}')$. Next, we randomly permute the $|\mathcal{X}\cup\mathcal{X}'|$ samples, and assign the first $|\mathcal{X}|$ samples to a set $\widetilde{\mathcal{X}}$ and the remaining $|\mathcal{X}'|$ samples to another set $\widetilde{\mathcal{X}}'$ (see Figure 10.2). Then we run the uLSIF-based PE divergence estimation procedure again using the randomly shuffled datasets $\widetilde{\mathcal{X}}$ and $\widetilde{\mathcal{X}}'$ and obtain a PE divergence estimate $\widehat{\mathrm{PE}}(\widetilde{\mathcal{X}},\widetilde{\mathcal{X}}')$. Note that $\widetilde{\mathcal{X}}$ and $\widetilde{\mathcal{X}}'$ can be regarded as being drawn from the same distribution. Thus,

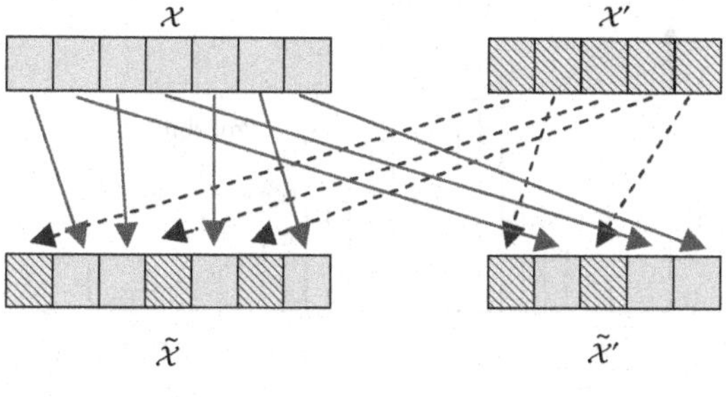

Figure 10.2. Randomly re-shuffling samples.

$\widehat{\text{PE}}(\widetilde{\mathcal{X}},\widetilde{\mathcal{X}}')$ would take a value close to zero. This random shuffling procedure is repeated many times, and the distribution of $\widehat{\text{PE}}(\widetilde{\mathcal{X}},\widetilde{\mathcal{X}}')$ under the null hypothesis (i.e., the two distributions are the same) is constructed. Finally, the p-value is approximated by evaluating the relative ranking of $\widehat{\text{PE}}(\mathcal{X},\mathcal{X}')$ in the distribution of $\widehat{\text{PE}}(\widetilde{\mathcal{X}},\widetilde{\mathcal{X}}')$.

This two-sample method is called the *least-squares two-sample test* (LSTT; Sugiyama et al., 2011c).

Suppose $|\mathcal{X}| = |\mathcal{X}'|$, and let F be the distribution function of $\widehat{\text{PE}}(\widetilde{\mathcal{X}},\widetilde{\mathcal{X}}')$. Let

$$\beta := \sup\{t \in \mathbb{R} | F(t) \leq 1-\alpha\}$$

be the upper 100α-percentile point of F (see Figure 10.3). If $P^* = P'^*$, it was shown (Sugiyama et al., 2011c) that

$$\text{Prob}\left(\widehat{\text{PE}}(\mathcal{X},\mathcal{X}') > \beta\right) \leq \alpha,$$

where Prob(e) denotes the probability of an event e.

This means that, for a given significance level α, the probability that $\widehat{\text{PE}}(\mathcal{X},\mathcal{X}')$ exceeds β is at most α when $P^* = P'^*$. Thus, when the null hypothesis is correct, it will be properly accepted with a specified probability.

Numerical Examples

Let the number of samples be $n = n' = 500$, and

$$\mathcal{X} = \{\boldsymbol{x}_i\}_{i=1}^{n} \overset{\text{i.i.d.}}{\sim} P^* = N(0,1),$$

$$\mathcal{X}' = \{\boldsymbol{x}'_j\}_{j=1}^{n'} \overset{\text{i.i.d.}}{\sim} P'^* = N(\mu,\sigma^2),$$

where $N(\mu,\sigma^2)$ denotes the normal distribution with mean μ and variance σ^2. We consider the following four setups:

(a) $(\mu,\sigma) = (0,1.3)$: P'^* has a larger standard deviation than P^*.
(b) $(\mu,\sigma) = (0,0.7)$: P'^* has a smaller standard deviation than P^*.
(c) $(\mu,\sigma) = (0.3,1)$: P^* and P'^* have different means.
(d) $(\mu,\sigma) = (0,1)$: P^* and P'^* are the same.

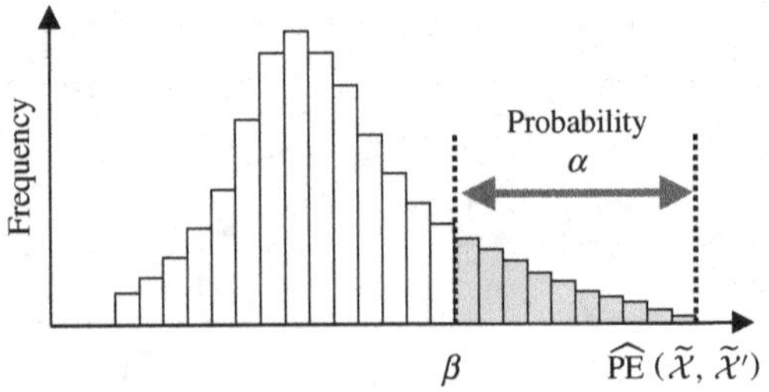

Figure 10.3. The role of the variables α and β.

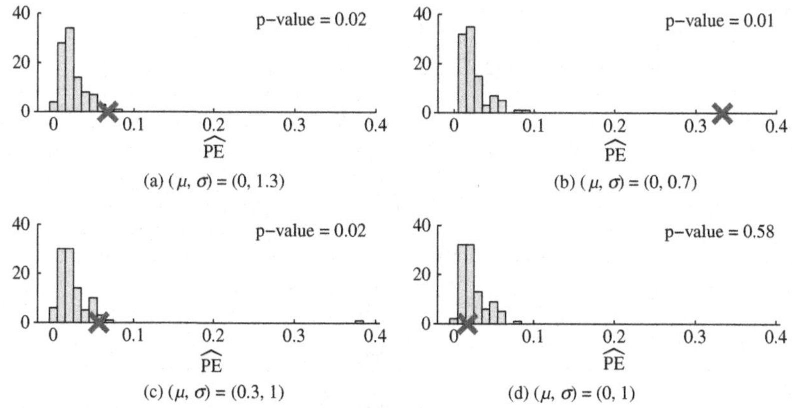

Figure 10.4. Histograms of $\widehat{\mathrm{PE}}(\widetilde{\mathcal{X}},\widetilde{\mathcal{X}}')$ (i.e., shuffled datasets) for the toy dataset. "×" indicates the value of $\widehat{\mathrm{PE}}(\mathcal{X},\mathcal{X}')$ (i.e., the original datasets).

Figure 10.4 depicts histograms of $\widehat{\mathrm{PE}}(\widetilde{\mathcal{X}},\widetilde{\mathcal{X}}')$ (i.e., shuffled datasets), showing that the profiles of the null distribution (i.e., the two distributions are the same) are rather similar to each other for the four cases. The values of $\widehat{\mathrm{PE}}(\mathcal{X},\mathcal{X}')$ (i.e., the original datasets) are also plotted in Figure 10.4 using the "×" symbol on the horizontal axis, showing that the p-values tend to be small when $P^* \neq P'^*$ and the p-value is large when $P^* = P'^*$. This is desirable behavior as a test.

Figure 10.5 depicts the means and standard deviations of p-values over 100 runs as functions of the sample size n $(= n')$, indicated by "plain." The graphs show that, when $P^* \neq P'^*$, the p-values tend to decrease as n increases. On the other hand, when $P^* = P'^*$, the p-values are almost unchanged and kept to relatively large values.

Figure 10.6 depicts the rate of accepting the null hypothesis (i.e., $P^* = P'^*$) over 100 runs when the significance level is set to 0.05 (i.e., the rate of p-values larger than 0.05). The graphs show that, when $P^* \neq P'^*$, the null hypothesis tends to be more frequently rejected as n increases. On the other hand, when $P^* = P'^*$, the null hypothesis is almost always accepted. Thus, the LSTT was shown to work properly for these toy datasets.

Choice of Numerator and Denominator

In LSTT, uLSIF was used for estimating the density-ratio function $r^*(\boldsymbol{x})$:

$$r^*(\boldsymbol{x}) = \frac{p^*(\boldsymbol{x})}{p'^*(\boldsymbol{x})}.$$

By definition, the *reciprocal* of the density-ratio $r^*(\boldsymbol{x})$,

$$\frac{1}{r^*(\boldsymbol{x})} = \frac{p'^*(\boldsymbol{x})}{p^*(\boldsymbol{x})},$$

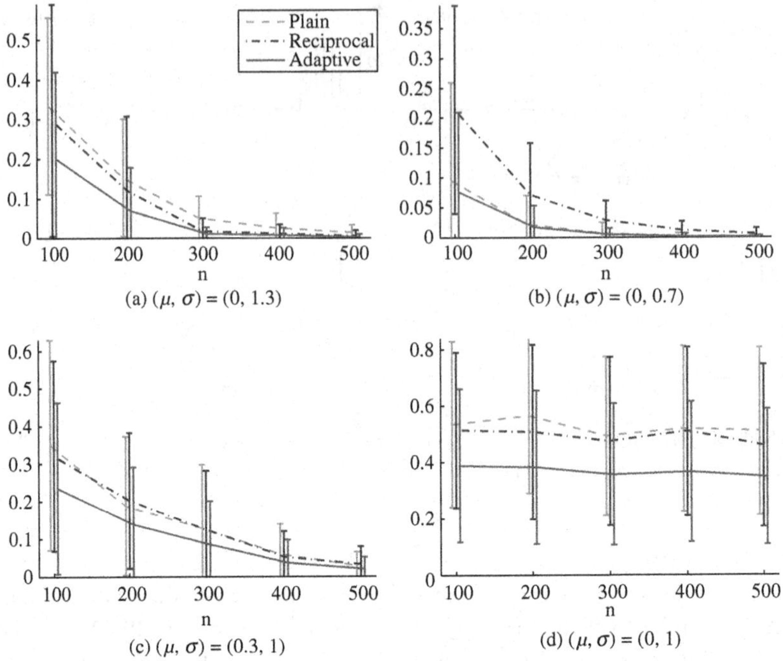

(a) $(\mu, \sigma) = (0, 1.3)$ (b) $(\mu, \sigma) = (0, 0.7)$

(c) $(\mu, \sigma) = (0.3, 1)$ (d) $(\mu, \sigma) = (0, 1)$

Figure 10.5. Means and standard deviations of p-values for the toy dataset.

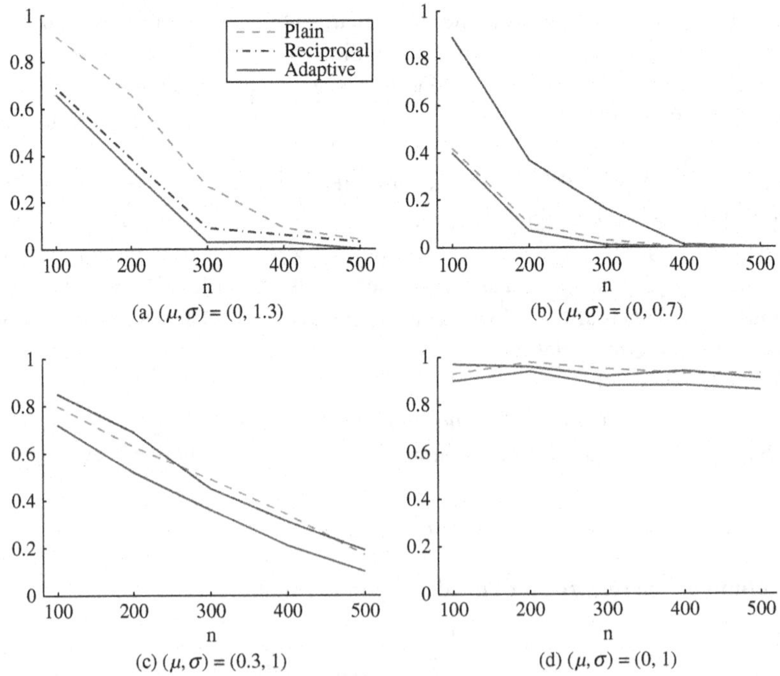

(a) $(\mu, \sigma) = (0, 1.3)$ (b) $(\mu, \sigma) = (0, 0.7)$

(c) $(\mu, \sigma) = (0.3, 1)$ (d) $(\mu, \sigma) = (0, 1)$

Figure 10.6. The rate of accepting the null hypothesis (i.e., $P^* = P'^*$) for the toy dataset under the significance level 0.05.

is also a density-ratio, assuming that $p^*(\boldsymbol{x}) > 0$ for all $\boldsymbol{x}$. This means that we can use uLSIF in two ways, estimating either the original density-ratio $r^*(\boldsymbol{x})$ or its reciprocal $1/r^*(\boldsymbol{x})$.

To illustrate this difference, we perform the same experiments as previously, but swap $\mathcal{X}$ and $\mathcal{X}'$. The obtained p-values and the acceptance rate are also included in Figures 10.5 and 10.6 as "reciprocal." In the experiments, we prefer to have smaller p-values when $P^* \neq P'^*$ and larger p-values when $P^* = P'^*$. The graphs show that, when $(\mu,\sigma) = (0,1.3)$, estimating the inverted density-ratio gives slightly smaller p-values and a significantly lower acceptance rate. On the other hand, when $(\mu,\sigma) = (0,0.7)$, reciprocal estimation yields larger p-values and a significantly higher acceptance rate. When $(\mu,\sigma) = (0.3,1)$ and $(\mu,\sigma) = (0,1)$, the 'plain' and 'reciprocal' methods result in similar p-values and thus similar acceptance rates. These experimental results imply that, if the plain and reciprocal approaches are adaptively chosen, the performance of the homogeneity test may be improved.

Figure 10.5 showed that, when $P^* = P'^*$ [i.e., $(\mu,\sigma) = (0,1)$], the p-values are large enough to reject the null hypothesis for both the plain and reciprocal approaches. Thus, the *type I error* (the rejection rate of correct null hypotheses, i.e., two distributions are judged to be different when they are actually the same) would be sufficiently small for both approaches, as illustrated in Figure 10.6.

Based on this observation, a strategy of choosing a smaller p-value between the plain and reciprocal approaches was proposed (Sugiyama et al., 2011c). This allows one to reduce the *type II error* (the acceptance rate of incorrect null hypotheses, i.e., two distributions are judged to be the same when they are actually different), and thus the *power* of the test can be enhanced.

The experimental results of this adaptive method are also included in Figures 10.5 and 10.6 as "adaptive." The results show that p-values obtained by the adaptive method are smaller than those obtained by the plain and reciprocal approaches. This provides significant performance improvement when $P^* \neq P'^*$. On the other hand, smaller p-values can be problematic when $P^* = P'^*$ because the acceptance rate can be lowered. However, as the experimental results show, the p-values are still large enough to accept the null hypothesis, and thus there is no critical performance degradation in this illustrative example.

A pseudo code of the "adaptive" LSTT method is summarized in Figures 10.7 and 10.8. Although the permutation test is computationally intensive, it can be easily parallelized using multi-processors/cores.

A MATLAB® implementation of LSTT is available from http://sugiyama-www.cs.titech.ac.jp/~sugi/software/LSTT/.

10.2.5 Relation to Existing Methods

The *maximum mean discrepancy* (MMD; Borgwardt et al., 2006; Gretton et al., 2007) is a kernel-based homogeneity test. Here, we review the definition of MMD and explain its basic properties.

Input: Two sets of samples $\mathcal{X} = \{\boldsymbol{x}_i\}_{i=1}^{n}$ and $\mathcal{X}' = \{\boldsymbol{x}'_j\}_{j=1}^{n'}$
Output: p-value $\widehat{p}$

$p_0 \longleftarrow \widehat{\mathrm{PE}}(\mathcal{X},\mathcal{X}')$; $\quad p'_0 \longleftarrow \widehat{\mathrm{PE}}(\mathcal{X}',\mathcal{X})$;
For $t = 1,\ldots,T$
  Randomly split $\mathcal{X} \cup \mathcal{X}'$ into $\widetilde{\mathcal{X}}$ of size $|\mathcal{X}|$ and $\widetilde{\mathcal{X}}'$ of size $|\mathcal{X}'|$;
  $p_t \longleftarrow \widehat{\mathrm{PE}}(\widetilde{\mathcal{X}},\widetilde{\mathcal{X}}')$; $\quad p'_t \longleftarrow \widehat{\mathrm{PE}}(\widetilde{\mathcal{X}}',\widetilde{\mathcal{X}})$;
End
$p \longleftarrow \frac{1}{T}\sum_{t=1}^{T} I(p_t > p_0)$; $\quad p' \longleftarrow \frac{1}{T}\sum_{t=1}^{T} I(p'_t > p'_0)$;
$\widehat{p} \longleftarrow \min(p,p')$;

Figure 10.7. Pseudo code of LSTT. Pseudo code of $\widehat{\mathrm{PE}}(\mathcal{X},\mathcal{X}')$ is given in Figure 10.8. $I(c)$ denotes the indicator function, i.e., $I(c) = 1$ if the condition c is true; otherwise $I(c) = 0$. When $|\widetilde{\mathcal{X}}| = |\widetilde{\mathcal{X}}'|$ (i.e., $n = n'$), $p'_t \longleftarrow \widehat{\mathrm{PE}}(\widetilde{\mathcal{X}}',\widetilde{\mathcal{X}})$ may be replaced by $p'_t \longleftarrow p_t$ because switching $\mathcal{X}$ and $\mathcal{X}'$ does not essentially affect the estimation of the PE divergence.

Input: Two sets of samples $\mathcal{X} = \{\boldsymbol{x}_i\}_{i=1}^{n}$ and $\mathcal{X}' = \{\boldsymbol{x}'_j\}_{j=1}^{n'}$
Output: PE divergence estimate $\widehat{\mathrm{PE}}(\mathcal{X},\mathcal{X}')$

Randomly split $\mathcal{X}$ into $\{\mathcal{X}_m\}_{m=1}^{M}$ and $\mathcal{X}'$ into $\{\mathcal{X}'_m\}_{m=1}^{M}$;
For each candidate of Gaussian width σ
  For $m = 1,\ldots,M$
    % $\boldsymbol{k}_\sigma(\boldsymbol{x}) = \left(1, \exp\left(-\frac{\|\boldsymbol{x}-\boldsymbol{x}_1\|^2}{2\sigma^2}\right),\ldots,\exp\left(-\frac{\|\boldsymbol{x}-\boldsymbol{x}_n\|^2}{2\sigma^2}\right)\right)^\top$
    $\widehat{\boldsymbol{G}}_m \longleftarrow \sum_{\boldsymbol{x}'\in\mathcal{X}'_m} \boldsymbol{k}_\sigma(\boldsymbol{x}')\boldsymbol{k}_\sigma(\boldsymbol{x}')^\top$; $\quad \widehat{\boldsymbol{g}}_m \longleftarrow \sum_{\boldsymbol{x}\in\mathcal{X}_m} \boldsymbol{k}_\sigma(\boldsymbol{x})$;
  End
  For each candidate of regularization parameter λ
    For $m = 1,\ldots,M$
      $\widehat{\boldsymbol{\theta}}_m \longleftarrow \left(\frac{1}{|\mathcal{X}'\backslash\mathcal{X}'_m|}\sum_{m'\neq m} \widehat{\boldsymbol{G}}_{m'} + \lambda \boldsymbol{I}_{n+1}\right)^{-1}\left(\frac{1}{|\mathcal{X}\backslash\mathcal{X}_m|}\sum_{m'\neq m}\widehat{\boldsymbol{g}}_{m'}\right)$;
      $\widehat{J}_m^{\mathrm{CV}}(\sigma,\lambda) \longleftarrow \frac{1}{2|\mathcal{X}'_m|}\widehat{\boldsymbol{\theta}}_m^\top \widehat{\boldsymbol{G}}_m \widehat{\boldsymbol{\theta}}_m - \frac{1}{|\mathcal{X}_m|}\widehat{\boldsymbol{\theta}}_m^\top \widehat{\boldsymbol{g}}_m$;
    End
    $\widehat{J}^{\mathrm{CV}}(\sigma,\lambda) \longleftarrow \frac{1}{M}\sum_{m=1}^{M} \widehat{J}_m^{\mathrm{CV}}(\sigma,\lambda)$;
  End
End
$(\widehat{\sigma},\widehat{\lambda}) \longleftarrow \mathrm{argmin}_{(\sigma,\lambda)}\, \widehat{J}^{\mathrm{CV}}(\sigma,\lambda)$;
$\widehat{\boldsymbol{h}} \longleftarrow \frac{1}{|\mathcal{X}|}\sum_{\boldsymbol{x}\in\mathcal{X}} \boldsymbol{k}_{\widehat{\sigma}}(\boldsymbol{x})$;
$\widehat{\boldsymbol{\theta}} \longleftarrow \left(\frac{1}{|\mathcal{X}'|}\sum_{\boldsymbol{x}'\in\mathcal{X}'} \boldsymbol{k}_{\widehat{\sigma}}(\boldsymbol{x}')\boldsymbol{k}_{\widehat{\sigma}}(\boldsymbol{x}')^\top + \widehat{\lambda}\boldsymbol{I}_{n+1}\right)^{-1}\widehat{\boldsymbol{h}}$;
$\widehat{\mathrm{PE}}(\mathcal{X},\mathcal{X}') \longleftarrow \frac{1}{2}\widehat{\boldsymbol{\theta}}^\top\widehat{\boldsymbol{h}} - \widehat{\boldsymbol{\theta}}^\top\left(\frac{1}{|\mathcal{X}'|}\sum_{\boldsymbol{x}'\in\mathcal{X}'} \boldsymbol{k}_{\widehat{\sigma}}(\boldsymbol{x}')\right) + \frac{1}{2}$;

Figure 10.8. Pseudo code of uLSIF-based PE divergence estimator.

MMD is an *integral probability metric* (Müller, 1997) defined as

$$\mathrm{MMD}(\mathcal{H}, P^*, P'^*) := \sup_{f \in \mathcal{H}} \left[\int f(\boldsymbol{x}) p^*(\boldsymbol{x}) \mathrm{d}\boldsymbol{x} - \int f(\boldsymbol{x}) p'^*(\boldsymbol{x}) \mathrm{d}\boldsymbol{x} \right],$$

where $\mathcal{H} : \mathbb{R}^d \to \mathbb{R}$ is some function class. When $\mathcal{H}$ is a unit ball in a *universal reproducing kernel Hilbert space* (universal RKHS; Steinwart, 2001) defined on a compact metric space, then $\mathrm{MMD}(\mathcal{H}, P^*, P'^*)$ vanishes if and only if $P^* = P'^*$. Gaussian RKHSs are examples of the universal RKHS.

Let $K(\boldsymbol{x},\boldsymbol{x}')$ be a reproducing kernel function. Then the reproducing property (Aronszajn, 1950) allows one to extract the value of a function $f \in \mathcal{H}$ at a point $\boldsymbol{x}$ by $f(\boldsymbol{x}) = \langle f, K(\cdot,\boldsymbol{x}) \rangle_{\mathcal{H}}$, where $\langle \cdot, \cdot \rangle_{\mathcal{H}}$ denotes the inner product in the RKHS $\mathcal{H}$. Let $\| \cdot \|_{\mathcal{H}}$ be the norm in $\mathcal{H}$. Then, one can explicitly express MMD in terms of the kernel function as

$$\begin{aligned}
&\mathrm{MMD}(\mathcal{H}, P^*, P'^*) \\
&= \sup_{\|f\|_{\mathcal{H}} \le 1} \left[\int \langle f, K(\cdot,\boldsymbol{x}) \rangle_{\mathcal{H}} p^*(\boldsymbol{x}) \mathrm{d}\boldsymbol{x} - \int \langle f, K(\cdot,\boldsymbol{x}) \rangle_{\mathcal{H}} p'^*(\boldsymbol{x}) \mathrm{d}\boldsymbol{x} \right] \\
&= \sup_{\|f\|_{\mathcal{H}} \le 1} \left\langle f, \int K(\cdot,\boldsymbol{x}) p^*(\boldsymbol{x}) \mathrm{d}\boldsymbol{x} - \int K(\cdot,\boldsymbol{x}) p'^*(\boldsymbol{x}) \mathrm{d}\boldsymbol{x} \right\rangle_{\mathcal{H}} \\
&= \left\| \int K(\cdot,\boldsymbol{x}) p^*(\boldsymbol{x}) \mathrm{d}\boldsymbol{x} - \int K(\cdot,\boldsymbol{x}) p'^*(\boldsymbol{x}) \mathrm{d}\boldsymbol{x} \right\|_{\mathcal{H}},
\end{aligned}$$

where the *Cauchy–Schwarz inequality* (Bachman and Narici, 2000) was used in the last equality. Furthermore, by using $K(\boldsymbol{x},\boldsymbol{x}') = \langle K(\cdot,\boldsymbol{x}), K(\cdot,\boldsymbol{x}') \rangle_{\mathcal{H}}$, the squared MMD can be expressed as

$$\begin{aligned}
\mathrm{MMD}^2(\mathcal{H}, P^*, P'^*) &= \left\| \int K(\cdot,\boldsymbol{x}) p^*(\boldsymbol{x}) \mathrm{d}\boldsymbol{x} - \int K(\cdot,\boldsymbol{x}) p'^*(\boldsymbol{x}) \mathrm{d}\boldsymbol{x} \right\|_{\mathcal{H}}^2 \\
&= \iint K(\boldsymbol{x},\boldsymbol{x}') p^*(\boldsymbol{x}) p^*(\boldsymbol{x}') \mathrm{d}\boldsymbol{x} \mathrm{d}\boldsymbol{x}' + \iint K(\boldsymbol{x},\boldsymbol{x}') p'^*(\boldsymbol{x}) p'^*(\boldsymbol{x}') \mathrm{d}\boldsymbol{x} \mathrm{d}\boldsymbol{x}' \\
&\quad - 2 \iint K(\boldsymbol{x},\boldsymbol{x}') p^*(\boldsymbol{x}) p'^*(\boldsymbol{x}) \mathrm{d}\boldsymbol{x} \mathrm{d}\boldsymbol{x}'.
\end{aligned}$$

This expression allows one to immediately obtain an empirical estimator – with i.i.d. samples $\mathcal{X} = \{\boldsymbol{x}_i\}_{i=1}^n$ following $p^*(\boldsymbol{x})$ and $\mathcal{X}' = \{\boldsymbol{x}'_j\}_{j=1}^{n'}$ following $p'^*(\boldsymbol{x})$, a consistent estimator of $\mathrm{MMD}^2(\mathcal{H}, P^*, P'^*)$ is given as

$$\begin{aligned}
\widehat{\mathrm{MMD}^2}(\mathcal{H}, \mathcal{X}, \mathcal{X}') &:= \frac{1}{n^2} \sum_{i,i'=1}^{n} K(\boldsymbol{x}_i,\boldsymbol{x}_{i'}) + \frac{1}{n'^2} \sum_{j,j'=1}^{n'} K(\boldsymbol{x}'_j,\boldsymbol{x}'_{j'}) \\
&\quad - \frac{2}{nn'} \sum_{i=1}^{n} \sum_{j=1}^{n'} K(\boldsymbol{x}_i,\boldsymbol{x}'_j).
\end{aligned}$$

By the same permutation test procedure as the one described in Section 10.2.4, one can compute p-values for $\widehat{\mathrm{MMD}^2}(\mathcal{H}, \mathcal{X}, \mathcal{X}')$. Furthermore, an asymptotic distribution of $\widehat{\mathrm{MMD}^2}(\mathcal{H}, \mathcal{X}, \mathcal{X}')$ under $P^* = P'^*$ can be obtained explicitly (Borgwardt et al., 2006; Gretton et al., 2007). This allows one to compute the p-values without resorting to the computationally intensive permutation procedure, which is an advantage of MMD over LSTT.

$\widehat{\mathrm{MMD}^2}(\mathcal{H}, \mathcal{X}, \mathcal{X}')$ depends on the choice of the universal RKHS $\mathcal{H}$. In the original MMD papers (Borgwardt et al., 2006; Gretton et al., 2007), the Gaussian RKHS with width set to the median distance between samples was used, which is a popular heuristic in the kernel method community (Schölkopf and Smola, 2002). Recently, an idea of using the universal RKHS yielding the maximum MMD value has been introduced (Sriperumbudur et al., 2009). In the experiments, we use this maximum MMD technique for choosing the universal RKHS, which was shown to work better than the median heuristic.

10.2.6 Numerical Examples

Here, the experimental performance of LSTT and MMD is compared.

We use binary classification datasets taken from the *IDA Repository* (Rätsch et al., 2001). For each dataset, we randomly split all the positive training samples into two disjoint sets, $\mathcal{X}$ and $\mathcal{X}'$, with $|\mathcal{X}| = |\mathcal{X}'|$.

We first investigate whether the test methods can correctly accept the null hypotheses (i.e., $\mathcal{X}$ and $\mathcal{X}'$ follow the same distribution). We use the Gaussian kernel both for LSTT and MMD. The Gaussian width and the regularization parameter in LSTT are determined by 5-fold cross-validation. The Gaussian width in MMD is chosen so that the MMD value is maximized. Because the permutation test procedures in LSTT and MMD are exactly the same, we are purely comparing the performance of the MMD and LSTT criteria in this experiment.

We investigate the rate of accepting the null hypothesis as functions of the relative sample size η for the significance level 0.05. The relative sample size η means that we use samples of size $\eta|\mathcal{X}|$ and $\eta|\mathcal{X}'|$ for homogeneity testing. The experimental results are plotted in Figure 10.9 by lines with "$\circ$" symbols. The results show that the both methods almost always accepted the null hypothesis correctly, meaning that the type I error (the rejection rate of correct null hypotheses, i.e., two distributions are judged to be different when they are actually the same) is small enough for both MMD and LSTT. However, MMD seems to perform slightly better than LSTT in terms of the type I error.

Next we replace a fraction of the samples in the set $\mathcal{X}'$ by randomly chosen negative training samples. Thus, while $\mathcal{X}$ contains only positive training samples, $\mathcal{X}'$ includes both positive and negative training samples. The experimental results are also plotted in Figure 10.9 by lines with "$\times$" symbols. The results show that LSTT tends to reject the null hypothesis more frequently than MMD for the *banana*, *ringnorm*, *splice*, *twonorm*, and *waveform* datasets. MMD works better than LSTT

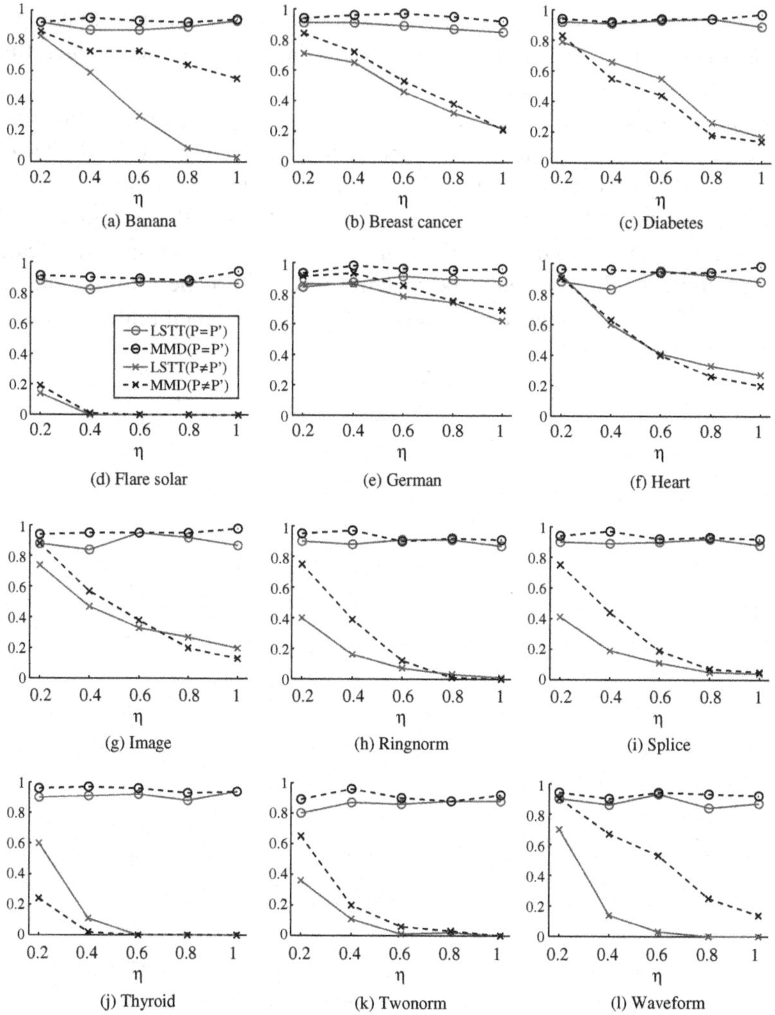

Figure 10.9. The rate of accepting the null hypothesis (i.e., $P^* = P'^*$) for IDA datasets under the significance level 0.05. η indicates the relative sample size we used in the experiments.

for the *thyroid* dataset, and the two methods are comparable for the other datasets. Overall, LSTT compares favorably with MMD in terms of the type II error (the acceptance rate of incorrect null-hypotheses, i.e., two distributions are judged to be the same when they are actually different).

10.2.7 Remarks

We explained a non-parametric method of testing homogeneity called the *least-squares two-sample test* (LSTT). Through experiments, the LSTT was shown to produce smaller type II error (the acceptance rate of incorrect null-hypotheses) than MMD, with a slightly larger type I error (the rejection rate of correct null hypotheses).

The performance of the LSTT relies on the accuracy of the density-ratio estimation. We adopted *unconstrained least-squares importance fitting* (uLSIF) because it possesses the optimal non-parametric convergence rate (Kanamori et al., 2011b) and optimal numerical stability (Kanamori et al., 2011c). uLSIF is computationally highly efficient thanks to the analytic-form solution, which is an attractive feature in the computationally demanding permutation test. Nevertheless, the permutation test is still time consuming, and hence speedup is an important future topic.

11

Mutual Information Estimation

For random variables $\boldsymbol{X}$ and $\boldsymbol{Y}$, *mutual information* (MI) is defined as follows[1] (Cover and Thomas, 2006):

$$\mathrm{MI}(\boldsymbol{X},\boldsymbol{Y}) := \iint p^*(\boldsymbol{x},\boldsymbol{y}) \log \frac{p^*(\boldsymbol{x},\boldsymbol{y})}{p^*(\boldsymbol{x})p^*(\boldsymbol{y})} \mathrm{d}\boldsymbol{x}\mathrm{d}\boldsymbol{y}. \tag{11.1}$$

MI can be regarded as the *Kullback–Leibler* (KL) divergence (Kullback and Leibler, 1951) from the joint density $p^*(\boldsymbol{x},\boldsymbol{y})$ to the product of marginals $p^*(\boldsymbol{x})p^*(\boldsymbol{y})$. This means that MI is zero if and only if

$$p^*(\boldsymbol{x},\boldsymbol{y}) = p^*(\boldsymbol{x})p^*(\boldsymbol{y}),$$

that is, $\boldsymbol{X}$ and $\boldsymbol{Y}$ are statistically independent. Therefore, MI can be used for detecting the statistical independence of random variables.

A variant of MI based on the *Pearson* (PE) divergence (Pearson, 1900) is given by

$$\mathrm{SMI}(\boldsymbol{X},\boldsymbol{Y}) := \frac{1}{2}\iint p^*(\boldsymbol{x})p^*(\boldsymbol{y}) \left(\frac{p^*(\boldsymbol{x},\boldsymbol{y})}{p^*(\boldsymbol{x})p^*(\boldsymbol{y})} - 1\right)^2 \mathrm{d}\boldsymbol{x}\mathrm{d}\boldsymbol{y}, \tag{11.2}$$

which is called the *squared-loss mutual information* (SMI). Similarly to MI, SMI is zero if and only if $\boldsymbol{X}$ and $\boldsymbol{Y}$ are statistically independent. Thus, SMI can also be used for detecting the statistical independence of random variables.

In this chapter we introduce methods of mutual information estimation based on density ratios and show their applications in machine learning. In Section 11.1, density-ratio methods of mutual information estimation are described. Then we show how the mutual information estimators may be utilized for solving *sufficient dimension reduction* (Suzuki and Sugiyama, 2010) in Section 11.2 and *independent component analysis* (Suzuki and Sugiyama, 2011) in Section 11.3. Note that

[1] To be precise, the density functions $p^*(\boldsymbol{x},\boldsymbol{y})$, $p^*(\boldsymbol{x})$, and $p^*(\boldsymbol{y})$ should have different names, e.g., $p^*_{\mathrm{XY}}(\boldsymbol{x},\boldsymbol{y})$, $p^*_{\mathrm{X}}(\boldsymbol{x})$, and $p^*_{\mathrm{Y}}(\boldsymbol{y})$. However, to simplify the notation, we use the same name p^* in this chapter.

the mutual information estimators can also be used for solving various machine learning tasks such as *independence testing* (Sugiyama and Suzuki, 2011), *variable selection* (Suzuki et al., 2009b), *clustering* (Kimura and Sugiyama, 2011; Sugiyama et al., 2011d), *object matching* (Yamada and Sugiyama, 2011a), and *causality learning* (Yamada and Sugiyama, 2010). For details, please refer to each reference.

11.1 Density-Ratio Methods of Mutual Information Estimation

In this section we describe methods of mutual information estimation based on density ratios. After an introduction in Section 11.1.1, we formulate the problem of mutual information estimation in Section 11.1.2. Then we describe an estimator of mutual information in Section 11.1.3 and an estimator of squared-loss mutual information in Section 11.1.4. The relation between density-ratio methods and other mutual information estimators is explained in Section 11.1.5, and numerical examples are provided in Section 11.1.6. Finally, the section is concluded in Section 11.1.7.

11.1.1 Introduction

A naive approach to estimating mutual information (MI) is to use nonparametric density estimation methods such as *kernel density estimation* (KDE; Fraser and Swinney, 1986); that is, the densities $p^*(\boldsymbol{x},\boldsymbol{y})$, $p^*(\boldsymbol{x})$, and $p^*(\boldsymbol{y})$ included in Eq. (11.1) are estimated separately from the samples, and the estimated densities are used for approximating MI. The bandwidth of the kernel functions may be optimized based on cross-validation (Härdle et al., 2004), and hence there is no open tuning parameter in this approach. However, density estimation is known to be a hard problem, and division by estimated densities tends to magnify the estimation error. Therefore, the KDE-based method may not be reliable in practice.

Another approach uses histogram-based density estimators with data-dependent partitions. In the context of estimating the KL divergence, histogram-based methods, which could be regarded as implicitly estimating the ratio $\frac{p^*(\boldsymbol{x},\boldsymbol{y})}{p^*(\boldsymbol{x})p^*(\boldsymbol{y})}$, have been studied thoroughly and their consistency has been established (Darbellay and Vajda, 1999; Wang et al., 2005; Silva and Narayanan, 2007). However, the rate of convergence seems to be unexplored at present, and such histogram-based methods seriously suffer from the *curse of dimensionality*. Thus, these methods may not be reliable in high-dimensional problems.

Based on the fact that MI can be expressed in terms of the entropies, the *nearest neighbor* distance has been used for approximating MI (Kraskov et al., 2004). Such a nearest neighbor approach was shown to perform better than the naive KDE-based approach (Khan et al., 2007), given that the number k of nearest neighbors is chosen appropriately – a small (large) k yields an estimator with a small (large) bias and a large (small) variance. However, appropriately determining the value of k so that the bias-variance trade-off is optimally controlled is not straightforward in the context of MI estimation. A similar nearest-neighbor idea has been applied to KL divergence estimation (Pérez-Cruz, 2008) in which consistency has been proved for finite k; this is an interesting result because KL divergence estimation is consistent even when density(-ratio) estimation is not consistent. However, the rate of convergence seems to still be an open research issue.

Approximating the entropies based on the *Edgeworth expansion* (EDGE) has also been explored in the context of MI estimation (Hulle, 2005). The EDGE method works well when the target density is close to Gaussian. However, if the target density is far from Gaussian, the EDGE method is no longer reliable.

In this section we consider an MI estimator based on the *KL importance estimation procedure* (KLIEP; Sugiyama et al., 2008; see also Chapter 5). This MI estimation method, called *maximum likelihood mutual information* (MLMI; Suzuki et al., 2008), can overcome the limitations of the previously mentioned approaches. MLMI does not involve density estimation but directly learns the density ratio

$$r^*(\boldsymbol{x},\boldsymbol{y}) := \frac{p^*(\boldsymbol{x},\boldsymbol{y})}{p^*(\boldsymbol{x})p^*(\boldsymbol{y})}$$

via maximum likelihood (ML) estimation.

Similarly, SMI defined by Eq. (11.2) can be estimated based on *unconstrained least-squares importance fitting* (uLSIF; Kanamori et al., 2009; see also Section 6.2.2). This SMI estimation method, called *least-squares mutual information* (LSMI; Suzuki et al., 2009b), provides an analytic-form SMI approximator that can be computed efficiently in the same way as uLSIF.

11.1.2 Problem Formulation

Here we formulate the problem of MI estimation.

Let $\mathcal{X} \subset \mathbb{R}^{d_x}$ and $\mathcal{Y} \subset \mathbb{R}^{d_y}$ be data domains, where d_x and d_y are the dimensionalities of $\mathcal{X}$ and $\mathcal{Y}$, respectively. Suppose we are given n independent and identically distributed (i.i.d.) paired samples

$$\{(\boldsymbol{x}_k,\boldsymbol{y}_k)\,|\,\boldsymbol{x}_k \in \mathcal{X},\ \boldsymbol{y}_k \in \mathcal{Y}\}_{k=1}^n$$

drawn from a joint distribution with density $p^*(\boldsymbol{x},\boldsymbol{y})$. Let $p^*(\boldsymbol{x})$ and $p^*(\boldsymbol{y})$ denote the marginal densities of $\boldsymbol{x}$ and $\boldsymbol{y}$, respectively. The goal is to estimate MI defined by Eq. (11.1) or SMI defined by Eq. (11.2) from the samples $\{(\boldsymbol{x}_k,\boldsymbol{y}_k)\}_{k=1}^n$.

In the methods described in the following, we estimate the density ratio $r^*(\boldsymbol{x},\boldsymbol{y})$ defined by

$$r^*(\boldsymbol{x},\boldsymbol{y}) := \frac{p^*(\boldsymbol{x},\boldsymbol{y})}{p^*(\boldsymbol{x})p^*(\boldsymbol{y})}.$$

Then MI can be approximated using a density-ratio estimator $\widehat{r}(\boldsymbol{x},\boldsymbol{y})$ as

$$\widehat{\mathrm{MI}}(\boldsymbol{X},\boldsymbol{Y}) := \frac{1}{n}\sum_{k=1}^{n}\log\widehat{r}(\boldsymbol{x}_k,\boldsymbol{y}_k). \tag{11.3}$$

Similarly, SMI can be approximated as

$$\widehat{\mathrm{SMI}}(\boldsymbol{X},\boldsymbol{Y}) := \frac{1}{2n}\sum_{k=1}^{n}\widehat{r}(\boldsymbol{x}_k,\boldsymbol{y}_k) - \frac{1}{2} \tag{11.4}$$

or

$$\widehat{\mathrm{SMI}}'(\boldsymbol{X},\boldsymbol{Y}) := -\frac{1}{2n}\sum_{k,k'=1}^{n}\widehat{r}(\boldsymbol{x}_k,\boldsymbol{y}_{k'})^2 + \frac{1}{n}\sum_{k'=1}^{n}\widehat{r}(\boldsymbol{x}_k,\boldsymbol{y}_k) - \frac{1}{2}, \tag{11.5}$$

where we use the fact that $\mathrm{SMI}(\boldsymbol{X},\boldsymbol{Y})$ can be equivalently expressed as

$$\begin{aligned}\mathrm{SMI}(\boldsymbol{X},\boldsymbol{Y}) &= \frac{1}{2}\iint p^*(\boldsymbol{x},\boldsymbol{y})r^*(\boldsymbol{x},\boldsymbol{y})\mathrm{d}\boldsymbol{x}\mathrm{d}\boldsymbol{y} - \frac{1}{2}\\ &= -\frac{1}{2}\iint p^*(\boldsymbol{x})p^*(\boldsymbol{y})r^*(\boldsymbol{x},\boldsymbol{y})^2\mathrm{d}\boldsymbol{x}\mathrm{d}\boldsymbol{y}\\ &\quad + \iint p^*(\boldsymbol{x},\boldsymbol{y})r^*(\boldsymbol{x},\boldsymbol{y})\mathrm{d}\boldsymbol{x}\mathrm{d}\boldsymbol{y} - \frac{1}{2}.\end{aligned}$$

11.1.3 Maximum Likelihood Mutual Information

Let us employ the *KL importance estimation procedure* (KLIEP; Sugiyama et al., 2008; see also Chapter 5) for learning the density-ratio model $r(\boldsymbol{x},\boldsymbol{y})$. The optimization criterion is given as follows:

$$\begin{aligned}&\max_{r}\ \frac{1}{n}\sum_{k=1}^{n}\log r(\boldsymbol{x}_k,\boldsymbol{y}_k)\\ &\text{s.t.}\ \frac{1}{n^2}\sum_{k,k'=1}^{n} r(\boldsymbol{x}_k,\boldsymbol{y}_{k'}) = 1 \text{ and } r(\boldsymbol{x},\boldsymbol{y}) \geq 0 \text{ for all } \boldsymbol{x},\boldsymbol{y}.\end{aligned}$$

Once a density-ratio estimator $\widehat{r}(\boldsymbol{x},\boldsymbol{y})$ is obtained, MI can be approximated by Eq. (11.3). This method is called *maximum likelihood mutual information* (MLMI; Suzuki et al., 2008).

As a density-ratio model $r(\boldsymbol{x},\boldsymbol{y})$, one may can choose from various models such as *linear/kernel* models (Section 5.2.1), *log-linear* models (Section 5.2.2), *Gaussian mixture* models (Section 5.2.3), and *probabilistic principal–component–analyzer mixture* models (Section 5.2.4).

A MATLAB® implementation of MLMI for linear/kernel models is available from http://sugiyama-www.cs.titech.ac.jp/~sugi/software/MLMI/.

11.1.4 Least-Squares Mutual Information

Let us employ *unconstrained least-squares importance fitting* (uLSIF; Kanamori et al., 2009; see also Section 6.2.2) for density-ratio estimation. We model the density ratio by a linear model:

$$r(\boldsymbol{x},\boldsymbol{y}) = \sum_{\ell=1}^{b} \theta_\ell \psi_\ell(\boldsymbol{x},\boldsymbol{y}) = \boldsymbol{\psi}(\boldsymbol{x},\boldsymbol{y})^\top \boldsymbol{\theta},$$

where $\boldsymbol{\psi}(\boldsymbol{x},\boldsymbol{y})$ ($\in \mathbb{R}^b$) is a non-negative basis function vector and $\boldsymbol{\theta}$ ($\in \mathbb{R}^b$) is a parameter vector. Let

$$\widehat{\boldsymbol{H}} := \frac{1}{n^2} \sum_{k,k'=1}^{n} \boldsymbol{\psi}(\boldsymbol{x}_k,\boldsymbol{y}_{k'})\boldsymbol{\psi}(\boldsymbol{x}_k,\boldsymbol{y}_{k'})^\top \quad \text{and} \quad \widehat{\boldsymbol{h}} := \frac{1}{n}\sum_{k=1}^{n} \boldsymbol{\psi}(\boldsymbol{x}_k,\boldsymbol{y}_k).$$

Then the uLSIF solution is given analytically as $\widehat{\boldsymbol{\theta}} = (\widehat{\boldsymbol{H}} + \lambda \boldsymbol{I}_b)^{-1}\widehat{\boldsymbol{h}}$, where λ (≥ 0) is the regularization parameter and $\boldsymbol{I}_b$ is the b-dimensional identity matrix.

Once a density-ratio estimator $\widehat{r}(\boldsymbol{x},\boldsymbol{y})$ is obtained, SMI can be approximated by Eq. (11.4) or Eq. (11.5). This method is called *least-squares mutual information* (LSMI; Suzuki et al., 2009b).

As basis functions one may use a Gaussian kernel model in the regression scenarios where $\boldsymbol{y}$ is continuous:

$$\psi_\ell(\boldsymbol{x},\boldsymbol{y}) = \exp\left(-\frac{\|\boldsymbol{x}-\boldsymbol{u}_\ell\|^2}{2\sigma^2}\right)\exp\left(-\frac{\|\boldsymbol{y}-\boldsymbol{v}_\ell\|^2}{2\sigma^2}\right),$$

where $\{(\boldsymbol{u}_\ell,\boldsymbol{v}_\ell)\}_{\ell=1}^{b}$ are Gaussian centers chosen randomly from $\{(\boldsymbol{x}_k,\boldsymbol{y}_k)\}_{k=1}^{n}$. In the classification scenario where $\boldsymbol{y}$ is categorical, the following Gaussian–delta kernel model would be useful:

$$\psi_\ell(\boldsymbol{x},\boldsymbol{y}) = \exp\left(-\frac{\|\boldsymbol{x}-\boldsymbol{u}_\ell\|^2}{2\sigma^2}\right)\delta(\boldsymbol{y}=\boldsymbol{v}_\ell),$$

where[2]

$$\delta(c) = \begin{cases} 1 & \text{if the condition } c \text{ is true,} \\ 0 & \text{otherwise.} \end{cases}$$

To these kernel basis functions we may also add a constant basis function $\psi_0(\boldsymbol{x},\boldsymbol{y}) = 1$.

A MATLAB® implementation of LSMI is available from http://sugiyama-www.cs.titech.ac.jp/~sugi/software/LSMI/.

11.1.5 Relation to Existing Methods

Here we discuss the characteristics of various approaches to mutual information estimation and a kernel-based independence measure.

[2] When the Gaussian-delta kernel is used, the matrix $\widehat{\boldsymbol{H}}$ becomes block-diagonal, given that the samples are sorted according to the class labels (Sugiyama et al., 2011d). Utilizing this block-diagonal structure, we can compute the solution $\widehat{\boldsymbol{\theta}} = (\widehat{\boldsymbol{H}} + \lambda \boldsymbol{I}_b)^{-1}\widehat{\boldsymbol{h}}$ more efficiently.

Kernel Density Estimation and Adaptive Histogram Methods

Kernel density estimation (KDE) is a non-parametric technique for estimating a density function $p^*(\boldsymbol{x})$ from its i.i.d. samples $\{\boldsymbol{x}_k\}_{k=1}^n$ (see Section 2.3.1). For the Gaussian kernel, KDE is expressed as

$$\widehat{p}(\boldsymbol{x}) = \frac{1}{n(2\pi\sigma^2)^{d_x/2}} \sum_{k=1}^{n} \exp\left(-\frac{\|\boldsymbol{x}-\boldsymbol{x}_k\|^2}{2\sigma^2}\right),$$

where d_x is the dimensionality of $\boldsymbol{x}$. The performance of KDE depends on the choice of the kernel width σ, and it can be optimized by *cross-validation* (see Section 2.3.3).

KDE-based estimations of MI can be performed using density estimators $\widehat{p}(\boldsymbol{x},\boldsymbol{y})$, $\widehat{p}(\boldsymbol{x})$, and $\widehat{p}(\boldsymbol{y})$ obtained from $\{(\boldsymbol{x}_k,\boldsymbol{y}_k)\}_{k=1}^n$, $\{\boldsymbol{x}_k\}_{k=1}^n$, and $\{\boldsymbol{y}_k\}_{k=1}^n$, respectively, as

$$\widehat{\mathrm{MI}}^{(\mathrm{KDE})}(\boldsymbol{X},\boldsymbol{Y}) := \frac{1}{n}\sum_{k=1}^{n} \log \frac{\widehat{p}(\boldsymbol{x}_k,\boldsymbol{y}_k)}{\widehat{p}(\boldsymbol{x}_k)\widehat{p}(\boldsymbol{y}_k)}.$$

However, density estimation is known to be a hard problem, and division by estimated densities may expand the estimation error. For this reason, the KDE-based approach may not be reliable in practice.

Histogram-based estimators with data-dependent partitions are more adaptive density estimation schemes. In the context of KL divergence estimation, the consistency properties of histogram-based methods, which may be regarded as implicitly estimating the ratio $\frac{p^*(\boldsymbol{x},\boldsymbol{y})}{p^*(\boldsymbol{x})p^*(\boldsymbol{y})}$, have been investigated in Wang et al. (2005) and Silva and Narayanan (2007). MI estimation following this line has been explored in Darbellay and Vajda (1999). However, such histogram-based methods may seriously suffer from the *curse of dimensionality*, and therefore they are not reliable in high-dimensional problems. Furthermore, the convergence rate seems to be unexplored as of yet.

Nearest Neighbor Method

If estimates of the entropies are obtained, MI can be estimated via the *MI–entropy identity* as

$$\mathrm{MI}(\boldsymbol{X},\boldsymbol{Y}) = H(\boldsymbol{X}) + H(\boldsymbol{Y}) - H(\boldsymbol{X},\boldsymbol{Y}),$$

where $H(\boldsymbol{X})$ denotes the entropy of $\boldsymbol{X}$:

$$H(\boldsymbol{X}) := -\int p^*(\boldsymbol{x}) \log p^*(\boldsymbol{x}) \mathrm{d}\boldsymbol{x}.$$

Thus, MI can be approximated if the entropies $H(\boldsymbol{X})$, $H(\boldsymbol{Y})$, and $H(\boldsymbol{X},\boldsymbol{Y})$ are estimated.

An entropy estimator that utilizes the nearest neighbor (NN) distance has been developed in Kraskov et al. (2004). Let us define the norm of $\boldsymbol{z} = (\boldsymbol{x},\boldsymbol{y})$ by

$\|z\|_z := \max\{\|x\|, \|y\|\}$, where $\|\cdot\|$ denotes the Euclidean norm. Let $\mathcal{N}_k(i)$ be the set of k-NN samples of $z_i = (x_i, y_i)$ with respect to the norm $\|\cdot\|_z$, and let

$$\epsilon_x(i) := \max\{\|x_i - x_j\| \mid (x_j, y_j) \in \mathcal{N}_k(i)\},$$

$$c_x(i) := |\{z_j \mid \|x_i - x_j\| \leq \epsilon_x(i)\}|,$$

$$\epsilon_y(i) := \max\{\|y_i - y_j\| \mid (x_j, y_j) \in \mathcal{N}_k(i)\},$$

$$c_y(i) := |\{z_j \mid \|y_i - y_j\| \leq \epsilon_y(i)\}|.$$

Then the NN-based MI estimator is given by

$$\widehat{\mathrm{MI}}^{(k\text{-NN})}(X, Y) := \Psi(k) + \Psi(n) - \frac{1}{k} - \frac{1}{n}\sum_{i=1}^{n}\Big[\Psi(c_x(i)) + \Psi(c_y(i))\Big],$$

where Ψ is the *digamma* function.

An advantage of the NN-based method is that it does not simply replace entropies with their estimates; it is designed to cancel the error of individual entropy estimates. A practical drawback of the NN-based approach is that the estimation accuracy depends on the value of k, and there seems to be no systematic strategy for choosing the value of k appropriately. Faivishevsky and Goldberger (2009, 2010) proposed taking the average over all k, by which an explicit choice of k becomes no longer necessary. Although this smoothed estimator was shown to work well in some cases, its theoretical validity is not clear.

Recently, a KL divergence estimator utilizing NN density estimation (see Section 2.3.2) was proposed in Pérez-Cruz (2008), and its consistency has been investigated. A notable property of this estimator is that the consistency of the density estimation is not necessary to establish the consistency of the KL divergence estimator. However, the rate of convergence still seems to be an open research issue.

Edgeworth Expansion Method

An entropy estimator based on the *Edgeworth (EDGE) expansion* was proposed in Hulle (2005). The basic idea is to approximate the entropy by that of the normal distribution and some additional higher order correction terms. More specifically, for a d-dimensional distribution, an estimator $\widehat{H}$ of the entropy H is given by

$$\widehat{H} = H_{\text{normal}} - \sum_{i=1}^{d}\frac{\kappa_{i,i,i}^2}{12} - \sum_{i,j=1, i\neq j}^{d}\frac{\kappa_{i,i,j}^2}{4} - \sum_{i,j,k=1, i<j<k}^{d}\frac{\kappa_{i,j,k}^2}{72},$$

where H_{normal} is the entropy of the normal distribution with a covariance matrix equal to the target distribution and $\kappa_{i,j,k}$ $(1 \leq i, j, k \leq d)$ is the standardized third cumulant of the target distribution. An estimate of MI can be obtained via the MI–entropy identity as

$$\widehat{\mathrm{MI}}^{(\text{EDGE})}(X, Y) := \widehat{H}(X) + \widehat{H}(Y) - \widehat{H}(X, Y).$$

In practice, all the cumulants should be estimated from samples.

If the underlying distribution is close to normal, the above approximation is accurate and the EDGE-based method works well. However, if the distributions are far from the normal distribution, the approximation error becomes large, and therefore the EDGE-based method is no longer reliable.

In principle, it is possible to include the fourth and even higher cumulants for reducing the estimation bias further. However, this in turn increases the estimation variance.

Hilbert–Schmidt Independence Criterion

We now describe a kernel-based independence measure called the *Hilbert–Schmidt independence criterion* (HSIC; Gretton et al., 2005, 2008), which is based on characteristic functions (see also Feuerverger, 1993; Kankainen, 1995).

Let $\mathcal{F}$ be a *reproducing kernel Hilbert space* (RKHS) with reproducing kernel $K(\boldsymbol{x},\boldsymbol{x}')$ (Aronszajn, 1950), and let $\mathcal{G}$ be another RKHS with reproducing kernel $L(\boldsymbol{y},\boldsymbol{y}')$. Let C_{xy} be a *cross-covariance operator* from $\mathcal{G}$ to $\mathcal{F}$, which is defined such that, for all $f \in \mathcal{F}$ and $g \in \mathcal{G}$,

$$\langle f, C_{\mathrm{xy}} g\rangle_{\mathcal{F}} = \iint \left(\left[f(\boldsymbol{x}) - \int f(\boldsymbol{x}) p^*(\boldsymbol{x})\mathrm{d}\boldsymbol{x}\right]\right.$$
$$\left. \times \left[g(\boldsymbol{y}) - \int g(\boldsymbol{y}) p^*(\boldsymbol{y})\mathrm{d}\boldsymbol{y}\right]\right) p^*(\boldsymbol{x},\boldsymbol{y})\mathrm{d}\boldsymbol{y}\mathrm{d}\boldsymbol{y},$$

where $\langle\cdot,\cdot\rangle_{\mathcal{F}}$ denotes the inner product in $\mathcal{F}$. Thus, C_{xy} can be expressed as

$$C_{\mathrm{xy}} := \iint \left(\left[K(\cdot,\boldsymbol{x}) - \int K(\cdot,\boldsymbol{x}) p^*(\boldsymbol{x})\mathrm{d}\boldsymbol{x}\right]\right.$$
$$\left. \otimes \left[L(\cdot,\boldsymbol{y}) - \int L(\cdot,\boldsymbol{y}) p^*(\boldsymbol{y})\mathrm{d}\boldsymbol{y}\right]\right) p^*(\boldsymbol{x},\boldsymbol{y})\mathrm{d}\boldsymbol{x}\mathrm{d}\boldsymbol{y},$$

where $\otimes$ denotes the *tensor product*, and we use the reproducing properties:

$$f(\boldsymbol{x}) = \langle f, K(\cdot,\boldsymbol{x})\rangle_{\mathcal{F}} \quad \text{and} \quad g(\boldsymbol{y}) = \langle g, L(\cdot,\boldsymbol{y})\rangle_{\mathcal{G}}.$$

The cross-covariance operator is a generalization of the *cross-covariance matrix* between random vectors. When $\mathcal{F}$ and $\mathcal{G}$ are *universal RKHSs* (Steinwart, 2001) defined on compact domains $\mathcal{X}$ and $\mathcal{Y}$, respectively, the largest singular value of C_{xy} is zero if and only if $\boldsymbol{x}$ and $\boldsymbol{y}$ are independent. Gaussian RKHSs are examples of the universal RKHS.

HSIC is defined as the the squared *Hilbert–Schmidt norm* (the sum of the squared singular values) of the cross-covariance operator C_{xy}:

$$\mathrm{HSIC}(P_{\mathrm{xy}}) := \iiiint K(\boldsymbol{x},\boldsymbol{x}')L(\boldsymbol{y},\boldsymbol{y}')p^*(\boldsymbol{x},\boldsymbol{y})p^*(\boldsymbol{x}',\boldsymbol{y}')\mathrm{d}\boldsymbol{x}\mathrm{d}\boldsymbol{y}\mathrm{d}\boldsymbol{x}\mathrm{d}\boldsymbol{y}'$$
$$+\left[\iint K(\boldsymbol{x},\boldsymbol{x}')p^*(\boldsymbol{x})p^*(\boldsymbol{x}')\mathrm{d}\boldsymbol{x}\mathrm{d}\boldsymbol{x}'\right]\left[\iint L(\boldsymbol{y},\boldsymbol{y}')p^*(\boldsymbol{y})p^*(\boldsymbol{y}')\mathrm{d}\boldsymbol{y}\mathrm{d}\boldsymbol{y}'\right]$$

$$-2\iint\left[\int K(\boldsymbol{x},\boldsymbol{x}')p^*(\boldsymbol{x}')\mathrm{d}\boldsymbol{x}'\right]\left[\int L(\boldsymbol{y},\boldsymbol{y}')p^*(\boldsymbol{y}')\mathrm{d}\boldsymbol{y}'\right]p^*(\boldsymbol{x},\boldsymbol{y})\mathrm{d}\boldsymbol{x}\mathrm{d}\boldsymbol{y}.$$

This expression allows one to obtain immediately an empirical estimator; with the i.i.d. samples $\mathcal{Z} = \{(\boldsymbol{x}_k,\boldsymbol{y}_k)\}_{k=1}^n$ following $p^*(\boldsymbol{x},\boldsymbol{y})$, a consistent estimator of $\mathrm{HSIC}(P_{\mathrm{xy}})$ is given as

$$\begin{aligned}\widehat{\mathrm{HSIC}}(\mathcal{Z}) &:= \frac{1}{n^2}\sum_{i,i'=1}^{n} K(\boldsymbol{x}_i,\boldsymbol{x}_{i'})L(\boldsymbol{y}_i,\boldsymbol{y}_{i'}) \\ &\quad + \frac{1}{n^4}\sum_{i,i',j,j'=1}^{n} K(\boldsymbol{x}_i,\boldsymbol{x}_{i'})L(\boldsymbol{y}_j,\boldsymbol{y}_{j'}) \\ &\quad - \frac{2}{n^3}\sum_{i,j,k=1}^{n} K(\boldsymbol{x}_i,\boldsymbol{x}_k)L(\boldsymbol{y}_j,\boldsymbol{y}_k) \\ &= \frac{1}{n^2}\mathrm{tr}(\boldsymbol{K}\boldsymbol{\Gamma}\boldsymbol{L}\boldsymbol{\Gamma}),\end{aligned}$$

where $\boldsymbol{K}_{i,i'} = K(\boldsymbol{x}_i,\boldsymbol{x}_{i'})$, $\boldsymbol{L}_{j,j'} = L(\boldsymbol{y}_i,\boldsymbol{y}_{i'})$, $\boldsymbol{\Gamma} = \boldsymbol{I}_n - \frac{1}{n}\boldsymbol{1}_n\boldsymbol{1}_n^\top$, $\boldsymbol{I}_n$ denotes the n-dimensional identity matrix, and $\boldsymbol{1}_n$ denotes the n-dimensional vector with all ones. Note that $\boldsymbol{\Gamma}$ corresponds to the "centering" matrix in the RKHS.

$\widehat{\mathrm{HSIC}}$ depends on the choice of the universal RKHSs $\mathcal{F}$ and $\mathcal{G}$. In the original HSIC papers (Gretton et al., 2005, 2008), the Gaussian RKHS with width set to the median distance between samples was used, which is a popular heuristic in the kernel method community (Schölkopf and Smola, 2002). However, there is no theoretical justification for this. On the other hand, the density-ratio methods are equipped with cross-validation, and thus all the tuning parameters such as the Gaussian width and the regularization parameter can be optimized in an objective and systematic way.

11.1.6 Numerical Examples

Here we experimentally illustrate the behavior of the MI estimators described in the previous subsection.

The task is to estimate MI between $x \in \mathbb{R}$ and $y \in \mathbb{R}$. We use the following four datasets (see Figure 11.1):

(a) Linear dependence: Y has a linear dependence on x as

$$X \sim N\left(0,\tfrac{1}{2}\right) \quad \text{and} \quad Y|X \sim N(3X,1),$$

where $N(\mu,\sigma^2)$ denotes the normal distribution with mean μ and variance σ^2.

(b) Non-linear dependence 1: Y has a quadratic dependence on X as

$$X \sim N(0,1) \quad \text{and} \quad Y|X \sim N(X^2,1).$$

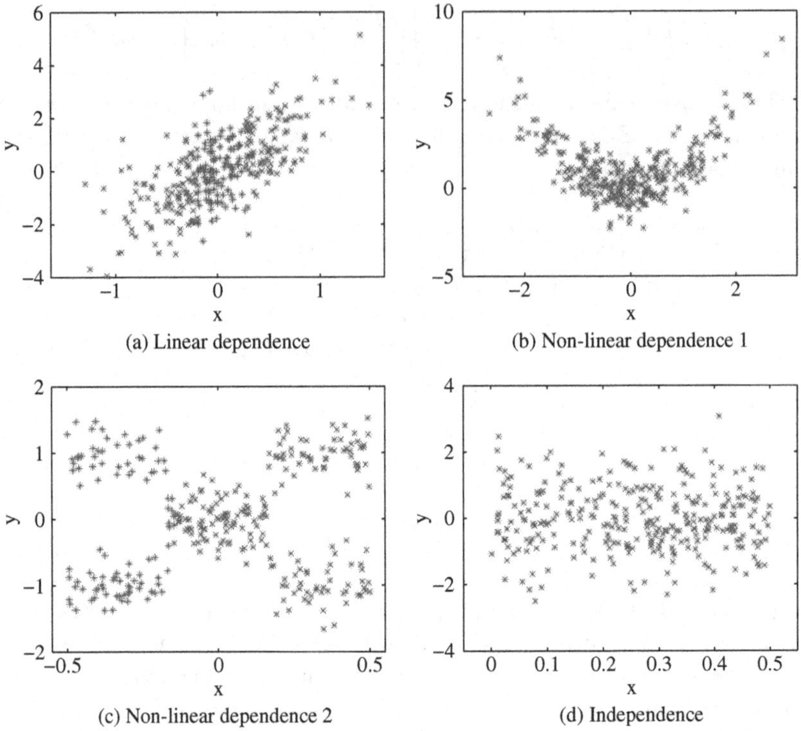

Figure 11.1. Datasets used in experiments.

(c) Non-linear dependence 2: Y has a lattice-structured dependence on X as

$$X \sim U\left(-\tfrac{1}{2}, \tfrac{1}{2}\right),$$

$$Y|X \sim \begin{cases} N\left(0, \frac{1}{3}\right) & \text{if } X \leq \left|\frac{1}{6}\right|, \\ \frac{1}{2}N\left(1, \frac{1}{3}\right) + \frac{1}{2}N\left(-1, \frac{1}{3}\right) & \text{otherwise,} \end{cases}$$

where $U(a,b)$ denotes the uniform distribution on (a,b).

(d) Independence: X and Y are independent each other as

$$Y \sim U\left(0, \tfrac{1}{2}\right) \quad \text{and} \quad Y|X \sim N(0,1).$$

We compare MLMI (with 5-fold cross-validation), KDE (with 5-fold cross-validation), KNN (with $k = 1, 5, 15$), and EDGE; the approximation error of an MI estimate $\widehat{\text{MI}}$ is measured by

$$\text{Error} := |\widehat{\text{MI}} - \text{MI}|.$$

Figure 11.2 depicts the approximation error averaged over 100 trials as a function of the sample size n. The symbol '$\circ$' on a line means that the corresponding method is the best in terms of the average error or is judged to be comparable to the best method by the *t-test* (Henkel, 1976) at the 1% significance level.

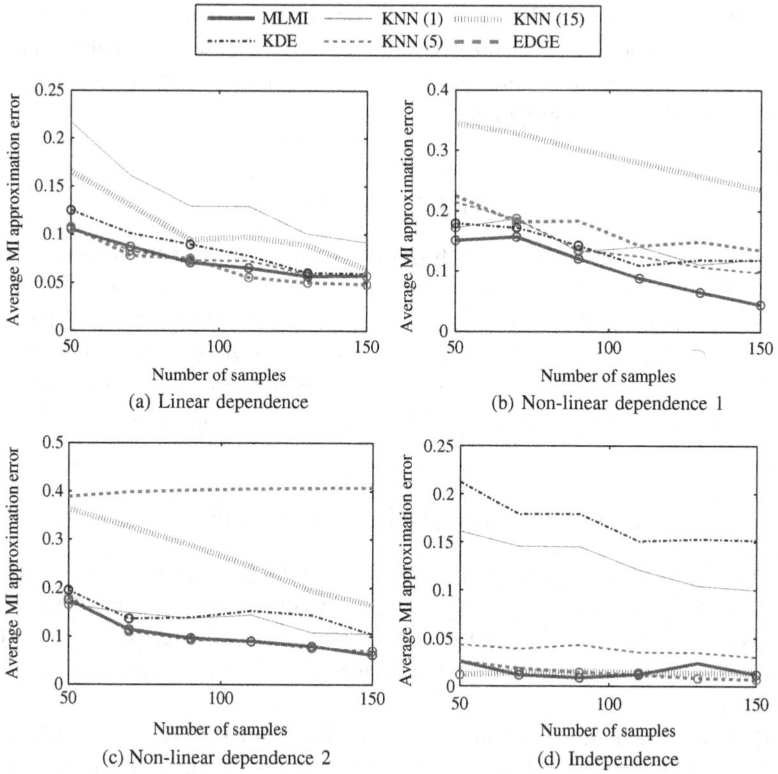

Figure 11.2. MI approximation error measured by $|\widehat{\mathrm{MI}} - \mathrm{MI}|$ averaged over 100 trials as a function of the sample size n. The symbol "o" on a line means that the corresponding method is the best in terms of the average error or is judged to be comparable to the best method by the t-test at the 1% significance level.

Figure 11.2 shows that (a), MLMI, KDE, KNN with $k = 5$, and EDGE perform well on the dataset (b), MLMI tends to outperform the other estimators on the dataset (c), MLMI and KNN with $k = 5$ show the best performance against the other methods on the dataset, and (d) MLMI, EDGE, and KNN with $k = 15$ perform well on the dataset.

KDE works moderately well on datasets (a)–(c) and performs poorly on dataset (d). This instability may be ascribed to division by estimated densities, which tends to magnify the estimation error. KNN seems to work well on all four datasets if the value of k is chosen optimally. However, there is no systematic model selection strategy for KNN (see Section 11.1.5), and hence KNN would be unreliable in practice. EDGE works well on datasets (a), (b), and (d), which posses high normality.[3] However, on dataset (c), where the normality of the target

[3] Note that, although the Edgeworth approximation is exact when the target distributions are precisely normal, the EDGE method still suffers from some estimation error because cumulants are estimated from samples.

distributions is low, the EDGE method performs poorly. In contrast, MLMI with cross-validation performs reasonably well for all four datasets in a stable manner.

These experimental results show that MLMI nicely compensates for the weaknesses of the other methods.

11.1.7 Remarks

In this section we described methods of mutual information approximation based on density-ratio estimation. The density-ratio methods have several useful properties; for example, they are single-shot procedures, density estimation is not involved, they are equipped with a cross-validation procedure for model selection, and the unique global solution can be computed efficiently. The numerical experiments illustrate the usefulness of the density-ratio approaches.

11.2 Sufficient Dimension Reduction

Feature selection is aimed at finding a subset of input features and *feature extraction* is aimed at finding a subspace (i.e., linear combinations) of input features. In this section we describe a particular framework of feature extraction called *sufficient dimension reduction* and describe a method based on density-ratio estimation.

After an introduction in Section 11.2.1, we formulate the problem of sufficient dimension reduction in Section 11.2.2. A sufficient dimension reduction method based on LSMI, called *least-squares dimension reduction* (LSDR; Suzuki and Sugiyama, 2010) is described in Section 11.2.3. Numerical examples are provided in Section 11.2.4, and the section is concluded in Section 11.2.5.

11.2.1 Introduction

The purpose of *dimension reduction* in supervised learning is to find a low-dimensional subspace of input features that has "sufficient" information for predicting output values. Supervised dimension reduction methods can be categorized broadly into two types – *wrappers* and *filters* (Guyon and Elisseeff, 2003). The wrapper approach performs dimension reduction specifically for a particular predictor, while the filter approach is independent of the choice of successive predictors.

If one wants to enhance the prediction accuracy, the wrapper approach is a suitable choice because predictors' characteristics can be taken into account in the dimension reduction phase. On the other hand, if one wants to interpret dimension-reduced features (e.g., in bioinformatics, computational chemistry, or brain-signal analysis), the filter approach is more appropriate because the extracted features are independent of the choice of successive predictors and therefore reliable in terms of interpretability. Here we focus on the filter approach.

A standard formulation of filter-type dimension reduction is *sufficient dimension reduction* (SDR), which is aimed at finding a low-rank projection matrix such that, given the relevant subspace of input features, the rest becomes conditionally independent of output values (Cook, 1998b; Chiaromonte and Cook, 2002; Li and Lu, 2008; Cook and Forzani, 2009; Fukumizu et al., 2009). A traditional dependency measure between random variables is the *Pearson correlation coefficient* (PCC). PCC can be used for detecting linear dependency, and hence it is useful for Gaussian data. However, the Gaussian assumption is rarely fulfilled in practice.

Recently, kernel-based dimension reduction has been studied to overcome the weakness of PCC. The *Hilbert–Schmidt independence criterion* (HSIC; Gretton et al., 2005; see also Section 11.1.5) utilizes *cross-covariance operators* on *universal* reproducing kernel Hilbert spaces (RKHSs; Steinwart, 2001). HSIC allows one to efficiently detect non-linear dependency by making use of the reproducing properties of RKHSs (Aronszajn, 1950), and its usefulness in feature selection scenarios has been demonstrated in Song et al. (2007b). However, HSIC has several weaknesses both theoretically and practically. Theoretically, HSIC evaluates the independence of random variables, not *conditional* independence. Thus, HSIC does not perform SDR in a strict sense. From a practical point of view, HSIC evaluates the covariance between random variables, not the correlation. This means that the change of input feature scaling affects the dimension reduction solution, which is not preferable in practice.

Kernel dimension reduction (KDR; Fukumizu et al., 2004) can overcome these weaknesses. KDR evaluates the *conditional covariance* using the kernel trick. Therefore, KDR directly performs SDR. KDR was demonstrated to outperform other dimension reduction schemes such as *canonical correlation analysis* (Hotelling, 1936), *partial least squares* (Wold, 1966; Goutis and Fearn, 1996; Durand and Sabatier, 1997; Reiss and Ogden, 2007), *sliced inverse regression* (Li, 1991; Bura and Cook, 2001; Cook and Ni, 2005; Zhu et al., 2006), and the *principal Hessian direction* (Li, 1992; Cook, 1998a; Li et al., 2000). The theoretical properties of KDR such as consistency have been studied thoroughly (Fukumizu et al., 2009). However, KDR still has a weakness in practice – the performance of KDR (and HSIC) depends on the choice of kernel parameters (e.g., the Gaussian width) and the regularization parameter. So far, there seems to be no systematic model selection method for KDR and HSIC.[4]

Another possible criterion for SDR is *mutual information* (MI; Cover and Thomas, 2006). MI may be employed directly in the context of SDR because maximizing MI between the output and a projected input leads to conditional

[4] In principle, it is possible to choose the Gaussian width and the regularization parameter by cross-validation (CV) over a successive predictor. However, this is not preferable for the following two reasons. The first is a significant increase of the computational cost. When CV is used, the tuning parameters in KDR (or HSIC) and hyperparameters in the target predictor (such as basis parameters and the regularization parameter) should be optimized at the same time. This results in a deeply nested CV procedure, and therefore this could be computationally very expensive. Another reason is that features extracted based on CV over a successive predictor are no longer independent of predictors. Thus, a merit of the filter approach (i.e., the obtained features are "reliable") is lost.

Table 11.1. Summary of existing and proposed dependency measures.

Methods	Non-linear dependence	Model selection	Distribution	Density estimation	Feature extraction
PCC	Not detectable	**Not necessary**	Gaussian	**Not involved**	**Possible**
HSIC	**Detectable**	Not available	**Free**	**Not involved**	**Possible**
KDR	**Detectable**	Not available	**Free**	**Not involved**	**Possible**
HIST	**Detectable**	**Available**	**Free**	Involved	Not available
KDE	**Detectable**	**Available**	**Free**	Involved	**Possible**
NN	**Detectable**	Not available	**Free**	**Not involved**	Not available
EDGE	**Detectable**	**Not necessary**	Near Gaussian	**Not involved**	**Possible**
MLMI	**Detectable**	**Available**	**Free**	**Not involved**	Not available
LSMI	**Detectable**	**Available**	**Free**	**Not involved**	**Possible**

independence of the output and input given the projected input. So far, a great deal of effort has been made to estimate MI accurately, as described in Section 11.1. MLMI has been shown to possess various practical advantages, as summarized in Table 11.1.

Thus, we want to employ the MLMI method for dimension reduction. However, this is not straightforward because the MLMI estimator is not explicit, that is, the MLMI estimator is defined implicitly as the solution of an optimization problem and is computed numerically. In the dimension reduction scenarios, the projection matrix needs to be optimized over an MI approximator. To cope with this problem, we adopt the *squared-loss MI* (SMI) defined by Eq. (11.2) as our independence measure and use its approximator *least-squares MI* (LSMI; see Section 11.1.4) for dimension reduction here. LSMI inherits the good properties of MLMI, and moreover it provides an *analytic* SMI estimator (see Table 11.1).

11.2.2 Problem Formulation

Here we formulate the problem of *sufficient dimension reduction* (SDR; Cook, 1998b; Chiaromonte and Cook, 2002; Li and Lu, 2008; Cook and Forzani, 2009; Fukumizu et al., 2009).

Let $\mathcal{X}$ ($\subset \mathbb{R}^d$) be the domain of input feature $\boldsymbol{x}$, and let $\mathcal{Y}$ be the domain of output data[5] $\boldsymbol{y}$. Let m ($\in \{1,\ldots,d\}$) be the dimensionality of the sufficient subspace. To search the sufficient subspace, we utilize the *Grassmann manifold* $\mathrm{Gr}_m^d(\mathbb{R})$, which is the set of all m-dimensional subspaces in $\mathbb{R}^d$ defined as

$$\mathrm{Gr}_m^d(\mathbb{R}) := \{\boldsymbol{W} \in \mathbb{R}^{m\times d} \mid \boldsymbol{W}\boldsymbol{W}^\top = \boldsymbol{I}_m\}/\sim, \tag{11.6}$$

where $^\top$ denotes the transpose, $\boldsymbol{I}_m$ is the m-dimensional identity matrix, and "$/\sim$" means that matrices sharing the same range are regarded as equivalent.

Let $\boldsymbol{W}^*$ be a projection matrix corresponding to a member of the Grassmann manifold Gr_m^d, and let $\boldsymbol{z}^*$ ($\in \mathbb{R}^m$) be the orthogonal projection of input $\boldsymbol{x}$ given by $\boldsymbol{W}^*$:

$$\boldsymbol{z}^* = \boldsymbol{W}^*\boldsymbol{x}.$$

Suppose that $\boldsymbol{z}^*$ satisfies

$$\boldsymbol{y} \perp\!\!\!\perp \boldsymbol{x} \mid \boldsymbol{z}^*. \tag{11.7}$$

That is, given the projected feature $\boldsymbol{z}^*$, the (remaining) feature $\boldsymbol{x}$ is conditionally independent of output $\boldsymbol{y}$ and thus can be discarded without sacrificing the predictability of $\boldsymbol{y}$.

Suppose that we are given n i.i.d. paired samples

$$\mathcal{D} = \{(\boldsymbol{x}_k, \boldsymbol{y}_k) \mid \boldsymbol{x}_k \in \mathcal{X},\ \boldsymbol{y}_k \in \mathcal{Y}\}_{k=1}^n$$

drawn from a joint distribution with density $p^*(\boldsymbol{x},\boldsymbol{y})$. The goal of SDR is, from data $\mathcal{D}$, to find a projection matrix whose range agrees with that of $\boldsymbol{W}^*$. For a projection matrix $\boldsymbol{W}$ ($\in \mathrm{Gr}_m^d(\mathbb{R})$) we write $\boldsymbol{z}_k = \boldsymbol{W}\boldsymbol{x}_k$. We assume that the reduced dimensionality m is known throughout this section.

11.2.3 Least-Squares Dimension Reduction

Here we describe a method of SDR based on least-squares density-ratio estimation.

Characterization of Sufficient Subspace by SMI

A direct approach to SDR is to determine $\boldsymbol{W}$ so that Eq. (11.7) is fulfilled. To this end, we adopt SMI as our criterion to be maximized with respect to $\boldsymbol{W}$:

$$\mathrm{SMI}(Y,Z) := \frac{1}{2}\int \left(\frac{p^*(\boldsymbol{y},\boldsymbol{z})}{p^*(\boldsymbol{y})p^*(\boldsymbol{z})} - 1\right)^2 p^*(\boldsymbol{y})p^*(\boldsymbol{z})\mathrm{d}\boldsymbol{y}\mathrm{d}\boldsymbol{z},$$

where $p^*(\boldsymbol{y},\boldsymbol{z})$ denotes the joint density of $\boldsymbol{y}$ and $\boldsymbol{z}$, and $p^*(\boldsymbol{y})$ and $p^*(\boldsymbol{z})$ denote the marginal densities of $\boldsymbol{y}$ and $\boldsymbol{z}$, respectively. $\mathrm{SMI}(Y,Z)$ allows one to evaluate the independence of $\boldsymbol{y}$ and $\boldsymbol{z}$ because $\mathrm{SMI}(Y,Z)$ vanishes if and only if

$$p^*(\boldsymbol{y},\boldsymbol{z}) = p^*(\boldsymbol{y})p^*(\boldsymbol{z}).$$

[5] $\mathcal{Y}$ can be multi-dimensional and either continuous (i.e., regression) or categorical (i.e., classification); structured outputs such as strings, trees, and graphs can also be handled in our framework, as long as kernel functions for structured data are available.

The rationale behind the use of SMI in the context of SDR relies on the following lemma.

Lemma 11.1 (Suzuki and Sugiyama, 2010) *Let $p^*(x,y|z)$, $p^*(x|z)$, and $p^*(y|z)$ be conditional densities. Then we have*

$$\begin{aligned}&\mathrm{SMI}(\boldsymbol{X},\boldsymbol{Y}) - \mathrm{SMI}(\boldsymbol{Z},\boldsymbol{Y})\\&= \frac{1}{2}\int\left(1-\frac{p^*(\boldsymbol{x},\boldsymbol{y}|\boldsymbol{z})}{p^*(\boldsymbol{x}|\boldsymbol{z})p^*(\boldsymbol{y}|\boldsymbol{z})}\right)^2 \frac{p^*(\boldsymbol{y},\boldsymbol{z})^2 p^*(\boldsymbol{x})}{p^*(\boldsymbol{z})^2 p^*(\boldsymbol{y})}\mathrm{d}\boldsymbol{x}\mathrm{d}\boldsymbol{y} \geq 0.\end{aligned}$$

Lemma 11.1 implies

$$\mathrm{SMI}(\boldsymbol{X},\boldsymbol{Y}) \geq \mathrm{SMI}(\boldsymbol{Z},\boldsymbol{Y}),$$

and the equality holds if and only if

$$p^*(\boldsymbol{x},\boldsymbol{y}|\boldsymbol{z}) = p^*(\boldsymbol{x}|\boldsymbol{z})p^*(\boldsymbol{y}|\boldsymbol{z}),$$

which is equivalent to Eq. (11.7). Thus, Eq. (11.7) can be achieved by maximizing $\mathrm{SMI}(\boldsymbol{Z},\boldsymbol{Y})$ with respect to $\boldsymbol{W}$; then the "sufficient" subspace can be identified.

SMI Approximation by LSMI

We want to find the projection matrix $\boldsymbol{W}$ that maximizes $\mathrm{SMI}(\boldsymbol{Z},\boldsymbol{Y})$. However, SMI is inaccessible in practice because densities $p^*(\boldsymbol{y},\boldsymbol{z})$, $p^*(\boldsymbol{y})$, and $p^*(\boldsymbol{z})$ are unknown. Thus, SMI needs to be estimated from data samples.

Here we use LSMI (see Section 11.1.4) for SMI approximation. An LSMI-based SMI estimator, $\widehat{\mathrm{SMI}}(\boldsymbol{Z},\boldsymbol{Y})$, is given as

$$\widehat{\mathrm{SMI}}(\boldsymbol{Z},\boldsymbol{Y}) = \widehat{\boldsymbol{h}}^\top\widehat{\boldsymbol{\theta}} - \frac{1}{2}\widehat{\boldsymbol{\theta}}^\top\widehat{\boldsymbol{H}}\widehat{\boldsymbol{\theta}} - \frac{1}{2},$$

where, for b being the number of basis functions used in LSMI, $\widehat{\boldsymbol{\theta}}$ $(\in\mathbb{R}^b)$, $\widehat{\boldsymbol{h}}$ $(\in\mathbb{R}^b)$, and $\widehat{\boldsymbol{H}}$ $(\in\mathbb{R}^{b\times b})$ are given by

$$\widehat{\boldsymbol{\theta}} = (\widehat{\boldsymbol{H}} + \lambda\boldsymbol{I}_b)^{-1}\widehat{\boldsymbol{h}}, \quad \widehat{h}_\ell = \frac{1}{n}\sum_{k=1}^{n}\phi_\ell^{\mathrm{y}}(\boldsymbol{y}_k)\phi_\ell^{\mathrm{y}}(\boldsymbol{z}_k),$$

$$\widehat{H}_{\ell,\ell'} = \frac{1}{n^2}\left(\sum_{k=1}^{n}\phi_\ell^{\mathrm{y}}(\boldsymbol{y}_k)\phi_{\ell'}^{\mathrm{y}}(\boldsymbol{y}_k)\right)\left(\sum_{k'=1}^{n}\phi_\ell^{\mathrm{z}}(\boldsymbol{z}_{k'})\phi_{\ell'}^{\mathrm{z}}(\boldsymbol{z}_{k'})\right),$$

$$\phi_\ell^{\mathrm{y}}(\boldsymbol{y}) = \begin{cases}\exp\left(-\frac{\|\boldsymbol{y}-\boldsymbol{u}_\ell\|^2}{2\sigma^2}\right) & \text{(regression)},\\ \delta(\boldsymbol{y}=\boldsymbol{u}_\ell) & \text{(classification)},\end{cases}$$

$$\phi_\ell^{\mathrm{z}}(\boldsymbol{z}) = \exp\left(-\frac{\|\boldsymbol{z}-\boldsymbol{v}_\ell\|^2}{2\sigma^2}\right), \quad \delta(c) = \begin{cases}1 & \text{if the condition } c \text{ is true},\\ 0 & \text{otherwise}.\end{cases}$$

λ (≥ 0) is the regularization parameter, σ is the kernel width, and $\{(\boldsymbol{u}_\ell,\boldsymbol{v}_\ell)\}_{\ell=1}^b$ are Gaussian centers chosen randomly from $\{(\boldsymbol{y}_k,\boldsymbol{z}_k)\}_{i=1}^n$; more precisely, we set

$\boldsymbol{u}_\ell := \boldsymbol{y}_{\tau(\ell)}$ and $\boldsymbol{v}_\ell := \boldsymbol{z}_{\tau(\ell)}$, where $\{\tau(\ell)\}_{\ell=1}^{b}$ are randomly chosen from $\{1,\ldots,n\}$ without replacement.

Sufficient Subspace Search

Finally, we show how LSMI is employed for dimension reduction. Because $\boldsymbol{W}$ is a projection matrix, dimension reduction involves an optimization problem over the Grassmann manifold $\mathrm{Gr}_m^d(\mathbb{R})$ [see Eq. (11.6)]. Here we employ a gradient ascent algorithm to find the maximizer of the LSMI approximator with respect to $\boldsymbol{W}$. After a few lines of calculations, we can show that the gradient is given by

$$\frac{\partial \widehat{\mathrm{SMI}}}{\partial W_{j,i}} = \frac{\partial \widehat{\boldsymbol{h}}^\top}{\partial W_{j,i}}(2\widehat{\boldsymbol{\theta}} - \widehat{\boldsymbol{\xi}}) - \widehat{\boldsymbol{\theta}}^\top \frac{\partial \widehat{\boldsymbol{H}}}{\partial W_{j,i}}\left(\frac{3}{2}\widehat{\boldsymbol{\theta}} - \widehat{\boldsymbol{\xi}}\right),$$

where, for $\boldsymbol{w}_\ell = (w_\ell^{(1)},\ldots,w_\ell^{(d)})^\top := \boldsymbol{x}_{\tau(\ell)}$,

$$\widehat{\boldsymbol{\xi}} = (\widehat{\boldsymbol{H}} + \lambda \boldsymbol{I}_b)^{-1}\widehat{\boldsymbol{H}}\widehat{\boldsymbol{\theta}},$$

$$\frac{\partial \widehat{h}_\ell}{\partial W_{j,i}} = -\frac{1}{n\sigma^2}\sum_{k=1}^{n}(z_k^{(j)} - v_\ell^{(j)})(x_k^{(i)} - w_\ell^{(i)})\exp\left(-\frac{\|\boldsymbol{z}_k - \boldsymbol{v}_{\ell'}\|^2}{2\sigma^2}\right)\phi_\ell^{\mathrm{y}}(\boldsymbol{y}_k),$$

$$\frac{\partial \widehat{H}_{\ell,\ell'}}{\partial W_{j,i}} = \left[\frac{1}{n}\sum_{k=1}^{n}\phi_\ell^{\mathrm{y}}(\boldsymbol{y}_k)\phi_{\ell'}^{\mathrm{y}}(\boldsymbol{y}_k)\right] \times \left[-\frac{1}{n\sigma^2}\sum_{k=1}^{n}\Big((z_k^{(j)} - v_\ell^{(j)})(x_k^{(i)} - w_\ell^{(i)}) + (z_k^{(j)} - v_{\ell'}^{(j)})(x_k^{(i)} - w_{\ell'}^{(i)})\Big) \times \exp\left(-\frac{\|\boldsymbol{z}_k - \boldsymbol{v}_\ell\|^2 + \|\boldsymbol{z}_k - \boldsymbol{v}_{\ell'}\|^2}{2\sigma^2}\right)\right].$$

In the Euclidean space, the ordinary gradient $\frac{\partial \widehat{\mathrm{SMI}}}{\partial \boldsymbol{W}}$ gives the steepest direction. However, on a manifold, the *natural gradient* (Amari, 1998) gives the steepest direction. The natural gradient $\nabla\widehat{\mathrm{SMI}}(\boldsymbol{W})$ is the projection of the ordinary gradient $\frac{\partial \widehat{\mathrm{SMI}}}{\partial \boldsymbol{W}}$ to the tangent space of the Grassmann manifold $\mathrm{Gr}_m^d(\mathbb{R})$ at $\boldsymbol{W}$. If the tangent space is equipped with the canonical metric $\langle \boldsymbol{G}_1, \boldsymbol{G}_2\rangle = \frac{1}{2}\mathrm{tr}(\boldsymbol{G}_1^\top \boldsymbol{G}_2)$, the natural gradient is given as follows (Edelman et al., 1998):

$$\nabla\widehat{\mathrm{SMI}}(\boldsymbol{W}) = \frac{\partial \widehat{\mathrm{SMI}}}{\partial \boldsymbol{W}} - \frac{\partial \widehat{\mathrm{SMI}}}{\partial \boldsymbol{W}}\boldsymbol{W}^\top \boldsymbol{W} = \frac{\partial \widehat{\mathrm{SMI}}}{\partial \boldsymbol{W}}\boldsymbol{W}_\perp^\top \boldsymbol{W}_\perp, \tag{11.8}$$

where $\boldsymbol{W}_\perp$ is any $(d-m)\times d$ matrix such that $[\boldsymbol{W}^\top\ \boldsymbol{W}_\perp^\top]$ is orthogonal. Then the *geodesic* from $\boldsymbol{W}$ to the direction of the natural gradient $\nabla\widehat{\mathrm{SMI}}(\boldsymbol{W})$ over $\mathrm{Gr}_d^m(\mathbb{R})$ can be expressed using t $(\in \mathbb{R})$ as

$$\boldsymbol{W}_t := \begin{bmatrix}\boldsymbol{I}_d & \boldsymbol{O}_{d-m}\end{bmatrix}\exp\left(t\begin{bmatrix}\boldsymbol{O}_m & \frac{\partial \widehat{\mathrm{SMI}}}{\partial \boldsymbol{W}}\boldsymbol{W}_\perp^\top \\ -\boldsymbol{W}_\perp \frac{\partial \widehat{\mathrm{SMI}}}{\partial \boldsymbol{W}}^\top & \boldsymbol{O}_{d-m}\end{bmatrix}\right)\begin{bmatrix}\boldsymbol{W} \\ \boldsymbol{W}_\perp\end{bmatrix},$$

where "exp" for a matrix denotes the *matrix exponential*; that is, for a square matrix $\boldsymbol{D}$, $\exp(\boldsymbol{D}) = \sum_{k=0}^{\infty}\frac{1}{k!}\boldsymbol{D}^k$. $\boldsymbol{O}_d$ is the $d\times d$ matrix with all zeros. Note that the derivative $\partial_t \boldsymbol{W}_t|_{t=0}$ coincides with the natural gradient (11.8); see Edelman et al. (1998) for a detailed derivation of the geodesic. Thus, line search along the

1. Initialize projection matrix $\boldsymbol{W}$.
2. Optimize Gaussian width σ and regularization parameter λ by CV.
3. Update $\boldsymbol{W}$ by $\boldsymbol{W} \leftarrow \boldsymbol{W}_t$, where t denotes the step size.
4. Repeat 2 and 3 until $\boldsymbol{W}$ converges.

Figure 11.3. The LSDR algorithm.

geodesic in the natural gradient direction is equivalent to finding the maximizer from $\{\boldsymbol{W}_t \mid t \geq 0\}$. For choosing the step size of each gradient update, we may use some approximate line search method such as *Armijo's rule* (Patriksson, 1999) or *backtracking line search* (Boyd and Vandenberghe, 2004).

The LSMI-based sufficient dimension reduction algorithm is called *least-squares dimension reduction* (LSDR). The entire algorithm is summarized in Figure 11.3. A MATLAB® implementation of LSDR is available from http://sugiyama-www.cs.titech.ac.jp/~sugi/software/LSDR/.

11.2.4 Numerical Examples

Here we experimentally investigate the performance of dimension reduction methods. In LSDR, Gaussian kernels are used as basis functions. We fix the number of basis functions to $b = \min(100, n)$ and choose the Gaussian width σ and the regularization parameter λ based on 5-fold CV with a grid search in terms of the density-ratio estimation error. We restart the natural gradient algorithm 10 times with random initial points, and choose the one that has the minimum CV score.

We use the following six artificial datasets (see Figure 11.4):

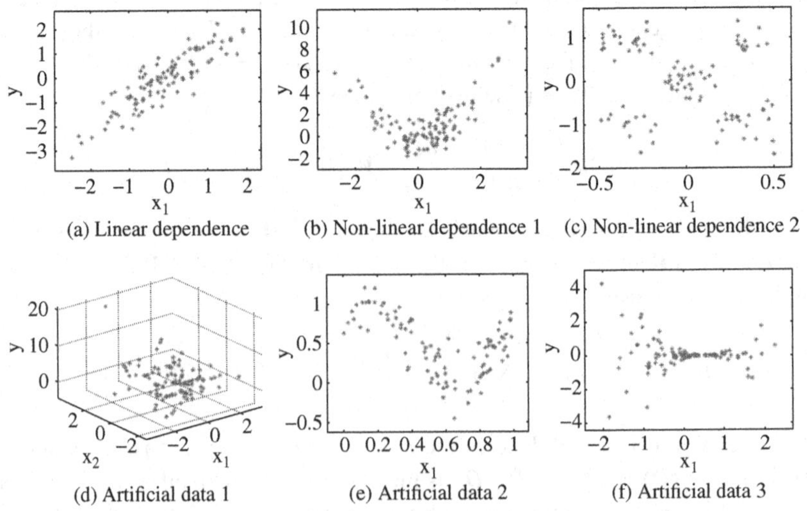

(a) Linear dependence (b) Non-linear dependence 1 (c) Non-linear dependence 2

(d) Artificial data 1 (e) Artificial data 2 (f) Artificial data 3

Figure 11.4. Artificial datasets.

(a) Linear dependence: $d = 5$ and $m = 1$: y has a linear dependence on $\boldsymbol{x}$ as

$$y = x^{(1)} + \epsilon, \quad \boldsymbol{x} \sim N(\boldsymbol{x}; \boldsymbol{0}_5, \boldsymbol{I}_5), \quad \text{and} \quad \epsilon \sim N\left(y; 0, \tfrac{1}{4}\right).$$

$x^{(i)}$ denotes the i-th element of the vector $\boldsymbol{x}$, $N(\boldsymbol{x}; \boldsymbol{\mu}, \boldsymbol{\Sigma})$ denotes the multivariate normal density with mean $\boldsymbol{\mu}$ and covariance matrix $\boldsymbol{\Sigma}$, $\boldsymbol{0}_d$ denotes the d-dimensional vector with all zeros, and $\boldsymbol{I}_d$ denotes the d-dimensional identity matrix. The optimal projection is given by $\boldsymbol{W}^* = (1\ 0\ 0\ 0\ 0)$.

(b) Non-linear dependence 1: $d = 5$ and $m = 1$. y has a quadratic dependence on $\boldsymbol{x}$ as

$$y = (x^{(1)})^2 + \epsilon, \quad \boldsymbol{x} \sim N(\boldsymbol{x}; \boldsymbol{0}_5, \boldsymbol{I}_5), \quad \text{and} \quad \epsilon \sim N(y; 0, 1).$$

The optimal projection is given by $\boldsymbol{W}^* = (1\ 0\ 0\ 0\ 0)$.

(c) Non-linear dependence 2: $d = 5$ and $m = 1$. y has a lattice-structured dependence on $\boldsymbol{x}$ as

$$\boldsymbol{x} \sim U(\boldsymbol{x}; [-\tfrac{1}{2}, \tfrac{1}{2}]^5)$$

$$y|\boldsymbol{x} \sim \begin{cases} N(y; 0, \frac{1}{4}) & \text{if } x^{(1)} \leq |\frac{1}{6}|, \\ \frac{1}{2}N(y; 1, \frac{1}{4}) + \frac{1}{2}N(y; -1, \frac{1}{4}) & \text{otherwise,} \end{cases}$$

where $U(\boldsymbol{x}; \mathcal{S})$ denotes the uniform density on the set $\mathcal{S}$. The optimal projection is given by $\boldsymbol{W}^* = (1\ 0\ 0\ 0\ 0)$.

(d) Artificial data 1: $d = 4$ and $m = 2$. y has a non-linear dependence on $\boldsymbol{x}$ as

$$y = \frac{x^{(1)}}{0.5 + (x^{(2)} + 1.5)^2} + (1 + x^{(2)})^2 + 0.4\epsilon,$$

$$\boldsymbol{x} \sim N(\boldsymbol{x}; \boldsymbol{0}_4, \boldsymbol{I}_4), \quad \text{and} \quad \epsilon \sim N(1; 0, 1).$$

The optimal projection is $\boldsymbol{W}^* = \begin{pmatrix} 1 & 0 & 0 & 0 \\ 0 & 1 & 0 & 0 \end{pmatrix}$.

(e) Artificial data 2: $d = 4$ and $m = 1$. y has a non-linear dependence on $\boldsymbol{x}$ as

$$y = \sin^2(\pi x^{(1)} + 1) + 0.4\epsilon,$$

$$\boldsymbol{x} \sim U(\boldsymbol{x}; [0, 1]^4 \setminus \{\boldsymbol{x} \in \mathbb{R}^4 \mid x^{(i)} \leq 0.7\ (i = 1, \ldots, 4)\}),$$

$$\epsilon \sim N(1; 0, 1).$$

The optimal projection is $\boldsymbol{W}^* = (1\ 0\ 0\ 0)$.

(f) Artificial data 3: $d = 10$ and $m = 1$. y has a non-linear dependence on $\boldsymbol{x}$ as

$$y = 0.5(x^{(1)} - 1)^2\epsilon, \quad \boldsymbol{x} \sim N(\boldsymbol{x}; \boldsymbol{0}_{10}, \boldsymbol{I}_{10}), \quad \text{and} \quad \epsilon \sim N(1; 0, 1).$$

The optimal projection is $\boldsymbol{W}^* = (1\ 0\ \cdots\ 0)$.

Let us compare the following methods.

- Least-squares dimension reduction (LSDR)
- Kernel dimension reduction (KDR; Fukumizu et al., 2009)

- The Hilbert–Schmidt independence criterion (HSIC; Gretton et al., 2005; see also Section 11.1.5)
- Sliced inverse regression (SIR; Li, 1991)
- Sliced average variance estimation (SAVE; Cook, 2000)
- Principal Hessian direction (Li, 1992, pHd)

In KDR and HSIC, the Gaussian width is set to the median sample distance, following the suggestions in the original papers (Fukumizu et al., 2009; Gretton et al., 2005). We use the dimension reduction package *dr* included in R for SIR, SAVE, and pHd. The principal directions estimated by SIR, SAVE, and pHd do not necessarily form an orthogonal system; that is, the matrix $\boldsymbol{F}$, each row of which corresponds to each principal direction, is not necessarily a projection matrix. To recover a projection matrix $\boldsymbol{W}$, we perform a singular decomposition of $\boldsymbol{F}$ as $\boldsymbol{F} = \boldsymbol{VSU}$ and set $\boldsymbol{W} = \boldsymbol{U}$.

We evaluate the performance of each method by

$$\|\widehat{\boldsymbol{W}}^\top \widehat{\boldsymbol{W}} - \boldsymbol{W}^{*\top} \boldsymbol{W}^*\|_{\text{Frobenius}}, \tag{11.9}$$

where $\|\cdot\|_{\text{Frobenius}}$ denotes the Frobenius norm, $\widehat{\boldsymbol{W}}$ is an estimated projection matrix, and $\boldsymbol{W}^*$ is an optimal projection matrix.

The performance of each method is summarized in Table 11.2, which describes the mean and standard deviation of the Frobenius-norm error (11.9) over 50 trials when the number of samples is $n = 100$. LSDR shows overall good performance; in particular, it performs the best for datasets (b), (c), and (e). KDR also tends to work reasonably well but it sometimes performs poorly; this seems to be caused by an inappropriate choice of the Gaussian kernel width, implying that the heuristic of using the median sample distance as the kernel width is not always appropriate. On the other hand, LSDR with CV performs stably well for various types of datasets.

Table 11.2. Mean (and standard deviation in the bracket) of the Frobenius-norm error (11.9) for toy datasets. The best method in terms of the mean error and comparable ones based on the t-test at the significance level 1% are indicated by boldface.

Dataset	d	m	LSDR	KDR	HSIC	SIR	SAVE	pHd
(a)	5	1	**.13(.05)**	**.13(.05)**	.17(.06)	**.11(.05)**	.37(.27)	.89(.12)
(b)	5	1	**.18(.14)**	**.23(.14)**	.35(.27)	.83(.19)	.31(.11)	.24(.07)
(c)	5	1	**.12(.05)**	.37(.31)	.70(.32)	.89(.14)	.48(.20)	.86(.12)
(d)	4	2	**.19(.10)**	**.16(.06)**	.19(.07)	.30(.15)	.44(.18)	.50(.18)
(e)	4	1	**.08(.05)**	.13(.04)	.17(.12)	.21(.10)	.34(.19)	.36(.14)
(f)	10	1	**.34(.11)**	**.37(.11)**	.45(.13)	.68(.22)	.91(.13)	.83(.12)

11.2.5 Remarks

In this section we described a method of sufficient dimension reduction (SDR) called *least-squares dimension reduction* (LSDR) that utilizes *least-squares mutual information* (LSMI). The LSDR method is advantageous over other approaches in several respects; for example, density estimation is not involved, it is distribution-free, and model selection by cross-validation is available. The numerical experiments show the usefulness of LSDR.

Although the LSMI solution is given analytically, sufficient subspace search involves non-convex optimization and the natural gradient method is still computationally demanding. Thus, improving the computation cost for a sufficient subspace search is an important future work. A heuristic for LSMI maximization is studied in Yamada et al. (2011c).

11.3 Independent Component Analysis

The purpose of *independent component analysis* (ICA; Hyvärinen et al., 2001) is to obtain a transformation matrix that separates mixed signals into statistically independent source signals. A direct approach to ICA is to find a transformation matrix such that the independence of separated signals is maximized under some independence measure such as *mutual information* (MI).

In this section we describe an ICA algorithm, called *least-squares ICA* (LICA; Suzuki and Sugiyama, 2011), that is based on *least-squares mutual information* (LSMI; see Section 11.1.4). After an introduction in Section 11.3.1, the ICA problem is formulated in Section 11.3.2. The LICA algorithm is described in Section 11.3.3, and numerical examples are shown in Section 11.3.4. Finally, the section is concluded in Section 11.3.5.

11.3.1 Introduction

Various approaches to evaluating the independence of random variables from samples have been explored so far. A naive approach is to estimate probability densities based on parametric or non-parametric density estimation methods. However, finding an appropriate parametric model is not easy without strong prior knowledge, and non-parametric estimation is not accurate in high-dimensional problems. Thus, this naive approach is not reliable in practice. Another approach is to approximate the *negentropy* (or negative entropy) based on the *Gram–Charlier expansion* (Cardoso and Souloumiac, 1993; Comon, 1994; Amari et al., 1996) or the *Edgeworth expansion* (Hulle, 2008). An advantage of this negentropy-based approach is that the hard task of density estimation is not directly involved. However, these expansion techniques are based on the assumption that the target density is close to normal and violation of this assumption can cause large approximation errors.

These approaches are based on the probability densities of signals. Another line of research that does not explicitly involve probability densities employs

Table 11.3. Summary of existing and proposed ICA methods.

	Hyperparameter selection	Distribution
Fast ICA (FICA) (Hyvaerinen, 1999)	**Not Necessary**	Not Free
Natural-gradient ICA (NICA) (Amari et al., 1996)	**Not Necessary**	Not Free
Kernel ICA (KICA) (Bach and Jordan, 2002)	Not Available	**Free**
Edgeworth-expansion ICA (EICA) (Hulle, 2008)	**Not Necessary**	Nearly normal
Least-squares ICA (LICA) (Suzuki and Sugiyama, 2011).	**Available**	**Free**

non-linear correlations – signals are statistically independent if and only if all non-linear correlations among the signals vanish. Following this line, computationally efficient algorithms have been developed based on a *contrast function* (Jutten and Herault, 1991; Hyvaerinen, 1999), which is an approximation of negentropy or mutual information. However, these methods require one to pre-specify non-linearities in the contrast function, and thus could be inaccurate if the predetermined non-linearities do not match the target distribution. To cope with this problem, the *kernel trick* (Schölkopf and Smola, 2002) has been applied in ICA, allowing one to evaluate all non-linear correlations in a computationally efficient manner (Bach and Jordan, 2002). However, its practical performance depends on the choice of kernels (more specifically, the Gaussian kernel width), and there seems to be no theoretically justified method to determine the kernel width (see also Fukumizu et al., 2009). This is a critical problem in *unsupervised learning* problems such as ICA.

In this section we describe an ICA algorithm based on density ratio estimation that can resolve the previously mentioned problems. The method is called *least-squares ICA* (LICA; Suzuki and Sugiyama, 2011). Characteristics of ICA methods are summarized in Table 11.3, highlighting the advantage of the LICA approach.

11.3.2 Problem Formulation

Suppose there is a d-dimensional random signal $\boldsymbol{x} = (x^{(1)},\dots,x^{(d)})^\top$ drawn from a distribution with density $p^*(\boldsymbol{x})$, where $x^{(1)},\dots,x^{(d)}$ are statistically independent of each other. Thus, $p^*(\boldsymbol{x})$ can be factorized as

$$p^*(\boldsymbol{x}) = p_1^*(x^{(1)}) \times \cdots \times p_d^*(x^{(d)}).$$

We cannot directly observe the *source* signal $\boldsymbol{x}$, but only a linearly mixed signal $\boldsymbol{y}$:

$$\boldsymbol{y} = (y^{(1)},\dots,y^{(d)})^\top := \boldsymbol{A}\boldsymbol{x},$$

where $\boldsymbol{A}$ is a $d \times d$ invertible matrix called the *mixing matrix*. The goal of ICA is, given samples of the mixed signals $\{\boldsymbol{y}_k\}_{k=1}^n$, to obtain a *demixing matrix* $\boldsymbol{W}$ that recovers the original source signal $\boldsymbol{x}$. We denote the demixed signal by $\boldsymbol{z}$:

$$\boldsymbol{z} = \boldsymbol{W}\boldsymbol{y}.$$

The ideal solution is $\boldsymbol{W} = \boldsymbol{A}^{-1}$, but we can only recover the source signals up to the permutation and scaling of components of $\boldsymbol{x}$ because of the *non-identifiability* of the ICA setup (Hyvärinen et al., 2001).

11.3.3 Least-Squares Independent Component Analysis

A direct approach to ICA is to determine $\boldsymbol{W}$ so that the components of $\boldsymbol{z}$ are as independent as possible. Here we adopt SMI as the independence measure:

$$\mathrm{SMI}(Z^{(1)}, \ldots, Z^{(d)}) := \frac{1}{2} \int \left(\frac{q^*(\boldsymbol{z})}{r^*(\boldsymbol{z})} - 1 \right)^2 r^*(\boldsymbol{z}) \mathrm{d}\boldsymbol{z}, \tag{11.10}$$

where $q^*(\boldsymbol{z})$ denotes the joint density of $\boldsymbol{z}$ and $r^*(\boldsymbol{z})$ denotes the product of marginal densities $q_1^*(z^{(1)}), \ldots, q_d^*(z^{(d)})$:

$$r^*(\boldsymbol{z}) = q_1^*(z^{(1)}) \times \cdots \times q_d^*(z^{(d)}).$$

SMI Approximation by LSMI

We want to find the demixing matrix $\boldsymbol{W}$ that minimizes $\mathrm{SMI}(Z^{(1)}, \ldots, Z^{(d)})$. However, SMI is inaccessible in practice because the densities $q^*(\boldsymbol{z})$ and $r^*(\boldsymbol{z})$ are unknown. Thus, SMI needs to be estimated from data samples.

Let us denote the demixed samples by

$$\{\boldsymbol{z}_k \mid \boldsymbol{z}_k = (z_k^{(1)}, \ldots, z_k^{(d)})^\top := \boldsymbol{W}\boldsymbol{y}_k\}_{k=1}^n.$$

Here we use LSMI (see Section 11.1.4) for SMI approximation. An LSMI-based SMI estimator, $\widehat{\mathrm{SMI}}(Z^{(1)}, \ldots, Z^{(d)})$, is given as

$$\widehat{\mathrm{SMI}}(Z^{(1)}, \ldots, Z^{(d)}) = \frac{1}{2} \widehat{\boldsymbol{h}}^\top \widehat{\boldsymbol{\theta}} - \frac{1}{2},$$

where

$$\widehat{\boldsymbol{\theta}} = (\widehat{\boldsymbol{H}} + \lambda \boldsymbol{I}_b)^{-1} \widehat{\boldsymbol{h}}, \quad \widehat{h}_\ell = \frac{1}{n} \sum_{k=1}^n \prod_{i=1}^d \exp\left(-\frac{(z_k^{(i)} - v_\ell^{(i)})^2}{2\sigma^2} \right),$$

$$\text{and} \quad \widehat{H}_{\ell,\ell'} = \frac{1}{n^d} \prod_{i=1}^d \left[\sum_{k=1}^n \exp\left(-\frac{(z_k^{(i)} - v_\ell^{(i)})^2 + (z_k^{(i)} - v_{\ell'}^{(i)})^2}{2\sigma^2} \right) \right].$$

b is the number of basis functions used in LSMI, and $\boldsymbol{I}_b$ denotes the b-dimensional identity matrix. Note that $\widehat{\boldsymbol{\theta}}$ and $\widehat{\boldsymbol{h}}$ are b-dimensional vectors and $\widehat{\boldsymbol{H}}$ is a $b \times b$ matrix. λ (≥ 0) is the regularization parameter in LSMI, σ is the kernel width, and

$\{\boldsymbol{v}_\ell | \boldsymbol{v}_\ell = (v_\ell^{(1)}, \ldots, v_\ell^{(d)})^\top\}_{\ell=1}^b$ are Gaussian centers randomly chosen from $\{\boldsymbol{z}_k\}_{k=1}^n$; more precisely, we set $\boldsymbol{v}_\ell := \boldsymbol{z}_{\tau(\ell)}$, where $\{\tau(\ell)\}_{\ell=1}^b$ are randomly chosen from $\{1, \ldots, n\}$ without replacement.

In the following we explain two algorithms, which are called *least-squares ICA* (LICA), for obtaining a minimizer of $\widehat{\text{SMI}}$ with respect to the demixing matrix $\boldsymbol{W}$– one is based on a *plain gradient* method (which is referred to as *PG-LICA*), and the other is based on a *natural gradient* method for whitened samples (which is referred to as *NG-LICA*). A MATLAB® implementation of LICA is available from http://www.simplex.t.u-tokyo.ac.jp/~s-taiji/software/LICA/.

Plain Gradient Algorithm: PG-LICA

Based on the plain gradient technique, an update rule of $\boldsymbol{W}$ is given by

$$\boldsymbol{W} \longleftarrow \boldsymbol{W} - \varepsilon \frac{\partial \widehat{\text{SMI}}}{\partial \boldsymbol{W}}, \tag{11.11}$$

where ε (> 0) is the step size. The gradient is given by

$$\frac{\partial \widehat{\text{SMI}}}{\partial W_{i,i'}} = \frac{\partial \widehat{\boldsymbol{h}}^\top}{\partial W_{i,i'}} \widehat{\boldsymbol{\theta}} - \frac{1}{2} \widehat{\boldsymbol{\theta}}^\top \frac{\partial \widehat{\boldsymbol{H}}}{\partial W_{i,i'}} \widehat{\boldsymbol{\theta}}, \tag{11.12}$$

where, for $\boldsymbol{u}_\ell = (u_\ell^{(1)}, \ldots, u_\ell^{(d)})^\top = \boldsymbol{y}_{\tau(\ell)}$ and $\boldsymbol{y}_k = (y_k^{(1)}, \ldots, y_k^{(d)})^\top$,

$$\frac{\partial \widehat{h}_\ell}{\partial W_{i,i'}} = -\frac{1}{n\sigma^2} \sum_{k=1}^n (z_k^{(i)} - v_\ell^{(i)})(y_k^{(i')} - u_\ell^{(i')}) \exp\left(-\frac{\|\boldsymbol{z}_k - \boldsymbol{v}_{i'}\|^2}{2\sigma^2}\right),$$

$$\begin{aligned}
\frac{\partial \widehat{H}_{\ell,\ell'}}{\partial W_{i,i'}} &= \frac{1}{n^{d-1}} \prod_{i'' \neq i} \left[\sum_{k=1}^n \exp\left(-\frac{(z_k^{(i'')} - v_\ell^{(i'')})^2 + (z_k^{(i'')} - v_{\ell'}^{(i'')})^2}{2\sigma^2}\right)\right] \\
&\quad \times \left[-\frac{1}{n\sigma^2} \sum_{k=1}^n \Big((z_k^{(i)} - v_\ell^{(i)})(y_k^{(i')} - u_\ell^{(i')}) + (z_k^{(i)} - v_{\ell'}^{(i)})(y_k^{(i')} - u_{\ell'}^{(i')})\Big)\right. \\
&\quad \left. \times \exp\left(-\frac{(z_k^{(i)} - v_\ell^{(i)})^2 + (z_k^{(i)} - v_{\ell'}^{(i)})^2}{2\sigma^2}\right)\right].
\end{aligned}$$

In ICA, the scale of components of $\boldsymbol{z}$ can be arbitrary. This implies that the above gradient updating rule can lead to a solution with poor scaling, which is not preferable from a numerical point of view. To avoid possible numerical instability, we normalize $\boldsymbol{W}$ at each gradient iteration as

$$W_{i,i'} \longleftarrow \frac{W_{i,i'}}{\sqrt{\sum_{i''=1}^d W_{i,i''}^2}}. \tag{11.13}$$

In practice, we may iteratively perform line searches along the gradient and optimize the Gaussian width σ and the regularization parameter λ by cross-validation (CV). A pseudo code of the PG-LICA algorithm is summarized in Figure 11.5.

1. Initialize demixing matrix $\boldsymbol{W}$ and normalize it by Eq. (11.13).
2. Optimize Gaussian width σ and regularization parameter λ by CV.
3. Compute gradient $\frac{\partial \widehat{\mathrm{SMI}}}{\partial \boldsymbol{W}}$ by Eq. (11.12).
4. Choose step-size t so that $\widehat{\mathrm{SMI}}$ [see Eq. (11.10)] is minimized.
5. Update $\boldsymbol{W}$ by Eq. (11.11).
6. Normalize $\boldsymbol{W}$ by Eq. (11.13).
7. Repeat steps 2–6 until $\boldsymbol{W}$ converges.

Figure 11.5. The LICA algorithm with plain gradient descent (PG-LICA).

Natural Gradient Algorithm for Whitened Data: NG-LICA

The second algorithm is based on a *natural gradient* technique (Amari, 1998).

Suppose the data samples are *whitened*, that is, samples $\{\boldsymbol{y}_k\}_{k=1}^n$ are transformed as

$$\boldsymbol{y}_k \longleftarrow \widehat{\boldsymbol{C}}^{-\frac{1}{2}} \boldsymbol{y}_k, \tag{11.14}$$

where $\widehat{\boldsymbol{C}}$ is the sample covariance matrix:

$$\widehat{\boldsymbol{C}} := \frac{1}{n}\sum_{k=1}^{n} (\boldsymbol{y}_k - \bar{\boldsymbol{y}})(\boldsymbol{y}_k - \bar{\boldsymbol{y}})^\top \quad \text{and} \quad \bar{\boldsymbol{y}} := \frac{1}{n}\sum_{k=1}^{n} \boldsymbol{y}_k.$$

Then it can be shown that a demixing matrix that eliminates the second-order correlation is an *orthogonal matrix* (Hyvärinen et al., 2001). Thus, for whitened data, the search space of $\boldsymbol{W}$ can be restricted to the *orthogonal group* $O(d)$ without loss of generality.

The *tangent space* of $O(d)$ at $\boldsymbol{W}$ is equal to the space of all matrices $\boldsymbol{U}$ such that $\boldsymbol{W}^\top \boldsymbol{U}$ is *skew symmetric*, that is, $\boldsymbol{U}\boldsymbol{W}^\top = -\boldsymbol{W}\boldsymbol{U}^\top$. The steepest direction on this tangent space, which is called the *natural gradient*, is given as follows (Amari, 1998):

$$\nabla\widehat{\mathrm{SMI}}(\boldsymbol{W}) := \frac{1}{2}\left(\frac{\partial \widehat{\mathrm{SMI}}}{\partial \boldsymbol{W}} - \boldsymbol{W}\frac{\partial \widehat{\mathrm{SMI}}}{\partial \boldsymbol{W}}^\top \boldsymbol{W}\right), \tag{11.15}$$

where the canonical metric $\langle \boldsymbol{G}_1, \boldsymbol{G}_2\rangle = \frac{1}{2}\mathrm{tr}(\boldsymbol{G}_1^\top \boldsymbol{G}_2)$ is adopted in the tangent space. Then the *geodesic* from $\boldsymbol{W}$ in the direction of the natural gradient over $O(d)$ can be expressed by $\boldsymbol{W}\exp\left(t\boldsymbol{W}^\top \nabla\widehat{\mathrm{SMI}}(\boldsymbol{W})\right)$, where $t \in \mathbb{R}$ and "exp" denotes the *matrix exponential*; that is, for a square matrix $\boldsymbol{D}$, $\exp(\boldsymbol{D}) = \sum_{k=0}^{\infty} \frac{1}{k!}\boldsymbol{D}^k$. Thus, when performing line searches along the geodesic in the natural gradient direction, the minimizer may be searched from the set

$$\left\{\boldsymbol{W}\exp\left(-t\boldsymbol{W}^\top \nabla\widehat{\mathrm{SMI}}(\boldsymbol{W})\right) \,\middle|\, t \geq 0\right\}; \tag{11.16}$$

that is, t is chosen such that $\widehat{\mathrm{SMI}}$ [see Eq. (11.10)] is minimized and $\boldsymbol{W}$ is updated as

$$\boldsymbol{W} \longleftarrow \boldsymbol{W}\exp\left(-t\boldsymbol{W}^\top \nabla\widehat{\mathrm{SMI}}(\boldsymbol{W})\right). \tag{11.17}$$

1. Whiten the data samples by Eq. (11.14).
2. Initialize demixing matrix $\boldsymbol{W}$ and normalize it by Eq. (11.13).
3. Optimize Gaussian width σ and regularization parameter λ by CV.
4. Compute the natural gradient $\nabla\widehat{\mathrm{SMI}}$ by Eq. (11.15).
5. Choose step size t such that $\widehat{\mathrm{SMI}}$ [see Eq. (11.10)] is minimized over the set (11.16).
6. Update $\boldsymbol{W}$ by Eq. (11.17).
7. Repeat steps 3–6 until $\boldsymbol{W}$ converges.

Figure 11.6. The LICA algorithm with natural gradient descent (NG-LICA).

Geometry and optimization algorithms on more general structures, such as the *Stiefel manifold*, were discussed in detail in Nishimori and Akaho (2005).

A pseudo code of the NG-LICA algorithm is summarized in Figure 11.6.

11.3.4 Numerical Examples

In this subsection we give some numerical examples. We compare LICA with KICA (Bach and Jordan, 2002), FICA (Hyvaerinen, 1999), and JADE (Cardoso and Souloumiac, 1993) on artificial and real datasets.

We use the following two-dimensional artificial datasets:

(a) Sub-sub-Gaussians: $p^*(\boldsymbol{x}) = U(x^{(1)}; -\frac{1}{2}, \frac{1}{2})U(x^{(2)}; -\frac{1}{2}, \frac{1}{2})$, where $U(x;a,b)$ $(a, b \in \mathbb{R}, a < b)$ denotes the uniform density on (a,b).

(b) Super-super-Gaussians: $p^*(\boldsymbol{x}) = L(x^{(1)}; 0, 1)L(x^{(2)}; 0, 1)$, where $L(x;\mu,v)$ $(\mu \in \mathbb{R}, v > 0)$ denotes the Laplace density with mean μ and variance v.

(c) Sub-super-Gaussians: $p^*(\boldsymbol{x}) = U(x^{(1)}; -\frac{1}{2}, \frac{1}{2})L(x^{(2)}; 0, 1)$.

We also use the *demosig* dataset available in the FastICA package[6] for MATLAB®, and *10halo*, *Sergio7*, *Speech4*, and *c5signals* datasets available in the ICALAB signal processing benchmark datasets[7] (Cichocki and Amari, 2003).

The *Amari index* (Amari et al., 1996) is used as the performance measure (smaller is better):

$$\text{Amari index} := \frac{1}{2d(d-1)} \sum_{i,i'=1}^{d} \left(\frac{|o_{i,i'}|}{\max_{i''} |o_{i,i''}|} + \frac{|o_{i,i'}|}{\max_{i''} |o_{i'',i'}|} \right) - \frac{1}{d-1},$$

[6] http://www.cis.hut.fi/projects/ica/fastica.

[7] http://www.bsp.brain.riken.jp/ICALAB/ICALABSignalProc/benchmarks/.

where $o_{i,i'} := [\widehat{\boldsymbol{W}}\boldsymbol{A}]_{i,i'}$ for an estimated demixing matrix $\widehat{\boldsymbol{W}}$. We use the publicly available MATLAB® codes for KICA,[8] FICA,[9] and JADE,[10] where default parameter settings are used. The hyperparameters σ and λ in LICA are chosen by 5-fold CV from the 10 values in $[0.1, 1]$ at regular intervals and the 10 values in $[0.001, 1]$ at regular intervals in log scale, respectively.

We randomly generate the mixing matrix $\boldsymbol{A}$ and source signals for artificial datasets and compute the Amari index between the true $\boldsymbol{A}$ and $\widehat{\boldsymbol{W}}^{-1}$ for $\widehat{\boldsymbol{W}}$ estimated by each method. As training samples, we use the first n samples for the *Sergio7* and *c5signals* datasets, and the n samples between the 1001th and $(1000{+}n)$-th intervals for the *10halo* and *Speech4* datasets. We test $n = 200$ and 500.

The performance of each method is summarized in Table 11.4, depicting the mean and standard deviation of the Amari index over 50 trials. NG-LICA shows overall good performance. KICA tends to work reasonably well for datasets (a), (b), (c), and *demosig*, but it performs poorly for the ICALAB datasets; this seems to be caused by an inappropriate choice of the Gaussian kernel width and local

Table 11.4. Means (and standard deviation in brackets) of the Amari index (smaller is better) for the benchmark datasets. The best method in terms of the mean Amari index and comparable ones based on the t-test at the significance level 1% are indicated by boldface.

dataset	n	NG-LICA	KICA	FICA	JADE
(a)	200	**0.05(0.03)**	**0.04(0.02)**	0.06(0.03)	**0.04(0.02)**
	500	**0.03(0.01)**	**0.03(0.01)**	**0.03(0.02)**	**0.02(0.01)**
(b)	200	**0.06(0.04)**	0.12(0.15)	0.16(0.20)	0.15(0.17)
	500	**0.04(0.03)**	**0.05(0.04)**	0.11(0.12)	**0.05(0.04)**
(c)	200	**0.08(0.05)**	**0.09(0.06)**	0.14(0.11)	0.13(0.09)
	500	**0.04(0.03)**	**0.04(0.03)**	0.09(0.08)	0.10(0.06)
demosig	200	**0.04(0.01)**	**0.05(0.11)**	0.08(0.05)	0.08(0.08)
	500	**0.02(0.01)**	**0.04(0.09)**	0.04(0.03)	0.04(0.02)
10halo	200	**0.29(0.02)**	0.38(0.03)	0.33(0.07)	0.36(0.00)
	500	**0.22(0.02)**	0.37(0.03)	**0.22(0.03)**	0.28(0.00)
Sergio7	200	**0.04(0.01)**	0.38(0.04)	0.05(0.02)	0.07(0.00)
	500	0.05(0.02)	0.37(0.03)	0.04(0.01)	**0.04(0.00)**
Speech4	200	**0.18(0.03)**	0.29(0.05)	0.20(0.03)	0.22(0.00)
	500	0.07(0.00)	0.10(0.04)	0.10(0.04)	**0.06(0.00)**
c5signals	200	0.12(0.01)	0.25(0.15)	**0.10(0.02)**	0.12(0.00)
	500	**0.06(0.04)**	0.07(0.06)	**0.04(0.02)**	0.07(0.00)

8 http://www.di.ens.fr/~fbach/kernel-ica/index.htm.
9 http://www.cis.hut.fi/projects/ica/fastica.
10 http://perso.telecom-paristech.fr/ cardoso/guidesepsou.html.

optima. On the other hand, FICA and JADE tend to work reasonably well for the ICALAB datasets but perform poorly for (a), (b), (c), and *demosig*; we conjecture that the contrast functions in FICA and the fourth-order statistics in JADE do not appropriately catch the non-Gaussianity of datasets (a), (b), (c), and *demosig*. Overall, the LICA algorithm compares favorably with other methods.

11.3.5 Remarks

In this section we explained an ICA method based on *squared-loss mutual information*. The method, called *least-squares ICA* (LICA), has several preferable properties; for example, it is distribution-free and hyperparameter selection by cross-validation is available.

Similarly to other ICA algorithms, the optimization problem involved in LICA is non-convex. Thus, it is practically very important to develop good heuristics for initialization and avoiding local optima in the gradient procedures, which is an open research topic to be investigated. Moreover, although the SMI estimator is analytic, the LICA algorithm is still computationally rather expensive because it requires one to solve linear equations and perform cross-validations. The computational issue needs to be addressed, for example, by vectorization and parallelization.

12

Conditional Probability Estimation

Estimating the conditional probability $p^*(\boldsymbol{y}|\boldsymbol{x})$ is a challenging problem, especially when the conditioning variable $\boldsymbol{x}$ is continuous. In this chapter we describe a density-ratio approach to conditional probability estimation. The key idea is that, by definition, the conditional probability $p^*(\boldsymbol{y}|\boldsymbol{x})$ can be expressed in terms of the density ratio of the joint density $p^*(\boldsymbol{x},\boldsymbol{y})$ and the marginal density $p^*(\boldsymbol{x})$:

$$p^*(\boldsymbol{y}|\boldsymbol{x}) = \frac{p^*(\boldsymbol{x},\boldsymbol{y})}{p^*(\boldsymbol{x})}. \tag{12.1}$$

In the following we cover the situation where the target variable $\boldsymbol{y}$ is continuous (i.e., *conditional density estimation*) in Section 12.1, and the situation where $\boldsymbol{y}$ is categorical (i.e., *probabilistic classification*) in Section 12.2. For both cases, computationally efficient algorithms can be derived based on the least-squares density-ratio fitting method described in Section 6.2.2.

12.1 Conditional Density Estimation

In this section we focus on the case where the target variable $\boldsymbol{y}$ is continuous, that is, *conditional density estimation* (Sugiyama et al., 2010b).

After an introduction in Section 12.1.1, we formulate the problem of conditional density estimation and describe the algorithm called *least-squares conditional density estimation* (LSCDE) in Section 12.1.2. Its relations to other conditional density estimators are reviewed in Section 12.1.3, and the performances of various conditional density estimators are compared experimentally in Section 12.1.4. Finally, the section is concluded in Section 12.1.5.

12.1.1 Introduction

Regression aims to estimate the conditional *mean* of output $\boldsymbol{y}$ given input $\boldsymbol{x}$ (see Section 1.1.1). When the conditional density $p^*(\boldsymbol{y}|\boldsymbol{x})$ is unimodal and symmetric, regression would be sufficient for analyzing the input–output dependency.

However, when the conditional distribution possesses *multi-modality* (e.g., inverse kinematics learning of a robot; see Bishop, 2006) or a highly skewed profile with *heteroscedastic noise* (e.g., biomedical data analysis; see Hastie et al., 2001), merely estimating the conditional mean may not be sufficient. In such cases, it would be more informative to estimate the conditional distribution itself. In this section we address the problem of estimating conditional densities when $\boldsymbol{x}$ and $\boldsymbol{y}$ are continuous and multi-dimensional.

When the conditioning variable $\boldsymbol{x}$ is discrete, estimating the conditional density $p^*(\boldsymbol{y}|\boldsymbol{x} = \widetilde{\boldsymbol{x}})$ from samples $\{(\boldsymbol{x}_k, \boldsymbol{y}_k)\}_{k=1}^n$ is straightforward – by using only samples that satisfy the condition, $\{\boldsymbol{y}_k | \boldsymbol{x}_k = \widetilde{\boldsymbol{x}}\}_{k=1}^n$, a standard density estimation method (see Section 2.2 and Section 2.3) gives an estimate of the conditional density. However, when the conditioning variable $\boldsymbol{x}$ is continuous, conditional density estimation is not straightforward because no sample matches exactlythe condition $\boldsymbol{x}_k = \widetilde{\boldsymbol{x}}$. A naive idea for coping with this problem is to use samples that *approximately* satisfy the condition (i.e., $\{\boldsymbol{y}_k | \boldsymbol{x}_k \approx \widetilde{\boldsymbol{x}}\}_{k=1}^n$), but such a naive method is not reliable in high-dimensional problems. Although slightly more sophisticated variants have been proposed based on weighted kernel density estimation (Fan et al., 1996; Wolff et al., 1999), they still share the same weakness.

The *mixture density network* (MDN; Bishop, 2006) uses a mixture of parametric density models for approximating conditional densities. The parameters in the density models are estimated by a neural network as functions of the input variable $\boldsymbol{x}$. MDN was shown to work well in experiments, although its training is time consuming and only a local optimal solution may be obtained due to the non-convexity of neural network learning. Similarly, a mixture of *Gaussian processes* (Rasmussen and Williams, 2006) was used for estimating conditional densities in Tresp (2001), where a mixture model was trained in a computationally efficient manner by an *expectation-maximization* algorithm (Dempster et al., 1977). However, because the optimization problem is still non-convex, one may only access a local optimal solution in practice.

The *kernel quantile regression* (KQR) method (Takeuchi et al., 2006; Li et al., 2007) allows one to predict the percentiles of the conditional distributions. This implies that solving KQR for all percentiles gives an estimate of the entire conditional *cumulative* distribution. KQR is formulated as a convex optimization problem, and therefore the unique global solution can be obtained. Furthermore, the entire solution path with respect to the percentile parameter can be computed, which allows highly efficient implementation (Takeuchi et al., 2009). However, the range of applications of KQR is limited to one-dimensional output, and solution path tracking could be numerically unstable in practice.

In this section we describe a method of conditional density estimation called *least-squares conditional density estimation* (LSCDE) that is applicable to multi-dimensional inputs and outputs. LSCDE is based on the fact that the conditional density can be expressed in terms of the ratio of the joint density $p^*(\boldsymbol{x},\boldsymbol{y})$ and the marginal density $p^*(\boldsymbol{x})$ [see Eq. (12.1)]. Then, the density ratio $p^*(\boldsymbol{x},\boldsymbol{y})/p^*(\boldsymbol{x})$ is directly estimated without having to estimate densities $p^*(\boldsymbol{x},\boldsymbol{y})$ and $p^*(\boldsymbol{x})$.

12.1.2 Problem Formulation and Solutions

Here we formulate the problem of conditional density estimation (i.e., the output variable $\boldsymbol{y}$ is continuous) and describe a density-ratio approach to conditional density estimation.

Formulation of Conditional Density Estimation

Let $\mathcal{X}$ ($\subset \mathbb{R}^{d_{\mathrm{x}}}$) and $\mathcal{Y}$ ($\subset \mathbb{R}^{d_{\mathrm{y}}}$) be input and output data domains, where d_{x} and d_{y} are the dimensionalities of the data domains, respectively. Let us consider a joint probability distribution on $\mathcal{X} \times \mathcal{Y}$ with probability density function $p^*(\boldsymbol{x},\boldsymbol{y})$, and suppose that we are given n i.i.d. paired samples of input $\boldsymbol{x}$ and output $\boldsymbol{y}$:

$$\{z_k | z_k = (\boldsymbol{x}_k, \boldsymbol{y}_k) \in \mathcal{X} \times \mathcal{Y}\}_{k=1}^{n}.$$

The goal is to estimate the conditional density $p^*(\boldsymbol{y}|\boldsymbol{x})$ from the samples $\{z_k\}_{k=1}^{n}$.

Our primary interest lies in the case where both variables $\boldsymbol{x}$ and $\boldsymbol{y}$ are continuous. In this case, conditional density estimation is not straightforward because no sample matches exactly the condition.

By definition, the conditional density $p^*(\boldsymbol{y}|\boldsymbol{x})$ can be expressed in terms of the following density ratio:

$$p^*(\boldsymbol{y}|\boldsymbol{x}) = \frac{p^*(\boldsymbol{x},\boldsymbol{y})}{p^*(\boldsymbol{x})},$$

where we assume $p^*(\boldsymbol{x}) > 0$ for all $\boldsymbol{x} \in \mathcal{X}$. In the following, *unconstrained least-squares importance fitting* (uLSIF; Kanamori et al., 2009; see also Section 6.2.2) is applied to the estimation of the above density ratio, and a practical algorithm of conditional density estimation called *least-squares conditional density estimation* (LSCDE; Sugiyama et al., 2010b) is given.

Least-Squares Conditional Density Estimation

The conditional density function $p^*(\boldsymbol{y}|\boldsymbol{x})$ is modeled as

$$p(\boldsymbol{y}|\boldsymbol{x};\boldsymbol{\theta}) := \sum_{\ell=1}^{b} \theta_\ell \psi(\boldsymbol{x},\boldsymbol{y}) = \boldsymbol{\psi}(\boldsymbol{x},\boldsymbol{y})^\top \boldsymbol{\theta},$$

where $\boldsymbol{\psi}(\boldsymbol{x},\boldsymbol{y})$ ($\in \mathbb{R}^b$) is a non-negative basis function vector and $\boldsymbol{\theta}$ ($\in \mathbb{R}^b$) is a parameter vector. Let

$$\widehat{\boldsymbol{H}} := \frac{1}{n}\sum_{k=1}^{n} \int \boldsymbol{\psi}(\boldsymbol{x}_k,\boldsymbol{y})\boldsymbol{\psi}(\boldsymbol{x}_k,\boldsymbol{y})^\top \mathrm{d}\boldsymbol{y}, \tag{12.2}$$

$$\widehat{\boldsymbol{h}} := \frac{1}{n}\sum_{k=1}^{n} \boldsymbol{\psi}(\boldsymbol{x}_k,\boldsymbol{y}_k).$$

Then the uLSIF solution is given analytically as follows (see Section 6.2.2):

$$\widehat{\boldsymbol{\theta}} = (\widehat{\boldsymbol{H}} + \lambda \boldsymbol{I}_b)^{-1}\widehat{\boldsymbol{h}},$$

where λ (≥ 0) is the regularization parameter and $\boldsymbol{I}_b$ is the b-dimensional identity matrix.

To assure that the solution is a conditional density (i.e., non-negative and integrated to one), we modify the solution as

$$\widehat{p}(\boldsymbol{y}|\boldsymbol{x}=\widetilde{\boldsymbol{x}}) = \frac{\boldsymbol{\psi}(\widetilde{\boldsymbol{x}},\boldsymbol{y})^\top \widetilde{\boldsymbol{\theta}}}{\int \boldsymbol{\psi}(\widetilde{\boldsymbol{x}},\boldsymbol{y}')^\top \widetilde{\boldsymbol{\theta}} \mathrm{d}\boldsymbol{y}'}, \tag{12.3}$$

where $\widetilde{\boldsymbol{\theta}} = \max(\boldsymbol{0}_b, \widehat{\boldsymbol{\theta}})$, $\boldsymbol{0}_b$ denotes the b-dimensional vector with all zeros, and the "max" operation for vectors is applied in an element-wise manner.

As basis functions, a Gaussian kernel model is practically useful. More specifically, suppose the variance of each element of $\{\boldsymbol{x}_k\}_{k=1}^n$ and $\{\boldsymbol{y}_k\}_{k=1}^n$ is normalized to one. Then, for $\boldsymbol{z} = (\boldsymbol{x}^\top, \boldsymbol{y}^\top)^\top$, the following Gaussian basis functions are used:

$$\psi_\ell(\boldsymbol{x},\boldsymbol{y}) = \exp\left(-\frac{\|\boldsymbol{z}-\boldsymbol{c}_\ell\|^2}{2\sigma^2}\right) = \exp\left(-\frac{\|\boldsymbol{x}-\boldsymbol{u}_\ell\|^2}{2\sigma^2}\right)\exp\left(-\frac{\|\boldsymbol{y}-\boldsymbol{v}_\ell\|^2}{2\sigma^2}\right),$$

where $\{\boldsymbol{c}_\ell | \boldsymbol{c}_\ell = (\boldsymbol{u}_\ell^\top, \boldsymbol{v}_\ell^\top)^\top\}_{\ell=1}^b$ are Gaussian centers randomly chosen from $\{\boldsymbol{z}_k | \boldsymbol{z}_k = (\boldsymbol{x}_k^\top, \boldsymbol{y}_k^\top)^\top\}_{k=1}^n$ without overlap. An advantage of this Gaussian kernel model is that the integrals with respect to $\boldsymbol{y}$ in $\widehat{\boldsymbol{H}}$ [see Eq. (12.2)] and in the normalization factor [see Eq. (12.3)] can be computed analytically as

$$\widehat{H}_{\ell,\ell'} = \frac{1}{n}\sum_{k=1}^n (\sqrt{\pi}\sigma)^{d_y} \exp\left(-\frac{2\|\boldsymbol{x}_k-\boldsymbol{u}_\ell\|^2+2\|\boldsymbol{x}_k-\boldsymbol{u}_{\ell'}\|^2+\|\boldsymbol{v}_\ell-\boldsymbol{v}_{\ell'}\|^2}{4\sigma^2}\right),$$

$$\int \boldsymbol{\psi}(\boldsymbol{x},\boldsymbol{y})^\top \widetilde{\boldsymbol{\theta}} \mathrm{d}\boldsymbol{y} = (\sqrt{2\pi}\sigma)^{d_y} \sum_{\ell=1}^b \widetilde{\theta}_\ell \exp\left(-\frac{\|\boldsymbol{x}-\boldsymbol{u}_\ell\|^2}{2\sigma^2}\right).$$

This method is called *least-squares conditional density estimation* (LSCDE; Sugiyama et al., 2010b). A MATLAB® implementation of LSCDE is available from http://sugiyama-www.cs.titech.ac.jp/~sugi/software/LSCDE/.

Cross-Validation for Model Selection

The practical performance of LSCDE depends on the choice of model parameters such as the basis functions $\boldsymbol{\psi}(\boldsymbol{x},\boldsymbol{y})$ and the regularization parameter λ.

Here we describe a *cross-validation* (CV) procedure for model selection. CV should be carried out in terms of the error metric used for evaluating the test performance. In the following we investigate two cases: the *squared (SQ) error* and the *Kullback–Leibler (KL) error*. The SQ error for a conditional density estimator $\widehat{p}(\boldsymbol{y}|\boldsymbol{x})$ is defined as

$$\mathrm{SQ}_0 := \frac{1}{2}\iint \left(\widehat{p}(\boldsymbol{y}|\boldsymbol{x}) - p^*(\boldsymbol{y}|\boldsymbol{x})\right)^2 p^*(\boldsymbol{x})\mathrm{d}\boldsymbol{x}\mathrm{d}\boldsymbol{y} = \mathrm{SQ} + C_{\mathrm{SQ}},$$

where

$$\mathrm{SQ} := \frac{1}{2}\iint (\widehat{p}(\boldsymbol{y}|\boldsymbol{x}))^2 p^*(\boldsymbol{x})\mathrm{d}\boldsymbol{x}\mathrm{d}\boldsymbol{y} - \iint \widehat{p}(\boldsymbol{y}|\boldsymbol{x}) p^*(\boldsymbol{x},\boldsymbol{y})\mathrm{d}\boldsymbol{x}\mathrm{d}\boldsymbol{y}$$

and C_{SQ} is the constant defined by $C_{\mathrm{SQ}} := \frac{1}{2}\iint p^*(\boldsymbol{y}|\boldsymbol{x})p^*(\boldsymbol{x},\boldsymbol{y})\mathrm{d}\boldsymbol{x}\mathrm{d}\boldsymbol{y}$. The KL error for a conditional density estimator $\widehat{p}(\boldsymbol{y}|\boldsymbol{x})$ is defined as

$$\mathrm{KL}_0 := \iint p^*(\boldsymbol{x},\boldsymbol{y}) \log \frac{p^*(\boldsymbol{x},\boldsymbol{y})}{\widehat{p}(\boldsymbol{y}|\boldsymbol{x})p^*(\boldsymbol{x})} \mathrm{d}\boldsymbol{x}\mathrm{d}\boldsymbol{y} = \mathrm{KL} + C_{\mathrm{KL}},$$

where

$$\mathrm{KL} := -\iint p^*(\boldsymbol{x},\boldsymbol{y}) \log \widehat{p}(\boldsymbol{y}|\boldsymbol{x})\mathrm{d}\boldsymbol{x}\mathrm{d}\boldsymbol{y}$$

and C_{KL} is the constant defined by $C_{\mathrm{KL}} := \iint p^*(\boldsymbol{x},\boldsymbol{y}) \log p^*(\boldsymbol{y}|\boldsymbol{x})\mathrm{d}\boldsymbol{x}\mathrm{d}\boldsymbol{y}$. The smaller the value of SQ or KL, the better the performance of the conditional density estimator $\widehat{p}(\boldsymbol{y}|\boldsymbol{x})$.

For the above performance measures, CV is carried out as follows. First, the samples $\mathcal{Z} := \{\boldsymbol{z}_k | \boldsymbol{z}_k = (\boldsymbol{x}_k, \boldsymbol{y}_k)\}_{k=1}^n$ are divided into K disjoint subsets $\{\mathcal{Z}_k\}_{k=1}^K$ of approximately the same size. Let $\widehat{p}_k$ be the conditional density estimator obtained using $\mathcal{Z}\backslash\mathcal{Z}_k$ (i.e., the estimator obtained without $\mathcal{Z}_k$). Then the target error values are approximated using the hold-out samples $\mathcal{Z}_k$ as

$$\widehat{\mathrm{SQ}}_{\mathcal{Z}_k} := \frac{1}{2|\mathcal{Z}_k|}\sum_{\widetilde{\boldsymbol{x}}\in\mathcal{Z}_k}\int (\widehat{p}_k(\boldsymbol{y}|\widetilde{\boldsymbol{x}}))^2\,\mathrm{d}\boldsymbol{y} - \frac{1}{|\mathcal{Z}_k|}\sum_{(\widetilde{\boldsymbol{x}},\widetilde{\boldsymbol{y}})\in\mathcal{Z}_k} \widehat{p}_k(\widetilde{\boldsymbol{y}}|\widetilde{\boldsymbol{x}}),$$

$$\widehat{\mathrm{KL}}_{\mathcal{Z}_k} := -\frac{1}{|\mathcal{Z}_k|}\sum_{(\widetilde{\boldsymbol{x}},\widetilde{\boldsymbol{y}})\in\mathcal{Z}_k} \log \widehat{p}_k(\widetilde{\boldsymbol{y}}|\widetilde{\boldsymbol{x}}),$$

where $|\mathcal{Z}_k|$ denotes the number of elements in the set $\mathcal{Z}_k$. This procedure is repeated for $k = 1,\ldots,K$ and their averages are computed:

$$\widehat{\mathrm{SQ}} := \frac{1}{K}\sum_{k=1}^{K}\widehat{\mathrm{SQ}}_{\mathcal{Z}_k} \quad \text{and} \quad \widehat{\mathrm{KL}} := \frac{1}{K}\sum_{k=1}^{K}\widehat{\mathrm{KL}}_{\mathcal{Z}_k}.$$

$\widehat{\mathrm{SQ}}$ and $\widehat{\mathrm{KL}}$ can be shown to be almost unbiased estimators of the true costs SQ and KL, respectively, where the "almost"-ness comes from the fact that the number of samples is reduced in the CV procedure as a result of data splitting (Luntz and Brailovsky, 1969; Schölkopf and Smola, 2002).

12.1.3 Relations to Existing Methods

Here we review other conditional density estimators and discuss their relations to LSCDE.

ϵ-Neighbor Kernel Density Estimation (ϵ-KDE)

For estimating the conditional density $p^*(\boldsymbol{y}|\boldsymbol{x})$, *ϵ-neighbor kernel density estimation* (ϵ-KDE) employs the standard kernel density estimator (see Section 2.3.1) using a subset of samples, $\{\boldsymbol{y}_k\}_{k\in\mathcal{I}_{\boldsymbol{x},\epsilon}}$ for some threshold ϵ (≥ 0), where $\mathcal{I}_{\boldsymbol{x},\epsilon}$ is the set of sample indices such that $\|\boldsymbol{x}_k - \boldsymbol{x}\| \leq \epsilon$.

In the case of Gaussian kernels, ϵ-KDE is expressed as

$$\widehat{p}(y|\boldsymbol{x}) = \frac{1}{|\mathcal{I}_{\boldsymbol{x},\epsilon}|} \sum_{k \in \mathcal{I}_{\boldsymbol{x},\epsilon}} N(\boldsymbol{y}; \boldsymbol{y}_k, \sigma^2 \boldsymbol{I}_{d_y}),$$

where $N(\boldsymbol{y}; \boldsymbol{\mu}, \boldsymbol{\Sigma})$ denotes the Gaussian density with mean $\boldsymbol{\mu}$ and covariance matrix $\boldsymbol{\Sigma}$. The threshold ϵ and the bandwidth σ may be chosen based on cross-validation (Härdle et al., 2004). ϵ-KDE is simple and easy to use, but it may not be reliable in high-dimensional problems. Slightly more sophisticated variants have been proposed based on weighted kernel density estimation (Fan et al., 1996; Wolff et al., 1999), but they may still share the same weaknesses.

Mixture Density Network (MDN)

The *mixture density network* (MDN) models the conditional density by a mixture of parametric densities (Bishop, 2006). In the case of the Gaussian density model, MDN is expressed as

$$\widehat{p}(y|\boldsymbol{x}) = \sum_{\ell=1}^{b} \pi_\ell(\boldsymbol{x}) N(\boldsymbol{y}; \boldsymbol{\mu}_\ell(\boldsymbol{x}), \sigma_\ell^2(\boldsymbol{x}) \boldsymbol{I}_{d_y}),$$

where $\pi_\ell(\boldsymbol{x})$ denotes the mixing coefficient such that

$$\sum_{\ell=1}^{b} \pi_\ell(\boldsymbol{x}) = 1 \quad \text{and} \quad 0 \leq \pi_\ell(\boldsymbol{x}) \leq 1 \quad \text{for all } \boldsymbol{x} \in \mathcal{X}.$$

All the parameters $\{\pi_\ell(\boldsymbol{x}), \boldsymbol{\mu}_\ell(\boldsymbol{x}), \sigma_\ell^2(\boldsymbol{x})\}_{\ell=1}^{b}$ are learned as a function of $\boldsymbol{x}$ by a neural network with regularized maximum-likelihood estimation. The number b of Gaussian components, the number of hidden units in the neural network, and the regularization parameter may be chosen based on cross-validation. MDN has been shown to work well, although its training is time consuming and only a local solution may be obtained due to the non-convexity of neural network learning.

Kernel Quantile Regression (KQR)

Kernel quantile regression (KQR) allows one to predict the 100τ-percentile of conditional distributions for a given τ ($\in (0,1)$) when y is one-dimensional (Takeuchi et al., 2006; Li et al., 2007). For the Gaussian kernel model

$$f_\tau(\boldsymbol{x}) = \sum_{k=1}^{n} \theta_{i,\tau} \phi_k(\boldsymbol{x}) + b_\tau,$$

where $\phi_k(\boldsymbol{x}) = \exp\left(-\frac{\|\boldsymbol{x}-\boldsymbol{x}_k\|^2}{2\sigma^2}\right)$, the parameters $\{\theta_{k,\tau}\}_{k=1}^{n}$ and b_τ are learned by

$$\min_{\{\theta_{k,\tau}\}_{k=1}^{n}, b_\tau} \left[\sum_{k=1}^{n} \rho_\tau(y_k - f_\tau(\boldsymbol{x}_k)) + \lambda \sum_{k,\ell=1}^{n} \phi_\ell(\boldsymbol{x}_k) \theta_{k,\tau} \theta_{\ell,\tau} \right],$$

where $\rho_\tau(\epsilon)$ denotes the *pin-ball loss* function defined by

$$\rho_\tau(\epsilon) = \begin{cases} (1-\tau)|\epsilon| & (\epsilon \le 0), \\ \tau|\epsilon| & (\epsilon > 0). \end{cases}$$

Thus, solving KQR for all $\tau \in (0,1)$ gives an estimate of the entire conditional distribution. The bandwidth σ and the regularization parameter λ may be chosen based on cross-validation.

A notable advantage of KQR is that the solution of KQR is *piece-wise linear* with respect to τ. Based on this fact, a *solution-path* algorithm that allows one to efficiently compute the solutions for all τ was developed (Takeuchi et al., 2009). This implies that the *conditional cumulative distribution* can be computed in a computationally efficient manner. However, solution-path tracking tends to be numerically unstable and the range of applications of KQR is limited to one-dimensional output y. Furthermore, some heuristic procedure is needed to convert conditional cumulative distributions to conditional densities, which can produce additional estimation errors.

12.1.4 Numerical Experiments

Here we investigate experimentally the performance of LSCDE and other conditional density estimators. In the experiments, we fix the number of basis functions in LSCDE to $b = \min(100, n)$, and choose the Gaussian width σ and the regularization parameter λ by cross-validation from $\sigma, \lambda \in \{0.01, 0.02, 0.05, 0.1, 0.2, 0.5, 1, 2, 5, 10\}$.

Illustrative Examples

First we illustrate how LSCDE behaves using toy datasets.

Let $d_\mathrm{x} = d_\mathrm{y} = 1$. Inputs $\{x_k\}_{k=1}^n$ are independently drawn from $U(-1,1)$, where $U(a,b)$ denotes the uniform distribution on (a,b). Outputs $\{y_k\}_{k=1}^n$ are generated by the following *heteroscedastic noise* model:

$$y_k = \mathrm{sinc}(2\pi x_k) + \frac{1}{8}\exp(1 - x_k) \cdot \varepsilon_k.$$

We test the following three different distributions for $\{\varepsilon_k\}_{i=1}^n$:

(a) Gaussian: $\varepsilon_k \overset{\text{i.i.d.}}{\sim} N(0,1)$

(b) Bimodal: $\varepsilon_k \overset{\text{i.i.d.}}{\sim} \frac{1}{2}N(-1, \frac{4}{9}) + \frac{1}{2}N(1, \frac{4}{9})$

(c) Skewed: $\varepsilon_k \overset{\text{i.i.d.}}{\sim} \frac{3}{4}N(0,1) + \frac{1}{4}N(\frac{3}{2}, \frac{1}{9})$

where "$\overset{\text{i.i.d.}}{\sim}$" denotes "independent and identically distributed" and $N(\mu, \sigma^2)$ denotes the Gaussian distribution with mean μ and variance σ^2. See Figure 12.1(a)–(c) for the true conditional densities and training samples of size $n = 200$. The estimated results are depicted in Figure 12.1(a)–(c), illustrating that LSCDE captures well heteroscedasticity, bimodality, and asymmetricity.

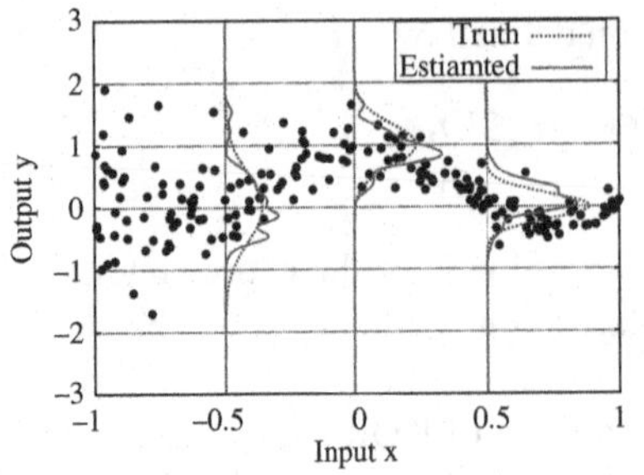

(a) Artificial dataset containing heteroscedastic Gaussian noise: $\varepsilon_k \overset{\text{i.i.d.}}{\sim} N(0,1)$

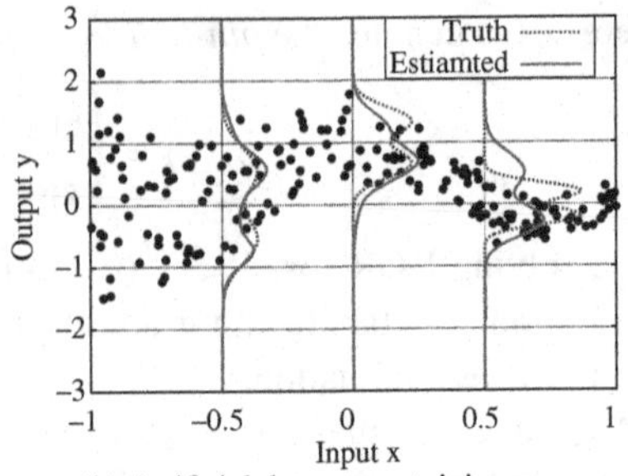

(b) Artificial dataset containing heteroscedastic bimodal Gaussian noise: $\varepsilon_k \overset{\text{i.i.d.}}{\sim} \frac{1}{2}N(-1, \frac{4}{9}) + \frac{1}{2}N(1, \frac{4}{9})$

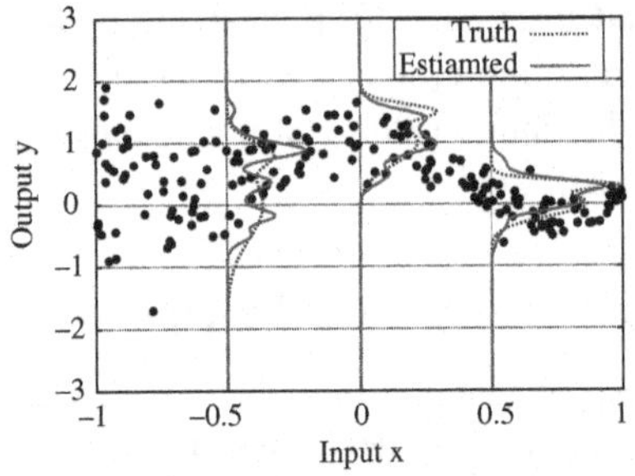

(c) Artificial dataset containing heteroscedastic bi modal Gaussian noise: $\varepsilon_k \overset{\text{i.i.d.}}{\sim} \frac{3}{4}N(0, 1) + \frac{1}{4}N(\frac{3}{2}, \frac{4}{9})$

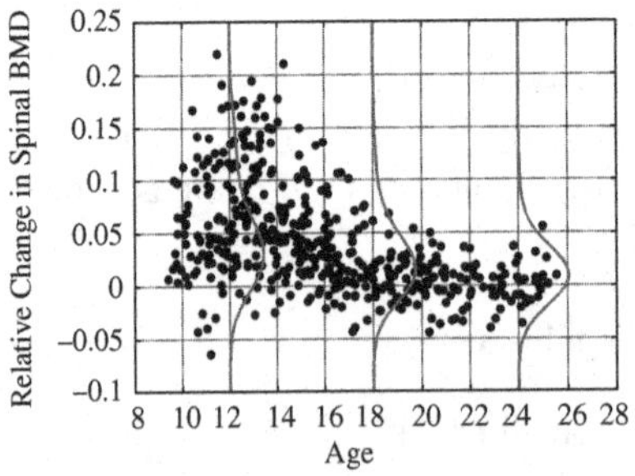

(d) Relative spinal bone mineral density measurements on North American adolescents (Hastie et al., 2001) having a heteroscedastic asymmetric conditional distribution

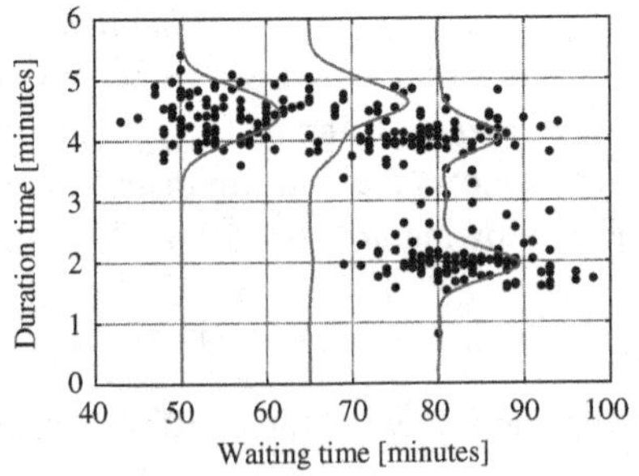

(e) The durations of eruptions of the Old Faithful Geyser (Weisberg, 1985) having a bimodal conditional distribution

Figure 12.1. Illustrative examples.

We also investigate the experimental performance of LSCDE using the following real datasets:

(d) ***Bone Mineral Density*** **dataset:** Relative spinal bone mineral density measurements on 485 North American adolescents (Hastie et al., 2001), having a heteroscedastic asymmetric conditional distribution.

(e) ***Old Faithful Geyser*** **dataset:** The durations of 299 eruptions of the Old Faithful Geyser (Weisberg, 1985), having a bimodal conditional distribution.

Figure 12.1 and (e) depict the results, showing that heteroscedastic and multi-modal structures are nicely revealed by LSCDE.

Benchmark Datasets

Next we apply LSCDE and the methods reviewed in Section 12.1.3 to the benchmark datasets accompanied with the R package (R Development Core Team, 2009), and evaluate their experimental performance. See Table 12.1 for the list of datasets.

In each dataset, 50% of the samples are chosen randomly for conditional density estimation and the rest are used for computing the estimation accuracy. The accuracy of a conditional density estimator $\widehat{p}(\boldsymbol{y}|\boldsymbol{x})$ is measured by the *negative log-likelihood for test samples* $\{\widetilde{\boldsymbol{z}}_k | \widetilde{\boldsymbol{z}}_k = (\widetilde{\boldsymbol{x}}_k, \widetilde{\boldsymbol{y}}_k)\}_{i=1}^{\widetilde{n}}$:

$$\mathrm{NLL} := -\frac{1}{\widetilde{n}} \sum_{i=1}^{\widetilde{n}} \log \widehat{p}(\widetilde{\boldsymbol{y}}_k | \widetilde{\boldsymbol{x}}_k). \tag{12.4}$$

Thus, the smaller the value of NLL, the better the performance of the conditional density estimator $\widehat{p}(\boldsymbol{y}|\boldsymbol{x})$.

We compare LSCDE, ϵ-KDE, MDN, and KQR. In addition, the *ratio of kernel density estimators* (RKDE) is also tested, which estimates the density ratio $p^*(\boldsymbol{x},\boldsymbol{y})/p^*(\boldsymbol{x})$ by first approximating the two densities $p^*(\boldsymbol{x},\boldsymbol{y})$ and $p^*(\boldsymbol{x})$ separately by kernel density estimation and then taking the ratio of the estimated densities. For model selection, we use cross-validation based on the Kullback–Leibler (KL) error (see Section 12.1.2), which is consistent with the above NLL. In MDN, cross-validation over three tuning parameters (the number of Gaussian components, the number of hidden units in the neural network, and the regularization parameter; see Section 12.1.3) is unbearably slow, and hence the number of Gaussian components is fixed to $b = 3$ and the other two tuning parameters are chosen by cross-validation.

The experimental results are summarized in Table 12.1. ϵ-KDE is computationally very efficient, but it tends to perform rather poorly. MDN works well, but it is computationally highly demanding. KQR performs well overall and is computationally slightly more efficient than LSCDE. However, its solution-path tracking algorithm is numerically rather unstable and solutions are not properly obtained for the *engel* and *cpus* datasets. RKDE does not perform well for all cases, implying that density-ratio estimation via density estimation is not reliable in practice.

Table 12.1. Experimental results on benchmark datasets ($d_y = 1$). The averages and the standard deviations of the NLL errors [see Eq. (12.4)] over 10 runs are described (smaller is better). The best method in terms of the mean error and comparable methods according to the t-test at the 5% significance level are specified by boldface. The mean computation time is normalized so that LSCDE is one.

Dataset	(n, d_x)	LSCDE	ϵ-KDE	MDN	KQR	RKDE
caution	(50,2)	**1.24 ± 0.29**	**1.25 ± 0.19**	**1.39 ± 0.18**	**1.73 ± 0.86**	17.11 ± 0.25
ftcollinssnow	(46,1)	**1.48 ± 0.01**	**1.53 ± 0.05**	**1.48 ± 0.03**	**2.11 ± 0.44**	46.06 ± 0.78
highway	(19,11)	**1.71 ± 0.41**	**2.24 ± 0.64**	7.41 ± 1.22	5.69 ± 1.69	15.30 ± 0.76
heights	(687,1)	**1.29 ± 0.00**	1.33 ± 0.01	**1.30 ± 0.01**	**1.29 ± 0.00**	54.79 ± 0.10
sniffer	(62,4)	**0.69 ± 0.16**	**0.96 ± 0.15**	**0.72 ± 0.09**	**0.68 ± 0.21**	26.80 ± 0.58
snowgeese	(22,2)	**0.95 ± 0.10**	1.35 ± 0.17	**2.49 ± 1.02**	**2.96 ± 1.13**	28.43 ± 1.02
ufc	(117,4)	**1.03 ± 0.01**	1.40 ± 0.02	**1.02 ± 0.06**	**1.02 ± 0.06**	11.10 ± 0.49
birthwt	(94,7)	**1.43 ± 0.01**	1.48 ± 0.01	**1.46 ± 0.01**	1.58 ± 0.05	15.95 ± 0.53
crabs	(100,6)	-0.07 ± 0.11	0.99 ± 0.09	**-0.70 ± 0.35**	**-1.03 ± 0.16**	12.60 ± 0.45
GAGurine	(157,1)	**0.45 ± 0.04**	0.92 ± 0.05	**0.57 ± 0.15**	**0.40 ± 0.08**	53.43 ± 0.27
geyser	(149,1)	**1.03 ± 0.00**	1.11 ± 0.02	1.23 ± 0.05	1.10 ± 0.02	53.49 ± 0.38
gilgais	(182,8)	0.73 ± 0.05	1.35 ± 0.03	**0.10 ± 0.04**	0.45 ± 0.15	10.44 ± 0.50
topo	(26,2)	**0.93 ± 0.02**	1.18 ± 0.09	2.11 ± 0.46	2.88 ± 0.85	10.80 ± 0.35
BostonHousing	(253,13)	0.82 ± 0.05	1.03 ± 0.05	**0.68 ± 0.06**	**0.48 ± 0.10**	17.81 ± 0.25
CobarOre	(19,2)	**1.58 ± 0.06**	**1.65 ± 0.09**	**1.63 ± 0.08**	6.33 ± 1.77	11.42 ± 0.51
engel	(117,1)	**0.69 ± 0.04**	1.27 ± 0.05	**0.71 ± 0.16**	N.A.	52.83 ± 0.16
mcycle	(66,1)	**0.83 ± 0.03**	1.25 ± 0.23	1.12 ± 0.10	**0.72 ± 0.06**	48.35 ± 0.79
BigMac2003	(34,9)	**1.32 ± 0.11**	**1.29 ± 0.14**	**2.64 ± 0.84**	**1.35 ± 0.26**	13.34 ± 0.52
UN3	(62,6)	**1.42 ± 0.12**	1.78 ± 0.14	**1.32 ± 0.08**	**1.22 ± 0.13**	11.43 ± 0.58
cpus	(104,7)	1.04 ± 0.07	1.01 ± 0.10	**-2.14 ± 0.13**	N.A.	15.16 ± 0.72
Time		1	0.004	267	0.755	0.089

Overall, LSCDE is a promising method for conditional density estimation in terms of its accuracy and computational efficiency.

Robot Transition Estimation

Finally, the problem of robot transition estimation is discussed. We use the pendulum robot and the Khepera robot simulators illustrated in Figure 12.2.

The *pendulum robot* consists of wheels and a pendulum hinged to the body. The state of the pendulum robot consists of angle θ and angular velocity $\dot{\theta}$ of the pendulum. The amount of torque τ applied to the wheels can be controlled, by which the robot can move left or right, and the state of the pendulum is changed to θ' and $\dot{\theta}'$. The task is to estimate $p^*(\theta',\dot{\theta}'|\theta,\dot{\theta},\tau)$, the transition probability density from state $(\theta,\dot{\theta})$ to state $(\theta',\dot{\theta}')$ by action τ.

The *Khepera robot* is equipped with two infrared sensors and two wheels. The infrared sensors h_L and h_R measure the distance to the left-front and right-front walls. The speed of the left and right wheels v_L and v_R can be controlled separately, by which the robot can move forward/backward and rotate left/right. The task is to estimate $p^*(h'_L,h'_R|h_L,h_R,v_L,v_R)$, where h'_L and h'_R are the next states.

The state transition of the pendulum robot is highly stochastic as a result of slipping, friction, or measurement errors with strong heteroscedasticity. Sensory inputs of the Khepera robot suffer from occlusions and contain highly heteroscedastic noise, and hence the transition probability density may possess multi-modality and heteroscedasticity. Thus, transition estimation of dynamic robots is a challenging task. Note that transition estimation is useful in *model-based reinforcement learning* (Sutton and Barto, 1998).

For both robots, 100 samples are used for conditional density estimation and an additional 900 samples are used for computing the NLL error [see Eq. (12.4)]. The number of Gaussian components is fixed to $b = 3$ in MDN, and all other tuning parameters are chosen by cross-validation based on the Kullback–Leibler (KL) error (see Section 12.1.2). Experimental results are summarized in Table 12.2, showing that LSCDE is promising in this challenging task of robot transition estimation.

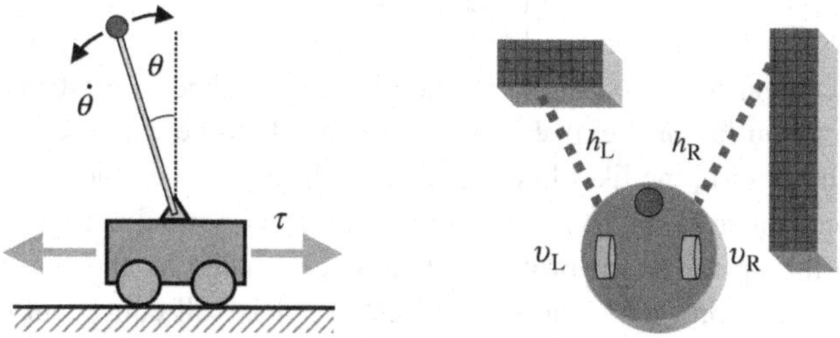

(a) Pendulumvrobot (b) Khepera robot

Figure 12.2. Illustration of robots used for experiments.

Table 12.2. Experimental results on robot transition estimation. The averages and the standard deviations of the NLL error [see Eq. (12.4)] over 10 runs are described (smaller is better). The best method in terms of the mean error and comparable methods according to the t-test at the 5% significance level are specified by boldface. The mean computation time is normalized so that LSCDE is one.

Dataset	LSCDE	ϵ-KDE	MDN	RKDE
Pendulum1	**1.27 ± 0.05**	2.04 ± 0.10	**1.44 ± 0.67**	11.24 ± 0.32
Pendulum2	**1.38 ± 0.05**	2.07 ± 0.10	**1.43 ± 0.58**	11.24 ± 0.32
Khepera1	**1.69 ± 0.01**	2.07 ± 0.02	**1.90 ± 0.36**	11.03 ± 0.03
Khepera2	**1.86 ± 0.01**	2.10 ± 0.01	**1.92 ± 0.26**	11.09 ± 0.02
Time	1	0.164	1134	0.431

12.1.5 Remarks

We described a density-ratio method for conditional density estimation called LSCDE. Experiments on benchmark and robot-transition datasets demonstrated the usefulness of LSCDE.

In LSCDE, a direct density-ratio estimation method based on the *squared distance* called *unconstrained least-squares importance fitting* (uLSIF; see Section 6.2.2) was applied to conditional density estimation. Similarly, applying the direct density-ratio estimation method based on the *KL importance estimation procedure* (KLIEP; see Chapter 5), we can obtain a *log-loss* variant of LSCDE. A valiant of the KLIEP method described in Section 5.2.2 uses a *log-linear* model (a.k.a. a *maximum entropy* model; Jaynes, 1957) for density-ratio estimation:

$$r(\boldsymbol{x},\boldsymbol{y}) := \frac{\exp(\boldsymbol{\psi}(\boldsymbol{x},\boldsymbol{y})^\top\boldsymbol{\theta})}{\int \exp(\boldsymbol{\psi}(\boldsymbol{x},\boldsymbol{y}')^\top\boldsymbol{\theta})\mathrm{d}\boldsymbol{y}'}.$$

Applying this log-linear KLIEP method to conditional density estimation is actually equivalent to maximum likelihood estimation of conditional densities for log-linear models[1]:

$$\max_{\boldsymbol{\theta}} \left[\sum_{k=1}^{n} \log r(\boldsymbol{x}_k, \boldsymbol{y}_k) \right].$$

A crucial fact regarding maximum likelihood conditional density estimation is that the normalization factor $\int \exp(\boldsymbol{\psi}(\boldsymbol{x},\boldsymbol{y}')^\top\boldsymbol{\theta})\mathrm{d}\boldsymbol{y}'$ needs to be explicitly included in the model; otherwise, the likelihood tends to infinity. On the other hand, LSCDE (based on the squared distance) does not require the normalization factor to be included in the optimization problem. This is evidenced by the fact that, without the normalization factor, the LSCDE estimator is still consistent (Sugiyama et al., 2010b). This contributes greatly to simplifying the optimization problem (see

[1] For *structured* output, it is particularly called a *conditional random field* (Lafferty et al., 2001).

Section 12.1.2), which results in an analytic-form solution that can be computed efficiently. This is a significant advantage of LSCDE over standard maximum likelihood conditional density estimation.

12.2 Probabilistic Classification

In this section we focus on conditional probability estimation with categorical output, that is, *probabilistic classification* (Sugiyama, 2010). After an introduction in Section 12.2.1, we describe a method of probabilistic classification based on density-ratio estimation called the *least-squares probabilistic classifier* (LSPC) in Section 12.2.2. The performance of LSPC and related methods is experimentally compared in Section 12.2.3, and the section is concluded in Section 12.2.4.

12.2.1 Introduction

The *support vector machine* (SVM; Cortes and Vapnik, 1995; Vapnik, 1998; see also Section 4.4) is a popular method for classification. Various computationally efficient algorithms for training SVMs with massive datasets have been developed so far and (e.g., Platt, 1999; Joachims, 1999; Chang and Lin, 2001; Collobert and Bengio., 2001; Suykens et al., 2002; Rifkin et al., 2003; Tsang et al., 2005; Fung and Mangasarian, 2005; Fan et al., 2005; Tang and Zhang, 2006; Joachims, 2006; Teo et al., 2007; Franc and Sonnenburg, 2009; and many other softwares available online). However, SVMs cannot provide the *confidence* of class prediction because they only learn the decision boundaries between different classes. To cope with this problem, several post-processing methods have been developed for approximately computing the *class-posterior probability* (Platt, 2000; Wu et al., 2004).

On the other hand, *logistic regression* (LR; see Section 4.2) is a classification algorithm that can naturally give the confidence of class prediction because it learns the class-posterior probabilities (Hastie et al., 2001). Recently, various efficient algorithms for training LR models specialized in *sparse* data have been developed (Koh et al., 2007; Fan et al., 2008).

Applying the *kernel trick* to LR as is done in SVMs, one can easily obtain a non-linear classifier with probabilistic outputs, called a *kernel logistic regression* (KLR). Because the kernel matrix is often *dense* (e.g., Gaussian kernels), the state-of-the-art LR algorithms for sparse data are not applicable to KLR. Thus, to train KLR classifiers, standard non-linear optimization techniques such as *Newton's method* (which results in *iteratively reweighted least squares*) and *quasi-Newton methods* such as the *Broyden–Fletcher–Goldfarb–Shanno* method seem to be commonly used in practice (Hastie et al., 2001; Minka, 2007). Although the performances of these general-purpose non-linear optimization techniques have been improved together with the evolution of computer environments in the last decade, computing the KLR solution is still challenging when the number of training samples is large. In this section we give an alternative probabilistic classification method that can be trained very efficiently.

The method we describe here is called the *least-squares probabilistic classifier* (LSPC). In LSPC, a linear combination of Gaussian kernels centered at training points is used as a model of class-posterior probabilities. Then this model is fitted to the true class-posterior probability by least squares.[2] An advantage of this linear least-squares formulation is that *consistency* is guaranteed without taking into account the normalization factor. In contrast, normalization is essential in the maximum likelihood LR formulation; otherwise, the likelihood tends to infinity. Thanks to the simplification brought by excluding the normalization factor from the optimization criterion, the globally optimal solution of LSPC can be computed *analytically* just by solving a system of linear equations.

Furthermore, the use of a linear combination of kernel functions in LSPC allows one to learn the parameters in a *class-wise* manner. This contributes significantly to further reducing the computational cost, particularly in multi-class classification scenarios.

12.2.2 Problem Formulation and Solutions

Here we formulate the problem of probabilistic classification and describe a method of probabilistic classification based on density-ratio estimation.

Formulation of Probabilistic Classification

Let $\mathcal{X}$ ($\subset \mathbb{R}^d$) be the input domain, where d is the dimensionality of the input domain. Let $\mathcal{Y} = \{1,\ldots,c\}$ be the set of labels, where c is the number of classes. Let us consider a joint probability distribution on $\mathcal{X} \times \mathcal{Y}$ with joint probability density $p^*(\boldsymbol{x}, y)$. Suppose that we are given n i.i.d. paired samples of input $\boldsymbol{x}$ and output y:

$$\{(\boldsymbol{x}_k, y_k) \in \mathcal{X} \times \mathcal{Y}\}_{k=1}^{n}.$$

The goal is to estimate the *class-posterior probability* $p^*(y|\boldsymbol{x})$ from the samples $\{(\boldsymbol{x}_k, y_k)\}_{k=1}^{n}$. The class-posterior probability allows one to classify test sample $\boldsymbol{x}$ to class $\widehat{y}$ with *confidence* $p^*(\widehat{y}|\boldsymbol{x})$:

$$\widehat{y} := \underset{y}{\operatorname{argmax}}\ p^*(y|\boldsymbol{x}).$$

Let us denote the marginal density of $\boldsymbol{x}$ by $p^*(\boldsymbol{x})$ and assume that it is strictly positive. Then, by definition, the class-posterior probability $p^*(y|\boldsymbol{x})$ can be expressed as

$$p^*(y|\boldsymbol{x}) = \frac{p^*(\boldsymbol{x}, y)}{p^*(\boldsymbol{x})}.$$

Here we apply *unconstrained least-squares importance fitting* (uLSIF; Kanamori et al., 2009; see also Section 6.2.2) to estimate the above density ratio and

[2] A least-squares formulation has been employed for improving the computational efficiency of SVMs (Suykens et al., 2002; Rifkin et al., 2003; Fung and Mangasarian, 2005). However, these approaches deal with deterministic classification, not probabilistic classification.

give a practical algorithm of probabilistic classification called the *least-squares probabilistic classifier* (LSPC; Sugiyama, 2010).

Least-Squares Probabilistic Classifier

We begin by describing the approach to learning the class-posterior probability $p^*(y|\boldsymbol{x})$ as a function of both $\boldsymbol{x}$ and y; that is, the class-posterior probabilities for all classes are learned simultaneously. Then we explain that this simultaneous learning problem can be decomposed into separate *class-wise* learning problems, which highly contributes to reducing the computational cost.

The class-posterior probability $p^*(y|\boldsymbol{x})$ is modeled as

$$p(y|\boldsymbol{x};\boldsymbol{\theta}) := \sum_{\ell=1}^{b} \theta_\ell \psi(\boldsymbol{x}, y) = \boldsymbol{\psi}(\boldsymbol{x}, y)^\top \boldsymbol{\theta},$$

where $\boldsymbol{\psi}(\boldsymbol{x}, y)$ $(\in \mathbb{R}^b)$ is a non-negative basis function vector and $\boldsymbol{\theta}$ $(\in \mathbb{R}^b)$ is a parameter vector. Let

$$\widehat{\boldsymbol{H}} := \frac{1}{n} \sum_{k=1}^{n} \sum_{y=1}^{c} \boldsymbol{\psi}(\boldsymbol{x}_k, y) \boldsymbol{\psi}(\boldsymbol{x}_k, y)^\top \quad \text{and} \quad \widehat{\boldsymbol{h}} := \frac{1}{n} \sum_{k=1}^{n} \boldsymbol{\psi}(\boldsymbol{x}_k, y_k).$$

Then the uLSIF solution is given analytically as follows (see Section 6.2.2):

$$\widehat{\boldsymbol{\theta}} = (\widehat{\boldsymbol{H}} + \lambda \boldsymbol{I}_b)^{-1} \widehat{\boldsymbol{h}}, \tag{12.5}$$

where λ (≥ 0) is the regularization parameter and $\boldsymbol{I}_b$ is the b-dimensional identity matrix.

To ensure that the output of LSPC is a probability, the outputs are normalized and the negative outputs are rounded up to zero as follows (Yamada et al., 2011a):

$$\widehat{p}(y|\boldsymbol{x} = \widetilde{\boldsymbol{x}}) = \frac{\max(0, \boldsymbol{\psi}(\widetilde{\boldsymbol{x}}, y)^\top \widehat{\boldsymbol{\theta}})}{\sum_{y'=1}^{c} \max(0, \boldsymbol{\psi}(\widetilde{\boldsymbol{x}}, y')^\top \widehat{\boldsymbol{\theta}})}.$$

This classification method is called the *least-squares probabilistic classifier* (LSPC).

Note that the way the solution is modified in LSPC is different from that in LSCDE (see Section 12.2.2): The negative output $\boldsymbol{\psi}(\widetilde{\boldsymbol{x}}, y)^\top \widehat{\boldsymbol{\theta}}$ is directly rounded up to zero in LSPC, whereas the negative elements of the parameter $\widehat{\boldsymbol{\theta}}$ are rounded up to zero in LSCDE. In the case of LSCDE, rounding up negative output is difficult because of the integration with respect to the output $\boldsymbol{y}$ included in the normalization factor [see Eq. (12.3)]. On the other hand, in the case of LSPC, the output y is discrete and thus directly rounding up negative output is possible. This direct rounding up was shown to be more accurate in experiments (Yamada et al., 2011a).

Basis Function Design

A naive choice of basis functions $\boldsymbol{\psi}(\boldsymbol{x}, y)$ would be a *kernel* model; that is, for some kernel function K',

$$p(y|\boldsymbol{x};\boldsymbol{\theta}) = \sum_{y'=1}^{c}\sum_{\ell=1}^{n} \theta_\ell^{(y')} K'(\boldsymbol{x},\boldsymbol{x}_\ell, y, y'), \tag{12.6}$$

which contains $c \times n$ parameters. For this model, the computational complexity for solving Eq. (12.5) is $\mathcal{O}(c^3n^3)$.

Let us now separate input $\boldsymbol{x}$ and output y and use the *delta kernel* for y (as in KLR):

$$p(y|\boldsymbol{x};\boldsymbol{\theta}) = \sum_{y'=1}^{c}\sum_{\ell=1}^{n} \theta_\ell^{(y')} K(\boldsymbol{x},\boldsymbol{x}_\ell)\delta_{y,y'},$$

where $K(\boldsymbol{x},\boldsymbol{x}')$ is a kernel function for $\boldsymbol{x}$ and $\delta_{y,y'}$ is the *Kronecker delta*; that is, $\delta_{y,y'} = 1$ if $y = y'$ and $\delta_{y,y'} = 0$ otherwise. This model choice actually allows us to speed up the computation of LSPC significantly because all of the calculations can be carried out *separately* in a class-wise manner. Indeed, this above model for class y is expressed as follows [see Figure 12.3(a)]:

$$p(y|\boldsymbol{x};\boldsymbol{\theta}) = \sum_{\ell=1}^{n} \theta_\ell^{(y)} K(\boldsymbol{x},\boldsymbol{x}_\ell). \tag{12.7}$$

Then the matrix $\widehat{\boldsymbol{H}}$ becomes block-diagonal, as illustrated in Figure 12.4. Thus, we only need to train a model with n parameters separately c times for each class y, by solving

$$(\widehat{\boldsymbol{H}}' + \lambda \boldsymbol{I}_n)\boldsymbol{\alpha}^{(y)} = \widetilde{\boldsymbol{h}}^{(y)},$$

where $\widehat{\boldsymbol{H}}'$ is the $n \times n$ matrix and $\widetilde{\boldsymbol{h}}^{(y)}$ is the n-dimensional vector defined as

$$\widehat{H}'_{\ell,\ell'} := \frac{1}{n}\sum_{i=1}^{n} K(\boldsymbol{x}_i,\boldsymbol{x}_\ell)K(\boldsymbol{x}_i,\boldsymbol{x}_{\ell'}) \quad \text{and} \quad \widetilde{h}_\ell^{(y)} := \frac{1}{n}\sum_{i=1}^{n} K(\boldsymbol{x}_i,\boldsymbol{x}_\ell)\delta_{y,y_i}.$$

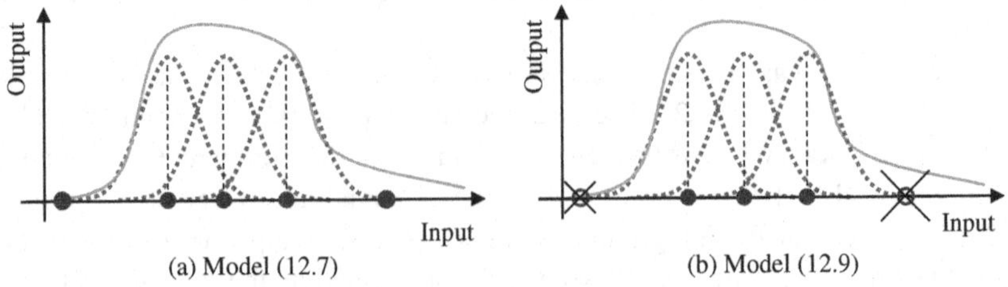

Figure 12.3. Gaussian kernel models for approximating class-posterior probabilities. (a) Locating Gaussian kernels at all samples. (b) Heuristic of reducing the number of basis functions – locate Gaussian kernels only at the samples of the target class.

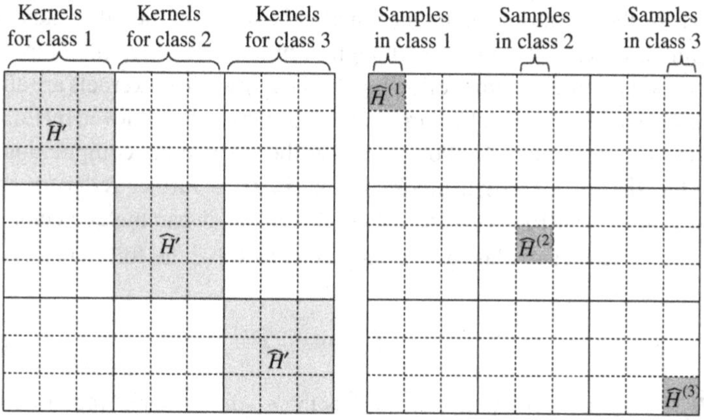

(a) Model (12.7) (b) Model (12.9)

Figure 12.4. Structure of matrix $\widehat{\boldsymbol{H}}$ for model (12.7) and model (12.9). The number of classes is $c = 3$. Suppose training samples $\{(\boldsymbol{x}_k, y_k)\}_{k=1}^n$ are sorted according to label y. Colored blocks are non-zero and others are zeros. For model (12.7) consisting of c sets of n basis functions, the matrix $\widehat{\boldsymbol{H}}$ becomes block-diagonal (with common block matrix $\widehat{\boldsymbol{H}}'$), and thus training can be carried out separately for each block. For model (12.9) consisting of c sets of n_y basis functions, the size of the target block is further reduced.

Because $\widehat{\boldsymbol{H}}'$ is common to all y, we only need to compute $(\widehat{\boldsymbol{H}}' + \lambda \boldsymbol{I}_n)^{-1}$ once. Then the computational complexity for obtaining the solution is $\mathcal{O}(n^3 + cn^2)$, which is smaller than the case with the general kernel model (12.6). Thus, this approach would be computationally efficient when the number of classes c is large.

Let us further reduce the number of kernels in model (12.7) by focusing on a kernel function $K(\boldsymbol{x},\boldsymbol{x}')$ that is "localized." Examples of such localized kernels include the popular *Gaussian kernel*:

$$K(\boldsymbol{x},\boldsymbol{x}') = \exp\left(-\frac{\|\boldsymbol{x}-\boldsymbol{x}'\|^2}{2\sigma^2}\right). \tag{12.8}$$

The key idea is to reduce the number of kernels by locating the kernels only at samples belonging to the *target* class [Figure 12.3(b)]:

$$p(y|\boldsymbol{x};\boldsymbol{\theta}) = \sum_{\ell=1}^{n_y} \theta_\ell^{(y)} K(\boldsymbol{x},\boldsymbol{x}_\ell^{(y)}), \tag{12.9}$$

where n_y is the number of training samples in class y and $\{\boldsymbol{x}_k^{(y)}\}_{k=1}^{n_y}$ is the training input samples in class y.

The rationale behind this model simplification is as follows. By definition, the class-posterior probability $p^*(y|\boldsymbol{x})$ takes large values in the regions where samples in class y are dense; conversely, $p^*(y|\boldsymbol{x})$ takes smaller values (i.e., close to zero) in the regions where samples in class y are sparse. When a non-negative function is approximated by a Gaussian kernel model, many kernels may be needed in the region where the output of the target function is large; on the other hand, only a small number of kernels would be enough in the region where the output of the target function is close to zero. Following this heuristic, many kernels are allocated in the region where $p^*(y|\boldsymbol{x})$ takes large values, which can be achieved by Eq. (12.9).

This model simplification allows us to further reduce the computational cost because the size of the target blocks in matrix $\widehat{\boldsymbol{H}}$ is further reduced, as illustrated in Figure 12.4(b). To learn the n_y-dimensional parameter vector $\boldsymbol{\theta}^{(y)} = (\theta_1^{(y)}, \ldots, \theta_{n_y}^{(y)})^\top$ for each class y, we only need to solve the following system of n_y linear equations:

$$(\widehat{\boldsymbol{H}}^{(y)} + \lambda \boldsymbol{I}_{n_y})\boldsymbol{\theta}^{(y)} = \widehat{\boldsymbol{h}}^{(y)}, \tag{12.10}$$

where $\widehat{\boldsymbol{H}}^{(y)}$ is the $n_y \times n_y$ matrix and $\widehat{\boldsymbol{h}}^{(y)}$ is the n_y-dimensional vector defined as

$$\widehat{H}_{\ell,\ell'}^{(y)} := \frac{1}{n}\sum_{k=1}^{n} K(\boldsymbol{x}_k, \boldsymbol{x}_\ell^{(y)}) K(\boldsymbol{x}_k, \boldsymbol{x}_{\ell'}^{(y)}), \tag{12.11}$$

$$\widehat{h}_\ell^{(y)} := \frac{1}{n}\sum_{k=1}^{n_y} K(\boldsymbol{x}_k^{(y)}, \boldsymbol{x}_\ell^{(y)}).$$

Let $\widehat{\boldsymbol{\theta}}^{(y)}$ be the solution of Eq. (12.10). Then the final solution is given by

$$\widehat{p}(y|\boldsymbol{x}) = \frac{\max\left(0, \sum_{\ell=1}^{n_y} \widehat{\theta}_\ell^{(y)} K(\boldsymbol{x}, \boldsymbol{x}_\ell^{(y)})\right)}{\sum_{y'=1}^{c} \max\left(0, \sum_{\ell=1}^{n_{y'}} \widehat{\theta}_\ell^{(y')} K(\boldsymbol{x}, \boldsymbol{x}_\ell^{(y')})\right)}.$$

For the simplified model (12.9), the computational complexity for obtaining the solution is $\mathcal{O}(cn_y^2 n)$; when $n_y = n/c$ for all y (i.e., *balanced* classification), this is equal to $\mathcal{O}(c^{-1}n^3)$. Thus, this approach is computationally highly efficient for multi-class problems.

A pseudo code of the simplest LSPC implementation for Gaussian kernels is summarized in Figure 12.5. A MATLAB® implementation of LSPC is available from http://sugiyama-www.cs.titech.ac.jp/~sugi/software/LSPC/.

12.2.3 Numerical Experiments

Here, we experimentally compare the performance of the following classification methods:

LSPC: LSPC with the simplified model (12.9)
LSPC(full): LSPC with the full model (12.7)
KLR: ℓ_2-penalized kernel logistic regression with Gaussian kernels (see Section 4.2)

For computing KLR, we used a MATLAB® implementation included in the *minFunc* package (Schmidt, 2005), which uses limited-memory *Broyden–Fletcher–Goldfarb–Shanno* (L-BFGS) updates with *Shanno–Phua scaling* in

Input: Labeled training samples $\{(\boldsymbol{x}_k, y_k\}_{k=1}^n$
(equivalently, $\{\boldsymbol{x}_k^{(y)}\}_{k=1}^{n_y}$ for class $y = 1,\ldots,c$)
Gaussian width σ, and regularization parameter λ;
Output: Class-posterior probability $\widehat{p}(y|\boldsymbol{x})$;

for $y = 1,\ldots,c$
  % $K(\boldsymbol{x},\boldsymbol{x}') = \exp\left(-\frac{\|\boldsymbol{x}-\boldsymbol{x}'\|^2}{2\sigma^2}\right)$
  $\widehat{H}_{\ell,\ell'}^{(y)} \longleftarrow \frac{1}{n}\sum_{k=1}^{n} K(\boldsymbol{x}_k,\boldsymbol{x}_\ell^{(y)})K(\boldsymbol{x}_k,\boldsymbol{x}_{\ell'}^{(y)})$ for $\ell,\ell' = 1,\ldots,n_y$;
  $\widehat{h}_\ell^{(y)} \longleftarrow \frac{1}{n}\sum_{k=1}^{n_y} K(\boldsymbol{x}_k^{(y)},\boldsymbol{x}_\ell^{(y)})$ for $\ell = 1,\ldots,n_y$;
  Solve linear equation $(\widehat{\boldsymbol{H}}^{(y)} + \lambda \boldsymbol{I}_{n_y})\boldsymbol{\theta}^{(y)} = \widehat{\boldsymbol{h}}^{(y)}$ and obtain $\widehat{\boldsymbol{\theta}}^{(y)}$;
end
$\widehat{p}(y|\boldsymbol{x}) \longleftarrow \frac{\max(0,\sum_{\ell=1}^{n_y}\widehat{\theta}_\ell^{(y)}K(\boldsymbol{x},\boldsymbol{x}_\ell^{(y)}))}{\sum_{y'=1}^{c}\max(0,\sum_{\ell=1}^{n_{y'}}\widehat{\theta}_\ell^{(y')}K(\boldsymbol{x},\boldsymbol{x}_\ell^{(y')}))}$

Figure 12.5. Pseudo code of LSPC for simplified model (12.9) with Gaussian kernel (12.8).

computing the step direction and a bracketing line search for a point satisfying the *strong Wolfe conditions* to compute the step size.

When data are fed to learning algorithms, the input samples are normalized in element-wise manner so that each element has mean zero and unit variance. The Gaussian width σ and the regularization parameter λ for all the methods are chosen based on 2-fold cross-validation from

$$\sigma \in \{\tfrac{1}{10}m, \tfrac{1}{5}m, \tfrac{1}{2}m, \tfrac{2}{3}m, m, \tfrac{3}{2}m, 2m, 5m, 10m\},$$
$$\lambda \in \{10^{-2}, 10^{-1.5}, 10^{-1}, 10^{-0.5}, 10^{0}\},$$

where $m := \text{median}(\{\|\boldsymbol{x}_k - \boldsymbol{x}_{k'}\|\}_{k,k'=1}^n)$.

We evaluate the classification accuracy and computation time of each method using the following multi-class classification datasets taken from the *LIBSVM* web page (Chang and Lin, 2001):

***satimage*:** Input dimensionality is 36 and the number of classes is 6.
***letter*:** Input dimensionality is 16 and the number of classes is 26.

We investigate the classification accuracy and computation time of LSPC, LSPC(full), and KLR. For given n and c, we randomly choose $n_y = \lfloor n/c \rfloor$ training samples from each class y, where $\lfloor t \rfloor$ is the largest integer not greater than t. In the first set of experiments, we fix the number of classes c to the original number shown above and change the number of training samples to $n = 100, 200, 500, 1000, 2000$. In the second set of experiments, we fix the number of training samples to $n = 1000$ and change the number of classes c – only samples in the first c classes in the dataset are used. The classification accuracy is evaluated using 100 test samples chosen randomly from each class. The computation time is measured by the CPU computation time required for training each classifier when the Gaussian width and the regularization parameter chosen by cross-validation are used.

The experimental results are summarized in Figures 12.6 and 12.7. The graphs on the left in Figure 12.6 show the misclassification errors. When n is increased, the misclassification error for all the methods tends to decrease and LSPC, LSPC(full), and KLR perform similarly well. The graphs on the right in Figure 12.6 show the computation times. When n is increased, the computation time tends to grow for all the methods, but LSPC is faster than KLR by two orders of magnitude. The graphs on the left in Figure 12.7 show that when c is increased, the misclassification error tends to increase for all the methods, and LSPC, LSPC(full), and KLR behave similarly well. The graphs on the right in Figure 12.7 show that when c is increased, the computation time of KLR tends to grow, whereas that of LSPC is kept constant or even tends to decrease slightly. This happens because the number of samples in each class decreases when c is increased, and the computation time of LSPC is governed by the number of samples in *each* class, not by the *total* number of samples (see Section 12.2.2).

Overall, the computation of LSPC was shown to be faster than that of KLR by two orders of magnitude, whereas LSPC and KLR were shown to be comparable to each other in terms of classification accuracy. LSPC and LSPC(full) were shown to possess similar classification performances, and thus LSPC with the simplified model (12.9) would be more preferable in practice.

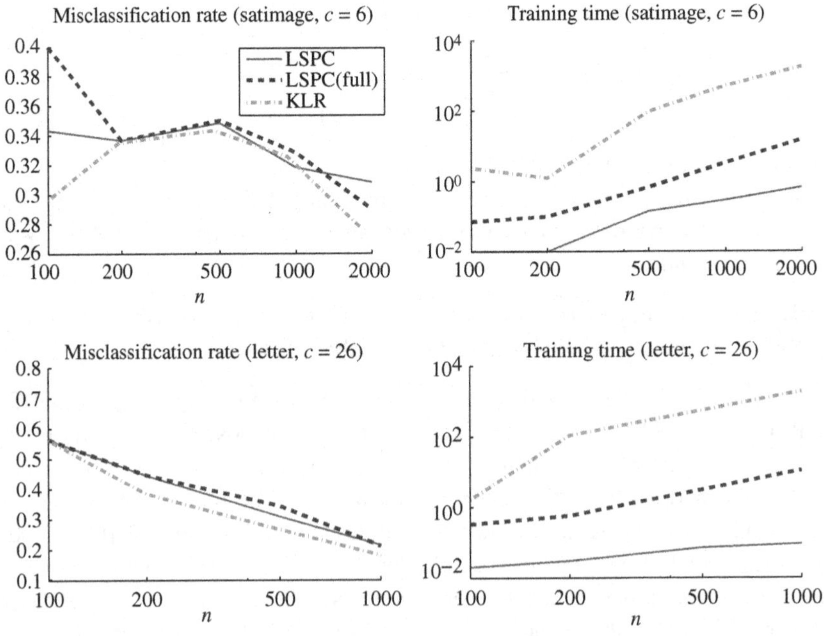

Figure 12.6. Misclassification rates (in percent, left) and computation times (in second, right) as functions of the number of training samples n. The two rows correspond to the *satimage*, and *letter* datasets, respectively.

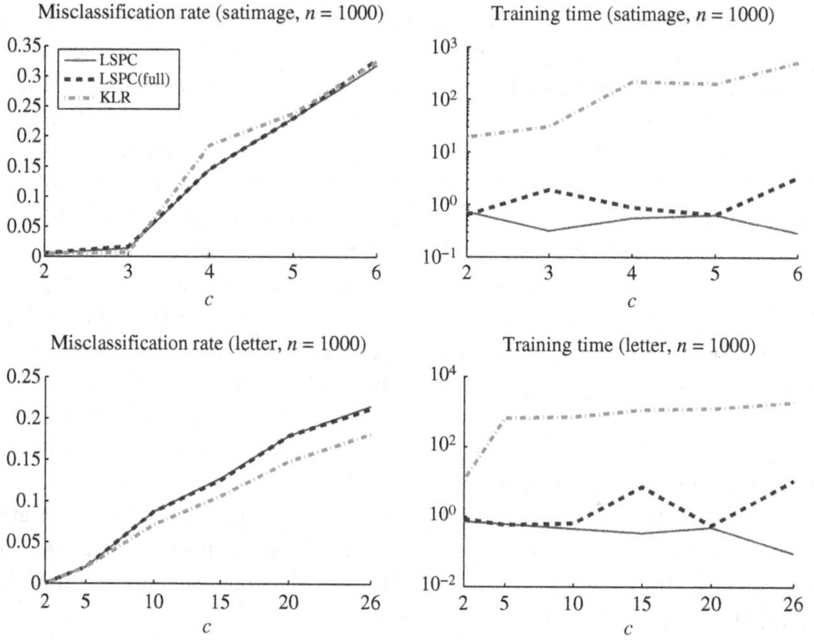

Figure 12.7. Misclassification rate (in percent, left) and computation time (in second, right) as functions of the number of classes c. From top to bottom, the graphs correspond to the 'mnist', 'usps', 'satimage', and 'letter' datasets.

12.2.4 Remarks

Recently, various efficient algorithms for computing the solution of logistic regressions have been developed for high-dimensional *sparse* data (Koh et al., 2007; Fan et al., 2008). However, for *dense* data, using standard non-linear optimization techniques such as Newton's method or quasi-Newton methods seem to be a common choice (Hastie et al., 2001; Minka, 2007). The performance of these general-purpose non-linear optimizers has been improved in the last decade, but computing the solution of logistic regressions for a large number of dense training samples is still a challenging problem.

In this section we described a probabilistic classification algorithm called a *least-squares probabilistic classifier* (LSPC). LSPC employs a linear combination of Gaussian kernels centered at training points for modeling the class-posterior probability, and the parameters are learned by least-squares class-posterior fitting. The notable advantages of LSPC are that its solution can be computed *analytically* just by solving a system of linear equations and training can be carried out separately in a class-wise manner. LSPC was shown experimentally to be faster than kernel logistic regression (KLR) in computation time by two orders of magnitude, with comparable accuracy.

The computational efficiency of LSPC was brought by the combination of appropriate model choice and loss function. More specifically, KLR uses a log-linear combination of kernel functions and its parameters are learned by regularized maximum likelihood. In this log-linear maximum likelihood formulation, normalization of the model is essential to avoid the likelihood diverging to infinity. Thus, the likelihood function tends to be complicated and numerically solving the optimization problem may be unavoidable. On the other hand, in LSPC, a linear combination of Gaussian kernel functions was used for modeling the class-posterior probability and its parameters were learned by regularized least-squares class-posterior fitting. This combination allows one to obtain the solution analytically. When Newton's method (more specifically, *iteratively reweighted least squares*) is used for learning the KLR model, a system of linear equations needs to be solved in *every* iteration until convergence (Hastie et al., 2001). On the other hand, LSPC requires that one solves a system of linear equations only once to obtain the global optimal solution.

It is straightforward to show that solutions for *all* regularization parameter values (i.e., the *regularization path*; see Efron et al., 2004; Hastie et al., 2004) can be computed efficiently in LSPC. Let us consider the eigendecomposition of the matrix $\widehat{\boldsymbol{H}}^{(y)}$ [see Eq. (12.11)]:

$$\widehat{\boldsymbol{H}}^{(y)} = \sum_{\ell=1}^{n_y} \gamma_\ell \boldsymbol{\psi}_\ell \boldsymbol{\psi}_\ell^\top,$$

where $\{\boldsymbol{\psi}_\ell\}_{\ell=1}^{n_y}$ are the eigenvectors of $\widehat{\boldsymbol{H}}^{(y)}$ associated with the eigenvalues $\{\gamma_\ell\}_{\ell=1}^{n_y}$. Then, the solution $\widehat{\boldsymbol{\theta}}^{(y)}$ can be expressed as

$$\widehat{\boldsymbol{\theta}}^{(y)} = (\widehat{\boldsymbol{H}}^{(y)} + \lambda \boldsymbol{I}_{n_y})^{-1} \widehat{\boldsymbol{h}}^{(y)} = \sum_{\ell=1}^{n_y} \frac{\widehat{\boldsymbol{h}}^\top \boldsymbol{\psi}_\ell}{\gamma_\ell + \lambda} \boldsymbol{\psi}_\ell.$$

Because $(\widehat{\boldsymbol{h}}^\top \boldsymbol{\psi}_\ell)\boldsymbol{\psi}_\ell$ is common to all λ, the solution $\widehat{\boldsymbol{\theta}}^{(y)}$ for all λ can be computed efficiently by eigendecomposing the matrix $\widehat{\boldsymbol{H}}^{(y)}$ *once* in advance. Although the eigendecomposition of $\widehat{\boldsymbol{H}}^{(y)}$ may be computationally slightly more demanding than solving a system of linear equations of the same size, this approach would be useful, for example, when computing the solutions for various values of λ in the cross-validation procedure.

When n_y is large, we may further reduce the computational cost and memory space by using only a subset of kernels. This would be a useful heuristic when a large number of samples are used for training. Another option for reducing the computation time when the number of samples is very large is the *stochastic gradient descent* method (Amari, 1967). That is, starting from some initial parameter value, gradient descent is carried out only for a randomly chosen *single* sample in each iteration. Because our optimization problem is convex, convergence to the global solution is guaranteed (in the probabilistic sense) by stochastic gradient descent.

Part IV

Theoretical Analysis of Density-Ratio Estimation

In this part we address theoretical aspects of density-ratio estimation.

In Chapter 13, we analyze the asymptotic properties of density-ratio estimation. We first establish the consistency and asymptotic normality of the KLIEP method (see Chapter 5) in Section 13.1, and we elucidate the asymptotic learning curve of the LSIF method (see Chapter 6) in Section 13.2. Then, in Section 13.3, we explain that the logistic regression method (see Chapter 4) achieves the minimum asymptotic variance when the parametric model is specified correctly. Finally, in Section 13.4, we compare theoretically the performance of density-ratio estimation methods, showing that separate density estimation (see Chapter 2) is favorable if correct density models are available, and direct density-ratio estimation is favorable otherwise.

In Chapter 14, the convergence rates of KLIEP (see Chapter 5) and uLSIF (see Chapter 6) are investigated theoretically under the non-parametric setup

In Chapter 15, a parametric method of a two-sample test is described, and its properties are analyzed. We derive an optimal estimator of the divergence in the sense of the asymptotic variance, which is based on parametric density-ratio estimation. Then we provide a statistic for two-sample tests based on the optimal divergence estimator, which is proved to dominate the existing empirical likelihood-score test.

Finally, in Chapter 16, the numerical stability of kernelized density-ratio estimators is analyzed. As shown in Section 7.2.2, the ratio fitting and the moment matching methods share the same solution in theory, although the optimization criteria are different. This fact may have a strong impact on the numerical stability and computational efficiency. We show that uLSIF has the smallest *condition numbers* among a class of estimators, implying that it would be numerically more reliable and computationally more efficient

Part IV

13

Parametric Convergence Analysis

In this chapter we theoretically elucidate the convergence properties of density-ratio estimation under the parameric setup. In Sections 13.1 and 13.2, we investigate the asymptotic behavior of the KLIEP method (see Chapter 5) and the LSIF method (see Chapter 6), respectively. Then, in Section 13.3, the optimality of the logistic regression method (see Chapter 4) is shown under the correctly specified parametric setup. Finally, in Section 13.4, we theoretically compare the performance of density-ratio estimation by density estimation (see Chapter 2), logistic regression (see Chapter 4), and Kullback–Leibler density-ratio fitting (see Chapter 5). The chapter is concluded in Section 13.5.

Let us recall the notation of our density-ratio estimation problem: Let $\mathcal{X}$ ($\subset \mathbb{R}^d$) be the data domain, and suppose we are given i.i.d. samples $\{\boldsymbol{x}_i^{\mathrm{nu}}\}_{i=1}^{n_{\mathrm{nu}}}$ drawn from a distribution P_{nu}^* with density $p_{\mathrm{nu}}^*(\boldsymbol{x})$ and i.i.d. samples $\{\boldsymbol{x}_j^{\mathrm{de}}\}_{j=1}^{n_{\mathrm{de}}}$ drawn from another distribution P_{de}^* with density $p_{\mathrm{de}}^*(\boldsymbol{x})$:

$$\{\boldsymbol{x}_i^{\mathrm{nu}}\}_{i=1}^{n_{\mathrm{nu}}} \overset{\text{i.i.d.}}{\sim} P_{\mathrm{nu}}^* \quad \text{and} \quad \{\boldsymbol{x}_j^{\mathrm{de}}\}_{j=1}^{n_{\mathrm{de}}} \overset{\text{i.i.d.}}{\sim} P_{\mathrm{de}}^*.$$

We assume that $p_{\mathrm{de}}^*(\boldsymbol{x})$ is strictly positive. The goal is to estimate the density ratio $r^*(\boldsymbol{x}) = p_{\mathrm{nu}}^*(\boldsymbol{x})/p_{\mathrm{de}}^*(\boldsymbol{x})$ based on the observed samples. In this chapter we focus on using a *parametric* model (i.e., a finite-dimensional model) for density-ratio estimation.

13.1 Density-Ratio Fitting under Kullback–Leibler Divergence

In this section we show the asymptotic normality of KLIEP in the parametric setup. All the proofs of the theorems in this subsection can be found in Sugiyama et al. (2008).

13.1.1 Preliminaries

We consider a linear parametric model with b basis functions $\{\varphi_\ell \mid \ell = 1,\ldots,b\}$. Letting $\boldsymbol{\varphi}(\boldsymbol{x}) := (\varphi_1(\boldsymbol{x}),\ldots,\varphi_b(\boldsymbol{x}))^\top$, we can express our parametric model $\mathcal{R}$ as

$$\mathcal{R} := \left\{\boldsymbol{\alpha}^\top \boldsymbol{\varphi} \mid \boldsymbol{\alpha} \geq \mathbf{0}\right\}.$$

For simplicity, we assume $n = n_{\mathrm{nu}} = n_{\mathrm{de}}$. Let $\widehat{r}_n$ be the density ratio estimated by KLIEP, which is given as the solution to the following optimization problem:

$$\widehat{r}_n := \underset{r\in\mathcal{R}}{\mathrm{argmax}} \left[\frac{1}{n}\sum_{i=1}^{n} \log(r(\boldsymbol{x}_i^{\mathrm{nu}}))\right] \quad \text{s.t. } \frac{1}{n}\sum_{j=1}^{n} r(\boldsymbol{x}_j^{\mathrm{de}}) = 1.$$

Let $\widehat{\boldsymbol{\alpha}}_n$ be the coefficient corresponding to $\widehat{r}_n$, that is, $\widehat{r}_n = \widehat{\boldsymbol{\alpha}}_n^\top \boldsymbol{\varphi}$, and let $\boldsymbol{\alpha}^*$ be the coefficient of the true density-ratio function:

$$r^* = \boldsymbol{\varphi}^\top \boldsymbol{\alpha}^* = \frac{p^*_{\mathrm{de}}}{p^*_{\mathrm{nu}}}.$$

For any function r, let us define P^*_{nu}, P^*_{de}, $\widehat{P}^*_{\mathrm{nu}}$, and $\widehat{P}^*_{\mathrm{de}}$ as

$$P^*_{\mathrm{nu}} r := \int r(\boldsymbol{x}) p^*_{\mathrm{nu}}(\boldsymbol{x}) \mathrm{d}\boldsymbol{x}, \quad P^*_{\mathrm{de}} r := \int r(\boldsymbol{x}) p^*_{\mathrm{de}}(\boldsymbol{x}) \mathrm{d}\boldsymbol{x},$$

$$\widehat{P}^*_{\mathrm{nu}} r := \frac{1}{n}\sum_{i=1}^{n} r(\boldsymbol{x}_i^{\mathrm{nu}}), \quad \widehat{P}^*_{\mathrm{de}} r := \frac{1}{n}\sum_{j=1}^{n} r(\boldsymbol{x}_j^{\mathrm{de}}).$$

We define the (generalized) Hellinger distance with respect to p^*_{de} as

$$h_{p^*_{\mathrm{de}}}(r, r') := \left(\int \left(\sqrt{r(\boldsymbol{x})} - \sqrt{r'(\boldsymbol{x})}\right)^2 p^*_{\mathrm{de}}(\boldsymbol{x}) \mathrm{d}\boldsymbol{x}\right)^{1/2},$$

where r and r' are non-negative measurable functions (not necessarily probability densities).

We assume the following conditions:

Assumption 13.1

1. *The density ratio r^* is bounded from both above and below:*

$$0 < \eta_0 \leq r^* \leq \eta_1$$

on the support of p^*_{nu}.

2. $\exists \epsilon^*, \xi^* > 0$ *such that*

$$\int \varphi_l(\boldsymbol{x}) p^*_{\mathrm{de}}(\boldsymbol{x}) \mathrm{d}\boldsymbol{x} \geq \epsilon^*, \quad \|\varphi_l\|_\infty \leq \xi^*, \quad (\forall \varphi_l \in \mathcal{F}).$$

3. $\int \boldsymbol{\varphi}(\boldsymbol{x})\boldsymbol{\varphi}(\boldsymbol{x})^\top p^*_{\mathrm{de}}(\boldsymbol{x})\mathrm{d}\boldsymbol{x} \succ O$ *(positive definite).*
4. *The model contains the true density-ratio function: $r^* \in \mathcal{R}$.*

Let $\psi(\boldsymbol{\alpha}) := \log(\boldsymbol{\alpha}^\top \boldsymbol{\varphi}(\boldsymbol{x}))$. Note that if $P^*_{\rm de}(\boldsymbol{\varphi}\boldsymbol{\varphi}^\top) \succ O$ is satisfied, then we obtain the following inequality for all $\boldsymbol{\beta} \neq \mathbf{0}$:

$$\begin{aligned}\boldsymbol{\beta}^\top \nabla^2 P^*_{\rm nu}\psi(\boldsymbol{\alpha}^*)\boldsymbol{\beta} &= \boldsymbol{\beta}^\top \nabla P^*_{\rm nu} \frac{\boldsymbol{\varphi}^\top}{\boldsymbol{\alpha}^\top\boldsymbol{\varphi}}\bigg|_{\boldsymbol{\alpha}=\boldsymbol{\alpha}^*}\boldsymbol{\beta} = -\boldsymbol{\beta}^\top P^*_{\rm nu}\frac{\boldsymbol{\varphi}\boldsymbol{\varphi}^\top}{(\boldsymbol{\varphi}^\top\boldsymbol{\alpha}^*)^2}\boldsymbol{\beta}\\ &= -\boldsymbol{\beta}^\top P^*_{\rm de}\frac{\boldsymbol{\varphi}\boldsymbol{\varphi}^\top}{(\boldsymbol{\varphi}^\top\boldsymbol{\alpha}^*)}\boldsymbol{\beta} \le -\boldsymbol{\beta}^\top P^*_{\rm de}(\boldsymbol{\varphi}\boldsymbol{\varphi}^\top)\boldsymbol{\beta}/\eta_1 < 0.\end{aligned}$$

Thus, $-\boldsymbol{\beta}^\top \nabla^2 P^*_{\rm nu}\psi(\boldsymbol{\alpha}^*)\boldsymbol{\beta}$ is also positive definite. Let

$$\boldsymbol{G}^* := -\nabla^2 P^*_{\rm nu}\psi(\boldsymbol{\alpha}^*) = P^*_{\rm nu}\nabla\psi(\boldsymbol{\alpha}^*)\nabla\psi(\boldsymbol{\alpha}^*)^\top \ (\succ O).$$

13.1.2 Consistency and Asymptotic Normality

We first give the $\sqrt{n}$-consistency result of $\widehat{\boldsymbol{\alpha}}_n/c_n$, where

$$c_n := (\widehat{P}^*_{\rm de} r^*)^{-1} = \left(\frac{1}{n}\sum_{j=1}^{n} r^*(\boldsymbol{x}^{\rm de}_j)\right)^{-1}.$$

Let $\|\cdot\|_{\boldsymbol{G}^*}$ denote a norm defined as

$$\|\boldsymbol{\alpha}\|^2_{\boldsymbol{G}^*} := \boldsymbol{\alpha}^\top \boldsymbol{G}^*\boldsymbol{\alpha}.$$

By the positivity of $\boldsymbol{G}^*$ there exist $0 < \xi_1 < \xi_2$ such that

$$\xi_1\|\boldsymbol{\alpha}\| \le \|\boldsymbol{\alpha}\|_{\boldsymbol{G}^*} \le \xi_2\|\boldsymbol{\alpha}\|. \tag{13.1}$$

Then we have the following lemma.

Lemma 13.2 *Under Assumption 13.1, the KLIEP estimator for a finite fixed-dimensional model satisfies*

$$\|\widehat{\boldsymbol{\alpha}}_n/c_n - \boldsymbol{\alpha}^*\| = \mathcal{O}_p(1/\sqrt{n}).$$

Remark. *From the relationship* (13.1)*, Lemma 13.2 also implies* $\|\widehat{\boldsymbol{\alpha}}_n/c_n - \boldsymbol{\alpha}^*\|_{\boldsymbol{G}^*} = \mathcal{O}_p(1/\sqrt{n})$, *which indicates*

$$h_{P^*_{\rm de}}(\widehat{r}_n, c_n r^*) = \mathcal{O}_p(1/\sqrt{n}).$$

Next we establish the asymptotic normality. Let

$$\begin{aligned}\mathcal{S} &:= \{\boldsymbol{\alpha} \mid P^*_{\rm de}(\boldsymbol{\alpha}^\top\boldsymbol{\varphi}) = 1, \boldsymbol{\alpha} \ge \mathbf{0}\},\\ \mathcal{S}_n &:= \{\boldsymbol{\alpha} \mid \widehat{P}^*_{\rm de}(\boldsymbol{\alpha}^\top\boldsymbol{\varphi}) = 1/c_n, \boldsymbol{\alpha} \ge \mathbf{0}\}.\end{aligned}$$

Note that $\boldsymbol{\alpha}^* \in \mathcal{S}$ and $\widehat{\boldsymbol{\alpha}}_n/c_n, \boldsymbol{\alpha}^* \in \mathcal{S}_n$. Let the approximating cones of $\mathcal{S}$ and $\mathcal{S}_n$ at $\boldsymbol{\alpha}^*$ be $\mathcal{C}$ and $\mathcal{C}_n$, respectively, where an approximating cone is defined as follows.

Definition 13.3 *Let $\mathcal{D}$ be a closed subset in $\mathbb{R}^k$ and $\boldsymbol{\theta} \in \mathcal{D}$ be a non-isolated point in $\mathcal{D}$. If there is a closed cone A that satisfies the following conditions, we define A as an approximating cone at $\boldsymbol{\theta}$:*

- *For an arbitrary sequence* $\boldsymbol{y}_i \in \mathcal{D} - \boldsymbol{\theta}$, $\boldsymbol{y}_i \to 0$,

$$\inf_{x \in A} \|\boldsymbol{x} - \boldsymbol{y}_i\| = o(\|\boldsymbol{y}_i\|).$$

- *For an arbitrary sequence* $\boldsymbol{x}_i \in A$, $\boldsymbol{x}_i \to 0$,

$$\inf_{y \in \mathcal{D} - \boldsymbol{\theta}} \|\boldsymbol{x}_i - \boldsymbol{y}\| = o(\|\boldsymbol{x}_i\|).$$

The ϵ-ball around $\boldsymbol{\alpha}$ is denoted by

$$\mathcal{B}(\boldsymbol{\alpha}, \epsilon) := \{\boldsymbol{\alpha}' \mid \|\boldsymbol{\alpha}' - \boldsymbol{\alpha}\| \leq \epsilon\}.$$

Now $\mathcal{S}$ and $\mathcal{S}_n$ are convex polytopes, so that the approximating cones at $\boldsymbol{\alpha}^*$ are also convex polytopes and

$$\mathcal{C} = \{\lambda(\boldsymbol{\alpha} - \boldsymbol{\alpha}^*) \mid \boldsymbol{\alpha} \in \mathcal{S} \cap \mathcal{B}(\boldsymbol{\alpha}^*, \epsilon),\ \lambda \geq 0\},$$
$$\mathcal{C}_n = \{\lambda(\boldsymbol{\alpha} - \boldsymbol{\alpha}^*) \mid \boldsymbol{\alpha} \in \mathcal{S}_n \cap \mathcal{B}(\boldsymbol{\alpha}^*, \epsilon),\ \lambda \geq 0\}$$

for a sufficiently small ϵ. There is no loss of generality if we assume $\alpha_{0,i} = 0$ $(i = 1, \ldots, j)$ and $\alpha_{0,i} > 0$ $(i = j+1, \ldots, b)$ for some j. Let $\nu_i := P_{\text{de}}^* \varphi_i$. Then the approximating cone $\mathcal{C}$ is spanned by $\boldsymbol{\mu}_i$ $(i = 1, \ldots, b-1)$ defined as

$$\boldsymbol{\mu}_1 := \begin{bmatrix} 1 \\ 0 \\ \vdots \\ 0 \\ -\frac{\nu_1}{\nu_{j+1}} \\ 0 \\ \vdots \\ 0 \end{bmatrix}, \ldots, \boldsymbol{\mu}_j := \begin{bmatrix} 0 \\ \vdots \\ 0 \\ 1 \\ -\frac{\nu_j}{\nu_{j+1}} \\ 0 \\ \vdots \\ 0 \end{bmatrix}, \boldsymbol{\mu}_{j+1} := \begin{bmatrix} 0 \\ \vdots \\ 0 \\ 0 \\ -\frac{\nu_{j+2}}{\nu_{j+1}} \\ 1 \\ \vdots \\ 0 \end{bmatrix}, \ldots, \boldsymbol{\mu}_{b-1} := \begin{bmatrix} 0 \\ \vdots \\ 0 \\ 0 \\ -\frac{\nu_b}{\nu_{j+1}} \\ 0 \\ \vdots \\ 1 \end{bmatrix}.$$

That is,

$$\mathcal{C} = \left\{ \sum_{i=1}^{j} \lambda_i \boldsymbol{\mu}_i + \sum_{i=j+1}^{b-1} \boldsymbol{\beta}_i \boldsymbol{\mu}_i \mid \lambda_i \geq 0, \boldsymbol{\beta}_i \in \mathbb{R} \right\}.$$

Then we obtain the asymptotic law of $\sqrt{n}(\widehat{\boldsymbol{\alpha}}_n / c_n - \boldsymbol{\alpha}^*)$.

Theorem 13.4 *Let* $Z \sim \mathcal{N}(0, \boldsymbol{G}^{*-1})$. *Then*

$$\sqrt{n}(\widehat{\boldsymbol{\alpha}}_n / c_n - \boldsymbol{\alpha}^*) \rightsquigarrow \operatorname*{argmin}_{\delta \in \mathcal{C}} \|\delta - Z\|_{\boldsymbol{G}^*} \quad \textit{(convergence in law)}.$$

In addition to Theorem 13.4, we can show the asymptotic law of $\sqrt{n}(\widehat{\boldsymbol{\alpha}}_n - \boldsymbol{\alpha}^*)$ as follows.

Theorem 13.5 *Let $Z \sim \mathcal{N}(0, \boldsymbol{G}^{*-1})$ and $Z' \sim \mathcal{N}(0, P^*_{\mathrm{de}}(r^* - 1)^2)$, where Z and Z' are independent. Then*

$$\sqrt{n}(\widehat{\boldsymbol{\alpha}}_n - \boldsymbol{\alpha}^*) \rightsquigarrow \operatorname*{argmin}_{\delta \in C} \|\delta - Z\|_{G^*} + \boldsymbol{\alpha}^* Z' \quad \text{(convergence in law)}.$$

Remark. *It can be easily checked that*

$$\boldsymbol{\mu}_i^\top \boldsymbol{G}^* \boldsymbol{\alpha}^* = 0 \quad (i = 1, \ldots, b-1).$$

Thus, Theorem 13.5 gives an orthogonal decomposition of the asymptotic law of $\sqrt{n}(\widehat{\boldsymbol{\alpha}}_n - \boldsymbol{\alpha}^*)$ to a parallel part and an orthogonal part to C. Moreover, if $p^*_{\mathrm{nu}} = p^*_{\mathrm{de}}$, then $r^* = 1$, so that the orthogonal part vanishes.

13.2 Density-Ratio Fitting under Squared Distance

In this section we elucidate the statistical properties of parametric density-ratio estimation under the squared distance, *least-squares importance fitting* (LSIF) introduced in Chapter 6.

13.2.1 Preliminaries

Let us model the density ratio $r^*(\boldsymbol{x}) = p^*_{\mathrm{nu}}(\boldsymbol{x})/p^*_{\mathrm{de}}(\boldsymbol{x})$ by the following linear model:

$$r(\boldsymbol{x}; \boldsymbol{\theta}) = \sum_{\ell=1}^{b} \theta_\ell \varphi_\ell(\boldsymbol{x}),$$

where $\varphi_1, \ldots, \varphi_b$ are basis functions and $\boldsymbol{\theta} = (\theta_1, \ldots, \theta_b)$ is the parameter vector. We assume that the basis functions are non-negative. Let $\widehat{\boldsymbol{H}}$ be the $b \times b$ matrix with the (ℓ, ℓ')-element

$$\widehat{H}_{\ell,\ell'} = \frac{1}{n_{\mathrm{de}}} \sum_{j=1}^{n_{\mathrm{de}}} \varphi_\ell(\boldsymbol{x}_j^{\mathrm{de}}) \varphi_{\ell'}(\boldsymbol{x}_j^{\mathrm{de}}),$$

and let $\widehat{\boldsymbol{h}}$ be the b-dimensional vector with the ℓ-th element

$$\widehat{h}_\ell = \frac{1}{n_{\mathrm{nu}}} \sum_{i=1}^{n_{\mathrm{nu}}} \varphi_\ell(\boldsymbol{x}_i^{\mathrm{nu}}).$$

Similarly, the elements of the $b \times b$ matrix $\boldsymbol{H}$ and the b-dimensional vector $\boldsymbol{h}$ are defined as

$$H_{\ell,\ell'} = \int \varphi_\ell(\boldsymbol{x}) \varphi_{\ell'}(\boldsymbol{x}) p^*_{\mathrm{de}}(\boldsymbol{x}) d\boldsymbol{x} \quad \text{and} \quad h_\ell = \int \varphi_\ell(\boldsymbol{x}) p^*_{\mathrm{nu}}(\boldsymbol{x}) d\boldsymbol{x},$$

which are obtained as the infinite sample limits of $\widehat{\boldsymbol{H}}$ and $\widehat{\boldsymbol{h}}$, respectively.

Suppose that the linear model $r(\boldsymbol{x};\boldsymbol{\theta})$ includes the true density ratio $r^*(\boldsymbol{x})$. Then, if the sample sizes n_{de} and n_{nu} tend to infinity, both the constrained LSIF (cLSIF; Section 6.2.1) and the unconstrained LSIF (uLSIF; Section 6.2.2) estimators will converge to $r^*(\boldsymbol{x})$. In the following we present the asymptotic properties of these estimators.

Let us consider the squared distance between two ratios, $r^*(\boldsymbol{x})$ and $r(\boldsymbol{x};\boldsymbol{\theta})$:

$$\begin{aligned} J_0(\boldsymbol{\theta}) &= \frac{1}{2}\int (r(\boldsymbol{x};\boldsymbol{\theta}) - r^*(\boldsymbol{x}))^2 p^*_{\mathrm{de}}(\boldsymbol{x})d\boldsymbol{x} \\ &= \frac{1}{2}\int r(\boldsymbol{x};\boldsymbol{\theta})^2 p^*_{\mathrm{de}}(\boldsymbol{x})d\boldsymbol{x} - \int r(\boldsymbol{x};\boldsymbol{\theta}) p^*_{\mathrm{nu}}(\boldsymbol{x})d\boldsymbol{x} + \frac{1}{2}\int r^*(\boldsymbol{x})^2 p^*_{\mathrm{de}}(\boldsymbol{x})d\boldsymbol{x}, \end{aligned}$$

where the last term is a constant and therefore can be safely ignored. Let us denote the first two terms by J:

$$\begin{aligned} J(\boldsymbol{\theta}) &= \frac{1}{2}\int r(\boldsymbol{x};\boldsymbol{\theta})^2 p^*_{\mathrm{de}}(\boldsymbol{x})d\boldsymbol{x} - \int r(\boldsymbol{x};\boldsymbol{\theta}) p^*_{\mathrm{nu}}(\boldsymbol{x})d\boldsymbol{x} \\ &= \frac{1}{2}\sum_{\ell,\ell'=1}^{b} \theta_\ell \theta_{\ell'} \int \varphi_\ell(\boldsymbol{x})\varphi_{\ell'}(\boldsymbol{x}) p^*_{\mathrm{de}}(\boldsymbol{x})d\boldsymbol{x} - \sum_{\ell=1}^{b} \theta_\ell \int \varphi_\ell(\boldsymbol{x}) p^*_{\mathrm{nu}}(\boldsymbol{x})d\boldsymbol{x} \\ &= \frac{1}{2}\boldsymbol{\theta}^\top \boldsymbol{H}\boldsymbol{\theta} - \boldsymbol{h}^\top\boldsymbol{\theta}. \end{aligned}$$

The accuracy of the estimated ratio $r(\boldsymbol{x};\widehat{\boldsymbol{\theta}})$ is measured by $J(\widehat{\boldsymbol{\theta}})$.

13.2.2 Asymptotic Properties of cLSIF

As shown in Section 6.2.1, the constrained LSIF (cLSIF) estimator is given as the optimal solution of the quadratic optimization problem

$$\max_{\boldsymbol{\theta}\in\mathbb{R}^b} \left[\frac{1}{2}\boldsymbol{\theta}^\top \widehat{\boldsymbol{H}}\boldsymbol{\theta} - \widehat{\boldsymbol{h}}^\top\boldsymbol{\theta} + \lambda \boldsymbol{1}_b^\top \boldsymbol{\theta}\right] \quad \text{s.t. } \boldsymbol{\theta} \geq \boldsymbol{0}_b, \tag{13.2}$$

where $\boldsymbol{0}_b$ and $\boldsymbol{1}_b$ are the b-dimensional vectors with all zeros and ones, respectively; the vector inequality $\boldsymbol{\theta} \geq \boldsymbol{0}_b$ is applied in an element-wise manner, that is, $\theta_\ell \geq 0$ for $\ell = 1,\ldots,b$. Denoting the optimal solution by $\widehat{\boldsymbol{\theta}} = (\widehat{\theta}_1,\ldots,\widehat{\theta}_b)$, we can express the estimated density ratio as $r(\boldsymbol{x};\widehat{\boldsymbol{\theta}})$.

To investigate the statistical properties of the cLSIF estimator, let us consider an "ideal" version of the problem (13.2):

$$\max_{\boldsymbol{\theta}\in\mathbb{R}^b} \left[\frac{1}{2}\boldsymbol{\theta}^\top \boldsymbol{H}\boldsymbol{\theta} - \boldsymbol{h}^\top\boldsymbol{\theta} + \lambda \boldsymbol{1}_b^\top \boldsymbol{\theta}\right] \quad \text{s.t. } \boldsymbol{\theta} \geq \boldsymbol{0}_b. \tag{13.3}$$

That is, $\widehat{\boldsymbol{H}}$ and $\widehat{\boldsymbol{h}}$ in Eq. (13.2) are replaced with $\boldsymbol{H}$ and $\boldsymbol{h}$, respectively. The optimal solution of Eq. (13.3) is denoted as $\boldsymbol{\theta}^* = (\theta^*_1,\ldots,\theta^*_b)$.

We prepare some notations. Let $\mathcal{A} \subset \{1,\ldots,b\}$ be the set of *active* indices of the optimal solution for the problem (13.3), that is,

$$\mathcal{A} = \{\ell \mid \theta^*_\ell = 0,\ \ell = 1,\ldots,b\}.$$

For the active set $\mathcal{A} = \{j_1, \ldots, j_{|\mathcal{A}|}\}$ with $j_1 < \cdots < j_{|\mathcal{A}|}$, let $\boldsymbol{E}$ be the $|\mathcal{A}| \times b$ indicator matrix with the (i, j_i)-th element

$$E_{i,j} = \begin{cases} 1 & j = j_i \in \mathcal{A}, \\ 0 & \text{otherwise,} \end{cases}$$

and $\boldsymbol{A} = \boldsymbol{H}^{-1} - \boldsymbol{H}^{-1}\boldsymbol{E}^\top(\boldsymbol{E}\boldsymbol{H}^{-1}\boldsymbol{E}^\top)^{-1}\boldsymbol{E}\boldsymbol{H}^{-1}$. For the functions $r(\boldsymbol{x})$ and $r'(\boldsymbol{x})$, let $\boldsymbol{C}_{r,r'}$ be the $b \times b$ covariance matrix with the (ℓ, ℓ')-th element being the covariance between $r(\boldsymbol{x})\varphi_\ell(\boldsymbol{x})$ and $r'(\boldsymbol{x})\varphi_{\ell'}(\boldsymbol{x})$ under the probability $p^*_{\mathrm{de}}(\boldsymbol{x})$, and the functions $r^*(\boldsymbol{x})$ and $v(\boldsymbol{x})$ denote

$$r^*(\boldsymbol{x}) = \sum_{\ell=1}^{b} \theta^*_\ell \varphi_\ell(\boldsymbol{x}) \quad \text{and} \quad v(\boldsymbol{x}) = \sum_{\ell=1}^{b} [\boldsymbol{A}\boldsymbol{1}_b]_\ell \varphi_\ell(\boldsymbol{x}).$$

In the following we also use $\boldsymbol{C}_{r^*,r^*}$ and $\boldsymbol{C}_{r^*,v}$ defined in the same way as was done previously. Let

$$f(n) = \omega(g(n))$$

denote that $f(n)$ asymptotically dominates $g(n)$; more precisely, for all $C > 0$, there exists n_0 such that

$$|Cg(n)| < |f(n)| \quad \text{for all } n > n_0.$$

Then we have the following theorem.

Theorem 13.6 *Assume that*

(a) *The optimal solution of the problem* (13.3) *satisfies the strict complementarity condition (Bertsekas et al., 2003).*
(b) n_{nu} *and* n_{de} *satisfy*

$$n_{\mathrm{nu}} = \omega(n_{\mathrm{de}}^2). \tag{13.4}$$

Then, for any $\lambda \geq 0$, *we have*

$$\mathbb{E}[J(\widehat{\boldsymbol{\theta}})] = J(\boldsymbol{\theta}^*) + \frac{1}{2n_{\mathrm{de}}}\mathrm{tr}(\boldsymbol{A}(\boldsymbol{C}_{w^*,w^*} - 2\lambda \boldsymbol{C}_{w^*,v})) + o\left(\frac{1}{n_{\mathrm{de}}}\right).$$

This theorem elucidates the *learning curve* (Amari et al., 1992) of cLSIF up to the order of $1/n_{\mathrm{de}}$.

13.2.3 Asymptotic Properties of uLSIF Estimator

Let the estimator $\widetilde{\boldsymbol{\theta}}$ be the optimal solution of

$$\min_{\boldsymbol{\theta} \in \mathbb{R}^b} \left[\frac{1}{2}\boldsymbol{\theta}^\top \widehat{\boldsymbol{H}}\boldsymbol{\theta} - \widehat{\boldsymbol{h}}^\top \boldsymbol{\theta} + \frac{\lambda}{2}\boldsymbol{\theta}^\top\boldsymbol{\theta}\right], \tag{13.5}$$

where λ (≥ 0) is the regularization parameter. Then the uLSIF estimator is defined as

$$\widehat{\boldsymbol{\theta}} = \max(\mathbf{0}_b, \widetilde{\boldsymbol{\theta}}) = \max(\mathbf{0}_b, (\widehat{\boldsymbol{H}} + \lambda \boldsymbol{I}_b)^{-1}\widehat{\boldsymbol{h}}),$$

where the "max" operation for a pair of vectors is applied in an element-wise manner.

To investigate statistical properties of the uLSIF estimator, we consider the "ideal" version of the problem (13.5). Let $\boldsymbol{\theta}^\circ$ be the optimal solution of the ideal problem:

$$\min_{\boldsymbol{\theta} \in \mathbb{R}^b} \left[\frac{1}{2}\boldsymbol{\theta}^\top \boldsymbol{H}\boldsymbol{\theta} - \boldsymbol{h}^\top \boldsymbol{\theta} + \frac{\lambda}{2}\boldsymbol{\theta}^\top \boldsymbol{\theta} \right]. \tag{13.6}$$

That is, $\boldsymbol{\theta}^\circ = (\boldsymbol{H} + \lambda \boldsymbol{I}_b)^{-1}\boldsymbol{h}$. Then the ideal solution $\boldsymbol{\theta}^*$ is given by

$$\boldsymbol{\theta}^* = \max(\mathbf{0}_b, \boldsymbol{\theta}^\circ) = \max(\mathbf{0}_b, (\boldsymbol{H} + \lambda \boldsymbol{I}_b)^{-1}\boldsymbol{h}).$$

Let $\mathcal{B} \subset \{1, \ldots, b\}$ be the set of negative indices of $\boldsymbol{\theta}^\circ$, that is,

$$\mathcal{B} = \{\ell \mid \theta^\circ_\ell < 0,\ \ell = 1, \ldots, b\}.$$

Let $\boldsymbol{D}$ be the b-dimensional diagonal matrix with the ℓ-th diagonal element

$$D_{\ell,\ell} = \begin{cases} 0 & \ell \in \mathcal{B}, \\ 1 & \text{otherwise.} \end{cases}$$

Let

$$r^*(\boldsymbol{x}) = \sum_{\ell=1}^{b} \theta^*_\ell \varphi_\ell(\boldsymbol{x}) \quad \text{and} \quad v(\boldsymbol{x}) = \sum_{\ell=1}^{b} [\boldsymbol{B}_\lambda^{-1}\boldsymbol{D}(\boldsymbol{H}\boldsymbol{\theta}^* - \boldsymbol{h})]_\ell \varphi_\ell(\boldsymbol{x}),$$

where $\boldsymbol{B}_\lambda = \boldsymbol{H} + \lambda \boldsymbol{I}_b$. Then we have the following theorem.

Theorem 13.7 *Assume that*

(a) *For the optimal solution of the problem* (13.6), *the condition* $\theta^\circ_\ell \neq 0$ *for* $\ell = 1, \ldots, b$ *holds.*
(b) n_{de} *and* n_{nu} *satisfy Eq.* (13.4).

Then, for any $\lambda \geq 0$, *we have*

$$\mathbb{E}[J(\widehat{\boldsymbol{\theta}})] = J(\boldsymbol{\theta}^*) + \frac{1}{2n_{\mathrm{de}}} \mathrm{tr}(\boldsymbol{B}_\lambda^{-1}\boldsymbol{D}\boldsymbol{H}\boldsymbol{D}\boldsymbol{B}_\lambda^{-1}\boldsymbol{C}_{r^*,r^*} + 2\boldsymbol{B}_\lambda^{-1}\boldsymbol{C}_{r^*,v}) + o\left(\frac{1}{n_{\mathrm{de}}}\right).$$

Theorem 13.7 elucidates the learning curve of uLSIF up to the order of n_{de}^{-1}.

13.3 Optimality of Logistic Regression

In this section we introduce Qin's (1998), result that is, a correctly specified logistic regression provides the optimal estimator for density ratios.

Let us model the density ratio $r^*(\boldsymbol{x}) = p^*_{\text{nu}}(\boldsymbol{x})/p^*_{\text{de}}(\boldsymbol{x})$ by the following parametric model:

$$r(\boldsymbol{x};\boldsymbol{\theta}) = \exp\{\theta_0 + \phi(\boldsymbol{x};\boldsymbol{\theta}_1)\},$$

where $\theta_0 \in \mathbb{R}$, $\boldsymbol{\theta}_1 \in \mathbb{R}^{b-1}$, $\boldsymbol{\theta} = (\theta_0, \boldsymbol{\theta}_1)$ is the b-dimensional parameter and $\phi(\boldsymbol{x};\boldsymbol{\theta}_1)$ is a real-valued function. We assume that the true density ratio $r^*(\boldsymbol{x})$ is realized by $r(\boldsymbol{x};\boldsymbol{\theta}^*)$ in the parametric model.

Here we consider the moment-matching estimator for density ratios. Let $\boldsymbol{\eta}(\boldsymbol{x};\boldsymbol{\theta}) \in \mathbb{R}^b$ be a vector-valued function, and let the estimator $\widehat{\boldsymbol{\theta}}_{\eta}$ be the solution of the equation

$$\frac{1}{n_{\text{de}}}\sum_{i=1}^{n_{\text{de}}} \boldsymbol{\eta}(\boldsymbol{x}_i^{\text{de}};\boldsymbol{\theta}) r(\boldsymbol{x}_i^{\text{de}};\boldsymbol{\theta}) = \frac{1}{n_{\text{nu}}}\sum_{j=1}^{n_{\text{nu}}} \boldsymbol{\eta}(\boldsymbol{x}_i^{\text{nu}};\boldsymbol{\theta}). \tag{13.7}$$

In the infinite sample limit, the Eq. (13.7) converges to

$$\int \boldsymbol{\eta}(\boldsymbol{x};\boldsymbol{\theta}) r(\boldsymbol{x};\boldsymbol{\theta}) p^*_{\text{de}}(\boldsymbol{x}) d\boldsymbol{x} = \int \boldsymbol{\eta}(\boldsymbol{x};\boldsymbol{\theta}) p^*_{\text{nu}}(\boldsymbol{x}) d\boldsymbol{x}, \tag{13.8}$$

and hence $\boldsymbol{\theta} = \boldsymbol{\theta}^*$ is a solution of Eq. (13.8). Under a mild assumption, the estimator $\widehat{\boldsymbol{\theta}}_{\eta}$ converge to $\boldsymbol{\theta}^*$; that is, the estimator has the statistical consistency. Qin (1998) proved that the moment function defined by

$$\boldsymbol{\eta}^*(\boldsymbol{x};\boldsymbol{\theta}) = \frac{1}{1 + n_{\text{nu}}/n_{\text{de}} \cdot r(\boldsymbol{x};\boldsymbol{\theta})} \nabla \log r(\boldsymbol{x};\boldsymbol{\theta}) \tag{13.9}$$

is optimal, where $\nabla \log r(\boldsymbol{x};\boldsymbol{\theta})$ denotes the b-dimensional gradient vector of $\log r(\boldsymbol{x};\boldsymbol{\theta})$. More precisely, the variance–covariance matrix $V(\widehat{\boldsymbol{\theta}}_{\eta^*})$ of the estimator $\widehat{\boldsymbol{\theta}}_{\eta^*}$ is asymptotically smaller than or equal to the variance–covariance matrix $V(\widehat{\boldsymbol{\theta}}_{\eta})$ of the other estimator $\widehat{\boldsymbol{\theta}}_{\eta}$ in the sense of the positive semi-definiteness of the matrix. This fact is summarized as follows.

Theorem 13.8 (Theorem 3 in Qin, 1998) *Suppose that the limit of $n_{\text{nu}}/n_{\text{de}}$ converges to a positive constant. For any vector-valued function $\boldsymbol{\eta}(\boldsymbol{x},\boldsymbol{\theta})$ with finite variance under p^*_{de} and p^*_{nu}, the difference of the asymptotic variance covariance matrix,*

$$\lim_{n_{\text{de}}\to\infty} n_{\text{de}}(V(\widehat{\boldsymbol{\theta}}_{\eta}) - V(\widehat{\boldsymbol{\theta}}_{\eta^*})),$$

is positive semi-definite, where $\boldsymbol{\eta}^*$ is defined by Eq. (13.9).

Because the probabilistic order of $\widehat{\boldsymbol{\theta}}_{\eta} - \boldsymbol{\theta}^*$ is usually $\mathcal{O}_p(1/\sqrt{n_{\text{de}}})$, the variance–covariance matrix is multiplied by the factor n_{de}, to the Theorem 13.8 guarantees that the estimator with $\boldsymbol{\eta}^*$ is optimal in the sense of the variance–covariance matrix of the estimator.

In the following we show that the optimal moment-matching estimator is derived from the maximum likelihood estimator of the logistic regression models. Let us assign a selector variable $y = \mathrm{nu}$ to samples drawn from $p^*_{\mathrm{nu}}(\boldsymbol{x})$ and $y = \mathrm{de}$ to samples drawn from $p^*_{\mathrm{de}}(\boldsymbol{x})$; that is, the two densities are written as

$$p^*_{\mathrm{nu}}(\boldsymbol{x}) = q^*(\boldsymbol{x}|y = \mathrm{nu}) \quad \text{and} \quad p^*_{\mathrm{de}}(\boldsymbol{x}) = q^*(\boldsymbol{x}|y = \mathrm{de}).$$

Suppose the marginal probability of y is defined as $q^*(\mathrm{nu})$ and $q^*(\mathrm{de})$. Then, according to the Bayes formula, the conditional probabilities $q^*(y = \mathrm{de}|\boldsymbol{x})$ and $q^*(y = \mathrm{nu}|\boldsymbol{x})$ are represented as

$$\begin{aligned} q^*(y = \mathrm{de}|\boldsymbol{x}) &= \frac{1}{1 + q^*(\mathrm{nu})/q^*(\mathrm{de}) \cdot q^*(\boldsymbol{x}|y = \mathrm{nu})/q^*(\boldsymbol{x}|y = \mathrm{de})} \\ &= \frac{1}{1 + q^*(\mathrm{nu})/q^*(\mathrm{de}) \cdot r^*(\boldsymbol{x})}, \\ q^*(y = \mathrm{nu}|\boldsymbol{x}) &= \frac{q^*(\mathrm{nu})/q^*(\mathrm{de}) \cdot r^*(\boldsymbol{x})}{1 + q^*(\mathrm{nu})/q^*(\mathrm{de}) \cdot r^*(\boldsymbol{x})}. \end{aligned}$$

Therefore, the statistical model

$$\begin{aligned} q(y = \mathrm{de}|\boldsymbol{x};\boldsymbol{\theta}) &= \frac{1}{1 + n_{\mathrm{nu}}/n_{\mathrm{de}} \cdot r(\boldsymbol{x};\boldsymbol{\theta})}, \\ q(y = \mathrm{nu}|\boldsymbol{x};\boldsymbol{\theta}) &= \frac{n_{\mathrm{nu}}/n_{\mathrm{de}} \cdot r(\boldsymbol{x};\boldsymbol{\theta})}{1 + n_{\mathrm{nu}}/n_{\mathrm{de}} \cdot r(\boldsymbol{x};\boldsymbol{\theta})}, \end{aligned} \tag{13.10}$$

is available to estimate the conditional probability, in which the ratio $q^*(\mathrm{nu})/q^*(\mathrm{de})$ is approximated by $\rho := n_{\mathrm{nu}}/n_{\mathrm{de}}$.

When the dataset

$$(\boldsymbol{x}^{\mathrm{de}}_i, \mathrm{de}),\ i = 1,\ldots,n_{\mathrm{de}} \quad \text{and} \quad (\boldsymbol{x}^{\mathrm{nu}}_j, \mathrm{nu}),\ j = 1,\ldots,n_{\mathrm{nu}},$$

is observed, the maximum likelihood estimator based on the model (13.10) is the maximizer of the log-likelihood function,

$$L(\boldsymbol{\theta}) = \sum_{i=1}^{n_{\mathrm{de}}} \log \frac{1}{1 + n_{\mathrm{nu}}/n_{\mathrm{de}} \cdot r(\boldsymbol{x}^{\mathrm{de}}_i;\boldsymbol{\theta})} + \sum_{j=1}^{n_{\mathrm{nu}}} \log \frac{n_{\mathrm{nu}}/n_{\mathrm{de}} \cdot r(\boldsymbol{x}^{\mathrm{nu}}_j;\boldsymbol{\theta})}{1 + n_{\mathrm{nu}}/n_{\mathrm{de}} \cdot r(\boldsymbol{x}^{\mathrm{nu}}_j;\boldsymbol{\theta})},$$

where

$$r(\boldsymbol{x},\boldsymbol{\theta}) = \exp\{\theta_0 + \boldsymbol{\theta}_1^\top \boldsymbol{\phi}(\boldsymbol{x})\}.$$

The extremal condition of the log-likelihood function is given as

$$\sum_{i=1}^{n_{\mathrm{de}}} \frac{\rho r(\boldsymbol{x}^{\mathrm{de}}_i;\boldsymbol{\theta})}{1 + \rho r(\boldsymbol{x}^{\mathrm{de}}_i;\boldsymbol{\theta})} \nabla \log r(\boldsymbol{x}^{\mathrm{de}}_i;\boldsymbol{\theta}) = \sum_{j=1}^{n_{\mathrm{nu}}} \frac{\rho}{1 + \rho r(\boldsymbol{x}^{\mathrm{nu}}_j;\boldsymbol{\theta})} \nabla \log r(\boldsymbol{x}^{\mathrm{nu}}_j;\boldsymbol{\theta}).$$

This equation is identical to Eq. (13.7) with $\eta = \eta^*$ up to a constant factor.

The logistic model (13.10) is closely related to the density ratio of $p^*_{\mathrm{nu}}(\boldsymbol{x})$ and $p^*_{\mathrm{de}}(\boldsymbol{x})$, and the maximum likelihood estimator of the logistic model is the asymptotically optimal estimator under some regularity condition. This is the main reason why the estimator with $\eta = \eta^*$ is optimal not only for the parameter of logistic regression models but also for the density-ratio models.

13.4 Accuracy Comparison

In this section we consider the following three methods of density-ratio estimation and compare their estimation accuracies (Kanamori et al., 2010):

(A) The numerator and denominator densities are separately estimated by the maximum likelihood estimation, and then the ratio of the estimated densities is computed (Chapter 2).
(B) The logistic regression classifier that discriminates denominator samples from numerator samples is learned, and then the ratio of the posterior probabilities is computed (Chapter 4).
(C) The density-ratio function is directly modeled and learned by minimizing the empirical Kullback–Leibler divergence (Chapter 5).

We first show that when the numerator and denominator densities are known to be members of the exponential family, (A) is better than (B) and (B) is better than (C). Then we show that once the model assumption is violated, (C) is better than (A) and (B). Thus, in practical situations where no exact model is available, (C) would be the most promising approach to density-ratio estimation.

Throughout this section, we assume $n = n_{\mathrm{nu}} = n_{\mathrm{de}}$.

13.4.1 Measure of Accuracy

Let us consider the *unnormalized Kullback–Leibler (UKL) divergence* (Cesa-Bianchi and Lugosi, 2006) from the true density $p^*_{\mathrm{nu}}(\boldsymbol{x})$ to its estimator $\widehat{r}(\boldsymbol{x})p^*_{\mathrm{de}}(\boldsymbol{x})$:

$$\mathrm{UKL}(p^*_{\mathrm{nu}}\|\widehat{r}\cdot p^*_{\mathrm{de}}) := \int p^*_{\mathrm{nu}}(\boldsymbol{x})\log\frac{p^*_{\mathrm{nu}}(\boldsymbol{x})}{\widehat{r}(\boldsymbol{x})p^*_{\mathrm{de}}(\boldsymbol{x})}\mathrm{d}\boldsymbol{x} - 1 + \int \widehat{r}(\boldsymbol{x})p^*_{\mathrm{de}}(\boldsymbol{x})\mathrm{d}\boldsymbol{x}. \qquad (13.11)$$

$\mathrm{UKL}(p^*_{\mathrm{nu}}(\boldsymbol{x})\|\widehat{r}(\boldsymbol{x})p^*_{\mathrm{de}}(\boldsymbol{x}))$ is non-negative for all $\widehat{r}$ and vanishes if and only if $\widehat{r} = r^*$. If $\widehat{r}(\boldsymbol{x})p^*_{\mathrm{de}}(\boldsymbol{x})$ is normalized to be a probability density function, that is, $\int \widehat{r}(\boldsymbol{x})p^*_{\mathrm{de}}(\boldsymbol{x})\mathrm{d}\boldsymbol{x} = 1$, then the unnormalized Kullback–Leibler divergence is reduced to the ordinary Kullback–Leibler divergence (Kullback and Leibler, 1951):

$$\mathrm{KL}(p^*_{\mathrm{nu}}\|\widehat{r}\cdot p^*_{\mathrm{de}}) := \int p^*_{\mathrm{nu}}(\boldsymbol{x})\log\frac{p^*_{\mathrm{nu}}(\boldsymbol{x})}{\widehat{r}(\boldsymbol{x})p^*_{\mathrm{de}}(\boldsymbol{x})}\mathrm{d}\boldsymbol{x}. \qquad (13.12)$$

In our theoretical analysis, we use the expectation of $\mathrm{UKL}(p^*_{\mathrm{nu}}\|\widehat{r}\cdot p^*_{\mathrm{de}})$ over $\{\boldsymbol{x}^{\mathrm{nu}}_i\}_{i=1}^n$ and $\{\boldsymbol{x}^{\mathrm{de}}_j\}_{j=1}^n$ as the measure of accuracy of a density-ratio estimator $\widehat{r}(\boldsymbol{x})$:

$$J(\widehat{r}) := \mathbb{E}\left[\mathrm{UKL}(p^*_{\mathrm{nu}}\|\widehat{r}\cdot p^*_{\mathrm{de}})\right], \tag{13.13}$$

where $\mathbb{E}$ denotes the expectation over $\{\boldsymbol{x}^{\mathrm{nu}}_i\}_{i=1}^n$ and $\{\boldsymbol{x}^{\mathrm{de}}_j\}_{j=1}^n$.

13.4.2 Density-Ratio Estimators

Here the three methods of density-ratio estimation we are dealing with are described in detail.

Ratio of Maximum Likelihood Density Estimators

When the parametric models for $p^*_{\mathrm{nu}}(\boldsymbol{x})$ and $p^*_{\mathrm{de}}(\boldsymbol{x})$ are prepared, the numerator and denominator densities are separately estimated and then the ratio of the estimated densities is computed. Suppose that two parametric models $p^*_{\mathrm{nu}}(\boldsymbol{x};\boldsymbol{\theta}_{\mathrm{nu}})$ and $p^*_{\mathrm{de}}(\boldsymbol{x};\boldsymbol{\theta}_{\mathrm{de}})$ for $p^*_{\mathrm{nu}}(\boldsymbol{x})$ and $p^*_{\mathrm{de}}(\boldsymbol{x})$ are defined as

$$\begin{aligned}
&\int p_{\mathrm{nu}}(\boldsymbol{x};\boldsymbol{\theta}_{\mathrm{nu}})\mathrm{d}\boldsymbol{x} = 1, \quad \forall \boldsymbol{\theta}_{\mathrm{nu}} \in \Theta_{\mathrm{nu}},\\
&p_{\mathrm{nu}}(\boldsymbol{x};\boldsymbol{\theta}_{\mathrm{nu}}) \geq 0, \quad \forall \boldsymbol{x} \in \mathcal{X}, \ \forall \boldsymbol{\theta}_{\mathrm{nu}} \in \Theta_{\mathrm{nu}},\\
&\int p_{\mathrm{de}}(\boldsymbol{x};\boldsymbol{\theta}_{\mathrm{de}})\mathrm{d}\boldsymbol{x} = 1 \quad \forall \boldsymbol{\theta}_{\mathrm{de}} \in \Theta_{\mathrm{de}},\\
&p_{\mathrm{de}}(\boldsymbol{x};\boldsymbol{\theta}_{\mathrm{de}}) \geq 0 \quad \forall \boldsymbol{x} \in \mathcal{X}, \ \forall \boldsymbol{\theta}_{\mathrm{de}} \in \Theta_{\mathrm{de}}.
\end{aligned}$$

Then the maximum likelihood estimators $\widehat{\boldsymbol{\theta}}_{\mathrm{nu}}$ and $\widehat{\boldsymbol{\theta}}_{\mathrm{de}}$ are computed separately from $\{\boldsymbol{x}^{\mathrm{nu}}_i\}_{i=1}^n$ and $\{\boldsymbol{x}^{\mathrm{de}}_j\}_{j=1}^n$:

$$\begin{aligned}
\widehat{\boldsymbol{\theta}}_{\mathrm{nu}} &:= \mathop{\mathrm{argmax}}_{\boldsymbol{\theta}_{\mathrm{nu}}\in\Theta_{\mathrm{nu}}}\left[\sum_{i=1}^n \log p_{\mathrm{nu}}(\boldsymbol{x}^{\mathrm{nu}}_i;\boldsymbol{\theta}_{\mathrm{nu}})\right],\\
\widehat{\boldsymbol{\theta}}_{\mathrm{de}} &:= \mathop{\mathrm{argmax}}_{\boldsymbol{\theta}_{\mathrm{de}}\in\Theta_{\mathrm{de}}}\left[\sum_{j=1}^n \log p_{\mathrm{de}}(\boldsymbol{x}^{\mathrm{de}}_j;\boldsymbol{\theta}_{\mathrm{de}})\right].
\end{aligned}$$

Note that the maximum likelihood estimators $\widehat{\boldsymbol{\theta}}_{\mathrm{nu}}$ and $\widehat{\boldsymbol{\theta}}_{\mathrm{de}}$ minimize the empirical Kullback–Leibler divergences from the true densities $p^*_{\mathrm{nu}}(\boldsymbol{x})$ and $p^*_{\mathrm{de}}(\boldsymbol{x})$ to their models $p_{\mathrm{nu}}(\boldsymbol{x};\boldsymbol{\theta}_{\mathrm{nu}})$ and $p_{\mathrm{de}}(\boldsymbol{x};\boldsymbol{\theta}_{\mathrm{de}})$, respectively:

$$\begin{aligned}
\widehat{\boldsymbol{\theta}}_{\mathrm{nu}} &= \mathop{\mathrm{argmin}}_{\boldsymbol{\theta}_{\mathrm{nu}}\in\Theta_{\mathrm{nu}}}\left[\frac{1}{n}\sum_{i=1}^n \log \frac{p^*_{\mathrm{nu}}(\boldsymbol{x}^{\mathrm{nu}}_i)}{p_{\mathrm{nu}}(\boldsymbol{x}^{\mathrm{nu}}_i;\boldsymbol{\theta}_{\mathrm{nu}})}\right],\\
\widehat{\boldsymbol{\theta}}_{\mathrm{de}} &= \mathop{\mathrm{argmin}}_{\boldsymbol{\theta}_{\mathrm{de}}\in\Theta_{\mathrm{de}}}\left[\frac{1}{n}\sum_{j=1}^n \log \frac{p^*_{\mathrm{de}}(\boldsymbol{x}^{\mathrm{de}}_j)}{p_{\mathrm{nu}}(\boldsymbol{x}^{\mathrm{de}}_j;\boldsymbol{\theta}_{\mathrm{de}})}\right].
\end{aligned}$$

Then the density-ratio estimator based on a separated maximum likelihood estimator is constructed by taking the ratio of the estimated densities:

$$\widehat{r}_{\mathrm{A}}(\boldsymbol{x}) := \frac{p_{\mathrm{nu}}(\boldsymbol{x};\widehat{\boldsymbol{\theta}}_{\mathrm{nu}})}{p_{\mathrm{de}}(\boldsymbol{x};\widehat{\boldsymbol{\theta}}_{\mathrm{de}})} \left(\frac{1}{n} \sum_{j=1}^{n} \frac{p_{\mathrm{nu}}(\boldsymbol{x}_j^{\mathrm{de}};\widehat{\boldsymbol{\theta}}_{\mathrm{nu}})}{p_{\mathrm{de}}(\boldsymbol{x}_j^{\mathrm{de}};\widehat{\boldsymbol{\theta}}_{\mathrm{de}})} \right)^{-1},$$

where the estimator is normalized so that $\frac{1}{n}\sum_{j=1}^{n} \widehat{r}_{\mathrm{A}}(\boldsymbol{x}_j^{\mathrm{de}}) = 1$.

Logistic Regression

Let us assign a selector variable $y = \mathrm{nu}$ to samples drawn from $p^*_{\mathrm{nu}}(\boldsymbol{x})$ and $y = \mathrm{de}$ to samples drawn from $p^*_{\mathrm{de}}(\boldsymbol{x})$; that is, the two densities are written as $p^*_{\mathrm{nu}}(\boldsymbol{x}) = q^*(\boldsymbol{x}|y = \mathrm{nu})$ and $p^*_{\mathrm{de}}(\boldsymbol{x}) = q^*(\boldsymbol{x}|y = \mathrm{de})$. Since

$$q^*(\boldsymbol{x}|y = \mathrm{nu}) = \frac{q^*(y = \mathrm{nu}|\boldsymbol{x})q^*(\boldsymbol{x})}{q^*(y = \mathrm{nu})},$$

$$q^*(\boldsymbol{x}|y = \mathrm{de}) = \frac{q^*(y = \mathrm{de}|\boldsymbol{x})q^*(\boldsymbol{x})}{q^*(y = \mathrm{de})},$$

the density ratio can be expressed in terms of y as

$$r^*(\boldsymbol{x}) = \frac{q^*(y = \mathrm{nu}|\boldsymbol{x})}{q^*(y = \mathrm{nu})} \frac{q^*(y = \mathrm{de})}{q^*(y = \mathrm{de}|\boldsymbol{x})} = \frac{q^*(y = \mathrm{nu}|\boldsymbol{x})}{q^*(y = \mathrm{de}|\boldsymbol{x})},$$

where we use $q^*(y = \mathrm{nu}) = q^*(y = \mathrm{de}) = 1/2$ based on the assumption that $n_{\mathrm{nu}} = n$.

The conditional probability $q^*(y|\boldsymbol{x})$ could be approximated by discriminating $\{\boldsymbol{x}_i^{\mathrm{nu}}\}_{i=1}^n$ from $\{\boldsymbol{x}_j^{\mathrm{de}}\}_{j=1}^n$ using a *logistic regression* classifier; that is, for a non-negative parametric function $r(\boldsymbol{x};\boldsymbol{\theta})$, the conditional probabilities $q^*(y = \mathrm{nu}|\boldsymbol{x})$ and $q^*(y = \mathrm{de}|\boldsymbol{x})$ are modeled by

$$q(y = \mathrm{nu}|\boldsymbol{x};\boldsymbol{\theta}) = \frac{r(\boldsymbol{x};\boldsymbol{\theta})}{1 + r(\boldsymbol{x};\boldsymbol{\theta})} \quad \text{and} \quad q(y = \mathrm{de}|\boldsymbol{x};\boldsymbol{\theta}) = \frac{1}{1 + r(\boldsymbol{x};\boldsymbol{\theta})}.$$

Then the maximum likelihood estimator $\widehat{\boldsymbol{\theta}}_{\mathrm{B}}$ is computed from $\{\boldsymbol{x}_i^{\mathrm{nu}}\}_{i=1}^n$ and $\{\boldsymbol{x}_j^{\mathrm{de}}\}_{j=1}^n$ as

$$\widehat{\boldsymbol{\theta}}_{\mathrm{B}} := \underset{\boldsymbol{\theta}\in\Theta}{\mathrm{argmax}} \left[\sum_{i=1}^{n} \log \frac{r(\boldsymbol{x}_i^{\mathrm{nu}};\boldsymbol{\theta})}{1 + r(\boldsymbol{x}_i^{\mathrm{nu}};\boldsymbol{\theta})} + \sum_{j=1}^{n} \log \frac{1}{1 + r(\boldsymbol{x}_j^{\mathrm{de}};\boldsymbol{\theta})} \right]. \tag{13.14}$$

Note that the maximum likelihood estimator $\widehat{\boldsymbol{\theta}}_{\mathrm{B}}$ minimizes the empirical Kullback–Leibler divergences from the true density $q^*(\boldsymbol{x}, y)$ to its estimator $q(y|\boldsymbol{x};\boldsymbol{\theta})q^*(\boldsymbol{x})$:

$$\widehat{\boldsymbol{\theta}}_{\mathrm{B}} = \underset{\boldsymbol{\theta}\in\Theta}{\mathrm{argmin}} \left[\frac{1}{2n} \sum_{i=1}^{n} \log \frac{q^*(\boldsymbol{x}_i^{\mathrm{nu}}, y = \mathrm{nu})}{q(y = \mathrm{nu}|\boldsymbol{x}_i^{\mathrm{nu}};\boldsymbol{\theta})q^*(\boldsymbol{x}_i^{\mathrm{nu}})} \right.$$

$$\left. + \frac{1}{2n} \sum_{j=1}^{n} \log \frac{q^*(\boldsymbol{x}_j^{\mathrm{de}}, y = \mathrm{de})}{q(y = \mathrm{de}|\boldsymbol{x}_j^{\mathrm{de}};\boldsymbol{\theta})q^*(\boldsymbol{x}_j^{\mathrm{de}})} \right].$$

Finally, the density-ratio estimator is constructed by taking the ratio of $q(y = \mathrm{nu}|\boldsymbol{x};\widehat{\boldsymbol{\theta}}_{\mathrm{B}})$ and $q(y = \mathrm{de}|\boldsymbol{x};\widehat{\boldsymbol{\theta}}_{\mathrm{B}})$ with proper normalization:

$$\widehat{r}_{\mathrm{B}}(\boldsymbol{x}) := \frac{q(y=\mathrm{nu}|\boldsymbol{x};\widehat{\boldsymbol{\theta}}_{\mathrm{B}})}{q(y=\mathrm{de}|\boldsymbol{x};\widehat{\boldsymbol{\theta}}_{\mathrm{B}})}\left(\frac{1}{n}\sum_{j=1}^{n}\frac{q(y=\mathrm{nu}|\boldsymbol{x}_j^{\mathrm{de}};\widehat{\boldsymbol{\theta}}_{\mathrm{B}})}{q(y=\mathrm{de}|\boldsymbol{x}_j^{\mathrm{de}};\widehat{\boldsymbol{\theta}}_{\mathrm{B}})}\right)^{-1}$$
$$= r(\boldsymbol{x};\widehat{\boldsymbol{\theta}}_{\mathrm{B}})\left(\frac{1}{n}\sum_{j=1}^{n} r(\boldsymbol{x}_j^{\mathrm{de}};\widehat{\boldsymbol{\theta}}_{\mathrm{B}})\right)^{-1}.$$

Empirical Unnormalized Kullback–Leibler Divergence

For the density-ratio function $r^*(\boldsymbol{x})$, a non-negative parametric model $r(\boldsymbol{x};\boldsymbol{\theta})$ is prepared. Then the following estimator $\widehat{\boldsymbol{\theta}}_{\mathrm{C}}$ is computed from $\{\boldsymbol{x}_i^{\mathrm{nu}}\}_{i=1}^n$ and $\{\boldsymbol{x}_j^{\mathrm{de}}\}_{j=1}^n$:

$$\widehat{\boldsymbol{\theta}}_{\mathrm{C}} := \underset{\boldsymbol{\theta}\in\Theta}{\mathrm{argmax}}\left[\sum_{i=1}^{n}\log r(\boldsymbol{x}_i^{\mathrm{nu}};\boldsymbol{\theta}) - \sum_{j=1}^{n} r(\boldsymbol{x}_j^{\mathrm{de}};\boldsymbol{\theta})\right]. \tag{13.15}$$

Note that $\widehat{\boldsymbol{\theta}}_{\mathrm{C}}$ minimizes the empirical unnormalized Kullback–Leibler divergence from the true density $p_{\mathrm{nu}}^*(\boldsymbol{x})$ to its estimator $\widehat{r}(\boldsymbol{x})p_{\mathrm{de}}^*(\boldsymbol{x})$:

$$\widehat{\boldsymbol{\theta}}_{\mathrm{C}} = \underset{\boldsymbol{\theta}\in\Theta}{\mathrm{argmin}}\left[\frac{1}{n}\sum_{i=1}^{n}\log\frac{p_{\mathrm{nu}}^*(\boldsymbol{x}_i^{\mathrm{nu}})}{\widehat{r}(\boldsymbol{x}_i^{\mathrm{nu}})p_{\mathrm{de}}^*(\boldsymbol{x}_i^{\mathrm{nu}})} - 1 + \frac{1}{n}\sum_{j=1}^{n}\widehat{r}(\boldsymbol{x}_j^{\mathrm{de}})\right].$$

Finally, the density-ratio estimator is obtained by

$$\widehat{r}_{\mathrm{C}}(\boldsymbol{x}) := r(\boldsymbol{x};\widehat{\boldsymbol{\theta}}_{\mathrm{C}})\left(\frac{1}{n}\sum_{j=1}^{n} r(\boldsymbol{x}_j^{\mathrm{de}};\widehat{\boldsymbol{\theta}}_{\mathrm{C}})\right)^{-1}.$$

13.4.3 Exponential Models for Densities and Ratios

For the densities $p_{\mathrm{nu}}^*(\boldsymbol{x})$ and $p_{\mathrm{de}}^*(\boldsymbol{x})$, we use the following *exponential model* (Lehmann and Casella, 1998):

$$p(\boldsymbol{x};\boldsymbol{\theta}) = h(\boldsymbol{x})\exp\left\{\boldsymbol{\theta}^\top\boldsymbol{\xi}(\boldsymbol{x}) - \varphi(\boldsymbol{\theta})\right\}, \quad \boldsymbol{\theta}\in\Theta, \tag{13.16}$$

where $h(\boldsymbol{x})$ is a *base measure*, $\boldsymbol{\xi}(\boldsymbol{x})$ is a *sufficient statistic*, $\varphi(\boldsymbol{\theta})$ is a *normalization factor*, and $^\top$ denotes the transpose of a vector. The exponential model includes various popular models as special cases, for example, the normal, exponential, gamma, chi-square, and beta distributions.

Correspondingly, we use the following exponential model for the density ratio $r^*(\boldsymbol{x})$:

$$r(\boldsymbol{x};\boldsymbol{\theta},\theta_0) = \exp\left\{\theta_0 + \boldsymbol{\theta}^\top\boldsymbol{\xi}(\boldsymbol{x})\right\}, \quad \theta\in\Theta,\ \theta_0\in\mathbb{R}. \tag{13.17}$$

Method (A): For the exponential model (13.16), the maximum likelihood estimators $\widehat{\boldsymbol{\theta}}_{\mathrm{nu}}$ and $\widehat{\boldsymbol{\theta}}_{\mathrm{de}}$ are given by

$$\widehat{\boldsymbol{\theta}}_{\mathrm{nu}} = \underset{\boldsymbol{\theta}_{\mathrm{nu}} \in \Theta}{\mathrm{argmax}} \left[\sum_{i=1}^{n} \boldsymbol{\theta}^\top \boldsymbol{\xi}(\boldsymbol{x}_i^{\mathrm{nu}}) - n\varphi(\boldsymbol{\theta}) \right],$$

$$\widehat{\boldsymbol{\theta}}_{\mathrm{de}} = \underset{\boldsymbol{\theta}_{\mathrm{de}} \in \Theta}{\mathrm{argmax}} \left[\sum_{j=1}^{n} \boldsymbol{\theta}^\top \boldsymbol{\xi}(\boldsymbol{x}_j^{\mathrm{de}}) - n\varphi(\boldsymbol{\theta}) \right],$$

where irrelevant constants are ignored. The density-ratio estimator $\widehat{r}_{\mathrm{A}}(\boldsymbol{x})$ for the exponential density model is expressed as

$$\widehat{r}_{\mathrm{A}}(\boldsymbol{x}) = \exp\left\{ \widehat{\boldsymbol{\theta}}_{\mathrm{A}}^\top \boldsymbol{\xi}(\boldsymbol{x}) \right\} \left(\frac{1}{n} \sum_{j=1}^{n} \exp\left\{ \widehat{\boldsymbol{\theta}}_{\mathrm{A}}^\top \boldsymbol{\xi}(\boldsymbol{x}_j^{\mathrm{de}}) \right\} \right)^{-1},$$

where $\widehat{\boldsymbol{\theta}}_{\mathrm{A}} := \widehat{\boldsymbol{\theta}}_{\mathrm{nu}} - \widehat{\boldsymbol{\theta}}_{\mathrm{de}}$. One may use other estimators such as

$$\widetilde{r}_{\mathrm{A}}(\boldsymbol{x}) = \exp\left\{ \widehat{\boldsymbol{\theta}}_{\mathrm{A}}^\top \boldsymbol{\xi}(\boldsymbol{x}) - \varphi(\widehat{\boldsymbol{\theta}}_{\mathrm{nu}}) + \varphi(\widehat{\boldsymbol{\theta}}_{\mathrm{de}}) \right\}$$

instead of $\widehat{r}_{\mathrm{A}}(\boldsymbol{x})$. However, we focus on $\widehat{r}_{\mathrm{A}}(\boldsymbol{x})$ here because the same normalization factor as $\widehat{r}_{\mathrm{A}}(\boldsymbol{x})$ appears in other methods, as is shown in the following. This fact facilitates the theoretical analysis.

Method (B): For the exponential model (13.17), the optimization problem (13.14) is expressed as

$$\begin{aligned}
&(\widehat{\boldsymbol{\theta}}_{\mathrm{B}}, \widehat{\theta}_{\mathrm{B},0}) \\
&= \underset{(\boldsymbol{\theta},\theta_0) \in \Theta \times \mathbb{R}}{\mathrm{argmax}} \left[\sum_{i=1}^{n} \log \frac{r(\boldsymbol{x}_i^{\mathrm{nu}};\boldsymbol{\theta},\theta_0)}{1 + r(\boldsymbol{x}_i^{\mathrm{nu}};\boldsymbol{\theta},\theta_0)} + \sum_{j=1}^{n} \log \frac{1}{1 + r(\boldsymbol{x}_j^{\mathrm{de}};\boldsymbol{\theta},\theta_0)} \right] \\
&= \underset{(\boldsymbol{\theta},\theta_0) \in \Theta \times \mathbb{R}}{\mathrm{argmax}} \left[\sum_{i=1}^{n} \log \frac{\exp\left\{\theta_0 + \boldsymbol{\theta}^\top \boldsymbol{\xi}(\boldsymbol{x}_i^{\mathrm{nu}})\right\}}{1 + \exp\left\{\theta_0 + \boldsymbol{\theta}^\top \boldsymbol{\xi}(\boldsymbol{x}_i^{\mathrm{nu}})\right\}} \right. \\
&\qquad \left. + \sum_{j=1}^{n} \log \frac{1}{1 + \exp\left\{\theta_0 + \boldsymbol{\theta}^\top \boldsymbol{\xi}(\boldsymbol{x}_j^{\mathrm{de}})\right\}} \right].
\end{aligned}$$

The density-ratio estimator $\widehat{r}_{\mathrm{B}}(\boldsymbol{x})$ for the exponential ratio model is expressed as

$$\widehat{r}_{\mathrm{B}}(\boldsymbol{x}) = \exp\left\{ \widehat{\boldsymbol{\theta}}_{\mathrm{B}}^\top \boldsymbol{\xi}(\boldsymbol{x}) \right\} \left(\frac{1}{n} \sum_{j=1}^{n} \exp\left\{ \widehat{\boldsymbol{\theta}}_{\mathrm{B}}^\top \boldsymbol{\xi}(\boldsymbol{x}_j^{\mathrm{de}}) \right\} \right)^{-1}.$$

Method (C): For the exponential model (13.17), the optimization problem (13.15) is expressed as

$$(\widehat{\boldsymbol{\theta}}_{\mathrm{C}}, \widehat{\theta}_{\mathrm{C},0}) = \underset{(\boldsymbol{\theta},\theta_0)\in\Theta\times\mathbb{R}}{\operatorname{argmax}} \left[\frac{1}{n}\sum_{i=1}^{n} \log r(\boldsymbol{x}_i^{\mathrm{nu}};\boldsymbol{\theta},\theta_0) - \frac{1}{n}\sum_{j=1}^{n} r(\boldsymbol{x}_j^{\mathrm{de}};\boldsymbol{\theta},\theta_0) \right]$$

$$= \underset{(\boldsymbol{\theta},\theta_0)\in\Theta\times\mathbb{R}}{\operatorname{argmax}} \left[\frac{1}{n}\sum_{i=1}^{n} (\theta_0 + \boldsymbol{\theta}^\top \boldsymbol{\xi}(\boldsymbol{x}_i^{\mathrm{nu}})) - \frac{1}{n}\sum_{j=1}^{n} \exp\left\{\theta_0 + \boldsymbol{\theta}^\top \boldsymbol{\xi}(\boldsymbol{x}_j^{\mathrm{de}})\right\} \right].$$

The density-ratio estimator $\widehat{r}_{\mathrm{C}}(\boldsymbol{x})$ for the exponential ratio model is expressed as

$$\widehat{r}_{\mathrm{C}}(\boldsymbol{x}) = \exp\left\{\widehat{\boldsymbol{\theta}}_{\mathrm{C}}^\top \boldsymbol{\xi}(\boldsymbol{x})\right\} \left(\frac{1}{n}\sum_{j=1}^{n} \exp\left\{\widehat{\boldsymbol{\theta}}_{\mathrm{C}}^\top \boldsymbol{\xi}(\boldsymbol{x}_j^{\mathrm{de}})\right\} \right)^{-1}.$$

13.4.4 Accuracy Analysis for Correctly Specified Exponential Models

Here we theoretically analyze the accuracy of the three previously mentioned density-ratio estimators under the assumption that the true densities $p^*_{\mathrm{nu}}(\boldsymbol{x})$ and $p^*_{\mathrm{de}}(\boldsymbol{x})$ both belong to the exponential family; that is, there exist $\boldsymbol{\theta}^*_{\mathrm{nu}} \in \Theta$ and $\boldsymbol{\theta}^*_{\mathrm{de}} \in \Theta$ such that $p^*_{\mathrm{nu}}(\boldsymbol{x}) = p(\boldsymbol{x};\boldsymbol{\theta}^*_{\mathrm{nu}})$ and $p^*_{\mathrm{de}}(\boldsymbol{x}) = p(\boldsymbol{x};\boldsymbol{\theta}^*_{\mathrm{de}})$. Because the ratio of the two exponential densities also belongs to the exponential model, this assumption implies that there exist $\boldsymbol{\theta}^* \in \Theta$ and $\theta_0^* \in \mathbb{R}$ such that

$$r^*(\boldsymbol{x}) = r(\boldsymbol{x};\boldsymbol{\theta}^*,\theta_0^*). \tag{13.18}$$

Note that it is straightforward to extend the current results to general parametric models, because we focus on the first-order asymptotics of the estimators. An arbitrary parametric model $p(\boldsymbol{x};\boldsymbol{\theta})$ has the same first-order asymptotics as the exponential model of the form

$$p_{\exp}(\boldsymbol{x};\boldsymbol{\theta}) \propto \exp\{\log p(\boldsymbol{x};\boldsymbol{\theta}^*) + (\boldsymbol{\theta}-\boldsymbol{\theta}^*)^\top \nabla \log p(\boldsymbol{x};\boldsymbol{\theta}^*)\}$$

around the parameter $\boldsymbol{\theta}^*$. Thus the same theoretical property holds.

First, we analyze the asymptotic behavior of $J(\widehat{r}_{\mathrm{A}})$.

Lemma 13.9 *$J(\widehat{r}_{\mathrm{A}})$ can be asymptotically expressed as*

$$J(\widehat{r}_{\mathrm{A}}) = \frac{1}{2n}\left[\dim\Theta + \mathrm{tr}(\boldsymbol{F}(\boldsymbol{\theta}^*_{\mathrm{nu}})\boldsymbol{F}(\boldsymbol{\theta}^*_{\mathrm{de}})^{-1}) + \mathrm{PE}(p^*_{\mathrm{de}} \| p^*_{\mathrm{nu}}) \right] + \mathcal{O}(n^{-3/2}),$$

where $\mathcal{O}(\cdot)$ denotes the asymptotic order. $\boldsymbol{F}(\boldsymbol{\theta})$ denotes the Fisher information matrix of the exponential model $p(\boldsymbol{x};\boldsymbol{\theta})$:

$$\boldsymbol{F}(\boldsymbol{\theta}) := \int \nabla \log p(\boldsymbol{x};\boldsymbol{\theta}) \nabla \log p(\boldsymbol{x};\boldsymbol{\theta})^\top p(\boldsymbol{x};\boldsymbol{\theta}) \mathrm{d}\boldsymbol{x},$$

where ∇ *denotes the partial differential operator with respect to* $\boldsymbol{\theta}$. $\mathrm{PE}(p\|q)$ *denotes the Pearson divergence of the two densities* p *and* q *and is defined as*

$$\mathrm{PE}(p\|q) := \frac{1}{2}\int \frac{(p(\boldsymbol{x}) - q(\boldsymbol{x}))^2}{p(\boldsymbol{x})}\mathrm{d}\boldsymbol{x}.$$

Next we investigate the asymptotic behavior of $J(\widehat{r}_{\mathrm{B}})$ and $J(\widehat{r}_{\mathrm{C}})$. Let y be the selector variable taking nu or de as defined in Section 13.4.2. The statistical model of the joint probability for $\boldsymbol{z} = (\boldsymbol{x}, y)$ is defined as

$$q(\boldsymbol{z};\boldsymbol{\theta},\theta_0) = q(y|\boldsymbol{x};\boldsymbol{\theta},\theta_0) \times \frac{p^*_{\mathrm{nu}}(\boldsymbol{x}) + p^*_{\mathrm{de}}(\boldsymbol{x})}{2}, \tag{13.19}$$

where $q(y|\boldsymbol{x};\boldsymbol{\theta},\theta_0)$ is the conditional probability of y such that

$$q(y=\mathrm{nu}|\boldsymbol{x};\boldsymbol{\theta},\theta_0) = \frac{r(\boldsymbol{x};\boldsymbol{\theta},\theta_0)}{1+r(\boldsymbol{x};\boldsymbol{\theta},\theta_0)} = \frac{\exp\{\theta_0 + \boldsymbol{\theta}^\top \boldsymbol{\xi}(\boldsymbol{x})\}}{1+\exp\{\theta_0 + \boldsymbol{\theta}^\top \boldsymbol{\xi}(\boldsymbol{x})\}},$$

$$q(y=\mathrm{de}|\boldsymbol{x};\boldsymbol{\theta},\theta_0) = \frac{1}{1+r(\boldsymbol{x};\boldsymbol{\theta},\theta_0)} = \frac{1}{1+\exp\{\theta_0 + \boldsymbol{\theta}^\top \boldsymbol{\xi}(\boldsymbol{x})\}}.$$

The Fisher information matrix of the model (13.19) is denoted as

$$\widetilde{\boldsymbol{F}}(\boldsymbol{\theta},\theta_0) \in \mathbb{R}^{(\dim\Theta+1)\times(\dim\Theta+1)},$$

and its inverse is expressed as

$$\widetilde{\boldsymbol{F}}(\boldsymbol{\theta},\theta_0)^{-1} = \begin{pmatrix} \boldsymbol{H}_{11}(\boldsymbol{\theta},\theta_0) & \boldsymbol{h}_{12}(\boldsymbol{\theta},\theta_0) \\ \boldsymbol{h}_{12}(\boldsymbol{\theta},\theta_0)^\top & h_{22}(\boldsymbol{\theta},\theta_0) \end{pmatrix},$$

where $\boldsymbol{H}_{11}(\boldsymbol{\theta},\theta_0)$ is a $(\dim\Theta) \times (\dim\Theta)$ matrix. Then we have the following lemmas.

Lemma 13.10 $J(\widehat{r}_{\mathrm{B}})$ *can be asymptotically expressed as*

$$J(\widehat{r}_{\mathrm{B}}) = \frac{1}{2n}\left[\mathrm{tr}(\boldsymbol{F}(\boldsymbol{\theta}^*_{\mathrm{nu}})\boldsymbol{H}_{11}(\boldsymbol{\theta}^*,\theta^*_0)) + \mathrm{PE}(p^*_{\mathrm{de}}\|p^*_{\mathrm{nu}})\right] + \mathcal{O}(n^{-3/2}),$$

where $(\boldsymbol{\theta}^*,\theta^*_0)$ *is defined in Eq.* (13.18).

Lemma 13.11 $J(\widehat{r}_{\mathrm{C}})$ *can be asymptotically expressed as*

$$J(\widehat{r}_{\mathrm{C}}) = \frac{1}{2n}\left[\dim\Theta + \mathrm{tr}(\boldsymbol{F}(\boldsymbol{\theta}^*_{\mathrm{nu}})^{-1}\boldsymbol{G}) + \mathrm{PE}(p^*_{\mathrm{de}}\|p^*_{\mathrm{nu}})\right] + \mathcal{O}(n^{-3/2}),$$

where $\boldsymbol{G} := \int r^*(\boldsymbol{x})(\boldsymbol{\xi}(\boldsymbol{x}) - \boldsymbol{\eta}_{\mathrm{nu}})(\boldsymbol{\xi}(\boldsymbol{x}) - \boldsymbol{\eta}_{\mathrm{nu}})^\top p^*_{\mathrm{nu}}(\boldsymbol{x})\mathrm{d}\boldsymbol{x}$ *and* $\boldsymbol{\eta}_{\mathrm{nu}} = \mathrm{E}_{\mathrm{nu}}[\boldsymbol{\xi}(\boldsymbol{x})]$.

Based on these lemmas, we compare the accuracy of the three methods. For the accuracy of (A) and (B), we have the following theorem.

Theorem 13.12 $J(\widehat{r}_{\mathrm{A}}) \leq J(\widehat{r}_{\mathrm{B}})$ *holds asymptotically.*

Thus method (A) is more accurate than method (B) in terms of the expected unnormalized Kullback–Leibler divergence (13.13). Theorem 13.12 may be regarded as an extension of the result for binary classification (Efron, 1975): estimating data-generating Gaussian densities by maximum likelihood estimation has higher statistical efficiency than logistic regression in terms of the classification error rate.

Next, we compare the accuracy of (B) and (C).

Theorem 13.13 $J(\widehat{r}_{\mathrm{B}}) \leq J(\widehat{r}_{\mathrm{C}})$ *holds asymptotically.*

Thus method (B) is more accurate than method (C) in terms of the expected unnormalized Kullback–Leibler divergence (13.13). This inequality is a direct consequence of Qin (1998) (see Section 13.3), where it was shown that method (B) has the smallest asymptotic variance in a class of semi-parametric estimators. It is easy to see that method (C) is included in the class.

Finally, we compare the accuracy of (A) and (C). From Theorems 13.12 and 13.13, we immediately have the following corollary.

Corollary 13.14 $J(\widehat{r}_{\mathrm{A}}) \leq J(\widehat{r}_{\mathrm{C}})$ *holds asymptotically.*

It was advocated that one should avoid solving more difficult intermediate problems when solving a target problem (Vapnik, 1998). This statement is sometimes referred to as *Vapnik's principle*, and the *support vector machine* (Cortes and Vapnik, 1995) would be a successful example of this principle; instead of estimating a data-generation model, it directly models the decision boundary, which is sufficient for pattern recognition.

If we follow Vapnik's principle, directly estimating the density ratio $r^*(\boldsymbol{x})$ would be more promising than estimating the two densities $p^*_{\mathrm{nu}}(\boldsymbol{x})$ and $p^*_{\mathrm{de}}(\boldsymbol{x})$, because knowing $p^*_{\mathrm{nu}}(\boldsymbol{x})$ and $p^*_{\mathrm{de}}(\boldsymbol{x})$ implies knowing $r^*(\boldsymbol{x})$, but not vice versa; indeed, $r^*(\boldsymbol{x})$ cannot be uniquely decomposed into $p^*_{\mathrm{nu}}(\boldsymbol{x})$ and $p^*_{\mathrm{de}}(\boldsymbol{x})$. Thus, at a glance, Corollary 13.14 is counterintuitive. However, Corollary 13.14 would be reasonable because method (C) does not make use of the knowledge that *each* density is exponential, but only the knowledge that their ratio is exponential. Thus method (A) can utilize the a priori model information more effectively. Thanks to the additional knowledge that both the densities belong to the exponential model, the intermediate problems (i.e., density estimation) were actually made easier in terms of Vapnik's principle.

13.4.5 Accuracy Analysis for Misspecified Exponential Models

Finally, we theoretically analyze the approximation error of the three density-ratio estimators for misspecified exponential models; that is, the true densities and ratio are not necessarily included in the exponential models. The unnormalized Kullback–Leibler divergence is employed to measure the approximation error.

First we study the convergence of method (A). Let $\overline{p}_{\mathrm{nu}}(\boldsymbol{x})$ and $\overline{p}_{\mathrm{de}}(\boldsymbol{x})$ be the projections of the true densities $p^*_{\mathrm{nu}}(\boldsymbol{x})$ and $p^*_{\mathrm{de}}(\boldsymbol{x})$ onto the model $p(\boldsymbol{x};\boldsymbol{\theta})$ in terms of the Kullback–Leibler divergence (13.12):

$$\overline{p}_{\mathrm{nu}}(\boldsymbol{x}) := p(\boldsymbol{x};\overline{\boldsymbol{\theta}}_{\mathrm{nu}}) \quad \text{and} \quad \overline{p}_{\mathrm{de}}(\boldsymbol{x}) := p(\boldsymbol{x};\overline{\boldsymbol{\theta}}_{\mathrm{de}}),$$

where

$$\overline{\boldsymbol{\theta}}_{\mathrm{nu}} := \operatorname*{argmin}_{\boldsymbol{\theta}\in\Theta} \int p^*_{\mathrm{nu}}(\boldsymbol{x}) \log \frac{p^*_{\mathrm{nu}}(\boldsymbol{x})}{p(\boldsymbol{x};\boldsymbol{\theta})} \mathrm{d}\boldsymbol{x},$$

$$\overline{\boldsymbol{\theta}}_{\mathrm{de}} := \operatorname*{argmin}_{\boldsymbol{\theta}\in\Theta} \int p^*_{\mathrm{de}}(\boldsymbol{x}) \log \frac{p^*_{\mathrm{de}}(\boldsymbol{x})}{p(\boldsymbol{x};\boldsymbol{\theta})} \mathrm{d}\boldsymbol{x}.$$

This means that $\overline{p}_{\mathrm{nu}}(\boldsymbol{x})$ and $\overline{p}_{\mathrm{de}}(\boldsymbol{x})$ are the optimal approximations to $p^*_{\mathrm{nu}}(\boldsymbol{x})$ and $p^*_{\mathrm{de}}(\boldsymbol{x})$ in the model $p(\boldsymbol{x};\boldsymbol{\theta})$ in terms of the Kullback–Leibler divergence. Let

$$\overline{r}_{\mathrm{A}}(\boldsymbol{x}) := \frac{\overline{p}_{\mathrm{nu}}(\boldsymbol{x})}{\overline{p}_{\mathrm{de}}(\boldsymbol{x})}.$$

Because the ratio of two exponential densities also belongs to the exponential model, there exists $\overline{\boldsymbol{\theta}}_{\mathrm{A}} \in \Theta$ such that $\overline{r}_{\mathrm{A}}(\boldsymbol{x}) = r(\boldsymbol{x};\overline{\boldsymbol{\theta}}_{\mathrm{A}},\bar{\theta}_{\mathrm{A},0})$. Then we have the following lemma.

Lemma 13.15 *$\widehat{r}_{\mathrm{A}}$ converges in probability to $\overline{r}_{\mathrm{A}}$ as $n \to \infty$.*

Next we investigate the convergence of method (B). Let $q^*(\boldsymbol{x},y)$ be the joint probability defined as

$$q^*(\boldsymbol{x},y) = q^*(y|\boldsymbol{x}) \times \frac{p^*_{\mathrm{nu}}(\boldsymbol{x}) + p^*_{\mathrm{de}}(\boldsymbol{x})}{2},$$

where $q^*(y|\boldsymbol{x})$ is the conditional probability of y such that

$$q^*(y=\mathrm{nu}|\boldsymbol{x}) = \frac{r^*(\boldsymbol{x})}{1+r^*(\boldsymbol{x})} \quad \text{and} \quad q^*(y=\mathrm{de}|\boldsymbol{x}) = \frac{1}{1+r^*(\boldsymbol{x})}.$$

The model (13.19) is used to estimate $q^*(\boldsymbol{x},y)$, and let $\overline{q}(\boldsymbol{x},y)$ be the projection of the true density $q^*(\boldsymbol{x},y)$ onto the model (13.19) in terms of the Kullback–Leibler divergence (13.12):

$$\overline{q}(\boldsymbol{x},y) := q(\boldsymbol{x},y;\overline{\boldsymbol{\theta}}_{\mathrm{B}},\bar{\theta}_{\mathrm{B},0}),$$

where

$$(\overline{\boldsymbol{\theta}}_{\mathrm{B}},\bar{\theta}_{\mathrm{B},0}) := \operatorname*{argmin}_{(\boldsymbol{\theta},\theta_0)\in\Theta\times\mathbb{R}} \int \sum_{y\in\{\mathrm{nu},\mathrm{de}\}} q^*(\boldsymbol{x},y) \log \frac{q^*(y|\boldsymbol{x})}{q(y|\boldsymbol{x};\boldsymbol{\theta},\theta_0)} \mathrm{d}\boldsymbol{x}.$$

This means that $\overline{q}(\boldsymbol{x},y)$ is the optimal approximation to $q^*(\boldsymbol{x},y)$ in the model

$$q(y|\boldsymbol{x};\boldsymbol{\theta},\theta_0)\frac{p^*_{\mathrm{nu}}(\boldsymbol{x}) + p^*_{\mathrm{de}}(\boldsymbol{x})}{2}$$

in terms of the Kullback–Leibler divergence. Letting $\bar{r}_{\mathrm{B}}(\boldsymbol{x}) := r(\boldsymbol{x};\bar{\boldsymbol{\theta}}_{\mathrm{B}},\bar{\theta}_{\mathrm{B},0})$, we have the following lemma.

Lemma 13.16 *$\widehat{r}_{\mathrm{B}}$ converges in probability to $\bar{r}_{\mathrm{B}}$ as $n \to \infty$.*

Finally, we study the convergence of method (C). Suppose that the model $r(\boldsymbol{x};\boldsymbol{\theta},\theta_0)$ in Eq. (13.17) is employed. Let $\bar{r}_{\mathrm{C}}(\boldsymbol{x})$ be the projection of the true density-ratio function $r^*(\boldsymbol{x})$ onto the model $r(\boldsymbol{x};\boldsymbol{\theta},\theta_0)$ in terms of the unnormalized Kullback–Leibler divergence (13.11):

$$\bar{r}_{\mathrm{C}}(\boldsymbol{x}) := r(\boldsymbol{x};\bar{\boldsymbol{\theta}}_{\mathrm{C}},\bar{\theta}_{\mathrm{C},0}),$$

where

$$(\bar{\boldsymbol{\theta}}_{\mathrm{C}},\bar{\theta}_{\mathrm{C},0}) := \underset{(\boldsymbol{\theta},\theta_0)\in\Theta\times\mathbb{R}}{\operatorname{argmin}} \left[\int p^*_{\mathrm{nu}}(\boldsymbol{x}) \log \frac{r^*(\boldsymbol{x})}{r(\boldsymbol{x};\boldsymbol{\theta},\theta_0)} \mathrm{d}\boldsymbol{x} \right.$$
$$\left. - 1 + \int p^*_{\mathrm{de}}(\boldsymbol{x}) r(\boldsymbol{x};\boldsymbol{\theta},\theta_0) \mathrm{d}\boldsymbol{x} \right].$$

This means that $\bar{r}_{\mathrm{C}}(\boldsymbol{x})$ is the optimal approximation to $r^*(\boldsymbol{x})$ in the model $r(\boldsymbol{x};\boldsymbol{\theta})$ in terms of the unnormalized Kullback–Leibler divergence. Then we have the following lemma.

Lemma 13.17 *$\widehat{r}_{\mathrm{C}}$ converges in probability to $\bar{r}_{\mathrm{C}}$ as $n \to \infty$.*

Based on these lemmas, we investigate the relation among the three methods. Lemma 13.17 implies that method (C) is consistent with the optimal approximation $\bar{r}_{\mathrm{C}}$. However, as we will show in the following, methods (A) and (B) are not consistent with the optimal approximation $\bar{r}_{\mathrm{C}}$ in general. Let us measure the deviation of a density-ratio function $\bar{r}'$ from $\bar{r}$ by

$$\mathrm{D}(\bar{r}',\bar{r}) := \int p^*_{\mathrm{de}}(\boldsymbol{x}) \left(\bar{r}'(\boldsymbol{x}) - \bar{r}(\boldsymbol{x})\right)^2 \mathrm{d}\boldsymbol{x}.$$

Then we have the following theorem.

Theorem 13.18 *For any $\bar{r}$ in the exponential model,*

$$\mathrm{D}(\bar{r},\bar{r}_{\mathrm{C}}) \geq \left| \int p^*_{\mathrm{de}}(\boldsymbol{x}) \bar{r}(\boldsymbol{x}) d\boldsymbol{x} - 1 \right|^2.$$

When the model is misspecified, $p^*_{\mathrm{de}}(\boldsymbol{x})\bar{r}_{\mathrm{A}}(\boldsymbol{x})$ and $p^*_{\mathrm{de}}(\boldsymbol{x})\bar{r}_{\mathrm{B}}(\boldsymbol{x})$ are not probability densities in general. Then Theorem 13.18 implies that methods (A) and (B) are not consistent with the optimal approximation $\bar{r}_{\mathrm{C}}$.

Because model misspecification is a usual situation in practice, method (C) is the most promising approach in density-ratio estimation.

Finally, for the consistency of method (A), we also have the following additional result.

Corollary 13.19 *If $p^*_{\mathrm{de}}(\boldsymbol{x})$ belongs to the exponential model* (13.16)*, that is, there exists $\overline{\boldsymbol{\theta}}_{\mathrm{de}} \in \Theta$ such that $p^*_{\mathrm{de}}(\boldsymbol{x}) = p(\boldsymbol{x};\overline{\boldsymbol{\theta}}_{\mathrm{de}})n$, then $\overline{r}_{\mathrm{A}} = \overline{r}_{\mathrm{C}}$ holds even when $p^*_{\mathrm{nu}}(\boldsymbol{x})$ does not belong to the exponential model* (13.16).

This corollary means that, as long as $p^*_{\mathrm{de}}(\boldsymbol{x})$ is correctly specified, method (A) is still consistent.

13.5 Remarks

In this chapter we analyzed the asymptotic properties of density-ratio estimators under the parametric setup.

We first elucidated the consistency and asymptotic normality of KLIEP (Chapter 5) in Section 13.1, and the asymptotic learning curve of cLSIF (Section 6.2.1) and uLSIF (Section 6.2.2) in Section 13.2. All of the methods were shown to achieve the $\sqrt{n}$-consistency, which is the optimal parametric convergence rate.

In Section 13.3 we considered the moment-matching approach to density-ratio estimation and introduced Qin's (1998) result: The logistic regression method (Chapter 4) achieves the minimum asymptotic variance under the correctly specified parametric setup. Thus, as long as the parametric model at hand is correctly specified, use of the logistic regression method is recommended.

Finally, in Section 13.4, we theoretically compared the performance of three density-ratio estimation methods:

(A) The density estimation method (Chapter 2)
(B) The logistic regression method (Chapter 4)
(C) The Kullback–Leibler divergence method (Chapter 5)

In Section 13.4.4, we first showed that when the numerator and denominator densities are known to be members of the exponential family, (A) is better than (B) and (B) is better than (C) in terms of the expected unnormalized Kullback–Leibler divergence. This implies that when correctly specified parametric density models are available for both the numerator and denominator densities, separate density estimation is more promising than direct density-ratio estimation. This is because direct density-ratio estimation *cannot* utilize the knowledge of each density, only the knowledge of their ratio. However, once the model assumption is violated, (C) is better than (A) and (B), as shown in Section 13.4.5. Thus, in practical situations where no exact model is available, (C) would be the most promising approach to density-ratio estimation.

In the next chapter we analyze statistical properties of density-ratio estimation under the non-parametric setup, which requires considerably different mathematical tools.

14

Non-Parametric Convergence Analysis

In this chapter we analyze the convergence properties of density-ratio estimators under a non-parametric setup. After summarizing the mathematical tools in Section 14.1, non-parametric convergence analyses for KLIEP (see Chapter 5) and uLSIF (see Chapter 6) are provided in Sections 14.2 and 14.3, respectively. Finally, Section 14.4 concludes the chapter.

We describe again the notation of our density-ratio estimation problem. We are given two sets of i.i.d. samples in the data domain $\mathcal{X}$ ($\subset \mathbb{R}^d$):

$$\{x_i^{\mathrm{nu}}\}_{i=1}^{n_{\mathrm{nu}}} \overset{\text{i.i.d.}}{\sim} P_{\mathrm{nu}}^* \quad \text{and} \quad \{x_j^{\mathrm{de}}\}_{j=1}^{n_{\mathrm{de}}} \overset{\text{i.i.d.}}{\sim} P_{\mathrm{de}}^*.$$

Let $p_{\mathrm{nu}}^*(x)$ and $p_{\mathrm{de}}^*(x)$ be the probability densities for the distributions P_{nu}^* and P_{de}^*, respectively. The goal is to estimate the density ratio $r^*(x) = p_{\mathrm{nu}}^*(x)/p_{\mathrm{de}}^*(x)$ based on the observed samples, where $p_{\mathrm{de}}^*(x)$ is assumed to be strictly positive. In this chapter we focus on using a *non-parametric* model (i.e., an infinite-dimensional model) for density-ratio estimation.

14.1 Mathematical Preliminaries

In this section we show the flow of the proof of the non-parametric convergence rates and prepare some basic mathematical devices.

As we will see, a uniform upper bound of *empirical processes* is used to derive the convergence rates. Roughly speaking, an empirical process of a function class $\mathcal{F}$ is a random process,

$$\mathcal{F} \ni f \mapsto \frac{1}{n}\sum_{i=1}^{n} f(x_i),$$

where $\{x_i\}_{i=1}^n$ are samples; its uniform upper bound is defined as

$$\sup_{f\in\mathcal{F}} \left| \frac{1}{n}\sum_{i=1}^{n} f(x_i) - \mathbb{E}[f] \right|,$$

where $\mathbb{E}$ denotes the expectation. To evaluate the uniform upper bound, quantities that represent the "complexity" of $\mathcal{F}$ are required. The *covering numbers* and *bracketing numbers* are commonly used complexity measures that will be introduced in Section 14.1.3. A key device to give the tail probability of the uniform upper bound is *Talagrand's concentration inequality*, which evaluates how the uniform upper bound of the empirical process concentrates around its expectation. Talagrand's concentration inequality will be explained in Section 14.1.5.

14.1.1 Outline

First we give an outline for deriving the convergence rates of non-parametrically estimated density ratios. Because the aim here is to give an intuitive explanation, mathematical preciseness is sacrificed to some extent.

Let $\mathcal{F}$ be a model that is a class of measurable functions. Let $\boldsymbol{x}_1,\ldots,\boldsymbol{x}_n$ be i.i.d. samples, and let P^* be an underlying probability measure generating $\boldsymbol{x}_i$. We denote an empirical risk of a function f for a loss function ℓ by

$$\widehat{P}^*\ell(f) := \frac{1}{n}\sum_{k=1}^{n}\ell(f(\boldsymbol{x}_k)).$$

The true risk of f with respect to the true probability measure P^* is written as

$$P^*\ell(f) := \int \ell(f(\boldsymbol{x}))p^*(\boldsymbol{x})\mathrm{d}\boldsymbol{x}.$$

We want to evaluate the convergence rate of the *excess risk*:

$$P^*\ell(\widehat{f}) - P^*\ell(f^*).$$

For simplicity, we assume that all elements of $\mathcal{F}$ are uniformly bounded from above; that is, there exists a constant M such that $\|f\|_\infty \le M$ $(\forall f \in \mathcal{F})$. In the following we consider the optimization problem

$$\widehat{f} = \operatorname*{argmin}_{f\in\mathcal{F}} \widehat{P}^*\ell(f).$$

Although there may be an additional regularization term in some methods such as uLSIF, we focus on the simplest situation here. We assume that f^* minimizes the true risk:

$$f^* = \operatorname*{argmin}_{f\in\mathcal{F}} P^*\ell(f).$$

A key technical ingredient to derive a tight convergence bound of the excess risk is the *localization technique* or the *pealing device*, which exploits a "distance" between $\widehat{f}$ and f^*. As the sample size increases, $\widehat{f}$ and f^* are likely to be close to each other, so that the asymptotic behavior of $\widehat{f}$ becomes similar to f^*. The localization technique utilizes such a property to bound the differences between the empirical and the true excess risks:

$$\widehat{P}^*(\ell(\widehat{f}) - \ell(f^*)) - P^*(\ell(\widehat{f}) - \ell(f^*)).$$

This allows us to obtain a tighter bound compared with dealing with $\widehat{f}$ and f^* independently. In the following we show an illustrative usage of the localization technique.

First we suppose that there exists a (pseudo) distance $d(\widehat{f}, f^*)$ such that

$$d(\widehat{f}, f^*) \geq \|\widehat{f} - f^*\|_{2,P^*}, \tag{14.1}$$

$$P^*(\ell(\widehat{f}) - \ell(f^*)) \geq d(\widehat{f}, f^*)^2, \tag{14.2}$$

where $\|\widehat{f} - f^*\|_{2,P}$ is the L_2-distance with respect to the probability measure P, and we ignore the difference in constant factors. This assumption can be achieved, for example, if there exists a constant $\delta > 0$ such that

$$\ell(z) - \ell(z_0) \geq (z - z_0)\ell'(z_0) + \frac{\delta}{2}(z - z_0)^2.$$

For $\mathcal{F}_\ell := \{\ell(f) \mid f \in \mathcal{F}\}$, its complexity is usually measured by the *covering number* or the *bracketing number*. Roughly speaking, the covering number and the bracketing number of $\mathcal{F}_\ell$ are large/small if the model $\mathcal{F}_\ell$ is complex/simple. To impose that the model $\mathcal{F}_\ell$ is not too complicated, we assume that there exists $0 < \gamma < 2$ such that one of the following two conditions is satisfied:

$$\log N_{[]}(\epsilon, \mathcal{F}_\ell, L_2(P^*)) = \mathcal{O}\left(\epsilon^{-\gamma}\right),$$

$$\sup_P \log N(\epsilon, \mathcal{F}_\ell, L_2(P)) = \mathcal{O}\left(\epsilon^{-\gamma}\right),$$

where $N_{[]}(\epsilon, \mathcal{F}_\ell, L_2(P))$ denotes the bracketing number of $\mathcal{F}_\ell$ (see Definition 14.4) and $N(\epsilon, \mathcal{F}_\ell, L_2(P))$ denotes the covering number of $\mathcal{F}_\ell$ with respect to the norm $L_2(P)$ (see Definition 14.3). In the last equation, the supremum is taken over all discrete probability measures (see Lemma 14.5).

Under the previously mentioned conditions about the covering number or the bracketing number, one can show that

$$\sup_{f \in \mathcal{F}: d(f, f^*) \leq \delta} (P^* - \widehat{P}^*)(\ell(f) - \ell(f^*)) \leq \mathcal{O}_p\left(\frac{\delta^{1-\frac{\gamma}{2}}}{\sqrt{n}}\right). \tag{14.3}$$

Condition (14.1) is used to prove this bound. Roughly speaking, the right-hand side comes from the so-called *Dudley integral* (see Lemmas 14.5 and 14.6):

$$\frac{1}{\sqrt{n}} \int_0^\delta \sqrt{\log N_{[]}(\epsilon, \mathcal{F}_\ell, L_2(P^*))} \mathrm{d}\epsilon \quad \text{or} \quad \frac{1}{\sqrt{n}} \int_0^\delta \sqrt{\sup_P \log N(\epsilon, \mathcal{F}_\ell, L_2(P))} \mathrm{d}\epsilon.$$

Equation (14.3) indicates that if $\widehat{f}$ is close to f^*, the stochastic behavior of $\widehat{f}$ is similar to f^*, so that noise $(P^* - \widehat{P}^*)(\ell(\widehat{f}) - \ell(f^*))$ of the risk becomes small.

The excess risk of the empirical risk minimizer $\widehat{f}$ can be bounded from above as

$$P^*(\ell(\widehat{f}) - \ell(f^*)) \leq (P^* - \widehat{P}^*)(\ell(\widehat{f}) - \ell(f^*)) \leq \mathcal{O}_p\left(\frac{d(\widehat{f}, f^*)^{1-\frac{\gamma}{2}}}{\sqrt{n}}\right), \tag{14.4}$$

where the second inequality follows from $\widehat{P}^*\ell(\widehat{f}) \leq \widehat{P}^*\ell(f^*)$ (recall that $\widehat{f}$ minimizes the empirical risk $\widehat{P}^*\ell$). On the other hand, by the assumption (14.2), the risk of $\widehat{f}$ is also bounded from below as

$$P^*(\ell(\widehat{f}) - \ell(f^*)) \geq d(\widehat{f}, f^*)^2. \tag{14.5}$$

Combining Eqs. (14.4) and (14.5), we observe that

$$d(\widehat{f}, f^*)^2 \leq P^*(\ell(\widehat{f}) - \ell(f^*)) \leq \mathcal{O}_p\left(\frac{d(\widehat{f}, f^*)^{1-\frac{\gamma}{2}}}{\sqrt{n}}\right).$$

Therefore, the convergence rate of the distance between $\widehat{f}$ and f^* can be evaluated by

$$d(\widehat{f}, f^*)^2 \leq \mathcal{O}_p\left(\frac{d(\widehat{f}, f^*)^{1-\frac{\gamma}{2}}}{\sqrt{n}}\right),$$

which implies that

$$d(\widehat{f}, f^*) = \mathcal{O}_p\left(n^{-\frac{1}{2+\gamma}}\right).$$

Consequently, we arrive at the convergence rate of the true risk of $\widehat{f}$:

$$P^*(\ell(\widehat{f}) - \ell(f^*)) \leq \mathcal{O}_p\left(\frac{d(\widehat{f}, f^*)^{1-\frac{\gamma}{2}}}{\sqrt{n}}\right) \leq \mathcal{O}_p\left(n^{-\frac{2}{2+\gamma}}\right).$$

This bound is called the *fast learning rate* (Koltchinskii, 2006; Bartlett et al., 2005).

14.1.2 Bernstein's and Hoeffding's Inequalities

The tail bound of the sum $\sum_{i=1}^n f(X_i)$ of a function f with independent random variables X_i is needed for analyzing the properties of non-parametric estimation such as the consistency and the convergence rate. *Bernstein's inequality* and *Hoeffding's inequality* give sub-Gaussian tail bounds of $\sum_{i=1}^n f(X_i)$.

For large n, the sum $\sum_{i=1}^n Y_i$ of independent variables with mean zero and a bounded range is approximately normally distributed with variance $v = \mathrm{var}(Y_1 + \cdots + Y_n)$. If the variables X_i have range $[-M, M]$, then Bernstein's inequality gives a tail bound $\exp[-x^2/(2v + (2Mx/3))]$ for variables $\sum_{i=1}^n Y_i$.

Proposition 14.1 (Bernstein's Inequality) *Let $Y_1, \ldots, Y_n$ be independent random variables with bounded range $[-M, M]$ and zero means. Then, for $v \geq \mathrm{Var}(Y_1 + \cdots + Y_n)$, where* Var *denotes the variance,*

$$\Pr(|Y_1 + \cdots + Y_n| > x) \leq 2\exp\left(-\frac{x^2}{2(v + Mx/3)}\right).$$

$\Pr(\cdot)$ *denotes the probability of an event.*

Hoeffding's inequality is simpler than Bernstein's, and gives the tail bound of $\sum_{i=1}^n Y_i$ of independent variables with range $[0,1]$ but unknown variance.

Proposition 14.2 (Hoeffding's Inequality) *Let $Y_1,\ldots,Y_n$ be independent random variables taking values in $[0,1]$, and let $\mu = \frac{1}{n}\sum_{i=1}^n \mathbb{E}[Y_i]$. Then, for $0 < t < 1-\mu$,*

$$\Pr\left(\frac{\sum_{i=1}^n Y_i}{n} - \mu \geq t\right) \leq \exp(-2nt^2).$$

14.1.3 Covering and Bracketing Numbers

Given a collection $\mathcal{F}$ of measurable functions, investigating the convergence rate of $\sup_{f\in\mathcal{F}} \left|\frac{1}{n}\sum_{i=1}^n f(X_i) - \mathbb{E}[f]\right|$ is key for analyzing of the convergence rate of non-parametric estimators. The convergence rate of $\sup_{f\in\mathcal{F}} \left|\frac{1}{n}\sum_{i=1}^n f(X_i) - \mathbb{E}[f]\right|$ depends on the complexity (size) of a class $\mathcal{F}$. A commonly used quantity to measure the complexity of a class $\mathcal{F}$ is the *entropy number*, which is the logarithm of the bracketing number or the covering number (see van der Vaart and Wellner, 1996, for details). Let $(\mathcal{F}, \|\cdot\|)$ be a subset of a normed space of real functions $f : \mathcal{X} \to \mathbb{R}$ on a domain $\mathcal{X}$. In the following we often use a subset of $L_2(P)$-space with respect to a probability measure P.

Definition 14.3 (Covering Number) *The* covering number *or the* ϵ-covering number $N(\epsilon, \mathcal{F}, \|\cdot\|)$ *is the minimal number of balls $\{g \mid \|f - g\| \leq \epsilon\}$ of radius ϵ and center f needed to cover a set $\mathcal{F}$. The centers of the balls need not belong to $\mathcal{F}$, but they should have finite norms. The* covering entropy *is the logarithm of the covering number.*

Definition 14.4 (Bracketing Number) *Given two functions l and u, the* bracket *$[l,u]$ is the set of all functions f with $l \leq f \leq u$. An ϵ-bracket is a* bracket $[l,u]$ *with $\|l - u\| \leq \epsilon$. The* bracketing number *or the* ϵ-bracketing number $N_{[]}(\epsilon, \mathcal{F}, \|\cdot\|)$ *is the minimal number of ϵ-brackets needed to cover $\mathcal{F}$. The upper and lower bounds u and l of the brackets need not belong to $\mathcal{F}$, but they should have finite norms. The* bracketing entropy *is the logarithm of the bracketing number.*

14.1.4 Uniform Upper Bounds

The entropy numbers give upper bounds of $\sup_{f\in\mathcal{F}} \left|\frac{1}{n}\sum_{i=1}^n f(X_i) - \mathbb{E}[f]\right|$. Let $\widehat{P}^*$ be an empirical measure of a sample of random elements $X_1,\ldots,X_n$; that is, $\widehat{P}^* = \frac{1}{n}\sum_{i=1}^n \delta_{X_i}$ of the Dirac measures at the observations. We use the abbreviation $Pf = \int f dP$ for a given measurable function f and a signed measure P. Let $\|P\|_{\mathcal{F}} = \sup\{|Pf| \mid f \in \mathcal{F}\}$. Then the following lemma holds.

Lemma 14.5 (Mendelson, 2002) *Let $\mathcal{F}$ be a class of functions such that $\|f\|_\infty \leq 1$ and $\sup_{f\in\mathcal{F}} \mathbb{E}f^2 \leq \delta^2$. Assume that there exist $K \geq 2$ and $0 < \gamma < 2$ such that*

$$\sup_P \log N(\epsilon, \mathcal{F}, L_2(P)) \leq \frac{K}{\epsilon^\gamma},$$

where "sup" is taken over all discrete probability measures. Then there exists a constant $C_{K,\gamma}$ such that

$$\mathbb{E}[\|\widehat{P}^* - P^*\|_{\mathcal{F}}] \leq C_{K,\gamma} \max\{n^{-1/2}\delta^{1-\gamma/2}, n^{-\frac{2}{2+\gamma}}\}.$$

By Lemma 3.4.2 of van der Vaart and Wellner (1996), we also have the following lemma.

Lemma 14.6 *Let $\mathcal{F}$ be a class of functions such that $\|f\|_\infty \leq 1$ and $\sup_{f \in \mathcal{F}} \mathbb{E} f^2 \leq \delta^2$. Then there exists a constant C such that*

$$\mathbb{E}[\|\widehat{P}^* - P^*\|_{\mathcal{F}}] \leq C\left(\frac{J(\mathcal{F},\delta,L_2(P^*))}{\sqrt{n}} + \frac{J(\mathcal{F},\delta,L_2(P^*))^2}{\delta^2 n}\right),$$

where

$$J(\mathcal{F},\delta,L_2(P^*)) := \int_0^\delta \sqrt{1+\log N_{[]}(\mathcal{F},\epsilon,L_2(P^*))}\mathrm{d}\epsilon.$$

It should be noted that the inequality shown in Lemma 14.5 is a uniform version of Hoeffding's inequality, and that of Lemma 14.6 is a uniform version of Bernstein's inequality.

14.1.5 Talagrand's Concentration Inequality

Our analysis in this chapter relies heavily on the inequality known as *Talagrand's concentration inequality* (Talagrand, 1996b,a). We utilize a version of Talagrand's concentration inequality that gives a uniform tail bound for the sum of i.i.d. random variables.

Let $\{X_i\}_{i=1}^n$ be a sample of i.i.d. random variables that take values on some space $\tilde{\mathcal{X}}$ and let P^* be an underlying probability measure generating X_i. Let $\mathcal{F}$ be a set of functions $\tilde{\mathcal{X}} \to [0,1]$ that is separable with respect to the L_∞-norm. The inequality associates the uniform tail bound (the tail bound of $\|\widehat{P}^* - P^*\|_{\mathcal{F}}$) with the expectation of $\|\widehat{P}^* - P^*\|_{\mathcal{F}}$, where the *diameter* of $\mathcal{F}$ is defined by $\sigma_{P^*}(\mathcal{F})^2 := \sup_{g\in\mathcal{F}}(P^*g^2 - (P^*g)^2)$.

The following bound is a version of Talagrand's concentration inequality, also known as *Bousquet's bound* (Bousquet, 2002), which plays a very important role in our analysis:

$$\Pr\left\{\|\widehat{P}^* - P^*\|_{\mathcal{F}} \geq \mathbb{E}\|\widehat{P}^* - P^*\|_{\mathcal{F}} + \sqrt{\frac{2t}{n}\left(\sigma_{P^*}(\mathcal{F})^2 + 2\mathbb{E}\|\widehat{P}^* - P^*\|_{\mathcal{F}}\right)} + \frac{t}{3n}\right\} \leq e^{-t}.$$

Bousquet's bound allows us to investigate the difference between the empirical risk and the true risk of an estimator. We can easily see that $\mathbb{E}\|\widehat{P}^* - P^*\|_{\mathcal{F}}$ and $\sigma_{P^*}(\mathcal{F})$ in Bousquet's bound can be replaced with other functions bounding from above. For example, upper bounds of $\mathbb{E}\|\widehat{P}^* - P^*\|_{\mathcal{F}}$ are available as indicated in Lemmas 14.5 and 14.6, and $\sigma_{P^*}(\mathcal{F})$ can be bounded by the $L_2(P^*)$-norm.

14.2 Non-Parametric Convergence Analysis of KLIEP

In this section we investigate convergence properties of the KLIEP algorithm (see Chapter 5) in a non-parametric setting.

We first give some mathematical notations in Section 14.2.1. Then we elucidate the non-parametric convergence rate of KLIEP under two different situations in Sections 14.2.2 and 14.2.3, respectively.

14.2.1 Preliminaries

For simplicity, we assume that the numbers of the numerator and denominator samples are the same, that is, $n = n_{\mathrm{nu}} = n_{\mathrm{de}}$. We note that this assumption is just for notational simplicity; in the absence of this assumption, the convergence rate is determined solely by the sample size with the slower rate.

For the two probability distributions $p^*_{\mathrm{nu}}(\boldsymbol{x})$ and $p^*_{\mathrm{de}}(\boldsymbol{x})$, we express the expectation of a function r as

$$P^*_{\mathrm{nu}}r := \int r(\boldsymbol{x})p^*_{\mathrm{nu}}(\boldsymbol{x})\mathrm{d}\boldsymbol{x} \quad \text{and} \quad P^*_{\mathrm{de}}r := \int r(\boldsymbol{x})p^*_{\mathrm{de}}(\boldsymbol{x})\mathrm{d}\boldsymbol{x}.$$

In a similar fashion we define the empirical distributions of p^*_{nu} and p^*_{de} by $\widehat{P}^*_{\mathrm{nu}}$ and $\widehat{P}^*_{\mathrm{de}}$, that is,

$$\widehat{P}^*_{\mathrm{nu}}r := \frac{1}{n}\sum_{i=1}^{n} r(\boldsymbol{x}^{\mathrm{nu}}_i) \quad \text{and} \quad \widehat{P}^*_{\mathrm{de}}r := \frac{1}{n}\sum_{j=1}^{n} r(\boldsymbol{x}^{\mathrm{de}}_j).$$

The set of basis functions is denoted by $\Phi := \{\varphi_\theta \mid \theta \in \Theta\}$, where Θ is some parameter or index set. Similarly, the set of basis functions at n samples is denoted using $\widehat{\Theta} \subseteq \Theta$ by $\widehat{\Phi} := \{\varphi_\theta \mid \theta \in \widehat{\Theta}\} \subset \Phi$, which can behave stochastically. The set of finite linear combinations of Φ with positive coefficients and its bounded subset are denoted by

$$\mathcal{R} := \left\{ \sum_{\ell} \alpha_\ell \varphi_{\theta_\ell} \;\middle|\; \alpha_\ell \geq 0,\ \varphi_{\theta_\ell} \in \Phi \right\},$$

$$\mathcal{R}^M := \{ r \in \mathcal{R} \mid \|r\|_\infty \leq M \},$$

and their subsets at n samples are denoted by

$$\mathcal{R}_n := \left\{ \sum_{\ell} \alpha_\ell \varphi_{\theta_\ell} \;\middle|\; \alpha_\ell \geq 0,\ \varphi_{\theta_\ell} \in \widehat{\Phi} \right\} \subset \mathcal{R},$$

$$\mathcal{R}^M_n := \{ r \in \mathcal{R}_n \mid \|r\|_\infty \leq M \} \subset \mathcal{R}^M.$$

Let $\widehat{\mathcal{R}}_n$ be the feasible set of KLIEP:

$$\widehat{\mathcal{R}}_n := \{ r \in \mathcal{R}_n \mid \widehat{P}^*_{\mathrm{de}} r = 1 \}.$$

Under the notations described above, the solution $\widehat{r}_n$ of (generalized) KLIEP is given as

$$\widehat{r}_n := \underset{r \in \widehat{\mathcal{R}}_n}{\mathrm{argmax}}\ \widehat{P}^*_{\mathrm{nu}} \log(r).$$

For simplicity, we assume that the optimal solution can be determined uniquely.

We define the (generalized) Hellinger distance with respect to p^*_{de} as

$$h_{p^*_{\mathrm{de}}}(r,r') := \left(\int \left(\sqrt{r(\boldsymbol{x})} - \sqrt{r'(\boldsymbol{x})} \right)^2 p^*_{\mathrm{de}}(\boldsymbol{x}) \mathrm{d}\boldsymbol{x} \right)^{1/2},$$

where r and r' are non-negative measurable functions (not restricted to be probability densities).

In Sections 14.2.2 and 14.2.3, we show two types of convergence analyses under different conditions. Although neither of the two conditions implies the other, the implications derived from the two analyses agree well with each other.

14.2.2 Convergence Analysis of KLIEP under L_2-Norm Covering and Bracketing Number Conditions

We now perform a theoretical analysis under the following assumptions (the proofs of the theorems in this subsection can be found in Sugiyama et al., 2008).

Assumption 14.7

1. *p^*_{nu} and p^*_{de} are absolutely continuous and satisfy*

$$0 < \eta_0 \leq r^*(\boldsymbol{x}) \leq \eta_1$$

for all $\boldsymbol{x}$ on the support of p^*_{nu} and p^*_{de}, where $r^*(\boldsymbol{x}) := p^*_{\mathrm{nu}}(\boldsymbol{x})/p^*_{\mathrm{de}}(\boldsymbol{x})$.

2. *There exist ϵ^*, $\xi^* > 0$, such that*

$$P^*_{\mathrm{de}}\varphi \geq \epsilon^*, \quad \|\varphi\|_\infty \leq \xi^*, \quad (\forall \varphi \in \Phi).$$

3. *Let $N(\epsilon, \Phi, \|\cdot\|)$ and $N_{[]}(\epsilon, \Phi, \|\cdot\|)$ be the ϵ-covering number and the ϵ-bracketing number of Φ with norm $\|\cdot\|$, respectively (see Definitions 14.3 and 14.4). For some constants $0 < \gamma < 2$ and K,*

$$\sup_P \log N(\epsilon, \mathcal{R}^M, L_2(P)) \leq K \left(\frac{M}{\epsilon} \right)^\gamma, \tag{14.6}$$

where the supremum is taken over all finitely discrete probability measures P, or

$$\log N_{[]}(\epsilon, \mathcal{R}^M, L_2(p^*_{\mathrm{de}})) \leq K \left(\frac{M}{\epsilon} \right)^\gamma. \tag{14.7}$$

The lower bound of r^* that appears in the first assumption will be used to ensure the existence of a Lipschitz continuous function that bounds the Hellinger distance from the true density ratio. The bound of r^* is needed only on the support of p^*_{nu} and p^*_{de}. The third assumption controls the complexity of the model. By this complexity assumption, we can bound the tail probability of the difference between the empirical risk and the true risk uniformly over the function class $\mathcal{R}^M$.

Then we have the following convergence bound for KLIEP.

Theorem 14.8 *Let* $\gamma_n := \max\{-\widehat{P}^*_{\mathrm{nu}} \log(\widehat{r}_n) + \widehat{P}^*_{\mathrm{nu}} \log(c_n r^*), 0\}$, *where* $c_n := (\widehat{P}^*_{\mathrm{de}} r^*)^{-1}$. *Then we have* $h_{P^*_{\mathrm{de}}}(r^*, \widehat{r}_n) = \mathcal{O}_p(n^{-\frac{1}{2+\gamma}} + \sqrt{\gamma_n})$.

The technical advantage of using the Hellinger distance instead of the Kullback–Leibler divergence is that the Hellinger distance is bounded from above by a Lipschitz continuous function. On the other hand, the Kullback–Leibler divergence is not Lipschitz continuous because $\log(x)$ diverges to $-\infty$ as $x \to 0$. This allows us to utilize the uniform convergence results of the empirical processes.

Remark. *If there exists* N *such that* $\forall n \geq N$, $r^* \in \mathcal{R}_n$, *then* $\gamma_n = 0$ $(\forall n \geq N)$. *In this setting,* $h_{P^*_{\mathrm{de}}}(r^*, \widehat{r}_n) = \mathcal{O}_p(n^{-\frac{1}{2+\gamma}})$.

From Theorem 14.8 we can derive another convergence theorem based on a different representation of the bias term as follows:

Theorem 14.9 *In addition to Assumption 14.7, if there exists* $r^*_n \in \widehat{\mathcal{R}}_n$ *such that, for some constant* c_0, $r^*(\boldsymbol{x})/r^*_n(\boldsymbol{x}) \leq c_0^2$ *for all* $\boldsymbol{x}$ *on the support of* p^*_{nu} *and* p^*_{de}, *then* $h_{P^*_{\mathrm{de}}}(r^*, \widehat{r}_n) = \mathcal{O}_p(n^{-\frac{1}{2+\gamma}} + h_{P^*_{\mathrm{de}}}(r^*, r^*_n))$.

In the following we evaluate more explicitly the convergence rate using an example.

Example 14.10 *Let* $d = 1$, *the support of* P^*_{nu} *be* $[0,1] \subseteq \mathbb{R}$, $\Phi = \{K_1(x, x') \mid x' \in [0,1]\}$, $\widehat{\Phi} = \{K_1(x, x^{\mathrm{nu}}_i) \mid i = 1, \ldots, n\}$, *and* $K_1(x, x') = \exp(-(x - x')^2/2)$. *Note that setting the Gaussian kernel variance to* 1 *is just for simplicity; essentially the same argument can be applied to an arbitrary Gaussian variance.*

Assume that P^*_{nu} *has a density* $p^*_{\mathrm{nu}}(x)$ *and there exists a constant* η_2 *such that* $p^*_{\mathrm{nu}}(x) \geq \eta_2 > 0$ $(\forall x \in [-1,1])$. *We also assume that the true density ratio* r^* *is a mixture of Gaussian kernels, that is,*

$$r^*(x) = \int K_1(x, x') \mathrm{d}P(x') \quad (\forall x \in [0,1]),$$

where P *is a positive finite measure whose support is contained in* $[0,1]$. *For a measure* P', *we define* $r_{P'}(x) := \int K_1(x, x') \mathrm{d}P'(x')$. *According to Lemma 3.1 of Ghosal and van der Vaart (2001), for every* $0 < \epsilon_n < 1/2$ *there exits a discrete positive finite measure* P' *on* $[0,1]$ *such that*

$$\|r^* - r_{P'}\|_\infty \leq \epsilon_n, \qquad P'([0,1]) = P([0,1]).$$

Let us divide $[0,1]$ *into bins with width* ϵ_n. *Then the number of sample points* x^{nu}_i *that fall in a bin is a binomial random variable. If* $\exp(-\eta_2 n \epsilon_n/4)/\epsilon_n \to 0$, *then the Chernoff bound*[1] *implies that the probability of the event*

$$W_n := \{\max_{x \in \mathrm{supp}(P')} \min_i |x - x_i^{\mathrm{nu}}| \leq \epsilon_n\}$$

converges to 1, where $\mathrm{supp}(P')$ *denotes the support of* P'*. This holds because the density* $p^*_{\mathrm{nu}}(x)$ *is bounded from below across the support.*

It holds that

$$\begin{aligned}
&|K_1(x,x_1) - K_1(x,x_2)| \\
&= \exp(-(x-x_1)^2/2)[1 - \exp(x(x_2 - x_1) + (x_1^2 - x_2^2)/2)] \\
&\leq \exp(-(x-x_1)^2/2)|x(x_2 - x_1) + (x_1^2 - x_2^2)/2| \\
&\leq \exp(-(x-x_1)^2/2)(|x - x_1||x_1 - x_2| + |x_1 - x_2|^2/2) \\
&\leq |x_1 - x_2|/\sqrt{e} + |x_1 - x_2|^2/2.
\end{aligned}$$

Thus, there exists $\tilde{\alpha}_i \geq 0$ $(i = 1, \ldots, n)$ *such that, for* $\tilde{r}^*_n := \sum_{i=1}^n \tilde{\alpha}_i K_1(x, x_i^{\mathrm{nu}})$,

$$\|\tilde{r}^*_n - r_{P'}\|_\infty \leq P'([0,1])(\epsilon_n/\sqrt{e} + \epsilon_n^2/2) = \mathcal{O}(\epsilon_n)$$

is satisfied on the event W_n*. Now, defining* $r^*_n := \tilde{r}^*_n/(\widehat{P}^*_{\mathrm{de}}\tilde{r}^*_n)$*, we have* $r^*_n \in \widehat{\mathcal{R}}_n$*.*

Set $\epsilon_n = 1/\sqrt{n}$*. Noticing*

$$\begin{aligned}
|1 - \widehat{P}^*_{\mathrm{de}}\tilde{r}^*_n| &= |1 - \widehat{P}^*_{\mathrm{de}}(\tilde{r}^*_n - r_{P'} + r_{P'} - r^* + r^*)| \\
&\leq \mathcal{O}(\epsilon_n) + |1 - \widehat{P}^*_{\mathrm{de}}r^*| = \mathcal{O}_p(1/\sqrt{n}),
\end{aligned}$$

we have $\|r^*_n - \tilde{r}^*_n\|_\infty = \|r^*_n\|_\infty |1 - \widehat{P}^*_{\mathrm{de}}\tilde{r}^*_n| = \mathcal{O}_p(1/\sqrt{n})$*. From the above discussion, we obtain* $\|r^*_n - r^*\|_\infty = \mathcal{O}_p(1/\sqrt{n})$*, which indicates that* $h_{P^*_{\mathrm{de}}}(r^*_n, r^*) = \mathcal{O}_p(1/\sqrt{n})$ *and that* $r^*/r^*_n \leq c_0^2$ *is satisfied with high probability.*

For the bias term in Theorem 14.8, set $\epsilon_n = C\log(n)/n$ *for sufficiently large* $C > 0$ *and replace* r^* *with* $c_n r^*$*. Then we obtain* $\gamma_n = \mathcal{O}_p(\log(n)/n)$*.*

As for the complexity of the model, a similar argument to Theorem 3.1 in Ghosal and van der Vaart (2001) gives

$$\log N(\epsilon, \mathcal{R}^M, \|\cdot\|_\infty) \leq K\left(\log\frac{M}{\epsilon}\right)^2$$

for $0 < \epsilon < M/2$*. This gives both conditions* (14.6) *and* (14.7) *of the third assumption in Assumption 14.7 for arbitrary small* $\gamma > 0$ *(but the constant* K *depends on* γ*). Thus, the convergence rate is evaluated as* $h_{P^*_{\mathrm{de}}}(r^*, \widehat{r}_n) = \mathcal{O}_p(n^{-1/(2+\gamma)})$ *for arbitrary small* $\gamma > 0$*.*

[1] Here we refer to the Chernoff bound as follows: Let $\{X_i\}_{i=1}^n$ be independent random variables taking values on 0 or 1. Then, for any $\delta > 0$,

$$\Pr\left(\sum_{i=1}^n X_i < (1-\delta)\sum_{i=1}^n \mathbb{E}[X_i]\right) < \exp\left(-\delta^2 \sum_{i=1}^n \mathbb{E}[X_i]/2\right).$$

14.2.3 Convergence Analysis of KLIEP under Hellinger Distance Bracketing Number Conditions

Here we provide another convergence analysis for KLIEP under different assumptions. We make the following assumptions instead of Assumption 14.7.

Assumption 14.11

1. *There exists a constant* $\eta^* < \infty$ *such that the true density ratio* r^* *is upper-bounded as* $r^*(\boldsymbol{x}) \leq \eta^*$ *for all* $\boldsymbol{x}$ *on the support of* p^*_{nu}.
2. *All basis functions are non-negative, and there exist constants* $\epsilon^*, \xi^* > 0$ *such that* $\forall \varphi \in \Phi$,

$$\int p^*_{\mathrm{de}}(\boldsymbol{x})\varphi(\boldsymbol{x})\mathrm{d}\boldsymbol{x} \geq \epsilon^*, \text{ and } \|\varphi\|_\infty \leq \xi^*.$$

3. *There exist constants* $0 < \gamma < 2$ *and* $K > 0$ *such that*

$$\log N_{[]}(\epsilon, \mathcal{R}^M, h_{P^*_{\mathrm{de}}}) \leq K \left(\frac{\sqrt{M}}{\epsilon}\right)^\gamma. \tag{14.8}$$

Note that only an upper bound on r^* is required in Assumption 14.11, whereas r^* was assumed to be bounded from both below and above in Assumption 14.7. Thus, Assumption 14.11 is weaker than Assumption 14.7 in terms of r^*.

Instead, the bracketing number condition (14.8) is with respect to the Hellinger distance $h_{P^*_{\mathrm{de}}}$, whereas the covering and bracketing number conditions in Eqs. (14.6) and (14.7) are with respect to the $L_2(p^*_{\mathrm{de}})$-norm. Typically, the bracketing condition with respect to the Hellinger distance is stronger and more difficult to check than that for the L_2-norm. The bracketing number for Gaussian mixture models with respect to the Hellinger distance is discussed in Ghosal and van der Vaart (2001).

Let r^*_n be the optimal function in $\widehat{\mathcal{R}}_n$:

$$r^*_n := \underset{r \in \widehat{\mathcal{R}}_n}{\mathrm{argmax}} \int p^*_{\mathrm{de}}(\boldsymbol{x}) \log r(\boldsymbol{x}) \mathrm{d}\boldsymbol{x}.$$

Then the following theorem and corollary establish the convergence rate of $\widehat{r}_n$.

Theorem 14.12 *If there exist constants* c_0 *and* c_1 *such that* r^*_n *satisfies*

$$\Pr\left(c_0 \leq \frac{r^*(\boldsymbol{x})}{r^*_n(\boldsymbol{x})} \leq c_1, \forall \boldsymbol{x}\right) \to 1 \quad as \quad n \to \infty,$$

then $h_{P^*_{\mathrm{de}}}(\widehat{r}_n, r^*) = \mathcal{O}_p(n^{-\frac{1}{2+\gamma}} + h_{P^*_{\mathrm{de}}}(r^*_n, r^*))$.

Corollary 14.13 *If there exists* N *such that* $\forall n \geq N$, $r^* \in \mathcal{R}_n$, *then* $h_{P^*_{\mathrm{de}}}(\widehat{r}_n, r^*) = \mathcal{O}_p(n^{-\frac{1}{2+\gamma}})$.

The main mathematical device used in Section 14.2.2 was to bound $h_{P^*_{\mathrm{de}}}(\widehat{r}_n, r^*_n)$ from above by the difference between the empirical mean and the expectation of

$\log(2r_n^*/(\widehat{r}_n + r_n^*))$. On the other hand, in the proof of the above results, $2\widehat{r}_n/(\widehat{r}_n + r_n^*)$ was used instead of $\log(2r_n^*/(\widehat{r}_n + r_n^*))$, which enabled us to replace the lower bound of r^* with the bounds of the ratio r^*/r_n^*. Then the convexity of $\widehat{\mathcal{R}}_n$ and the bracketing number condition with respect to the Hellinger distance were utilized to establish the above proof (see Section 7 of van de Geer, 2000). The complete proof can be found in Suzuki et al. (2011).

14.3 Convergence Analysis of KuLSIF

In this section, following Kanamori et al. (2011b), we study the non-parametric convergence properties of uLSIF (see Chapter 6).

We first give some mathematical notations in Section 14.3.1. Then we elucidate the non-parametric convergence rate of uLSIF under two different situations in Sections 14.2.2 and 14.2.3, respectively.

14.3.1 Preliminaries

For simplicity, we assume that the numbers of numerator and denominator samples are the same, that is, $n = n_{\mathrm{nu}} = n_{\mathrm{de}}$. We note that this assumption is just for notational simplicity; in the absence of this assumption, the convergence rate is determined solely by the sample size with a slower rate.

Given a probability distribution P and a random variable $h(X)$, we denote the expectation of $h(X)$ under P by $\int h\mathrm{d}P$ or $\int h(\boldsymbol{x})P(\mathrm{d}\boldsymbol{x})$. Let $\|\cdot\|_\infty$ be the infinity norm, and let $\|\cdot\|_P$ be the L_2-norm under the probability P, that is, $\|h\|_P^2 = \int |h|^2 \mathrm{d}P$. For a *reproducing kernel Hilbert space* (RKHS) $\mathcal{R}$ (Schölkopf and Smola, 2002), the inner product and the norm on $\mathcal{R}$ are denoted as $\langle\cdot,\cdot\rangle_{\mathcal{R}}$ and $\|\cdot\|_{\mathcal{R}}$, respectively.

Let $\mathcal{R}$ be an RKHS endowed with the kernel $K(\boldsymbol{x},\boldsymbol{x}')$, and let the estimated density ratio $\widehat{r}_n$ be defined as the minimizer of the following minimization problem:

$$\widehat{g} := \underset{r\in\mathcal{R}}{\operatorname{argmin}} \left[\frac{1}{2n}\sum_{j=1}^{n} r(\boldsymbol{x}_j^{\mathrm{de}})^2 - \frac{1}{n}\sum_{i=1}^{n} r(\boldsymbol{x}_i^{\mathrm{nu}}) + \frac{\lambda}{2}\|r\|_{\mathcal{R}}^2 \right]. \tag{14.9}$$

In practice, the truncated estimator $\widehat{g}_+ = \max\{\widehat{g}, 0\}$ may be preferable. The estimation procedure of $\widehat{g}$ or $\widehat{g}_+$ based on Eq. (14.9) is called uLSIF (Chapter 6).

The non-negativity condition $r \geq 0$ may be added to the problem (14.9), although the computation will become hard (see Section 6.2.1). When the sample size is large, the estimator $\widehat{g}$ obtained by Eq. (14.9) will automatically be a non-negative function. Thus, the estimators $\widehat{g}$ and $\widehat{g}_+$ are asymptotically equivalent to the one obtained by imposing the non-negative constraint on the problem (14.9). For a small sample size, however, the estimator $\widehat{g}$ can take a negative value, and the rounding-up post-processing in $\widehat{g}$ may yield some statistical bias. In non-parametric density estimation, non-negative estimators cannot be unbiased

(Rosenblatt, 1956), and the same fact may hold in non-parametric density-ratio estimation.

14.3.2 Convergence Analysis of uLSIF under Bracketing Number Conditions

Here we elucidate the convergence rate of the uLSIF estimators $\widehat{g}$ and $\widehat{g}_+$ based on bracketing numbers.

Theorem 14.14 (Convergence rate of uLSIF) *Assume that the domain $\mathcal{X}$ is compact. Let $\mathcal{R}$ be an RKHS with a Gaussian kernel. Suppose that $p^*_{\mathrm{nu}}/p^*_{\mathrm{de}} = r^* \in \mathcal{R}$ and $\|r^*\|_{\mathcal{R}} < \infty$. Set the regularization parameter $\lambda = \lambda_n$ so that*

$$\lim_{n\to\infty} \lambda_n = 0 \quad \textit{and} \quad \lambda_n^{-1} = O(n^{1-\delta}) \quad (n \to \infty),$$

where δ is an arbitrary number satisfying $0 < \delta < 1$. Then the estimators $\widehat{r}_n$ and $\widehat{g}_+$ satisfy

$$\|\widehat{g}_+ - r^*\|_{P^*_{\mathrm{nu}}} \le \|\widehat{g} - r^*\|_{P^*_{\mathrm{nu}}} = O_p(\lambda_n^{1/2}),$$

where $\|\cdot\|_{P^*_{\mathrm{nu}}}$ is the L_2-norm under the probability P^*_{nu}.

By choosing small $\delta > 0$, this convergence rate will get close to the convergence rate for parametric models, $O(1/\sqrt{n})$.

Remark. *Although Theorem 14.14 focuses on the Gaussian kernel, extending it to other kernels is straightforward. Let $\mathcal{X}$ be a probability space, and let K be a kernel function over $\mathcal{X} \times \mathcal{X}$ such that $\sup_{\boldsymbol{x}\in\mathcal{X}} K(\boldsymbol{x},\boldsymbol{x}) < \infty$. We assume that the bracketing entropy $\log N_{[]}(\delta, \mathcal{H}_M, P^*_{\mathrm{nu}})$ is bounded above by $O(M/\delta)^\gamma$, where $0 < \gamma < 2$. Then we obtain*

$$\|\widehat{g}_+ - r^*\|_{P^*_{\mathrm{nu}}} \le \|\widehat{g} - r^*\|_{P^*_{\mathrm{nu}}} = O_p(\lambda_n^{1/2}),$$

where $\lambda_n^{1/2} = O(n^{1-\delta})$ with $1 - 2/(2+\gamma) < \delta < 1$.

14.3.3 Convergence Analysis of uLSIF under Kernel Spectrum Conditions

In Section 14.3.2, the convergence rate of uLSIF was shown based on bracketing numbers. Here, we explore an alternative way to reveal the convergence rate of uLSIF based on the *spectrum* of the kernel function. The proofs of the theorems in this subsection can be found in Sugiyama et al. (2011c).

Using the condition of the kernel spectrum, a much simpler proof is possible for deriving the convergence rate. In fact, instead of the uniform bounds (Lemmas 14.5 and 14.6), the proof based on the kernel spectrum only requires Bernstein's inequality on Hilbert spaces. This is because, with the spectrum condition, we can fully make use of the analytic solution of uLSIF. A similar idea was applied to *kernel ridge regression* in Caponnetto and de Vito (2007).

By *Mercer's theorem* (Mercer, 1909), the kernel $K(\boldsymbol{x},\boldsymbol{x}')$ has the following spectrum decomposition with respect to p^*_{de}:

$$K(\boldsymbol{x},\boldsymbol{x}') = \sum_{k=1}^{\infty} e_k(\boldsymbol{x})\mu_k e_k(\boldsymbol{x}'),$$

where $\{e_k\}_{k=1}^{\infty}$ is an orthogonal system in $L_2(p^*_{\mathrm{de}})$; that is, $\mathbb{E}_{p^*_{\mathrm{de}}}[e_k^2] = 1$ and $\mathbb{E}_{p^*_{\mathrm{de}}}[e_k e_{k'}] = 0$ for all $k \neq k'$.

We assume the following conditions.

Assumption 14.15

1. $\sup_{\boldsymbol{x}\in\mathbb{R}^d} K(\boldsymbol{x},\boldsymbol{x}) \leq 1$.
2. *The true density ratio* $p^*_{\mathrm{nu}}/p^*_{\mathrm{de}}$ *is contained in* $\mathcal{R}$, *that is,* $p^*_{\mathrm{nu}}/p^*_{\mathrm{de}} = r^* \in \mathcal{R}$.
3. *There exists a constant* $0 < \gamma < 1$ *such that the spectrum* μ_k *of the kernel decays as* $\mu_k \leq ck^{-\frac{2}{\gamma}}$ *for some positive constant c.*

The first condition is used to ensure that

$$|f(\boldsymbol{x})| \leq |\langle f, K(\cdot,\boldsymbol{x})\rangle_{\mathcal{R}}| \leq \|f\|_{\mathcal{R}}\sqrt{\langle K(\boldsymbol{x},\cdot), K(\cdot,\boldsymbol{x})\rangle_{\mathcal{R}}} \leq \|f\|_{\mathcal{R}}$$

for all $f \in \mathcal{R}$. The third condition is important for controlling the complexity of the model $\mathcal{R}$. The main message of this condition is that the constant γ represents the "complexity" of the model $\mathcal{R}$. It is easy to see that the spectrum decays rapidly if γ is small. Then the situation gets close to a finite-dimensional case, and thus the model becomes simple. In fact, if the kernel is linear, that is, $K(\boldsymbol{x},\boldsymbol{x}') = \boldsymbol{x}^\top\boldsymbol{x}'$, then $\mu_k = 0$ for all $k > d$ (this corresponds to the situation where γ is arbitrarily small). We note that there is a clear relation between the spectrum condition and the covering number condition (Steinwart et al., 2009); that is, $\mu_k \sim ck^{-\frac{2}{\gamma}}$ if and only if $N(\epsilon, \mathcal{B}_{\mathcal{R}}, L_2(p^*_{\mathrm{de}})) \sim \epsilon^{-\gamma}$, where $\mathcal{B}_{\mathcal{R}}$ is the unit ball in $\mathcal{R}$. However, dealing directly with the spectrum condition gives a tighter bound because the spectrum condition allows us to avoid using the uniform bounds.

Then we have the following theorem.

Theorem 14.16 *Under Assumption 14.15, if we set* $\lambda_n = \left(\frac{\log n}{n}\right)^{2/(2+\gamma)}$, *then we have*

$$\|\widehat{r}_n - r^*\|_{L_2(p^*_{\mathrm{de}})} = \mathcal{O}_p\left(\left(\frac{\log n}{n}\right)^{\frac{1}{2+\gamma}}\right),$$

where γ $(0 < \gamma < 1)$ *is a constant in the third condition of Assumption 14.15.*

The above convergence rate agrees with the *mini-max optimal rate* up to the $\log(n)$ factor. It is easy to see that, if γ is small (i.e., the model $\mathcal{R}$ is simple), the convergence rate becomes faster.

Finally, we investigate the convergence rate of an uLSIF-based Pearson divergence estimator (see Section 10.2.3),

$$\widehat{\mathrm{PE}} := \frac{1}{2n}\sum_{i=1}^{n}\widehat{r}_n(\boldsymbol{x}_i^{\mathrm{nu}}) - \frac{1}{n}\sum_{j=1}^{n}\widehat{r}_n(\boldsymbol{x}_j^{\mathrm{de}}) + \frac{1}{2},$$

to the true Pearson divergence:

$$\begin{aligned}\mathrm{PE} &:= \frac{1}{2}\int\left(\frac{p_{\mathrm{nu}}^*(\boldsymbol{x})}{p_{\mathrm{de}}^*(\boldsymbol{x})} - 1\right)^2 p_{\mathrm{de}}^*(\boldsymbol{x})\mathrm{d}\boldsymbol{x}\\ &= \frac{1}{2}\int r^*(\boldsymbol{x})p_{\mathrm{nu}}^*(\boldsymbol{x})\mathrm{d}\boldsymbol{x} - \int r^*(\boldsymbol{x})p_{\mathrm{de}}^*(\boldsymbol{x})\mathrm{d}\boldsymbol{x} + \frac{1}{2},\end{aligned}$$

where $r^*(\boldsymbol{x})$ is the density-ratio function defined by $r^*(x) = \frac{p_{\mathrm{nu}}^*(x)}{p_{\mathrm{de}}^*(x)}$.

Theorem 14.17 *Assume that the constant function 1 is contained in $\mathcal{R}$, that is, $1 \in \mathcal{R}$. Then, under Assumption 14.15, if we set $\lambda_n = (\log n/n)^{2/(2+\gamma)}$, we have*

$$|\widehat{\mathrm{PE}} - \mathrm{PE}| = \mathcal{O}_p\left((\log n/n)^{\frac{2}{2+\gamma}} + C(\log n/n)^{\frac{1}{2+\gamma}}\right), \tag{14.10}$$

where γ $(0 < \gamma < 1)$ is a constant determined by the third condition of Assumption 14.15, and $C := \sqrt{\int (r^*(\boldsymbol{x}) - 1)^2\, p_{\mathrm{de}}^*(\boldsymbol{x})\mathrm{d}\boldsymbol{x}}$.

The assumption that the constant function 1 is contained in $\mathcal{R}$ is not essential and just for simplicity. Indeed, even if this assumption is not satisfied, the same result holds by considering a model $r(\boldsymbol{x}) + b$ where $r \in \mathcal{R}$ and $b \in \mathbb{R}$.

Theorem 14.17 means that the convergence rate of $\widehat{\mathrm{PE}}$ to PE is $(\log n/n)^{\frac{1}{2+\gamma}}$ in general. However, when the two distributions P_{nu}^* and P_{de}^* are the same, $r^*(\boldsymbol{x}) = 1$ and thus $C = 0$. Then, the $\mathcal{O}_p\left((\log n/n)^{\frac{1}{2+\gamma}}\right)$ term in Eq. (14.10) disappears, and therefore the uLSIF-based Pearson divergence estimator possesses an even faster convergence rate $\mathcal{O}_p\left((\log n/n)^{\frac{2}{2+\gamma}}\right)$. This property is brought about by the introduction of the constant function in the model. See Chapter 15 for a similar property in the parametric setting.

14.4 Remarks

In this chapter we investigated the non-parametric convergence rate of KLIEP and uLSIF. In the case of a parametric estimation, the convergence rate was shown to be $n^{-1/2}$ (see Chapter 13). On the other hand, the convergence rate in a non-parametric estimation was shown to be slightly slower than $n^{-1/2}$ (depending on the complexity of the function space used for estimation). Thus, parametric estimations achieve faster convergence rates than non-parametric estimations. However, non-parametric methods can handle infinite-dimensional models, which would be more flexible and powerful than the parametric approach.

The parametric analysis in Chapter 13 provided an explicit expression of the coefficients of leading terms. On the other hand, the non-parametric analysis is far more complex than the parametric analysis, and even state-of-the-art mathematical tools are not precise enough to reveal the coefficients of leading terms explicitly in the non-parametric setup.

15

Parametric Two-Sample Test

The goal of a two-sample test is to, given two sets of samples, test whether the probability distributions behind the samples are equivalent. In Section 10.2 we described a practical two-sample method based on non-parametric density-ratio estimation. In this chapter we study two-sample tests for parametric density-ratio models.

After an introduction in Section 15.1, basic materials for parametric density-ratio estimation and divergence estimation are summarized in Sections 15.2 and 15.3, respectively. Then we derive the optimal divergence estimator in the sense of the asymptotic variance in Section 15.4 and give a two-sample test statistic based on the optimal divergence estimator in Section 15.5. Finally, numerical examples are shown in Section 15.6, and the chapter is concluded in Section 15.7.

15.1 Introduction

We study a two-sample homogeneity test under semi-parametric density-ratio models, where an estimator of density ratios is exploited to obtain a test statistic. For two probability densities $p^*_{\mathrm{nu}}(\boldsymbol{x})$ and $p^*_{\mathrm{de}}(\boldsymbol{x})$ over a probability space $\mathcal{X}$, the density ratio $r^*(\boldsymbol{x})$ is defined as the ratio of these densities, that is,

$$r^*(\boldsymbol{x}) := \frac{p^*_{\mathrm{nu}}(\boldsymbol{x})}{p^*_{\mathrm{de}}(\boldsymbol{x})}.$$

Qin (1998) studied the inference problem of density ratios under retrospective sampling plans and proved that in the sense of Godambe (1960), the estimating function obtained from the prospective likelihood is optimal in a class of unbiased estimating functions for semi-parametric density-ratio models. In a similar fashion, a semi-parametric density-ratio estimators based on logistic regression were studied in Cheng and Chu (2004).

Density-ratio estimation is closely related to the estimation of divergences. A divergence is a discrepancy measure between pairs of multivariate probability densities, and the *Ali–Silvey–Csiszár* (ASC) divergence (a.k.a. the f*-divergence*;

see Ali and Silvey, 1966; Csiszár, 1967) is a class of divergences based on the ratio of two probability densities. For a strictly convex function f such that $f(1) = 0$, the ASC divergence from $p^*_{\mathrm{nu}}(\boldsymbol{x})$ to $p^*_{\mathrm{de}}(\boldsymbol{x})$ is defined as

$$\mathrm{ASC}_f(p^*_{\mathrm{nu}} \| p^*_{\mathrm{de}}) := \int p^*_{\mathrm{de}}(\boldsymbol{x}) f\left(\frac{p^*_{\mathrm{nu}}(\boldsymbol{x})}{p^*_{\mathrm{de}}(\boldsymbol{x})}\right) \mathrm{d}\boldsymbol{x}. \tag{15.1}$$

Because f is strictly convex, the ASC divergence is non-negative and takes zero if and only if $p^*_{\mathrm{nu}} = p^*_{\mathrm{de}}$. Popular divergences such as the Kullback–Leibler (KL) divergence (Kullback and Leibler, 1951), the Hellinger distance, and the Pearson divergence (Pearson, 1900) are included in the class of ASC divergences. In statistics, machine learning, and information theory, the ASC divergence is often employed as a metric between probability distributions, even though the divergence does not necessarily satisfy the definition of the metric such as symmetry.

A typical approach to divergence estimation uses non-parametric density estimators (Qing et al., 2006). Another approach exploits a conjugate expression of the function f in the context of one-sample problems (Broniatowski and Keziou, 2009; Keziou, 2003a) and two-sample problems (Keziou and Leoni-Aubin, 2005). Furthermore, a kernel-based estimator of the ASC divergence with a non-parametric density-ratio model was developed (Nguyen et al., 2010).

Once a divergence between two probability densities is estimated, the homogeneity test can be conducted. In a two-sample homogeneity test, the null hypothesis is represented as

$$H_0 : p^*_{\mathrm{nu}} = p^*_{\mathrm{de}},$$

and its complementary alternative is given by

$$H_1 : p^*_{\mathrm{nu}} \neq p^*_{\mathrm{de}}.$$

If an estimate of $\mathrm{ASC}_f(p^*_{\mathrm{nu}} \| p^*_{\mathrm{de}})$ is beyond some threshold, the null hypothesis is rejected and the alternative hypothesis is accepted. Keziou (2003b) and Keziou and Leoni-Aubin (2005) studied the homogeneity test using an ASC divergence estimator with semi-parametric density-ratio models. On the other hand, Fokianos et al. (2001) proposed a more direct, *Wald-type score test* derived from the empirical likelihood estimator of density ratios. In this chapter we discuss the optimality of ASC divergence estimators and investigate the relation between the test statistic based on an ASC divergence estimator and the Wald-type score test derived from an empirical likelihood estimator.

15.2 Estimation of Density Ratios

In this section we introduce the method of estimating density ratios proposed in Qin (1998) and investigate its theoretical properties.

15.2.1 Formulation

Suppose that two sets of samples are independently generated from each probability:

$$\boldsymbol{x}_1^{\mathrm{nu}}, \ldots, \boldsymbol{x}_{n_{\mathrm{nu}}}^{\mathrm{nu}} \overset{\text{i.i.d.}}{\sim} p_{\mathrm{nu}}^* \quad \text{and} \quad \boldsymbol{x}_1^{\mathrm{de}}, \ldots, \boldsymbol{x}_{n_{\mathrm{de}}}^{\mathrm{de}} \overset{\text{i.i.d.}}{\sim} p_{\mathrm{de}}^*.$$

Let us denote a model for the density ratio by $r(\boldsymbol{x};\boldsymbol{\theta})$, where $\boldsymbol{\theta} \in \boldsymbol{\Theta} \subset \mathbb{R}^d$ is the parameter. We assume that the model is correctly specified; that is, there exists $\boldsymbol{\theta}^* \in \boldsymbol{\Theta}$ such that the true density ratio is represented as

$$r^*(\boldsymbol{x}) = \frac{p_{\mathrm{nu}}^*(\boldsymbol{x})}{p_{\mathrm{de}}^*(\boldsymbol{x})} = r(\boldsymbol{x};\boldsymbol{\theta}^*).$$

The model for the density ratio $r^*(\boldsymbol{x})$ is regarded as a semi-parametric model for probability densities. That is, even if $r(\boldsymbol{x};\boldsymbol{\theta}^*) = p_{\mathrm{nu}}^*(\boldsymbol{x})/p_{\mathrm{de}}^*(\boldsymbol{x})$ is specified, there are still infinite degrees of freedom for the probability densities p_{nu}^* and p_{de}^*.

15.2.2 Moment-Matching Estimator

Qin (1998) proposed a moment-matching method for density-ratio estimation. Let $\boldsymbol{\phi}(\boldsymbol{x};\boldsymbol{\theta}) \in \mathbb{R}^d$ be a vector-valued function from $\mathcal{X} \times \boldsymbol{\Theta}$ to $\mathbb{R}^d$, and let the *estimating function* $\boldsymbol{Q}_{\boldsymbol{\phi}}$ be defined as

$$\boldsymbol{Q}_{\boldsymbol{\phi}}(\boldsymbol{\theta}) := \frac{1}{n_{\mathrm{de}}} \sum_{j=1}^{n_{\mathrm{de}}} r(\boldsymbol{x}_j^{\mathrm{de}};\boldsymbol{\theta})\boldsymbol{\phi}(\boldsymbol{x}_j^{\mathrm{de}};\boldsymbol{\theta}) - \frac{1}{n_{\mathrm{nu}}} \sum_{i=1}^{n_{\mathrm{nu}}} \boldsymbol{\phi}(\boldsymbol{x}_i^{\mathrm{nu}};\boldsymbol{\theta}).$$

Because $p_{\mathrm{nu}}^*(\boldsymbol{x}) = r(\boldsymbol{x};\boldsymbol{\theta}^*)p_{\mathrm{de}}^*(\boldsymbol{x})$, the expectation of $\boldsymbol{Q}_{\boldsymbol{\phi}}(\boldsymbol{\theta})$ over observed samples vanishes at $\boldsymbol{\theta} = \boldsymbol{\theta}^*$. In addition, the estimation function $\boldsymbol{Q}_{\boldsymbol{\phi}}(\boldsymbol{\theta})$ converges to its expectation in the large sample limit. Thus, the estimator $\widehat{\boldsymbol{\theta}}$ defined as a solution of the estimating equation,

$$\boldsymbol{Q}_{\boldsymbol{\phi}}(\widehat{\boldsymbol{\theta}}) = \boldsymbol{0},$$

has the statistical consistency under some mild assumption. See Qin (1998) for details. In the following we give a sufficient condition for the consistency and the asymptotic normality of $\widehat{\boldsymbol{\theta}}$.

The previously mentioned moment-matching framework includes various density-ratio estimators (Keziou, 2003b; Keziou and Leoni-Aubin, 2005, 2008; Nguyen et al., 2010; Sugiyama et al., 2008; Kanamori et al., 2009); that is, these estimators with a finite-dimensional model $r(\boldsymbol{x};\boldsymbol{\theta})$ can all be represented as a moment-matching estimator. However, these methods were originally intended to be used with non-parametric kernel models. On the other hand, kernel density estimators can also be exploited as another approach to density-ratio estimation (Ćwik and Mielniczuk, 1989; Jacoba and Oliveirab, 1997; Bensaid and Fabre, 2007).

15.2.3 Asymptotic Properties

Before presenting the asymptotic results we prepare some notations. Let $\mathrm{E}_{\mathrm{nu}}[\cdot]$ and $\mathrm{V}_{\mathrm{nu}}[\cdot]$ be the expectation and the variance (or the variance-covariance matrix for multi-dimensional random variables) under the probability p^*_{nu}, respectively. We define $\mathrm{E}_{\mathrm{de}}[\cdot]$ and $\mathrm{V}_{\mathrm{de}}[\cdot]$ in the same way for the probability p^*_{de}. The expectation and the variance by the joint probability of all samples, $\boldsymbol{x}_i^{\mathrm{nu}}$ $(i=1,\dots,n_{\mathrm{nu}})$ and $\boldsymbol{x}_j^{\mathrm{de}}$ $(j=1,\dots,n_{\mathrm{de}})$, are denoted by $\mathbb{E}[\cdot]$ and $\mathbb{V}[\cdot]$, respectively. The covariance matrix between two random variables with respect to the joint probability of all samples is denoted as $\mathrm{Cov}[\cdot,\cdot]$. For a sequence of random variables X_n, we denote the convergence in distribution to X by $X_n \xrightarrow{\mathrm{d}} X$ and the convergence in probability to X by $X_n \xrightarrow{\mathrm{p}} X$. We also use the probabilistic orders $O_p(\cdot)$ and $o_p(\cdot)$. See van der Vaart and Wellner (1996) for their precise definitions. For a vector-valued function

$$\boldsymbol{\phi}(\boldsymbol{x};\boldsymbol{\theta}) = (\phi_1(\boldsymbol{x};\boldsymbol{\theta}),\dots,\phi_d(\boldsymbol{x};\boldsymbol{\theta}))^\top,$$

let $\mathcal{L}[\boldsymbol{\phi}(\boldsymbol{x};\boldsymbol{\theta})]$ be the linear space

$$\mathcal{L}[\boldsymbol{\phi}(\boldsymbol{x};\boldsymbol{\theta})] = \left\{ \sum_{k=1}^{d} a_k\, \phi_k(\boldsymbol{x};\boldsymbol{\theta}) \;\middle|\; a_1,\dots,a_d \in \mathbb{R} \right\}.$$

Let ρ and m be

$$\rho = \frac{n_{\mathrm{nu}}}{n_{\mathrm{de}}} \quad \text{and} \quad m = \frac{1}{1/n_{\mathrm{nu}} + 1/n_{\mathrm{de}}} = \frac{n_{\mathrm{nu}} n_{\mathrm{de}}}{n_{\mathrm{nu}} + n_{\mathrm{de}}},$$

and let $\boldsymbol{U}_{\boldsymbol{\phi}}$ be the d-by-d matrix defined by

$$\boldsymbol{U}_{\boldsymbol{\phi}}(\boldsymbol{\theta}) = \mathrm{E}_{\mathrm{nu}}[\boldsymbol{\phi}(\boldsymbol{x};\boldsymbol{\theta}) \nabla \log r(\boldsymbol{x};\boldsymbol{\theta})^\top],$$

where $\boldsymbol{\phi}(\boldsymbol{x};\boldsymbol{\theta})$ is a d-dimensional vector-valued function. Suppose that $\boldsymbol{U}_{\boldsymbol{\phi}}(\boldsymbol{\theta})$ is non-degenerate in the vicinity of $\boldsymbol{\theta} = \boldsymbol{\theta}^*$. In the following, the notation ρ is also used as the large sample limit of $n_{\mathrm{nu}}/n_{\mathrm{de}}$, and we assume that $0 < \rho < \infty$ holds even in the limit.

According to Section 5 of van der Vaart (1998), the following assumptions are required for establishing the consistency of density-ratio estimation based on moment matching[1]:

Assumption 15.1 (Consistency of $\widehat{\boldsymbol{\theta}}$)

1. *The estimator $\widehat{\boldsymbol{\theta}} \in \boldsymbol{\theta}$ such that $\boldsymbol{Q}_{\boldsymbol{\phi}}(\widehat{\boldsymbol{\theta}}) = 0$ exists.*
2. *$\boldsymbol{\phi}(x;\boldsymbol{\theta})$ and $r(x;\boldsymbol{\theta})$ satisfy*

$$\sup_{\boldsymbol{\theta}\in\Theta} \left\| \frac{1}{n_{\mathrm{nu}}} \sum_{i=1}^{n_{\mathrm{nu}}} \boldsymbol{\phi}(\boldsymbol{x}_i^{\mathrm{nu}};\boldsymbol{\theta}) - \mathrm{E}_{\mathrm{nu}}[\boldsymbol{\phi}(\boldsymbol{x};\boldsymbol{\theta})] \right\| \xrightarrow{\mathrm{p}} 0,$$

[1] Similar assumptions for one-sample problems have been studied in Broniatowski and Keziou (2009).

$$\sup_{\theta\in\Theta}\left\|\frac{1}{n_{\mathrm{de}}}\sum_{j=1}^{n_{\mathrm{de}}}\boldsymbol{\phi}(\boldsymbol{x}_j^{\mathrm{de}};\boldsymbol{\theta})r(\boldsymbol{x}_j^{\mathrm{de}};\boldsymbol{\theta})-\mathrm{E}_{\mathrm{de}}[\boldsymbol{\phi}(\boldsymbol{x};\boldsymbol{\theta})r(\boldsymbol{x};\boldsymbol{\theta})]\right\|\stackrel{\mathrm{p}}{\longrightarrow}0.$$

3. *For any* $\varepsilon > 0$,

$$\inf_{\boldsymbol{\theta}:\|\boldsymbol{\theta}-\boldsymbol{\theta}^*\|\geq\varepsilon}\left\|\mathrm{E}_{\mathrm{nu}}[\boldsymbol{\phi}(\boldsymbol{x};\boldsymbol{\theta})]-\mathrm{E}_{\mathrm{de}}[\boldsymbol{\phi}(\boldsymbol{x};\boldsymbol{\theta})r(\boldsymbol{x};\boldsymbol{\theta})]\right\|>0$$

holds.

Note that item 15.1 in Assumption 15.1 and the triangle inequality lead to the *uniform convergence* of $\boldsymbol{Q}_\phi$:

$$\sup_{\boldsymbol{\theta}\in\Theta}\Big|\|\boldsymbol{Q}_\phi(\boldsymbol{\theta})\|-\|\mathbb{E}[\boldsymbol{Q}_\phi(\boldsymbol{\theta})]\|\Big|\stackrel{\mathrm{p}}{\longrightarrow}0.$$

Similarly, the following assumptions are required for establishing the asymptotic normality of density-ratio estimation based on moment matching (see Section 5 of van der Vaart, 1998, for details):

Assumption 15.2 (Asymptotic normality of $\widehat{\boldsymbol{\theta}}$)

1. *The estimator of the density ratio,* $\widehat{\boldsymbol{\theta}}$, *exists and is consistent.*
2. *The expectations*

$$\mathrm{E}_{\mathrm{nu}}[\|\boldsymbol{\phi}(\boldsymbol{x};\boldsymbol{\theta}^*)\|^2],\quad \mathrm{E}_{\mathrm{nu}}[\|\nabla\boldsymbol{\phi}(\boldsymbol{x};\boldsymbol{\theta}^*)\|],$$
$$\mathrm{E}_{\mathrm{de}}[\|\boldsymbol{\phi}(\boldsymbol{x};\boldsymbol{\theta}^*)r(\boldsymbol{x};\boldsymbol{\theta}^*)\|^2],\quad \textit{and}\quad \mathrm{E}_{\mathrm{de}}[\|\nabla(\boldsymbol{\phi}(\boldsymbol{x};\boldsymbol{\theta}^*)r(\boldsymbol{x};\boldsymbol{\theta}^*))\|]$$

are finite. In the vicinity of $\boldsymbol{\theta}^*$, *each element of the second derivatives of* $\boldsymbol{\phi}(\boldsymbol{x};\boldsymbol{\theta})$ *and* $\boldsymbol{\phi}(\boldsymbol{x};\boldsymbol{\theta})r(\boldsymbol{x};\boldsymbol{\theta})$ *with respect to* $\boldsymbol{\theta}$ *is dominated by a* p^*_{nu}*-integrable function and a* p^*_{de}*-integrable function, respectively.*
3. *The matrix* $\boldsymbol{U}_\phi(\boldsymbol{\theta})$ *is non-singular in the vicinity of* $\boldsymbol{\theta}=\boldsymbol{\theta}^*$.

Under Assumption 15.2, the asymptotic expansion of the estimating equation $\boldsymbol{Q}_\phi(\widehat{\boldsymbol{\theta}})=\boldsymbol{0}$ around $\boldsymbol{\theta}=\boldsymbol{\theta}^*$ yields the following convergence in distribution:

$$\begin{aligned}\sqrt{m}(\widehat{\boldsymbol{\theta}}-\boldsymbol{\theta}^*)&=-\sqrt{m}\boldsymbol{U}_\phi^{-1}\boldsymbol{Q}_\phi+o_p(1)\\&\stackrel{\mathrm{d}}{\longrightarrow}N_d\left(\boldsymbol{0},\,\boldsymbol{U}_\phi^{-1}\frac{\rho\mathrm{V}_{\mathrm{de}}[r\boldsymbol{\phi}]+\mathrm{V}_{\mathrm{nu}}[\boldsymbol{\phi}]}{\rho+1}(\boldsymbol{U}_\phi^\top)^{-1}\right),\end{aligned}\tag{15.2}$$

where the functions are evaluated at $\boldsymbol{\theta}=\boldsymbol{\theta}^*$ and $N_d(\boldsymbol{\mu},\boldsymbol{\Sigma})$ denotes the d-dimensional normal distribution with mean $\boldsymbol{\mu}$ and covariance matrix $\boldsymbol{\Sigma}$. The asymptotic variance above is derived from the equalities

$$\mathbb{E}[\boldsymbol{Q}_\phi]=\boldsymbol{0}\quad\text{and}\quad m\cdot\mathbb{E}[\boldsymbol{Q}_\phi\boldsymbol{Q}_\phi^\top]=\frac{\rho\mathrm{V}_{\mathrm{de}}[r\boldsymbol{\phi}]+\mathrm{V}_{\mathrm{nu}}[\boldsymbol{\phi}]}{\rho+1}.$$

Qin (1998) showed that the prospective likelihood minimizes the asymptotic variance in the class of moment-matching estimators. More precisely, for the density-ratio model

$$r(\boldsymbol{x};\boldsymbol{\theta}) = \exp\{\alpha + \phi(\boldsymbol{x};\boldsymbol{\beta})\}, \quad \boldsymbol{\theta} = (\alpha, \boldsymbol{\beta}^\top)^\top \in \mathbb{R} \times \mathbb{R}^{d-1},$$

the vector-valued function $\boldsymbol{\phi}_{\mathrm{opt}}$ defined by

$$\boldsymbol{\phi}_{\mathrm{opt}}(\boldsymbol{x};\boldsymbol{\theta}) = \frac{1}{1+\rho r(\boldsymbol{x};\boldsymbol{\theta})} \nabla \log r(\boldsymbol{x};\boldsymbol{\theta}) \qquad (15.3)$$

minimizes the asymptotic variance (15.2).

15.3 Estimation of ASC Divergence

In this section we introduce estimators of the ASC divergence (15.1) based on density-ratio estimation.

15.3.1 Estimation Based on Conjugate Representation

For $r^*(\boldsymbol{x}) := p^*_{\mathrm{nu}}(\boldsymbol{x})/p^*_{\mathrm{de}}(\boldsymbol{x})$, the ASC divergence can be represented as the expectation of $f(r^*(\boldsymbol{x}))$ over $p^*_{\mathrm{de}}(\boldsymbol{x})$:

$$\mathrm{ASC}_f(p^*_{\mathrm{nu}} \| p^*_{\mathrm{de}}) = \int p^*_{\mathrm{de}}(\boldsymbol{x}) f\big(r^*(\boldsymbol{x})\big)\mathrm{d}\boldsymbol{x}.$$

A conjugate representation of the function f is useful in the ASC divergence estimation (Broniatowski and Keziou, 2009; Keziou, 2003a,b; Keziou and Leoni-Aubin, 2005, 2008; Nguyen et al., 2010). More specifically, for a convex function f, the conjugate function of f is defined as

$$f^*(w) := \sup_{r \in \mathbb{R}} \{rw - f(r)\}.$$

Under a mild assumption on f (Rockafellar, 1970), it holds that

$$f(r) = \sup_{w \in \mathbb{R}} \{rw - f^*(w)\} = rf'(r) - f^*(f'(r)). \qquad (15.4)$$

Substituting Eq. (15.4) into the ASC divergence, we have

$$\mathrm{ASC}_f(p^*_{\mathrm{nu}} \| p^*_{\mathrm{de}}) = \sup_{w} \left\{ \int p^*_{\mathrm{nu}}(\boldsymbol{x}) w(\boldsymbol{x}) \mathrm{d}\boldsymbol{x} - \int p^*_{\mathrm{de}}(\boldsymbol{x}) f^*(w(\boldsymbol{x}))\mathrm{d}\boldsymbol{x} \right\}, \qquad (15.5)$$

where the supremum is taken over all measurable functions and the supremum is attained at $w(\boldsymbol{x}) = f'(r^*(\boldsymbol{x}))$. Based on Eq. (15.5), one can consider the ASC divergence estimator $\widehat{\mathrm{ASC}}_f$ by replacing the expectations with their empirical averages:

$$\widehat{\mathrm{ASC}}_f := \sup_{\boldsymbol{\theta} \in \Theta} \left\{ \frac{1}{n_{\mathrm{nu}}} \sum_{i=1}^{n_{\mathrm{nu}}} f'(r(\boldsymbol{x}^{\mathrm{nu}}_i;\boldsymbol{\theta})) - \frac{1}{n_{\mathrm{de}}} \sum_{j=1}^{n_{\mathrm{de}}} f^*(f'(r(\boldsymbol{x}^{\mathrm{de}}_j;\boldsymbol{\theta}))) \right\}. \qquad (15.6)$$

The parameter attaining the supremum of $\widehat{\mathrm{ASC}}_f$ satisfies the extremal condition,

$$\frac{1}{n_{\mathrm{nu}}}\sum_{i=1}^{n_{\mathrm{nu}}}\nabla(f'(r(\boldsymbol{x}_i^{\mathrm{nu}};\boldsymbol{\theta}))) - \frac{1}{n_{\mathrm{de}}}\sum_{j=1}^{n_{\mathrm{de}}} r(\boldsymbol{x}_i^{\mathrm{de}};\boldsymbol{\theta})\nabla(f'(r(\boldsymbol{x}_j^{\mathrm{de}};\boldsymbol{\theta}))) = \mathbf{0},$$

where the identity $(f^*)'(f'(r)) = r$ is used. This is equivalent to the moment-matching estimator with

$$\boldsymbol{\phi}(\boldsymbol{x};\boldsymbol{\theta}) = \nabla(f'(r(\boldsymbol{x};\boldsymbol{\theta}))) = f''(r(\boldsymbol{x};\boldsymbol{\theta}))\nabla r(\boldsymbol{x};\boldsymbol{\theta}).$$

15.3.2 Extension to General Decomposition

Here we generalize the previously mentioned ASC divergence estimator.

In the ASC divergence estimator in the previous subsection, the density ratio was first estimated by the moment matching estimator with $\boldsymbol{\phi}(\boldsymbol{x};\boldsymbol{\theta}) = f''(r(\boldsymbol{x};\boldsymbol{\theta}))\nabla r(\boldsymbol{x};\boldsymbol{\theta})$. Then, the estimated density ratio $r(\boldsymbol{x};\widehat{\boldsymbol{\theta}})$ was substituted into the expression of the ASC divergence derived from the decomposition

$$f(r) = rf'(r) - f^*(f'(r)).$$

Here, we consider moment-matching estimators with $\boldsymbol{\phi}(\boldsymbol{x};\boldsymbol{\theta})$ for any decomposition of the function f such as

$$f(r) = r f_{\mathrm{nu}}(r) + f_{\mathrm{de}}(r).$$

Note that the decomposition (15.4) corresponds to

$$f_{\mathrm{nu}}(r) = f'(r) \quad \text{and} \quad f_{\mathrm{de}}(r) = -f^*(f'(r)).$$

Then, because of $r^*(\boldsymbol{x}) = p^*_{\mathrm{nu}}(\boldsymbol{x})/p^*_{\mathrm{de}}(\boldsymbol{x})$, the ASC divergence (15.1) is represented as

$$\mathrm{ASC}_f(p^*_{\mathrm{nu}} \| p^*_{\mathrm{de}}) = \int p^*_{\mathrm{nu}}(\boldsymbol{x}) f_{\mathrm{nu}}(r^*(\boldsymbol{x}))\mathrm{d}\boldsymbol{x} + \int p^*_{\mathrm{de}}(\boldsymbol{x}) f_{\mathrm{de}}(r^*(\boldsymbol{x}))\mathrm{d}\boldsymbol{x}.$$

Its empirical version provides the following estimate of the ASC divergence:

$$\widehat{\mathrm{ASC}}_f = \frac{1}{n_{\mathrm{de}}}\sum_{j=1}^{n_{\mathrm{de}}} f_{\mathrm{de}}(r(\boldsymbol{x}_j^{\mathrm{de}};\widehat{\boldsymbol{\theta}})) + \frac{1}{n_{\mathrm{nu}}}\sum_{i=1}^{n_{\mathrm{nu}}} f_{\mathrm{nu}}(r(\boldsymbol{x}_i^{\mathrm{nu}};\widehat{\boldsymbol{\theta}})), \tag{15.7}$$

where the parameter $\widehat{\boldsymbol{\theta}}$ is estimated based on the estimating function $\boldsymbol{Q}_{\boldsymbol{\phi}}$. In Section 15.4, we study the optimal choices of $\boldsymbol{\phi}$, f_{nu}, and f_{de}.

We may consider a wider class of ASC divergence estimators than the estimator of the form Eq. (15.7). For example, one may exploit non-parametric estimators of probability densities to estimate the ASC divergence. However, the estimator (15.7) has the advantage that its simple "plug-in" nature allows us to easily analyze its statistical properties. For this reason, we focus on the estimator (15.7) in the next section.

15.4 Optimal Estimator of ASC Divergence

In this section we derive the optimal estimator of the ASC divergence in the sense of the asymptotic variance (Godambe, 1960).

15.4.1 Preliminaries

For the model $r(\boldsymbol{x};\boldsymbol{\theta})$ and the function $f(r)$, we assume the following conditions.

Assumption 15.3

1. *The model* $r(\boldsymbol{x};\boldsymbol{\theta})$ *includes the constant function* 1.
2. *For any* $\boldsymbol{\theta} \in \boldsymbol{\Theta}$, $1 \in \mathcal{L}[\nabla \log r(\boldsymbol{x};\boldsymbol{\theta})]$ *holds.*
3. f *is third-order differentiable and strictly convex, and it satisfies* $f(1) = f'(1) = 0$.

Standard models of density ratios may satisfy items 1 and 2 of Assumption 15.3. Furthermore, we assume the following conditions to justify the asymptotic expansion of the estimator $\widehat{\mathrm{ASC}}_f$ defined in Eq. (15.7).

Assumption 15.4 (Asymptotic expansion of $\widehat{\mathrm{ASC}}_f$)

1. *For the estimator* $\widehat{\boldsymbol{\theta}}$, $\sqrt{m}(\widehat{\boldsymbol{\theta}} - \boldsymbol{\theta}^*)$ *converges in distribution to a centered multivariate normal distribution.*
2. *For the decomposition*

$$f(r) = f_{\mathrm{de}}(r) + r f_{\mathrm{nu}}(r),$$

suppose that

$$\mathrm{E}_{\mathrm{de}}[|f_{\mathrm{de}}(r(\boldsymbol{x};\boldsymbol{\theta}^*))|^2], \quad \mathrm{E}_{\mathrm{de}}[\|\nabla f_{\mathrm{de}}(r(\boldsymbol{x};\boldsymbol{\theta}^*))\|],$$
$$\mathrm{E}_{\mathrm{nu}}[|f_{\mathrm{nu}}(r(\boldsymbol{x};\boldsymbol{\theta}^*))|^2], \quad \textit{and} \quad \mathrm{E}_{\mathrm{nu}}[\|\nabla f_{\mathrm{nu}}(r(\boldsymbol{x};\boldsymbol{\theta}^*))\|]$$

are finite. In the vicinity of $\boldsymbol{\theta}^*$, *the second derivatives of* $f_{\mathrm{nu}}(r(\boldsymbol{x};\boldsymbol{\theta}))$ *and* $f_{\mathrm{de}}(r(\boldsymbol{x};\boldsymbol{\theta}))$ *with respect to* $\boldsymbol{\theta}$ *are dominated by a* p^*_{nu}*-integrable function and a* p^*_{de}*-integrable function, respectively.*
3. *The expectation*

$$\mathrm{E}_{\mathrm{nu}}[f'(r(\boldsymbol{x};\boldsymbol{\theta}^*) - f_{\mathrm{nu}}(r(\boldsymbol{x};\boldsymbol{\theta}^*))\nabla \log r(\boldsymbol{x};\boldsymbol{\theta}^*)]$$

exists.

Under Assumption 15.4, the *delta method* is available (see Section 3 of van der Vaart, 1998, for details).

15.4.2 Analysis of Asymptotic Variance

Here we compare the asymptotic variance of two estimators for the ASC divergence: One is the estimator $\widehat{\mathrm{ASC}}_f$ derived from the moment-matching estimator with $\boldsymbol{\phi}(\boldsymbol{x};\boldsymbol{\theta})$ and the decomposition $f(r) = f_{\mathrm{de}}(r) + r f_{\mathrm{nu}}(r)$, and the other is the estimator $\overline{\mathrm{ASC}}_f$ defined by the density-ratio estimator with $\overline{\boldsymbol{\phi}}(\boldsymbol{x};\boldsymbol{\theta})$ and the decomposition $f(r) = \overline{f_{\mathrm{de}}}(r) + r\overline{f_{\mathrm{nu}}}(r)$.

To compare the variances of these estimators, we consider the formula

$$\begin{aligned}
0 &\leq \mathbb{V}[\widehat{\mathrm{ASC}}_f - \overline{\mathrm{ASC}}_f] \\
&= \mathbb{V}[\widehat{\mathrm{ASC}}_f] - \mathbb{V}[\overline{\mathrm{ASC}}_f] - 2\,\mathrm{Cov}[\widehat{\mathrm{ASC}}_f - \overline{\mathrm{ASC}}_f, \overline{\mathrm{ASC}}_f].
\end{aligned}$$

Suppose that the third term vanishes for any $\widehat{\mathrm{ASC}}_f$. Then we have

$$\mathbb{V}[\overline{\mathrm{ASC}}_f] \leq \mathbb{V}[\widehat{\mathrm{ASC}}_f]$$

for any $\widehat{\mathrm{ASC}}_f$. This implies that the estimator $\overline{\mathrm{ASC}}_f$ is asymptotically optimal in terms of the variance.

In the following we compute the covariance $\mathrm{Cov}[\widehat{\mathrm{ASC}}_f - \overline{\mathrm{ASC}}_f, \overline{\mathrm{ASC}}_f]$. Let the vectors $\boldsymbol{c}(\boldsymbol{\theta}), \overline{\boldsymbol{c}}(\boldsymbol{\theta}) \in \mathbb{R}^d$ be

$$\begin{aligned}
\boldsymbol{c}(\boldsymbol{\theta}) &= \mathrm{E}_{\mathrm{nu}}[\{f'(r(\boldsymbol{x};\boldsymbol{\theta})) - f_{\mathrm{nu}}(r(\boldsymbol{x};\boldsymbol{\theta}))\}\nabla \log r(\boldsymbol{x};\boldsymbol{\theta})], \\
\overline{\boldsymbol{c}}(\boldsymbol{\theta}) &= \mathrm{E}_{\mathrm{nu}}[\{f'(r(\boldsymbol{x};\boldsymbol{\theta})) - \overline{f_{\mathrm{nu}}}(r(\boldsymbol{x};\boldsymbol{\theta}))\}\nabla \log r(\boldsymbol{x};\boldsymbol{\theta})].
\end{aligned}$$

Then, under Assumptions 15.3 and 15.4, the following equality holds:

$$\begin{aligned}
&m(1+\rho^{-1}) \cdot \mathrm{Cov}[\widehat{\mathrm{ASC}}_f - \overline{\mathrm{ASC}}_f, \overline{\mathrm{ASC}}_f] \\
&= \mathrm{E}_{\mathrm{nu}}\Big[\{\overline{f_{\mathrm{nu}}}(r^*) - f_{\mathrm{nu}}(r^*) + \overline{\boldsymbol{c}}^\top \boldsymbol{U}_{\overline{\boldsymbol{\phi}}}^{-1}\overline{\boldsymbol{\phi}} - \boldsymbol{c}^\top \boldsymbol{U}_{\boldsymbol{\phi}}^{-1}\boldsymbol{\phi}\} \\
&\qquad \times \{f(r^*) - (r^* + \rho^{-1})(\overline{f_{\mathrm{nu}}}(r^*) + \overline{\boldsymbol{c}}^\top \boldsymbol{U}_{\overline{\boldsymbol{\phi}}}^{-1}\overline{\boldsymbol{\phi}})\}\Big] + o(1),
\end{aligned} \tag{15.8}$$

where r^* denotes the true density ratio $r^*(x) = r(\boldsymbol{x};\boldsymbol{\theta}^*)$, and the functions in Eq. (15.8) are evaluated at $\boldsymbol{\theta} = \boldsymbol{\theta}^*$.

The next theorem shows a sufficient condition that the covariance $\mathrm{Cov}[\widehat{\mathrm{ASC}}_f - \overline{\mathrm{ASC}}_f, \overline{\mathrm{ASC}}_f]$ vanishes.

Theorem 15.5 *Suppose Assumptions 15.3 and 15.4 hold for the decomposition of f, and suppose that $\overline{\boldsymbol{\phi}}(\boldsymbol{x};\boldsymbol{\theta})$, $\overline{f_{\mathrm{nu}}}(r(\boldsymbol{x};\boldsymbol{\theta}))$, and $\overline{f_{\mathrm{de}}}(r(\boldsymbol{x};\boldsymbol{\theta}))$ satisfy*

$$\begin{aligned}
&f(r(\boldsymbol{x};\boldsymbol{\theta})) - (r(\boldsymbol{x};\boldsymbol{\theta}) + \rho^{-1})(\overline{f_{\mathrm{nu}}}(r(\boldsymbol{x};\boldsymbol{\theta})) + \overline{\boldsymbol{c}}^\top \boldsymbol{U}_{\overline{\boldsymbol{\phi}}}^{-1}\overline{\boldsymbol{\phi}}(\boldsymbol{x};\boldsymbol{\theta})) \\
&\in \mathcal{L}[\nabla \log r(\boldsymbol{x};\boldsymbol{\theta})]
\end{aligned} \tag{15.9}$$

for all $\boldsymbol{\theta} \in \boldsymbol{\Theta}$. Then the estimator $\overline{\mathrm{ASC}}_f$ with $\overline{\boldsymbol{\phi}}(\boldsymbol{x};\boldsymbol{\theta})$ and the decomposition $f(r) = \overline{f_{\mathrm{de}}}(r) + r\overline{f_{\mathrm{nu}}}(r)$ satisfies

$$\lim_{m\to\infty} m\mathbb{V}[\overline{\mathrm{ASC}}_f] \leq \lim_{m\to\infty} m\mathbb{V}[\widehat{\mathrm{ASC}}_f].$$

This means that $\overline{\mathrm{ASC}}_f$ uniformly attains the minimum asymptotic variance in terms of the ASC divergence estimation.

Proof Recall that

$$U_{\overline{\phi}} = \mathrm{E}_{\mathrm{nu}}[\overline{\phi}(x;\theta)\nabla \log r(x;\theta)^\top].$$

For any p^*_{nu} and p^*_{de} such that $p^*_{\mathrm{nu}}(x)/p^*_{\mathrm{de}}(x) = r(x;\theta^*)$, we have

$$\begin{aligned}
&\mathrm{E}_{\mathrm{nu}}\left[\{\overline{f_{\mathrm{nu}}}(r^*) - f_{\mathrm{nu}}(r^*) + \overline{c}^\top U_{\overline{\phi}}^{-1}\overline{\phi} - c^\top U_{\phi}^{-1}\phi\}\nabla \log r(x;\theta^*)^\top\right]\\
&= \mathrm{E}_{\mathrm{nu}}\left[\{\overline{f_{\mathrm{nu}}}(r(x;\theta^*)) - f_{\mathrm{nu}}(r(x;\theta^*))\}\nabla \log r(x;\theta^*)^\top\right]\\
&\quad + \overline{c}^\top U_{\overline{\phi}}^{-1}U_{\overline{\phi}} - c^\top U_{\phi}^{-1}U_{\phi}\\
&= \mathrm{E}_{\mathrm{nu}}\left[\{\overline{f_{\mathrm{nu}}}(r(x;\theta^*)) - f_{\mathrm{nu}}(r(x;\theta^*))\}\nabla \log r(x;\theta)^\top\right] + \overline{c}^\top - c^\top\\
&= 0.
\end{aligned}$$

Hence, when Eq. (15.9) holds, we have

$$m(1+\rho^{-1})\cdot \mathrm{Cov}[\widehat{\mathrm{ASC}}_f - \overline{\mathrm{ASC}}_f, \overline{\mathrm{ASC}}_f] = o(1)$$

for any $\widehat{\mathrm{ASC}}_f$. □

15.4.3 Examples of Optimal Estimators

In the following corollaries we present sufficient conditions for fulfilling Eq. (15.9).

Corollary 15.6 *Under Assumptions 15.3 and 15.4, suppose that*

$$f(r(x;\theta)) - (r(x;\theta)+\rho^{-1})\overline{f_{\mathrm{nu}}}(r(x;\theta)) \in \mathcal{L}[\nabla \log r(x;\theta)] \tag{15.10}$$

holds for all $\theta \in \Theta$. Then the function $\overline{\phi} = \phi_{\mathrm{opt}}$ defined in Eq. (15.3) *and the decomposition $f(r) = \overline{f_{\mathrm{de}}}(r) + r\overline{f_{\mathrm{nu}}}(r)$ satisfy the condition* (15.9).

Proof We see that the condition (15.10) and the equality

$$(r(x;\theta)+\rho^{-1})\phi_{\mathrm{opt}}(x;\theta) = \rho^{-1}\nabla \log r(x;\theta)$$

ensure the condition (15.9). □

Based on Corollary 15.6, we see that the estimator defined from

$$f_{\mathrm{de}}(r) = \frac{f(r)}{1+\rho r}, \quad f_{\mathrm{nu}}(r) = \frac{\rho f(r)}{1+\rho r}, \quad \text{and} \quad \phi(x;\theta) = \phi_{\mathrm{opt}}(x;\theta) \tag{15.11}$$

leads to an optimal estimator of the ASC divergence. In the optimal estimator, the function f is decomposed according to the ratio of the logistic model, $1/(1+\rho r)$ and $\rho r/(1+\rho r)$.

In the following we show another sufficient condition.

Corollary 15.7 *Under Assumptions 15.3 and 15.4, suppose that, for the model $r(x;\theta)$ and $\overline{\phi}(x;\theta)$,*

$$f(r(x;\theta)) - (r(x;\theta)+\rho^{-1})f'(r(x;\theta)) \in \mathcal{L}[\nabla \log r(x;\theta)]$$

and

$$f'(r(\boldsymbol{x};\boldsymbol{\theta})) - \overline{f_{\mathrm{nu}}}(r(\boldsymbol{x};\boldsymbol{\theta})) \in \mathcal{L}[\overline{\boldsymbol{\phi}}(x;\boldsymbol{\theta})]$$

hold for all $\boldsymbol{\theta} \in \boldsymbol{\Theta}$. *Then the decomposition* $f(r) = \overline{f_{\mathrm{de}}}(r) + r\overline{f_{\mathrm{nu}}}(r)$ *and the vector-valued function* $\overline{\boldsymbol{\phi}}(\boldsymbol{x};\boldsymbol{\theta})$ *satisfy Eq.* (15.9).

Proof When

$$f'(r(\boldsymbol{x};\boldsymbol{\theta})) - \overline{f_{\mathrm{nu}}}(r(\boldsymbol{x};\boldsymbol{\theta})) \in \mathcal{L}[\overline{\boldsymbol{\phi}}(\boldsymbol{x};\boldsymbol{\theta})],$$

there exists a vector $\boldsymbol{b} \in \mathbb{R}^d$ such that

$$f'(r(\boldsymbol{x};\boldsymbol{\theta})) - \overline{f_{\mathrm{nu}}}(r(\boldsymbol{x};\boldsymbol{\theta})) = \boldsymbol{b}^\top \overline{\boldsymbol{\phi}}(\boldsymbol{x};\boldsymbol{\theta}).$$

Recall that

$$\overline{\boldsymbol{c}}(\boldsymbol{\theta}) = \mathrm{E}_{\mathrm{nu}}[\{f'(r(\boldsymbol{x};\boldsymbol{\theta})) - \overline{f_{\mathrm{nu}}}(r(\boldsymbol{x};\boldsymbol{\theta}))\}\nabla \log r(\boldsymbol{x};\boldsymbol{\theta})]$$

and

$$\boldsymbol{U}_{\overline{\boldsymbol{\phi}}}(\boldsymbol{\theta}) = \mathrm{E}_{\mathrm{nu}}[\overline{\boldsymbol{\phi}} \nabla \log r(\boldsymbol{x};\boldsymbol{\theta})^\top].$$

Then

$$\overline{\boldsymbol{c}}^\top \boldsymbol{U}_{\overline{\boldsymbol{\phi}}}^{-1} = \boldsymbol{b}^\top$$

holds. Hence, we have

$$\overline{\boldsymbol{c}}^\top \boldsymbol{U}_{\overline{\boldsymbol{\phi}}}^{-1} \overline{\boldsymbol{\phi}}(\boldsymbol{x};\boldsymbol{\theta}) = \boldsymbol{b}^\top \overline{\boldsymbol{\phi}}(\boldsymbol{x};\boldsymbol{\theta}) = f'(r(\boldsymbol{x};\boldsymbol{\theta})) - \overline{f_{\mathrm{nu}}}(r(\boldsymbol{x};\boldsymbol{\theta})),$$

and we can confirm that Eq. (15.9) holds under the assumption. □

We consider the decomposition derived from the conjugate representation

$$f(r) = -f^*(f'(r)) + rf'(r).$$

That is,

$$f_{\mathrm{de}}(r) = -f^*(f'(r)) \quad \text{and} \quad f_{\mathrm{nu}}(r) = f'(r),$$

where f^* is the conjugate function of f. For the conjugate representation, the second condition in Corollary 15.7 is always satisfied, because $f'(r) - f_{\mathrm{nu}}(r) = 0$ holds. Then the decomposition based on the conjugate representation leads to an optimal estimator when the model $r(\boldsymbol{x};\boldsymbol{\theta})$ and the function f satisfy

$$f(r(\boldsymbol{x};\boldsymbol{\theta})) - (r(\boldsymbol{x};\boldsymbol{\theta}) + \rho^{-1})f'(r(\boldsymbol{x};\boldsymbol{\theta})). \in \mathcal{L}[\nabla \log r(\boldsymbol{x};\boldsymbol{\theta})]. \qquad (15.12)$$

Later we will show some more specific examples.

As shown previously, the conjugate representation leads to an optimal estimator, if Eq. (15.12) holds. However, there exists a pair of the function f and the model $r(\boldsymbol{x};\boldsymbol{\theta})$ that does not satisfy Eq. (15.12), as shown in Example 15.8 later. In this case, the optimality of the estimator based on the conjugate representation is not guaranteed. On the other hand, the decomposition (15.11) always leads to an optimal estimator without specific conditions on $f(r)$ and $r(\boldsymbol{x};\boldsymbol{\theta})$, as long as the asymptotic expansion is valid.

In the following we show some examples in which Corollary 15.6 or Corollary 15.7 is applicable to constructing the optimal estimator.

Example 15.8 *Let the model be*

$$r(\boldsymbol{x};\boldsymbol{\theta}) = \exp\{\boldsymbol{\theta}^\top \boldsymbol{\phi}(\boldsymbol{x})\}, \boldsymbol{\theta} \in \mathbb{R}^d$$

with $\boldsymbol{\phi}(\boldsymbol{x}) = (\phi_1(\boldsymbol{x}),\ldots,\phi_d(\boldsymbol{x}))^\top$ *and* $\phi_1(\boldsymbol{x}) = 1$. *Then* $\mathcal{L}[\nabla \log r(\boldsymbol{x};\boldsymbol{\theta})]$ *is spanned by* $1, \phi_2(\boldsymbol{x}),\ldots,\phi_d(\boldsymbol{x})$. *The ASC divergence with*

$$f(r) = -\log r + r - 1$$

leads to the KL divergence. Let

$$f_{\mathrm{de}}(r) = -\log r - 1 \quad \textit{and} \quad f_{\mathrm{nu}}(r) = 1.$$

Then we can confirm that Eq. (15.10) *is satisfied. Hence, the function* $\boldsymbol{\phi} = \boldsymbol{\phi}_{\mathrm{opt}}$ *and the above decomposition lead to an optimal estimator of the KL divergence.*

We see that there is redundancy for the decomposition of f. *Indeed, for any constants* $c_0, c_1 \in \mathbb{R}$, *the function* $c_0 + c_1 \log r(\boldsymbol{x};\boldsymbol{\theta})$ *is included in* $\mathcal{L}[\nabla \log r(\boldsymbol{x};\boldsymbol{\theta})]$. *Hence the decomposition*

$$f_{\mathrm{nu}}(r) = \frac{r + c_1 \log r + c_0}{r + \rho^{-1}} \quad \textit{and} \quad f_{\mathrm{de}}(r) = r - \log r - 1 - r f_{\mathrm{nu}}(r)$$

with $\overline{\boldsymbol{\phi}} = \boldsymbol{\phi}_{\mathrm{opt}}$ *also leads to an optimal estimator. The decomposition in Eq.* (15.11) *is realized by setting* $c_0 = -1$ *and* $c_1 = -1$.

Next we consider the conjugate expression of the KL divergence. For $f(r) = -\log r + r - 1$ *and* $r(\boldsymbol{x};\boldsymbol{\theta}) = \exp\{\boldsymbol{\theta}^\top \boldsymbol{\phi}(\boldsymbol{x})\}$, *we have*

$$\begin{aligned} &f(r(\boldsymbol{x};\boldsymbol{\theta})) - (r(\boldsymbol{x};\boldsymbol{\theta}) + \rho^{-1}) f'(r(\boldsymbol{x};\boldsymbol{\theta})) \\ &\quad = -\boldsymbol{\theta}^\top \boldsymbol{\phi}(\boldsymbol{x}) - \rho^{-1} + \rho^{-1} \exp\{-\boldsymbol{\theta}^\top \boldsymbol{\phi}(\boldsymbol{x})\}. \end{aligned}$$

In general, the function $\exp\{-\boldsymbol{\theta}^\top \boldsymbol{\phi}(\boldsymbol{x})\}$ *is not represented by the linear combination of* $\phi_1(\boldsymbol{x}),\ldots,\phi_d(\boldsymbol{x})$, *and thus the condition in Corollary 15.7 does not hold. This means that the conjugate expression of the KL divergence is not optimal in general.*

Let us compare numerically the optimal estimator using Eq. (15.11) with the estimator defined based on the conjugate representation of the KL divergence for the model

$$r(x;\boldsymbol{\theta}) = \exp\{\alpha + \beta x\}, \boldsymbol{\theta} = (\alpha, \beta)^\top \in \mathbb{R}^2.$$

We estimate the KL divergence from $N(0,1)$ to $N(\mu,1)$ for $\mu = 0.1$, 0.5, 0.9, 1.3, and 1.7. The sample size is set to $n_{\mathrm{nu}} = n_{\mathrm{de}} = 50$, and the averaged values of the square error $m(\widehat{\mathrm{ASC}}_f - \mathrm{ASC}_f)^2$ over 1000 runs are computed. Table 15.1 summarizes the numerical results, showing that the optimal estimator outperforms the estimator using the conjugate representation.

We now give more examples.

Table 15.1. Mean square error $m\mathbb{E}[(\widehat{\mathrm{ASC}}_f - \mathrm{ASC}_f)^2]$ for the KL divergence is shown ($n_{\mathrm{nu}} = n_{\mathrm{de}} = 50$). p^*_{nu} and p^*_{de} are set to $N(0,1)$ and $N(\mu,1)$, respectively.

μ	0.1	0.5	0.9	1.3	1.7
Optimal estimator	0.038	0.299	1.119	2.502	5.276
Conjugate representation	0.040	0.381	1.480	4.125	9.553

Example 15.9 *Let the model be*

$$r(\boldsymbol{x};\boldsymbol{\theta}) = \exp\{\boldsymbol{\theta}^\top \boldsymbol{\phi}(x)\}, \boldsymbol{\theta} \in \mathbb{R}^d$$

with $\boldsymbol{\phi}(\boldsymbol{x}) = (\phi_1(\boldsymbol{x}),\ldots,\phi_d(\boldsymbol{x}))^\top$ *and* $\phi_1(\boldsymbol{x}) = 1$. *Then the linear space* $\mathcal{L}[\nabla \log r(\boldsymbol{x};\boldsymbol{\theta})]$ *is spanned by* $\{\phi_1(\boldsymbol{x}),\ldots,\phi_d(\boldsymbol{x})\}$ *and thus* $\mathcal{L}[\nabla \log r(\boldsymbol{x};\boldsymbol{\theta})]$ *includes the function of the form*

$$c_0 + c_1 \log r(\boldsymbol{x};\boldsymbol{\theta}) \ \textit{for}\ c_0, c_1 \in \mathbb{R}.$$

Let the convex function $f(r)$ *be*

$$f(r) = \frac{1}{1+\rho}\log\frac{1+\rho}{1+\rho r} + r\frac{\rho}{1+\rho}\log\frac{r(1+\rho)}{1+\rho r} \tag{15.13}$$

for $\rho > 0$. *Then the corresponding ASC divergence is reduced to mutual information:*

$$\int p^*_{\mathrm{de}}(\boldsymbol{x}) f\left(\frac{p^*_{\mathrm{nu}}(\boldsymbol{x})}{p^*_{\mathrm{de}}(\boldsymbol{x})}\right)\mathrm{d}\boldsymbol{x} = \int \sum_{y=\mathrm{nu},\mathrm{de}} p(\boldsymbol{x},y)\log\frac{p(\boldsymbol{x},y)}{p(\boldsymbol{x})p(y)}\mathrm{d}\boldsymbol{x},$$

where y *is the binary random variable taking* nu *or* de; *the joint probability of* $\boldsymbol{x}$ *and* y *is defined as*

$$p(\boldsymbol{x},\mathrm{nu}) = p^*_{\mathrm{nu}}(\boldsymbol{x})\frac{\rho}{1+\rho} \quad \textit{and} \quad p(\boldsymbol{x},\mathrm{de}) = p^*_{\mathrm{de}}(\boldsymbol{x})\frac{1}{1+\rho}.$$

The equality $p^*_{\mathrm{nu}} = p^*_{\mathrm{de}}$ *implies that the conditional probability* $p(\boldsymbol{x}|y)$ *is independent of* y. *Thus, mutual information becomes zero if and only if* $p^*_{\mathrm{nu}} = p^*_{\mathrm{de}}$ *holds. For any moment-matching estimator, we can confirm that the following decomposition satisfies the condition in Corollary 15.7:*

$$f_{\mathrm{de}}(r) = \frac{1}{1+\rho}\log\frac{1+\rho}{1+\rho r} \quad \textit{and} \quad f_{\mathrm{nu}}(r) = \frac{\rho}{1+\rho}\log\frac{r(1+\rho)}{1+\rho r}. \tag{15.14}$$

Note that this decomposition with the model $r(\boldsymbol{x};\boldsymbol{\theta}) = \exp\{\boldsymbol{\theta}^\top\boldsymbol{\phi}(\boldsymbol{x})\}$ *also satisfies the condition in Corollary 15.6. As pointed out in Keziou and Leoni-Aubin (2005, 2008), the decomposition above is derived from the conjugate expression of Eq.* (15.13). *Thus, in this example, we are presenting that the above estimator is also optimal in mutual information estimation.*

Example 15.10 *Let*

$$r(\boldsymbol{x};\boldsymbol{\theta}) = 1 + \boldsymbol{\theta}^\top \boldsymbol{\phi}(\boldsymbol{x})$$

and $\boldsymbol{\phi}_1(\boldsymbol{x}) = 1$. *The subspace* $\mathcal{L}[\nabla \log r(\boldsymbol{x};\boldsymbol{\theta})]$ *is spanned by*

$$\{\phi_1(\boldsymbol{x};\boldsymbol{\theta})/r(\boldsymbol{x};\boldsymbol{\theta}),\ldots,\phi_d(\boldsymbol{x};\boldsymbol{\theta})/r(\boldsymbol{x};\boldsymbol{\theta})\},$$

and thus $\mathcal{L}[\nabla \log r(\boldsymbol{x};\boldsymbol{\theta})]$ *includes the function of the form*

$$c_0 + c_1/r(\boldsymbol{x};\boldsymbol{\theta}) \text{ for } c_0, c_1 \in \mathbb{R}.$$

Let the convex function f *be*

$$f(r) = \frac{1}{\rho+1}\left(r - 1 + (1+\rho r)\log\frac{1+\rho r}{r(1+\rho)}\right)$$

for $\rho > 0$. *Then the corresponding ASC divergence is expressed as*

$$\int p^*_{\mathrm{de}}(\boldsymbol{x}) f\left(\frac{p^*_{\mathrm{nu}}(\boldsymbol{x})}{p^*_{\mathrm{de}}(\boldsymbol{x})}\right)\mathrm{d}\boldsymbol{x} = \mathrm{KL}\left(\frac{p^*_{\mathrm{de}} + \rho\, p^*_{\mathrm{nu}}}{1+\rho}\,\middle\|\, p^*_{\mathrm{nu}}\right),$$

where KL *denotes the Kullback–Leibler divergence.*

Corollary 15.6 assures that the decomposition

$$f_{\mathrm{de}}(r) = \frac{1}{\rho+1}\left(\frac{r-1}{1+\rho r} + \log\frac{1+\rho r}{r(1+\rho)}\right),$$

$$f_{\mathrm{nu}}(r) = \frac{\rho}{\rho+1}\left(\frac{r-1}{1+\rho r} + \log\frac{1+\rho r}{r(1+\rho)}\right)$$

and the moment-matching estimator with $\boldsymbol{\phi} = \boldsymbol{\phi}_{\mathrm{opt}}$ *lead to an optimal estimator for the above ASC divergence. On the other hand, from Corollary 15.7, we can confirm that the decomposition derived from the conjugate expression,*

$$f_{\mathrm{de}}(r) = \frac{1}{1+\rho}\log\frac{1+\rho r}{r(1+\rho)},$$

$$f_{\mathrm{nu}}(r) = f'(r) = \frac{1}{r(1+\rho)}\left(r - 1 + \rho r \log\frac{1+\rho r}{r(1+\rho)}\right),$$

leads to another optimal estimator.

15.5 Two-Sample Test Based on ASC Divergence Estimation

Based on the ASC divergence estimator $\widehat{\mathrm{ASC}}_f$, we can conduct a two-sample homogeneity test with hypotheses

$$H_0 : p^*_{\mathrm{nu}} = p^*_{\mathrm{de}} \quad\text{and}\quad H_1 : p^*_{\mathrm{nu}} \neq p^*_{\mathrm{de}}. \tag{15.15}$$

When the null hypothesis H_0 is true, the ASC divergence $\mathrm{ASC}_f(p^*_{\mathrm{nu}} \| p^*_{\mathrm{de}})$ is zero; otherwise, $\mathrm{ASC}_f(p^*_{\mathrm{nu}} \| p^*_{\mathrm{de}})$ takes a positive value. Thus, in a practical two-sample test, the null hypothesis may be rejected if $\widehat{\mathrm{ASC}}_f > t$, where the threshold t is determined from the *significance level*.

In this section we first derive an asymptotic distribution of $\widehat{\mathrm{ASC}}_f$ under the null hypothesis H_0 in Eq. (15.15), that is,

$$\frac{p^*_{\mathrm{nu}}(\boldsymbol{x})}{p^*_{\mathrm{de}}(\boldsymbol{x})} = r(\boldsymbol{x};\boldsymbol{\theta}^*) = 1.$$

Then we give a test statistic based on the asymptotic distribution and analyze its *power* (the acceptance rate of correct null-hypotheses, i.e., two distributions are judged to be the same when they actually are the same).

15.5.1 ASC-Based Test

Let us consider the optimal estimator $\widehat{\mathrm{ASC}}_f$ defined in Eq. (15.11). The asymptotic distribution of the optimal estimator is given by the following theorem.

Theorem 15.11 (Kanamori et al., 2011a) *Let* $p^*_{\mathrm{nu}}(\boldsymbol{x})/p^*_{\mathrm{de}}(\boldsymbol{x}) = r(\boldsymbol{x};\boldsymbol{\theta}^*) = 1$. *Suppose that Assumptions 15.3 and 15.4 hold, and that the third-order derivatives of* $f_{\mathrm{nu}}(r(\boldsymbol{x};\boldsymbol{\theta}))$ *and* $f_{\mathrm{de}}(r(\boldsymbol{x};\boldsymbol{\theta}))$ *with respect to* $\boldsymbol{\theta}$ *are dominated by a* p^*_{de}*-integrable function in the vicinity of* $\boldsymbol{\theta}^*$. *We assume that the d-by-d symmetric matrix* $\boldsymbol{U}_{\phi_{\mathrm{opt}}}(\boldsymbol{\theta})$ *is non-degenerate in the vicinity of* $\boldsymbol{\theta} = \boldsymbol{\theta}^*$. *Let* $\widehat{\mathrm{ASC}}_f$ *be the estimator defined by Eq.* (15.11). *Then we have*

$$\frac{2m}{f''(1)}\widehat{\mathrm{ASC}}_f \stackrel{\mathrm{d}}{\longrightarrow} \chi^2_{d-1},$$

where χ^2_{d-1} *denotes the chi-square distribution with* $d-1$ *degrees of freedom.*

Based on this theorem, the null hypothesis $H_0 : p^*_{\mathrm{nu}} = p^*_{\mathrm{de}}$ is rejected if

$$\widehat{\mathrm{ASC}}_f \geq \frac{f''(1)}{2m}\chi^2_{d-1}(1-\alpha), \tag{15.16}$$

where $\chi^2_{d-1}(1-\alpha)$ is the chi-square $100(1-\alpha)$ percent point function with $d-1$ degrees of freedom. We refer to the homogeneity test based on Eq. (15.16) with the optimal choice (15.11) as the $\widehat{\mathrm{ASC}}_f$*-based test*.

A standard approach to a two-sample homogeneity test is to exploit an asymptotic distribution of the empirical likelihood estimator $\widehat{\boldsymbol{\theta}}$. Under the model

$$r(\boldsymbol{x};\boldsymbol{\theta}) = \exp\{\alpha + \phi(\boldsymbol{x};\boldsymbol{\beta})\},\ \boldsymbol{\theta} = (\alpha, \boldsymbol{\beta}^\top)^\top \in \mathbb{R}\times\mathbb{R}^{d-1} \tag{15.17}$$

with $\phi(\boldsymbol{x},\boldsymbol{\beta}) \in \mathbb{R}$, Fokianos et al. (2001) pointed out that the asymptotic distribution of the empirical likelihood estimator $\widehat{\boldsymbol{\theta}} = (\widehat{\alpha}, \widehat{\boldsymbol{\beta}}^\top)^\top \in \mathbb{R}\times\mathbb{R}^{d-1}$ under the null hypothesis $p^*_{\mathrm{nu}} = p^*_{\mathrm{de}}$ is given by

$$\sqrt{m}(\widehat{\boldsymbol{\beta}} - \boldsymbol{\beta}^*) \stackrel{\mathrm{d}}{\longrightarrow} N_{d-1}(\boldsymbol{0}, \mathrm{V}_{\mathrm{nu}}[\nabla_{\boldsymbol{\beta}}\phi]^{-1}),$$

where $\boldsymbol{\theta}^* = (\alpha^*, \boldsymbol{\beta}^{*\top})^\top$ and $\nabla_{\boldsymbol{\beta}}\phi$ is the $(d-1)$-dimensional gradient vector of $\phi(\boldsymbol{x};\boldsymbol{\beta})$ at $\boldsymbol{\beta} = \boldsymbol{\beta}^*$ with respect to the parameter $\boldsymbol{\beta}$. Then the null hypothesis is rejected if the *Wald-type test statistic*,

$$S = m(\widehat{\boldsymbol{\beta}} - \boldsymbol{\beta}^*)^\top \widehat{V}_{\mathrm{nu}}[\nabla_{\boldsymbol{\beta}}\phi](\widehat{\boldsymbol{\beta}} - \boldsymbol{\beta}^*), \tag{15.18}$$

is larger than $\chi^2_{d-1}(1-\alpha)$, where $\widehat{V}_{\mathrm{nu}}[\nabla_{\boldsymbol{\beta}}\phi]$ is a consistent estimator of $\mathrm{V}_{\mathrm{nu}}[\nabla_{\boldsymbol{\beta}}\phi]$. The homogeneity test based on the statistic S is referred to as the *empirical likelihood-score test*. Fokianos et al. (2001) studied the statistical properties of the empirical likelihood-score test through numerical experiments and reported that the power of the empirical likelihood-score test is comparable to the standard t-test and the ASC-based test under parametric models.

An alternative test statistic is given by the *empirical likelihood-ratio test*. Let $\ell(\boldsymbol{\theta})$ be

$$\ell(\boldsymbol{\theta}) = \sum_{j=1}^{n_{\mathrm{de}}} \log \frac{1}{\rho r(\boldsymbol{x}_j^{\mathrm{de}};\boldsymbol{\theta}) + 1} + \sum_{i=1}^{n_{\mathrm{nu}}} \log \frac{\rho r(\boldsymbol{x}_i^{\mathrm{nu}};\boldsymbol{\theta})}{\rho r(\boldsymbol{x}_i^{\mathrm{nu}};\boldsymbol{\theta}) + 1}.$$

Then the empirical likelihood-ratio test uses the statistic

$$R := 2 \max_{\boldsymbol{\theta} \in \Theta} \{\ell(\boldsymbol{\theta}) - \ell(\boldsymbol{\theta}^*)\}. \tag{15.19}$$

It is shown that, under the null hypothesis $r^*(\boldsymbol{x}) = 1$, the statistic R converges in distribution to the chi-square distribution with $d-1$ degrees of freedom (Keziou and Leoni-Aubin, 2008).

Note that the empirical likelihood-ratio test is closely related to mutual information. Indeed, the mutual information estimator $\widehat{\mathrm{ASC}}_f$ derived from Eqs. (15.6) and (15.13) is related to R defined in Eq. (15.19) as follows (Keziou and Leoni-Aubin, 2008):

$$R = 2(n_{\mathrm{nu}} + n_{\mathrm{de}})\widehat{\mathrm{ASC}}_f.$$

Example 15.9 guarantees that $\widehat{\mathrm{ASC}}_f$ attains the minimum asymptotic variance in mutual information estimation.

15.5.2 Power Analysis

Here we analyze the power function of an $\widehat{\mathrm{ASC}}_f$-based test and compare it with those of other methods. More specifically, we show that the power of the $\widehat{\mathrm{ASC}}_f$-based test is not less than that of the empirical likelihood-score test under the setup of *local alternatives*, where the distributions p^*_{nu} and p^*_{de} vary according to the sample size.

We assume the following conditions.

Assumption 15.12

1. *f is third-order differentiable and strictly convex, and it satisfies $f(1) = f'(1) = 0$.*

2. *The density-ratio model* $r(\boldsymbol{x};\boldsymbol{\theta})$ *is represented by Eq.* (15.17), *and the true density-ratio is given by* $r(\boldsymbol{x};\boldsymbol{\theta}^*) = 1$. *Note that, for any* $\boldsymbol{\theta} \in \boldsymbol{\Theta}$, $1 \in \mathcal{L}[\nabla \log r(\boldsymbol{x};\boldsymbol{\theta})]$ *holds.*
3. *For a fixed probability density* $p(\boldsymbol{x})$, *we assume* $p^*_{\mathrm{de}}(\boldsymbol{x}) = p(\boldsymbol{x})$. *Let* ${p^*_{\mathrm{nu}}}^{(m)}$ *be the probability density given by*

$$ {p^*_{\mathrm{nu}}}^{(m)}(\boldsymbol{x}) = p^*_{\mathrm{de}}(\boldsymbol{x}) r(\boldsymbol{x};\boldsymbol{\theta}_m), $$

where the parameter $\boldsymbol{\theta}_m$ *is defined as*

$$ \boldsymbol{\theta}_m = \boldsymbol{\theta}^* + \frac{1}{\sqrt{m}} \boldsymbol{h}_m \qquad (15.20) $$

for $\boldsymbol{h}_m \in \mathbb{R}^d$ *such that* $\lim_{m\to\infty} \boldsymbol{h}_m = \boldsymbol{h} \in \mathbb{R}^d$.

Then the following theorem holds.

Theorem 15.13 (Kanamori et al., 2011a) *Let* $\boldsymbol{M}(\boldsymbol{\theta})$ *be the matrix defined as*

$$ \boldsymbol{M}(\boldsymbol{\theta}) = \mathrm{E}_{\mathrm{de}}[\nabla \log r(\boldsymbol{x};\boldsymbol{\theta}) \nabla \log r(\boldsymbol{x};\boldsymbol{\theta})^\top]. $$

Under Assumption 15.12 and some additional regularity conditions (see Kanamori et al., 2011a, for details), the power function of the $\widehat{\mathrm{ASC}}_f$*-based test with significance level* α *is asymptotically given as*

$$ \Pr\left\{ Y \geq \chi^2_{d-1}(1-\alpha) \right\}, $$

where $\Pr(\cdot)$ *denotes the probability of an event and* Y *is the random variable following the non-central chi-square distribution with* $d-1$ *degrees of freedom and non-centrality parameter* $\boldsymbol{h}^\top \boldsymbol{M}(\boldsymbol{\theta}^*)\boldsymbol{h}$. *Moreover, the asymptotic power function of the empirical likelihood-score test (15.18) is the same.*

Theorem 15.13 implies that, under the local alternative (15.20), the power function of the $\widehat{\mathrm{ASC}}_f$-based test does not depend on the choice of the ASC divergence, and that the empirical likelihood-score test has the same power as the $\widehat{\mathrm{ASC}}_f$-based test.

Next we consider the power function under model misspecification.

Theorem 15.14 (Kanamori et al., 2011a) *We assume that the density ratio* ${p^*_{\mathrm{nu}}}^{(m)}/p^*_{\mathrm{de}}$ *is not realized by the model* $r(\boldsymbol{x};\boldsymbol{\theta})$, *and that* ${p^*_{\mathrm{nu}}}^{(m)}$ *is represented as*

$$ {p^*_{\mathrm{nu}}}^{(m)}(\boldsymbol{x}) = p^*_{\mathrm{de}}(\boldsymbol{x}) \left(r(\boldsymbol{x};\boldsymbol{\theta}_m) + \frac{s_m(\boldsymbol{x}) + \varepsilon_m}{\sqrt{m}} \right), $$

where $s_m(\boldsymbol{x})$ *satisfies* $\mathrm{E}_{\mathrm{de}}[s_m(\boldsymbol{x})] = 0$ *and* $\lim_{m\to\infty} \varepsilon_m = \varepsilon$. *Suppose that all of the items in Assumption 15.12 hold except the definition of* ${p^*_{\mathrm{nu}}}^{(m)}(x)$. *We further assume some additional regularity conditions (see Kanamori et al., 2011a, for details). Then, under the setup of the local alternatives, the power function of the* $\widehat{\mathrm{ASC}}_f$*-based test is larger than or equal to that of the empirical likelihood-score test.*

Theorems 15.13 and 15.14 indicate that the $\widehat{\mathrm{ASC}}_f$-based test is more powerful than the empirical likelihood-score test regardless of whether the model $r(\boldsymbol{x};\boldsymbol{\theta})$ is correct or slightly misspecified.

See Section 11.4.2 of Lehmann (1986) for a more detailed explanation on the asymptotic theory under local alternatives.

15.6 Numerical Studies

In this section numerical results are reported for illustrating the adequacy of the above asymptotic theory for a finite-sample inference.

15.6.1 Setup

We examine two ASC divergences for a two-sample homogeneity test. One is the KL divergence defined by $f(r) = r - 1 - \log(r)$ as shown in Example 15.8, and the test statistic is derived from the optimal choice (15.11). This is referred to as the *KL-based test*. The other is mutual information defined by Eq. (15.13), and the estimator $\widehat{\mathrm{ASC}}_f$ is derived from the optimal decomposition (15.11) and the moment-matching estimator $\boldsymbol{\phi} = \boldsymbol{\phi}_{\mathrm{opt}}$. This is referred to as the *MI-based test.*

In addition, the empirical likelihood-ratio test (15.19) is also attempted. As shown in Keziou and Leoni-Aubin (2005, 2008), the statistic of the empirical likelihood-ratio test is equivalent to the estimator of mutual information using the conjugate representation (15.14) and the moment-matching estimator $\boldsymbol{\phi} = \boldsymbol{\phi}_{\mathrm{opt}}$. Thus, the MI-based test and the empirical likelihood-ratio test share the same moment-matching estimator, but the ways in which the function f is decomposed are different.

We further compare these methods with the empirical likelihood-score test (15.18) proposed by Fokianos et al. (2001), and the Hotelling T^2-test. The null hypothesis of the test is $H_0 : p^*_{\mathrm{nu}} = p^*_{\mathrm{de}}$, and the alternative is $H_1 : p^*_{\mathrm{nu}} \neq p^*_{\mathrm{de}}$. The *type I error* (the rejection rate of the correct null hypotheses, i.e., two distributions are judged to be different when they are actually the same) and the power function (the acceptance rate of the correct null hypotheses, i.e., two distributions are judged to be the same when they actually are the same) of these tests are numerically computed.

15.6.2 Type I Error

First we assume that the null hypothesis $p^*_{\mathrm{nu}} = p^*_{\mathrm{de}}$ is correct and compute the type I error.

The following three cases are examined:

(a) The distributions of p^*_{nu} and p^*_{de} are given as a one-dimensional exponential distribution with rate parameter 0.1 or 1.

(b) The distributions of p^*_{nu} and p^*_{de} are given as the ten-dimensional normal distribution $N_{10}(0, \boldsymbol{I}_{10})$, where $\boldsymbol{I}_{10}$ denotes the 10-dimensional identity matrix.

(c) Each element of the 10-dimensional vector $\boldsymbol{x} \in \mathbb{R}^{10}$ is i.i.d. from the t-distribution with 10 degrees of freedom.

For the k-dimensional vector $\boldsymbol{x} = (x_{(1)}, \ldots, x_{(k)})^\top$, the semi-parametric model for the density ratio is defined as

$$r(\boldsymbol{x};\boldsymbol{\theta}) = \exp\left\{\alpha + \sum_{\ell=1}^{k} \left(\beta_\ell x_{(\ell)} + \beta_{k+\ell} x_{(\ell)}^2\right)\right\} \tag{15.21}$$

with the $(2k+1)$-dimensional parameter $\boldsymbol{\theta} = (\alpha, \beta_1, \ldots, \beta_{2k})^\top$. The sample size is set to $n_{\text{nu}} = n_{\text{de}}$ and is varied from 10 to 100 for one-dimensional random variables and from 100 to 1000 for 10-dimensional random variables.

The significance level of the test is set to 0.05, and the type I error is averaged over 1000 runs. For each of the above three cases, the averaged type I errors of the KL-based test, the MI-based test, the empirical likelihood-ratio test, and the empirical likelihood-score test are shown in Table 15.2.

For case (a), the type I error of the empirical likelihood-score test is larger than the significance level even with a large sample size. On the other hand, the type I errors of the KL-based test, the MI-based test, and the empirical likelihood-ratio test are close to the significance level for a large sample size. For case (b), the type I error of all methods converges to the significance level with a modest sample size. For case (c), the type I error of the empirical likelihood-score test is larger than the significance level, even with a large sample size. On the other hand, the type I error of the other tests is close to the significance level with a moderate sample size.

15.6.3 Power Function

Next we compute the power functions of the KL-based test, the MI-based test, the empirical likelihood-ratio test, the empirical likelihood-score test, and the Hotelling T^2-test. In the numerical simulations, $p^*_{\text{nu}}(\boldsymbol{x})$ is fixed and $p^*_{\text{de}}(\boldsymbol{x})$ is varied by changing the parameters in the distribution such as the rate parameter, the mean parameter, and the scale parameter.

We consider the following setups:

(A) $p^*_{\text{nu}}(\boldsymbol{x})$ is defined as the 10-dimensional standard normal distribution, or the 10-dimensional t-distribution with 5 degrees of freedom. The sample $\boldsymbol{x}^{\text{de}} = (x^{\text{de}}_{(1)}, \ldots, x^{\text{de}}_{(10)})$ corresponding to p^*_{de} is generated as

$$x^{\text{de}}_{(\ell)} = x_{(\ell)} + \mu, \quad \ell = 1, \ldots, 10, \tag{15.22}$$

where $\boldsymbol{x} = (x_{(1)}, \ldots, x_{(10)})$ is drawn from p^*_{nu}. That is, the mean parameter $\mu \in \mathbb{R}$ is added to each element of $\boldsymbol{x} \in \mathbb{R}^{10}$. Hence, $p^*_{\text{nu}} = p^*_{\text{de}}$ holds for $\mu = 0$.

Table 15.2. Averaged type I errors over 1000 runs are shown as functions of the number of samples. The significance level is set to 0.05. In the table, "KL," "MI," "Ratio," and "Score" denote the KL-based test, the MI-based test, the empirical likelihood-ratio test, and the empirical likelihood-score test, respectively.

(a) One-dimensional exponential distribution with rate parameter 0.1

n_{nu}	KL	MI	Ratio	Score
10	0.177	0.084	0.084	0.206
50	0.095	0.067	0.067	0.124
100	0.085	0.059	0.059	0.104

(a′) One-dimensional exponential distribution with rate parameter 1

n_{nu}	KL	MI	Ratio	Score
10	0.170	0.083	0.083	0.203
50	0.099	0.068	0.068	0.134
100	0.092	0.067	0.067	0.107

(b) 10-dimensional standard normal distribution

n_{nu}	KL	MI	Ratio	Score
100	0.152	0.102	0.102	0.200
500	0.058	0.051	0.051	0.059
1000	0.062	0.058	0.058	0.069

(c) 10-dimensional t-distribution with 10 degrees of freedom

n_{nu}	KL	MI	Ratio	Score
100	0.179	0.092	0.092	0.244
500	0.084	0.073	0.073	0.114
1000	0.063	0.056	0.056	0.078

(B) $p^*_{\mathrm{nu}}(\boldsymbol{x})$ is defined in the same way as (A), and the sample $\boldsymbol{x}^{\mathrm{de}} = (x^{\mathrm{de}}_{(1)}, \ldots, x^{\mathrm{de}}_{(10)})$ corresponding to p^*_{de} is generated as

$$x^{\mathrm{de}}_{(\ell)} = \sigma \times x_{(\ell)}, \quad \ell = 1, \ldots, 10, \tag{15.23}$$

where $\boldsymbol{x} = (x_{(1)}, \ldots, x_{(10)})$ is drawn from p^*_{nu}. That is, the scale parameter $\sigma > 0$ is multiplied to each element of $\boldsymbol{x} \in \mathbb{R}^{10}$. Hence, the null hypothesis $p^*_{\mathrm{nu}} = p^*_{\mathrm{de}}$ corresponds to $\sigma = 1$.

In both cases the sample size is set to $n_{\mathrm{nu}} = n_{\mathrm{de}} = 500$ and the density-ratio model (15.21) with $k = 10$ is used. When p^*_{nu} and p^*_{de} are the normal distributions, the density-ratio model (15.21) includes the true density ratio. However, when they are the t-distributions, the true ratio $r^*(\boldsymbol{x})$ resides outside of the model (15.21). In all simulations, the significance level is set to 0.05, and the power functions are averaged over 1000 runs.

Table 15.3 shows the numerical results for setup (A). The mean parameter μ in Eq. (15.22) is varied from -0.1 to 0.1. When both p^*_{nu} and p^*_{de} are the normal distributions, the powers of the KL-based test, the MI-based test, the empirical likelihood-ratio test, and the empirical likelihood-score test almost coincide with each other. On the other hand, the power of the Hotelling T^2-test is slightly larger than the others. This is natural because the Hotelling T^2-test was designed to work well under a normal distribution. For the t-distribution with 5 degrees of freedom,

Table 15.3. Averaged power functions over 1000 runs for the setup (A), i.e., the mean is shifted by μ. $n_{\mathrm{nu}} = n_{\mathrm{de}} = 500$ and the significance level is set to 0.05. In the table, "KL," "MI," "Ratio," "Score," and "Hotelling" denote the KL-based test, the MI-based test, the empirical likelihood-ratio test, the empirical likelihood-score test, and the Hotelling T^2-test, respectively.

10-dimensional standard normal distribution (model is correctly specified)

μ	KL	MI	Ratio	Score	Hotelling
−0.10	0.905	0.900	0.900	0.908	0.955
−0.08	0.716	0.696	0.696	0.720	0.814
−0.06	0.386	0.358	0.358	0.389	0.480
−0.04	0.168	0.155	0.155	0.185	0.210
−0.02	0.112	0.096	0.096	0.123	0.105
0.00	0.071	0.061	0.061	0.080	0.046
0.02	0.089	0.081	0.081	0.106	0.080
0.04	0.187	0.161	0.161	0.203	0.206
0.06	0.421	0.395	0.395	0.429	0.508
0.08	0.709	0.686	0.686	0.706	0.812
0.10	0.875	0.861	0.861	0.873	0.945

10-dimensional t-distribution with 5 degrees of freedom (model is misspecified)

μ	KL	MI	Ratio	Score	Hotelling
−0.10	0.707	0.671	0.671	0.740	0.726
−0.08	0.509	0.439	0.439	0.554	0.532
−0.06	0.348	0.273	0.273	0.413	0.298
−0.04	0.186	0.135	0.135	0.272	0.143
−0.02	0.126	0.083	0.083	0.224	0.085
0.00	0.118	0.076	0.076	0.203	0.056
0.02	0.132	0.087	0.087	0.233	0.062
0.04	0.183	0.130	0.130	0.257	0.137
0.06	0.335	0.274	0.274	0.391	0.294
0.08	0.511	0.449	0.449	0.559	0.523
0.10	0.724	0.676	0.676	0.733	0.781

the power of the empirical likelihood-score test around $\mu = 0$ is much larger than the significance level, 0.05. This means that the empirical likelihood-score test is not conservative and will lead to a high false-positive rate. The powers of the MI-based test and the empirical likelihood-ratio test are close to the significance level around $\mu = 0$ and are comparable to the Hotelling T^2-test.

Table 15.4 shows the averaged power functions for setup (B), where the scale parameter σ in Eq. (15.23) is varied from 0.9 to 1.1. The results show that the

Table 15.4. Averaged power functions over 1000 runs for the setup (B), i.e., the standard deviation is changed by σ. $n_{\mathrm{nu}} = n_{\mathrm{de}} = 500$ and the significance level is set to 0.05. In the table, "KL," "MI," "Ratio," "Score," and "Hotelling" denote the KL-based test, the MI-based test, the empirical likelihood-ratio test, the empirical likelihood-score test, and the Hotelling T^2-test, respectively.

10-dimensional standard normal distribution (model is correctly specified)

σ	KL	MI	Ratio	Score	Hotelling
0.90	0.998	0.999	0.999	0.995	0.051
0.92	0.960	0.967	0.967	0.905	0.069
0.94	0.725	0.761	0.761	0.578	0.037
0.96	0.319	0.356	0.356	0.206	0.053
0.98	0.088	0.093	0.093	0.063	0.047
1.00	0.068	0.057	0.057	0.069	0.054
1.02	0.156	0.118	0.118	0.217	0.057
1.04	0.404	0.315	0.315	0.512	0.060
1.06	0.762	0.687	0.687	0.837	0.059
1.08	0.975	0.955	0.955	0.991	0.051
1.10	0.999	0.997	0.997	0.999	0.044

10-dimensional t-distribution with 5 degrees of freedom (model is misspecified)

σ	KL	MI	Ratio	Score	Hotelling
0.90	0.819	0.870	0.870	0.484	0.054
0.92	0.560	0.638	0.638	0.250	0.061
0.94	0.265	0.329	0.329	0.117	0.048
0.96	0.159	0.188	0.188	0.103	0.054
0.98	0.113	0.109	0.109	0.121	0.051
1.00	0.129	0.076	0.076	0.208	0.052
1.02	0.213	0.097	0.097	0.374	0.051
1.04	0.331	0.177	0.177	0.544	0.052
1.06	0.544	0.314	0.314	0.749	0.053
1.08	0.740	0.531	0.531	0.898	0.039
1.10	0.903	0.762	0.762	0.964	0.044

Hotelling T^2-test completely fails because it relies on the difference of the means, but the means are the same in setup (B). The results also show that the power function of the empirical likelihood-score test takes the minimum value at σ less than 1. Such a biased result is caused by the fact that the estimated variance, $\widehat{V}_{\mathrm{nu}}$, based on the empirical likelihood-score estimator, tends to take slightly smaller values than the true variance. The powers of the MI-based test and the empirical likelihood-ratio test are close to the significance level around $\sigma = 1$, whereas that of the KL-based test is slightly larger than the significance level around $\sigma = 1$.

Overall, these numerical results show that when the model $r(\boldsymbol{x};\boldsymbol{\theta})$ is specified correctly, the powers of the KL-based test, the MI-based test, the empirical likelihood-ratio test, and the empirical likelihood-score test are highly comparable to each other. This tendency agrees well with Theorem 15.13.

On the other hand, the empirical likelihood-score test has a large type I error and its power is biased when the model is misspecified. The MI-based test and the empirical likelihood-ratio test have comparable powers to the other methods, and their type I error is well controlled.

15.7 Remarks

In this chapter we discussed a two-sample homogeneity test under the semi-parametric density-ratio models. We first showed that the moment-matching estimator introduced in Qin (1998) provides an optimal estimator of the ASC divergence with appropriate decomposition of the function f. We then gave a test statistic for a two-sample homogeneity test using the optimal ASC divergence estimator. We showed that the power function of the $\widehat{\mathrm{ASC}}_f$-based test does not depend on the choice of the ASC divergence up to the first order under the local alternative setup. Furthermore, the $\widehat{\mathrm{ASC}}_f$-based test and the empirical likelihood-score test (Fokianos et al., 2001) were shown to have asymptotically the same power. For misspecified density-ratio models, we showed that the $\widehat{\mathrm{ASC}}_f$-based test usually has greater power than the empirical likelihood-score test.

In numerical studies, the MI-based test and the empirical likelihood-ratio test gave the most reliable results. It is also notable that their powers were comparable to that of the Hotelling T^2-test even under the normal case. We experimentally observed that the null distributions of the MI-based test and the empirical likelihood-ratio test are approximated by the asymptotic distribution more accurately than that of the KL-based test, although the first-order asymptotic theory provided in Section 15.5 does not explain this empirical fact. Higher order asymptotic theory may be needed to better understand this tendency.

Although we focused on estimators of the form (15.7) in this chapter, a variety of estimators is available for divergence estimation. Along this line of research, remaining future works are to study the optimal estimator among *all* estimators of the ASC divergence and to specify how large the class of estimators (15.7) is among all estimators.

16

Non-Parametric Numerical Stability Analysis

As shown in Chapter 7, kernelized versions of unconstrained least-squares density-ratio estimation (i.e., uLSIF given in Chapter 6) and moment matching (i.e., KMM given in Chapter 3) share the same solution in theory. However, their optimization criteria are substantially different. In this chapter, we analyze their numerical stabilities and computational efficiencies through *condition numbers* (Kanamori et al., 2011c).

The framework of condition number analysis is described in Section 16.1, and then the relation between uLSIF and KMM is discussed in Section 16.2. In Section 16.3, we show that uLSIF possesses a smaller condition number than KMM, which implies that uLSIF is numerically more reliable and computationally more efficient than KMM. Then, in Section 16.4, we show that uLSIF has the smallest condition number among all ratio-fitting estimators. Finally, in Section 16.5, we compare condition numbers and computational efficiencies through numerical experiments. The chapter is concluded in Section 16.6.

16.1 Preliminaries

In this section we describe the density-ratio estimators that will be analyzed in this chapter.

First, let us briefly review the problem formulation and notation. Consider two probability densities $p^*_{\mathrm{nu}}(\boldsymbol{x})$ and $p^*_{\mathrm{de}}(\boldsymbol{x})$ on a probability space $\mathcal{X}$. We assume $p^*_{\mathrm{de}}(\boldsymbol{x}) > 0$ for all $\boldsymbol{x} \in \mathcal{X}$. Suppose that we are given two sets of i.i.d. samples,

$$\boldsymbol{x}_1^{\mathrm{nu}}, \ldots, \boldsymbol{x}_{n_{\mathrm{nu}}}^{\mathrm{nu}} \overset{\text{i.i.d.}}{\sim} p^*_{\mathrm{nu}} \quad \text{and} \quad \boldsymbol{x}_1^{\mathrm{de}}, \ldots, \boldsymbol{x}_{n_{\mathrm{de}}}^{\mathrm{de}} \overset{\text{i.i.d.}}{\sim} p^*_{\mathrm{de}}. \tag{16.1}$$

Our goal is to estimate the density ratio $r^*(\boldsymbol{x}) = \frac{p^*_{\mathrm{nu}}(\boldsymbol{x})}{p^*_{\mathrm{de}}(\boldsymbol{x})}$ based on the observed samples (16.1).

16.1.1 Kernel Mean Matching

The *kernel mean matching* (KMM) method allows us to directly obtain an estimate of $r^*(\boldsymbol{x})$ at $\boldsymbol{x}_1^{\mathrm{de}},\ldots,\boldsymbol{x}_{n_{\mathrm{de}}}^{\mathrm{de}}$ without going through density estimation (see Chapter 3).

The basic idea of KMM is to minimize the mean discrepancy between samples drawn from p_{nu}^* and p_{de}^* in a *universal reproducing kernel Hilbert space* (universal RKHS; Steinwart, 2001). We describe the definition of universal kernel and universal RKHS in the following.

Definition 16.1 (Definition 4.52 in Steinwart, 2001) *A continuous kernel K on a compact metric space $\mathcal{X}$ is called universal if the RKHS $\mathcal{R}$ of K is dense in the set of all continuous functions on $\mathcal{X}$; that is, for every continuous function g on $\mathcal{X}$ and all $\varepsilon > 0$, there exists $f \in \mathcal{R}$ such that $\|f - g\|_\infty < \varepsilon$, where $\|\cdot\|_\infty$ denotes the infinity norm. The corresponding RKHS is called a universal RKHS.*

The Gaussian kernel is an example of a universal kernel. Let $\mathcal{R}$ be a universal RKHS endowed with the kernel function $K : \mathcal{X} \times \mathcal{X} \to \mathbb{R}$. For any $\boldsymbol{x} \in \mathcal{X}$, the function $K(\cdot,\boldsymbol{x})$ is an element of $\mathcal{R}$. Suppose that the ture density-ratio function $r^*(\boldsymbol{x})$ is included in the RKHS $\mathcal{R}$. Then, it was shown that the solution of the following optimization problem agrees with r^* (Huang et al., 2007; Gretton et al., 2009):

$$\min_{r\in\mathcal{R}} \frac{1}{2}\left\| \int r(\boldsymbol{x})K(\cdot,\boldsymbol{x})p_{\mathrm{de}}^*(\boldsymbol{x})\mathrm{d}\boldsymbol{x} - \int K(\cdot,\boldsymbol{x})p_{\mathrm{nu}}^*(\boldsymbol{x})\mathrm{d}\boldsymbol{x} \right\|_{\mathcal{R}}^2$$

$$\text{s.t.} \int r(\boldsymbol{x})p_{\mathrm{de}}^*(\boldsymbol{x})\mathrm{d}\boldsymbol{x} = 1 \text{ and } r \geq 0,$$

where $\|\cdot\|_{\mathcal{R}}$ denotes the norm in the RKHS $\mathcal{R}$.

Indeed, when $r = r^*$, the above loss function vanishes. An empirical version of this problem is reduced to the following convex quadratic program:

$$\min_{r_1,\ldots,r_{n_{\mathrm{de}}}} \left[\frac{1}{2n_{\mathrm{de}}} \sum_{j,j'=1}^{n_{\mathrm{de}}} r_j r_{j'} K(\boldsymbol{x}_j^{\mathrm{de}},\boldsymbol{x}_{j'}^{\mathrm{de}}) - \frac{1}{n_{\mathrm{nu}}} \sum_{i=1}^{n_{\mathrm{nu}}}\sum_{j=1}^{n_{\mathrm{de}}} r_j K(\boldsymbol{x}_j^{\mathrm{de}},\boldsymbol{x}_i^{\mathrm{nu}}) \right]$$

$$\text{s.t.} \left| \frac{1}{n_{\mathrm{de}}} \sum_{j=1}^{n_{\mathrm{de}}} r_j - 1 \right| \leq \epsilon \text{ and } 0 \leq r_1,\ldots,r_{n_{\mathrm{de}}} \leq B. \tag{16.2}$$

The tuning parameters $B \geq 0$ and $\epsilon \geq 0$ control the regularization effects. The solution $\widehat{r}_1,\ldots,\widehat{r}_{n_{\mathrm{de}}}$ is an estimate of the density ratio at the samples from p_{de}^*, that is, $r^*(\boldsymbol{x}_1^{\mathrm{de}}),\ldots,r^*(\boldsymbol{x}_{n_{\mathrm{de}}}^{\mathrm{de}})$. Note that KMM does not estimate the entire density-ratio function r^* on $\mathcal{X}$, only its values at sample points.

16.1.2 M-Estimator Based on ASC Divergence

An estimator of the density ratio based on the *Ali–Silvey–Csiszár* (ASC) divergence (a.k.a. the *f-divergence*) described in Section 7.3.1 is reviewed here.

Let $f : \mathbb{R} \to \mathbb{R}$ be a convex function. Then the ASC divergence from p^*_{nu} to p^*_{de} is defined as follows (Ali and Silvey, 1966; Csiszár, 1967):

$$\mathrm{ASC}_f(p^*_{\mathrm{nu}} \| p^*_{\mathrm{de}}) := \int f\left(\frac{p^*_{\mathrm{nu}}(\boldsymbol{x})}{p^*_{\mathrm{de}}(\boldsymbol{x})}\right) p^*_{\mathrm{de}}(\boldsymbol{x})\mathrm{d}\boldsymbol{x}. \tag{16.3}$$

Let the *conjugate dual function* g of f be

$$g(z) := \sup_{u\in\mathbb{R}}\{zu - f(u)\} = -\inf_{u\in\mathbb{R}}\{f(u) - zu\}.$$

When f is a convex function, we also have

$$f(u) = -\inf_{z\in\mathbb{R}}\{g(z) - uz\}. \tag{16.4}$$

See Section 12 of Rockafellar (1970) for details. Substituting Eq. (16.4) into Eq. (16.3), we obtain the following expression of the ASC divergence:

$$\mathrm{ASC}_f(p^*_{\mathrm{nu}} \| p^*_{\mathrm{de}}) = -\inf_r \left[\int g(r(\boldsymbol{x}))p^*_{\mathrm{de}}(\boldsymbol{x})\mathrm{d}\boldsymbol{x} - \int r(\boldsymbol{x})p^*_{\mathrm{nu}}(\boldsymbol{x})\mathrm{d}\boldsymbol{x}\right], \tag{16.5}$$

where the infimum is taken over all measurable functions $r : \mathcal{X} \to \mathbb{R}$. The infimum is attained at the function r such that

$$\frac{p^*_{\mathrm{nu}}(\boldsymbol{x})}{p^*_{\mathrm{de}}(\boldsymbol{x})} = g'(r(\boldsymbol{x})), \tag{16.6}$$

where g' is the derivative of g. Approximating Eq. (16.5) with the empirical distributions, we obtain the empirical loss function. This estimator is referred to as the *M-estimator* of the density ratio. An M-estimator based on the Kullback–Leibler divergence is derived from $g(z) = -1 - \log(-z)$.

When an RKHS $\mathcal{R}$ is employed as a statistical model, the M-estimator is given by

$$\inf_{r\in\mathcal{R}} \left[\frac{1}{n_{\mathrm{de}}}\sum_{j=1}^{n_{\mathrm{de}}} g(r(\boldsymbol{x}^{\mathrm{de}}_j)) - \frac{1}{n_{\mathrm{nu}}}\sum_{i=1}^{n_{\mathrm{nu}}} r(\boldsymbol{x}^{\mathrm{nu}}_i) + \frac{\lambda}{2}\|r\|^2_{\mathcal{R}}\right], \tag{16.7}$$

where the regularization term $\frac{\lambda}{2}\|r\|^2_{\mathcal{R}}$ with the regularization parameter λ is introduced to avoid overfitting. Using the solution $\widehat{r}$ of the above optimization problem, a density-ratio estimator is given by $g'(\widehat{r}(\boldsymbol{x}))$ [see Eq. (16.6)].

16.1.3 Kernel uLSIF

Let us consider a kernelized variant of uLSIF (which we refer to as *kernel uLSIF*; KuLSIF), which will be shown to possess good theoretical properties. Here we formalize the KuLSIF algorithm and briefly show its fundamental properties. Then, in the following sections, we analyze the numerical stability and computational efficiency of KuLSIF.

The KuLSIF optimization problem is given as Eq. (16.7) with $g(u) = u^2/2$:

$$\min_{r \in \mathcal{R}} \left[\frac{1}{2n_{\mathrm{de}}} \sum_{j=1}^{n_{\mathrm{de}}} r(\boldsymbol{x}_j^{\mathrm{de}})^2 - \frac{1}{n_{\mathrm{nu}}} \sum_{i=1}^{n_{\mathrm{nu}}} r(\boldsymbol{x}_i^{\mathrm{nu}}) + \frac{\lambda}{2} \|r\|_{\mathcal{R}}^2 \right]. \tag{16.8}$$

For an infinite-dimensional RKHS $\mathcal{R}$, Eq. (16.8) is an infinite-dimensional optimization problem and thus is computationally intractable. However, the *representer theorem* (Kimeldorf and Wahba, 1971) is applicable to RKHSs, which shows that the estimator $\widehat{r}$ always lies in a finite-dimensional subspace of $\mathcal{R}$:

Theorem 16.2 *A solution of Eq. (16.8) is of the form*

$$\widehat{r}(\boldsymbol{x}) = \sum_{j=1}^{n_{\mathrm{de}}} \alpha_i K(\boldsymbol{x}, \boldsymbol{x}_j^{\mathrm{de}}) + \sum_{i=1}^{n_{\mathrm{nu}}} \beta_i K(\boldsymbol{x}, \boldsymbol{x}_i^{\mathrm{nu}}),$$

where $\alpha_1, \ldots, \alpha_{n_{\mathrm{de}}}, \beta_1, \ldots, \beta_{n_{\mathrm{nu}}} \in \mathbb{R}$.

Moreover, for KuLSIF, the parameters $\alpha_1, \ldots, \alpha_{n_{\mathrm{de}}}, \beta_1, \ldots, \beta_{n_{\mathrm{nu}}}$ can be estimated analytically. Let $\boldsymbol{K}_{\mathrm{de,de}}$, $\boldsymbol{K}_{\mathrm{de,nu}}$, and $\boldsymbol{K}_{\mathrm{nu,nu}}$ be the Gram matrices, that is, $[\boldsymbol{K}_{\mathrm{de,de}}]_{j,j'} = K(\boldsymbol{x}_j^{\mathrm{de}}, \boldsymbol{x}_{j'}^{\mathrm{de}})$, $[\boldsymbol{K}_{\mathrm{de,nu}}]_{j,i} = K(\boldsymbol{x}_j^{\mathrm{de}}, \boldsymbol{x}_i^{\mathrm{nu}})$, and $[\boldsymbol{K}_{\mathrm{nu,nu}}]_{i,i'} = K(\boldsymbol{x}_i^{\mathrm{nu}}, \boldsymbol{x}_{i'}^{\mathrm{nu}})$, where $j, j' = 1, \ldots, n_{\mathrm{de}}$ and $i, i' = 1, \ldots, n_{\mathrm{nu}}$. Then, for KuLSIF, the parameters $\boldsymbol{\alpha} = (\alpha_1, \ldots, \alpha_{n_{\mathrm{de}}})^\top$ and $\boldsymbol{\beta} = (\beta_1, \ldots, \beta_{n_{\mathrm{nu}}})^\top$ in the estimator $\widehat{r}$ can be optimized analytically as follows.

Theorem 16.3 (Analytic solution of KuLSIF) *Suppose that the regularization parameter λ is strictly positive. Then the KuLSIF solutions $\widehat{\boldsymbol{\alpha}}$ and $\widehat{\boldsymbol{\beta}}$ are given as*

$$\widehat{\boldsymbol{\alpha}} = -\frac{1}{n_{\mathrm{nu}}\lambda} \left(\boldsymbol{K}_{\mathrm{de,de}} + n_{\mathrm{de}} \lambda \boldsymbol{I}_{n_{\mathrm{de}}} \right)^{-1} \boldsymbol{K}_{\mathrm{de,nu}} \boldsymbol{1}_{n_{\mathrm{nu}}}, \tag{16.9}$$

$$\widehat{\boldsymbol{\beta}} = \frac{1}{n_{\mathrm{nu}}\lambda} \boldsymbol{1}_{n_{\mathrm{nu}}}, \tag{16.10}$$

where $\boldsymbol{I}_n$ is the n-dimensional identity matrix and $\boldsymbol{1}_n$ are the n-dimensional vectors with all ones.

Remark. *It can be shown that the solution $\widehat{\boldsymbol{\beta}}$ is given by Eq. (16.10) for any ASC divergence (16.7) [but $\widehat{\boldsymbol{\alpha}}$ is not given by Eq. (16.9) in general]. The density-ratio estimator based on the ASC divergence is given by solving the following optimization problem:*

$$\inf_{\alpha_1, \ldots, \alpha_{n_{\mathrm{de}}} \in \mathbb{R}} \left[\frac{1}{n_{\mathrm{de}}} \sum_{j=1}^{n_{\mathrm{de}}} g(r(\boldsymbol{x}_j^{\mathrm{de}})) - \frac{1}{n_{\mathrm{nu}}} \sum_{i=1}^{n_{\mathrm{nu}}} r(\boldsymbol{x}_i^{\mathrm{nu}}) + \frac{\lambda}{2} \|r\|_{\mathcal{R}}^2 \right], \tag{16.11}$$

where $r(\boldsymbol{x}) = \sum_{j=1}^{n_{\mathrm{de}}} \alpha_j K(\boldsymbol{x}, \boldsymbol{x}_j^{\mathrm{de}}) + \frac{1}{n_{\mathrm{nu}}\lambda} \sum_{i=1}^{n_{\mathrm{nu}}} K(\boldsymbol{x}, \boldsymbol{x}_i^{\mathrm{nu}})$.

When $g(z) = z^2/2$, the problem (16.11) is reduced to

$$\min_{\boldsymbol{\alpha} \in \mathbb{R}^{n_{\mathrm{de}}}} \left[\frac{1}{2} \boldsymbol{\alpha}^\top \left(\frac{1}{n_{\mathrm{de}}} \boldsymbol{K}_{\mathrm{de,de}}^2 + \lambda \boldsymbol{K}_{\mathrm{de,de}} \right) \boldsymbol{\alpha} + \frac{1}{n_{\mathrm{nu}} n_{\mathrm{de}} \lambda} \boldsymbol{1}_{n_{\mathrm{nu}}}^\top \boldsymbol{K}_{\mathrm{de,nu}}^\top \boldsymbol{K}_{\mathrm{de,de}} \boldsymbol{\alpha} \right], \tag{16.12}$$

where the term independent of the parameter $\boldsymbol{\alpha}$ is dropped. This is the optimization criterion for KuLSIF.

For a positive definite matrix $\boldsymbol{A}$, the solution of a linear equation $\boldsymbol{Ax} = \boldsymbol{b}$ is given as the minimizer of $\frac{1}{2}\boldsymbol{x}^\top \boldsymbol{Ax} - \boldsymbol{b}^\top \boldsymbol{x}$. Applying this fact to Eq. (16.9), we can obtain the solution $\widehat{\boldsymbol{\alpha}}$ for KuLSIF by solving the following optimization problem:

$$\min_{\alpha \in \mathbb{R}^{n_{\mathrm{de}}}} \left[\frac{1}{2} \boldsymbol{\alpha}^\top \left(\frac{1}{n_{\mathrm{de}}} \boldsymbol{K}_{\mathrm{de,de}} + \lambda \boldsymbol{I}_{n_{\mathrm{de}}} \right) \boldsymbol{\alpha} + \frac{1}{n_{\mathrm{nu}} n_{\mathrm{de}} \lambda} \boldsymbol{1}_{n_{\mathrm{nu}}}^\top \boldsymbol{K}_{\mathrm{de,nu}}^\top \boldsymbol{\alpha} \right]. \tag{16.13}$$

In the following, the estimator obtained by solving the optimization problem (16.13) is referred to as *reduced-KuLSIF* (R-KuLSIF). Although KuLSIF and R-KuLSIF share the same optimal solution, their loss functions are different [cf. Eq.(16.12)]. As shown in the following, this difference yields significant improvement of the numerical stability and computational efficiency.

16.2 Relation between KuLSIF and KMM

In this section we investigate the relation between KuLSIF and KMM. In Section 16.2.1 we reformulate KuLSIF and KMM and compare their loss functions. Then, in Section 16.2.2, we extend the comparison of the loss functions to general ASC divergences.

16.2.1 Loss Functions of KuLSIF and KMM

We assume that the true density ratio $r^* = p^*_{\mathrm{nu}}/p^*_{\mathrm{de}}$ is included in the RKHS $\mathcal{R}$. As shown in Section 16.1.3, the loss function of KMM on $\mathcal{R}$ is defined as

$$L_{\mathrm{KMM}}(r) := \frac{1}{2} \|\boldsymbol{\phi}(r)\|^2_{\mathcal{R}},$$

where

$$\boldsymbol{\phi}(r) := \int K(\cdot, \boldsymbol{x}) r(\boldsymbol{x}) p^*_{\mathrm{de}}(\boldsymbol{x}) \mathrm{d}\boldsymbol{x} - \int K(\cdot, \boldsymbol{x}) p^*_{\mathrm{nu}}(\boldsymbol{x}) \mathrm{d}\boldsymbol{x} \in \mathcal{R}.$$

In the estimation phase, an empirical approximation of L_{KMM} is optimized in the KMM algorithm. On the other hand, the (unregularized) loss function of KuLSIF is given by

$$L_{\mathrm{KuLSIF}}(r) := \frac{1}{2} \int r(\boldsymbol{x})^2 p^*_{\mathrm{de}}(\boldsymbol{x}) \mathrm{d}\boldsymbol{x} - \int r(\boldsymbol{x}) p^*_{\mathrm{nu}}(\boldsymbol{x}) \mathrm{d}\boldsymbol{x}.$$

Both L_{KMM} and L_{KuLSIF} are minimized at the true density ratio $r^* \in \mathcal{R}$. Although some linear constraints may be introduced in the optimization phase, we study the optimization problems of L_{KMM} and L_{KuLSIF} without constraints. This is because when the sample size tends to infinity, the optimal solutions of L_{KMM} and L_{KuLSIF} without constraints automatically satisfy the required constraints, such as $\int r(\boldsymbol{x}) p^*_{\mathrm{de}}(\boldsymbol{x}) \mathrm{d}\boldsymbol{x} = 1$ and $r \geq 0$.

We consider the extremal condition of $L_{\mathrm{KuLSIF}}(r)$ at r^*. Substituting $r = r^* + \delta \cdot v$ for $\delta \in \mathbb{R}$ and $v \in \mathcal{R}$ into $L_{\mathrm{KuLSIF}}(r)$, we have

$$\begin{aligned}
&L_{\mathrm{KuLSIF}}(r^* + \delta v) - L_{\mathrm{KuLSIF}}(r^*) \\
&= \delta \left\{ \int r^*(\boldsymbol{x}) v(\boldsymbol{x}) p^*_{\mathrm{de}}(\boldsymbol{x}) \mathrm{d}\boldsymbol{x} - \int v(\boldsymbol{x}) p^*_{\mathrm{nu}}(\boldsymbol{x}) \mathrm{d}\boldsymbol{x} \right\} + \frac{\delta^2}{2} \int v(\boldsymbol{x})^2 p^*_{\mathrm{de}}(\boldsymbol{x}) \mathrm{d}\boldsymbol{x}.
\end{aligned}$$

Because $L_{\mathrm{KuLSIF}}(r^* + \delta v)$ is minimized at $\delta = 0$, the derivative of $L_{\mathrm{KuLSIF}}(r^* + \delta v)$ at $\delta = 0$ vanishes, that is,

$$\int r^*(\boldsymbol{x}) v(\boldsymbol{x}) p^*_{\mathrm{de}}(\boldsymbol{x}) \mathrm{d}\boldsymbol{x} - \int v(\boldsymbol{x}) p^*_{\mathrm{nu}}(\boldsymbol{x}) \mathrm{d}\boldsymbol{x} = 0.$$

Using the reproducing property of the kernel function K, we can express the above equality in terms of $\boldsymbol{\phi}(r^*)$ as:

$$\begin{aligned}
&\int r^*(\boldsymbol{x}) v(\boldsymbol{x}) p^*_{\mathrm{de}}(\boldsymbol{x}) \mathrm{d}\boldsymbol{x} - \int v(\boldsymbol{x}) p^*_{\mathrm{nu}}(\boldsymbol{x}) \mathrm{d}\boldsymbol{x} \\
&= \int r^*(\boldsymbol{x}) \langle K(\cdot, \boldsymbol{x}), v \rangle_{\mathcal{R}} p^*_{\mathrm{de}}(\boldsymbol{x}) \mathrm{d}\boldsymbol{x} - \int \langle K(\cdot, \boldsymbol{x}), v \rangle_{\mathcal{R}} p^*_{\mathrm{nu}}(\boldsymbol{x}) \mathrm{d}\boldsymbol{x} \\
&= \left\langle \int K(\cdot, \boldsymbol{x}) r^*(\boldsymbol{x}) p^*_{\mathrm{de}}(\boldsymbol{x}) \mathrm{d}\boldsymbol{x} - \int K(\cdot, \boldsymbol{x}) p^*_{\mathrm{nu}}(\boldsymbol{x}) \mathrm{d}\boldsymbol{x},\ v \right\rangle_{\mathcal{R}} \\
&= \langle \boldsymbol{\phi}(r^*),\ v \rangle_{\mathcal{R}} = 0, \qquad (16.14)
\end{aligned}$$

where $\langle \cdot, \cdot \rangle_{\mathcal{R}}$ denotes the inner product in the RKHS $\mathcal{R}$. Because Eq. (16.14) holds for arbitrary $v \in \mathcal{R}$, we have $\boldsymbol{\phi}(r^*) = 0$.

The above expression implies that $\boldsymbol{\phi}(r)$ is the *Gâteaux derivative* (see Section 4.2 of Zeidler, 1986) of L_{KuLSIF} at $r \in \mathcal{R}$; that is,

$$\frac{\mathrm{d}}{\mathrm{d}\delta} L_{\mathrm{KuLSIF}}(r + \delta \cdot v)\big|_{\delta=0} = \langle \boldsymbol{\phi}(r), v \rangle_{\mathcal{R}}$$

holds for all $v \in \mathcal{R}$. See Section 16.2.2 for the definition of the Gâteaux derivative. Let $\mathrm{D}L_{\mathrm{KuLSIF}}$ $(= \boldsymbol{\phi})$ be the Gâteaux derivative of L_{KuLSIF} over the RKHS $\mathcal{R}$. Then the equality $L_{\mathrm{KMM}}(r) = \frac{1}{2} \|\mathrm{D}L_{\mathrm{KuLSIF}}(r)\|^2_{\mathcal{R}}$ holds. Note that a similar relation also holds for the M-estimator based on the Kullback–Leibler divergence with log-linear models (Tsuboi et al., 2009).

Now we illustrate the relation between KuLSIF and KMM by showing an analogous optimization example in the Euclidean space. Let $h : \mathbb{R}^d \to \mathbb{R}$ be a differentiable function, and consider the optimization problem $\min_{\boldsymbol{x} \in \mathbb{R}^d} h(\boldsymbol{x})$. At the optimal solution $\boldsymbol{x}^*$, the extremal condition $\nabla h(\boldsymbol{x}^*) = 0$ should hold, where ∇h is the gradient of h. Thus, instead of minimizing h, minimizing $\|\nabla h(\boldsymbol{x})\|^2$ also provides the minimizer of h. This actually corresponds to the relation between

KuLSIF and KMM:

$$\text{KuLSIF} \iff \min_{x \in \mathbb{R}^d} h(x),$$

$$\text{KMM} \iff \min_{x \in \mathbb{R}^d} \frac{1}{2}\|\nabla h(x)\|^2.$$

In other words, to find the solution of the equation $\phi(r) = 0$, KMM tries to minimize the norm of $\phi(r)$. The "dual" expression of $\phi(r) = 0$ is given as

$$\langle \phi(r), v \rangle_{\mathcal{R}} = 0, \quad {}^{\forall} v \in \mathcal{R}. \tag{16.15}$$

By "integrating" $\langle \phi(r), v \rangle_{\mathcal{R}}$, we obtain the loss function L_{KuLSIF}.

16.2.2 Generalization to ASC Divergence

The discussion in the previous subsection can be extended to the general ASC divergence approach. The loss function of the M-estimator (Nguyen et al., 2010) is defined by

$$L_g(r) = \int g(r(x)) p^*_{\text{de}}(x)\mathrm{d}x - \int r(x) p^*_{\text{nu}}(x)\mathrm{d}x, \quad r \in \mathcal{R}.$$

The Gâteaux derivative of L_g over $\mathcal{R}$ is defined as the function $\mathrm{D}L_g : \mathcal{R} \to \mathcal{R}$ such that

$$\lim_{\delta \to 0} \frac{1}{\delta}\left[L_g(r + \delta \cdot v) - L_g(r)\right] = \langle \mathrm{D}L_g(r), v \rangle_{\mathcal{R}}, \quad {}^{\forall} v \in \mathcal{R}.$$

Then the following theorem holds.

Theorem 16.4 *Suppose that g is the once continuously differentiable and convex function, and that the kernel function K of the RKHS $\mathcal{R}$ satisfies* $\sup_{x \in \mathcal{X}} K(x,x) < \infty$. *Suppose that, for any $r \in \mathcal{R}$, $g(r)$ and $g'(r)$ are integrable with respect to the probability $p^*_{\text{de}}(x)$. Then, the following assertions hold.*

1. *The Gâteaux derivative of L_g is given as*

$$\mathrm{D}L_g(r) = \int K(\cdot, x) g'(r(x)) p^*_{\text{de}}(x)\mathrm{d}x - \int K(\cdot, x) p^*_{\text{nu}}(x)\mathrm{d}x.$$

2. *Let $L_{g\text{-}KMM} : \mathcal{R} \to \mathbb{R}$ be*

$$L_{g\text{-}KMM}(r) = \frac{1}{2}\|\mathrm{D}L_g(r)\|^2_{\mathcal{R}},$$

and suppose that $r^*(x) = p^*_{\text{nu}}(x)/p^*_{\text{de}}(x)$ is represented by $r^* = g'(r_g)$ for some $r_g \in \mathcal{R}$. Then, r_g is the minimizer of both L_g and $L_{g\text{-}KMM}$.

The quadratic function $g(z) = z^2/2$ and a bounded kernel satisfy the assumption of Theorem 16.4. Indeed, for any bounded kernel, the inequality $|r(x)| \leq$

$\|r\|_{\mathcal{R}} \sup_{x\in\mathcal{X}} \sqrt{K(x,x)} < \infty$ holds, and thus $r^2/2$ and r are integrable with respect to the probability p^*_{de}.

On the other hand, for the function $g(z) = -1 - \log(-z)$ [and $g'(z) = -1/z$], which leads to the M-estimator using the Kullback–Leibler divergence, the Gâteaux derivative of L_g is given as

$$\mathrm{D}L_g(r) = -\int K(\cdot,x)\frac{1}{r(x)}p^*_{\mathrm{de}}(x)\mathrm{d}x - \int K(\cdot,x)p^*_{\mathrm{nu}}(x)\mathrm{d}x.$$

In this case, the functional $\mathrm{D}L_g(r)$ is not necessarily defined for all $r \in \mathcal{R}$; for example, $\mathrm{D}L_g(r)$ does not exist for $r = 0$.

Nevertheless, the second statement in Theorem 16.4 is still valid for the Kullback–Leibler divergence. Suppose that there exists an $r_g \in \mathcal{R}$ such that $r^* = -1/r_g$. Then there exists a positive constant $c > 0$ such that $r^* \geq c > 0$, because $|r_g(x)| \leq \|r_g\|_{\mathcal{R}} \sup_{x\in\mathcal{X}} \sqrt{K(x,x)} < \infty$ holds. The condition that r^* is bounded below by a positive constant is assumed when the Kullback–Leibler divergence is used in the estimator (Nguyen et al., 2010; Sugiyama et al., 2008). On the other hand, for the quadratic function $g(z) = z^2/2$, such an assumption is not required.

16.3 Condition Number Analysis

In this section we investigate *condition numbers* in density-ratio estimation. We first introduce the basic concept and fundamental properties of the condition number in Section 16.3.1. Then, in Section 16.3.2, we analyze the condition numbers of various density-ratio estimators.

16.3.1 Condition Numbers

The *condition number* plays a crucial role in *numerical analysis* and *optimization* (Demmel, 1997; Luenberger and Ye, 2008; Sankar et al., 2006).

The condition number of a symmetric positive definite matrix A is defined by $\lambda_{\max}/\lambda_{\min}$ (≥ 1), where $\lambda_{\max}$ and $\lambda_{\min}$ are the maximal and minimal eigenvalues of A, respectively. The condition number of A is denoted by $\kappa(A)$. More generally, the condition number for a non-symmetric (i.e., rectangular) matrix is defined through singular values.

Round-Off Error in Numerical Analysis

The condition number governs the *round-off error* of the solution of a linear equation.

Let us consider a linear equation $Ax = b$. The matrix A with a large condition number results in a large upper bound on the relative error of the solution x. More precisely, in the perturbed linear equation

$$(A + \delta A)(x + \delta x) = b + \delta b,$$

the relative error of the solution is given as follows (Section 2.2 of Demmel, 1997):

$$\frac{\|\delta x\|}{\|x\|} \leq \frac{\kappa(A)}{1-\kappa(A)\|\delta A\|/\|A\|}\left(\frac{\|\delta A\|}{\|A\|}+\frac{\|\delta b\|}{\|b\|}\right).$$

Hence, smaller condition numbers are preferable in numerical computations.

Convergence Rate in Optimization

The condition number provides an upper bound of the convergence rate for optimization algorithms.

Let us consider a minimization problem $\min_{x \in \mathbb{R}^n} h(x)$, where $h : \mathbb{R}^n \to \mathbb{R}$ is a differentiable function and x^* is a local optimal solution. We consider an iterative algorithm that generates a sequence $\{x_i\}_{i=1}^{\infty}$. In various iterative algorithms, the sequence is generated by

$$x_{i+1} = x_i - S_i^{-1} \nabla h(x_i), \quad i = 1, \ldots,$$

where S_i is a symmetric positive definite matrix that is an approximation of the *Hessian matrix* of h at x^*, that is, $S_i \approx \nabla^2 h(x^*)$. Then, under a mild assumption, the sequence $\{x_i\}_{i=1}^{\infty}$ converges to x^*. Practical numerical techniques such as *scaling* and *pre-conditioning* are also incorporated in this form with a certain choice of S_i.

According to the *modified Newton-method theorem* (Section 10.1 of Luenberger and Ye, 2008), the convergence rate of such iterative algorithms is given as

$$\|x_k - x^*\| = O\left(\prod_{i=1}^{k} \frac{\kappa_i - 1}{\kappa_i + 1}\right), \tag{16.16}$$

where κ_i is the condition number of $S_i^{-1/2}(\nabla^2 h(x^*))S_i^{-1/2}$. Although the modified Newton-method theorem was shown only for convex quadratic functions in Luenberger and Ye (2008), the rate-of-convergence behavior is essentially the same for general non-quadratic objective functions. Regarding non-quadratic functions, details are presented in Section 8.6 of Luenberger and Ye (2008). Equation (16.16) implies that the convergence rate of the sequence $\{x_i\}_{i=1}^{\infty}$ is fast if the condition numbers $\kappa_i, i = 1, \ldots$ are small.

When the condition number of the Hessian matrix $\nabla^2 h(x^*)$ is large, there is a trade-off between the numerical accuracy and the convergence rate in optimization. Let us illustrate this trade-off using the following examples:

- When the *Newton method* is employed, S_k is given as $\nabla^2 h(x_k)$. Because of the continuity of $\nabla^2 h$, if $\kappa(\nabla^2 h(x^*))$ is large, the condition number of $S_k = \nabla^2 h(x_k)$ will also be large and thus the numerical computation of $S_k^{-1} \nabla h(x_k)$ will become unstable.
- When the *quasi-Newton methods* such as the *Broyden–Fletcher–Goldfarb–Shanno* (BFGS) method and the *Davidon–Fletcher–Powell* method (Luenberger and Ye, 2008) are employed, S_k or S_k^{-1} is successively computed based on the information of the gradient. If $\kappa(\nabla^2 h(x^*))$ is large, $\kappa(S_k)$ is also likely

to be large, and thus the numerical computation of $\boldsymbol{S}_k^{-1}\nabla h(\boldsymbol{x}_k)$ will not be reliable. This implies that the round-off error caused by nearly singular Hessian matrices significantly affects the accuracy of the quasi-Newton methods. Consequently, $\boldsymbol{S}_k^{-1}\nabla h(\boldsymbol{x}_k)$ is not guaranteed to be a proper descent direction of the objective function h.

In optimization problems with large condition numbers, the numerical computation tends to be unreliable. To avoid numerical instability, the Hessian matrix is often modified so that $\boldsymbol{S}_k$ has a moderate condition number. For example, in the optimization toolbox in MATLAB®, gradient descent methods are implemented by the function `fminunc`. The default method in `fminunc` is the BFGS method with an update through the *Cholesky factorization* of $\boldsymbol{S}_k$ (not $\boldsymbol{S}_k^{-1}$). Even if the positive definiteness of $\boldsymbol{S}_k$ is violated by the round-off error, the Cholesky factorization immediately detects the negativity of the eigenvalues and the positive definiteness of $\boldsymbol{S}_k$ is recovered by adding a correction term. When the modified Cholesky factorization is used, the condition number of $\boldsymbol{S}_k$ is guaranteed to be bounded above by some constant. See Moré and Sorensen (1984) for details.

16.3.2 Condition Number Analysis of Density-Ratio Estimation

Here we analyze the condition numbers of KuLSIF and KMM.

Preliminaries

Let us consider the optimization problems of KuLSIF and KMM on an RKHS $\mathcal{R}$ endowed with a kernel function K over a set $\mathcal{X}$. Given the samples (16.1), the optimization problems of KuLSIF and KMM are defined as

$$\text{(KuLSIF)} \quad \min_{r\in\mathcal{R}} \left[\frac{1}{2n_{\mathrm{de}}}\sum_{j=1}^{n_{\mathrm{de}}}(r(\boldsymbol{x}_j^{\mathrm{de}}))^2 - \frac{1}{n_{\mathrm{nu}}}\sum_{i=1}^{n_{\mathrm{nu}}} r(\boldsymbol{x}_i^{\mathrm{nu}}) + \frac{\lambda}{2}\|r\|_{\mathcal{R}}^2\right],$$

$$\text{(KMM)} \quad \min_{r\in\mathcal{R}} \frac{1}{2}\|\widehat{\boldsymbol{\phi}}(r)+\lambda r\|_{\mathcal{R}}^2,$$

where $\widehat{\boldsymbol{\phi}}(r)=\frac{1}{n_{\mathrm{de}}}\sum_{j=1}^{n_{\mathrm{de}}} K(\cdot,\boldsymbol{x}_j^{\mathrm{de}})r(\boldsymbol{x}_j^{\mathrm{de}})-\frac{1}{n_{\mathrm{nu}}}\sum_{i=1}^{n_{\mathrm{nu}}} K(\cdot,\boldsymbol{x}_i^{\mathrm{nu}})$. Here, $\widehat{\boldsymbol{\phi}}(r)+\lambda r$ is the Gâteaux derivative of the loss function for KuLSIF including the regularization term. In the original KMM method, the density-ratio values at denominator samples $\boldsymbol{x}_1^{\mathrm{de}},\ldots,\boldsymbol{x}_{n_{\mathrm{de}}}^{\mathrm{de}}$ are optimized (Huang et al., 2007). Here we consider its *inductive* variant; that is, the entire density-ratio function $r^*=p_{\mathrm{nu}}^*/p_{\mathrm{de}}^*$ on $\mathcal{X}$ is estimated using the loss function of KMM.

According to Theorem 16.3, the optimal solution of equation (KuLSIF) is given as a form of

$$\widehat{r}=\sum_{j=1}^{n_{\mathrm{de}}}\alpha_j K(\cdot,\boldsymbol{x}_j^{\mathrm{de}})+\frac{1}{n_{\mathrm{nu}}\lambda}\sum_{i=1}^{n_{\mathrm{nu}}} K(\cdot,\boldsymbol{x}_i^{\mathrm{nu}}).$$

Note that the optimal solution of equation (KMM) is also given by the same form. Thus, the variables to be optimized in (KuLSIF) and (KMM) are $\alpha_1,\ldots,\alpha_{n_{\mathrm{de}}}$.

Condition Number Analysis of KuLSIF, KMM, and R-KuLSIF

Now we investigate the numerical efficiencies of (KuLSIF) and (KMM).

When we solve the minimization problem $\min_{\boldsymbol{x}} h(\boldsymbol{x})$, it is not recommended to minimize the norm of the gradient $\min_{\boldsymbol{x}} \|\nabla h(\boldsymbol{x})\|^2$, because the problem $\min_{\boldsymbol{x}} \|\nabla h(\boldsymbol{x})\|^2$ generally has a larger condition number than $\min_{\boldsymbol{x}} h(\boldsymbol{x})$ (Luenberger and Ye, 2008, Section 8.7). For example, let h be the convex quadratic function defined as $h(\boldsymbol{x}) = \frac{1}{2}\boldsymbol{x}^\top \boldsymbol{A}\boldsymbol{x} - \boldsymbol{b}^\top \boldsymbol{x}$ with a positive definite matrix $\boldsymbol{A}$. Then the condition number of the Hessian matrix is given by $\kappa(\boldsymbol{A})$, where $\kappa(\boldsymbol{A})$ denotes the condition number of $\boldsymbol{A}$. On the other hand, the Hessian matrix of the function $\|\nabla h(\boldsymbol{x})\|^2 = \|\boldsymbol{A}\boldsymbol{x} - \boldsymbol{b}\|^2$ is given by $\kappa(\boldsymbol{A}^2) = \kappa(\boldsymbol{A})^2$; that is, the condition number is squared and thus becomes larger or unchanged (recall that the condition number is larger than or equal to one). In the following we show that the same argument applies to equations (KuLSIF) and (KMM).

The Hessian matrices of the objective functions of equations (KuLSIF) and (KMM) are given as

$$\boldsymbol{H}_{\text{KuLSIF}} = \frac{1}{n_{\text{de}}}\boldsymbol{K}_{\text{de,de}}^2 + \lambda \boldsymbol{K}_{\text{de,de}},$$

$$\boldsymbol{H}_{\text{KMM}} = \frac{1}{n_{\text{de}}^2}\boldsymbol{K}_{\text{de,de}}^3 + \frac{2\lambda}{n_{\text{de}}}\boldsymbol{K}_{\text{de,de}}^2 + \lambda^2 \boldsymbol{K}_{\text{de,de}}.$$

$\boldsymbol{H}_{\text{KuLSIF}}$ is derived from Eq. (16.12), and $\boldsymbol{H}_{\text{KMM}}$ is given by a direct computation based on (KMM). Then we obtain

$$\kappa(\boldsymbol{H}_{\text{KuLSIF}}) = \kappa(\boldsymbol{K}_{\text{de,de}})\kappa\left(\frac{1}{n_{\text{de}}}\boldsymbol{K}_{\text{de,de}} + \lambda \boldsymbol{I}_{n_{\text{de}}}\right),$$

$$\kappa(\boldsymbol{H}_{\text{KMM}}) = \kappa(\boldsymbol{K}_{\text{de,de}})\kappa\left(\frac{1}{n_{\text{de}}}\boldsymbol{K}_{\text{de,de}} + \lambda \boldsymbol{I}_{n_{\text{de}}}\right)^2.$$

Because the condition number is larger than or equal to one, the inequality

$$\kappa(\boldsymbol{H}_{\text{KuLSIF}}) \le \kappa(\boldsymbol{H}_{\text{KMM}})$$

always holds. This implies that the convergence rate of KuLSIF will be faster than that of KMM, when an iterative optimization algorithm is used.

In the R-KuLSIF (16.13), the Hessian matrix of the objective function is given by

$$\boldsymbol{H}_{\text{R-KuLSIF}} = \frac{1}{n_{\text{de}}}\boldsymbol{K}_{\text{de,de}} + \lambda \boldsymbol{I}_{n_{\text{de}}},$$

and thus the condition number of $\boldsymbol{H}_{\text{R-KuLSIF}}$ satisfies

$$\kappa(\boldsymbol{H}_{\text{R-KuLSIF}}) \le \kappa(\boldsymbol{H}_{\text{KuLSIF}}) \le \kappa(\boldsymbol{H}_{\text{KMM}}).$$

Therefore, the R-KuLSIF has an advantage in the efficiency and the robustness of numerical computation. This theoretical analysis will be illustrated numerically in Section 16.5.

Condition Number Analysis of M-Estimators

According to Theorem 16.4, we expect that the condition number of the M-estimator based on L_g will be smaller than that of KMM based on $L_{g\text{-KMM}}$, which is investigated here.

Let the Hessian matrices at the optimal solutions $\widehat{r}$ be $\boldsymbol{H}_{g\text{-div}}$ for L_g and $\boldsymbol{H}_{g\text{-KMM}}$ for $L_{g\text{-KMM}}$, respectively. Then we have

$$\begin{aligned}\boldsymbol{H}_{g\text{-div}} =& \frac{1}{n}\boldsymbol{K}_{\text{de,de}}\boldsymbol{D}_{g,\widehat{r}}\boldsymbol{K}_{\text{de,de}} + \lambda\boldsymbol{K}_{\text{de,de}} \\ =& \boldsymbol{K}_{\text{de,de}}^{1/2}\left(\frac{1}{n}\boldsymbol{K}_{\text{de,de}}^{1/2}\boldsymbol{D}_{g,\widehat{r}}\boldsymbol{K}_{\text{de,de}}^{1/2} + \lambda\boldsymbol{I}_{n_{\text{de}}}\right)\boldsymbol{K}_{\text{de,de}}^{1/2}, \\ \boldsymbol{H}_{g\text{-KMM}} =& \boldsymbol{K}_{\text{de,de}}^{1/2}\left(\frac{1}{n}\boldsymbol{K}_{\text{de,de}}^{1/2}\boldsymbol{D}_{g,\widehat{r}}\boldsymbol{K}_{\text{de,de}}^{1/2} + \lambda\boldsymbol{I}_{n_{\text{de}}}\right)^2\boldsymbol{K}_{\text{de,de}}^{1/2},\end{aligned} \tag{16.17}$$

where $\boldsymbol{D}_{g,\widehat{r}}$ is the $n \times n$ diagonal matrix with the j-th diagonal element given by $g''(\widehat{r}(\boldsymbol{x}_j^{\text{de}}))$, and g'' denotes the second-order derivative of g. Hence, using the inequality $\kappa(\boldsymbol{A}^{1/2}\boldsymbol{B}\boldsymbol{A}^{1/2}) \le \kappa(\boldsymbol{A})\kappa(\boldsymbol{B})$ for any positive definite matrices $\boldsymbol{A}$ and $\boldsymbol{B}$ (Horn and Johnson, 1985, Section 5.8), we have

$$\begin{aligned}\kappa(\boldsymbol{H}_{g\text{-div}}) \le& \kappa(\boldsymbol{K}_{\text{de,de}})\kappa\left(\frac{1}{n}\boldsymbol{K}_{\text{de,de}}^{1/2}\boldsymbol{D}_{g,\widehat{r}}\boldsymbol{K}_{\text{de,de}}^{1/2} + \lambda\boldsymbol{I}_{n_{\text{de}}}\right), \\ \kappa(\boldsymbol{H}_{g\text{-KMM}}) \le& \kappa(\boldsymbol{K}_{\text{de,de}})\kappa\left(\frac{1}{n}\boldsymbol{K}_{\text{de,de}}^{1/2}\boldsymbol{D}_{g,\widehat{r}}\boldsymbol{K}_{\text{de,de}}^{1/2} + \lambda\boldsymbol{I}_{n_{\text{de}}}\right)^2.\end{aligned}$$

The upper bounds of the condition number suggest that the M-estimator based on L_g is more preferable than that with $L_{g\text{-KMM}}$.

16.4 Optimality of KuLSIF

In this section we study the condition number of the Hessian matrix associated with the minimization problem in the ASC divergence approach (see Section 16.2.2). More specifically, we show that KuLSIF is optimal among all M-estimators based on the ASC divergence under a mini-max evaluation and a probabilistic evaluation of the condition number.

Mini-Max Evaluation

We assume that a universal RKHS $\mathcal{R}$ endowed with a kernel function K on a compact set $\mathcal{X}$ is used to estimate r^*. The M-estimator based on the ASC divergence is obtained by solving the problem (16.11). As shown in Eq. (16.17), the Hessian matrix of the loss function at the optimal solution $\widehat{r}$ is given by

$$\frac{1}{n}\boldsymbol{K}_{\text{de,de}}\boldsymbol{D}_{g,\widehat{r}}\boldsymbol{K}_{\text{de,de}} + \lambda\boldsymbol{K}_{\text{de,de}}.$$

The condition number of the Hessian matrix is denoted by

$$\kappa_0(\boldsymbol{D}_{g,\widehat{r}}) := \kappa\left(\frac{1}{n}\boldsymbol{K}_{\text{de,de}}\boldsymbol{D}_{g,\widehat{r}}\boldsymbol{K}_{\text{de,de}} + \lambda\boldsymbol{K}_{\text{de,de}}\right).$$

In KuLSIF, the equality $g'' = 1$ holds, and thus the condition number is given by $\kappa_0(\boldsymbol{I}_{n_{\mathrm{de}}})$. In the following we analyze the relation between $\kappa_0(\boldsymbol{I}_{n_{\mathrm{de}}})$ and $\kappa_0(\boldsymbol{D}_{g,\widehat{r}})$.

Theorem 16.5 (Mini-max evaluation) *Suppose that $\mathcal{R}$ is a universal RKHS and $\boldsymbol{K}_{\mathrm{de,de}}$ is non-singular, and let c be a positive constant. Then*

$$\inf_{\substack{g:\mathbb{R}\to\mathbb{R},\\ g''((g')^{-1}(1))=c}} \sup_{r\in\mathcal{R}} \kappa_0(\boldsymbol{D}_{g,r}) = \kappa_0(c\boldsymbol{I}_{n_{\mathrm{de}}}) \tag{16.18}$$

holds, where the infimum is taken over all convex second-order continuously differentiable functions such that $g''((g')^{-1}(1)) = c$.

When $r^* = 1$ (i.e., $p^*_{\mathrm{nu}} = p^*_{\mathrm{de}}$), the Hessian matrices are approximately the same for any function g such that $g''((g')^{-1}(1)) = c$. More precisely, when $\lambda = 0$, $n_{\mathrm{nu}} = n_{\mathrm{de}}$, and $\boldsymbol{x}^{\mathrm{nu}}_i = \boldsymbol{x}^{\mathrm{de}}_i$ $(i = 1,\dots,n_{\mathrm{nu}})$ hold in Eq. (16.11), the estimator satisfies $g'(\widehat{r}(\boldsymbol{x}^{\mathrm{de}}_j)) = 1$ and $g''(\widehat{r}(\boldsymbol{x}^{\mathrm{de}}_j)) = c$ for all $j = 1,\dots,n_{\mathrm{de}}$. Then the Hessian matrix is equal to $\frac{c}{n_{\mathrm{nu}}}\boldsymbol{K}^2_{\mathrm{de,de}}$. The constraint on g in Theorem 16.5 [i.e., $g''((g')^{-1}(1)) = c$] works as a kind of calibration at the density ratio $r^* = 1$.

Under such a calibration, Theorem 16.5 shows that the quadratic function $g(z) = cz^2/2$ is optimal in the mini-max sense. This feature is brought about by the fact that the condition number of KuLSIF does not depend on the optimal solution. Because both sides of Eq. (16.18) depend on the samples $\boldsymbol{x}^{\mathrm{de}}_1,\dots,\boldsymbol{x}^{\mathrm{de}}_{n_{\mathrm{de}}}$, KuLSIF achieves the mini-max solution in terms of the condition number for *each* observation.

Probabilistic Evaluation

Next we study the probabilistic evaluation of the condition number. As shown in Eq. (16.17), the Hessian matrix at the estimated function $\widehat{g}$ is given as

$$\boldsymbol{H}_{g\text{-div}} = \frac{1}{n}\boldsymbol{K}_{\mathrm{de,de}}\boldsymbol{D}_{g,\widehat{r}}\boldsymbol{K}_{\mathrm{de,de}} + \lambda\boldsymbol{K}_{\mathrm{de,de}},$$

where the diagonal elements of $\boldsymbol{D}_{g,\widehat{r}}$ are given by $g''(\widehat{r}(\boldsymbol{x}^{\mathrm{de}}_1)),\dots,g''(\widehat{r}(\boldsymbol{x}^{\mathrm{de}}_{n_{\mathrm{de}}}))$, and $\widehat{r}$ is the minimizer of Eq. (16.11). Let us define the random variable $T_{n_{\mathrm{de}}}$ as

$$T_{n_{\mathrm{de}}} = \max_{j=1,\dots,n_{\mathrm{de}}} g''(\widehat{r}(\boldsymbol{x}^{\mathrm{de}}_j)) \geq 0. \tag{16.19}$$

Let $F_{n_{\mathrm{de}}}$ be the distribution function of $T_{n_{\mathrm{de}}}$. More precisely, $T_{n_{\mathrm{de}}}$ and $F_{n_{\mathrm{de}}}$ depend not only on n_{de} but also on n_{nu} through $\widehat{g}$. However, here we consider the case where n_{nu} is fixed to a finite number, or n_{nu} may be a function of n_{de}. Then, $T_{n_{\mathrm{de}}}$ and $F_{n_{\mathrm{de}}}$ depend only on n_{de}.

In the following we first compute the distribution of the condition number $\kappa(\boldsymbol{H}_{g\text{-div}})$. Then we investigate the relation between the function g and the distribution of the condition number $\kappa(\boldsymbol{H}_{g\text{-div}})$. We need to study the eigenvalues and condition numbers of random matrices. For the *Wishart distribution*, the probability distribution of condition numbers has been investigated, for example, by Edelman (1988) and Edelman and Sutton (2005). Recently, the condition numbers of matrices perturbed by additive Gaussian noise have been investigated by the method called *smoothed analysis* (Sankar et al., 2006; Spielman and Teng, 2004; Tao and Vu, 2007). However, the randomness involved in the matrix $\boldsymbol{H}_{g\text{-div}}$ is different from that in existing smoothed analysis studies.

Theorem 16.6 (Probabilistic evaluation) *Let $\mathcal{R}$ be an RKHS endowed with a kernel function $K : \mathcal{X} \times \mathcal{X} \to \mathbb{R}$ satisfying the following boundedness condition:*

$$0 < \inf_{\boldsymbol{x},\boldsymbol{x}' \in \mathcal{X}} K(\boldsymbol{x},\boldsymbol{x}'), \qquad \sup_{\boldsymbol{x},\boldsymbol{x}' \in \mathcal{X}} K(\boldsymbol{x},\boldsymbol{x}') < \infty.$$

Assume that the Gram matrix $\boldsymbol{K}_{\text{de,de}}$ is almost surely positive definite in terms of the probability measure P^*_{de}. Suppose that there exist sequences $s_{n_{\text{de}}}$ and $t_{n_{\text{de}}}$ such that

$$\lim_{n_{\text{de}}\to\infty} s_{n_{\text{de}}} = \infty, \quad \lim_{n_{\text{de}}\to\infty} F_{n_{\text{de}}}(s_{n_{\text{de}}}) = 0, \quad \textit{and} \quad \lim_{n_{\text{de}}\to\infty} F_{n_{\text{de}}}(t_{n_{\text{de}}}/U) = 1,$$

where $U = \sup_{\boldsymbol{x},\boldsymbol{x}' \in \mathcal{X}} K(\boldsymbol{x},\boldsymbol{x}')$. Furthermore, suppose that $\limsup_{n_{\text{de}}\to\infty} E[g''(\widehat{r}(X_1))] < \infty$ holds, and that, for the regularization parameter $\lambda = \lambda_{n_{\text{de}}} > 0$, the bounded condition $\limsup_{n_{\text{de}}\to\infty} \lambda_{n_{\text{de}}} < \infty$ is satisfied. Then, for any small $\nu > 0$, we have

$$\lim_{n_{\text{de}}\to\infty} \Pr\left(s_{n_{\text{de}}}^{1-\nu} \leq \kappa(\boldsymbol{H}_{g\text{-div}}) \leq \kappa(\boldsymbol{K}_{\text{de,de}}) \left(1 + t_{n_{\text{de}}}/\lambda_{n_{\text{de}}}\right)\right) = 1, \tag{16.20}$$

where the probability $\Pr(\cdot)$ is defined for the distribution of all samples $\boldsymbol{x}^{\text{nu}}_1, \ldots, \boldsymbol{x}^{\text{nu}}_{n_{\text{nu}}}, \boldsymbol{x}^{\text{de}}_1, \ldots, \boldsymbol{x}^{\text{de}}_{n_{\text{de}}}$.

Remark. *The Gaussian kernel on a compact set $\mathcal{X}$ meets the condition of Theorem 16.6 under a mild assumption on the probability p^*_{de}. Suppose that $\mathcal{X}$ is included in the ball $\{\boldsymbol{x} \in \mathbb{R}^d \mid \|\boldsymbol{x}\| \leq R\}$. Then, for $K(\boldsymbol{x},\boldsymbol{x}') = \exp\{-\gamma\|\boldsymbol{x}-\boldsymbol{x}'\|^2\}$ with $\boldsymbol{x},\boldsymbol{x}' \in \mathcal{X}$ and $\gamma > 0$, we have $e^{-4\gamma R^2} \leq K(\boldsymbol{x},\boldsymbol{x}') \leq 1$. If the distribution P^*_{de} of samples $\boldsymbol{x}^{\text{de}}_1, \ldots, \boldsymbol{x}^{\text{de}}_{n_{\text{de}}}$ is absolutely continuous with respect to the Lebesgue measure, the Gram matrix of the Gaussian kernel is almost surely positive definite because $\boldsymbol{K}_{\text{de,de}}$ is positive definite if $\boldsymbol{x}^{\text{de}}_j \neq \boldsymbol{x}^{\text{de}}_{j'}$ for $j \neq j'$.*

When g is the quadratic function $g(z) = z^2/2$, the distribution function $F_{n_{\text{de}}}$ is given by $F_{n_{\text{de}}}(t) = \mathbf{1}[t \geq 1]$, where $\mathbf{1}[\cdot]$ is the indicator function. Hence, the sequence $s_{n_{\text{de}}}$ defined in Theorem 16.6 does not exist. Nevertheless, by choosing $t_{n_{\text{de}}} = 1$, the upper bound of $\kappa(\boldsymbol{H}_{g\text{-div}})$ with $g(z) = z^2/2$ is asymptotically given as $\kappa(\boldsymbol{K}_{\text{de,de}})(1 + \lambda^{-1}_{n_{\text{de}}})$.

On the other hand, for the M-estimator with the Kullback–Leibler divergence (Nguyen et al., 2010), the function g is defined by $g(z) = -1 - \log(-z)$, $z < 0$, and thus $g''(z) = 1/z^2$ holds. Then we have $T_{n_{\text{de}}} = \max_{j=1,\ldots,n_{\text{de}}} (\widehat{r}(\boldsymbol{x}^{\text{de}}_j))^{-2}$. However, we note that $(\widehat{r}(\boldsymbol{x}^{\text{de}}_j))^2$ can take a very small value for the Kullback–Leibler divergence, which yields that the order of $T_{n_{\text{de}}}$ is larger than a constant and thus $t_{n_{\text{de}}}$ diverges to infinity. This simple analysis indicates that KuLSIF is more preferable than the M-estimator with the Kullback–Leibler divergence in the sense of numerical stability and computational efficiency.

Next we derive an approximation of the inequality in Eq. (16.20). The random variables $g''(\widehat{r}(\boldsymbol{x}_j^{\mathrm{de}}))$, $j = 1,\ldots,n_{\mathrm{de}}$ are correlated to each other, because the estimator $\widehat{r}$ depends on all samples $\boldsymbol{x}_1^{\mathrm{nu}},\ldots,\boldsymbol{x}_{n_{\mathrm{nu}}}^{\mathrm{nu}},\boldsymbol{x}_1^{\mathrm{de}},\ldots,\boldsymbol{x}_{n_{\mathrm{de}}}^{\mathrm{de}}$. The estimator $\widehat{r}$ approximates the function $r_g^* \in \mathcal{R}$ such that $p_{\mathrm{nu}}^*(\boldsymbol{x})/p_{\mathrm{de}}^*(\boldsymbol{x}) = g'(r_g^*(\boldsymbol{x}))$, and we expect that $\widehat{r}$ will converge to r_g^* when the sample size tends to infinity. Hence, the approximation that $g''(\widehat{r}(\boldsymbol{x}_j^{\mathrm{de}}))$, $j = 1,\ldots,n_{\mathrm{de}}$ are independent of each other will be acceptable in the large sample limit. Under such an approximation, the distribution function $F_{n_{\mathrm{de}}}(t)$ is given by $(\bar{F}(t))^{n_{\mathrm{de}}}$, where $\bar{F}$ is the distribution function of each $g''(\widehat{r}(\boldsymbol{x}_j^{\mathrm{de}}))$. Based on this intuition, we have the following proposition.

Proposition 16.7 (Approximated bound) *Suppose the kernel function K and the regularization parameter $\lambda = \lambda_{n_{\mathrm{de}}}$ satisfy the same condition as Theorem 16.6. For the distribution function $F_{n_{\mathrm{de}}}$ of the random variable $T_{n_{\mathrm{de}}}$, we assume that there exist distribution functions $\bar{F}_0$ and $\bar{F}_1$ such that the following conditions are satisfied:*

1. *For large n_{de}, the inequality $(\bar{F}_0(t))^{n_{\mathrm{de}}} \le F_{n_{\mathrm{de}}}(t) \le (\bar{F}_1(t))^{n_{\mathrm{de}}}$ holds for all $t > 0$.*
2. *Let $G_0 := 1 - \bar{F}_0$ and $G_1 := 1 - \bar{F}_1$. Then both $G_0(t)$ and $G_1(t)$ have the inverse functions $G_0^{-1}(t)$ and $G_1^{-1}(t)$ for small $t > 0$. Furthermore, $\lim_{t\to+0} G_1^{-1}(t) = \infty$ holds.*

Then, for any small $\eta > 0$ and any small $\nu > 0$, we have

$$\lim_{n_{\mathrm{de}}\to\infty} \Pr\Bigg(\{G_1^{-1}(n_{\mathrm{de}}^{-1+\eta})\}^{1-\nu} \le \kappa(\boldsymbol{H}_{g\text{-}div})$$
$$\le \kappa(\boldsymbol{K}_{\mathrm{de,de}})\left(1 + U\lambda_{n_{\mathrm{de}}}^{-1} G_0^{-1}(n_{\mathrm{de}}^{-1-\eta})\right)\Bigg) = 1,$$

where $U = \sup_{\boldsymbol{x},\boldsymbol{x}'} K(\boldsymbol{x},\boldsymbol{x}') < \infty$.

Remark. *Suppose that $F_{n_{\mathrm{de}}}(t)$ is approximated by $(F(t))^{n_{\mathrm{de}}}$ and let $G(t) = 1 - F(t)$. Then Proposition 16.7 implies that, for large n_{de}, the inequality*

$$\{G^{-1}(n_{\mathrm{de}}^{-1+\eta})\}^{1-\nu} \le \kappa(\boldsymbol{H}_{g\text{-}div})$$
$$\le \kappa(\boldsymbol{K}_{\mathrm{de,de}})\left(1 + U\lambda_{n_{\mathrm{de}}}^{-1} G^{-1}(n_{\mathrm{de}}^{-1-\eta})\right) \tag{16.21}$$

holds with high probability. In KuLSIF, the function g is given as $g(z) = z^2/2$. Then the corresponding distribution function of each diagonal element in $\boldsymbol{D}_{g,\widehat{g}}$ is given by $F_{\mathrm{KuLSIF}}(t) = \mathbf{1}[t \ge 1]$, and thus $G_{\mathrm{KuLSIF}}(t) = 1 - F_{\mathrm{KuLSIF}}(t) = \mathbf{1}[t < 1]$. In all M-estimators except KuLSIF, the diagonal elements of $\boldsymbol{D}_{g,\widehat{g}}$ can take various positive values. We can regard the diagonal elements of $\boldsymbol{D}_{g,\widehat{g}}$ as a typical realization of random variables with the distribution function $F(t)$. When the distribution function F is close to F_{KuLSIF}, the function $G = 1 - F$ is also close to G_{KuLSIF}. Then, as illustrated in Figure 16.1, the function G^{-1} will take small values. As a result, we can expect that the condition number of KuLSIF will be smaller than that

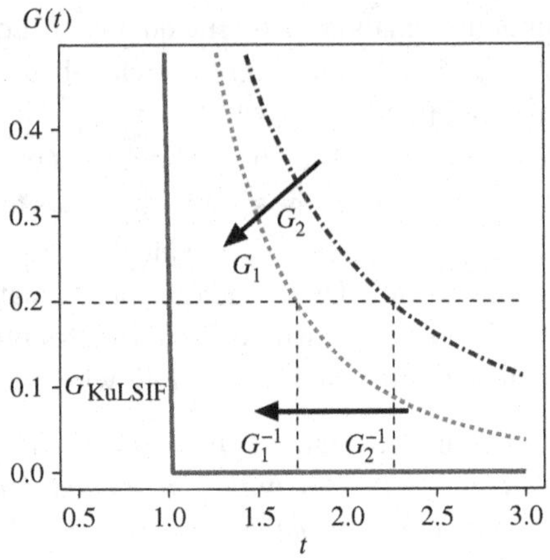

Figure 16.1. If the function $G_1(t)$ is closer to $G_{\mathrm{KuLSIF}}(t)$ $(=0)$ than $G_2(t)$ for large t, then $G_1^{-1}(z)$ takes a smaller value than $G_2^{-1}(z)$ for small z.

of other M-estimators. In Section 16.5, we further investigate this issue through numerical experiments.

Example 16.8 *Let $\bar{F}_\gamma(t)$ be*

$$\bar{F}_\gamma(t) = \begin{cases} 0 & (0 \leq t < 1), \\ 1 - t^{-\gamma} & (1 \leq t). \end{cases}$$

Suppose that $F_{n_{\mathrm{de}}}(t)$ is approximated by $(\bar{F}_\gamma(t))^{n_{\mathrm{de}}}$. The distribution function $F_{\mathrm{KuLSIF}}(t) = \mathbf{1}[t \geq 1]$ defined in Remark 16.4 is represented as $\mathbf{1}[t \geq 1] = \lim_{\gamma \to \infty} \bar{F}_\gamma(t)$ except at $t = 1$. Then, $G_\gamma(t) = 1 - \bar{F}_\gamma(t)$ is given by

$$G_\gamma(t) = \begin{cases} 1 & (0 \leq t < 1), \\ t^{-\gamma} & (1 \leq t). \end{cases}$$

For small $z > 0$, the inverse function $G_\gamma^{-1}(z)$ is given as $G_\gamma^{-1}(z) = z^{-1/\gamma}$. Hence, for small η and small ν, the inequality (16.21) is reduced to

$$n_{\mathrm{de}}{}^{(1-\eta)(1-\nu)/\gamma} \leq \kappa(\boldsymbol{H}_{g\text{-}div}) \leq \kappa(\boldsymbol{K}_{\mathrm{de,de}})\left(1 + U\lambda_{n_{\mathrm{de}}}^{-1} n_{\mathrm{de}}{}^{(1+\eta)/\gamma}\right).$$

Both upper and lower bounds in this inequality are monotone decreasing with respect to γ.

Example 16.9 *Let $\bar{F}_\gamma(t)$ be*

$$\bar{F}_\gamma(t) = \frac{1}{1 + e^{-\gamma(t-1)}}, \quad t \geq 0.$$

Suppose that $F_{n_{\mathrm{de}}}(t)$ is approximated by $(\bar{F}_\gamma(t))^{n_{\mathrm{de}}}$. The distribution function $F_{\mathrm{KuLSIF}}(t) = \mathbf{1}[t \geq 1]$ is represented as $\mathbf{1}[t \geq 1] = \lim_{\gamma \to \infty} \bar{F}_\gamma(t)$ except at $t = 1$.

The function $G_\gamma(t) = 1 - \bar{F}_\gamma(t)$ is given by $G_\gamma(t) = \frac{1}{1+e^{\gamma(t-1)}}$ for $t \geq 0$. For small z, the inverse function $G_\gamma^{-1}(z)$ is given as $G_\gamma^{-1}(z) = 1 + \frac{1}{\gamma}\log\frac{1-z}{z}$. Hence, for small η and small ν, the inequality (16.21) is reduced to

$$\left(\frac{1-\eta}{\gamma}\log\frac{n_{\mathrm{de}}}{2}\right)^{1-\nu} \leq \kappa(\boldsymbol{H}_{g\text{-}div})$$
$$\leq \kappa(\boldsymbol{K}_{\mathrm{de,de}})\left(1 + \frac{U}{\lambda_{n_{\mathrm{nu}},n_{\mathrm{de}}}}\left(1 + \frac{1+\eta}{\gamma}\log n_{\mathrm{de}}\right)\right).$$

The upper and lower bounds in this inequality are monotone decreasing with respect to γ.

Finally, we review briefly the idea of *smoothed analysis* (Spielman and Teng, 2004) and discuss its relation to the above analysis. Let us consider the expected computation cost $E_P[c(X)]$, where $c(X)$ is the cost of an algorithm for the input X, and $E_P[\cdot]$ denotes the expectation with respect to a probability P over the input space. Let $\mathcal{P}$ be a set of probabilities on the input space. In a smoothed analysis, the performance of an algorithm is measured by $\max_{P\in\mathcal{P}} E_P[c(X)]$, where the set of Gaussian distributions is a popular choice as $\mathcal{P}$. On the other hand, in our theoretical analysis, we considered the probabilistic order of condition numbers as a measure of the computation cost. Thus, roughly speaking, the loss function achieving $\min_g \max_{p^*_{\mathrm{nu}},p^*_{\mathrm{de}}} O_p(\kappa(\boldsymbol{H}_{g\text{-div}}))$ will be the optimal choice in our analysis, where the sample distributions p^*_{nu} and p^*_{de} vary in an appropriate set of distributions. This means that our concern is not only to compute the worst-case computation cost but also to find the optimal loss function or tuning parameters in the algorithm.

Remark. *We summarize the theoretical results on condition numbers. Let $\boldsymbol{H}_{g\text{-}div}$ be the Hessian matrix (16.17) of the M-estimator. Then the following inequalities hold:*

$$\kappa(\boldsymbol{H}_{\mathrm{R-KuLSIF}}) \leq \kappa(\boldsymbol{K}_{\mathrm{de,de}}) \leq \kappa(\boldsymbol{H}_{\mathrm{KuLSIF}}) \leq \kappa(\boldsymbol{H}_{\mathrm{KMM}}),$$
$$\kappa(\boldsymbol{H}_{\mathrm{KuLSIF}}) = \sup_{r\in\mathcal{R}} \kappa(\boldsymbol{H}_{\mathrm{KuLSIF}}) \leq \sup_{r\in\mathcal{R}} \kappa(\boldsymbol{H}_{g\text{-}div}).$$

Recall that $\boldsymbol{K}_{\mathrm{de,de}}$ is the Hessian matrix of the original fixed-design KMM method (which estimates the density-ratio values only at denominator samples), and $\boldsymbol{H}_{\mathrm{KMM}}$ is its inductive variant that estimates the entire density-ratio function using the loss function of KMM.

Based on a probabilistic evaluation, the inequality

$$\kappa(\boldsymbol{H}_{\mathrm{KuLSIF}}) \leq \kappa(\boldsymbol{H}_{g\text{-}div})$$

also holds with high probability, although the probabilistic order of $T_{n_{\mathrm{de}}}$ in Eq. (16.19) is left unexplored.

Overall, R-KuLSIF was shown to be advantageous in numerical computations.

16.5 Numerical Examples

In this section we investigate experimentally the relation between the condition number and the convergence rate in the optimization of density-ratio estimators.

16.5.1 Artificial Datasets

In the inductive KMM method, the Hessian matrix is given by

$$\boldsymbol{H}_{\text{KMM}} = \frac{1}{n_{\text{de}}^2}\boldsymbol{K}_{\text{de,de}}^3 + \frac{2\lambda}{n_{\text{de}}}\boldsymbol{K}_{\text{de,de}}^2 + \lambda^2\boldsymbol{K}_{\text{de,de}}.$$

In the M-estimator based on the ASC divergence, the Hessian matrix involved in the optimization problem is given as

$$\boldsymbol{H} = \frac{1}{n}\boldsymbol{K}_{\text{de,de}}\boldsymbol{D}_{g,r}\boldsymbol{K}_{\text{de,de}} + \lambda\boldsymbol{K}_{\text{de,de}} \in \mathbb{R}^{n_{\text{de}}\times n_{\text{de}}}. \tag{16.22}$$

For the Kullback–Leibler divergence, we have $f(u) = -\log u$ and $g(z) = -1 - \log(-z)$, $z < 0$, and thus $g'(z) = -1/z$ and $g''(z) = 1/z^2$ hold for $z < 0$. Thus, for the optimal solution $r_g(\boldsymbol{x})$ under the population distribution, we have

$$g''(r_g(\boldsymbol{x})) = g''((g')^{-1}(r^*(\boldsymbol{x}))) = r^*(\boldsymbol{x})^2.$$

Then the Hessian matrix at the target function r_g is given as

$$\boldsymbol{H}_{\text{KL}} = \frac{1}{n_{\text{de}}}\boldsymbol{K}_{\text{de,de}}\text{diag}(r^*(\boldsymbol{x}_1^{\text{de}})^2, \ldots, r^*(\boldsymbol{x}_{n_{\text{de}}}^{\text{de}})^2)\boldsymbol{K}_{\text{de,de}} + \lambda\boldsymbol{K}_{\text{de,de}}.$$

On the other hand, the Hessian matrix of KuLSIF is given by

$$\boldsymbol{H}_{\text{KuLSIF}} = \frac{1}{n_{\text{de}}}\boldsymbol{K}_{\text{de,de}}^2 + \lambda\boldsymbol{K}_{\text{de,de}},$$

and the Hessian matrix of R-KuLSIF is given by

$$\boldsymbol{H}_{\text{R-KuLSIF}} = \frac{1}{n_{\text{de}}}\boldsymbol{K}_{\text{de,de}} + \lambda\boldsymbol{I}_{n_{\text{de}}}.$$

Here, the condition numbers of the Hessian matrices $\boldsymbol{H}_{\text{KMM}}, \boldsymbol{H}_{\text{KL}}, \boldsymbol{H}_{\text{KuLSIF}}$, and $\boldsymbol{H}_{\text{R-KuLSIF}}$ are compared numerically. In addition, the condition number of $\boldsymbol{K}_{\text{de,de}}$ is also included in the comparison. Up to the constraints in Eq. (16.2), the condition number of $\boldsymbol{K}_{\text{de,de}}$ corresponds to the KMM estimator defined by Eq. (16.2) that estimates the density-ratio values only at denominator samples.

The probability densities p_{nu}^* and p_{de}^* are set to the normal distribution on the 10-dimensional Euclidean space with the unit variance–covariance matrix $\boldsymbol{I}_{10}$. The mean vectors of p_{nu}^* and p_{de}^* are set to $0 \times \mathbf{1}_{10}$ and $\mu \times \mathbf{1}_{10}$, respectively. We test $\mu = 0.2$ or $\mu = 0.5$. Note that the mean value μ affects only $\kappa(\boldsymbol{H}_{\text{KL}})$. In the kernel-based estimators, we use the Gaussian kernel with width $\sigma = 2$ or $\sigma = 4$. Note that $\sigma = 4$ is close to the median of the distance between samples $\|\boldsymbol{x}_j^{\text{de}} - \boldsymbol{x}_{j'}^{\text{de}}\|$;

using the median distance as the kernel width is a popular heuristics (Schölkopf and Smola, 2002).

The sample size is increased under $n_{\mathrm{nu}} = n_{\mathrm{de}}$ in the first set of experiments, whereas n_{nu} is fixed to 50 and n_{de} is varied from 20 to 500 in the second set of experiments. The regularization parameter λ is set to $\lambda_{n_{\mathrm{nu}},n_{\mathrm{de}}} = \min(n_{\mathrm{nu}}, n_{\mathrm{de}})^{-0.9}$, which meets the assumption in Theorem 14.14.

Table 16.1 shows the average condition numbers over 1000 runs. In each setup, samples $\boldsymbol{x}_1^{\mathrm{de}}, \ldots, \boldsymbol{x}_{n_{\mathrm{de}}}^{\mathrm{de}}$ are randomly generated and the condition number is computed. The table shows that the condition number of R-KuLSIF is much smaller than the condition numbers for the other methods for all cases. Thus it is expected that the convergence speed of R-KuLSIF in optimization is faster than in the other methods and that R-KuLSIF is robust against numerical degeneracy. It is also noteworthy that $\kappa(\boldsymbol{H}_{\text{R-KuLSIF}})$ is smaller than $\kappa(\boldsymbol{K}_{\mathrm{de,de}})$ – this is because the identity matrix in $\boldsymbol{H}_{\text{R-KuLSIF}}$ prevents the smallest eigenvalue from becoming extremely small.

Next we investigate the number of iterations and computation times required for obtaining the solutions of R-KuLSIF, KuLSIF, the inductive KMM (simply referred to as KMM from here on), and the M-estimator with the Kullback–Leibler divergence (KL). We also include in the comparison the computation time required for solving the linear equation of R-KuLSIF, which is denoted as R-KuLSIF(direct). The probability densities p_{nu}^* and p_{de}^* are essentially the same as in the previous experiment, but the mean vector of p_{nu}^* is set to $0.5 \times \mathbf{1}_{10}$. The number of samples from each probability distribution is set to $n_{\mathrm{nu}} = n_{\mathrm{de}} = 100, \ldots, 6000$, and the regularization parameter is defined by $\lambda = \min(n_{\mathrm{nu}}, n_{\mathrm{de}})^{-0.9}$. The kernel parameter σ is set to the median of $\|\boldsymbol{x}_j^{\mathrm{de}} - \boldsymbol{x}_{j'}^{\mathrm{de}}\|$. To solve the optimization problems in the M-estimators and KMM, we use two optimization methods: the BFGS quasi-Newton method implemented in the `optim` function in R (R Development Core Team, 2009) and the steepest descent method. Furthermore, for R-KuLSIF(direct), we use the `solve` function in R.

Tables 16.2 and 16.3 show the average number of iterations and the average computation times for solving the optimization problems over 50 runs. For the steepest descent method, the maximum number of iterations was limited to 4000, and the KL method reached the limit. The numerical results indicate that the number of iterations in optimization is highly correlated with the condition numbers of the Hessian matrices in Table 16.1.

Although the practical computational time would depend on various issues such as stopping rules, our theoretical results in Section 16.4 were shown to be in good agreement with the empirical results obtained from artificial datasets. We also observed that numerical optimization methods such as the quasi-Newton method are competitive with numerical algorithms for solving linear equations using the *LU decomposition* or the *Cholesky decomposition*, especially when the sample size n_{de} is large (note that the number of parameters is n_{de} in the kernel-based methods). This implies that our theoretical result will be useful in large sample cases, which are common situations in practical applications.

Table 16.1. Average condition numbers of the Hessian matrices over 1000 runs. The top two tables show the condition numbers for $n_{nu} = n_{de}$ and $\sigma = 2, 4$, whereas the bottom one shows the result when the sample size from p^*_{nu} is fixed to $n_{nu} = 50$ and σ is set to 4.

kernel width: $\sigma = 2$, sample size: $n_{nu} = n_{de}$

n_{nu}, n_{de}	$K_{de,de}$	$H_{R\text{-}KuLSIF}$	H_{KuLSIF}	H_{KMM}	H_{KL} $\mu = 0.2$	H_{KL} $\mu = 0.5$
20	1.6e+01	3.8e+00	6.4e+01	2.7e+02	9.0e+01	1.4e+03
50	7.1e+01	8.1e+00	5.9e+02	5.1e+03	7.6e+02	4.8e+03
100	2.6e+02	1.5e+01	4.1e+03	6.5e+04	5.0e+03	2.7e+04
200	1.1e+03	3.0e+01	3.4e+04	1.0e+06	4.2e+04	1.6e+05
300	2.9e+03	4.4e+01	1.3e+05	5.7e+06	1.6e+05	5.8e+05
400	5.9e+03	5.8e+01	3.4e+05	2.0e+07	4.2e+05	1.5e+06
500	1.0e+04	7.3e+01	7.5e+05	5.5e+07	9.2e+05	3.1e+06

kernel width: $\sigma = 4$, sample size: $n_{nu} = n_{de}$

n_{nu}, n_{de}	$K_{de,de}$	$H_{R\text{-}KuLSIF}$	H_{KuLSIF}	H_{KMM}	H_{KL} $\mu = 0.2$	H_{KL} $\mu = 0.5$
20	4.3e+02	1.2e+01	5.2e+03	6.3e+04	6.9e+03	2.8e+04
50	4.2e+03	2.8e+01	1.2e+05	3.4e+06	1.6e+05	7.7e+05
100	3.1e+04	5.5e+01	1.7e+06	9.6e+07	2.4e+06	1.2e+07
200	2.6e+05	1.1e+02	2.8e+07	3.1e+09	3.9e+07	2.1e+08
300	1.0e+06	1.6e+02	1.7e+08	2.7e+10	2.3e+08	1.2e+09
400	3.0e+06	2.1e+02	6.3e+08	1.4e+11	8.7e+08	5.0e+09
500	6.5e+06	2.7e+02	1.7e+09	4.6e+11	2.4e+09	1.3e+10

kernel width: $\sigma = 4$, sample size: $n_{nu} = 50$

n_{de}	$K_{de,de}$	$H_{R\text{-}KuLSIF}$	H_{KuLSIF}	H_{KMM}	H_{KL} $\mu = 0.2$	H_{KL} $\mu = 0.5$
20	4.3e+02	9.4e+00	4.1e+03	3.9e+04	5.4e+03	2.3e+04
50	4.3e+03	2.0e+01	8.7e+04	1.8e+06	1.2e+05	5.6e+05
100	3.2e+04	2.0e+01	6.4e+05	1.3e+07	8.7e+05	4.5e+06
200	2.6e+05	2.0e+01	5.3e+06	1.1e+08	7.2e+06	3.9e+07
300	1.0e+06	2.0e+01	2.1e+07	4.2e+08	2.8e+07	1.4e+08
400	2.9e+06	2.0e+01	5.8e+07	1.2e+09	7.9e+07	4.3e+08
500	6.6e+06	2.0e+01	1.3e+08	2.7e+09	1.8e+08	8.8e+08

16.5.2 Benchmark Datasets

Finally, we apply density-ratio estimation to benchmark datasets and compare the computation costs in a more practical setup.

We consider the problem of *inlier-based outlier detection* for finding irregular samples in a dataset ("evaluation dataset") based on another dataset ("model dataset") that contains only regular samples (see Section 10.1). We use

Table 16.2. The average computation times and the average numbers of iterations in the BFGS method over 50 runs.

	$n_{de} = n_{nu} = 100$		$n_{de} = n_{nu} = 300$	
Estimator	Comp. time (sec.)	Number of iterations	Comp. time (sec.)	Number of iterations
R-KuLSIF	0.01	18.3	0.06	17.0
KuLSIF	0.03	45.8	0.13	38.7
KMM	0.63	372.0	10.95	366.8
KL	0.07	98.6	0.61	159.3
R-KuLSIF(direct)	0.001	–	0.01	–

	$n_{de} = n_{nu} = 1000$		$n_{de} = n_{nu} = 6000$	
Estimator	Comp. time (sec.)	Number of iterations	Comp. time (sec.)	Number of iterations
R-KuLSIF	1.44	23.0	71.69	30.7
KuLSIF	2.25	38.4	107.79	47.3
KMM	51.83	453.7	1091.69	373.1
KL	27.63	329.1	2718.89	669.2
R-KuLSIF(direct)	0.46	–	87.06	–

Table 16.3. The average computation times and the average numbers of iterations in the steepest descent method over 50 runs. ">" means that the actual computation time is longer than the number described in the table.

	$n_{de} = n_{nu} = 300$		$n_{de} = n_{nu} = 700$	
Estimator	Comp. time (sec.)	Number of iterations	Comp. time (sec.)	Number of iterations
R-KuLSIF	0.50	33.7	4.46	49.0
KuLSIF	10.16	487.5	78.21	640.4
KMM	31.43	806.1	281.75	1389.5
KL	> 111.83	over 4000	> 539.72	> 4000

the IDA binary classification datasets (Rätsch et al., 2001), which consist of positive/negative and training/test samples. We allocate all positive training samples for the model dataset and assign all positive test samples and 5% of negative test samples to the evaluation dataset. Thus, we regard the positive samples as inliers and the negative samples as outliers. The density ratio $r^*(\boldsymbol{x})$ is defined as the probability density of the model dataset over that of the evaluation dataset. Then the true density ratio is approximately equal to one in inlier regions and takes small values around outliers.

Table 16.4 shows the average computation times and the average numbers of iterations over 20 runs for the *image* and *splice* datasets and over 50 runs for the

Table 16.4. The average computation times and the average numbers of iterations for the IDA benchmark datasets. The BFGS quasi-Newton method in the `optim` function of the R environment is used to obtain numerical solutions. For each dataset, the numbers in the upper row denote the the computation time (sec.), and the numbers in the lower row denote the numbers of iterations of the quasi-Newton update.

Data	# samples	R-KuLSIF	KuLSIF	KMM	KL	R-KuLSIF (direct)
b-cancer	$n_{\mathrm{de}} = 27$	0.008	0.012	0.356	0.013	0.001
	$n_{\mathrm{nu}} = 58$	13.1	30.8	398.7	29.8	–
thyroid	$n_{\mathrm{de}} = 30$	0.008	0.015	0.500	0.015	0.001
	$n_{\mathrm{nu}} = 39$	14.1	39.8	579.2	36.1	–
heart	$n_{\mathrm{de}} = 49$	0.010	0.016	0.474	0.021	0.001
	$n_{\mathrm{nu}} = 76$	14.0	35.0	394.1	42.4	–
german	$n_{\mathrm{de}} = 98$	0.02	0.03	1.70	0.05	0.002
	$n_{\mathrm{nu}} = 217$	15.5	39.1	405.2	48.8	–
diabetes	$n_{\mathrm{de}} = 113$	0.02	0.04	2.20	0.07	0.002
	$n_{\mathrm{nu}} = 170$	14.8	44.3	414.1	65.3	–
f-solar	$n_{\mathrm{de}} = 242$	0.05	0.11	7.90	0.24	0.01
	$n_{\mathrm{nu}} = 367$	14.7	30.8	213.7	61.1	–
image	$n_{\mathrm{de}} = 631$	0.85	2.19	85.11	6.02	0.15
	$n_{\mathrm{nu}} = 740$	22.1	61.3	439.5	135.3	–
titanic	$n_{\mathrm{de}} = 771$	0.98	0.96	18.66	1.11	0.28
	$n_{\mathrm{nu}} = 43$	20.7	16.4	70.2	19.7	–
splice	$n_{\mathrm{de}} = 1153$	1.66	3.59	197.08	6.50	0.84
	$n_{\mathrm{nu}} = 483$	15.0	28.8	450.8	49.9	–
waveform	$n_{\mathrm{de}} = 1745$	4.06	3.96	195.89	5.95	2.50
	$n_{\mathrm{nu}} = 132$	20.3	17.7	305.4	28.2	–
banana	$n_{\mathrm{de}} = 2404$	11.51	10.77	179.28	14.18	6.69
	$n_{\mathrm{nu}} = 217$	28.4	23.2	194.1	30.6	–
ringnorm	$n_{\mathrm{de}} = 3807$	18.27	12.77	365.14	29.97	24.92
	$n_{\mathrm{nu}} = 207$	20.3	13.5	214.5	31.7	–
twonorm	$n_{\mathrm{de}} = 3846$	22.10	15.70	351.96	30.14	26.69
	$n_{\mathrm{nu}} = 207$	22.2	13.2	183.9	26.9	–

other datasets. In the same way as the simulations in Section 16.5.1, we compare R-KuLSIF, KuLSIF, the inductive variant of KMM (KMM), and the M-estimator with the Kullback–Leibler divergence (KL). In addition, the computation time for solving the linear equation of R-KuLSIF is also shown as "direct." For the optimization, we use the BFGS method implemented in the `optim` function in R (R Development Core Team, 2009), and for R-KuLSIF(direct) we use the `solve` function in R. The kernel parameter σ is determined based on the median of $\|\boldsymbol{x}_j^{\mathrm{de}} - \boldsymbol{x}_{j'}^{\mathrm{de}}\|$, which is computed by the function *sigest* in the *kernlab* library (Karatzoglou et al., 2004). The number of samples is shown in the second column, and the regularization parameter is defined by $\lambda = \min(n_{\mathrm{nu}}, n_{\mathrm{de}})^{-0.9}$.

The numerical results show that the number of iterations agrees well with the theoretical analysis when the sample size is balanced, that is, n_{nu} and n_{de} are comparable. On the other hand, for the *titanic*, *waveform*, *banana*, *ringnorm*, and *twonorm* datasets, the number of iterations of each method is almost the same except KMM. In these datasets, n_{nu} is much smaller than n_{de}, and thus the second term, $\lambda \boldsymbol{K}_{\mathrm{de,de}}$, in the Hessian matrix (16.22) for the M-estimator will govern the convergence property, because the order of λ is larger than $O(n_{\mathrm{de}}^{-1})$. This tendency can be explained by Eq. (16.20); that is, a large λ provides a small upper bound of $\kappa(\boldsymbol{H})$.

Next, we more systematically investigate the number of iterations when n_{nu} and n_{de} are comparable. We use the *titanic*, *waveform*, *banana*, *ringnorm*, and *twonorm* datasets. In the first set of experiments, the evaluation dataset consists of all positive test samples, and the model dataset is defined by all negative test samples. Therefore, the true density ratio may be far from the constant function $r^*(\boldsymbol{x}) = 1$. The upper half of Table 16.5 summarizes the results, showing that R-KuLSIF keeps the computation costs low for all cases. This again agrees well with our theoretical analysis. In the second set of experiments, both model samples and evaluation samples are taken randomly from all test samples. Thus, the target density ratio is the constant function $r^*(\boldsymbol{x}) = 1$. The lower half of Table 16.5 summarizes the results, showing that the number of iterations for the KL method is significantly smaller than that shown in the upper half of Table 16.5. This is because the condition number of the Hessian matrix (16.22) is likely to be small when the true density ratio r^* is close to the constant function. Nevertheless, R-KuLSIF is still a preferable approach even when the target density ratio is constant. Furthermore, it is noteworthy that the computation time of R-KuLSIF is comparable to a direct method such as the Cholesky decomposition when the sample size is more than about 3000.

16.6 Remarks

In this chapter we investigated the numerical stability and computational efficiency of kernel-based density-ratio estimation via conditional number analysis. In Section 16.3 we showed that, although KuLSIF and KMM share the same

Table 16.5. The average computation times and the average numbers of iterations for balanced samples, i.e., n_{nu} and n_{de} are comparable. We use the *titanic*, *waveform*, *banana*, *ringnorm*, and *twonorm* datasets in the IDA benchmark repository. In the upper table, the evaluation dataset consists of all positive test samples and the model dataset is defined by all negative test samples; i.e., the two datasets follow highly different distributions and thus the true density-ratio function is far from constant. In the lower table, the evaluation dataset and the model dataset are both randomly generated from all test samples; i.e., the two datasets follow the same distribution and thus the true density-ratio function is constant. The BFGS quasi-Newton method in the *optim* function of the R environment is used to obtain numerical solutions. For each dataset, the numbers in the upper row denote the computation time (sec.), and the numbers in the lower row denote the number of iterations of the quasi-Newton update.

Data	# samples	R-KuLSIF	KuLSIF	KMM	KL	R-KuLSIF (direct)
titanic	$n_{de} = 668$	0.88	0.91	11.82	2.16	0.16
	$n_{nu} = 1383$	20.7	23.7	101.1	51.8	–
waveform	$n_{de} = 1515$	5.89	21.28	276.11	89.44	1.60
	$n_{nu} = 3085$	30.1	126.1	627.4	413.3	–
banana	$n_{de} = 2159$	12.85	34.62	262.20	205.67	4.86
	$n_{nu} = 2741$	32.6	96.7	356.5	444.6	–
ringnorm	$n_{de} = 3457$	20.04	23.63	640.22	644.00	17.19
	$n_{nu} = 3543$	25.4	33.0	471.0	599.2	–
twonorm	$n_{de} = 3496$	22.36	29.64	345.52	554.64	18.56
	$n_{nu} = 3504$	25.9	38.8	234.1	546.1	–

Data	# samples	R-KuLSIF	KuLSIF	KMM	KL	R-KuLSIF (direct)
titanic	$n_{de} = 1026$	1.34	1.79	24.89	2.71	0.53
	$n_{nu} = 1025$	16.5	21.1	97.5	31.6	–
waveform	$n_{de} = 2300$	9.84	20.73	504.84	67.72	5.42
	$n_{nu} = 2300$	24.5	58.5	683.8	149.5	–
banana	$n_{de} = 2450$	12.56	17.81	214.08	36.92	6.61
	$n_{nu} = 2450$	27.3	40.5	256.9	74.0	–
ringnorm	$n_{de} = 3500$	18.54	18.63	521.44	239.50	18.86
	$n_{nu} = 3500$	21.8	21.5	335.1	190.4	–
twonorm	$n_{de} = 3500$	19.00	25.30	589.04	173.46	17.45
	$n_{nu} = 3500$	23.6	31.8	410.3	172.0	–

solution, KuLSIF possesses a smaller condition number than KMM. Then, in Section 16.4, we showed that KuLSIF has the smallest condition number among all ratio-fitting estimators. Thus, from the viewpoint of condition numbers, KuLSIF is the numerically most reliable and computationally most efficient method. The numerical experiments in Section 16.5 showed that the practical convergence behavior of optimization is explained well by our theoretical analysis of condition numbers of the Hessian matrix.

Part V

Conclusions

17

Conclusions and Future Directions

In this book we described a new approach to machine learning based on *density-ratio estimation*. This density-ratio approach offers a novel research paradigm in the field of machine learning and data mining from theory and algorithms to application.

In Part II, various methods for density-ratio estimation were described, including methods based on separate estimations of numerator and denominator densities (Chapter 2), moment matching between numerator and denominator samples (Chapter 3), probabilistic classifications of numerator and denominator samples (Chapter 4), density fitting between numerator and denominator densities (Chapter 5), and direct fitting of a density-ratio model to the true density-ratio (Chapter 6). We also gave a unified framework of density-ratio estimation in Chapter 7, which accommodates the various methods described above and is substantially more general – as an example, a robust density-ratio estimator was derived. Finally, in Chapter 8, we described methods that combine density-ratio estimation with dimensionality reduction. Among various density-ratio estimators, the *unconstrained least-squares importance fitting* (uLSIF) method described in Chapter 6 would be most useful practically because of its high computational efficiency by an analytic-form solution, the availability of cross-validation for model selection, its wide applicability to various machine learning tasks (Part III), and its superior convergence and numerical properties (Part IV).

In Part III we covered the usage of density-ratio estimators in various machine learning tasks that were categorized into four groups. In Chapter 9 we described applications of density ratios to importance sampling tasks such as non-stationarity/domain adaptation and multi-task learning. Combining domain adaptation and multi-task learning, which has high practical importance, may also be possible in a similar way. In Chapter 10 we showed applications of density-ratio estimations to distribution comparison tasks such as outlier detection and two-sample homogeneity tests. Change detection in a time series can also be formulated as a distribution comparison task, to which density-ratio estimators can also be applied. In Chapter 11 methods for mutual information approximations via density-ratio estimation and their application to supervised dimensionality reduction and independent component analysis were shown. In addition to these applications, mutual information estimators can be used for solving various importance tasks including feature selection, clustering, object matching, independence test, and causality learning. Finally, in Chapter 12, density-ratio estimation was used for approximating conditional densities and conditional probabilities, which provided computationally efficient algorithms.

In Part IV we studied theoretically the properties of density-ratio estimators. In Chapters 13 and 14, the asymptotic behavior of parametric and non-parametric density-ratio estimators was elucidated. In Chapter 15, properties of a parametric two-sample test were investigated. Finally, in Chapter 16, the numerical stability of density-ratio estimators was analyzed.

Because many important machine learning tasks were shown to be tackled via density-ratio estimation, it will be promising to make further efforts to improve the accuracy and computational efficiency of density-ratio estimation. We expect that the general framework provided in Chapter 7 is useful for exploring new density-ratio estimators. Further development for coping with high dimensionality beyond the methods described in Chapter 8 will also be a challenging research topic.

We also expect that more applications will be found in each of the four categories of machine learning tasks described in Part III. Completely new categories of machine learning tasks that can be solved by density-ratio estimation could also be explored beyond the above four categories. A key challenge along this line would be to go beyond the *plain* density ratio:

$$r^*(\boldsymbol{x}) := \frac{p^*_{\mathrm{nu}}(\boldsymbol{x})}{p^*_{\mathrm{de}}(\boldsymbol{x})}.$$

For example, considering more elaborate quantities such as the *relative density ratio* (Yamada et al., 2011b),

$$r^*_\alpha(\boldsymbol{x}) := \frac{p^*_{\mathrm{nu}}(\boldsymbol{x})}{\alpha p^*_{\mathrm{nu}}(\boldsymbol{x}) + (1-\alpha)p^*_{\mathrm{de}}(\boldsymbol{x})} \quad \text{for } 0 \leq \alpha \leq 1,$$

and the *conditional density ratio*,

$$r^*(\boldsymbol{y}|\boldsymbol{x}) := \frac{p^*_{\mathrm{nu}}(\boldsymbol{y}|\boldsymbol{x})}{p^*_{\mathrm{de}}(\boldsymbol{y}|\boldsymbol{x})},$$

would be a promising direction to be pursued.

Beyond sophisticated algorithmic implementations of density-ratio estimations, state-of-the-art computing paradigms such as the *field-programmable gate array* (FPGA), *multi-core processors*, and *cloud computing* would no doubt be promising directions for handling massive-scale and distributed real-world data. Securing the *privacy* of the data gathered from multiple confidential sources would also be an important issue to be incorporated.

It is a big challenge to apply density-ratio methods to various real-world data analyses such as image and video processing, speech and music analyses, natural language processing, sensory data analysis, web data mining, robot and system control, financial data analysis, bioinformatics, computational chemistry, and brain science. We believe that machine learning techniques will play a central role in next-generation data-processing paradigms such as *cyber physical systems*. Density-ratio methods could be a key tool in such scenarios.

Finally, various implementations of density-ratio methods are available from http://sugiyama-www.cs.titech.ac.jp/~sugi/software/.

We hope that these software packages are useful for developing new machine learning techniques and exploring novel application areas.

Symbols and Abbreviations

$\boldsymbol{x}$	Input variable
$\mathcal{X}$	Domain of input $\boldsymbol{x}$
d	Dimensionality of input $\boldsymbol{x}$
$\mathbb{E}$	Expectation
$p^*_{\mathrm{nu}}(\boldsymbol{x})$	Probability density function in the numerator of the ratio
$p^*_{\mathrm{de}}(\boldsymbol{x})$	Probability density function in the denominator of the ratio
$p_{\mathrm{nu}}(\boldsymbol{x})$	Model of $p^*_{\mathrm{nu}}(\boldsymbol{x})$
$p_{\mathrm{de}}(\boldsymbol{x})$	Model of $p^*_{\mathrm{de}}(\boldsymbol{x})$
$\widehat{p}_{\mathrm{nu}}(\boldsymbol{x})$	Estimator of $p^*_{\mathrm{nu}}(\boldsymbol{x})$
$\widehat{p}_{\mathrm{de}}(\boldsymbol{x})$	Estimator of $p^*_{\mathrm{de}}(\boldsymbol{x})$
$r^*(\boldsymbol{x})$	Density ratio $p^*_{\mathrm{nu}}(\boldsymbol{x})/p^*_{\mathrm{de}}(\boldsymbol{x})$
$\widehat{r}(\boldsymbol{x})$	Estimator of $r^*(\boldsymbol{x})$
$r(\boldsymbol{x})$	Model of $r^*(\boldsymbol{x})$
i.i.d.	Independent and identically distributed
$\{\boldsymbol{x}^{\mathrm{nu}}_i\}_{i=1}^{n_{\mathrm{nu}}}$	Set of n_{nu} i.i.d. samples following $p^*_{\mathrm{nu}}(\boldsymbol{x})$
$\{\boldsymbol{x}^{\mathrm{de}}_j\}_{j=1}^{n_{\mathrm{de}}}$	Set of n_{de} i.i.d. samples following $p^*_{\mathrm{de}}(\boldsymbol{x})$
$\boldsymbol{\phi}(\boldsymbol{x})$, $\boldsymbol{\psi}(\boldsymbol{x})$	Basis functions
$\boldsymbol{\Phi}_{\mathrm{nu}}$, $\boldsymbol{\Psi}_{\mathrm{nu}}$	Design matrices for numerator samples
$\boldsymbol{\Phi}_{\mathrm{de}}$, $\boldsymbol{\Psi}_{\mathrm{de}}$	Design matrices for denominator samples
$K(\boldsymbol{x},\boldsymbol{x}')$	Kernel function
λ	Regularization parameter
$^\top$	Transpose
$\boldsymbol{0}_n$	n-dimensional vector with all zeros
$\boldsymbol{1}_n$	n-dimensional vector with all ones
$\boldsymbol{0}_{n\times n'}$	$n \times n'$ matrix with all zeros
$\boldsymbol{1}_{n\times n'}$	$n \times n'$ matrix with all ones
$\boldsymbol{I}_n$	n-dimensional identity matrix

$\mathbb{R}$	Set of all real numbers
$N(\cdot;\mu,\sigma^2)$	Gaussian density with mean μ and variance σ^2
$N(\cdot;\boldsymbol{\mu},\boldsymbol{\Sigma})$	Multi-dimensional Gaussian density with mean $\boldsymbol{\mu}$ and covariance matrix $\boldsymbol{\Sigma}$

AIC	Akaike information criterion
ASC	Ali–Silvey–Csiszár divergence
BA	Basu's power divergence
BIC	Bayesian information criterion
BR	Bregman divergence
cLSIF	Constrained LSIF
CV	Cross-validation
IWCV	Importance-weighted cross-validation
KDE	Kernel density estimation
KL	Kullback–Leibler divergence
KLIEP	Kullback–Leibler importance estimation procedure
KMM	Kernel mean matching
KuLSIF	Kernel uLSIF
LR	Logistic regression
LSIF	Least-squares importance fitting
MAP	Maximum a posteriori
MI	Mutual information
ML	Maximum likelihood
MSC	Mean square contingency
NNDE	Nearest neighbor density estimation
PE	Pearson divergence
SMI	Squared-loss mutual information
SVM	Support vector machine
UKL	Unnormalized Kullback–Leibler divergence
uLSIF	Unconstrained LSIF

References

Agakov, F., and Barber, D. 2006. Kernelized Infomax Clustering. Pages 17–24 of: Weiss, Y., Schölkopf, B., and Platt, J. (eds), *Advances in Neural Information Processing Systems 18*. Cambridge, MA: MIT Press.

Aggarwal, C. C., and Yu, P. S. (eds). 2008. *Privacy-Preserving Data Mining: Models and Algorithms*. New York: Springer.

Akaike, H. 1970. Statistical Predictor Identification. *Annals of the Institute of Statistical Mathematics*, **22**, 203–217.

Akaike, H. 1974. A New Look at the Statistical Model Identification. *IEEE Transactions on Automatic Control*, **AC-19**(6), 716–723.

Akaike, H. 1980. Likelihood and the Bayes Procedure. Pages 141–166 of: Bernardo, J. M., DeGroot, M. H., Lindley, D. V., and Smith, A. F. M. (eds), *Bayesian Statistics*. Valencia, Spain: Valencia University Press.

Akiyama, T., Hachiya, H., and Sugiyama, M. 2010. Efficient Exploration through Active Learning for Value Function Approximation in Reinforcement Learning. *Neural Networks*, **23**(5), 639–648.

Ali, S. M., and Silvey, S. D. 1966. A General Class of Coefficients of Divergence of One Distribution from Another. *Journal of the Royal Statistical Society, Series B*, **28**(1), 131–142.

Amari, S. 1967. Theory of Adaptive Pattern Classifiers. *IEEE Transactions on Electronic Computers*, **EC-16**(3), 299–307.

Amari, S. 1998. Natural Gradient Works Efficiently in Learning. *Neural Computation*, **10**(2), 251–276.

Amari, S. 2000. Estimating Functions of Independent Component analysis for Temporally Correlated Signals. *Neural Computation*, **12**(9), 2083–2107.

Amari, S., and Nagaoka, H. 2000. *Methods of Information Geometry*. Providence, RI: Oxford University Press.

Amari, S., Fujita, N., and Shinomoto, S. 1992. Four Types of Learning Curves. *Neural Computation*, **4**(4), 605–618.

Amari, S., Cichocki, A., and Yang, H. H. 1996. A New Learning Algorithm for Blind Signal Separation. Pages 757–763 of: Touretzky, D. S., Mozer, M. C., and Hasselmo, M. E. (eds), *Advances in Neural Information Processing Systems 8*. Cambridge, MA: MIT Press.

Anderson, N., Hall, P., and Titterington, D. 1994. Two-Sample Test Statistics for Measuring Discrepancies between Two Multivariate Probability Density Functions Using Kernel-based Density Estimates. *Journal of Multivariate Analysis*, **50**, 41–54.

Ando, R. K., and Zhang, T. 2005. A Framework for Learning Predictive Structures from Multiple Tasks and Unlabeled Data. *Journal of Machine Learning Research*, **6**, 1817–1853.

Antoniak, C. 1974. Mixtures of Dirichlet Processes with Applications to Bayesian Nonparametric Problems. *The Annals of Statistics*, **2**(6), 1152–1174.

Aronszajn, N. 1950. Theory of Reproducing Kernels. *Transactions of the American Mathematical Society*, **68**, 337–404.

Bach, F., and Harchaoui, Z. 2008. DIFFRAC: A Discriminative and Flexible Framework for Clustering. Pages 49–56 of: Platt, J. C., Koller, D., Singer, Y., and Roweis, S. (eds), *Advances in Neural Information Processing Systems 20*. Cambridge, MA: MIT Press.

Bach, F., and Jordan, M. I. 2002. Kernel Independent Component Analysis. *Journal of Machine Learning Research*, **3**, 1–48.

Bach, F., and Jordan, M. I. 2006. Learning Spectral Clustering, with Application to Speech Separation. *Journal of Machine Learning Research*, **7**, 1963–2001.

Bachman, G., and Narici, L. 2000. *Functional Analysis*. Mineola, NY: Dover Publications.

Bakker, B., and Heskes, T. 2003. Task Clustering and Gating for Bayesian Multitask Learning. *Journal of Machine Learning Research*, **4**, 83–99.

Bartlett, P., Bousquet, O., and Mendelson, S. 2005. Local Rademacher Complexities. *The Annals of Statistics*, **33**, 1487–1537.

Basseville, M., and Nikiforov, V. 1993. *Detection of Abrupt Changes: Theory and Application*. Englewood Cliffs, NJ: Prentice-Hall, Inc.

Basu, A., Harris, I. R., Hjort, N. L., and Jones, M. C. 1998. Robust and Efficient Estimation by Minimising a Density Power Divergence. *Biometrika*, **85**(3), 549–559.

Baxter, J. 1997. A Bayesian/Information Theoretic Model of Learning to Learn via Mutiple Task Sampling. *Machine Learning*, **28**, 7–39.

Baxter, J. 2000. A Model of Inductive Bias Learning. *Journal of Artificail Intelligence Research*, **12**, 149–198.

Belkin, M., and Niyogi, P. 2003. Laplacian Eigenmaps for Dimensionality Reduction and Data Representation. *Neural Computation*, **15**(6), 1373–1396.

Bellman, R. 1961. *Adaptive Control Processes: A Guided Tour*. Princeton, NJ: Princeton University Press.

Ben-David, S., and Schuller, R. 2003. Exploiting Task Relatedness for Multiple Task Learning. Pages 567–580 of: *Proceedings of the Sixteenth Annual Conference on Learning Theory (COLT2003)*.

Ben-David, S., Gehrke, J., and Schuller, R. 2002. A Theoretical Framework for Learning from a Pool of Disparate Data Sources. Pages 443–449 of: *Proceedings of The Eighth ACM SIGKDD International Conference on Knowledge Discovery and Data Mining (KDD2002)*.

Bensaid, N., and Fabre, J. P. 2007. Optimal Asymptotic Quadratic Error of Kernel Estimators of Radon-Nikodym Derivatives for Strong Mixing Data. *Journal of Nonparametric Statistics*, **19**(2), 77–88.

Bertsekas, D., Nedic, A., and Ozdaglar, A. 2003. *Convex Analysis and Optimization*. Belmont, MA: Athena Scientific.

Best, M. J. 1982. *An Algorithm for the Solution of the Parametric Quadratic Programming Problem*. Tech. rept. 82–24. Faculty of Mathematics, University of Waterloo.

Biau, G., and Györfi, L. 2005. On the Asymptotic Properties of a Nonparametric l1-test Statistic of Homogeneity. *IEEE Transactions on Information Theory*, **51**(11), 3965–3973.

Bickel, P. 1969. A Distribution Free Version of the Smirnov Two Sample Test in the p-variate Case. *The Annals of Mathematical Statistics*, **40**(1), 1–23.

Bickel, S., Brückner, M., and Scheffer, T. 2007. Discriminative Learning for Differing Training and Test Distributions. Pages 81–88 of: *Proceedings of the 24th International Conference on Machine Learning (ICML2007)*.

Bickel, S., Bogojeska, J., Lengauer, T., and Scheffer, T. 2008. Multi-Task Learning for HIV Therapy Screening. Pages 56–63 of: McCallum, A., and Roweis, S. (eds), *Proceedings of 25th Annual International Conference on Machine Learning (ICML2008)*.

Bishop, C. M. 1995. *Neural Networks for Pattern Recognition*. Oxford, UK: Clarendon Press.

Bishop, C. M. 2006. *Pattern Recognition and Machine Learning*. New York: Springer.

Blanchard, G., Kawanabe, M., Sugiyama, M., Spokoiny, V., and Müller, K.-R. 2006. In Search of Non-Gaussian Components of a High-dimensional Distribution. *Journal of Machine Learning Research*, **7**(Feb.), 247–282.

Blei, D. M., and Jordan, M. I. 2006. Variational Inference for Dirichlet Process Mixtures. *Bayesian Analysis*, **1**(1), 121–144.

Bolton, R. J., and Hand, D. J. 2002. Statistical Fraud Detection: A Review. *Statistical Science*, **17**(3), 235–255.

Bonilla, E., Chai, K. M., and Williams, C. 2008. Multi-Task Gaussian Process Prediction. Pages 153–160 of: Platt, J. C., Koller, D., Singer, Y., and Roweis, S. (eds), *Advances in Neural Information Processing Systems 20*. Cambridge, MA: MIT Press.

Borgwardt, K. M., Gretton, A., Rasch, M. J., Kriegel, H.-P., Schölkopf, B., and Smola, A. J. 2006. Integrating Structured Biological Data by Kernel Maximum Mean Discrepancy. *Bioinformatics*, **22**(14), e49–e57.

Bousquet, O. 2002. A Bennett Concentration Inequality and its Application to Suprema of Empirical Process. *Note aux Compte Rendus de l'Académie des Sciences de Paris*, **334**, 495–500.

Boyd, S., and Vandenberghe, L. 2004. *Convex Optimization*. Cambridge, UK: Cambridge University Press.

Bradley, A. P. 1997. The Use of the Area under the ROC Curve in the Evaluation of Machine Learning Algorithms. *Pattern Recognition*, **30**(7), 1145–1159.

Bregman, L. M. 1967. The Relaxation Method of Finding the Common Point of Convex Sets and Its Application to the Solution of Problems in Convex Programming. *USSR Computational Mathematics and Mathematical Physics*, **7**, 200–217.

Breunig, M. M., Kriegel, H.-P., Ng, R. T., and Sander, J. 2000. LOF: Identifying Density-Based Local Outliers. Pages 93–104 of: Chen, W., Naughton, J. F., and Bernstein, P. A. (eds), *Proceedings of the ACM SIGMOD International Conference on Management of Data*.

Brodsky, B., and Darkhovsky, B. 1993. *Nonparametric Methods in Change-Point Problems*. Dordrecht, the Netherlands: Kluwer Academic Publishers.

Broniatowski, M., and Keziou, A. 2009. Parametric Estimation and Tests through Divergences and the Duality Technique. *Journal of Multivariate Analysis*, **100**, 16–26.

Buhmann, J. M. 1995. Data Clustering and Learning. Pages 278–281 of: Arbib, M. A. (ed), *The Handbook of Brain Theory and Neural Networks*. Cambridge, MA: MIT Press.

Bura, E., and Cook, R. D. 2001. Extending Sliced Inverse Regression. *Journal of the American Statistical Association*, **96**(455), 996–1003.

Caponnetto, A., and de Vito, E. 2007. Optimal Rates for Regularized Least-Squares Algorithm. *Foundations of Computational Mathematics*, **7**(3), 331–368.

Cardoso, J.-F. 1999. High-Order Contrasts for Independent Component Analysis. *Neural Computation*, **11**(1), 157–192.

Cardoso, J.-F., and Souloumiac, A. 1993. Blind Beamforming for Non-Gaussian Signals. *Radar and Signal Processing, IEE Proceedings-F*, **140**(6), 362–370.

Caruana, R., Pratt, L., and Thrun, S. 1997. Multitask Learning. *Machine Learning*, **28**, 41–75.

Cesa-Bianchi, N., and Lugosi, G. 2006. *Prediction, Learning, and Games*. Cambridge, UK: Cambridge University Press.

Chan, J., Bailey, J., and Leckie, C. 2008. Discovering Correlated Spatio-Temporal Changes in Evolving Graphs. *Knowledge and Information Systems*, **16**(1), 53–96.

Chang, C. C., and Lin, C. J. 2001. *LIBSVM: A Library for Support Vector Machines*. Tech. rept. Department of Computer Science, National Taiwan University. http://www.csie.ntu.edu.tw/~cjlin/libsvm/.

Chapelle, O., Schölkopf, B., and Zien, A. (eds). 2006. *Semi-Supervised Learning*. Cambridge, MA: MIT Press.

Chawla, N. V., Japkowicz, N., and Kotcz, A. 2004. Editorial: Special Issue on Learning from Imbalanced Data Sets. *ACM SIGKDD Explorations Newsletter*, **6**(1), 1–6.

Chen, S.-M., Hsu, Y.-S., and Liaw, J.-T. 2009. On Kernel Estimators of Density Ratio. *Statistics*, **43**(5), 463–479.

Chen, S. S., Donoho, D. L., and Saunders, M. A. 1998. Atomic Decomposition by Basis Pursuit. *SIAM Journal on Scientific Computing*, **20**(1), 33–61.

Cheng, K. F., and Chu, C. K. 2004. Semiparametric Density Estimation under a Two-sample Density Ratio Model. *Bernoulli*, **10**(4), 583–604.

Chiaromonte, F., and Cook, R. D. 2002. Sufficient Dimension Reduction and Graphics in Regression. *Annals of the Institute of Statistical Mathematics*, **54**(4), 768–795.

Cichocki, A., and Amari, S. 2003. *Adaptive Blind Signal and Image Processing: Learning Algorithms and Applications*. New York: Wiley.

Cohn, D. A., Ghahramani, Z., and Jordan, M. I. 1996. Active Learning with Statistical Models. *Journal of Artificial Intelligence Research*, **4**, 129–145.

Collobert, R., and Bengio., S. 2001. SVMTorch: Support Vector Machines for Large-Scale Regression Problems. *Journal of Machine Learning Research*, **1**, 143–160.

Comon, P. 1994. Independent Component Analysis, A New Concept? *Signal Processing*, **36**(3), 287–314.

Cook, R. D. 1998a. Principal Hessian Directions Revisited. *Journal of the American Statistical Association*, **93**(441), 84–100.

Cook, R. D. 1998b. *Regression Graphics: Ideas for Studying Regressions through Graphics*. New York: Wiley.

Cook, R. D. 2000. SAVE: A Method for Dimension Reduction and Graphics in Regression. *Communications in Statistics – Theory and Methods*, **29**(9), 2109–2121.

Cook, R. D., and Forzani, L. 2009. Likelihood-Based Sufficient Dimension Reduction. *Journal of the American Statistical Association*, **104**(485), 197–208.

Cook, R. D., and Ni, L. 2005. Sufficient Dimension Reduction via Inverse Regression. *Journal of the American Statistical Association*, **100**(470), 410–428.

Cortes, C., and Vapnik, V. 1995. Support-Vector Networks. *Machine Learning*, **20**, 273–297.

Cover, T. M., and Thomas, J. A. 2006. *Elements of Information Theory*. 2nd edn. Hoboken, NJ: Wiley.

Cramér, H. 1946. *Mathematical Methods of Statistics*. Princeton, NJ: Princeton University Press.

Craven, P., and Wahba, G. 1979. Smoothing Noisy Data with Spline Functions: Estimating the Correct Degree of Smoothing by the Method of Generalized Cross-Validation. *Numerische Mathematik*, **31**, 377–403.

Csiszár, I. 1967. Information-Type Measures of Difference of Probability Distributions and Indirect Observation. *Studia Scientiarum Mathematicarum Hungarica*, **2**, 229–318.

Ćwik, J., and Mielniczuk, J. 1989. Estimating Density Ratio with Application to Discriminant Analysis. *Communications in Statistics: Theory and Methods*, **18**(8), 3057–3069.

Darbellay, G. A., and Vajda, I. 1999. Estimation of the Information by an Adaptive Partitioning of the Observation Space. *IEEE Transactions on Information Theory*, **45**(4), 1315–1321.

Davis, J., Kulis, B., Jain, P., Sra, S., and Dhillon, I. 2007. Information-Theoretic Metric Learning. Pages 209–216 of: Ghahramani, Z. (ed), *Proceedings of the 24th Annual International Conference on Machine Learning (ICML2007)*.

Demmel, J. W. 1997. *Applied Numerical Linear Algebra*. Philadelphia, PA: Society for Industrial and Applied Mathematics.

Dempster, A. P., Laird, N. M., and Rubin, D. B. 1977. Maximum Likelihood from Incomplete Data via the EM Algorithm. *Journal of the Royal Statistical Society, series B*, **39**(1), 1–38.

Dhillon, I. S., Guan, Y., and Kulis, B. 2004. Kernel K-Means, Spectral Clustering and Normalized Cuts. Pages 551–556 of: *Proceedings of the Tenth ACM SIGKDD International Conference on Knowledge Discovery and Data Mining*. New York: ACM Press.

Donoho, D. L., and Grimes, C. E. 2003. Hessian Eigenmaps: Locally Linear Embedding Techniques for High-Dimensional Data. Pages 5591–5596 of: *Proceedings of the National Academy of Arts and Sciences*.

Duda, R. O., Hart, P. E., and Stork, D. G. 2001. *Pattern Classification*. 2nd edn. New York: Wiley.

Duffy, N., and Collins, M. 2002. Convolution Kernels for Natural Language. Pages 625–632 of: Dietterich, T. G., Becker, S., and Ghahramani, Z. (eds), *Advances in Neural Information Processing Systems 14*. Cambridge, MA: MIT Press.

Durand, J., and Sabatier, R. 1997. Additive Splines for Partial Least Squares Regression. *Journal of the American Statistical Association*, **92**(440), 1546–1554.

Edelman, A. 1988. Eigenvalues and Condition Numbers of Random Matrices. *SIAM Journal on Matrix Analysis and Applications*, **9**(4), 543–560.

Edelman, A., and Sutton, B. D. 2005. Tails of Condition Number Distributions. *SIAM Journal on Matrix Analysis and Applications*, **27**(2), 547–560.

Edelman, A., Arias, T. A., and Smith, S. T. 1998. The Geometry of Algorithms with Orthogonality Constraints. *SIAM Journal on Matrix Analysis and Applications*, **20**(2), 303–353.

Efron, B. 1975. The Efficiency of Logistic Regression Compared to Normal Discriminant Analysis. *Journal of the American Statistical Association*, **70**(352), 892–898.

Efron, B., and Tibshirani, R. J. 1993. *An Introduction to the Bootstrap*. New York: Chapman & Hall/CRC.

Efron, B., Hastie, T., Johnstone, I., and Tibshirani, R. 2004. Least Angle Regression. *The Annals of Statistics*, **32**(2), 407–499.

Elkan, C. 2011. Privacy-Preserving Data Mining via Importance Weighting. In C. Dimitrakakis, A. Gkoulalas-Divanis, A. Mitrokotsa, V. S. Verykios, and Y. Saygin (Eds.): *Privacy and Security Issues in Data Mining and Machine Learning*, 15–21, Berlin: Springer.

Evgeniou, T., and Pontil, M. 2004. Regularized Multi-Task Learning. Pages 109–117 of: *Proceedings of the Tenth ACM SIGKDD International Conference on Knowledge Discovery and Data Mining (KDD2004)*.

Faivishevsky, L., and Goldberger, J. 2009. ICA based on a Smooth Estimation of the Differential Entropy. Pages 433–440 of: Koller, D., Schuurmans, D., Bengio, Y., and Bottou, L. (eds), *Advances in Neural Information Processing Systems 21*. Cambridge, MA: MIT Press.

Faivishevsky, L., and Goldberger, J. 2010 (Jun. 21–25). A Nonparametric Information Theoretic Clustering Algorithm. Pages 351–358 of: Joachims, A. T., and Fürnkranz, J. (eds), *Proceedings of 27th International Conference on Machine Learning (ICML2010)*.

Fan, H., Zaïane, O. R., Foss, A., and Wu, J. 2009. Resolution-Based Outlier Factor: Dtecting the Top-n Most Outlying Data Points in Engineering Data. *Knowledge and Information Systems*, **19**(1), 31–51.

Fan, J., Yao, Q., and Tong, H. 1996. Estimation of Conditional Densities and Sensitivity Measures in Nonlinear Dynamical Systems. *Biometrika*, **83**(1), 189–206.

Fan, R.-E., Chen, P.-H., and Lin, C.-J. 2005. Working Set Selection Using Second Order Information for Training SVM. *Journal of Machine Learning Research*, **6**, 1889–1918.

Fan, R.-E., Chang, K.-W., Hsieh, C.-J., Wang, X.-R., and Lin, C.-J. 2008. LIBLINEAR: A Library for Large Linear Classification. *Journal of Machine Learning Research*, **9**, 1871–1874.

Fedorov, V. V. 1972. *Theory of Optimal Experiments*. New York: Academic Press.

Fernandez, E. A. 2005. *The dprep Package*. Tech. rept. University of Puerto Rico.

Feuerverger, A. 1993. A Consistent Test for Bivariate Dependence. *International Statistical Review*, **61**(3), 419–433.

Fisher, R. A. 1936. The Use of Multiple Measurements in Taxonomic Problems. *Annals of Eugenics*, **7**(2), 179–188.

Fishman, G. S. 1996. *Monte Carlo: Concepts, Algorithms, and Applications*. Berlin, Germany: Springer-Verlag.

Fokianos, K., Kedem, B., Qin, J., and Short, D. A. 2001. A Semiparametric Approach to the One-Way Layout. *Technometrics*, **43**, 56–64.

Franc, V., and Sonnenburg, S. 2009. Optimized Cutting Plane Algorithm for Large-Scale Risk Minimization. *Journal of Machine Learning Research*, **10**, 2157–2192.

Fraser, A. M., and Swinney, H. L. 1986. Independent Coordinates for Strange Attractors from Mutual Information. *Physical Review A*, **33**(2), 1134–1140.

Friedman, J., and Rafsky, L. 1979. Multivariate Generalizations of the Wald-Wolfowitz and Smirnov Two-Sample Tests. *The Annals of Statistics*, **7**(4), 697–717.

Friedman, J. H. 1987. Exploratory Projection Pursuit. *Journal of the American Statistical Association*, **82**(397), 249–266.

Friedman, J. H., and Tukey, J. W. 1974. A Projection Pursuit Algorithm for Exploratory Data Analysis. *IEEE Transactions on Computers*, **C-23**(9), 881–890.

Fujimaki, R., Yairi, T., and Machida, K. 2005. An Approachh to Spacecraft Anomaly Detection Problem Using Kernel Feature Space. Pages 401–410 of: *Proceedings of the 11th ACM SIGKDD International Conference on Knowledge Discovery and Data Mining (KDD2005)*.

Fujisawa, H., and Eguchi, S. 2008. Robust Parameter Estimation with a Small Bias against Heavy Contamination. *Journal of Multivariate Analysis*, **99**(9), 2053–2081.

Fukumizu, K. 2000. Statistical Active Learning in Multilayer Perceptrons. *IEEE Transactions on Neural Networks*, **11**(1), 17–26.

Fukumizu, K., Bach, F. R., and Jordan, M. I. 2004. Dimensionality Reduction for Supervised Learning with Reproducing Kernel Hilbert Spaces. *Journal of Machine Learning Research*, **5**(Jan), 73–99.

Fukumizu, K., Bach, F. R., and Jordan, M. I. 2009. Kernel Dimension Reduction in Regression. *The Annals of Statistics*, **37**(4), 1871–1905.

Fukunaga, K. 1990. *Introduction to Statistical Pattern Recognition*. 2nd edn. Boston, MA: Academic Press, Inc.

Fung, G. M., and Mangasarian, O. L. 2005. Multicategory Proximal Support Vector Machine Classifiers. *Machine Learning*, **59**(1–2), 77–97.

Gao, J., Cheng, H., and Tan, P.-N. 2006a. A Novel Framework for Incorporating Labeled Examples into Anomaly Detection. Pages 593–597 of: *Proceedings of the 2006 SIAM International Conference on Data Mining*.

Gao, J., Cheng, H., and Tan, P.-N. 2006b. Semi-Supervised Outlier Detection. Pages 635–636 of: *Proceedings of the 2006 ACM symposium on Applied Computing*.

Gärtner, T. 2003. A Survey of Kernels for Structured Data. *SIGKDD Explorations*, **5**(1), S268–S275.

Gärtner, T., Flach, P., and Wrobel, S. 2003. On Graph Kernels: Hardness Results and Efficient Alternatives. Pages 129–143 of: Schölkopf, B., and Warmuth, M. (eds), *Proceedings of the Sixteenth Annual Conference on Computational Learning Theory*.

Ghosal, S., and van der Vaart, A. W. 2001. Entropies and Rates of Convergence for Maximum Likelihood and Bayes Estimation for Mixtures of Normal Densities. *Annals of Statistics*, **29**, 1233–1263.

Globerson, A., and Roweis, S. 2006. Metric Learning by Collapsing Classes. Pages 451–458 of: Weiss, Y., Schölkopf, B., and Platt, J. (eds), *Advances in Neural Information Processing Systems 18*. Cambridge, MA: MIT Press.

Godambe, V. P. 1960. An Optimum Property of Regular Maximum Likelihood Estimation. *Annals of Mathematical Statistics*, **31**, 1208–1211.

Goldberger, J., Roweis, S., Hinton, G., and Salakhutdinov, R. 2005. Neighbourhood Components Analysis. Pages 513–520 of: Saul, L. K., Weiss, Y., and Bottou, L. (eds), *Advances in Neural Information Processing Systems 17*. Cambridge, MA: MIT Press.

Golub, G. H., and Loan, C. F. Van. 1996. *Matrix Computations*. Baltimore, MD: Johns Hopkins University Press.

Gomes, R., Krause, A., and Perona, P. 2010. Discriminative Clustering by Regularized Information Maximization. Pages 766–774 of: Lafferty, J., Williams, C. K. I., Zemel, R., Shawe-Taylor, J., and Culotta, A. (eds), *Advances in Neural Information Processing Systems 23*. Cambridge, MA: MIT Press.

Goutis, C., and Fearn, T. 1996. Partial Least Squares Regression on Smooth Factors. *Journal of the American Statistical Association*, **91**(434), 627–632.

Graham, D. B., and Allinson, N. M. 1998. Characterizing Virtual Eigensignatures for General Purpose Face Recognition. Pages 446–456 of: *Computer and Systems Sciences*. NATO ASI Series F, vol. 163. Berlin, Germany: Springer.

Gretton, A., Bousquet, O., Smola, A., and Schölkopf, B. 2005. Measuring Statistical Dependence with Hilbert-Schmidt Norms. Pages 63–77 of: Jain, S., Simon, H. U., and Tomita, E. (eds), *Algorithmic Learning Theory*. Lecture Notes in Artificial Intelligence. Berlin, Germany: Springer-Verlag.

Gretton, A., Borgwardt, K. M., Rasch, M., Schölkopf, B., and Smola, A. J. 2007. A Kernel Method for the Two-Sample-Problem. Pages 513–520 of: Schölkopf, B., Platt, J., and Hoffman, T. (eds), *Advances in Neural Information Processing Systems 19*. Cambridge, MA: MIT Press.

Gretton, A., Fukumizu, K., Teo, C. H., Song, L., Schölkopf, B., and Smola, A. 2008. A Kernel Statistical Test of Independence. Pages 585–592 of: Platt, J. C., Koller, D., Singer, Y., and Roweis, S. (eds), *Advances in Neural Information Processing Systems 20*. Cambridge, MA: MIT Press.

Gretton, A., Smola, A., Huang, J., Schmittfull, M., Borgwardt, K., and Schölkopf, B. 2009. Covariate Shift by Kernel Mean Matching. Chap. 8, pages 131–160 of: Quiñonero-Candela, J., Sugiyama, M., Schwaighofer, A., and Lawrence, N. (eds), *Dataset Shift in Machine Learning*. Cambridge, MA: MIT Press.

Guralnik, V., and Srivastava, J. 1999. Event Detection from Time Series Data. Pages 33–42 of: *Proceedings of the 5th ACM SIGKDD International Conference on Knowledge Discovery and Data Mining (KDD1999)*.

Gustafsson, F. 2000. *Adaptive Filtering and Change Detection*. Chichester, UK: Wiley.

Guyon, I., and Elisseeff, A. 2003. An Introduction to Variable Feature Selection. *Journal of Machine Learning Research*, **3**, 1157–1182.

Hachiya, H., Akiyama, T., Sugiyama, M., and Peters, J. 2009. Adaptive Importance Sampling for Value Function Approximation in Off-policy Reinforcement Learning. *Neural Networks*, **22**(10), 1399–1410.

Hachiya, H., Sugiyama, M., and Ueda, N. 2011a. Importance-Weighted Least-Squares Probabilistic Classifier for Covariate Shift Adaptation with Application to Human Activity Recognition. *Neurocomputing*. To appear.

Hachiya, H., Peters, J., and Sugiyama, M. 2011b. Reward Weighted Regression with Sample Reuse. *Neural Computation*, **23**(11), 2798–2832.

Hall, P., and Tajvidi, N. 2002. Permutation Tests for Equality of Distributions in Highdimensional Settings. *Biometrika*, **89**(2), 359–374.

Härdle, W., Müller, M., Sperlich, S., and Werwatz, A. 2004. *Nonparametric and Semiparametric Models*. Berlin, Germany: Springer.

Hartigan, J. A. 1975. *Clustering Algorithms*. New York: Wiley.

Hastie, T., and Tibshirani, R. 1996a. Discriminant Adaptive Nearest Neighbor Classification. *IEEE Transactions on Pattern Analysis and Machine Intelligence*, **18**(6), 607–615.

Hastie, T., and Tibshirani, R. 1996b. Discriminant Analysis by Gaussian mixtures. *Journal of the Royal Statistical Society, Series B*, **58**(1), 155–176.

Hastie, T., Tibshirani, R., and Friedman, J. 2001. *The Elements of Statistical Learning: Data Mining, Inference, and Prediction*. New York: Springer.

Hastie, T., Rosset, S., Tibshirani, R., and Zhu, J. 2004. The Entire Regularization Path for the Support Vector Machine. *Journal of Machine Learning Research*, **5**, 1391–1415.

He, X., and Niyogi, P. 2004. Locality Preserving Projections. Pages 153–160 of: Thrun, S., Saul, L., and Schölkopf, B. (eds), *Advances in Neural Information Processing Systems 16*. Cambridge, MA: MIT Press.

Heckman, J. J. 1979. Sample Selection Bias as a Specification Error. *Econometrica*, **47**(1), 153–161.

Henkel, R. E. 1976. *Tests of Significance*. Beverly Hills, CA: Sage.

Hido, S., Tsuboi, Y., Kashima, H., Sugiyama, M., and Kanamori, T. 2011. Statistical Outlier Detection Using Direct Density Ratio Estimation. *Knowledge and Information Systems*, **26**(2), 309–336.

Hinton, G. E., and Salakhutdinov, R. R. 2006. Reducing the Dimensionality of Data with Neural Networks. *Science*, **313**(5786), 504–507.

Hodge, V., and Austin, J. 2004. A Survey of Outlier Detection Methodologies. *Artificial Intelligence Review*, **22**(2), 85–126.

Hoerl, A. E., and Kennard, R. W. 1970. Ridge Regression: Biased Estimation for Nonorthogonal Problems. *Technometrics*, **12**(3), 55–67.

Horn, R., and Johnson, C. 1985. *Matrix Analysis*. Cambridge, UK: Cambridge University Press.

Hotelling, H. 1936. Relations between Two Sets of Variates. *Biometrika*, **28**(3–4), 321–377.

Hotelling, H. 1951. A Generalized T Test and Measure of Multivariate Dispersion. Pages 23–41 of: *Proceedings of the 2nd Berkeley Symposium on Mathematical Statistics and Probability*. Berkeley: University of California Press.

Hoyer, P. O., Janzing, D., Mooij, J. M., Peters, J., and Schölkopf, B. 2009. Nonlinear Causal Discovery with Additive Noise Models. Pages 689–696 of: Koller, D., Schuurmans, D., Bengio, Y., and Bottou, L. (eds), *Advances in Neural Information Processing Systems 21*. Cambridge, MA: MIT Press.

Huang, J., Smola, A., Gretton, A., Borgwardt, K. M., and Schölkopf, B. 2007. Correcting Sample Selection Bias by Unlabeled Data. Pages 601–608 of: Schölkopf, B., Platt, J., and Hoffman, T. (eds), *Advances in Neural Information Processing Systems 19*. Cambridge, MA: MIT Press.

Huber, P. J. 1985. Projection Pursuit. *The Annals of Statistics*, **13**(2), 435–475.

Hulle, M. M. Van. 2005. Edgeworth Approximation of Multivariate Differential Entropy. *Neural Computation*, **17**(9), 1903–1910.

Hulle, M. M. Van. 2008. Sequential Fixed-Point ICA Based on Mutual Information Minimization. *Neural Computation*, **20**(5), 1344–1365.

Hyvaerinen, A. 1999. Fast and Robust Fixed-Point Algorithms for Independent Component Analysis. *IEEE Transactions on Neural Networks*, **10**(3), 626.

Hyvärinen, A., Karhunen, J., and Oja, E. 2001. *Independent Component Analysis*. New York: Wiley.

Ide, T., and Kashima, H. 2004. Eigenspace-Based Anomaly Detection in Computer Systems. Pages 440–449 of: *Proceedings of the 10th ACM SIGKDD International Conference on Knowledge Discovery and Data Mining (KDD2004)*.

Ishiguro, M., Sakamoto, Y., and Kitagawa, G. 1997. Bootstrapping Log Likelihood and EIC, an Extension of AIC. *Annals of the Institute of Statistical Mathematics*, **49**, 411–434.

Jacoba, P., and Oliveirab, P. E. 1997. Kernel Estimators of General Radon-Nikodym Derivatives. *Statistics*, **30**, 25–46.

Jain, A. K., and Dubes, R. C. 1988. *Algorithms for Clustering Data*. Englewood Cliffs, NJ: Prentice Hall.

Jaynes, E. T. 1957. Information Theory and Statistical Mechanics. *Physical Review*, **106**(4), 620–630.

Jebara, T. 2004. Kernelized Sorting, Permutation and Alignment for Minimum Volume PCA. Pages 609–623 of: *17th Annual Conference on Learning Theory (COLT2004)*.

Jiang, X., and Zhu, X. 2009. vEye: Behavioral Footprinting for Self-Propagating Worm Detection and Profiling. *Knowledge and Information Systems*, **18**(2), 231–262.

Joachims, T. 1999. Making Large-Scale SVM Learning Practical. Pages 169–184 of: Schölkopf, B., Burges, C. J. C., and Smola, A. J. (eds), *Advances in Kernel Methods—Support Vector Learning*. Cambridge, MA: MIT Press.

Joachims, T. 2006. Training Linear SVMs in Linear Time. Pages 217–226 of: *ACM SIGKDD International Conference on Knowledge Discovery and Data Mining (KDD2006)*.

Jolliffe, I. T. 1986. *Principal Component Analysis*. New York: Springer-Verlag.

Jones, M. C., Hjort, N. L., Harris, I. R., and Basu, A. 2001. A Comparison of Related Density-based Minimum Divergence Estimators. *Biometrika*, **88**, 865–873.

Jordan, M. I., Ghahramani, Z., Jaakkola, T. S., and Saul, L. K. 1999. An Introduction to Variational Methods for Graphical Models. *Machine Learning*, **37**(2), 183.

Jutten, C., and Herault, J. 1991. Blind Separation of Sources, Part I: An Adaptive algorithm Based on Neuromimetic Architecture. *Signal Processing*, **24**(1), 1–10.

Kanamori, T. 2007. Pool-Based Active Learning with Optimal Sampling Distribution and its Information Geometrical Interpretation. *Neurocomputing*, **71**(1–3), 353–362.

Kanamori, T., and Shimodaira, H. 2003. Active Learning Algorithm Using the Maximum Weighted Log-Likelihood Estimator. *Journal of Statistical Planning and Inference*, **116**(1), 149–162.

Kanamori, T., Hido, S., and Sugiyama, M. 2009. A Least-squares Approach to Direct Importance Estimation. *Journal of Machine Learning Research*, **10**(Jul.), 1391–1445.

Kanamori, T., Suzuki, T., and Sugiyama, M. 2010. Theoretical Analysis of Density Ratio Estimation. *IEICE Transactions on Fundamentals of Electronics, Communications and Computer Sciences*, **E93-A**(4), 787–798.

Kanamori, T., Suzuki, T., and Sugiyama, M. 2011a. f-Divergence Estimation and Two-Sample Homogeneity Test under Semiparametric Density-Ratio Models. *IEEE Transactions on Information Theory*. To appear.

Kanamori, T., Suzuki, T., and Sugiyama, M. 2011b. Statistical Analysis of Kernel-Based Least-Squares Density-Ratio Estimation. *Machine Learning*. To appear.

Kanamori, T., Suzuki, T., and Sugiyama, M. 2011c. Kernel-Based Least-Squares Density-Ratio Estimation II. Condition Number Analysis. *Machine Learning*. submitted.

Kankainen, A. 1995. *Consistent Testing of Total Independence Based on the Empirical Characteristic Function*. Ph.D. thesis, University of Jyväskylä, Jyväskylä, Finland.

Karatzoglou, A., Smola, A., Hornik, K., and Zeileis, A. 2004. kernlab—An S4 Package for Kernel Methods in R. *Journal of Statistical Planning and Inference*, **11**(9), 1–20.

Kashima, H., and Koyanagi, T. 2002. Kernels for Semi-Structured Data. Pages 291–298 of: *Proceedings of the Nineteenth International Conference on Machine Learning*.

Kashima, H., Tsuda, K., and Inokuchi, A. 2003. Marginalized Kernels between Labeled Graphs. Pages 321–328 of: *Proceedings of the Twentieth International Conference on Machine Learning*.

Kato, T., Kashima, H., Sugiyama, M., and Asai, K. 2010. Conic Programming for Multi-Task Learning. *IEEE Transactions on Knowledge and Data Engineering*, **22**(7), 957–968.

Kawahara, Y., and Sugiyama, M. 2011. Sequential Change-Point Detection Based on Direct Density-Ratio Estimation. *Statistical Analysis and Data Mining*. To appear.

Kawanabe, M., Sugiyama, M., Blanchard, G., and Müller, K.-R. 2007. A New Algorithm of Non-Gaussian Component Analysis with Radial Kernel Functions. *Annals of the Institute of Statistical Mathematics*, **59**(1), 57–75.

Ke, Y., Sukthankar, R., and Hebert, M. 2007. Event Detection in Crowded Videos. Pages 1–8 of: *Proceedings of the 11th IEEE International Conference on Computer Vision (ICCV2007)*.

Keziou, A. 2003a. Dual Representation of ϕ-Divergences and Applications. *Comptes Rendus Mathématique*, **336**(10), 857–862.

Keziou, A. 2003b. *Utilisation Des Divergences Entre Mesures en Statistique Inferentielle*. Ph.D. thesis, UPMC University. in French.

Keziou, A., and Leoni-Aubin, S. 2005. Test of Homogeneity in Semiparametric Two-sample Density Ratio Models. *Comptes Rendus Mathématique*, **340**(12), 905–910.

Keziou, A., and Leoni-Aubin, S. 2008. On Empirical Likelihood for Semiparametric Two-Sample Density Ratio Models. *Journal of Statistical Planning and Inference*, **138**(4), 915–928.

Khan, S., Bandyopadhyay, S., Ganguly, A., and Saigal, S. 2007. Relative Performance of Mutual Information Estimation Methods for Quantifying the Dependence among Short and Noisy Data. *Physical Review E*, **76**, 026209.

Kifer, D., Ben-David, S, and Gehrke, J. 2004. Detecting Change in Data Streams. Pages 180–191 of: *Proceedings of the 30th International Conference on Very Large Data Bases (VLDB2004)*.

Kimeldorf, G. S., and Wahba, G. 1971. Some Results on Tchebycheffian Spline Functions. *Journal of Mathematical Analysis and Applications*, **33**(1), 82–95.

Kimura, M., and Sugiyama, M. 2011. Dependence-Maximization Clustering with Least-Squares Mutual Information. *Journal of Advanced Computational Intelligence and Intelligent Informatics*, **15**(7), 800–805.

Koh, K., Kim, S.-J., and Boyd, S. P. 2007. An Interior-point Method for Large-Scale l_1-Regularized Logistic Regression. *Journal of Machine Learning Research*, **8**, 1519–1555.

Kohonen, T. 1988. Learning Vector Quantization. *Neural Networks*, **1**(Supplementary 1), 303.

Kohonen, T. 1995. *Self-Organizing Maps*. Berlin, Germany: Springer.

Koltchinskii, V. 2006. Local Rademacher Complexities and Oracle Inequalities in Risk Minimization. *The Annals of Statistics*, **34**, 2593–2656.

Kondor, R. I., and Lafferty, J. 2002. Diffusion Kernels on Graphs and Other Discrete Input Spaces. Pages 315–322 of: *Proceedings of the Nineteenth International Conference on Machine Learning*.

Konishi, S., and Kitagawa, G. 1996. Generalized Information Criteria in Model Selection. *Biometrika*, **83**(4), 875–890.

Korostelëv, A. P., and Tsybakov, A. B. 1993. *Minimax Theory of Image Reconstruction*. New York: Springer.

Kraskov, A., Stögbauer, H., and Grassberger, P. 2004. Estimating Mutual Information. *Physical Review E*, **69**(6), 066138.

Kullback, S. 1959. *Information Theory and Statistics*. New York: Wiley.

Kullback, S., and Leibler, R. A. 1951. On Information and Sufficiency. *Annals of Mathematical Statistics*, **22**, 79–86.

Kurihara, N., Sugiyama, M., Ogawa, H., Kitagawa, K., and Suzuki, K. 2010. Iteratively-Reweighted Local Model Fitting Method for Adaptive and Accurate Single-Shot Surface Profiling. *Applied Optics*, **49**(22), 4270–4277.

Lafferty, J., McCallum, A., and Pereira, F. 2001. Conditional Random Fields: Probabilistic Models for Segmenting and Labeling Sequence Data. Pages 282–289 of: *Proceedings of the 18th International Conference on Machine Learning*.

Lagoudakis, M. G., and Parr, R. 2003. Least-Squares Policy Iteration. *Journal of Machine Learning Research*, **4**, 1107–1149.

Lapedriza, À., Masip, D., and Vitrià, J. 2007. A Hierarchical Approach for Multi-task Logistic Regression. Pages 258–265 of: Mart, J., Bened, J. M., Mendonga, A. M., and Serrat, J. (eds), *Proceedings of the 3rd Iberian Conference on Pattern Recognition and Image Analysis, Part II*. Lecture Notes in Computer Science, vol. 4478. Berlin, Germany: Springer-Verlag.

Larsen, J., and Hansen, L. K. 1996. Linear Unlearning for Cross-Validation. *Advances in Computational Mathematics*, **5**, 269–280.

Latecki, L. J., Lazarevic, A., and Pokrajac, D. 2007. Outlier Detection with Kernel Density Functions. Pages 61–75 of: *Proceedings of the 5th International Conference on Machine Learning and Data Mining in Pattern Recognition*.

Lee, T.-W., Girolami, M., and Sejnowski, T. J. 1999. Independent Component Analysis Using an Extended Infomax Algorithm for Mixed Subgaussian and Supergaussian Sources. *Neural Computation*, **11**(2), 417–441.

Lehmann, E. L. 1986. *Testing Statistical Hypotheses*. 2nd edn. New York: Wiley.

Lehmann, E. L., and Casella, G. 1998. *Theory of Point Estimation*. 2nd edn. New York: Springer.

Li, K. 1991. Sliced Inverse Regression for Dimension Reduction. *Journal of the American Statistical Association*, **86**(414), 316–342.

Li, K. 1992. On Principal Hessian Directions for Data Visualization and Dimension Reduction: Another Application of Stein's Lemma. *Journal of the American Statistical Association*, **87**(420), 1025–1039.

Li, K. C., Lue, H. H., and Chen, C. H. 2000. Interactive Tree-structured Regression via Principal Hessian Directions. *Journal of the American Statistical Association*, **95**(450), 547–560.

Li, L., and Lu, W. 2008. Sufficient Dimension Reduction with Missing Predictors. *Journal of the American Statistical Association*, **103**(482), 822–831.

Li, Q. 1996. Nonparametric Testing of Closeness between Two Unknown Distribution Functions. *Econometric Reviews*, **15**(3), 261–274.

Li, Y., Liu, Y., and Zhu, J. 2007. Quantile Regression in Reproducing Kernel Hilbert Spaces. *Journal of the American Statistical Association*, **102**(477), 255–268.

Li, Y., Kambara, H., Koike, Y., and Sugiyama, M. 2010. Application of Covariate Shift Adaptation Techniques in Brain Computer Interfaces. *IEEE Transactions on Biomedical Engineering*, **57**(6), 1318–1324.

Lin, Y. 2002. Support Vector Machines and the Bayes Rule in Classification. *Data Mining and Knowledge Discovery*, **6**(3), 259–275.

Lodhi, H., Saunders, C., Shawe-Taylor, J., Cristianini, N., and Watkins, C. 2002. Text Classification Using String Kernels. *Journal of Machine Learning Research*, **2**, 419–444.

Luenberger, D., and Ye, Y. 2008. *Linear and Nonlinear Programming*. Reading, MA: Springer.

Luntz, A., and Brailovsky, V. 1969. On Estimation of Characters Obtained in Statistical Procedure of Recognition. *Technicheskaya Kibernetica*, **3**. in Russian.

MacKay, D. J. C. 2003. *Information Theory, Inference, and Learning Algorithms*. Cambridge, UK: Cambridge University Press.

MacQueen, J. B. 1967. Some Methods for Classification and Analysis of Multivariate Observations. Pages 281–297 of: *Proceedings of the 5th Berkeley Symposium on Mathematical Statistics and Probability*, vol. 1. Berkeley: University of California Press.

Mallows, C. L. 1973. Some Comments on C_P. *Technometrics*, **15**(4), 661–675.

Manevitz, L. M., and Yousef, M. 2002. One-Class SVMs for Document Classification. *Journal of Machine Learning Research*, **2**, 139–154.

Meila, M., and Heckerman, D. 2001. An Experimental Comparison of Model-Based Clustering Methods. *Machine Learning*, **42**(1/2), 9.

Mendelson, S. 2002. Improving the Sample Complexity Using Global Data. *IEEE Transactions on Information Theory*, **48**(7), 1977–1991.

Mercer, J. 1909. Functions of Positive and Negative Type and Their Connection with the Theory of Integral Equations. *Philosophical Transactions of the Royal Society of London*, **A-209**, 415–446.

Micchelli, C. A., and Pontil, M. 2005. Kernels for Multi-Task Learning. Pages 921–928 of: Saul, L. K., Weiss, Y., and Bottou, L. (eds), *Advances in Neural Information Processing Systems 17*. Cambridge, MA: MIT Press.

Minka, T. P. 2007. *A Comparison of Numerical Optimizers for Logistic Regression*. Tech. rept. Microsoft Research.

Moré, J. J., and Sorensen, D. C. 1984. Newton's Method. In: Golub, G. H. (ed), *Studies in Numerical Analysis*. Washington, DC: Mathematical Association of America.

Mori, S., Sugiyama, M., Ogawa, H., Kitagawa, K., and Irie, K. 2011. Automatic Parameter Optimization of the Local Model Fitting Method for Single-shot Surface Profiling. *Applied Optics*, **50**(21), 3773–3780.

Müller, A. 1997. Integral Probability Metrics and Their Generating Classes of Functions. *Advances in Applied Probability*, **29**, 429–443.

Murad, U., and Pinkas, G. 1999. Unsupervised Profiling for Identifying Superimposed Fraud. Pages 251–261 of: *Proceedings of the 5th ACM SIGKDD International Conference on Knowledge Discovery and Data Mining (KDD1999)*.

Murata, N., Yoshizawa, S., and Amari, S. 1994. Network Information Criterion — Determining the Number of Hidden Units for an Artificial Neural Network Model. *IEEE Transactions on Neural Networks*, **5**(6), 865–872.

Ng, A. Y., Jordan, M. I., and Weiss, Y. 2002. On Spectral Clustering: Analysis and An Algorithm. Pages 849–856 of: Dietterich, T. G., Becker, S., and Ghahramani, Z. (eds), *Advances in Neural Information Processing Systems 14*. Cambridge, MA: MIT Press.

Nguyen, X., Wainwright, M. J., and Jordan, M. I. 2010. Estimating Divergence Functionals and the Likelihood Ratio by Convex Risk Minimization. *IEEE Transactions on Information Theory*, **56**(11), 5847–5861.

Nishimori, Y., and Akaho, S. 2005. Learning Algorithms Utilizing Quasi-geodesic Flows on the Stiefel Manifold. *Neurocomputing*, **67**, 106–135.

Oja, E. 1982. A Simplified Neuron Model as a Principal Component Analyzer. *Journal of Mathematical Biology*, **15**(3), 267–273.

Oja, E. 1989. Neural Networks, Principal Components and Subspaces. *International Journal of Neural Systems*, **1**, 61–68.

Patriksson, M. 1999. *Nonlinear Programming and Variational Inequality Problems*. Dordrecht, the Netherlands: Kluwer Academic.

Pearl, J. 2000. *Causality: Models, Reasning and Inference*. New York: Cambridge University Press.

Pearson, K. 1900. On the Criterion That a Given System of Deviations from the Probable in the Case of a Correlated System of Variables Is Such That It Can Be Reasonably

Supposed to Have Arisen from Random Sampling. *Philosophical Magazine Series 5*, **50**(302), 157–175.

Pérez-Cruz, F. 2008. Kullback-Leibler Divergence Estimation of Continuous Distributions. Pages 1666–1670 of: *Proceedings of IEEE International Symposium on Information Theory*.

Platt, J. 1999. Fast Training of Support Vector Machines Using Sequential Minimal Optimization. Pages 169–184 of: Schölkopf, B., Burges, C. J. C., and Smola, A. J. (eds), *Advances in Kernel Methods—Support Vector Learning*. Cambridge, MA: MIT Press.

Platt, J. 2000. Probabilities for SV Machines. In: Smola, A. J., Bartlett, P. L., Schölkopf, B., and Schuurmans, D. (eds), *Advances in Large Margin Classifiers*. Cambridge, MA: MIT Press.

Plumbley, M. D. 2005. Geometrical Methods for Non-Negative ICA: Manifolds, Lie Groups and Toral Subalgebras. *Neurocomputing*, **67**(Aug.), 161–197.

Press, W. H., Flannery, B. P., Teukolsky, S. A., and Vetterling, W. T. 1992. *Numerical Recipes in C*. 2nd edn. Cambridge, UK: Cambridge University Press.

Pukelsheim, F. 1993. *Optimal Design of Experiments*. New York: Wiley.

Qin, J. 1998. Inferences for Case-control and Semiparametric Two-sample Density Ratio Models. *Biometrika*, **85**(3), 619–630.

Qing, W., Kulkarni, S. R., and Verdu, S. 2006. A Nearest-Neighbor Approach to Estimating Divergence between Continuous Random Vectors. Pages 242–246 of: *Proceedings of IEEE International Symposium on Information Theory*.

Quadrianto, N., Smola, A. J., Song, L., and Tuytelaars, T. 2010. Kernelized Sorting. *IEEE Transactions on Pattern Analysis and Machine Intelligence*, **32**, 1809–1821.

Quiñonero-Candela, J., Sugiyama, M., Schwaighofer, A., and Lawrence, N. (eds). 2009. *Dataset Shift in Machine Learning*. Cambridge, MA: MIT Press.

R Development Core Team. 2009. *R: A Language and Environment for Statistical Computing*. R Foundation for Statistical Computing, Vienna, Austria. http://www.r-project.org.

Rao, C. 1945. Information and the Accuracy Attainable in the Estimation of Statistical Parameters. *Bulletin of the Calcutta Mathematics Society*, **37**, 81–89.

Rasmussen, C. E., and Williams, C. K. I. 2006. *Gaussian Processes for Machine Learning*. Cambridge, MA: MIT Press.

Rätsch, G., Onoda, T., and Müller, K.-R. 2001. Soft Margins for AdaBoost. *Machine Learning*, **42**(3), 287–320.

Reiss, P. T., and Ogden, R. T. 2007. Functional Principal Component Regression and Functional Partial Least Squares. *Journal of the American Statistical Association*, **102**(479), 984–996.

Rifkin, R., Yeo, G., and Poggio, T. 2003. Regularized Least-Squares Classification. Pages 131–154 of: Suykens, J. A. K., Horvath, G., Basu, S., Micchelli, C., and Vandewalle, J. (eds), *Advances in Learning Theory: Methods, Models and Applications*. NATO Science Series III: Computer & Systems Sciences, vol. 190. Amsterdam, the Netherlands: IOS Press.

Rissanen, J. 1978. Modeling by Shortest Data Description. *Automatica*, **14**(5), 465–471.

Rissanen, J. 1987. Stochastic Complexity. *Journal of the Royal Statistical Society, Series B*, **49**(3), 223–239.

Rockafellar, R. T. 1970. *Convex Analysis*. Princeton, NJ: Princeton University Press.

Rosenblatt, M. 1956. Remarks on some nonparametric estimates of a density function. *Annals of Mathematical Statistics*, **27**, 832–837.

Roweis, S., and Saul, L. 2000. Nonlinear Dimensionality Reduction by Locally Linear Embedding. *Science*, **290**(5500), 2323–2326.

Sankar, A., Spielman, D. A., and Teng, S.-H. 2006. Smoothed Analysis of the Condition Numbers and Growth Factors of Matrices. *SIAM Journal on Matrix Analysis and Applications*, **28**(2), 446–476.

Saul, L. K., and Roweis, S. T. 2003. Think Globally, Fit Locally: Unsupervised Learning of Low Dimensional Manifolds. *Journal of Machine Learning Research*, **4**(Jun), 119–155.

Schapire, R., Freund, Y., Bartlett, P., and Lee, W. Sun. 1998. Boosting the Margin: A New Explanation for the Effectiveness of Voting Methods. *Annals of Statistics*, **26**, 1651–1686.

Scheinberg, K. 2006. An Efficient Implementation of an Active Set Method for SVMs. *Journal of Machine Learning Research*, **7**, 2237–2257.

Schmidt, M. 2005. *minFunc*. http://people.cs.ubc.ca/~schmidtm/Software/minFunc.html.
Schölkopf, B., and Smola, A. J. 2002. *Learning with Kernels*. Cambridge, MA: MIT Press.
Schölkopf, B., Smola, A., and Müller, K.-R. 1998. Nonlinear Component Analysis as a Kernel Eigenvalue Problem. *Neural Computation*, **10**(5), 1299–1319.
Schölkopf, B., Platt, J. C., Shawe-Taylor, J., Smola, A. J., and Williamson, R. C. 2001. Estimating the Support of a High-Dimensional Distribution. *Neural Computation*, **13**(7), 1443–1471.
Schwarz, G. 1978. Estimating the Dimension of a Model. *The Annals of Statistics*, **6**, 461–464.
Shi, J., and Malik, J. 2000. Normalized Cuts and Image Segmentation. *IEEE Transactions on Pattern Analysis and Machine Intelligence*, **22**(8), 888–905.
Shibata, R. 1981. An Optimal Selection of Regression Variables. *Biometrika*, **68**(1), 45–54.
Shibata, R. 1989. Statistical Aspects of Model Selection. Pages 215–240 of: Willems, J. C. (ed), *From Data to Model*. New York: Springer-Verlag.
Shimodaira, H. 2000. Improving Predictive Inference under Covariate Shift by Weighting the Log-Likelihood Function. *Journal of Statistical Planning and Inference*, **90**(2), 227–244.
Silva, J., and Narayanan, S. 2007. Universal Consistency of Data-Driven Partitions for Divergence Estimation. Pages 2021–2025 of: *Proceedings of IEEE International Symposium on Information Theory*.
Simm, J., Sugiyama, M., and Kato, T. 2011. Computationally Efficient Multi-task Learning with Least-Squares Probabilistic Classifiers. *IPSJ Transactions on Computer Vision and Applications*, **3**, 1–8.
Smola, A., Song, L., and Teo, C. H. 2009. Relative Novelty Detection. Pages 536–543 of: van Dyk, D., and Welling, M. (eds), *Proceedings of Twelfth International Conference on Artificial Intelligence and Statistics (AISTATS2009)*. JMLR Workshop and Conference Proceedings, vol. 5.
Song, L., Smola, A., Gretton, A., and Borgwardt, K. 2007a. A Dependence Maximization View of Clustering. Pages 815–822 of: Ghahramani, Z. (ed), *Proceedings of the 24th Annual International Conference on Machine Learning (ICML2007)*.
Song, L., Smola, A., Gretton, A., Borgwardt, K. M., and Bedo, J. 2007b. Supervised Feature Selection via Dependence Estimation. Pages 823–830 of: Ghahramani, Z. (ed), *Proceedings of the 24th Annual International Conference on Machine Learning (ICML2007)*.
Spielman, D. A., and Teng, S.-H. 2004. Smoothed Analysis of Algorithms: Why the Simplex Algorithm Usually Takes Polynomial Time. *Journal of the ACM*, **51**(3), 385–463.
Sriperumbudur, B., Fukumizu, K., Gretton, A., Lanckriet, G., and Schölkopf, B. 2009. Kernel Choice and Classifiability for RKHS Embeddings of Probability Distributions. Pages 1750–1758 of: Bengio, Y., Schuurmans, D., Lafferty, J., Williams, C. K. I., and Culotta, A. (eds), *Advances in Neural Information Processing Systems 22*. Cambridge, MA: MIT Press.
Steinwart, I. 2001. On the Influence of the Kernel on the Consistency of Support Vector Machines. *Journal of Machine Learning Research*, **2**, 67–93.
Steinwart, I., Hush, D., and Scovel, C. 2009. Optimal Rates for Regularized Least Squares Regression. Pages 79–93 of: *Proceedings of the Annual Conference on Learning Theory*.
Stone, M. 1974. Cross-validatory Choice and Assessment of Statistical Predictions. *Journal of the Royal Statistical Society, Series B*, **36**, 111–147.
Storkey, A., and Sugiyama, M. 2007. Mixture Regression for Covariate Shift. Pages 1337–1344 of: Schölkopf, B., Platt, J. C., and Hoffmann, T. (eds), *Advances in Neural Information Processing Systems 19*. Cambridge, MA: MIT Press.
Student. 1908. The Probable Error of A Mean. *Biometrika*, **6**, 1–25.
Sugiyama, M. 2006. Active Learning in Approximately Linear Regression Based on Conditional Expectation of Generalization Error. *Journal of Machine Learning Research*, **7**(Jan.), 141–166.
Sugiyama, M. 2007. Dimensionality Reduction of Multimodal Labeled Data by Local Fisher Discriminant Analysis. *Journal of Machine Learning Research*, **8**(May), 1027–1061.
Sugiyama, M. 2009. On Computational Issues of Semi-supervised Local Fisher Discriminant Analysis. *IEICE Transactions on Information and Systems*, **E92-D**(5), 1204–1208.
Sugiyama, M. 2010. Superfast-Trainable Multi-Class Probabilistic Classifier by Least-Squares Posterior Fitting. *IEICE Transactions on Information and Systems*, **E93-D**(10), 2690–2701.

Sugiyama, M., and Kawanabe, M. 2012. *Machine Learning in Non-Stationary Environments: Introduction to Covariate Shift Adaptation*. Cambridge, MA: MIT Press. to appear.

Sugiyama, M., and Müller, K.-R. 2002. The Subspace Information Criterion for Infinite Dimensional Hypothesis Spaces. *Journal of Machine Learning Research*, **3**(Nov.), 323–359.

Sugiyama, M., and Müller, K.-R. 2005. Input-Dependent Estimation of Generalization Error under Covariate Shift. *Statistics & Decisions*, **23**(4), 249–279.

Sugiyama, M., and Nakajima, S. 2009. Pool-based Active Learning in Approximate Linear Regression. *Machine Learning*, **75**(3), 249–274.

Sugiyama, M., and Ogawa, H. 2000. Incremental Active Learning for Optimal Generalization. *Neural Computation*, **12**(12), 2909–2940.

Sugiyama, M., and Ogawa, H. 2001a. Active Learning for Optimal Generalization in Trigonometric Polynomial Models. *IEICE Transactions on Fundamentals of Electronics, Communications and Computer Sciences*, **E84-A**(9), 2319–2329.

Sugiyama, M., and Ogawa, H. 2001b. Subspace Information Criterion for Model Selection. *Neural Computation*, **13**(8), 1863–1889.

Sugiyama, M., and Ogawa, H. 2003. Active Learning with Model Selection—Simultaneous Optimization of Sample Points and Models for Trigonometric Polynomial Models. *IEICE Transactions on Information and Systems*, **E86-D**(12), 2753–2763.

Sugiyama, M., and Rubens, N. 2008. A Batch Ensemble Approach to Active Learning with Model Selection. *Neural Networks*, **21**(9), 1278–1286.

Sugiyama, M., and Suzuki, T. 2011. Least-Squares Independence Test. *IEICE Transactions on Information and Systems*, **E94-D**(6), 1333–1336.

Sugiyama, M., Kawanabe, M., and Müller, K.-R. 2004. Trading Variance Reduction with Unbiasedness: The Regularized Subspace Information Criterion for Robust Model Selection in Kernel Regression. *Neural Computation*, **16**(5), 1077–1104.

Sugiyama, M., Ogawa, H., Kitagawa, K., and Suzuki, K. 2006. Single-shot Surface Profiling by Local Model Fitting. *Applied Optics*, **45**(31), 7999–8005.

Sugiyama, M., Krauledat, M., and Müller, K.-R. 2007. Covariate Shift Adaptation by Importance Weighted Cross Validation. *Journal of Machine Learning Research*, **8**(May), 985–1005.

Sugiyama, M., Suzuki, T., Nakajima, S., Kashima, H., von Bünau, P., and Kawanabe, M. 2008. Direct Importance Estimation for Covariate Shift Adaptation. *Annals of the Institute of Statistical Mathematics*, **60**(4), 699–746.

Sugiyama, M., Kanamori, T., Suzuki, T., Hido, S., Sese, J., Takeuchi, I., and Wang, L. 2009. A Density-ratio Framework for Statistical Data Processing. *IPSJ Transactions on Computer Vision and Applications*, **1**, 183–208.

Sugiyama, M., Kawanabe, M., and Chui, P. L. 2010a. Dimensionality Reduction for Density Ratio Estimation in High-dimensional Spaces. *Neural Networks*, **23**(1), 44–59.

Sugiyama, M., Takeuchi, I., Suzuki, T., Kanamori, T., Hachiya, H., and Okanohara, D. 2010b. Least-squares Conditional Density Estimation. *IEICE Transactions on Information and Systems*, **E93-D**(3), 583–594.

Sugiyama, M., Idé, T., Nakajima, S., and Sese, J. 2010c. Semi-supervised Local Fisher Discriminant Analysis for Dimensionality Reduction. *Machine Learning*, **78**(1–2), 35–61.

Sugiyama, M., Suzuki, T., and Kanamori, T. 2011a. Density Ratio Matching under the Bregman Divergence: A Unified Framework of Density Ratio Estimation. *Annals of the Institute of Statistical Mathematics*. To appear.

Sugiyama, M., Yamada, M., von Bünau, P., Suzuki, T., Kanamori, T., and Kawanabe, M. 2011b. Direct Density-ratio Estimation with Dimensionality Reduction via Least-squares Hetero-distributional Subspace Search. *Neural Networks*, **24**(2), 183–198.

Sugiyama, M., Suzuki, T., Itoh, Y., Kanamori, T., and Kimura, M. 2011c. Least-Squares Two-Sample Test. *Neural Networks*, **24**(7), 735–751.

Sugiyama, M., Yamada, M., Kimura, M., and Hachiya, H. 2011d. On Information-Maximization Clustering: Tuning Parameter Selection and Analytic Solution. In: *Proceedings of 28th International Conference on Machine Learning (ICML2011)*, 65–72.

Sutton, R. S., and Barto, G. A. 1998. *Reinforcement Learning: An Introduction*. Cambridge, MA: MIT Press.

Suykens, J. A. K., Gestel, T. Van, Brabanter, J. De, Moor, B. De, and Vandewalle, J. 2002. *Least Squares Support Vector Machines*. Singapore: World Scientific Pub. Co.

Suzuki, T., and Sugiyama, M. 2010. Sufficient Dimension Reduction via Squared-loss Mutual Information Estimation. Pages 804–811 of: Teh, Y. W., and Tiggerington, M. (eds), *Proceedings of the Thirteenth International Conference on Artificial Intelligence and Statistics (AISTATS2010)*. JMLR Workshop and Conference Proceedings, vol. 9.

Suzuki, T., and Sugiyama, M. 2011. Least-Squares Independent Component Analysis. *Neural Computation*, **23**(1), 284–301.

Suzuki, T., Sugiyama, M., Sese, J., and Kanamori, T. 2008. Approximating Mutual Information by Maximum Likelihood Density Ratio Estimation. Pages 5–20 of: Saeys, Y., Liu, H., Inza, I., Wehenkel, L., and de Peer, Y. Van (eds), *Proceedings of ECML-PKDD2008 Workshop on New Challenges for Feature Selection in Data Mining and Knowledge Discovery 2008 (FSDM2008)*. JMLR Workshop and Conference Proceedings, vol. 4.

Suzuki, T., Sugiyama, M., and Tanaka, T. 2009a. Mutual Information Approximation via Maximum Likelihood Estimation of Density Ratio. Pages 463–467 of: *Proceedings of 2009 IEEE International Symposium on Information Theory (ISIT2009)*.

Suzuki, T., Sugiyama, M., Kanamori, T., and Sese, J. 2009b. Mutual Information Estimation Reveals Global Associations between Stimuli and Biological Processes. *BMC Bioinformatics*, **10**(1), S52.

Suzuki, T., Sugiyama, M., and Tanaka, Toshiyuki. 2011. Mutual Information Approximation via Maximum Likelihood Estimation of Density Ratio. in preparation.

Takeuchi, I., Le, Q. V., Sears, T. D., and Smola, A. J. 2006. Nonparametric Quantile Estimation. *Journal of Machine Learning Research*, **7**, 1231–1264.

Takeuchi, I., Nomura, K., and Kanamori, T. 2009. Nonparametric Conditional Density Estimation Using Piecewise-linear Solution Path of Kernel Quantile Regression. *Neural Computation*, **21**(2), 533–559.

Takeuchi, K. 1976. Distribution of Information Statistics and Validity Criteria of Models. *Mathematical Science*, **153**, 12–18. in Japanese.

Takimoto, M., Matsugu, M., and Sugiyama, M. 2009. Visual Inspection of Precision Instruments by Least-Squares Outlier Detection. Pages 22–26 of: *Proceedings of The Fourth International Workshop on Data-Mining and Statistical Science (DMSS2009)*.

Talagrand, M. 1996a. New Concentration Inequalities in Product Spaces. *Inventiones Mathematicae*, **126**, 505–563.

Talagrand, M. 1996b. A New Look at Independence. *The Annals of Statistics*, **24**, 1–34.

Tang, Y., and Zhang, H. H. 2006. Multiclass Proximal Support Vector Machines. *Journal of Computational and Graphical Statistics*, **15**(2), 339–355.

Tao, T., and Vu, V. H. 2007. The Condition Number of a Randomly Perturbed Matrix. Pages 248–255 of: *Proceedings of the Thirty-Ninth Annual ACM Symposium on Theory of Computing*. New York: ACM.

Tax, D. M. J., and Duin, R. P. W. 2004. Support Vector Data Description. *Machine Learning*, **54**(1), 45–66.

Tenenbaum, J. B., de Silva, V., and Langford, J. C. 2000. A Global Geometric Framework for Nonlinear Dimensionality Reduction. *Science*, **290**(5500), 2319–2323.

Teo, C. H., Le, Q., Smola, A., and Vishwanathan, S. V. N. 2007. A Scalable Modular Convex Solver for Regularized Risk Minimization. Pages 727–736 of: *ACM SIGKDD International Conference on Knowledge Discovery and Data Mining (KDD2007)*.

Tibshirani, R. 1996. Regression Shrinkage and Subset Selection with the Lasso. *Journal of the Royal Statistical Society, Series B*, **58**(1), 267–288.

Tipping, M. E., and Bishop, C. M. 1999. Mixtures of Probabilistic Principal Component Analyzers. *Neural Computation*, **11**(2), 443–482.

Tresp, V. 2001. Mixtures of Gaussian Processes. Pages 654–660 of: Leen, T. K., Dietterich, T. G., and Tresp, V. (eds), *Advances in Neural Information Processing Systems 13*. Cambridge, MA: MIT Press.

Tsang, I., Kwok, J., and Cheung, P.-M. 2005. Core Vector Machines: Fast SVM Training on Very Large Data Sets. *Journal of Machine Learning Research*, **6**, 363–392.

Tsuboi, Y., Kashima, H., Hido, S., Bickel, S., and Sugiyama, M. 2009. Direct Density Ratio Estimation for Large-scale Covariate Shift Adaptation. *Journal of Information Processing*, **17**, 138–155.

Ueki, K., Sugiyama, M., and Ihara, Y. 2011. Lighting Condition Adaptation for Perceived Age Estimation. *IEICE Transactions on Information and Systems*, **E94-D**(2), 392–395.

van de Geer, S. 2000. *Empirical Processes in M-Estimation*. Cambridge, UK: Cambridge University Press.

van der Vaart, A. W. 1998. *Asymptotic Statistics*. Cambridge, UK: Cambridge University Press.

van der Vaart, A. W., and Wellner, J. A. 1996. *Weak Convergence and Empirical Processes. with Applications to Statistics*. New York: Springer-Verlag.

Vapnik, V. N. 1998. *Statistical Learning Theory*. New York: Wiley.

Wahba, G. 1990. *Spline Models for Observational Data*. Philadelphia, PA: Society for Industrial and Applied Mathematics.

Wang, Q., Kulkarmi, S. R., and Verdú, S. 2005. Divergence Estimation of Contiunous Distributions Based on Data-Dependent Partitions. *IEEE Transactions on Information Theory*, **51**(9), 3064–3074.

Watanabe, S. 2009. *Algebraic Geometry and Statistical Learning Theory*. Cambridge, UK: Cambridge University Press.

Weinberger, K., Blitzer, J., and Saul, L. 2006. Distance Metric Learning for Large Margin Nearest Neighbor Classification. Pages 1473–1480 of: Weiss, Y., Schölkopf, B., and Platt, J. (eds), *Advances in Neural Information Processing Systems 18*. Cambridge, MA: MIT Press.

Weisberg, S. 1985. *Applied Linear Regression*. New York: John Wiley.

Wichern, G., Yamada, M., Thornburg, H., Sugiyama, M., and Spanias, A. 2010 (Mar. 14–19). Automatic Audio Tagging Using Covariate Shift Adaptation. Pages 253–256 of: *Proceedings of 2010 IEEE International Conference on Acoustics, Speech, and Signal Processing (ICASSP2010)*.

Wiens, D. P. 2000. Robust Weights and Designs for Biased Regression Models: Least Squares and Generalized M-Estimation. *Journal of Statistical Planning and Inference*, **83**(2), 395–412.

Williams, P. M. 1995. Bayesian Regularization and Pruning Using a Laplace Prior. *Neural Computation*, **7**(1), 117–143.

Wold, H. 1966. Estimation of Principal Components and Related Models by Iterative Least Squares. Pages 391–420 of: Krishnaiah, P. R. (ed), *Multivariate Analysis*. New York: Academic Press.

Wolff, R. C. L., Yao, Q., and Hall, P. 1999. Methods for Estimating a Conditional Distribution Function. *Journal of the American Statistical Association*, **94**(445), 154–163.

Wu, T.-F., Lin, C.-J., and Weng, R. C. 2004. Probability Estimates for Multi-Class Classification by Pairwise Coupling. *Journal of Machine Learning Research*, **5**, 975–1005.

Xu, L., Neufeld, J., Larson, B., and Schuurmans, D. 2005. Maximum Margin Clustering. Pages 1537–1544 of: Saul, L. K., Weiss, Y., and Bottou, L. (eds), *Advances in Neural Information Processing Systems 17*. Cambridge, MA: MIT Press.

Xue, Y., Liao, X., Carin, L., and Krishnapuram, B. 2007. Multi-Task Learning for Classification with Dirichlet Process Priors. *Journal of Machine Learning Research*, **8**, 35–63.

Yamada, M., and Sugiyama, M. 2009. Direct Importance Estimation with Gaussian Mixture Models. *IEICE Transactions on Information and Systems*, **E92-D**(10), 2159–2162.

Yamada, M., and Sugiyama, M. 2010. Dependence Minimizing Regression with Model Selection for Non-Linear Causal Inference under Non-Gaussian Noise. Pages 643–648 of: *Proceedings of the Twenty-Fourth AAAI Conference on Artificial Intelligence (AAAI2010)*. Atlanta, GA: AAAI Press.

Yamada, M., and Sugiyama, M. 2011a. Cross-Domain Object Matching with Model Selection. Pages 807–815 in Gordon, G., Dunson, D., and Dudík, M. (eds), *Proceedings of the Fourteenth International Conference on Artificial Intelligence and Statistics, JMLR Workshop and Conference Proceedings,* vol. 15.

Yamada, M., and Sugiyama, M. 2011b. Direct Density-Ratio Estimation with Dimensionality Reduction via Hetero-Distributional Subspace Analysis. Pages 549–554 of: *Proceedings of the Twenty-Fifth AAAI Conference on Artificial Intelligence (AAAI2011)*. San Francisco: AAAI Press.

Yamada, M., Sugiyama, M., Wichern, G., and Simm, J. 2010a. Direct Importance Estimation with a Mixture of Probabilistic Principal Component Analyzers. *IEICE Transactions on Information and Systems*, **E93-D**(10), 2846–2849.

Yamada, M., Sugiyama, M., and Matsui, T. 2010b. Semi-supervised Speaker Identification under Covariate Shift. *Signal Processing*, **90**(8), 2353–2361.

Yamada, M., Sugiyama, M., Wichern, G., and Simm, J. 2011a. Improving the Accuracy of Least-Squares Probabilistic Classifiers. *IEICE Transactions on Information and Systems*, **E94-D**(6), 1337–1340.

Yamada, M., Suzuki, T., Kanamori, T., Hachiya, H., and Sugiyama, M. 2011b. *Relative Density-Ratio Estimation for Robust Distribution Comparison*. To appear in "Advances in Neural Information Processing Systems," vol. 24.

Yamada, M., Niu, G., Takagi, J., and Sugiyama, M. 2011c. Computationally Efficient Sufficient Dimension Reduction via Squared-Loss Mutual Information. Pages 247–262 of: C.-N. Hsu and W. S. Lee (eds.), *Proceedings of the Third Asian Conference on Machine Learning (ACML 2011)*, JMLR Workshop and Conference Proceedings, vol. 20.

Yamanishi, K., and Takeuchi, J. 2002. A Unifying Framework for Detecting Outliers and Change Points from Non-Stationary Time Series Data. Pages 676–681 of: *Proceedings of the 8th ACM SIGKDD International Conference on Knowledge Discovery and Data Mining (KDD2002)*.

Yamanishi, K., Takeuchi, J., Williams, G., and Milne, P. 2004. On-Line Unsupervised Outlier Detection Using Finite Mixtures with Discounting Learning Algorithms. *Data Mining and Knowledge Discovery*, **8**(3), 275–300.

Yamazaki, K., Kawanabe, M., Watanabe, S., Sugiyama, M., and Müller, K.-R. 2007. Asymptotic Bayesian Generalization Error When Training and Test Distributions Are Different. Pages 1079–1086 of: Ghahramani, Z. (ed), *Proceedings of 24th International Conference on Machine Learning (ICML2007)*.

Yankov, D., Keogh, E., and Rebbapragada, U. 2008. Disk Aware Discord Discovery: Finding Unusual Time Series in Terabyte Sized Datasets. *Knowledge and Information Systems*, **17**(2), 241–262.

Yokota, T., Sugiyama, M., Ogawa, H., Kitagawa, K., and Suzuki, K. 2009. The Interpolated Local Model Fitting Method for Accurate and Fast Single-shot Surface Profiling. *Applied Optics*, **48**(18), 3497–3508.

Yu, K., Tresp, V., and Schwaighofer, A. 2005. Learning Gaussian Processes from Multiple Tasks. Pages 1012–1019 of: *Proceedings of the 22nd International Conference on Machine Learning (ICML2005)*. New York: ACM.

Zadrozny, B. 2004. Learning and Evaluating Classifiers under Sample Selection Bias. Pages 903–910 of: *Proceedings of the Twenty-First International Conference on Machine Learning (ICML2004)*. New York: ACM.

Zeidler, E. 1986. *Nonlinear Functional Analysis and Its Applications, I: Fixed-Point Theorems*. New York: Springer-Verlag.

Zelnik-Manor, L., and Perona, P. 2005. Self-Tuning Spectral Clustering. Pages 1601–1608 of: Saul, L. K., Weiss, Y., and Bottou, L. (eds), *Advances in Neural Information Processing Systems 17*. Cambridge, MA: MIT Press.

Zhu, L., Miao, B., and Peng, H. 2006. On Sliced Inverse Regression with High-Dimensional Covariates. *Journal of the American Statistical Association*, **101**(474), 630–643.

Index

Printed in the United States
By Bookmasters